"The last line of the national anthem poses a question. Francis Scott Key asks whether the flag still flies over the land of the free. Never before has the question been so prescient and the answer so tentative. I can recall when conservatives and liberals would argue over tax and foreign policy but never over the essence of America. Days long gone. Our schools, mainstream media, pop culture, multinational corporations, and the growing cult of multiculturalism form an unholy alliance with the purpose of carrying out Barack Obama's intention to 'thoroughly transform America.' No one can articulate that threat better than Michelle Malkin. The solutions are elusive, but all depend on first understanding the reality and nature of those subsidizing the barbarians who are now past our gate."

—**TOM TANCREDO**, **former Colorado GOP congressman, 2008 presidential candidate, and We Build The Wall, Inc. advisory board member**

"The beautiful and brilliant Michelle Malkin has long been a joy to American patriots. Her brutal analysis of the political economy of the Treason Lobby, which is promoting reckless mass immigration to obliterate the historic American nation, breaks new ground."

—**PETER BRIMELOW**, **author of** *Alien Nation* **and founder of VDARE.com**

"Malkin is one of the pioneers of the modern conservative movement and one of the leaders in harnessing the Internet to fight for the cause. Yet, while most of the new leaders have become distracted or have even lost their way, Malkin is still holding down the fort. While everyone is focused on the daily soap opera of politics, the left has stolen the foundation of this country right before our own eyes—the sovereignty of we the people to determine who comes into this country. We now have a government of, by, and for foreign nationals rather than one that represents American citizens. Malkin inspired a new generation of activists to defend American sovereignty by fighting open borders in the 1990s. The fight is the same today, but the enemies are slightly different, and the consequences are graver. With *Open Borders Inc.*, Malkin uses her skill as one of the few effective, veteran investigative journalists on the right to issue one final clarion call on behalf of We the People."

—**DANIEL HOROWITZ,** author of *Stolen Sovereignty*

"Once again, Michelle Malkin brings us hard-hitting facts and incisive analysis—all thoroughly documented. She exposes the immigration anarchy agenda of the radical leftists, establishment opportunists, 'philanthropic' phonies, cottage industry 'humanitarians,' media propagandists, smear artists, and race hustlers. Ms. Malkin delivers facts, history, documentation, and context like no other. Her work is essential reading."

—**CHRISTOPHER J. FARRELL,** Director of Investigations & Research, Judicial Watch

"Michelle Malkin is not a pretty little Filipino girl. That's just what she looks like. Her personality is more like Charles Bronson in *Death Wish*. When the alt-left's chant of 'No borders—No Wall—No USA at all' went mainstream, Michelle went ballistic, and this book is a veritable fireball of finely tuned arguments that beautifully counter the new wave of anti-Americanism. If any book could save America from itself, this is it."

—**GAVIN MCINNES,** co-founder of VICE, founder of Proud Boys, host of FreeSpeech.TV

Open Borders Inc.

MICHELLE MALKIN

OPEN BORDERS INC.

WHO'S FUNDING AMERICA'S DESTRUCTION?

REGNERY
PUBLISHING
A Division of Salem Media Group

Regnery® is a registered trademark of Salem Communications Holding Corporation

Cataloging-in-Publication data on file with the Library of Congress

ISBN 978-1-62157-971-7
ebook ISBN 978-1-62157-978-6

Published in the United States by
Regnery Publishing
A Division of Salem Media Group
300 New Jersey Ave NW
Washington, DC 20001
www.Regnery.com

Manufactured in the United States of America

10 9 8 7 6 5 4 3 2 1

Books are available in quantity for promotional or premium use. For information on discounts and terms, please visit our website: www.Regnery.com.

*For the brave men and women of the U.S. Border Patrol and
U.S. Immigration and Customs Enforcement Agency*

*For the Angel Families and the memories of their loved ones
sacrificed at the altar of open borders*

*For my patriotic friends and allies dwelling in the
Valley of the Banned*

I hereby declare, on oath, that I absolutely and entirely renounce and abjure all allegiance and fidelity to any foreign prince, potentate, state, or sovereignty of whom or which I have heretofore been a subject or citizen; that **I will support and defend the Constitution and laws of the United States of America against all enemies, foreign and domestic;** *that I will bear true faith and allegiance to the same; that I will bear arms on behalf of the United States when required by the law; that I will perform noncombatant service in the Armed Forces of the United States when required by the law; that I will perform work of national importance under civilian direction when required by the law; and that I take this obligation freely without any mental reservation or purpose of evasion; so help me God.*

— *Oath of Allegiance to the United States of America*[1]

CONTENTS

PREFACE   xv

Introduction
**THE MAKE AMERICA DISAPPEAR AGENDA
(MADA)**   xix

OPEN BORDERS INC: BY THE NUMBERS   xli

Part 1: All Enemies Foreign

Chapter One
**SIN FRONTERAS: ALL ABOARD THE CARAVAN
CARTEL**   1

Chapter Two
**GEORGE SOROS:
THE CEO OF OPEN BORDERS INC.**   39

Chapter Three
**UNHOLY ALLIANCE: THE POPE, CATHOLIC
BISHOPS, AND AMNESTY PROFITEERS**   83

Chapter Four
**WRETCHED REFUSE:
THE REFUGEE RESETTLEMENT RACKET**   109

Part 2: All Enemies Domestic

Chapter Five
**THE A-TEAM: ABOLISH ICE, ANTIFA,
AND SANCTUARY ANARCHISTS**   143

Chapter Six
**HATE MACHINE: THE SOUTHERN POVERTY
LAW CENTER**   183

Chapter Seven
**HOLLYWOOD OR HOLLYWALL? INSIDE THE
FORTRESS OF CELEBRITY HYPOCRISY**   237

Chapter Eight
**FACT CHECK: TRUE, THE LIBERAL MEDIA
HATES AMERICA**   273

Conclusion
BORDER DEFENDERS' ACTION PLAN   295

Appendix A
**PUEBLO SIN FRONTERAS PRESS RELEASE
AND DEMAND LETTER**   301

Appendix B
**SOROSWORLD: INTERNATIONAL ALPHABET
SOUP OF NGOs**   305

Appendix C
SOROS'S ALIEN BAR ASSOCIATION   313

Appendix D
**AMERICAN SJWs, SHARIA ENFORCERS,
AND SPEECH POLICE**   317

Appendix E
CORPORATE HANDMAIDENS   319

Appendix F
**CATHOLIC CAMPAIGN FOR HUMAN
DEVELOPMENT'S AMNESTY PROMOTERS**   331

Appendix G
60 OF THE WORLD'S FINEST REFUJIHADIS   337

Appendix H
**TOP 10 REFUGEE DESTINATIONS BY STATE
AND METRO AREA (2008-2017)**   349

Appendix I
REFUGEE RESETTLEMENT HIJACKERS   351

APPENDIX J
**TIMELINE OF ANTIFA VIOLENCE AND
ABOLISH ICE VIGILANTISM**   353

Map A   357
Map B   365

ACKNOWLEDGMENTS   367
NOTES   369
INDEX   463

PREFACE

As I was finishing last-minute edits to this manuscript in mid-summer 2019, open-borders anarchy in America reached a boiling point:

- A 21-year-old Syrian Muslim refugee, Mustafa Mousab Alowemer, was arrested in Pittsburgh and charged with plotting to bomb a Christian church in the name of ISIS. He had relocated to the U.S. at taxpayer expense under the refugee resettlement program in 2016.[1]

- In Portland, Oregon, independent journalist Andy Ngo was hospitalized with brain bleeding after being beaten by an Antifa mob.[2] Portland is a militant sanctuary city for illegal aliens. Its far left mayor, Ted Wheeler, issued stand down orders to the police during Antifa/anti-ICE demonstrations in 2018[3] and vowed to resist President Trump's deportation enforcement initiative in July 2019.[4]

- In Tacoma, Washington, longtime Puget Sound anarchist and Antifa member Willem Van Spronsen—armed with a rifle and incendiary devices—ambushed a federal immigration detention center. He hurled flaming objects at vehicles and buildings, and attempted to ignite a propane tank, before being fatally shot by police. Spronsen had previously been arrested at a protest at the same facility for tackling a law enforcement officer while carrying a collapsible baton and knife. Spronsen's "I am Antifa" manifesto echoed Democrat Representative Alexandria Ocasio-Cortez's attack on ICE detention facilities as "concentration camps."[5] CNN had aired a documentary cheerleading Pacific Northwest anarchists in May; Van Spronsen appeared several times on the show.[6] Fellow anarchists brazenly celebrated their fallen "comrade" with "Rest in power" eulogies.[7] Antifa agitators justified his violence on social media[8]—where countless peaceful conservatives and nationalists have been de-platformed in a 2020 election cycle purge. Antifa's domestic terrorists have been championed by Muslim Democrat Keith Ellison on the left[9] and Utah GOP Senator Mitt Romney on the Never Trump right.[10]

- The *New York Times* escalated hatred of homeland security employees with an op-ed by a foreign academic calling on the public to wage a "social shame" campaign against Border Patrol officers—including publicly naming them, likening them to Nazis, and endorsing punishment of attorneys who provide legal representation to law enforcement officials and other personnel at immigration detention facilities.[11]

- In Houston and Los Angeles, in clear violation of federal law prohibiting the aiding and abetting of illegal immigration, several churches defiantly opened their doors to illegal aliens hiding from President Trump's enforcement actions against deportation evaders. The Catholic archbishop of Chicago accused ICE of "terroriz[ing] communities."[12] Los Angeles Mayor Eric Garcetti posted a video announcement, with the L.A. police chief by his side, informing citizens that the city would "not be coordinating with ICE."[13]

- With our borders collapsing and sanctuary cities operating with impunity, the Center for Immigration Studies' Todd Bensman reported that "as many as 35,000" Africans were headed our way through the Darien Gap between South America and North America.[14] Border officials in the Del Rio sector reported they had caught 1,000 Haitians in less than a month, 80 percent of which were family units drawn by the kiddie catch-and-release magnet.[15]

- In my adopted home state of Colorado, militant agitators tore down an American flag at an Aurora illegal alien detention facility and hoisted a Mexican flag overhead. The orchestrated demonstrations against President Trump's deportation enforcement actions were sponsored by a multitude of left-wing groups I investigated for this book, including the Council on American Islamic Relations and Women's March (funded directly and indirectly by billionaire George Soros); United We Dream (which provides grants to Soros affiliates); and RAICES (an outgrowth of the Southwest sanctuary church movement). Even more shocking: one of the top "hosts" of these rabble-rousing anti-ICE protests held across the country was the Lutheran Immigration and Refugee Service—which is a designated federal refugee resettlement agency that receives more than 96 percent of its funding from public tax dollars.

The America my parents taught me never to take for granted is disappearing before our eyes. It is fast becoming a no-go zone for patriots. I wrote *Open Borders Inc.* to arm fellow citizens with vital information about the financiers of our nation's downfall and their vile, violent foot soldiers. I pray that you will be compelled to read, digest, share, and *use* it to defend our beloved nation under God.

Michelle Malkin

July 2019

INTRODUCTION

THE MAKE AMERICA DISAPPEAR AGENDA (MADA)

"YO NO CREO EN FRONTERAS"
(Translation: "I don't believe in borders")
—*T-shirt worn by former Democratic National Committee deputy*
chair, first Muslim member of Congress, and current Minnesota state
Attorney General Keith Ellison[1]

"The crucial issue of our time is how to overcome the
obstacles posed by national sovereignty to the pursuit of
the common interest."
—*Billionaire George Soros*[2]

"A person who thinks only about building walls,
wherever they may be, and not building bridges,
is not Christian."
—*Pope Francis*[3]

"We need to fight back against the criminalization of immigrants and those crossing the border."[4]
—*Somalian refugee and Democrat Representative Ilhan Omar*[5] *of Minnesota's 5th district, terrorist recruiting capital of the nation*[6]

"Display signs with messages like 'Migration is Beautiful' and 'No Human Being is Illegal.'"
—*Southern Poverty Law Center, Teaching Tolerance guide for K–12 educators*[7]

"This is not about simply the abolition of ICE, but the decolonization of North America."
—*Anarchist declaration on Antifa digital network, "It's Going Down"*[8]

"Mata, viola, controla." ("Kill, rape, control.")
—*Motto of illegal alien gang MS-13*[9]

I fear for my country and I fear for our freedom to speak up for it.

After exercising my First Amendment rights for a living over the past quarter-century, I never thought I'd have to say such a thing out loud. I'm not merely worried. I'm terrified. During the past year, as I worked furiously to complete this manuscript (my seventh in seventeen years), I have witnessed friends and allies stripped of their platforms, reputations, and voices. Some can no longer communicate on social media. Others cannot gather peacefully at hotel conferences to discuss their ideas. Still others are now forbidden from doing business with their banks, payment processors, online retailers, and even ridesharing services. Many have gone underground to protect themselves and their families. They are mocked, defamed, and ostracized on airwaves and in public spaces. They face a daily barrage of dehumanizing lies, violence, and death threats—all in the name of eradicating "hate." As I found out firsthand in May 2019, you can be censored by Silicon Valley simply for protesting the censorship of the un-personed![10] A month later, Google/YouTube declared in June 2019 that it is now "hate speech" to criticize any individual based on his or her "immigration status."[11]

Why is this happening? Who is behind it? What is the objective of the destabilizers and de-platformers? The quotations from Minnesota Attorney General Keith Ellison, left-wing billionaire George Soros, Pope Francis, Democrat Congresswoman Ilhan Omar of Minnesota, so-called "Antifa" operatives, the Southern Poverty Law Center indoctrinators, and the violent MS-13 criminal enterprise spell it all out quite clearly. The foreign and domestic enemies of America do not believe in borders (no matter how many times their sympathizers in the media deny it[12]). National sovereignty is an "obstacle" to be ended, not defended. Walls are "un-Christian" (except for the centuries-old fortifications that surround the Vatican and hallowed churches around the world, of course.) Border-trespassing is a human right. Dissent is "hate." Chaos and destruction are the ultimate goals.

It may seem paradoxical at this pivotal moment in American political history, with a president in office who is more vocal than any other on fundamental issues of sovereignty and self-determination, that America First voices are being stifled. Squelched. Silenced. But it makes perfect sense. Globalists are doing everything in their power to deny President Donald Trump reelection in 2020. The caravan cartel hates him. George Soros, the Pope, and the United Nations consider him an evil threat to their billion-dollar migration and refugee enterprises. Antifa wants him dead. The Southern Poverty Law Center and Silicon Valley want to purge every last one of his supporters from the public square. They see the pendulum swinging towards nationalists across Europe and Asia amid an open-borders backlash in Britain, France, Italy, Poland, Hungary, and even India.[13] Cultural Marxists and Big Tech social justice warriors cannot compete on a level playing field of ideas, so they are rigging the game to prevent online Trump supporters from influencing voters and correcting false narratives. On the ground, as I have warned, we are not at peace, or rather, the radical Left is not at peace with us. This hatred long predated Donald Trump, and unless we unite against it, this hatred will consume our country. From the comfort of TV green rooms, Beltway back rooms, corporate boardrooms, and conference ballrooms, it may not look like civil war is imminent. But threats and outright violence against ordinary, law-abiding people are now regularized features, not random bugs, of political life in these dis-United States. College students are being punched,[14] elderly citizens are being assaulted,[15] MAGA hat wearers are being kicked off planes[16] and assaulted in school hallways[17] and restaurants,[18] conservative speakers are being mobbed and Molotov-cocktailed,[19] ICE agents and their families are being targeted, and pro-Trump moms[20] on social media are being monitored and doxxed.[21]

You and I have watched in outrage as thousands of "migrant caravan" travelers swarm our southern border in unprecedented numbers—all the while cursing President Trump as the "Anti-Christ"[22] as their supporters back in their native land burn our flag.[23] Hostile forces enable these masses to make their journey equipped with smart phones, transported by buses, escorted by "humanitarian" guides or ruthless coyotes, and sheltered every step of the way.

You and I have watched in outrage as hundreds of cities, counties, and states ruled by Democrats and corporate elites openly defy federal immigration agents to provide sanctuary for millions of illegal aliens who provide an unrelenting supply of cheap labor and eventually (after the inevitable bipartisan amnesties) cheap votes.

You and I have watched in outrage as tens of thousands of impoverished and unassimilated refugees from Third World and radical Muslim countries are redistributed across our heartland without the consent of the governed—creating cultural ghettos and terror recruitment hot spots that weaponize America's good grace and blind generosity against us.

Too many Americans are afraid to say it out loud: not all migrants and refugees are welcome here. Muslim extremist refugees seeking to wage jihad on our soil and kill all infidels are not welcome here. Anti-American refugees seeking to transform our society and culture into a Balkanized hell are not welcome here. Misogynist refugees who treat their (multiple) wives as second-class citizens and subjugate their daughters (who are vulnerable to "honor killings" for the slightest transgressions) are not welcome here. Jobless migrants and uneducated refugees seeking to soak up our tax dollars and send remittances back home while griping about our lack of generosity are not welcome here. In Democrat-controlled sanctuaries, where taxpayers are fed up with crime, homelessness, and literal human waste piling up on the streets, even anti-Trump Hollywood liberals like Cher have complained that their homeland "isn't taking care of its own."[24]

What has our "welcoming" culture wrought? It has produced obnoxious ingrates like Congresswoman Ilhan Omar, a Somalian refugee who was awarded a tax-subsidized golden path to U.S. citizenship, only to make a career out of denigrating the 9/11 terrorist attacks,[25] demonizing immigration enforcement officers,[26] and proclaiming that she brings the "perspective of a foreigner" to her coveted seat on the U.S. House Foreign Affairs Committee.[27] If *I* questioned her loyalties, I'd risk getting banned on social media or TV. But since she has thrown her own American allegiance under the bus, can we all question her patriotism now?

Instead of an attitude of gratitude, which my legal immigrant parents inculcated in me, Omar exhibits a toxic defiance, arrogance, and resentment that typifies the new generation of open-borders beneficiaries. She represents the Entitled Other. Assimilation is not in her vocabulary. Respect for our common culture is an alien concept. So is respect for our campaign finance and tax rules. In June 2019, the Minnesota state Campaign Finance and Public Disclosure Board ordered Omar to reimburse nearly $4,000 in improper spending.[28] More troubling, Omar has evaded questions about her bizarre marriage license history[29] documenting that she is betrothed to a man that social media,[30] photographic evidence, and other biographical data strongly suggests is her brother[31]— while at the same time living with a different man she describes as her "husband" and father of her three children.[32] The Minnesota board discovered that Omar filed at least two joint tax returns with one "husband" while legally married to the other.[33] The usual deflections (racist, sexist, Islamophobe!) have proven effective with the lazy enablers of the mainstream media.[34]

Sob stories are always easier to tell and sell than nailing down pesky details about whether, why, and how she gamed our immigration system. Propaganda journalists preferred to spill tons of ink on Congresswoman Omar's illegal alien guest for the State of the Union in 2019; she fit the anti-Trump, anti-America narrative to a tee. Linda Clark "has lived here over eighteen years," Omar lamented, "and there's no reason she should be taken from her family." An estimated 22,000 Liberians have settled in Minnesota.[35] Ahead of the annual address to Congress in January, Omar blasted President Trump for "threatening to deport" Clark and "thousands of Liberians for no reason other than hate."[36] Clark in turn echoed her radical host's heated rhetoric, calling Trump White House efforts to reform the Temporary Protected Status and Deferred Enforced Departure programs "hateful" and castigating Trump "for deliberately targeting people like me."[37]

Of course, there is a very simple reason that Omar's State of the Union guest and hundreds of thousands like her from ten different countries have been threatened with deportation. They were allowed to enter, stay, and work here because of the extraordinary generosity of the United States of America. And now, after decades of our government's largesse, their time is finally up. The Temporary Protected Status[38] (TPS) and Deferred Enforced Departure[39] (DED) programs were established as part of the Immigration Act of 1990, signed by President George H. W. Bush. The idea was to create an orderly way to deal compassionately with foreigners who could not return to their home countries due to natural disasters, hurricanes, environmental catastrophes, civil war, epidemics, and other "extraordinary and temporary conditions." An estimated 250,000 illegal immigrants from El Salvador first won TPS golden tickets after an earthquake struck the country in January 2001. In addition, about 60,000 illegal immigrant Haitians received TPS after earthquakes in their homeland in 2010. An estimated 80,000 illegal immigrant Hondurans and Nicaraguans have been here since 1998—when Hurricane Mitch hit their homeland. Several hundred Somalis remain in the country with TPS first granted in 1991, along with some 700 Sudanese who first secured TPS benefits in 1997. About 7,000 Syrians have been granted TPS status since 2016, along with 1,500 Yemenis.[40]

TPS designees won three-year renewable passes to live and work here, travel freely, and enjoy immunity from detention or deportation. Participants were originally required to provide proof that they arrived here on an eligible date, had committed no more than two misdemeanors and no felonies, and maintained a continuous presence in the country. But the programs are dangerously rife with unchecked document fraud, including unknown numbers of TPS winners who have used multiple aliases and faked their country of origin to qualify. And without a fully functioning biometric entry–exit database in place to track temporary foreign visitors, there's no way to track all the TPS enrollees.

You rarely hear about this massive illegal alien and family importation plan in the news. There are no dramatic visuals of women and children crying at the border, no photo ops at our broken fences and bits of new wall. But it is permanent pipelines like TPS that flood our cities and corrode our foundations indiscriminately. If Congresswoman Omar has fixed her attention on it, you know it is part of the plan. An entire army of "community activists" like her State of the Union guest Linda Clark have risen up to defend their turf. Imagine the cultural and political impact of nearly 400,000 TPS beneficiaries spread across key battleground states winning amnesty, a path to citizenship, and a road to the voting booth. As I've reported repeatedly over the past quarter-century, these "temporary" amnesties have become endless, interminable residency plans for unlawful border crossers, visa overstayers, and deportation evaders from around the world. They are not, and never were, entitled to be here. Entry into our country is a privilege, not a right. That is not "hateful." It is the stance that every modern, industrialized sovereign nation must take toward non-citizens in order to survive.

Trump was the first commander in chief to challenge the temporary-in-name-only farce since the creation of the program. At least 3,700 Liberians like Clark have been here since 1991 on TPS because of civil wars that ended sixteen years ago. President Bill Clinton first ordered Deferred Enforced Departure (discretionary deportation delays) for this group in 1999, arguing that Liberia was still unstable. Nineteen years later, after multiple extensions by Presidents George W. Bush and Barack Obama, Trump finally determined that it was safe for these guests to return to their homeland.

But instead of thanks and farewell, the beneficiaries of our country's humanitarian TPS and DED policies like Linda Clark and their Democratic enablers like Congresswoman Omar cling bitterly and hurl invectives at leaders who take our laws and borders seriously. Clark now leads the charge as a community organizer for black immigrants demanding sanctuary policies and local government-funded legal defense funds for illegal aliens challenging deportation decisions.[41] The disgruntled "victims" have a phalanx of American Civil Liberties Union lawyers helping them sue to avoid deportation and a phalanx of open-borders journalists to drum up public sympathy for their plights. One of the key groups lobbying on the issue, Alianza Americas, went door-to-door hunting for TPS recipients in San Francisco, Los Angeles, Houston, Miami, Nashville, Minneapolis, Raleigh-Durham, and Henderson, North Carolina.[42] Alianza is a George Soros-funded grantee of the International Migration Initiative. There were fifteen different plaintiffs dragooned into two separate lawsuits filed on behalf of TPS aliens by the ACLU of California and the National Day Laborer Organizing Network,[43] both with financial ties to SorosWorld, as you'll learn in chapter two.

In March 2019, the Trump White House gave in after relentless bitching and moaning from immigration expansionists and extended TPS for Liberians until March 2020.[44] The White House similarly caved on TPS extensions for illegals from South Sudan, Sudan, El Salvador, Haiti, and Nicaragua[45] after Trump's cancellation of the programs was blocked by Obama appointee Judge Edward Chen in one of the two ACLU lawsuits against Trump's Department of Homeland Security. Chen is a former lawyer for the open-borders, Soros-funded American Civil Liberties Union in San Francisco.[46] Even though federal statute plainly limits judicial review of the executive branch's TPS-related designations, Judge Chen found a way to override the president's prerogative. He cited his personal belief that President Trump harbored "animus against non-white, non-European immigrants in violation of Equal Protection guaranteed by the Constitution" based on, among other things, Trump's likening of illegal alien MS-13 gang members to snakes.[47] (That's a rather mild and generous comparison, if you ask me.)

With thousands of illegal aliens pouring across the border every day, and thousands more with lobbying groups fighting furiously on Capitol Hill and in our courts for amnesty benefits and deportation immunity, I know you are wondering:

What other nation in the world has been so recklessly tolerant of foreign grumblers, agitators, and grifters overstaying their welcome and seizing political power?

More broadly, who sponsored these floods of unassimilated foreigners?

Who organized them?

Who's providing them with legal services, work permits, employment protections, housing, foster care, college tuition benefits, and even abortion entitlements?

Who profits? Who pays?

Like you, I've grown increasingly frustrated with mainstream media coverage of the most central and existential issue of our time. I'm sick of the bias, the pandering, the tiptoeing, and virtue signaling. I'm fed up with the liberal smear machine that tars all immigration enforcement officials and advocates as racists and xenophobes, while deifying all illegal aliens and refugees as saints and martyrs. I'm exasperated by Two Minutes Hate sessions on CNN by hysterical tools like Chris Cuomo (who compared heroic American soldiers landing at D-Day to degenerate Antifa thugs[48])—or Jim Acosta and Ana Navarro, who pin all the blame for "separated families" on President Trump and none of it on the illegal alien parents themselves or the open-borders infrastructure that created irresistible magnets drawing them here in the first place. I'm impatient with hasty three-minute Fox News segments on the southern border siege that barely scratch the surface of the who, what, where, when, and why of the migrant crisis.

This book is a deep-dive dossier of the funders and foot soldiers of immigration anarchy here and around the globe. There are no commercial interruptions, no shouting matches, no censors. Just names and numbers, facts and research, maps and data, aggregated in one handy place for those of you who want answers, accountability, and change.

The most shocking revelation herein is not how much time and money militant "progressives" and socialists dedicate to the destruction of America. What will turn your stomach and boil your blood is how much of *your own money* is being used to rob you, your children, and grandchildren of the blessings of liberty. I'm not just talking about the billions in tax dollars spent on illegal alien services, refugee resettlement, meddling international bodies, sovereignty-sabotaging non-governmental agencies, and foreign aid. (Speaking of which: in May 2019, the governments of Mexico and Central America demanded that Americans cough up nearly $6 billion in "investments" to cure the chronic poverty and corruption that plague the region,[49] while they sit back and watch their citizens collect billions of dollars in remittances sent home by illegal aliens in the United States.)

I'm also talking about the money you may have unknowingly contributed to "humanitarian" organizations, churches and other faith-based groups, corporations, and political entities that effectively aid and abet worldwide smuggling and trafficking rackets. They have feel-good names like "Save the Children," "Doctors Without Borders, "Catholic Charities," "Hope Not Hate," and "No More Deaths." Don't be fooled. They are risking lives, not saving them. They are creating "pull factors" that lure desperate people into danger, and dump dangerous masses on strained villages and towns from Turkey to Italy to Columbus, Ohio, to Nashville, Tennessee, to the Twin Cities, Minnesota, and all points in between. These are not soul-saving campaigns, as you'll see in chapter three. These are money-making missions.

Eager to prove their own anti-Trump credentials with the John Lennon-addled "Imagine there's no country" crowd, American companies are putting Americans last and refugees first: Starbucks vowed to hire ten thousand refugees; Airbnb offered them free housing; and Lyft helped subsidize left-wing legal efforts to fight President Trump's refugee moratorium and enhanced visa-holder vetting. Enough pandering a day keeps the left-wing boycotters away. But all these helpers and handmaidens are nowhere to be found, of course, when untold numbers among the "wretched refuse" imported to our soil turn out to be America-hating jihadists and criminals. (In chapter four, you'll meet *sixty* of the world's finest refujihadis.)

As longtime readers know, the safety and security of the United States have long been *leitmotifs* of my life's work. My first book, *Invasion,* published in 2002, exposed how border failures and systemic non-enforcement of our visa program rules created a national security crisis that led to the 9/11 terrorist attacks. A key argument in *Invasion*—that our porous borders give cover to conniving jihadists—was again confirmed straight from the horse's mouth in June 2019 when researchers from the International Center for the Study of Violent Extremism learned from a Canadian jihadist serving in the Islamic State caliphate that "there was at least one ISIS plot for their cadres to travel from Syria to penetrate the U.S. southern border, by infiltrating migration routes via the U.S.-Mexico border."[50] My last book, *Sold Out,* which I co-authored in 2015 with former American computer-programmer-turned-labor-lawyer John Miano, documented how Big Business and Big Government created an economic crisis by exploiting the H-1B tech worker visa program and other foreign employment visas for cheap labor. *Open Borders Inc.* completes a trilogy of my immigration tomes—three individual works tethered together by my personal love of country and journalistic imperative to expose those who seek to tear it down.

In my reporting on the civilizational threat that uncontrolled immigration and demographic conquest pose to our nation-state, I have hammered a recurrent theme: movers, shakers, and major donors of *both* establishment political parties in Washington have conspired to keep our borders loose, enforcement weak, oversight toothless, and opposition marginalized. In *Invasion,* I called out both Clinton identity-politics ideologues and Bush amnesty-peddlers, Democrat lobbyists for the travel industry and GOP kowtowers to Saudi Arabia, for enabling foreign jihadists. In *Sold Out,* I name-checked billionaires Bill Gates, Mark Zuckerberg, and Michael Bloomberg on the left and Rupert Murdoch and Sheldon Adelson on the right for betraying American tech workers in favor of low-wage Chinese and Indian programmers (Republican Congressman Paul Ryan and political activist Grover Norquist came in for blame too). The good news, of course, is that the 2016 presidential election disrupted open-borders business as usual with the victory of Donald J. Trump, the populist businessman beholden to no one. The bad news? The Beltway Swamp Force is still strong—inside and outside the White House.

When you follow the money, you find the truth. If we have any chance of defeating what I call the Make America Disappear Agenda, the *whole* truth must be confronted unflinchingly.

Some truths are more obvious than others. For instance, what was once the loony open-borders fringe has become the center of the Democratic Party. While *New York Times* "fact-checker" Linda Qiu scoffed that "No, Democrats don't want open borders,"[51] former Vice President and 2020 Democratic presidential candidate Joe Biden declared that America has an "obligation" to provide healthcare to everyone on our soil "regardless of whether they are documented or undocumented."[52] Oh, and never mind the pesky technicalities of U.S. citizenship. Biden considers the millions of illegal aliens living and working in our country "already Americans."[53] Senator Kamala Harris of California, another 2020 Democratic presidential hopeful, wants Medicare for all illegal aliens[54] and repeal of the congressional hiring ban on illegals.[55] A bevy of 2020 presidential wannabes jumped on the extremist Abolish ICE bandwagon in the summer of 2018, including Democratic Senators Kamala Harris, Elizabeth Warren, Kirsten Gillibrand, and socialist Bernie Sanders. 2020 presidential dark horse and former Obama Housing and Urban Development secretary Julian Castro wants to decriminalize border jumping;[56] Castro's fellow Texas Democrat and 2020 presidential aspirant Beto O'Rourke has similarly proposed decriminalizing fraudulent asylum claimants looking to game the system at the southern border.[57] And at a Capitol Hill event sponsored by George Soros-funded MoveOn.org, the America-trashing trio of social justice divas and congresswomen, Ilhan Omar, Alexandria Ocasio-Cortez, and Rashida Tlaib, demanded that their fellow Democrats defund and destroy ICE, which they lambasted as an agency "systematically violating human rights" and guilty of "torture."[58] To righteous applause, Ocasio-Cortez babbled incoherently about the "right of human mobility. Because it is a right. It is a right. Because we are standing on native land, and Latino people are descendants of native people. And we cannot be told and criminalized simply for our identity or our status. Period."[59] Did someone order a word *ensalada* with geographically illiterate *reconquista* dressing on the side? Welcome to the leading light and future of the Democratic Party.

This left-wing clown-car spectacle of mental midgets would be entertaining if our nation's survival weren't at stake. Mocking Bozo Biden, Cover Boy Beto, Alexandria Open-O-Borderz, and the Progressive Hamas Caucus is just too easy and expedient. Far more threatening are the Big Business alliances of bipartisan treachery that lead from George Soros to the Koch Brothers to the American Conservative Union to the White House. Let me connect some disturbing dots for you.

As I report extensively in chapter one on the caravan cartel, Soros funds a vast constellation of identity-politics groups spreading false narratives about President Trump's border-enforcement and visa-vetting measures. One of the key "social change" organizations subsidized by Soros money is the Tides Foundation, which funds the work of illegal alien Filipino "journalist" Jose Antonio Vargas. (Vargas is now embedded in Hollywood circles, as I discuss in chapter seven.) In the summer of 2018, Vargas, a Pulitzer Prize-winner formerly with the *Washington Post*, disseminated a viral photo of a young Latino boy in a cage, which he peddled as a symbol of President Trump's cruel family separation policies. "This is what happens when a government believes people are 'illegal,'" he raged. "Kids in cages."[60] Vargas's post garnered more than 24,000 retweets. It was complete and total fake news. The image came from the Facebook page of a militant Latino group called the Brown Berets, who stuffed several children in pens as props in a staged open-borders protest. Vargas still has his blue check-marked verified Twitter account to this day and the false and defamatory tweet remains on the site.

Now, you would think the Right would want nothing to do with such a serial fraudster as Vargas. Long before his phony open-borders attack on the Trump White House, Vargas had admitted using a phony passport with a fake name, a fake green card, a bogus Social Security number, falsified federal I-9 employment eligibility forms,[61] and a fraudulent Oregon driver's license to obtain prestigious journalism jobs and remain illegally in the country. No matter. The Charles Koch Institute, a giant in conservative philanthropic circles, joined with liberal BuzzFeed in 2013 during the "Gang of Eight" amnesty push to sponsor an "immigration summit" in which Vargas played a marquee role as a discussion moderator.[62] (A decade ago, I was a speaker on the Koch-funded Americans for Prosperity circuit. But you won't see me at any Koch immigration summits, because conservative Filipino-American journalists who oppose open borders take a back seat to liberal, lawbreaking Filipino journalists whose racial and ethnic-focused amnesty advocacy dutifully serves Big Business interests over the national interest.)

Charles Koch, who likened Trump to a Nazi in 2016, teamed up with leftist Apple CEO Tim Cook to lobby for legalizing hundreds of thousands of so-called DREAMers.[63] (Cook, as you'll learn in chapter six, is a top financial donor and partner in the Southern Poverty Law Center's campaign to smear and silence immigration hawks, anti-jihad activists, and other American patriots.) The Koch-founded LIBRE Initiative, a Latino identity-politics activist outfit, helps illegal aliens obtain driver's licenses[64] and spearheaded a seven-figure ad blitz rewarding open-borders Democrats and Republicans carrying water for the DREAMers.[65] What thanks do Koch and the GOP get? As you'll see in chapter two, the Soros-funded DREAMers use partisan mob tactics to obstruct the Right, from disrupting the Brett Kavanaugh Supreme Court confirmation hearings to shutting down airports over the Trump foreign travel restrictions.

In 2005, Koch Industries hired Bush administration operative Matt Schlapp to head its D.C. lobbying operation.[66] In 2009, Schlapp founded lobbying firm Cove Strategies with his wife, Mercedes. In 2014, he was elected chairman of the American Conservative Union to oversee the annual Conservative Political Action Conference (CPAC).[67] In 2017, Mercedes Schlapp was named senior White House communications adviser.[68] While the missus left the family lobbying shop, Matt Schlapp reaped the benefits of his intimate ties to the White House. The year his wife headed to the West Wing, Cove Strategies under Schlapp's reign raked in more than $1 million in lobbying income;[69] in 2018, the Schlapps' firm made nearly $1.3 million;[70] and in the first five months of 2019, the business had already pulled in $420,000.[71] Among its top clients: the Seasonal Employment Alliance, a business association singularly dedicated to busting the caps on the H-2B visa program for temporary, low-skilled, non-agricultural workers.[72] (If you've ever wondered why it's so difficult for your teenage kids to get summer jobs at your local resort or amusement park, you can thank the H-2B program.) In February 2018, the alliance held a "fly-in" lobbying event in D.C. for members to pressure Congress to expand their cheap labor pipeline;[73] out-of-towners reportedly received a sweetheart discount at the Trump hotel.[74] In February 2019, journalist Peter D'Abrosca of the conservative Big League Politics news site reported that Mercedes Schlapp blocked Angel Moms, a group for parents of children killed by illegal alien criminals, from meeting with President Trump to express their opposition to a budget bill that shortchanged border wall funding.[75] In March 2019, despite adopting a "Hire American" job agenda, the Trump Department of Homeland Security raised the H-2B limit by 30,000 visas to a record high of 96,000.[76] Scores of those visas have gone to laborers at Trump's Mar-a-Lago hotel in Florida.[77]

All of this swampy business came to a climax after my CPAC 2019 speech sounding the alarm on open borders, in which I blasted Republican failures to control overall levels of both legal and illegal immigration. When I returned to the backstage VIP area, a man in a business suit approached me ... to pester me about the need to lift the H-2B visa cap! Ordinary citizens don't have access to the exclusive, roped-off areas. But deep-pocketed donors and corporate lobbyists do. The very next day, after heaping effusive praise on the Schlapps, President Trump gave a speech in which he sounded more like a Koch lobbyist than an America First champion. "We need an immigration policy that's going to be great for our corporations and our great companies," he insisted. "We need workers to come in" from abroad legally, he told stunned conservative immigration hawks, and he ad-libbed that America would welcome them all "in the largest numbers ever."[78] Out: America First. In: Cove Strategies First.

The unseemly conflict of interest in Matt Schlapp conducting his cheap-labor lobbying business and running CPAC while his wife works in the White House is classic D.C. access-trading.[79] Once the premiere gathering for the rank-and-file base of the conservative movement, CPAC has become an elitist pay-for-play operation that reflects the Open Borders Inc. agenda—not the grass roots. It's time to cancel this outdated and out-of-touch Beltway institution that marginalizes the youthful energy of millennial nationalists (some of whom were banned from the event in 2019), and which has long shunned and shunted immigration hawks unafraid to call out the Big Business influence on the party establishment. Anti-jihad investigative journalist Laura Loomer was banned from the conference for questioning why Right Wing Watch, Soros-backed People for the American Way, and CNN's Oliver Darcy (all left-wing operatives masquerading as journalists) were granted media credentials to sit and trash conservatives all day long.[80] CPAC punished her for "harassing" (translation: challenging) the propagandists.[81]

In chapter five, you'll learn much more about the insidious and bloody activities of what I call the A-Team of Open Borders Inc.: Abolish ICE, Antifa, and sanctuary anarchists. One of the anti-ICE doxxers was New York University adjunct professor Sam Lavigne, who worked at a Microsoft-supported program for the Tisch School of the Arts Interactive Telecommunications Program. I asked Microsoft spokeswoman Alexis Bridgewater whether the company approved of Lavigne posting the private information of 1,600 ICE employees—endangering the agents and exposing their families to potential harassment and harm. This was the bland response: "Thank you for your patience as I looked into your request. I have connected with my most appropriate colleagues, and unfortunately, we are unable to accommodate your request at this time. I apologize for any inconvenience this may cause."[82]

Microsoft couldn't even be bothered to provide a response. By not taking a side between violence-inciting, privacy-invading tech elites in the university system and rank-and-file immigration enforcement agents and their families, Microsoft *has* taken a side—standing squarely with the destructive forces on Open Borders Inc. You'll learn more about my interactions with PayPal, Apple, and other corporate flacks apathetic about their roles in enabling a left-wing witch hunt against peaceful, patriotic American citizens. The madness is beyond parody (but certainly very familiar if you read my third book, *Unhinged*).

You know who *is* safe from harm and free to speak at a venue full of conservative activists he despises? Self-avowed Communist Van Jones, who took CPAC's main stage to chatter away about criminal justice reform with former Koch lobbyist Schlapp. Jones's Color of Change group is dedicated to censoring and sabotaging right-leaning groups for championing the free market, opposing radical Islam, and exposing open borders. In 2012, I reported on how the group pressured Pepsi, McDonald's, Intuit, and other companies to cut ties to the mainstream American Legislative Exchange Council (ALEC), a half-century-old association of state legislators who believe in "the Jeffersonian principles of free markets, limited government, federalism, and individual liberty."[83] What was ALEC's crime? Drafting model legislation on voter ID to protect election integrity, immigration enforcement measures, and self-defense legislation to strengthen Second Amendment rights.[84] Color of Change and the Southern Poverty Law Center use the same playbook to marginalize and criminalize mainstream conservatives, anti-jihad groups, and immigration hawks as "hate groups" and push us out of the public square. As you'll see in chapter six, they conspire with payment processors and Silicon Valley to deprive sovereignty advocates of their livelihoods. They align with far-left "journalists" and violent anarchist groups to erase our borders by erasing those who speak out for our borders.

It's not a conspiracy theory that supposedly "mainstream" reporters actively promote Antifa and appear deeply embedded in their movement. In May 2019, online extremism researcher Dr. Eoin Lenihan published results of a data-mapping study and linguistic analysis involving nearly sixty thousand Antifa or Antifa-associated Twitter accounts and their overlapping connections with verified Twitter accounts of journalists—of which fifteen were journalists who work regularly with national-level news outlets. Lenihan found that of all fifteen verified national-level journalists in his research team's subset, "We couldn't find a single article, by any of them, that was markedly critical of Antifa in any way. In all cases, their work in this area consisted primarily of downplaying Antifa violence while advancing Antifa talking points, and in some cases quoting Antifa extremists as if they were impartial experts."[85] After Antifa harassed him for a week on Twitter following publication of his findings, Dr. Lenihan tweeted a warning on May 20, 2019, to Twitter CEO Jack Dorsey: "@jack, there is a massive Antifa problem on your platform."

Nine days later, Dr. Lenihan's whistle-blowing Twitter account was suspended.[86] Chapter 8 will plunge deeper into the cesspool that Lenihan investigated.

Once you start down the money trail of *Open Borders Inc.*, you'll be angered by how much taxpayers have been forced to prop up their own persecutors. Take JPMorgan Chase. As I will show you in chapter six, the financial giant threw its support to the leftist Southern Poverty Law Center and has shut down accounts of peaceful conservatives deemed "alt-right." At a shareholders' meeting in May 2019, David Almasi, vice president of the conservative-leaning National Center for Public Policy Research, protested the "de-banking" campaign by bringing a copy of George Orwell's *1984* for JPMorgan CEO Jamie Dimon.[87] "If Jamie Dimon can't absolutely guarantee that Chase Bank won't ever discriminate against conservatives," Almasi told the *New York Post*, "conservatives should consider banking elsewhere." Unfortunately for customers who choose to walk away from Chase, we can't get back any of the hundreds of millions of dollars of taxpayer subsidies that the company received as part of the government's Troubled Asset Relief Program that it spent on luxury jets and a luxury airport hangar renovation.[88] JPMorgan reaped a total of $25 billion in bailout funds under the Bush administration.

First, they splurge. Then, they purge. All at our expense.

How to Make America Disappear in Ten Steps

In 2003, former Colorado governor Dick Lamm delivered a pithy, viral speech on the bipartisan elites' plan to destroy America—from inventing multiculturalism, to establishing an unassimilated underclass, to promoting diversity above all else, enforcing victimology, and obstructing immigration enforcement.[89] This book updates and fleshes out many of those themes by immersing you in the identities, movements, patrons, and battle plans of the ground troops of Open Borders Inc.

How do you make America disappear?

Step One: Brainwash the children. Feed them "Teaching Tolerance" propaganda peddled by the Southern Poverty Law Center: "Display signs with messages like 'Migration is Beautiful' and 'No Human Being is Illegal.'"[90] Teach them to despise any form of enforcement. Instruct them to reject parents who value tradition, assimilation, and the rule of law. Bully those who think independently. Manipulate images of child migrants at every opportunity. Use them as human shields to prevent rational discussion of the consequences of open borders. Photograph and record them crying. Crying stifles dissent. Exploit the deaths of children at the border to incite hatred of the Border Patrol, ICE, and President Trump. Blame everyone but the parents, because blaming illegal aliens for anything equals hate!

Step Two: Infiltrate the churches. Use guilt to pressure good people to abet the Vatican's pursuit of power around the world. Twist the words of the Bible to defend reckless sanctuary policies and the lucrative refugee resettlement racket. Rake in billions of dollars to help Catholic operators of shelters across Mexico and Central America. Keep the Church's books closed and the borders open.

Step Three: Find a foreign billionaire hostile to America (it's easy if you try). Get him to fund a vast network of faith-based and secular non-profit "charities" so large that it is impossible to track all their work, spending, and coordination among themselves and with meddling international agencies and foreign governments. Deny, deny, deny that the network exists. Smear all who shed light on the network as racists, xenophobes, and anti-Semites. Repeat loudly and often.

Step Four: Sow constant fear and division by promoting multiculturalism and diversity in universities, the media, and Hollywood twenty-four hours a day, seven days a week. Reward victimhood. Punish "white privilege." Make it a thought crime to be proud of our country. Turn patriotism into "hate-riotism." Equate all peaceful nationalists with violent "white supremacists," even if they're yellow, brown, or black. Activate the social justice network against pro-sovereignty free speech online. De-platform all effective dissent from open borders.

Step Five: Invoke the Statue of Liberty over the U.S. Constitution in every immigration debate. Hijack the definition of "Who We Are" as a country. Obliterate the true meaning of "refugee" to facilitate the passage of migrant caravans full of job-seekers across our border. Create a refugee resettlement racket under the guise of humanitarianism that enriches the operators while burdening local communities with the crime, conflict, and costs of refugee dumps sponsored by the United Nations. Scream *"raaacist!"* if anyone complains.

Step Six: Take over law schools and never let go. Train legions of immigration lawyers, law clerks, and future men and women in black robes to embrace a ruinous combination of open borders and judicial supremacism. Fund legal foundations and non-profits to challenge every exercise of the president's plenary powers to enforce immigration laws. Create an illegal alien bar association to secure constitutional rights and due process for foreigners who have no right to be here. Permanently erase any distinction between alien and citizen.

Step Seven: Co-opt the Republican Party establishment. Exploit the statist U.S. Chamber of Commerce's and the agricultural lobby's thirst for cheap labor. Ally with Never Trumpers to prevent the southern border wall from ever being completed. Quietly lobby for cheap worker visa increases and mini-amnesties while the American public is distracted by non-essential partisan bickering.

Step Eight: Normalize violence against sovereignty activists. Spread "Punch a Nazi" memes on TV shows and in social media. Collaborate with open-borders journalists to downplay bloodthirsty anarchist movements and hype "hate crimes" reports by well-funded grievance-mongering operations (such as the Southern Poverty Law Center and the Council on American-Islamic Relations). "Doxx," defame, and harass grassroots activists and social media influencers to keep them on the margins of the public square.

Step Nine: Ban the following words, phrases, and concepts from acceptable discourse on immigration: invasion, illegal, alien, MS-13, crime, disease, fraud, Soros, chain migration, mob, animals, sharia, 9/11, Constitution, Make America Great Again, and, of course, open borders.

Step Ten: Prevent Americans from investigating the profiteers and engineers behind the "global migration crisis." Brand them as dangerous conspiracy nuts and push them off every available platform. Do not let them follow the money.

When you follow the money, you find the truth.

OPEN BORDERS INC.: BY THE NUMBERS

The making of America's "majority minority future"[1]

Total U.S. population: **325.7 million**[2]

Number of foreign-born individuals in the U.S.: **44.5 million** (1 in every 7.3 people or 13.7 percent of the population; the highest in 107 years.)[3]

Annual number of new green cards issued: **1.1 million**[4]

Estimated number of immigrants admitted over 35 years due to chain migration: **20 million**[5]

Estimated number of illegal aliens in the U.S.: **11 million**[6]–**17 million to 22.8 million–30 million**[7]

Illegal aliens granted Obama DACA protection from deportation and work permits: **800,000**

Estimated number of illegal visa overstayers in the U.S.: **4.5 million– 6 million**[8]

Estimated annual cost of illegal immigration to taxpayers (local, state, and federal): **$16 billion**[9]–**$54.5 billion**[10]

Number of people smuggled across Mexico to southern U.S. border every year: **800,000**[11]

Annual revenue from southern border smuggling enterprise: **$3.7 billion and $4.2 billion**[12]

Total number of illegal unaccompanied alien children (UAC) served in HHS tax-subsidized shelters: **340,000**[13]

Annual budget for HHS illegal alien children's housing (2017): **$1.4 billion**[14]

Total number of refugees settled in the U.S. since 1975: **3 million**[15]

Annual number of green cards issued to refugees/asylees: **146,000**[16]

Total annual humanitarian spending by U.S.: **$8 billion**[17]

State Department contractors' earnings per refugee resettled: **$2,125–$4,000 per refugee** for

initial reception and placement[18]

State Department annual spending on refugee processing and resettlement: **$545 million**[19]

Estimated total cost of resettling refugees over five years (including welfare, education, housing, and cash assistance): **$8.8 billion**[20]

Number of pending affirmative[21] asylum cases at end of 2018: Approx. **492,000 individuals.**[22]

Asylum backlog in U.S. immigration court system (2018): **348,000 individuals.**[23]

George Soros net worth: **$25.2 billion**[24]

Wealth transfer to Open Society Foundations announced in 2017: **$18 billion**[25]

OSF "immigrant rights" budget (1997-2013): **$100 million**

Anti-Trump speech policing initiative based on SPLC smear reports: **$10 million**[26]

OSF 2018 budget: **$1 billion**[27]

OSF 2018 spending on "migration" issues: **$63.3 million**[28]

Equity investments in "businesses that benefit migrants:" **$500 million**[29]

Catholic Church

Annual parish income: **$11.9 billion**[30]

U.S. Conference of Catholic Bishops total annual operating revenues, gains, and other support: **$274 million**[31]

Government contracts and grant revenue 2017: **$72 million**

Collection fees on refugee loans 2017: **$3.5 million**

Estimated total government refugee resettlement subsidies 2008-2017: **$534.7 million**

Catholic Campaign for Human Development

Spending on amnesty lobbying 2013: **$3.5 million**

Grants "to empower immigrant communities" 2014: **$4 million**

Catholic Legal Immigration Network, Inc. (CLINIC) annual budget (2017): **$12.8 million**

Catholic Relief Services annual revenue (2017): **$1 billion**[32]

Catholic Charities annual revenue (2016): **$3.8 billion**[33]

Revenue from government sources (2016): **$1.2 billion**

Remittances (money transfers) sent from illegal and legal alien workers in the U.S. to Mexico in 2018: **$34 billion**[34]

Percentage of population of Guatemala now living in the U.S.: **6.6 percent**[35]

Percentage of population of Honduras now living in the U.S.: **9.2 percent**[36]

Percentage of population of El Salvador now living in the U.S. **22 percent**[37]

U.S. Census projection of population change by 2060: **78.2 million people**[38]

Number of people projected to arrive in the U.S. via net international migration by 2060: **46.4 foreigners**[39]

Number of states with majority minority populations: 5 (**California, New Mexico, Hawaii, Texas,**[40] **and Nevada**[41])

Dates that next five states are projected to become majority minority: **Maryland (2020); Arizona (2023); Georgia (2025); Florida (2028); Alaska (2030).**[42]

Percent of congressional districts with foreign-born population above the national average that went Democrat: **Nearly 90 percent.**[43]

Election year in which Hispanic voters will replace black voters as largest potential minority voting bloc: **2020.**[44]

Fraction of U.S. voters who will have been foreign born in 2020 election: **1 in 10.**[45]

Date that America is projected to become a majority minority country: **2045.**[46]

CHAPTER ONE

SIN FRONTERAS: ALL ABOARD THE CARAVAN CARTEL

Amnesty begets amnesty. Immigration anarchy breeds more anarchy. Sanctioned lawlessness spawns ever more militant, entitled outlaws.

Irineo Mujica (also known as Irineo Mujica Azrate) is a dual Mexican-American citizen and a direct beneficiary of our suicidal amnesty policies. How has he repaid our generosity? By dedicating his life to erasing our borders and facilitating the very same mass lawbreaking that our nation's first mass amnesty was supposed to stop. As a lead organizer and the Mexico director of Pueblo Sin Fronteras, the trans-border trafficking outfit masquerading as a humanitarian group, Mujica is the man to whom *USA Today* gave singular credit for orchestrating floods of illegal aliens coming across our southern border.[1] "Perhaps no single person is more responsible for the huge caravans of migrants headed for the United States than Mujica," the newspaper gushed. He's been an open-borders travel agent and shelter operator for more than fifteen years.[2] Border Patrol and intelligence agents have documented Mujica's travel and interactions along the Arizona-Mexico border, including phone calls with Central American illegal aliens and a van filled with "items related to illegal border crossings, such as black water jugs and identification cards belonging to people who had been removed from the United States."[3] Shortly after President Trump announced plans to impose tariffs on Mexico in retaliation for the government's failures to control illegal alien surges in June 2019, Mexican authorities arrested Mujica and a colleague, Cristobal Sanchez, but later freed them citing insufficient evidence. "Human rights" journalist Madeleine Wattenbarger blamed the arrest on "right-wing media."[4]

Who enabled Irineo Mujica? In 1986, President Ronald Reagan signed the disastrous Immigration Reform and Control Act (IRCA), granting a path to citizenship to 2.7 million illegal aliens in exchange for purported border and interior enforcements. "It's high time we regained control of our borders," Reagan asserted at the time, "and this bill will do it."[5] Thanks to cheap-labor Republicans and cheap-vote Democrats, however, the legislation was followed by unprecedented illegal immigration—and seven more legislative amnesties between 1986 and 2000,[6] supplemented by President Barack Obama's administrative amnesties for upwards of four million illegal alien "youth" and their parents,[7] plus multiple extensions of the Temporary Protected Status program for an additional 300,000 illegal aliens.[8] Within a year of IRCA's passage, illegal immigration broke all previous records, skyrocketing to 800,000 per year. The "reform" and "control" parts of the Immigration Reform and Control Act vanished like mirages in the Sonoran Desert. *Adios.* Mujica, born in the Mexican state of Michoacán, says he and his family were farm workers who secured green cards through one of the agricultural amnesties embedded in IRCA.[9]

Various media accounts report that Mujica came to the United States at age thirteen to help pay for his sister's "quinceañera" (fifteenth birthday celebration) because his parents were too poor.[10] He says he grew up in Phoenix, where he joined an older brother. Were his family's 1986 amnesty claims legitimate? Who knows? I reached out to Mujica through the Pueblo Sin Fronteras Facebook page. Neither he nor the group replied.[11] This much is undeniable: both the Special Agricultural Workers (SAW) and Replenishment Agricultural Workers (RAW) programs—buried in IRCA at the behest of agribusiness interests—were plagued by fraud thanks to flimsy eligibility requirements and fake document mills run by unscrupulous labor contractors.[12] SAW applicants needed to prove they had been working illegally for ninety days; RAW applicants only needed to meet a twenty-day threshold. By comparison, the IRCA amnesty for non-agricultural workers required proof of residency for a five-year period. This led to a bumper crop of outlandish, phony farmworker claims that slipped through the cracks of overwhelmed immigration bureaucrats. As David North, a former top Labor Department official and immigration scholar who reviewed IRCA implementation for the Ford Foundation, reported: "There were countless anecdotes of fur-coat wearing Europeans seeking SAW status in Manhattan, applicants who contended that the cotton they harvested was purple, or that cherries were dug out of the ground, or that one used a ladder to pick strawberries. Often the temporary INS staffers handling the SAW applications were as clueless about agriculture as some of the applicants."[13] (Among the most notorious phony winners of the 1986 agricultural amnesty program I noted in *Invasion*: convicted 1993 World Trade Center bomber Mahmud Abouhalima, who arrived in the U.S. on a tourist visa in 1986, overstayed illegally, and fraudulently claimed to have worked on a farm in South Carolina to win his IRCA green card.[14])

With his farm workers' green card in hand, Mujica told a public radio reporter that he studied photojournalism and spent time in Minnesota before becoming a so-called "human rights defender."[15] He trained with George Soros–funded Doctors Without Borders, learning to administer first aid and heal foot wounds.[16] In 2008, he rode *"La Bestia*," the Mexican freight train network hijacked by Central American illegal aliens to get to the U.S., and photographed the journey. Amnesty International led an outcry after Mexican immigration officials accused Mujica of being a human trafficker.[17] How dare anybody get that wacky idea! In 2011, Mujica organized a protest caravan of five hundred marchers dubbed *"Paso a Paso Hacia La Paz"* ("Step by Step Towards Peace")[18] to drum up sympathy for migrants making dangerous journeys to the U.S.-Mexico southern border from southeastern Mexico near the Guatemalan border and from Guatemala City via bus and train through the southern Mexican states of Chiapas and Oaxaca.[19] It was one of three major caravans that year.

Embedded among the human rights radicals and family members of missing migrants from El Salvador, Honduras, and Guatemala were illegal alien laborers like construction worker Wilfredo from El Salvador, who told a reporter: "I want to reach Nuevo Laredo and pay a coyote (people smuggler) to cross the (Mexican-U.S. border) there."[20] He and other marchers on a quest for jobs chanted: "Migrants are not criminals, we are international workers." In other words: not desperate asylum seekers, not refugees escaping persecution or civil war.

The star of Mujica's 2011 Step by Step caravan was Mexican illegal alien deportee and sanctuary activist Elvira Arellano, who met the marchers at the "La 72" shelter in Tenosique, Mexico, near the Guatemalan border. Arellano had crossed the border illegally into the U.S. in the 1990s, was deported, then subsequently snuck back to the U.S, and lived in Washington State in 1997. Five years later, she was arrested for working at Chicago's O'Hare Airport with a fake Social Security number during the post-9/11 Operation Tarmac security sweep. She holed up at the Adalberto United Methodist Church in the Windy City in 2006 to avoid deportation and became the face of the long-festering illegal alien sanctuary movement in America. *Time* magazine named her a "Person of the Year."[21] (Living in the shadows is a terrible plight.) While awaiting her hearing, Arellano became a powerful illegal alien community organizer. She formed the non-profit illegal alien activist group La Familia Latina Unida and became co-chair of Centro Sin Fronteras, a sister organization founded by Emma Lozano, wife of Adalberto United Methodist Church's radical pastor, Walter "Slim" Coleman. He heads Familia Latina Unida Ministries[22] while Lozano serves as pastor at another Chicago sanctuary church, Lincoln United Methodist. Arellano was deported back to Mexico with her U.S.-born seven-year-old son in 2007, but she crossed the border again illegally for the third time as part of a protest caravan in 2014 with a new infant son on her back. She was released in San Diego, claimed asylum, and won a reprieve from deportation in 2017 despite her multiple illegal reentries after previous deportations and document fraud.[23]

The resistance apple doesn't fall far from the outlaw tree: Arellano's oldest son, Saul, is an outspoken anti-Trump amnesty-for-illegal-aliens advocate.[24] Only the best and brightest!

Arellano's La Familia Latina Unida and Lozano's Centro Sin Fronteras spawned Irineo Mujica's Pueblo Sin Fronteras, which at one point shared the same physical address as both the Adalberto United Methodist Church and La Familia Latina Unida: 2176 West Division Street, Chicago, Illinois.[25] Centro Sin Fronteras is headquartered at the Lincoln United Methodist Church on 2009 W. 22nd Place, where the vast majority of the congregation are illegal aliens and refugees.[26]

In 2014, while Arellano snuck her way back into America, Mujica and other "human rights defenders" organized a series of marches and protests across Mexico. Franciscan Friar Tomás González, director of the La 72 migrant shelter, led the annual Viacrucis Migrante, modeled after the Catholic stations of the cross during Holy Week, complete with biblical costumery and prop crosses.[27] The goal of Friar González and other Catholic priests sponsoring the event: to "establish the right for people to travel freely through Mexico, the abolishment of the National Institute of Migration" (Mexico's immigration enforcement agency), and "the guaranteed safety of all migratory routes."[28] That, my friends, is the essence of open borders. A reported 1,200 Central American illegal alien participants converged in Mexico City, and untold numbers of them successfully trespassed into the U.S.[29] A second caravan dubbed "the Caravan for Dialogue" soon departed from the Hermanos en el Camino (Brothers on the Path) migrant shelter in Ixtepec, Oaxaca, founded by Mexican Catholic priest Father Alejandro Solalinde Guerra. Among their demands: removal of security barriers and posts to prevent illegals from hopping on and off the La Bestia freight trains.[30] Mujica helped spearhead a third protest—a week-long hunger strike—in Mexico City in August 2014, where Pueblo Sin Fronteras conceived the idea of building a shelter in Chahuites, Oaxaca, known as Centro de Ayuda Humanitaria (the Center for Humanitarian Aid).[31] Mujica has founded a total of seven migrant shelters across Mexico.[32]

All of this planning, organization, and coordination was documented by Alex Mensing, who participated behind and in front of the camera on a video project extolling the Central American and Mexican "migrant defense movement" and the creation of the Collective of Defenders of Migrants and Refugees (CODEMIRE), in 2015.[33] Mensing is described by Frontline Defenders, a Dublin, Ireland-based human rights group, as a "member of Pueblo Sin Fronteras since 2014."[34] Frontline Defenders, which distributes grants and promotes featured human rights defenders, lists George Soros's Open Society Foundations among its donors.[35]

So, let's review: The 1986 amnesty allowed immigration outlaw Irineo Mujica to remain in America, get an education, earn a living, and establish himself as an illegal alien advocate on both sides of the border. He joined forces with defiant illegal alien deportee Elvira Arellano, who has been agitating against American sovereignty since her document-fraud arrest in 2002. During the Obama years, multiple caravans coalesced in Mexico, enabling untold numbers of Central American and Mexican illegal aliens to breach our borders—all with the aid and comfort of Catholic priests, Vatican-subsidized shelters, European NGOs, and Soros satellites. Pueblo Sin Fronteras has been explicit about its agenda for years: "Our mission is to provide shelter and safety to migrants and refugees in transit, accompany them in their journey, and together demand respect for our human rights."[36] The table was set for the most audacious caravan to date declared by Pueblo Sin Fronteras in March 2018—once again timed for Holy Week and the Easter season. This one was dubbed the 2018 Refugee Caravan ("Migrantes en la Lucha"). Two of the main points of media contact for the "collective" behind the caravan were Irineo Mujica and Alex Mensing. A Facebook post announced the plan and the demands, including that the U.S. and Mexico both "open the borders to us because we are as much citizens as the people of the countries where we are and/or travel" and "that deportations, which destroy families, come to an end." [See Appendix A.][37]

Open Borders Inc. motto: ask not what you can do for your country, but what you can demand of the countries you invade.

With their grandiose, Marxist-tinged manifestos, video hagiographies, and years of pilot caravan projects under their belts, the coordinators of the spring 2018 caravan were ready for prime time. The organizers were seasoned. The support network was wide and deep. Sympathetic media were geared up for the ride. When the second Pueblo Sin Fronteras-supported wave of at least four thousand illegal aliens struck the southern border in the fall of 2018, the media was quick to deny that there was any concerted effort to organize and transport the illegals, because "no group has claimed responsibility for organizing this week's caravan."[38] All hell broke loose after President Trump had the audacity to call the full-scale assault on our borders what it was: Not a mass "visit." Not a "protest." Not an "exodus." But a premeditated invasion.

Let's delve even deeper into the vast galaxy of enablers, propagandists, and legal vultures who are cashing in on the caravan cartel.

Shelters in Place

To fully appreciate the manufacturing of the 2018–2019 invasions of our southern border, you must first understand this: Pueblo Sin Fronteras is just one cog in the well-oiled, illegal-alien-caravan-generating machine. Let's start with what open-borders advocates themselves call their "Underground Railroad" of migrant safe houses that extend across Central America, through Mexico, and up and into the U.S.[39] We've touched on a few of the shelters (*casas de migrantes* or *albergues*) providing lodging, medical care, and sustenance to marchers across Mexico. This sprawling network of aid stations has been in place for years, bolstered by global interests, left-wing activists, and religious institutions that advocate for illegal aliens.

In 2012, for example, the United Nations' International Organization for Migration (IOM) in Mexico[40] signed "cooperation agreements" with three migrant shelters along Mexico's southern border to support their work assisting "irregulars" traveling through the Mexican states of Chiapas and Oaxaca on their way to the U.S. The IOM pact guaranteed supplies of medicine, hygiene products, construction materials, as well as therapy services and legal training at the previously mentioned Hermanos en el Camino shelter, along with the Catholic-run Hogar de la Misericordia shelter and Jesus el Buen Pastor del Pobre y el Migrante shelter. IOM extended similar aid to nine other migrant shelters in the northern and central parts of Mexico, from Chihuahua, Sonora, and Tamaulipas along the northern border to San Luis Potosi, Veracruz, and Tlaxcala in the center of the country.

Guess who subsidized the IOM shelter support program? The U.S. State Department's Bureau of Population, Refugees and Migration. In other words: you and me.

If you're Catholic, your collection plate dollars are most likely contributing to these and other shelters run by Jesuits, Franciscans, and Scalabrinian missionaries scattered across Mexico. The La 72 shelter in Tenosique is run by Franciscans. The El Caminante shelter in Palenque is overseen by Catholic nuns. The Scalabrinians operate Casa del Migrante in Tijuana and have managed an entire shelter ministry network since 1999.[41]

On the southern border of Mexico in Chiapas, the city of Tapachula is the first entry point for Central Americans headed to the U.S. There, the Fray Matías de Córdova Human Rights Center provides "comprehensive support" to illegal alien travelers, including legal consultations, monitoring detention centers, and offering "online resources, art and social activities, job training, and basic social services to migrants."[42] The group has received nearly $200,000 from the liberal MacArthur Foundation to "improve access to justice and services for the migrant population" in Chiapas.[43] Also in Tapachula, the Jesuit Refugee Service (JRS) opens its churches and pastoral centers to provide shelter, monetary aid, voluntary aid, and emergency assistance. Its team of lawyers, psychologists, social workers, and Jesuit clergy spread from Tapachula to Comalapa and Mexico City. JRS staff served as sherpas for the 2018 caravan marchers and liaisons with the U.N. High Commissioner for Refugees (UNCHR).[44]

There's no shortage of travel guides through the expansive network of Catholic volunteers. JRS is part of a binational coalition called the Kino Border Initiative (KBI) stationed in Nogales, Arizona, and Nogales, Sonora, Mexico, since 2009. Along with JRS, the partners who provide "direct humanitarian assistance and accompaniment" with migrants on the trespassing path are: the California Province of the Society of Jesus, the Missionary Sisters of the Eucharist, the Mexican Province of the Society of Jesus, the Diocese of Tucson and the Diocese of Nogales.[45] KBI members operate soup kitchens and first aid stations, in addition to overnight shelters and caravan escort services.

Médecins Sans Frontiéres (MSF)/Doctors Without Borders facilitates illegal immigration at our southern doorstep as well as across the Mediterranean Sea, as you'll see in chapter two. Since 2012, the group boasts, its activists have been providing medical care and mental health care in Mexico to migrants and refugees from Honduras, Guatemala, and El Salvador moving along the migratory route up through Mexico toward the U.S. MSF personnel are on the scene at migrant shelters and mobile clinics that parallel La Bestia railway lines. In addition, the organization opened a comprehensive health center in Mexico City in 2016 for caravan participants.[46] Psychologists, medical doctors, and social workers are at the ready, along with staff who provide a full range of caravan concierge services: "guidance, information on the migrant route and legal rights," plus "referrals to second and third level medical and mental health service providers." MSF workers treat "dehydration, skin infections, fatigue, acute stress, anxiety and depression," injuries from traveling on top of freight trains, and "injuries from violent incidents."[47]

If only my crappy Obamacare-era health insurance plan were half as generous.

The Mexico City region hosts a multitude of *casas de migrantes*. The El Samaritano migrant house provides meals, baths, medical care, and phone services. It is conveniently located along the train tracks, and has become an inevitable magnet for narcotics and human trafficking. "We will be here until the last migrant passes through," El Samaritano's Sister Rosa Bogado vowed to a *Miami Herald* reporter.[48] At Casa Mambré, a special LGBTQI unit houses transgender migrants who receive separate shelter and psychotherapy services.[49] Casa Tochán (which means "our house" in Nahuatl) teaches guests how to do woodwork and sell artisan crafts. Families bunking at CAFEMIN (Casa de Acogida, Formación y Empoderamiento de la Mujer y Internacional y Nacional, or "House for Shelter, Training and Empowerment of International and National Women") bake bread and receive asylum advice.[50] Casa del Migrante de Saltillo is gated and has "stunning" mountain views and close proximity to the train tracks. It provides three free meals a day and sells additional snacks and calling cards. Canada, the Netherlands, and the European Union provide donations to the migrant shelter.[51]

Next up: Yelp ratings and TripAdvisor reviews for illegal alien shelters? (I say this only half tongue in cheek. There is already a site called Contratados.org, which is billed as a Yelp or TripAdvisor-style tool that "lets migrant workers rate their experience of recruiters or employers online, by voicemail or by text message."[52])

The Mexican Government's Illegal Alien Welcoming Committee

You've heard of beta males, right? They're the emasculated weaklings who lack physical confidence and avoid conflict at all costs. Well, meet the appropriately named Los Grupos Beta ("the Beta Groups"). Funded by the Mexican government's National Institute of Migration, the trained officers of Grupos Beta are like our version of the Border Patrol—except they don't believe in enforcing borders and they don't have arms or equipment for patrolling. Instead, they act as a toothless welcoming committee that incentivizes and perpetuates illegal immigration.

The agency's motto is "vocation, humanitarianism, and loyalty." Translation: The Betas don't conduct arrests or deportations, just searches and rescues, emergency medical services, shelter referrals, and social and legal consultations. The agents also install thirty-three-foot-high "orientation" towers in the desert for lost and distressed migrants that beam strobe lights across a six-mile range. The beacons are equipped with a roof and water tank.[53] Once rescued by Betas wearing bright orange vests driving customized orange all-terrain vehicles, illegal aliens can take advantage of cell phones and discounted bus tickets offered by the government helpers.[54] For the migrant who can't quite find the right Fodor's guide to crossing the desert, the Betas generously published a thirty-two-page comic-style handbook (*Guía del Migrante Mexicano*)[55] with practical tips ("Thick clothing increases your weight when wet, and this makes it difficult to swim or float") and evasion techniques ("Avoid attracting attention, at least while you are arranging your stay or documents to live in the United States.... The best formula is to not alter your routine of going from work to home.")[56] Open-borders sympathizers praise the group as a compassionate provider of humanitarian aid. In practice, these feckless Betas serve as human trafficking co-conspirators luring migrants to danger and death.

In the Gulf Coast state of Veracruz, the governor initially offered shuttle service to caravan travelers before rescinding the offer due to a "water shortage" in his city.[57] But the border state of Coahuila provided its own brand of welcome wagon to caravan invaders in February 2019, when regional officials procured scores of buses with the help of private companies to transport 1,700 Honduran migrants through the Mexican interior to our southern border.[58] All aboard!

You've Got AOL!

"Al Otro Lado" means "on the other side" in Spanish. The 501(c)(3) non-profit of the same name serves illegal aliens on both sides of the U.S. border, with offices in Los Angeles and Tijuana. Co-founder Esmeralda Flores was stationed at the Casa del Migrante shelter in Tijuana as an attorney for a Mexican human rights group. While attending a legal training session in Los Angeles, she met Nora Phillips, a staff attorney at another open-borders group called CARECEN (Central American Resource Center). Their alliance spawned Al Otro Lado (AOL), a "binational, direct legal services organization serving indigent deportees, migrants, and refugees in Tijuana."[59] They help deportees sue to get back into the U.S. They've sued the Trump administration over asylum reform. They host large-scale "know your rights" seminars in Mexico and connect illegal aliens in detention with potential housing arrangements. AOL collaborates with the National Lawyers Guild to host *charlas* (chat sessions) in Tijuana to help illegal aliens navigate the asylum racket. The group also provides technical assistance to Mexican lawyers and takes advantage of volunteer help from attorneys, law professors, and law students from across the U.S. Make no mistake: putting illegal alien rights above American sovereignty pays. AOL's donation solicitation serves as an informative rate sheet for the group's booming legal enterprise:

- $5,000 pays for one refugee clinic, providing legal orientation for up to fifty refugee families
- $60,000 pays for one full-time legal assistant, drastically increasing program capacity and
- $90,000 pays for one full-time attorney representing dozens of refugee families in court [60]

In February 2019, Phillips and a colleague were denied entry into Mexico and detained for several hours. The lawyers accused the U.S. of directing Mexican government officials to "flag" them.[61] Phillips told *The Intercept* that it "was just literally hell on earth."[62] No, dear, not "literally." The left-wing publication decried homeland security monitoring of "journalists" and "advocates" including members of AOL and Pueblo Sin Fronteras, ominously reporting that it had "uncovered a pattern of heightened U.S. law enforcement scrutiny aimed at individuals with a proximity to the migrant caravans."[63] I'm glad somebody's watching out for *our side*. Our laws are clear, even if all the legal eagles at Al Otro Lado ignore it at their Tijuana chats and seminars with foreign clients: 8 U.S. Code Section 1324 makes it a felony to knowingly bring or attempt to bring aliens across the border illegally; to knowingly conceal, harbor, or shield them from detection in reckless disregard for the law; and to engage in any conspiracy or to aid and abet such acts.[64] Open-borders aiders and abettors deserve far more scrutiny than they're getting.

Off to the RAICES

The Refugee and Immigrant Center for Education and Legal Services (RAICES) is a 501(c)(3) nonprofit that "promotes justice by providing free and low-cost legal services to underserved immigrant children, families, and refugees in Central and South Texas."[65] Now the largest immigration nonprofit in Texas, with offices in Austin, Corpus Christi, Dallas, Fort Worth, Houston, and San Antonio, the group grew out of the Sanctuary movement of the 1980s and 1990s among Quakers, Catholics, and liberal evangelical Christians who criminally assisted and sheltered Central American illegal aliens with the help of more than five hundred congregations nationwide. Founding Sanctuary movement leader Jim Corbett "personally smuggled two hundred Salvadorians to safety in the U.S."[66] Another original Sanctuary movement activist, Jack Elder of San Antonio's Casa Oscar Romera refugee shelter in the Rio Grande Valley, was arrested twice for transporting illegal alien border-crossers.[67] Yet another founding father of the Sanctuary movement, John Fife, harbored an estimated fifteen thousand Central American illegal aliens through his Southside Presbyterian Church in Tucson, Arizona from 1982 to 1992, and founded No More Deaths in 2004 to continue sabotaging the border[68] under the guise of "humanitarian work" and "resistance."[69]

Now, RAICES coordinates pro bono legal representation for illegal aliens as part of the CARA Family Detention Project, whose partners include the Catholic Legal Immigration Network, the American Immigration Council, and the American Immigration Lawyers Association. The organization became the cause celebre of Hollywood bleeding hearts and Silicon Valley moguls in June 2018 after open-borders media outlets turned "Crying Girl"—Getty Images photographer John Moore's image of a two-year-old Honduran girl allegedly separated from her mother by cruel Border Patrol agents[70]—into a viral fundraising phenomenon.[71] Airbnb executive Dave Willner and his wife Charlotte posted a donation appeal on Facebook, which was circulated widely on Twitter by musicians, comedians, screenwriters, and other Hollywood hypocrites ensconced behind their high walls in Beverly Hills while working to knock down America's (see chapter seven). Within one month, RAICES had raked in an astounding $30 million[72]—all based on a caravan clickbait lie (chapter seven will also show you how Hollywood helped to perpetrate the Crying Girl hoax). The money will go to bond out detained illegal aliens—fueling the catch-and-release machinery—and to supplement the already well-funded resettlement services for unaccompanied minors and their families.

There's an App for That

Give me your poor, your tired, your huddled masses, yearning to recharge their smartphones. Not quite how I remember the Emma Lazarus poem. How about you? Like me, you may have noticed that while open-borders media advocates keep telling us of the impoverished desperation of caravan marchers, their photos and videos keep showing us large crowds of migrants with fists full of smartphones,[73] earbuds, and power cords in hand[74] to facilitate their border-trespassing and stay in touch with friends and family along the way. These oppressed travelers now use Facebook and WhatsApp (owned by Facebook) to coordinate their journeys. As Abbdel Camargo, an anthropologist at the College of the Southern Border in Mexico, explained to the Associated Press, "The social networks have had an empowering role in this new way of migrating."[75] Indeed, NGOs, advocacy groups, and financial institutions have created an array of free apps to "help." The U.N.'s International Organization for Migration offers MigApp on Google Play and Apple's App Store with information and "assistance to migrate safely."[76] The app features weather and crime alerts, medical clinic appointment scheduling, and money transfer services (more on that in a moment). Just to make Silicon Valley's sympathies clear: an app that aids and abets illegal immigration and human smuggling is approved on Google Play and Apple's App Store, but social media app Gab—a free speech-promoting micro-blogging tool used by anti-open borders activists and deemed unacceptably "alt-right"—is banned.[77]

The International Committee of the Red Cross's WhatsApp alerts provide "advice on how to avoid and prevent accidents, illness and being separated from family members," as well as a means "to share the geo-location of a shelter or send specific advice or alerts in the event of unexpected situations."[78] United We Dream's Notifica app is also available on Google Play and the Apple App Store. It gives illegal alien travelers a "help button" to alert friends, family, lawyers, media propagandists, and others in case of detention or encounters with law enforcement.[79]

Border saboteurs have used technology for decades to help undermine immigration enforcement. Ricardo Dominguez created a crowd-sourced website-jamming network in the 1990s called FloodNet, "which allowed anyone with an internet connection to gum up the official sites of the US Border Patrol, White House, G8, Mexican embassy, and others, rendering them inaccessible," *Vice* reported.[80] He then introduced the Transborder Immigrant Tool in 2009 using cheap thirty-dollar Motorola cell phones equipped with a free GPS applet to help illegal aliens navigate desert routes, locate water stations, and determine their proximity to highways.[81] An expert consulted by the U.N. High Commissioner for Refugees (UNHCR) lauded "how smart phones and social media have revolutionized" migration, allowing refugees to bypass "legal means" of finding agents that "take a long time" and instead use the "dark digital underworld" for "facilitating access to agents and smugglers" through "encrypted Facebook and WhatsApp channels."[82]

Move over, Uber, Viber, and Tumblr. Here comes Smugglr!

Kiddie Catch, Release, and Cash In

Speaking of smuggling, let's get to the bottom of the "unaccompanied alien minors" racket. The scandal isn't that President Trump is tearing children out of parents' arms. The true moral outrage is that a transnational network of open-borders opportunists has created a de facto illegal alien child smuggling ring operating in plain sight under the guise of family reunification and phony "refugee resettlement."

Just as the shelter network is central to incentivizing Central American caravans to trek across Mexico, government-funded housing in the U.S. serves as a powerful magnet for families and smugglers to send children alone on the treacherous journey to our southern border. Thanks to a landmark class-action settlement in 1997 between open-borders groups and the Clinton administration, known as the *Flores v. Reno* Settlement Agreement, the feds created new rights and standards for shelter care for illegal alien minors. Clinton immigration bureaucrats agreed to provide food, clothing, personal grooming items, medical and dental care, family planning services, academic classes, "appropriate reading materials in languages other than English for use" during the minor's recreational times, "at least one hour a day of large muscle activity," "structured leisure time activities," social work, group counseling, "access to religious services of the minor's choice," "legal services information regarding the availability of free legal assistance, the right to be represented by counsel," "the right to a deportation or exclusion hearing," and "the right to apply for political asylum."[83]

After the 9/11 terrorist attacks, President Bush signed the Homeland Security Act of 2002 transferring responsibility for unaccompanied alien children (UACs) from immigration enforcement agencies to the Department of Health and Human Services' Office of Refugee Resettlement (HHS/ORR). In 2008, the William Wilberforce Trafficking Victims Protection Reauthorization Act was signed into law at the end of the

Bush administration. Intended to stop child sex trafficking and named after the nineteenth-century British abolitionist, the act gave children from non-contiguous countries (countries other than Mexico and Canada) full immigration court hearing privileges instead of being summarily turned away. (Thanks, Dubya!) Word spread to Central America that if illegal alien parents in the U.S. could shell out for smugglers ("coyotes") to guide their unaccompanied children across the border, the kids would "end up in immigration limbo with little threat of deportation—all the while getting a decent education."[84]

I call it "Kiddie Catch, Release, and Cash In."

Within seventy-two hours of arrival on American soil, eligible UACs are turned over to HHS/ORR, which pays private operators to provide the illegal alien children immediate shelter and integrate them into communities "in the least restrictive setting that is in the best interest of the child."[85] The HHS/ORR grantees, who receive hundreds of millions of dollars in government contracts, provide a wealth of social, medical, educational, and legal services to alien youths while they await adjudication of their cases in the hopelessly overwhelmed and backlogged immigration court system,[86] which I documented extensively in *Invasion*. HHS now operates a sprawling network of 100 state-licensed shelters in 17 states[87] and has provided care to a total of more than 340,000 children.[88] (For perspective: that's a population roughly equivalent to the city of Anaheim, California, or Aurora, Colorado.) In fiscal year 2014 alone, the unaccompanied children program's total operating budget for care and placement was nearly $912 million, serving 58,000 children in a variety of shelters, foster care units, residential treatment centers, and medium- and high-security facilities.[89] In 2017, the budget was $1.4 billion.[90] The Capital Research Center's analysis of grant data for that year found that 40,810 UACs[91] were referred to 48 different organizations providing shelter services at a cost of over $34,000 for each child; dividing that number by the average length of stay in 2017 (48 days) yielded a cost of over $700 per day, per individual, according to the center.[92] The big kahunas in the alien minor shelter business are Texas-based Baptist

Child and Family Services (BCFS) and Texas-based Southwest Key Programs. In 2017, BCFS received $228 million to serve UACs;[93] Southwest Key received $286 million to serve UACs.[94] According to the Capital Research Center, government funding accounted for 90 and 99 percent of the two nonprofits' budgets respectively.[95]

Secular and private for-profit groups have also carved out niches in the illegal alien kid-care industry. So have local governments. At one such HHS facility run by Yolo County, California, where residents stayed an average of sixty-two days in 2016, illegal alien children receive access to anger management training, meditation classes, "bi-weekly yoga," movie nights, "board games, computer games, and Kinect games on the Xbox 360, ping-pong, and air hockey" before being transferred to group homes, reunified with parents or sponsors, or repatriated[96] back to their home countries.[97] An estimated 96 percent of unaccompanied minors released to a sponsor were released to a family member already here in the U.S in 2014; nearly 60 percent were parents or legal guardians.[98] A Freedom of Information Act request by the Associated Press revealed that a whopping 80 percent of the seventy-one thousand mostly Central American children resettled in the U.S. between February 2014 and September 2015 were sent to illegal alien sponsors; another 6 percent were placed with illegal alien adults who had temporary protected status; and 1 percent were placed with illegal aliens in deportation proceedings.[99] Sponsor families automatically receive at least six months of "post-release" services and benefits (such as "psycho-educational support" and "low cost or pro bono immigration legal assistance")—paid for by taxpayers and provided by the Lutheran Immigration and Refugee Service (LIRS) and the United States Conference of Catholic Bishops (USCCB) for the past quarter-century.[100]

The William Wilberforce Trafficking Victims Protection Reauthorization Act also authorized HHS to create and fund a "Child Advocate" program, which provides legal advocates who accompany UACs to immigration court proceedings to "make recommendations regarding the best interest of the child with respect to custody, care, legal representation, and other issues to immigration judges, asylum officers, and federal agencies, including ORR."[101] The Young Center for Immigrant Children's Rights, based at the University of Chicago Law School and backed by the open-borders Tides Foundation, holds the exclusive contract with HHS/ORR to run the Child Advocate program.[102] Additionally, as a result of the *Flores* agreement, ORR contracts with the Vera Institute and the U.S. Committee for Refugees and Immigrants (which subcontract to other non-profits) to provide "Know Your Rights" seminars and legal screening for UACs.[103] George Soros's Open Society Institute (OSI) provided at least $200,000 to the Vera Institute, which was founded by OSI trustee Herbert Sturz.[104] (We'll delve more into the activities of the U.S. Committee for Refugees and Immigrants, which has helped resettle thousands of UACs, refugees, and Special Immigrant Visa recipients, in Chapter 4.[105])

Immigration scholar and *Stolen Sovereignty* author Daniel Horowitz summed up the scheme enabled by the William Wilberforce Trafficking Victims Protection Reauthorization Act: "A statute that was designed to protect victims of sex trafficking who were truly destitute and without parents in this country is now being abused to fund a circuitous smuggling operation in which illegal immigrant parents smuggle in their own children."[106]

In June 2012, President Obama announced his Deferred Action for Childhood Arrivals (DACA) executive order granting amnesty to illegal alien youth who had arrived in the U.S. by 2007 before age sixteen. In November 2014, Obama expanded the mass deportation pardons to a wider group of illegal aliens who had been in the country since 2010, extended the work authorization grace period from two to three years, and created the Deferred Action for Parents of Americans and Lawful Permanent Residents (DAPA) for illegal alien parents of anchor babies and green card-holding children.[107] Texas sued to stop DAPA, which was never implemented as a result of a federal court injunction, and the White House rescinded it in June 2017.[108] But approximately 800,000 illegal aliens have received DACA protection and work permits so far while that program is tied up in litigation and President Trump's planned phaseout remains in limbo.[109] The details mattered little to lawbreaking families around the world who got wind of the ongoing promise of amnesty on the backs of their children. Former ambassador to the Organization of American States Roger F. Noriega testified before the Senate Homeland Security and Governmental Affairs Committee in 2015 that "brazen radio advertising campaigns" across Central America by coyotes spread word of *permisos* (free passes) to minors reaching U.S. territory.[110] Widespread publicity about President Obama's executive DACA and DAPA amnesties fueled the child alien smuggling fire.

Escaping violence is the standard open-borders talking point to explain the Central American exodus. The American Civil Liberties Union blamed "domestic violence and gang brutality."[111] The United Nations likewise decried "horrific gang violence."[112] Democratic presidential candidate and former El Paso, Texas, Congressman "Beto" O'Rourke cited "brutality" and "violence"[113] as the driving factors. There's no question that the "Northern Triangle" countries of Central America (Guatemala, Honduras, and El Salvador) are among the most violent in the world. But homicide rates have either fluctuated (in El Salvador) or fallen significantly (in Guatemala and Honduras) since Obama's DACA and DAPA programs were announced.[114] Matthew Sussis of the Center for Immigration Studies reported that Honduran murder rates have fallen by over half since 2011; Guatemala's homicide rate has similarly declined.[115] Moreover, the migrants themselves refute the "fleeing violence" narrative: an International Organization for Migration poll of more than 3,200 Guatemalan households in 2016, highlighted by the Center for Immigration Studies' Kausha Luna, reported that 91 percent of migrants surveyed had moved to the U.S. for economic reasons (jobs, homes, income boosts)—while only 0.3 percent blamed violence, 0.2 percent cited extortion, and 0.2 percent attributed their decision to gangs.[116]

One Guatemalan smuggler told journalist Richard Pollock: "Obama has helped us with the children because they're able to stay

in the United States. That's the reason so many children are coming."[117]
The smuggler described a transcontinental network of 5,000 coyotes
and recruiters working in cahoots with former and current Guatemalan
officials to transport thousands of illegal aliens and their children in
anticipation of amnesty, jobs, free public education, and welfare.[118]
According to the United Nations Office on Drugs and Crime (UNODC),
upwards of 820,000 people per year are smuggled along the land route
through Mexico to North America.[119] Between 200,000 and 400,000
of them are now from Central America.[120] This smuggling enterprise
generated between $3.7 billion and $4.2 billion per year in revenue in
2016. Smuggling fees are estimated at $5,000 per head for Mexicans
and an average of $7,000 per head for Central Americans.[121] Children
receive discounted rates. Some smugglers offer special "VIP packages"
like the $10,000 option for a single adult to be driven all the way to
Houston or the $6,000 adult-and-child bargain deal with a drop-off
at a South Texas riverbank.[122]

Drug cartels controlling huge swaths of the U.S.-Mexico border grab
their own piece of the pie through *derecho de piso* ("right of passage"),
a tax paid by smugglers to use routes under the drug traffickers' control.
Failure to pay can result in torture or execution of the smugglers or the
illegal immigrants themselves.[123] Center for Immigration Studies fellow
Andrew Arthur pointed to a March 2019 article from the *Texas Tribune*
reporting on the Gulf Cartel's smuggling surcharge of "$1,000 to $1,500
per person to let migrants cross its territory."[124] The RAND Corporation
estimated revenue from *derecho de piso* at anywhere between $30 mil-
lion to $180 million in 2017.[125]

Federal judge Andrew Hanen of the Southern District of Texas—
apparently one of the few judges in the entire U.S. who believes our
country's laws should be enforced—blew the lid off the Obama administration's deplorable role as child smuggling facilitators in a scathing
ruling on the case of *U.S. v. Mirtha Veronica Nava-Martinez*. Nava-
Martinez, a resident alien, was an admitted human trafficker caught at
the border trying to smuggle an El Salvadoran minor into the U.S. using

a birth certificate that belonged to one of Nava-Martinez's daughters. The transaction had been arranged by the minor's illegal alien mother living in Virginia.[126] She paid $6,000 up front on an $8,000 fee. After Nava-Martinez and the child were caught, the Department of Homeland Security did not arrest the mother. Instead, DHS "delivered the child to her" in Virginia, "thus successfully completing the mission of the criminal conspiracy.... Instead of enforcing the laws of the United States, the Government took direct steps to help the individuals who violated it."[127]

Judge Hanen noted that the Nava-Martinez case was the fourth that had come before his court in which illegal alien parents had paid smugglers to bring minor children across the border and the U.S. government had abetted the operations. He called the federal government's actions "dangerous" and "unconscionable" for inducing parents to jeopardize their own children's safety by turning them over to strangers engaged in criminal activity and risking their lives in the desert—not to mention the impact of helping "fund the illegal drug cartels which are a very real danger for both citizens of this country and Mexico."[128] Indeed, Judge Hanen warned, "the government is not only allowing them to fund the illegal and evil activities of these cartels, but is also inspiring them to do so."[129]

In the early Obama years, only a handful of unaccompanied minors entered the U.S. from El Salvador, Guatemala, and Honduras. The numbers have exploded since then. In fiscal year 2014, more unaccompanied children from El Salvador crossed our southern border than the combined total of the previous five years. The same is true for unaccompanied children from Guatemala and Honduras. The increase in Guatemalan unaccompanied alien children and family units was especially striking. As mentioned previously, the smuggling network in that country is vast and said to involve both former and current government officials. Despite DHS officials paying visits to Guatemalan villages warning them against fraudulent claims by coyotes,[130] impoverished families were not deterred. Smugglers advertised illusory charter buses that would reunite customers with relatives in the U.S.[131]

An estimated 980,000 Guatemalans, legal and illegal, already live in the U.S. In May 2019, a Guatemalan newspaper, *Prensa Libre*, reported that in a recent survey conducted by the Association for Research and Social Studies and Barometro de las Americas, 39.2 percent of Guatemalans told pollsters they would like to leave the country, and of that number 85 percent said they would like to move to the United States. Out of a population of 16 million in Guatemala, that translates to 5 million of its impoverished citizens wanting to crash our gates. And "if the same percentage of people who would like to come here from Guatemala hold that view in El Salvador and Honduras," Daniel Horowitz calculates, "that would be roughly 10.7 million people ready to march north under the right circumstances."[132] An El Paso Intelligence Center report in May 2014 revealed that 219 of 230 unaccompanied children and border-crossing families in the Rio Grande Valley told the Border Patrol their primary reason for migrating to the United States was that they believed U.S. immigration laws granted free passes or *permisos* to unaccompanied children or to adult females from Central America traveling with minors.[133] A majority of migrants interviewed by El Paso Sector Border Patrol agents indicated they planned to surrender to U.S. authorities because they were informed that they would likely be released. Put on your shocked faces again: in May 2019, the acting chief of U.S. Immigration and Customs Enforcement's deportation branch reported to Congress that a whopping 87 percent of illegal alien families caught and released after crossing the border are failing to show up for their hearings.[134]

Another immigration magnet switched on when President Obama created the Central American Minors Refugee/Parole Program (CAM) in November 2014 for children of Central American parents living in the U.S. The pretext of the scheme was to spare children left behind in Central America the dangerous land journey to get here by declaring them "refugees" in their native countries and then flying them to the U.S. at U.N./State Department expense. Those determined not to meet the definition of "refugee" would be granted entry into the country through "parole" and be allowed to remain while awaiting adjudication of their cases in American immigration courts. The Obama administration implemented the program after meeting with the presidents of El Salvador, Guatemala, and Honduras and promoting the concept that America had a "shared responsibility" with Central America to address the region's violence, drug trafficking, and migrant outflow.[135] "Shared responsibility" meant putting the burden on Americans to take in tens of thousands of new illegal aliens on top of the millions already here, while Central American leaders lectured us about the need to show even more "humanitarian" compassion and demanded even more foreign aid than the nearly half-billion allocated to Central America and Mexico in 2014 (plus an additional $650 million for a regional security initiative since 2008).[136]

Under CAM, only families from the Northern Triangle of Central America qualified for the new joint initiative of the State Department and Department of Homeland Security. As originally proposed, only parents who were here *legally* from those countries could petition for their children; DNA testing was required. But the definition of "lawful" included *illegal* aliens from Central America here in America who had secured de facto amnesty through "temporary protected status," "deferred enforced departure" enrollment, and "deferred action."[137] Make no mistake. This program provided a blanket amnesty extension and path to green cards and citizenship under the phony guise of addressing a "humanitarian" crisis. By law, the federal government's immigration "parole" authority is intended to be used "sparingly" only for "compelling" and "urgent medical, family, and related needs" on a "case-by-case basis."[138] Instead, CAM brazenly encouraged a rush to the U.S. to take advantage of an amnesty program created administratively with no input from Congress and no support from the American public.

To create thousands of Special Immigrant Juvenile (SIJ) visas for these instant "refugees," the Obama White House hijacked a Special Immigrant Visa program (EB-4/I-360) created for religious workers,

Iraqi and Afghan translators, and interpreters who assisted U.S. military forces, and international organization workers.[139] Toward the end of the Obama presidency, the number of SIJ applications and approvals exploded. Since President Trump came into office, however, there has been a sharp reduction in the number of approved applications.[140] You can well imagine what the trend line would have looked like had Hillary Clinton won office.

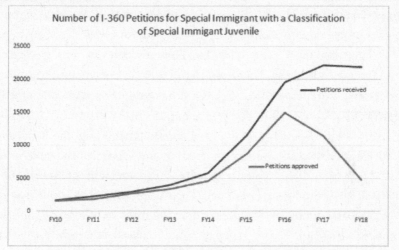

Number of I-360 Petitions for Special Immigrant with a Classification of Special Immigrant Juvenile

Here's the kicker: SIJ applicants are only eligible if they have been abused, neglected, or abandoned by parents or guardians[141]—yet as we have seen, the majority of Central American minors entering the U.S. are reunited with, yep, their illegal alien parents (untold numbers of whom paid smugglers to get them here). Family reunification is a disqualifier for the SIJ visa, but it's the central goal of the CAM racket, and illegal alien sponsors/petitioners are the instigators. Seasoned immigration lawyers, keenly aware of the chronic green-card backlog, are lobbying the feds to grant "deferred action" (deportation reprieves and work permits) to SIJ applicants in limbo.[142]

Thomas Homan, former acting director of ICE, told immigration analyst and author Daniel Horowitz that gangbangers have been among the CAM refugee/parole beneficiaries. "[I]n one operation against

MS-13," he disclosed to Horowitz, 40 percent of those caught were unaccompanied alien children resettled through this very program designed for refugees. "Many that entered the U.S. were already gang members or soon became gang members after arriving in the U.S.," Homan told Horowitz, who added that we've "witnessed a spike in MS-13 growth over the past few years as a result of the influx of Central American teens in 2014. One can only imagine the degree of danger our country is in from the exponentially higher number of teens coming in under the same circumstances."[143]

Mercifully, the Trump State Department stopped granting parole to CAM refugee/parole applicants in August 2017 and terminated the whole program in November 2017. But the flow of unaccompanied alien children into the U.S. during the first six months of FY 2019 was unabated. An estimated 62 percent of all aliens apprehended along the Southwest border were unaccompanied alien children and aliens traveling in "family units" (alleged parents or legal guardians traveling with children); those groups constituted 48 percent of all aliens deemed inadmissible at the ports of entry along that border.[144] In May 2019, ICE released another flabbergasting figure: the agency revealed that 168,000 family members over the previous four months had been released. "We've released four times as many people as we're able to arrest on annual basis," acting ICE director Matt Albence told reporters.[145]

The surge of "family units" bringing children across the border was further incentivized by the Obama administration, a liberal California judge, and the Ninth Circuit Court of Appeals. Remember the aforementioned *Flores* Settlement Agreement, which set standards for detention and care of illegal alien children? In July 2015, Central District of California federal judge Dolly Gee sided with liberal immigration advocates, who had sued to stop detention of parents and children at three immigrant family detention centers in Karnes, Texas; Dilley, Texas; and Berks, Pennsylvania. Judge Gee reinterpreted the *Flores* agreement to require that *all* illegal alien children be released from federal custody if they were not being held in licensed, non-locked down, HHS-approved facilities (which includes the three named facilities). Judge Gee also determined that all illegal alien children should be released from such facilities, whether they came here unaccompanied or with an alleged parent. Further, Judge Gee ruled, illegal alien parents who crossed the border with their children and were taken into custody together after being caught trespassing the border as a family unit (as opposed to presenting themselves at a port of entry claiming asylum) must all be released together *within twenty days*.[146] In 2016, a panel of the Ninth Circuit Court of Appeals upheld Gee's determination that all illegal alien children be released, but reversed her parental release decree.[147] Meanwhile, in May 2019, another set of liberal lawyers filed suit demanding the release of up to 2,350 unaccompanied minors in a Florida detention center.

Republican Senator Ron Johnson of Wisconsin, chairman of the Senate Committee on Homeland Security and Governmental Affairs, publicized a stark graphic that illustrates acting DHS secretary Kevin McAleenan's blunt conclusion that the *Flores* settlement "has been the essential driver, frankly, for the increase in family units."[148] Rule of human nature confirmed: people respond to incentives.

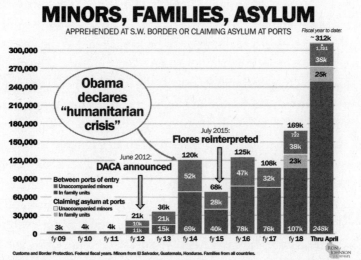

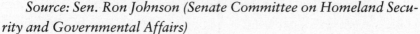

Source: Sen. Ron Johnson (Senate Committee on Homeland Security and Governmental Affairs)

Even as the Trump administration sought to push back the tide of Central American unaccompanied minors and adults hauling children to the border to game the system through ongoing court battles and attempted implementation of a "zero-tolerance" crackdown on trespassers at the border,[149] families from around the world clamored to take advantage of kiddie catch-and-release. At the end of May 2019, border patrol agents caught 116 illegal aliens with children from Angola, Cameroon, and the Congo near Del Rio, Texas. "Bring a child, get released," one border official summed it up for the *Washington Times*.[150] In the Border Patrol's Del Rio Sector, family unit apprehensions are up 374 percent compared to 2018.[151] In the El Paso Sector, family unit apprehensions are up a flabbergasting 1,816 percent.[152]

Where there's a will, there's always a perverse way to exploit the children. At the border, the promise of amnesty is the mother of invention. In spring 2019, Border Patrol agents discovered a "recycled" illegal alien kid who had been used by at least three "families" of unrelated adults attempting to get into the U.S. from Mexico.[153] Back and forth, the minor would travel across the border each time with a new set of "relatives." He was not alone. The *Arizona Daily Star* uncovered the scheme of fake "father" Maynor Velasquez Molina, who paid $130 to the family of an eight-year-old boy so he could pretend the boy was his son when they entered the United States. The fraudster showed Border Patrol agents a Guatemalan birth certificate to prove the boy was his son, the paper reported, but four days later agents determined the claim was false. Velasquez Molina said "he was told that it was easier to get into the United States with a child," according to a criminal complaint.[154]

"In just a couple of weeks, we've interviewed 256 family units and identified 65 fraudulent families. Almost 3 out of every 10 families we've interviewed have become fraudulent," acting ICE director Matthew Albence told Breitbart in May 2019.[155] The practice is orchestrated by transnational criminal organizations, agents said, to increase their smuggling profits.[156] One Guatemalan woman in South Carolina recycled children 13 times for payments of $1,500 each.[157] More than 3,100 illegal border-crossers were caught making false claims about their ages and family relations in 2019.[158] A rapid DNA testing pilot program run in April 2019 determined that 30 percent of suspicious "families" apprehended at the border in McAllen and El Paso, Texas, were fraudulent.[159]

The costs to U.S. taxpayers are considerable, including transportation, room, board, and guardian services to reunite unaccompanied children with their illegal alien "parents" or family members who initiated the smuggling operations. Look at just one sector: for the first half of FY 2019, the Yuma Sector Border Patrol spent more than $1 million on humanitarian costs for families and unaccompanied alien children in U.S. custody, compared to $340,000 for all of FY 2018, according to U.S. Customs and Border Protection. These costs include food, diapers, clothes, baby formula, and other items.[160] But some innocent American families have paid a far higher price—in bloodshed and lost lives. One nineteen-year-old Honduran classified as an unaccompanied minor, Edwin (or "Eswin") Mejia, crossed the southern border illegally in May 2013 near Nogales, Arizona, was moved to a temporary HHS shelter in Los Angeles, was released to an illegal alien sponsor in Tennessee (his older brother), and then allegedly killed twenty-one-year-old Iowan Sarah Root while driving drunk in January 2016.[161] He was released on bond, then absconded, and he remains a fugitive on the ICE Most Wanted list.[162]

I repeat: Amnesty begets amnesty. Immigration anarchy breeds more anarchy. Sanctioned lawlessness spawns ever more militant, entitled outlaws.

At a Senate Homeland Security and Governmental Affairs Committee hearing in April 2019, Senator Ron Johnson released figures showing that between July 2018 and January 2019, 23,445 unaccompanied children were released to sponsors. Of those sponsors, nearly 70 percent did not have legal status in the United States. In fact, 21 were under final orders to be removed from the country, 6 were denied asylum and were appealing to a federal court, and nearly 3 percent were in removal proceedings to be kicked out of the country.[163] Center for Immigration

Studies fellow Andrew Arthur observed, "Adding just those categories together, more than 81.5 percent of all UAC sponsors had no status or were facing the prospect of removal. Interestingly, 1,006 sponsors were listed as 'other,' an unclear identifier given the fact that U.S. citizens, lawful permanent residents, and even aliens with certain nonimmigrant statuses were individually identified. In addition, 958 (4 percent) of those sponsors had Temporary Protected Status (TPS). The aliens in that status are in an extremely uncertain position as relates to the immigration laws of the United States."[164]

According to a legal source who briefed me on the CAM scam, the farce is compounded by the fact that while the program's beneficiaries awaited court proceedings, President Obama put them in a "subsidized holding pattern until a visa was available or until they'd established a continued presence for another program."[165] Those subsidies include foster care payments under the federal Title IV-E foster care program. Several states, including California, Massachusetts, Michigan, New Jersey, and Oregon, have carved out exceptions to federal prohibitions so that illegal alien sponsors can be compensated for foster care of illegal alien youths.[166]

In April 2019, HHS secretary Alex Azar reported that the Office of Refugee Resettlement anticipated that it would run out of funding for its UAC program by the end of the year, after spending a total of $1.3 billion so far on illegal alien resettlement and child welfare operations. Azar announced a total of $831 million in diverted funds from other HHS programs to fill the gap.[167] Those funds for illegal alien families were transferred from HHS programs designed to help Americans, including Head Start, Centers for Disease Control and Prevention initiatives, cancer prevention, and Alzheimer's care.[168]

There's nothing humanitarian about robbing Americans to pay an out-of-control, transnational illegal alien smuggling ring fueled by illegal alien parents who consciously chose to separate their own families in the first place and endanger their own children by entrusting them to lawless smugglers, who paid off drug cartels to get across the southern border.

Worst of all, the entire enterprise was aided by the U.S. Department of Homeland Security, paid for by you and me, all in the name of "keeping families together."

Banking on Illegals

I've reported on the shameless illegal alien pandering of Big American Banks for nearly twenty years. Just months after the 9/11 terrorist attacks in 2001, for example, Wells Fargo, U.S. Bancorp, Firstar Bank, Harris Bank, Union Bank, and U.S. branches of the Puerto Rico-based Banco Popular all announced plans to loosen identification guidelines for Mexican customers looking to open American checking or savings accounts. Banks usually require foreign customers to show passports as a primary form of identification, with credit cards and Social Security numbers or federal taxpayer ID numbers as backup documents. But after heavy lobbying from the Mexican government and Latino activists, Wells Fargo led the financial industry's move to accept the ID card issued by Mexican consulate offices known as *matrícula consular*. Any Mexican national living abroad (translation: any *illegal* Mexican immigrant living in the U.S.) was now able to get the card by simply supplying proof of Mexican citizenship, such as a birth certificate or voting card. No other secondary ID was required if a Wells Fargo customer signed a residency form from the Internal Revenue Service—which vowed not to share it with immigration enforcement officials.[169]

In 2007, the *Wall Street Journal* reported that Bank of America was rolling out new credit cards "to customers without Social Security numbers—typically illegal immigrants."[170] Its first testing grounds were fifty-one branches in Los Angeles County, home to the largest concentration of illegal aliens in the U.S. In response to concerns about the national security implications and open-borders endorsement of the program, Brian Tuite, the bank's director of Latin America card operations and one of the architects of the program, bleated, "These people are coming here for quality of life, and they deserve somebody to give them a chance to achieve that quality of life."[171] It didn't matter to Bank of (Illegal Aliens in) America that offering open-borders credit cards violated multiple federal laws prohibiting the "encouraging or inducing unauthorized aliens to enter the United States, and engaging in a conspiracy or aiding and abetting" such inducements under Title 8 U.S.C. Section 1324(a).[172] And it didn't seem to matter to the federal government, either. The Internal Revenue Service continues to issue "individual taxpayer identification numbers" (ITINs) to illegal alien laborers, who can then use the numbers to open bank accounts that enable them to buy homes, establish credit histories, and borrow funds to start businesses. Several credit unions specialize in services for illegal aliens, such as the Latino Credit Union and Self-Help Credit Union, which offer tailored loans for DACA recipients.[173]

But the biggest cash prizes milked from caravan migrants and other illegal alien workers are, of course, remittances—the money transfers sent by workers in the U.S. back to their native homelands. The United States is the largest source of remittance money on the planet.[174] World Bank reported that a record $34 billion in remittances from both legal and illegal workers in America went to Mexico in 2018[175]—a nearly 11 percent jump over the previous year. Guatemala, El Salvador, and Honduras raked in total remittances of nearly $20 billion in 2018, a 25 percent increase from 2016.[176] The Federation for American Immigration Reform estimated that the U.S. loses approximately $150 billion to remittances sent overseas. Remittances from the U.S. to the Northern Triangle of Central America transfer $16.1 billion to El Salvador, Guatemala, and Honduras. Those governments are dependent on the legions of illegal and legal alien workers dispersed abroad. Remittances sent to El Salvador are equal to 20 percent of its GDP; Guatemala, 11 percent; and Honduras, 18.8 percent.[177] According to the Spanish banking group, BBVA, the average amount sent to Mexico by U.S. workers is about $1,900 per family (or 36,000 pesos) annually, with 98 percent of those remittances sent by electronic fund transfer.[178] "That's a significant amount of income in a country where 7 million workers earn minimum wage and about half of the population lives below the national poverty line," a BBVA analyst noted. The financial group offers migrants a money transfer app called Tuyyo "to quickly forward funds to Mexico by phone using a debit or credit card for a flat fee of $5.49 per transfer."[179]

Such peer-to-peer apps are giving traditional service providers for sending remittances, such as Western Union, a run for illegal aliens' money. Western Union, the granddaddy of money transfer services, handled 268 million consumer transactions in 2016 worth $80 billion,[180] holds about 20 percent of the Mexican remittance market share,[181] and unveiled its own digital transfer app for Mexicans in September 2018.[182] The business of illegal alien money transfers is big business: in 2017, the aggregate cost of sending remittances was about $30 billion.[183] Old-line money-transfer operators charge steep fees averaging about 7 percent of the amount sent.[184] Among the plethora of competitors and disrupters jockeying in the migrant money market to peel away customers with lower transaction fees are:

- Wells Fargo
- MoneyGram
- Ria
- Circle
- Xoom
- Abra
- PayPal[185]
- TransferWise
- WorldRemit

Many of the newcomers are integrating with Facebook Messenger, Viber, and WeChat. WorldRemit, a start-up founded by a Somalian former United Nations official with venture capital backing from Facebook, Spotify, Netflix, and Slack, is closing in on 600,000 transfers per month, according to *Fast Company*.[186] A survey of remittance senders found that nearly 16 percent used cryptocurrency to get money to family and friends, who spent the transfers mostly on food, household goods, housing, medicine, clothes, and education.[187]

In April 2019, the Trump administration reportedly floated a plan to tax remittances.[188] But at the time of publication of this book, floating had not turned into *doing*. In case you were wondering why the federal government hasn't cracked down on such illegal immigration-promoting remittance enterprises, get this: the Federal Reserve itself runs its own remittance service in conjunction with Banco de México[189] and has heavily promoted the program with Spanish-language flyers and brochures since it was created by President George W. Bush in 2005. It's not just Mexico and Central American governments that have direct financial incentives to encourage illegal aliens to break laws, cross borders, take jobs, and earn illicit wages in the U.S. in order to send money home. The Fed's Directo a México allows customers without Social Security numbers (translation: illegal aliens) to wire money through the Fed to Mexico's central bank—and to allow both legal and illegal alien customers to open accounts at participating banks and credit unions in the U.S. or Mexico.[190]

Judicial Watch investigators first exposed Directo a México's pandering marketing materials in 2006. One item in a frequently-asked-questions section asked: "If I return to Mexico or am deported, will I lose the money in my bank account?" "No. The money still belongs to you and can easily be accessed at an ATM in Mexico using your debit card," was the chirpy answer. "In short," Judicial Watch concluded, "the U.S. created this special banking system specifically for illegal aliens and tens of billions of dollars have streamed through it."[191]

I discovered in my research of the program that our government has actively collaborated with the Institute for Mexicans Abroad (*Instituto de los Mexicanos en el Exterior*, or IME), an agency of Mexico's Foreign Ministry that supports its illegal alien workers around the world, to market Directo a México specifically to "translocal migrant networks" or *corredores financieros* within the U.S.[192] An IME official told Marymount University sociologist Matt Bakker that the agency identified a target customer base of "migrants from Tarímbaro, Michoacán" in St. Paul, Minnesota, and recruited them as potential remitters through the Fed's program by holding a "community event" at a local credit union. "There was a merry-go-round and everything," the official bragged, including a "satellite connection" back in Tarímbaro so relatives could connect with each other.[193] The promotional campaign led by U.S. and Mexican government officials was facilitated by the local Mexican consulate and led to upwards of one hundred new customers in its first three months.[194] The two governments worked together to target fifteen more financial corridors of illegal alien workers in California, Florida, Illinois, Indiana, Kentucky, Michigan, Minnesota, and Texas, with sister cities in nine Mexican states.[195] Free video conferencing between migrant families in the U.S. and their relatives back in Mexico was a main attraction. By 2010, more than four hundred banks and credit unions signed up for Directo a México. Bakker, a champion of the program, expressed disappointment at its limited use by illegal aliens, given the enormous effort of both governments to attract customers. But statistics provided by Banco de México show a steady stream of business in the past five years, with roughly forty thousand transactions generated each month totaling roughly $20 million to $27 million per month.[196]

Your government, ladies and gentlemen, once again hard at work facilitating and profiting off illegal immigration instead of ending it.

A Global Conspiracy

From long-standing Catholic shelters and Doctors Without Borders clinics across Mexico, to binational immigration lawyers embedded on both sides of the adjudication process, to travel guides peddling navigational apps, to smugglers, drug cartels, and document fakers, to MS-13 and other alien gangs, to foster care providers and other social welfare contractors, to foreign government and non-governmental officials, multinational banks, money transfer organizations, tech start-ups, and the Federal Reserve, this much is clear:

The open-borders conspiracy enabling unrelenting waves of migrant outlaws is a colossal, profit-seeking venture cloaked in humanitarian virtue.

There's more than a grain of truth to Pueblo Sin Fronteras's protestations that it alone is not responsible for engineering the illegal alien influx. But the spontaneous combustion theory of the caravans is nonsense on stilts on a Segway. Moreover, the firsthand reporting from multiple observers on both sides of the border confirms that Pueblo Sin Fronteras organized, induced, and lied to migrants every step of the way. Independent documentarian Ami Horowitz spoke directly with Pueblo Sin Fronteras organizers "clad in black T-shirts and colored vests" in November 2018 who mobilized supply chains, organized "Know Your Rights" sessions, and trained "folks on how to deal with the press."[197] *La Razón*, a Mexican newspaper, reported that some human rights activists had criticized Pueblo Sin Fronteras and specifically Irineo Mujica for "inciting members of the migrant caravan to generate violence on the northern border of Mexico."[198] *Mexico News Daily* quoted one migrant assailing Pueblo Sin Fronteras because they "took advantage of us" and "they used us in a horrific way."[199]

Heritage Foundation researchers Ana Rosa Quintana and David Inserra interviewed migrants housed at Magdalena Mixhuca Olympic Park in Mexico City from November 4 to 10, 2018, as well as caravan leaders and American lawyers providing asylum counseling. Quintana and Inserra discovered that Pueblo Sin Fronteras told caravan participants they were intermediaries and guides who "would call local governments and let them know they were en route with the caravan and media, essentially coercing them, nongovernmental organizations, and civil society groups into providing the migrants with food, clothing, shelter, and medical care."[200]

Pueblo Sin Fronteras advised marchers not to accept Mexico's asylum offer and pumped up their expectations with false claims that the United Nations would be responsible for them once they reached the U.S. "Statements echoing this sentiment were routinely told to the migrants, compelling vulnerable people to continue along the dangerous journey," the Heritage fact finders reported. "This point should highlight that caravan leaders are not interested in the well-being of the migrants, but in their own broader objectives, whether financial or political." Quintana also identified Honduras's radical leftist Libre Party as a destabilizing force "generating turmoil and instability" and called out former Libre Party legislator Bartolo Fuentes as one of the fall 2018 caravan instigators in San Pedro Sula, Honduras;[201] he was arrested after entering Guatemala illegally.[202]

In March 2019, Mexico's interior minister Olga Cordero warned that "the mother of all caravans" was forming in Honduras.[203] Cordero condemned Pueblo Sin Fronteras for recruiting migrants, which elicited yet more denials of responsibility from the group for its key role in abetting multinational invasion. Instead, Pueblo Sin Fronteras accused the Mexican official of promoting a "discourse of fear and crisis" that "spreads criminalizing, racist and xenophobic sentiment against migrants."[204] Sound familiar? These are the very accusations that Mexican officials themselves have hurled at American citizens standing up for our nation's laws, while Mexican consular offices agitated on behalf of unlimited illegal alien amnesties to cash in on $34 billion in remittances.

Playing the race card to distract from the open-borders agenda is straight from the Open Society handbook, authored by a single billionaire with a terrifying amount of power over the citizens of every sovereign nation in the world. You may know his influence is far-reaching, but you have no idea just how pernicious and pervasive it truly is.

CHAPTER TWO

GEORGE SOROS: THE CEO OF OPEN BORDERS INC.

It's not a conspiracy "theory." It's a conspiracy *truth*: Hungarian-born billionaire George Soros is the mastermind of mass-migration chaos. He is the center of the globalist galaxy. He is the undisputed heavyweight, central financier, and chief executive officer of Open Borders Inc. What American citizens need to know is that while Soros can plausibly deny *directly* subsidizing any specific or single caravan attempting to violate our borders, his elaborate network of nonprofit grantees and sub-grantees around the world serve as advocates, activists, organizers, lawyers, and enablers for illegal alien and refugee influxes.

In November 2018, George Soros's Open Society Foundations denied they had anything to do with steering the redistribution and resettlement of trespassers into our country: "Neither our founder George Soros nor Open Society is involved in the migrant caravan. We have never funded nor directed people to migrate. We support humane approaches to immigration that respect the law and borders."[1]

Soros-funded media operatives likewise decried such accusations. "Conspiracy theories about Soros aren't just false. They're anti-Semitic," fumed Talia Lavin in an October 2018 op-ed for the *Washington Post*.

Her tagline identified her as "a writer and researcher based in Brooklyn."[2] What the *Post* originally neglected[3] to mention is that she had been hired by Soros-funded left-wing smear machine Media Matters for America "as a researcher on far-right extremism and the alt-right" in July 2018[4] after being fired from her job as a *New Yorker* fact-checker. Lavin had falsely accused double amputee Justin Gaertner, a combat-wounded war veteran and computer forensic analyst for the U.S. Immigration and Customs Enforcement agency, of sporting a "Nazi" tattoo. It was a Maltese Cross symbolizing his platoon in Afghanistan.[5] Fake news, real harm. In SorosWorld, that's grounds for a promotion![6]

Not to be outdone, Adam Serwer penned an article for *The Atlantic* claiming "Trump's caravan hysteria" sparked a massacre.[7] The piece outrageously blamed the Pittsburgh Tree of Life synagogue shootings in 2018 on White House criticism of the Central American illegal alien influx. It did so even though the crazed gunman was politically opposed to President Trump.[8] As I'll show you in nauseating detail in chapter six on the Soros-supported Southern Poverty Law Center and its partners, marginalizing peaceful, non-leftist speech by American patriots is a textbook Soros-style tactic. Wait a second. Did I just baselessly accuse Serwer of carrying water for Soros? Am I a conspiracist making an unjust accusation against a purportedly mainstream journalist? Nope, just telling the truth. Serwer's tagline on the widely cited and disseminated screed identified him as "a staff writer at *The Atlantic*, where he covers politics." But what *The Atlantic* failed to disclose is that Serwer was a former hit man for Soros-funded Media Matters for America in 2006 and 2007, where he whipped up fear and loathing of conservative talk radio and TV hosts in scores of blog posts.[9]

Salon.com echoed the echo chamber in June 2019 with a sweeping smear of conservative critics of Soros. According to Salon.com, conservative "attacks" on the sovereignty-bashing billionaire as a leader of the "globalist elite" are "thinly coded anti-Semitic propaganda."[10]

The evidence of Soros's impact on immigration policy in the U.S. and around the world is incontrovertible. Through Soros's gargantuan Open Society Foundations (formerly the Open Society Institute), which he has subsidized with his hedge fund fortune since 1979, the border-eroding billionaire helps facilitate the destruction of sovereign nations step by step, stealth activist by stealth activist, disruptive protest by disruptive protest, radical conference by radical conference, refugee resettlement by refugee resettlement, illegal alien caravan by illegal alien caravan. From 1983 to the present, Soros's Open Society has spent more than $14 billion on everything from gun control to police-bashing to international climate change regulations to electoral meddling to erasing borders and national identity.[11] Leaked Open Society Foundations board meeting notes from 2014 reported that between 1997 and 2013, Open Society Foundations had invested more than $100 million in "immigrant rights."[12] In 2017, Soros funneled nearly $18 billion from his family financial empire to Open Society Foundations in a move that, according to the *Wall Street Journal,* "transforms both the philanthropy he founded and the investment firm supplying its wealth."[13] The transfer represents 72 percent of his total fortune, estimated at nearly $25 billion. In 2018, the Open Society Foundation's budget topped $1 billion, an increase of $65 million from the year prior, which includes a "doubling of funds we are devoting to work on migration" to $63.3 million.[14] That figure does not include an additional $500 million Soros committed to "equity investments in businesses that benefit migrants."[15]

Open Society Foundations Spending 2017–2018, in millions of U.S. dollars

	2017 (amount spent)	2018 (budget)
Asylum & Protection	3.4	3.5
Democratic Practice	0.8	1.8
Economic Governance & Advancement	0.2	24.4
Program-Related Investments	-	20.0
Education	6.2	5.7
Health & Rights	1.3	1.5
Human Rights Movements & Institutions	1.3	2.8
Inclusion & Integration	8.0	11.0
Justice Reform & the Rule of Law	0.9	2.1
Labor Migration	2.7	2.3
Migration Policy and Enforcement	8.9	7.8
Other	0.7	0.4
Total	24.4	63.3

Source: Open Society Foundations, 2018 Budget Overview

In America, Soros is well known for his financial support of anti-war activism, MoveOn.org's defense of Bill Clinton during impeachment, Hillary Clinton's failed presidential campaign, left-wing websites that attack conservative media, police-bashing Black Lives Matter, Latino voter turnout, and lobbying for Obamacare.[16] Immediately after the 2016 election, sore-loser Soros earmarked $10 million to combat what he characterized as violence caused by President Trump's "harsh rhetoric and policy proposals during the 2016 presidential campaign."[17] The alleged "hate crimes" epidemic, of course, was perpetuated and hyped[18] by the Soros-supported Southern Poverty Law Center (SPLC), which is directly cited as the impetus for Soros's $10 million anti-Trump initiative.[19] SPLC is the recipient of at least $75,000 from Soros's Foundation to Promote Open Society.[20] That may not seem like much money to advance his agenda, but it's the extraordinary, synergistic power that Soros has leveraged over the years with his myriad social justice investments that is key to his success. SPLC's partners in the Soros-directed anti-Trump initiative include the Soros-funded Center for American Progress (recipient of an estimated $10.7 million from Soros's Open Foundations), Free Press, ($2 million),[21] National Hispanic Media Coalition (at least $300,000),[22] Color of Change ($550,000),[23] and forty other groups. This dizzying array of organizations, all working lockstep together and singing from the same "Right-Wing Speech = Hate Speech = Violence" hymnbook, keeps Trump supporters and immigration hawks constantly on the defensive and under siege. The existence of scores of affiliated groups, grantees, and sub-grantees crusading against "hate" confers the illusion of a "grassroots" movement, but the ideological and financial fuel tanks trace back to one source: George Soros and Open Society.

Many citizens became woke to Soros's involvement in fomenting border chaos after waves of illegal alien invaders in so-called "caravans" clambered over our decrepit walls in the first two years of the Trump administration. But even supposedly "conservative" media outlets have refused to expose the full extent of Soros's Open Society agenda, non-governmental organizations, and governmental co-conspirators with their army of Open Society Foundations employees operating in forty-nine offices in forty-three countries around the world.[24] In October 2018, Chris Farrell, investigations and research director of the indispensable Judicial Watch, was banned from Fox News for sharing his firsthand report from the southern border—including his conversations with sources high up in the Guatemalan government—about the left-wing groups "receiving money from the Soros-occupied State Department" to facilitate migrant movements. He was banned for telling the truth.[25] Through multiple public records lawsuits, Farrell and Judicial Watch have delved extensively into the State Department's partnerships and overlapping interests with Open Society officials in Romania,[26] Macedonia,[27] Colombia,[28] and Guatemala.[29]

We need more exposure of the Soros racket, not less.

Open Society Foundations' top brass in the U.S. will be familiar to readers of my previous book *Culture of Corruption* and my nationally syndicated columns. Soros tapped Patrick Gaspard to become president of the OSF network in September 2017. He's the former Service Employees International Union (SEIU) chief lobbyist who served as national political director for Barack Obama's 2008 presidential campaign and transition deputy director of personnel. During the 2004 election cycle, he led the radical, left-wing Soros-funded group, America Coming Together (ACT) as national field director. SEIU poured $23 million of workers' dues money into ACT in its failed attempt to put former Massachusetts Democrat Senator John Kerry in the White House. Under Gaspard's tenure at ACT, the get-out-the-vote group employed convicted felons as canvassers and committed campaign finance violations that led to a $775,000 fine by the Federal Election Commission—the third largest civil penalty levied in the panel's history.[30] Gaspard was appointed White House political director shortly after Election Day 2008.[31] Gaspard's admirers and aides called him the "glue man"[32] because he holds liberal interest groups together. He moved up to senior presidential aide, executive director of the Democratic

National Committee, and U.S. ambassador to South Africa before returning to his far-left, Sorosian roots. In 2018, he announced "new leadership"
with the appointment of his Obama White House pal Cecilia Muñoz to
chair the board of OSF's U.S. Programs. But everything "new" is recycled
again.

Like Gaspard, Muñoz is a longtime alum of SorosWorld, having
spent nearly twenty years at the Soros-funded, illegal alien amnesty-
promoting National Council of La Raza ("The Race"), which is now
known as UnidosUS, and having previously served on the boards of OSF,
the Soros-backed National Immigration Forum, the Soros-backed Center
for Community Change, and the Atlantic Philanthropies (previously run
by Gara LaMarche, the former U.S. Programs director of OSF and current head of the Soros-funded dark money group of liberal millionaires
and billionaires, Democracy Alliance).[33] During Muñoz's tenure at La
Raza, the militant group promoted drivers' licenses and in-state college-
tuition breaks for illegal aliens; lobbied for amnesty through executive
orders; opposed cooperative immigration-enforcement efforts between
local, state, and federal authorities; and opposed a secure fence along the
southern border. Mexico's Institute for Mexicans Abroad rewarded
Muñoz with its Ohtli Award for her service. As we'll see in chapter 6,
the group also pressured TV and cable-news networks to keep immigration-enforcement proponents off the airwaves. (Have I mentioned how
marginalizing peaceful, non-leftist speech by American patriots is a
textbook Soros operative tactic?)

Make no mistake: open borders are a prerequisite for Soros's vision
of an "open society." Like a horse and carriage, you can't have one without the other. Don't take my word for it. Take his. In 2006, Soros's
foundation published *Keeping America Open* on the tenth anniversary
of its U.S-based philanthropic programs. Question: open to whom?
Answer: as many potential future Democratic voters from foreign countries as possible. Among Soros's key "achievements": funding the $50
million Emma Lazarus Fund in 1996 to sign up millions of amnestied
illegal aliens for naturalization classes and voter registration. Also on the

Open Society Foundations' anniversary celebration list: undermining bipartisan welfare reform measures[34]—signed by President Clinton and supported by the GOP—which restricted means-tested public aid to new immigrants for five years.[35] Soros blasted the effort as "a mean-spirited attack on immigrants" contrary to the spirit of "the Statue of Liberty" and "the American Dream,"[36] ignoring the plain fact that financial self-sufficiency tests to exclude aliens "liable to become a public charge" have been on the books in America since 1885 and upheld by the U.S. Supreme Court. In its decision, the Court noted the internationally accepted principle that "every sovereign nation has the power, as inherent in sovereignty, and essential to self-preservation, to forbid the entrance of foreigners within its dominions, or to admit them only in such cases and upon such conditions as it may see fit to prescribe."[37] The Emma Lazarus Fund subsidized a constellation of "immigrants' rights" groups that successfully lobbied for restoration of $16 billion in welfare benefits for aliens.[38]

Soros advocates transformative governance for the planet in his 1998 book, *The Crisis of Global Capitalism*: "To stabilize and regulate a truly global economy," he urged, "we need some global system of political decision-making." While he disingenuously acknowledged that it is neither "feasible nor desirable" to "abolish the existence of states," he insisted that "the sovereignty of states must be subordinated to international law and international institutions."[39] Remember that. The "crucial issue of our time," Soros wrote, is "how to overcome the obstacles posed by national sovereignty to the pursuit of the common interest."[40] In 2009, Soros penned a *Foreign Policy* essay that opens brazenly: "Sovereignty is an anachronistic concept originating in bygone times."[41] And in 2015, trading barbs with his nationalist nemesis Viktor Orbán, prime minister of Hungary, Soros sneered that Orbán's prioritizing of "national borders" was an "obstacle" to the Open Society grand plan to "protect refugees."[42]

Responding to Orbán for singling out his outsized influence on the world's immigration and refugee policies, Soros accused the Hungarian leader of "employing anti-Semitic tropes reminiscent of the 1930s" against him.[43] Soros is a Jewish Holocaust survivor. Soros is a global financier. So is Orbán's critique "anti-Semitic?" Here's the truth: in 2017, Orbán's ruling party, Fidesz, launched an informational campaign about the European Left's open-borders agenda with billboards featuring Soros's face and the caption, "Let's not let Soros have the last laugh."[44] The broadside came as Hungary refused to accept the European Union-directed mass relocation of Muslim refugees.[45] Orbán connected the dots between the refugee resettlement agenda at the EU's Brussels headquarters and the activism of Soros-funded non-governmental organizations inside and outside Hungary[46] that assist illegal and mass immigration. Soros is "someone who has a plan" that is "threatening Europe's peace and future," Orbán warned.[47] After winning a third term in office in 2018, Orbán successfully pushed for a package of immigration-reform laws criminalizing non-governmental organizations funded by Soros that facilitated fraudulent asylum claims.[48] This is not antisemitism. This is what a country looks like when it is serious about enforcing its laws against aiding and abetting illegal immigration!

Now, remember Soros's explicit view of sovereignty as an "obstacle" to "international law and international institutions"? That's what this battle is about: power, not bigotry. Two top Open Society officials demanded that the European Union sanction Hungary for cracking down on smuggling conspirators, tightening asylum procedures, and punishing open-borders non-governmental organizations (NGOs) that conspire to undermine immigration enforcement. Kersty McCourt, senior advocacy officer at the Open Society Justice Initiative, and Natacha Kazatchkine, head of the EU internal policy team for the Open Society European Policy Institute, called for the EU to "suspend Hungary's voting rights" in the EU as retaliation against its "anti-migrant legislation" that led Soros's Open Society Foundations to withdraw from Hungary.[49] Following their boss's cue, the Soros flacks then played the antisemitism card. They accused Fidesz members of waging a campaign "dangerously reminiscent of the campaign against Jewish establishments of the 1930s"[50]—because they posted stickers on the office doors of Budapest "human rights groups" that labeled each as a "pro-migration organization," which of course they are. In September 2018, Soros announced plans to sue Hungary over its asylum-reform laws in the European Court of Human Rights.[51] The Orbán administration remained defiant against the governance meddlers: "The Soros organization attacks the Stop Soros package with all possible means as the legislation stands in the way of illegal immigration. The aim of George Soros and organizations supported by him is to flood Europe with migrants."[52]

Soros and his acolytes use Hungary's past failure to protect Jews[53] during World War II as an argument against immigration control. But Orbán has forged a close alliance with Israel's Prime Minister Benjamin Netanyahu and America's President Trump (who welcomed Orbán to the White House in May 2019) precisely because of the existential threat that uncontrolled masses of migrants pose to peace and safety, especially to Jews in Europe. Netanyahu called Orbán a "true friend to Israel" and said they bonded personally because "both understand that the threat of radical Islam is a real one."[54] Trump endorsed Orbán's stance against open borders, praising him for a "tremendous job" in having "kept your country safe."[55] As the Hungarian prime minister trenchantly pointed out, the "enmity against Jews and against Israel is carried into our societies by migration" of the very Muslim population that Soros wants to foist on his native land and other industrialized Western nations.[56] Orbán's call to his countrymen to combat the vast Soros network was not rooted in hatred of Jews, but in love of country. In a speech, marking the 170th anniversary of the 1848 Hungarian Revolution, he exhorted his fellow citizens to remember the necessity of guarding Hungary's sovereignty:

> We are up against media outlets maintained by foreign concerns and domestic oligarchs, professional hired activists, troublemaking protest organisers, and a chain of NGOs financed by an international speculator, summed up by and

embodied in the name "George Soros." This is the world we must fight with in order to defend that which is ours.[57]

If we care about *our* homeland, we cannot and must not cower in fear of baseless smears meant to silence all dissent. We must bring the hidden faces, organizations, and partners of Open Borders Inc. out of the shadows. Heading into the 2020 presidential election, SorosWorld agitators will be fighting as fiercely here in America against immigration hawks and pro-sovereignty groups as they have been in Hungary and across Europe. Soros told global elites at the World Economic Forum in Davos, Switzerland, in 2018 that President Trump is a "danger to the world."[58] He vowed to the *Washington Post* to "redouble" his efforts against the "America First" agenda of the White House because, "the bigger the danger, the bigger the threat, the more I feel engaged to confront it."[59] In 2016, Soros spent at least $25 million supporting Hillary Clinton and other Democrats. The mogul poured $15 million into the 2018 midterm election cycle[60] and an estimated $10 million on far-left district attorney candidates across the country over the past four years.[61] Soros is also a key member of the secretive Democracy Alliance, a club of "progressive" billionaires, who have reportedly budgeted a total of $275 million to defeat Trump, according to confidential documents obtained by the *Washington Free Beacon's* Joe Schofstall in April 2019.[62]

Former Trump adviser and sovereignty champion Steve Bannon is right: "Soros is vilified because he is effective."[63] To defend the president and our country effectively requires more than just a superficial inkling of Soros's worldwide enterprise. It requires an informed knowledge of just how far-reaching the Open Society network has spread—and how its border-busters work in concert with speech-squelchers to eliminate political opposition and activist dissent. President Trump called out the Soros-funded extremists who disrupted Judge Brett Kavanaugh's Supreme Court nomination hearings in an October 2018 tweet:[64]

The very rude elevator screamers are paid professionals only looking to make Senators look bad. Don't fall for it! Also, look at all of the professionally made identical signs. Paid for by Soros and others. These are not signs made in the basement from love! #Troublemakers

President Trump was immediately labeled, you guessed it, "anti-Semitic" by the *New York Times*' Paul Krugman,[65] the *New York Times*' Jamelle Bouie,[66] the *Washington Post*'s E. J. Dionne,[67] and the left-wing website, ThinkProgress.[68] But as you'll learn in this chapter, Trump's characterization of the anti-Kavanaugh rent-a-mob and its ties to Soros was spot-on. I repeat: It's not a conspiracy "theory." It's a conspiracy *truth*.

Asked later that same month whether the Central American illegal alien caravans laying siege to our border were underwritten by "someone," including Soros, Trump answered: "I don't know who, but I wouldn't be surprised. A lot of people say yes."[69] Yes, we do. Chapter 1 showed you exactly which forces and whose funds fuel the coordinated caravans striking our southern border. Now, we'll broaden the focus to include the mass migration crisis besieging Europe. Our fates are inextricably intertwined. If Hungary can "Stop Soros," so can we. When sovereign nations stand together, we can be the "obstacles" to the architects of global governance that Soros expressly wishes to "subordinate" to "international law and international institutions." The following is a fully sourced compendium of the Soros-backed international organizations, U.S. satellites, faith-based flunkies, propaganda arms, speech monitors, and corporate conspirators who imperil the independence of Western nation-states. As Soros increases his focus on finding local and state officials to do his bidding (district attorneys, secretaries of states, and most recently, open-borders mayors through the OSF-sponsored Mayors Migration Council[70]), this guide will be helpful in identifying the activist groups seemingly coming out of nowhere to push refugees, sanctuary policies, amnesty, and phony anti-"hate" speech campaigns in your backyards.

I've broken out separate notable categories of Soros grantees in Appendices B–E. My dossier on SorosWorld is by no means exhaustive, but it can certainly feel exhausting! If the thought of all these professional protesters, influencers, ideologues, and thought-police working against America First keeps you up late at night, join the club. Then join the battle. *This is the world we must fight with in order to defend that which is ours.*

Global Meddlers

The big hypocrisy of Open Society Foundations is that while it purports to promote transparency, its colossal network encompasses a bewildering array of "dark money" groups that shield donors and key financial data. An alphabet soup of programs and initiatives doles out OSF grants to 501(c)(4) social welfare organizations that are exempt from federal income taxes and may engage in political lobbying and campaign activities. The grantees in turn dole out grants to their own set of grantees. There isn't just one bouncing ball to follow. There's an entire Olympic stadium full of them.

One internal OSF document posted by the hacker site DCLeaks in 2016[71] helpfully demonstrates the coordination between OSF, NGOs, the U.N., churches, and academic institutions. The "Migration Governance and Enforcement Portfolio Review," prepared internally in May 2016 by Anna Crowley and Katin Rosin, reports that OSF's International Migration Initiative (IMI)[72] provided forty grants to twenty-two organizations in a two-year review period from 2014 to 2016, totaling more than $8.2 million. Their mission: combating the "rise of the radical right and growing intolerance towards migrants" by capitalizing on the Muslim refugee crisis ("the new normal") and deploying its partners to promote OSF's "common advocacy agenda" on behalf of "global migration governance." See Appendix B-1 for a list of key global grantees from the international alphabet soup of Soros NGOs.

Soros's IMI reviewers were particularly delighted with the payoff on their investment in the Columbia Global Policy Initiative in New York City, where the secretariat for U.N. secretary general's Special Representative on International Migration Peter Sutherland is based. OSF officials praised Sutherland for taking "advantage of momentum created by the current [refugee] crisis to shape conversations about rethinking migration governance" at U.N. and Obama administration summits on migrants and refugees. Pairing Sutherland with the IMI-funded Migrant Policy Initiative (the purportedly "neutral voice" that wrote Sutherland's papers) gave OSF double the lobbying power at elitist policy-shaping meetings. Sutherland, a Big Business honcho who held top positions at Goldman Sachs and BP, has blasted sovereignty defenders in Europe and the U.K. as "xenophobic."[73] At a House of Lords subcommittee hearing on migration, he insisted the European Union should "do its best to undermine" the "homogeneity" of European nation-states in favor of "open," "multicultural states"[74] in which migrants choose them—and not the other way around. Remember: national self-determination is the pesky "obstacle" in the path to Soros's open society.

Maria Teresa Rojas, Open Society Foundations' program director for the International Migration Initiative, was previously director of the U.S. immigrant rights portfolio, deputy director of the U.S. Justice Fund, and associate director for communications for OSF. She sits on the migration advisory board of another heavy-hitting Soros NGO, the International Organization for Migration (IOM).[75] It's known around the world as "the migration agency." IOM began as a post-World War II refugee resettlement operation in Europe and now boasts an annual operating budget of an estimated $1.5 billion, with more than ten thousand employees around the globe providing services to "persons who require international migration assistance."[76] In September 2016, IOM and several partners hosted a Concordia Summit. The event was a "private sector forum on migration and refugees" sponsored by OSF and featuring

George Soros as keynote speaker.[77] (It was at this event that Soros first publicly discussed his $500 million investment in "startups, established companies, social-impact initiatives, and businesses founded by migrants and refugees themselves.")[78]

IOM became an office of the United Nations in 2016, with 173 member states signing on to the agency's mantra: "migration is inevitable, necessary, and desirable—if well governed."[79]

Necessary and desirable for whom? For the facilitators of illegal migration, sure. For the countries that become the designated dumping grounds, not so much. At the end of 2018,[80] IOM served as a travel agency to the world's stateless travelers and border-trespassers—transporting more than 284,000 refugees and migrants by plane, bus, or ship to new frontiers. IOM purchases the tickets; here in the U.S., the State Department's Bureau for Population, Refugees, and Migration covers the transportation costs and grants loans to the refugees. Designated refugee resettlement agencies (as you'll see in Chapter 4) get their own cut when they collect on the interest-free loans. The repayments are then used to cover the costs of future refugee travel. IOM has its own network of satellite offices in Chicago, JFK Airport, Los Angeles, Miami, and Newark, and provides assistance to refugees arriving at these designated ports of entry.[81]

IOM and OSF also co-organized a conference of "global mayors" in December 2018 to lobby for the U.N. Global Compact for Safe, Orderly and Regular Migration and the U.N Global Compact on Refugees.[82] The mayors then issued a statement uniting behind sanctuary spaces for illegal aliens ("irregular" is their politically correct term); asserting a role over immigration policy to challenge every nation-state's prerogative to exercise primary authority over its border and interior enforcement; and committing to "shaping a better narrative on migration" (translation: spreading open-borders propaganda which glorifies all aliens and de-emphasizes ill effects on the economy, health and welfare, national security, and public safety).[83] This Mayors Migration Council, in other words, is a Soros-sponsored collection of "obstacles" to federal enforcement of borders and immigration law. It won't shock you to know that radical Democratic mayors from America's largest illegal alien sanctuary spaces—L.A.'s Eric Garcetti and New York City's Bill de Blasio (also a 2020 Democratic presidential candidate)—are key players on the council. (Soros endorsed de Blasio for mayor.[84])

Let's follow another Soros tentacle that reaches from overseas into our backyards. At the bottom of the Mayors Migration Council's website is a little emblem that reads "C40 Cities." The two groups are "strategic partners," "committed to urgent action on climate change, while increasing the health, well-being and economic opportunities of urban citizens." It's the open-borders agenda married to the radical green agenda, or as they put it, "the intertwined challenges of migration and climate change in cities."[85] If you live in Austin, Boston, Chicago, Houston, New Orleans, Philadelphia, Portland, San Francisco, Seattle, or Washington, D.C., your mayor is also signed on as a proxy lobbyist for this Open Society/Open Borders initiative.

SorosWorld has even penetrated the Deep South, where far-left Democrat Mayor Ted Terry of Clarkston, Georgia, has turned his town of thirteen thousand into a "city of migration." Nicknamed the "Ellis Island of the South," Clarkston is now home to a fabricated category of "climate change refugees" from around the world. Yes, "climate change refugees." Basically, anywhere the sun is too bright, wind is too strong, or tide is too high qualifies as having "extreme weather."[86] Terry and his supporters do admit that "legally, there's no such thing as a 'climate change refugee.'"[87] But that hasn't stopped the Soros propaganda machine from laying the groundwork for expanding refugee protections to untold millions of people who can't adapt to their environments. IOM now claims that "one person was displaced each second, on average, by a climate or weather-related event worldwide between 2008 and 2016."[88] The Soros propagandists have made the issue so hot (pun intended) that 2020 Democratic presidential candidate Beto O'Rourke spotlighted the plight of manufactured "climate change refugees" in his campaign kickoff in March 2019. "If you think 300,000 immigrants and asylum-seekers apprehended on the southern border is a problem—and I don't necessarily think that it is," O'Rourke opined, "the kind of migration and refugee flows that we will see when entire bands of this world are no longer habitable will be a crisis of a different magnitude altogether. We face catastrophe and crisis on this planet, even if we were to stop emitting carbon today right now at this moment."[89] Please go first, Beto, and cease emitting carbon today. The rest of us would welcome a sanctuary from open-borders hot air. Fellow 2020 Democratic presidential candidate Jay Inslee added his own hot air, calling for a climate refugee rescue plan that includes "increasing annual refugee admissions to 110,000" and "withdrawing U.S. military personnel from the border."[90]

Feel-Good Smugglers at Sea

You've probably heard of the noble charity called Save the Children. In the United States, the nonprofit helped poor children in Appalachia during the Great Depression. More recently, the group has helped feed hungry toddlers in Africa and teaches inner-city kindergarteners to read. My son, a talented young musician, even served as a Save the Children youth ambassador in 2012 and performed at the Social Good Summit held in conjunction with the United Nations General Assembly meeting in New York.[91] Like most Americans, I had no idea that a group supposedly dedicated to saving children actually aids and abets a criminal operation that endangers the lives of children and their families.

In Europe, the organization is notorious for its role as a boat operator for illegal immigrants, mostly from Libya, who are crossing the Mediterranean to get to Italy's southern shores. A video on the group's website depicts a crying child wrapped in a foil blanket aboard Save the Children's *Vos Hestia*, a former tugboat, based at the port of Sicily.[92] The NGO claims to have rescued 435 such children "fleeing bullets, poverty, persecution, and the growing impact of climate change." But reporter Nicholas Farrell reported in *The Spectator* in 2017 that the *Vos Hestia* and a fleet of other NGO-operated charity vessels were conducting unauthorized search-and-rescue missions in territorial waters involving migrants who were in no way "in distress" and hardly "children." Farrell observed that "the vast majority of migrants from Libya are young men paying the equivalent of 1,000 each to people smugglers in what they see as a calculated risk to reach a better life in Europe." The NGO vessel operators are "now under investigation by Sicilian magistrates for possible collusion with people smugglers." One magistrate stated, "We have evidence that there are direct contacts between certain NGOs and people traffickers in Libya."[93] After initially denying that it had ever entered Libyan waters, Save the Children admitted it had done so "on a highly exceptional basis" in "coordination" with the Italian coast guard.[94] While claiming "to be saving lives," Farrell concluded, "what they really are doing is colluding—either intentionally or not—in a people-trafficking operation" that provided a "pick-up service a few miles off Libya."[95] Save the Children listed Open Society Foundations as one of its "most generous foundation partners" in 2017.[96] The OSF grant database shows donations to Save the Children projects totaling at least $675,000 since 2016.[97]

Here's another noble-sounding charity known around the world: Médicins Sans Frontiéres (MSF), also known as Doctors Without Borders. Founded in France in 1971 by health professionals seeking to provide charity medical care around the world, MSF is known for rushing to hot spots vulnerable to natural disasters and endemic diseases. But they've also become mobile hospital operators for illegal aliens trekking from the Middle East, Africa, and Central America. MSF condemns the U.S. and Europe for "closing their borders" and "enacting inhumane policies" to deter asylum abuse and protect their own citizens.[98] No shock there. Their name is "Doctors *Without Borders*," after all. Like Save the Children, MSF operated five vessels that transported migrants across the Central Mediterranean between May 2015 and December 2018: *Phoenix* (in partnership with an open-borders NGO based in Malta, the Migrant Offshore Aid Station); *Dignity I*; *Bourbon Argos*; *Prudence*; and *Aquarius* (in partnership with another open-borders NGO based in France, SOS Méditerranée).

When Italian authorities cracked down on the lawless fleets and shut down several of the boats, OSF decried "deterrence" measures and defended the charity boats because "standing back is not an option."[99] (Never mind that the European Union itself, which had sponsored its own rescue boat operation in 2014 called *Mare Nostrum*, canceled it after concluding that the service ended up being a "pull factor" luring migrants to risk their lives at sea.[100] Or that left-wing French president Emmanuel Macron conceded that "in the end we are playing into the hands of smugglers by reducing the risks of the journey."[101] Or that the Italian commander of the EU's anti-trafficking operation reported that the NGO boats' floodlights were attracting smugglers' migrant-crammed dinghies to them at night.[102]) On the defensive, Doctors Without Borders official Stefano Argenziano accused the Italian government of implementing "a deliberate plan to stop the migration flow."[103] How dare they! At the Intergovernmental Conference on the Global Compact on Migration, Doctors Without Borders's international president Joanne Liu attacked Italy's exercise of sovereignty through judicial and investigative channels as a "concerted, sinister campaign of legal challenges and administrative obstacles" (there's that favorite word of George Soros again: "obstacles")[104] to their vision of a borderless world. The group terminated all of its boat operations in December 2018, but continues on land providing "shelter, water, sanitation, and essential relief items at reception centres, informal settlements, and transit camps" across Europe—more "pull factors" drawing migrants by the thousands across dangerous seas.

While OSF officials adamantly assert that they "do not fund search and rescue operations in the Mediterranean," the Soros Foundations singled out MSF as one of its designated NGO partners, with whom they have developed special "alliances in pursuing crucial parts of the open society agenda."[105] (See Appendix B-3 for more Soros-backed European refugee travel agents and public relations propagandists.)

OSF doesn't just fund nonprofits running sea taxi and tour guide services to migrants. It also funds support groups that raise money for what is essentially a smuggling operation. Avaaz means "voice" in Farsi and several other languages. It's also the name of a New York-based nonprofit that claims to have "51,689,681" followers[106] comprising a "global web movement to bring people-powered politics to decision-making everywhere." Among its "victories": Avaazers donated "nearly a million dollars to fund life-saving missions at sea and protection programmes" for refugees.[107] IRS 990 forms for the group from 2016 document that Avaaz "funded costs of a month of rescue missions in the Mediterranean and provided additional funds for aid missions in the Greek Islands."[108] Avaaz was founded in 2007 by Res Publica, "a global civic advocacy group," along with the Clinton-era agitation army MoveOn.org. NGO Monitor, a watchdog group, reported that Res Publica received grants totaling $250,000 from the Soros Open Society Institute in 2008.[109] MoveOn.org scooped up $2.5 million from Soros in 2003 and another $1.5 million grant from Soros in 2004. Open Society Foundations infused Res Publica with $600,000 in 2009, which it passed on to Avaaz for "general support" and "climate change" work.[110] In 2017, the group hoovered up more than $20 million in revenue.[111] Because of its nonprofit 501(c)(4) status, Avaaz is not required to reveal its donors, so its claim to be fully funded by small-dollar donors cannot be verified.

What we do know: Avaaz's 2017 Form 990 lists "fighting hate and division in politics and media" and opposing "the hate and division encouraged by Trump-style politics" among its primary activities. Translation: meddling in elections "to prevent the far-Right from taking power" in France, the Netherlands, and across Europe, as well as opposing Rupert Murdoch's bid to take over Sky News.[112]

What we also know: Avaaz funneled a whopping $380,000 into the failed Virginia Democratic gubernatorial campaign of radical progressive and former Virginia congressman Tom Perriello, who just happens to be one of Avaaz's co-founders, a former Obama State Department official, and the current executive director of the Open Society Foundations' U.S. Programs.[113]

"People-powered politics" sure pays...for the people running it.

The World's Speech Cops

Because you can't have enough acronym-clogged networks all marching in lockstep to advance "a civil society vision for a transformative agenda for human mobility, migration and development," OSF joined with the European Union, other Soros-funded NGOs, and the governments of Australia, Canada, Sweden, Germany, the Netherlands, Switzerland, Turkey, Bangladesh, and the United Arab Emirates to form yet another coalition called the Migration and Development Civil Society Network (MADE).[114] The network's international steering committee and top planners are listed in Appendix B-2. The network devoted most of its time and energy the past decade lobbying for passage of the U.N. Global Compact for Safe, Orderly and Regular Migration[115]—a founding document of Open Borders Inc. along with the companion U.N. Global Compact on Refugees. MADE network partners coordinated talking points and strategy on lobbying for the compact's "pathways to regular movement and status" and "access to rights and services regardless of status,"[116] while working to "bridge the gap" between "regular and irregular migrants" (by obliterating the legal differences between the two, of course).[117]

The non-binding migration treaty was endorsed by the U.N. General Assembly in December 2018 by a vote of 152 to 5 over the forceful objection of President Trump and the U.S., which was joined in opposition by the Czech Republic, Hungary, Israel, and Poland. A dozen countries abstained: Algeria, Australia, Austria, Bulgaria, Chile, Italy, Latvia, Libya, Liechtenstein, Romania, Singapore, and Switzerland. Two dozen more didn't vote at all. Undaunted and claiming victory, Soros-funded activists hired an "independent consultant" to plot the next step: implementation! As usual, framing all opposition as bigotry is a top priority. The consultant pinpointed the need to hire a communications expert to "address negative narratives on migration, including by developing communications and advocacy strategies at various levels (states, politicians, media) to combat racism, xenophobia and discrimination."[118]

For all their bloated talk of taking power from the elites and putting it in the hands of the people, Open Society zealots show unfettered contempt for actual popular sentiment. When ordinary Italians expressed anger and frustration over the impact of mass migration, the elitist solution was to create NGOs that would rectify public wrongthink through media propaganda. Left-wing Italian journalists from the National Council of Journalists (CNOG) and the National Federation of Italian Press collaborated with the Office of the United Nations High Commissioner for Refugees (UNHCR) to create a "code of conduct on migrants, asylum-seekers, refugees and victims of trafficking" in force since June 2008. The code is known as the Rome Charter (Associazione Carta di Roma).

Soros's OSF is a major sponsor of the Rome Charter because, its leaders explained, "We also believe that the Italian society has the right to know the facts about migration, and consequently we support those actors that seek to present facts and evidence on how migration is caused, how it affects societies, and which policies bring the best solutions." As OSF describes it, the Rome Charter "organizes training for media professionals in the correct use of a fair terminology on immigration and minorities" along with the "Italian Civil Liberties Coalition's web platform, called #OpenMigration, which provides data, infographics, commentary, news reporting, and analysis on migration trends, and legal and policy developments."[119] The charter's governmental and non-governmental partners enlisted Italian academics to give the endeavor the air of "scientific" objectivity,[120] but biased birds of a feather flock together. The Rome Charter's working guidelines are based on a framework created by an Italian government agency called the Ufficio Nazionale Antidiscriminazioni Razziali (UNAR or "National Office against Racial Discrimination"). The obstacle facing #OpenMigration, you see, is that opposition to it is rooted in racism and insufficient appreciation for, you guessed it, "diversity."

Guidelines for application of the Rome Charter advise journalists to avoid mentioning the nationality of migrants to avoid "negative consequences on social cohesion"; "counter the unsubstantiated notion of an 'invasion'"; hire more "journalists of migrant origin"; and subject themselves to a "diversity checklist," including political correctness litmus tests such as these:

- Do I mention ethnicity if it is not relevant to the story?
- Do I actively try to recruit colleagues who will bring a diversity of perspective into the newsroom?
- Am I sure that I am using the correct terms?[121]

To enforce the "correct" language, the Rome Charter's glossary for journalists decrees that the Italian term for "clandestine" ("illegal" in English) "has an extremely negative meaning" and use of "this highly stigmatising term" should be avoided—even if it is accurate.[122] These aren't just recommendations. As the association's president explained, "This is not good advice but a code of deontology whose violation implies sanctions for journalists." In 2017, an estimated twenty journalists had reportedly committed wrongthink and wrongwrite.[123] The Rome Charter Association happily reported that Greece, Spain, and Bulgaria were coming up with similar language codes and implementation handbooks.

HOPE Not Hate (HNH) is another speech-policing nonprofit that has received multiple grants through the OSF's European "Fund to Counter Xenophobia." HNH bills itself as a "positive antidote to the politics of hate" and claims to oppose "fascism" and "racism."[124] There's not much "hope" in HNH's message, but plenty of hate for those it accuses of "hate"—namely white people, Christians, and the "far Right." The contempt is explicit. HNH's "leading expert" Matthew Collins, for example, tweeted out a link to a 2016 *Washington Post* piece titled "White Christian America Is Dying" with the tolerant comment: "And now for some good news."[125]

The Soros-supported agenda is destruction by any means necessary, wrapped in a cloak of sanctimony and tolerance. Think of the operatives at HNH as the brass knuckles of the global speech police. Operationally, HNH is the European equivalent of the "hate"-weaponizing Southern Poverty Law Center (SPLC), also supported by Soros. In the United States, the OSF sponsors Communities Against Hate, a national initiative that gathers rumors and anecdotes of "hate crimes" for a database to help "address the disturbing spike in hate incidents across the United States," with the statistics dutifully inflated by SPLC researchers and regurgitated by a complaisant media.[126] (Other participants and partners are listed in Appendix D.)

In Britain, HNH "researchers" issue reports on extremism that British open-borders journalists obligingly parrot without challenge. A "progressive" journalist-turned-agitator, Nick Lowles, heads the group. Under his leadership, the group called for banning "far right" and "Nazi" books on Amazon and at British bookstores, which resulted in scores of publications disappearing from store shelves. HNH's gloating press release that celebrated this censorship boasted of the group's commitment to "free speech."[127]

HNH's collaborations with anti-borders, anti-Right media are not empty speculation. English anti-jihad activist Tommy Robinson produced a documentary alleging how a liberal BBC journalist, John Sweeney, had lured one of Robinson's former employees to snitch on him, loosened her up with liquor, and coached her on negative talking points about Robinson that he guaranteed would end up on his BBC segment (titled "Tommy Takedown") if she delivered them satisfactorily.[128] The former employee, Lucy Brown, wore a hidden camera for Robinson's undercover investigation, which alleged intimate coordination between HNH and the BBC. Brown claims HNH offered her £5,000 to cooperate.[129] Robinson and Brown have been incessant targets of HNH. Just days after screening the documentary, Robinson was banned from Facebook and Instagram for allegedly using "dehumanizing language" and engaging in "organized hate."[130] It was another victory for the speech-squelching saboteurs who, according to former operative Dan Hodges, had "used every dirty, underhand, low down, unscrupulous trick in the book" to defeat their political opponents.[131]

Human Rights and Wrongs

One of the most well-known human rights watchdogs on the planet is Human Rights Watch (HRW). Its international footprint spans 100 countries and 450 employees. The NGO boasted total assets of $233 million in 2018.[132] In 2010, George Soros announced a $100 million donation to the group to "expand and deepen" its presence globally.[133] It was a financial windfall and public relations coup for the group, which had come under fire by one of its own co-founders, Bob Bernstein, for its obsessive anti-Israel bias and gullibility in spreading unverified Palestinian accounts of human rights abuses. "Why does HRW seem so credulous of civilian witnesses in places like Gaza but so sceptical of anyone in a uniform?" Bernstein challenged.[134] There was also the shocking revelation that HRW's lead military writer was a creepily enthusiastic collector of Nazi memorabilia.[135] Then there were the fundraising forays in Saudi Arabia.[136] After investigating the unsavory alliance with the House of Saud's notorious human rights abusers, *The Atlantic* writer Jeffrey Goldberg concluded, "It appears as if Human Rights Watch, in the pursuit of dollars, has compromised its integrity."[137]

Undaunted, HRW has relentlessly bashed America for immigration enforcement at the state and federal level. In 2010, the group waged war on Arizona after Governor Jan Brewer signed into law Senate Bill 1070, which sought to enforce federal immigration law and outlaw sanctuary policies in the state. HRW claimed that the state had violated the International Convention on the Elimination of All Forms of Racial Discrimination, and of course found a ready ally in President Obama's Justice Department.[138] HRW has continually demonized Border Patrol and ICE agents for doing their jobs at the southern border,[139] and in March 2019 called for reducing the federal detention and enforcement budget in favor of protecting illegal aliens' "due process" rights, providing "know your rights" services," and supplying the influx of border-trespassers with attorneys.[140] Another of HRW's co-founders, Aryeh Neier, was a long-time lawyer for the American Civil Liberties Union. He served as executive director of HRW and was president of the Open Society Foundations for nineteen years.

Rent-a-Mob: Loudmouths for Hire

Make the Road is a community-organizing front group that storms the streets and legislative chambers on behalf of illegal aliens in New York with posters defiantly asserting "#HereToStay," "Trump is not my president," and "#MeltICE." Since President Trump was elected, the group has "led or co-led most of the post-election mobilizations in New York City to drive broader immigrant rights resistance." The professional mob marched to Trump Tower a week after Election Day 2016 to put the White House on notice that the "resistance" had arrived, and spearheaded the so-called "spontaneous" protests that purportedly grew "out of nowhere"[141] at John F. Kennedy Airport over President Trump's national security travel restrictions. A left-wing *Daily Beast* reporter noted, "From the moment Trump defeated Hillary Clinton in the general election," Make the Road had "been anticipating and mapping out their battle plans for Trump's orders on deportations, bans, and detention. So when you heard about a large crowd at an airport in the past few days yelling catchy slogans like 'FUCK TRUMP, FUCK PENCE, THIS COUNTRY'S BUILT ON IMMIGRANTS,' it was no 'spontaneous' outpouring of support. It was the result of a lot of unseen work and man hours."[142]

No space is safe. Make the Road activists turned up at JPMorgan Chase CEO Jamie Dimon's Upper East Side home to protest the bank's corporate holdings in private detention facilities[143] as part of a "Corporate Backers of Hate" campaign targeting financial institutions. On May Day 2017, Make the Road led thousands nationwide holding signs that read "THIS LAND IS FOR EVERYONE. NO BORDERS," "Not One More Deportation," "No One is Illegal," "Sanctuary for All," and "NO BAN NO WALL RESIST."[144]

Make the Road organizers lead "Know Your Rights" training sessions for day laborers, sign up amnestied illegal aliens for naturalization and voter registration, push for extending voting privileges to non-citizens, and lobby for sanctuary cities. After years of pressure from Make the Road, the New York legislature passed a state version of the "DREAM Act," providing $27 million in government funding, program awards, and in-state tuition benefits to illegal aliens[145]—while children of military Gold Star Families, whose parents died while serving their country, were denied a similar benefits package.[146]

Open Society Foundations granted Make the Road $140,000 in 2009;[147] up to $700,000 in 2011;[148] $24,000 in 2016 to help organize a "National Day Laborer Network" with the Center for Popular Democracy (CPD);[149] and $70,000 to "educate immigrants about current immigration policy, and build a network of volunteer non-immigrant advocates for immigrant rights" in 2017.[150] While illegal alien activists present the public face on the streets for Make the Road, the Center for Popular Democracy's staff and founders pull the puppet strings. The *Washington Free Beacon*'s Joe Schoffstall reported on the incestuous ties and money-shuffling between the two groups:[151]

- Andrew Friedman, Center for Popular Democracy (CPD) co-executive director, co-founded Make the Road New York in 1997 and serves on the board of Make the Road and Make the Road Action Fund.
- Ana Maria Archila, another co-executive director of CPD, also served as co-executive director of Make the Road. A partisan operative and anti-Trump resistance loyalist, she infamously confronted GOP Senator Jeff Flake in an elevator during Judge Brett Kavanaugh's Supreme Court nomination hearings and used the confrontation to drum up

    more donations for CPD.[152] (If she had ceased shrieking for a second, the liberal Flake might have had time to soothe her anger with reassurances that when it comes to open borders, she and he are on the same side.)

- Javier Valdes, co-executive director of Make the Road, is board chair of the Center for Popular Democracy.

Open Society entities bestowed CPD with $130,000 in 2014;[153] $1,164,500 in 2015;[154] and an additional $705,000 in 2016.[155] Between 2012 and 2014, the two groups have traded hundreds of thousands of grants with each other, as well as other Soros-backed groups, including UnidosUS/National Council of La Raza. CPD's action arm unveiled an astonishing $80 million dark-money network in 2017 to mobilize new voters for 2020 and flip six state legislatures.[156] The CPD board includes two members[157] who organized for the defunct and disgraced Association of Community Organizations for Reform Now (ACORN) community organizing racket, and CPD's federation of local groups includes many old ACORN chapters. Supplementing the Soros subsidies are massive grants and contributions from the government. Influence Watch reported that on its 2014 tax returns, Make the Road disclosed receiving more than $5 million in government grants among its $13.4 million in total revenues—approximately 37 percent of the group's revenues in that year.[158]

    Every time Make the Road/CPD political theater disrupts public business and undermines our safety, remember, New Yorkers: you're paying for it twice over.

Casa de Soros

    How do you spell astroturf agitation in Spanish? The same way you spell it in English: S-O-R-O-S. Founded in 1985, illegal alien advocacy group CASA de Maryland claims an active membership of more than twelve thousand who specialize in "resistance and protest."[159] During the

Bush and Obama years, CASA provided training sessions to illegal workers on evading deportation, lobbied for mass amnesty and in-state tuition discounts for illegal aliens, crusaded for drivers' licenses for illegal aliens, and fought Arizona's Senate Bill 1070. CASA opposes enforcement of deportation orders; has protested post–9/11 coordination of local, state, and national criminal databases; and produced a "know your rights" propaganda pamphlet for illegal aliens depicting federal immigration agents as armed bullies making babies cry. In 2006, CASA de Maryland threatened to protest at the schools of children whose parents belonged to the pro-immigration enforcement group, the Minutemen—and then headed into the Montgomery County, Maryland, public schools to recruit junior amnesty protesters who were offered school credits for traveling with CASA de Maryland to march on Washington.[160]

In 2016–2017 alone, CASA de Maryland took in $370,000 from OSF;[161] according to its IRS Form 990 for 2017, the nonprofit reported total revenues topping $9.9 million.[162] Influence Watch, the Capital Research Center's watchdog website, noted a 2011 *Washington Post* profile that reported "nearly half" of CASA's $6 million budget came from "local, state and federal appropriations" and that contributors named in its 2017 annual report include "several federal agencies, the state governments of Maryland and Virginia, and local government agencies within those states."[163] Next to Soros and taxpayers, the most noteworthy (or rather, notorious) donor to CASA in its history is CITGO, the repressive Venezuelan government's oil company, which showered $1 million on its community development programs. CASA cheered the gift from then-dictator Hugo Chavez's regime as the most generous "corporate investment" in its history.[164]

Anti-Trump action through marches, protests, and legal filings is now the centerpiece of CASA de Maryland's agenda. CASA's highest-ranking alumnus is Thomas E. Perez, chairman of the Democratic National Committee and former Obama labor secretary and Justice Department Civil Rights Division chief. He is a far-Left, race-baiting[165] lawyer and activist who served as a trustee and board member for the

Center for American Progress (recipient of $10.7 million from Soros's Open Foundations), and volunteered for CASA before joining its board and then becoming its president. As chairman of the Democratic National Committee, Perez shrieked that Republicans "don't give a shit" about people[166] while parroting the moldy, oldy open-borders mantra that "No human being is illegal."[167]

Compared to CASA, the Mexican American Legal Defense and Educational Fund (MALDEF) looks positively staid. The group marked its fiftieth anniversary in 2019. "Whether on the streets or in schools, in boardrooms or living rooms, in legislative chambers or courthouses right up to the U.S. Supreme Court," the group boasts, it has earned its reputation as the "civil rights law firm of the Latino community." In 2016, Soros's Foundations gave MALDEF $700,000. MALDEF leaders spearheaded the drive to get "ICE out of communities,"[168] likened ICE agents to terrorists,[169] took to the streets to protest against Hollywood's alleged lack of Latino representation ("We're asking, we're demanding" to be hired, they shouted[170]), and are suing American companies (Bank of America and Proctor & Gamble) on behalf of two illegal aliens who claim that the companies' refusal to hire them because of their outlaw immigration status constitutes "illegal discrimination."[171]

MALDEF is just one of a plethora of Soros-sponsored legal groups that constitute what I call the Illegal Alien Bar Association. (See Appendix C for a breakdown of the top pro bono lawyers' groups that leave no alien plaintiff behind.)

One of the new kids on the Latino social justice warrior block cut from the same identity-politics cloth as CASA and MALDEF is United We Dream (UWD). Claiming a membership of four hundred thousand, UWD bills itself as the "largest immigrant, youth-led community in the country" with an emphasis on "the undocumented." The group operates a "MigraWatch hotline," a "Deportation Defense" team, and a store[172] hawking "Undocumented Students Are Here to Stay" and "Unafraid Educator" T-shirts. Members have occupied congressional offices. They've barraged Twitter with messages condemning rank-and-file Border Patrol and ICE agents as a "dangerous and racist cancer on the liberties of all people."[173] UWD reported total revenue of $15.5 million in 2017, five times the amount it pulled in the year prior.[174] The activist group shared the wealth, plowing grants back into fellow Soros-supported agitation operations, including more than $63,000 to Make the Road in 2017 for DREAMer project work, $5,500 to MALDEF, and grants of $25,500 each to Catholic charities chapters in Venice, Florida; Tulsa, Oklahoma; and Indianapolis, Indiana.[175] The National Immigration Law Center was a financial sponsor for the group from 2008 to 2013.[176] *Time* magazine honored United We Dream co-founder and executive director (also a Make the Road alumna) Cristina Jiménez as one of its Most Influential People in the World in 2018.[177] An illegal alien from Ecuador, Jiménez has also won a MacArthur Foundation "Genius Grant" Fellowship,[178] been named to *Forbes*'s "30 under 30 in Law and Policy," been designated one of "40 under 40 Young Leaders Who Are Solving Problems of Today and Tomorrow" by the *Chronicle of Philanthropy*, and won honors as one of "50 Fearless Women" by *Cosmopolitan*.[179] Wielding bullhorns and blocking streets while supposedly being forced to "live in the shadows" has its privileges.

Jiménez sits on the advisory board of another Soros-tied constellation of identity politics-focused nonprofits called the Emergent Fund, which has raised at least $500,000 to combat "immediate threats" to immigrant groups and "people of color," according to Joe Schoffstall of the *Washington Free Beacon*.[180] Additionally, the Open Society Policy Center reported the following immigration-related lobbying expenditures of U.S.-based grantees in 2018:[181]

- Alliance San Diego Mobilization Fund—$150,000
- America's Voice—$575,000
- American Immigration Council—$35,000
- Care in Action—$500,000
- Light of Freedom Ballot Initiative—$500,000
- MomsRising—$200,000

- National Immigration Forum Action Fund—$150,000
- NEO Action Fund—$605,000
- PICO Action Fund—$40,000

The Muslim Grievance-Mongerers

The pot-stirring, unindicted terror co-conspirators of the Council on American-Islamic Relations, known for promoting fake hate crimes,[182] received a total of $366,000 from the Open Society Foundations to launch new anti-hate crimes campaigns, "shift the narrative surrounding the American Muslim community," and conduct "rapid response safety workshops at mosques."[183] The Islamic Society of North America (ISNA), a front group also named unindicted co-conspirators by federal prosecutors in the Holy Land Foundation terror financing case, was part of a network of Muslim Brotherhood entities conducting "a kind of grand jihad" bent on "eliminating and destroying the Western civilization from within ...so that it is eliminated and Allah's religion is made victorious over all other religions."[184] In 2016, ISNA received $50,000 from OSF to "mobilize the faith community to push back against anti-refugee backlash.[185] Civilization-destroying birds of a feather flock together!

In June 2018, hundreds of Muslims led by a small nonprofit named Muslim Advocates converged on the Supreme Court steps to protest President Trump's national security travel restrictions. They were joined by prominent Democrats on Capitol Hill, including Senators Richard Blumenthal of Connecticut, Cory Booker of New Jersey, Mazie Hirono of Hawaii, and Jeff Merkley of Oregon, and Representatives André Carson of Indiana, Debbie Dingell of Michigan, Sheila Jackson Lee of Texas, Joe Kennedy III of Massachusetts, Barbara Lee of California, Jan Schakowsky of Illinois, and Nydia Velázquez of New York. Muslim Advocates has pressured groups as various as Twitter, Uber, and Marriott Hotels in efforts to stifle free speech and oppose Donald Trump.[186]

DCLeaks documents revealed that Open Society Foundations injected $1.8 million into Muslim Advocates' budget between 2008 and 2015.[187] Executive director Farhana Khera maintained close ties with the Obama White House; the Investigative Project on Terrorism reported that visitor logs tracked her meeting there with officials at least eleven times.[188] In December 2018, Muslim Advocates led a pressure campaign with thirty-two other "civil rights" groups urging Facebook's Mark Zuckerberg and Sheryl Sandberg to step down and for new leadership to crack down on purported "white nationalists and hate groups."[189] The coalition included an ever-widening array of social justice groups, many of which were Soros satellites. (See Appendix D for the full list.)

At least one non-Muslim religious group has collected Soros money to shill for the Muslim public relations drive. Lutheran Social Services of South Dakota received $20,000 from Open Society Foundations in 2017 to "produce a media campaign to raise awareness about refugee and Muslim communities."[190] As if "awareness" of the Islamophobia complainers hasn't been raised enough.

Hijacking the News

In 2010, George Soros announced a $1 million donation to Media Matters for America (MMFA) to "more widely publicize the challenge Fox News poses to civil and informed discourse in our democracy."[191] During the Obama years, MMFA "researchers" met regularly with the White House, along with the Soros-funded Center for American Progress,[192] to assist Obama White House communications director Anita Dunn in waging political war on Fox.[193] Now, MMFA occupies itself with pouncing on every pro-immigration enforcement opinion voiced on the network as akin to white supremacy.[194] Sample of MMFA's self-echo chamber on Twitter:

- Fox News peddles for voter suppression with Kansas Secretary of State Kris Kobach, who has ties to white supremacy[195]

- Full-blown white supremacy on Fox: Tucker Carlson guest defends white supremacists and claims that Hispanics in Arizona represent the end of American society[196]
- Fox News is regularly airing blatant white nationalist propaganda
- Tucker Carlson promoted a white nationalist social media app on Fox News yesterday[197]
- On CNN, @GoAngelo [Media Matters president Angelo Carusone] highlights the rise of white nationalist rhetoric on Fox News[198]
- The source for Fox News' anti-refugee fear-mongering is a white nationalist writer[199]

Oh, and the loudest loudmouths denying that SorosWorld exists? Soros-funded Media Matters, of course. Its "director of media intelligence," Lis Power, called on Fox to "get Jeanine Pirro off the air" for simply mentioning Soros's name in a fiery, truthful monologue about open borders.[200] MMFA's official Twitter account repeated and broadened the complaint in October 2018: "Fox personalities repeatedly pushed conspiracy theories about George Soros and migrant caravans. Will the network do anything about them?"[201] MMFA then successfully planted the Soros criticism = bigotry/antisemitism meme[202] that led to Judicial Watch investigative director Chris Farrell getting booted for bringing Soros facts to the Fox News table.

The National Hispanic Media Coalition (NHMC) teamed up with MMFA to target immigration hawk Lou Dobbs during his tenure at CNN and regularly attacks conservative media and their consumers as racist. The "coalition" consists of the National Latino Media Council, the National Hispanic Leadership Agenda, and the Leadership Conference on Civil and Human Rights (LCCHR). A Daily Caller investigation unearthed internal memos bragging that "as part of the Drop Dobbs campaign, Media Matters produced and was prepared to run an advertisement against Ford Motor Company on Spanish Language stations."[203]

Without disclosing its behind the scenes coordination, Media Matters then touted a study by NHMC purporting to show that "Fox News viewers hold more anti-immigrant, anti-Latino opinions."[204] In 2016, OSF handed the NHMC $300,000 for "general support."[205]

Center for Media Justice (CMJ) is an Oakland-based "nationally recognized organizing hub representing the media policy interests and building the cultural leadership of hundreds of social justice groups across the United States." It organizes the Media Action Grassroots Network (MAG-Net) to train an army of social justice warriors on the internet. Their mission? To "create media and cultural conditions that strengthen movements for racial justice, economic equity, and human rights."[206] In practice, this means haranguing left-wing Facebook for not being sufficiently intolerant of conservative voices on its platform and failing to censor critics of George Soros[207]—or hectoring journalists or commentators for using the terms "savages," "illegals," or "terrorists" to describe "people of color."[208] "Social justice" is the redistribution of wealth and economic "rights." "Media justice" is the redistribution of speech and First Amendment rights. CMJ and its allies target conservative opponents on talk radio, cable TV, and on the web as purveyors of "hate" who need to be managed or censored.[209] For Soros "progressives" who cloak their ambitions in the mantle of "fairness" and "equity," it's all about control. It's always about control. In 2016, OSF granted CMJ $450,000.[210]

When it comes to racial agitation, the radical activist group Color of Change is second to none. It bills itself as "the nation's largest online racial justice organization." Founded by disgraced 9/11 Truther, anti-police agitator, Occupy movement promoter, and former Obama green-jobs czar Van Jones, Color of Change never lets a crisis go to waste. The group used Hurricane Katrina to condemn America as institutionally racist, helped perpetuate director Spike Lee and Nation of Islam leader Louis Farrakhan's wild conspiracy theories about government-engineered black genocide in New Orleans, and exploited the Trayvon Martin shooting to attack the conservative American Legislative Exchange Council

(ALEC), a four-decade-old association of state legislators who believe in "the Jeffersonian principles of free markets, limited government, federalism, and individual liberty." Color of Change's pressure campaign and boycott efforts led several corporate giants to cave and cut ties with ALEC, including McDonald's, Wendy's, Mars Inc., Coca-Cola, PepsiCo, Kraft Foods, Intuit, Blue Cross Blue Shield Association, Reed Elsevier (owner of LexisNexis), American Traffic Solutions, and Arizona Public Service.[211]

Color of Change also joined the "net neutrality" battle and more recently allied with OSF grantees Muslim Advocates and the Center for Media Justice to browbeat Facebook into conducting a "civil rights and safety audit" after the Silicon Valley giant partnered with the conservative Heritage Foundation—unacceptable heresy to the Soros mob—to review liberal bias at the company.[212] Acting as a Soros force multiplier, Color of Change joined the Soros-funded Immigrant Legal Resource Center to lobby the Associated Press not to use the accurate phrase "chain migration" to describe the indiscriminate policy of allowing green card holders or legal U.S. residents to sponsor a family member's immigration. New immigrants can sponsor their entire extended families in an endless, yes, chain: parents, spouses, adult children and their children, and siblings and their children. Scholars have used the term for decades, but since President Trump announced his intention to end the practice, SorosWorld has sought to demonize the reformers as "hard-liners" guilty of prejudice.[213] Color of Change pressured media outlets to drop the phrase "chain migration" and cited Soros-funded Media Matters to attack Fox News for using the term "295 times in 2017, compared to zero times in 2016 and three times in 2015."[214] Grievance-mongering paid off. The Associated Press bowed and issued guidance warning its journalists to "avoid the term."[215]

Most notoriously, Color of Change pounced after the Unite the Right/Antifa chaos in Charlottesville, Virginia, to spearhead a pressure campaign called "Blood Money" against financial institutions including Mastercard, Amazon, PayPal, Discover, American Express, Visa, and

Stripe.[216] The speech-squelchers bragged that their pressure helped "push PayPal and Mastercard to remove their services from dozens of hate sites, and to create internal policies to stop profiting from bigotry"—policies shaped, as we'll see later, by Soros-backed entities redefining conservative dissent as "hate." OSF has bestowed Color of Change with grants amounting to at least $550,000 since 2009.[217]

Founded by socialist University of Illinois Urbana-Champaign professor Robert McChesney in 2003, the nonprofit Free Press and its advocacy arm, Free Press Action Fund, are organized around "net neutrality"—a "progressive" plan to expand regulatory authority over the internet while cloaking their online power grab in the rhetoric of civil rights and technological "access" for "people of color." In 2009, OSF gave the group $350,000 for general support[218] of its agenda to "change the media to transform democracy to realize a just society."[219] A conservative Media Research Center analysis tallied Free Press's total OSF haul at $2,210,000 between 2000 and 2013.[220] Barack Obama and his Federal Communications Commission embraced the rhetoric of net neutrality and its preferred government takeover of the internet with convoluted rules governing internet service providers, bandwidth use, content, prices, and even disclosure details on internet speeds. Obama FCC commissioner Michael Copps proclaimed, "Universal access to broadband needs to be seen as a civil right." The Trump administration's FCC preferred a free internet and repealed "net neutrality" rules in December 2017.[221] Soros-funded Free Press and the National Hispanic Media Coalition joined other astroturf "media justice" groups and tech companies in a lawsuit against the FCC to restore the regulatory regime.[222]

On immigration, Free Press occupies itself coaching liberal journalists on how to cover the migrant caravan. First, never say "migrant caravan" because it is "a term that dehumanizes, criminalizes and sensationalizes the Central American refugees to stir up racism and fear" ("migrant exodus" is now the proper euphemism).[223] Also out: "invasion" (there goes my first book!) and "crossing" the border ("presenting" is the acceptable term).[224] Free Press has created guides and dispatched activists to newsrooms to "help journalists and newsrooms disrupt oppression in the way they do their work."[225]

Disruption is indeed the name of the game.

Corporate Catalysts

Let us now return to George Soros's September 2016 decision to earmark $500 million from his Soros Economic Development Fund for "startups, established companies, social-impact initiatives and businesses founded by migrants and refugees themselves."[226] Any profits, he wrote in his op-ed for the *Wall Street Journal* (yes, the very same newspaper that declared "There shall be open borders"[227]) will go to fund programs at the Open Society Foundations.[228] An estimated $100 million of the gift will be invested. So far, according to investment publication *Impact Alpha*, $8 million has been earmarked for GroFin's Nomou Jordan Fund (along with $400,000 in technical assistance) to finance and support small businesses in Jordan, hard-hit by massive numbers of Syrian refugees. Another $3 million will be invested in Humanity United's Working Capital fund, "which backs early stage companies with innovations to boost transparency and protect workers, including migrants and refugees, in global supply chains."[229] Refugees, the investment report noted, are being eyed for their potential as "investable" resources.[230]

With Soros's latest half-billion dollar investment in private-sector profiteers of global migration chaos, Open Borders Inc. is now a completely self-perpetuating racket. Here are some of the corporate names and investment funds cashing in:

- *Mastercard/Mastercard Aid Network:* The financial services giant now markets itself as a "future-forward technology company moving 'beyond borders' to a 'World Without Cash.'"[231] In 2017, the credit card company announced a new partnership with George Soros called Humanity Ventures to use its payment, data, and identity tools to help migrants and refugees "connect to the formal economy."[232] Ajay Banga, president and CEO of Mastercard, hailed the alliance in a press release: "We can have transformational impact by scaling our business-driven organization to leverage innovation, on-the-ground experience and long-term capital investments." Mastercard publicized a potential $50 million investment from Soros, who decried migrants' inability "to gain access to financial, healthcare and government services." Soros praised Mastercard's ability to "create products that serve vulnerable communities," showing "how private capital can play a constructive role in solving social problems."[233]

Indeed, the Mastercard Aid Network has already partnered with many of the Soros-backed NGOs facilitating border-busting. The company produced special chip-enabled, prepaid cards to be doled out to migrants and refugees allowing them to acquire food, medicine, or shelter from participating groups or vendors. Open Society–funded Save the Children used the system in Yemen to distribute aid. In addition to prepaid cards, the system offers capabilities for sending money to mobile wallets, bank accounts, and ATMs. Open Society partner Mercy Corps[234] deployed Mastercard prepaid debit cards ($235 for families; $78 for individuals) as part of a pilot program to an estimated four hundred participants from Syria, Iraq, and Afghanistan traveling through Serbia. Mercy Corps and Mastercard added similar debit card cash programs to nearly four thousand refugees in seven camps and shelters in Greece.[235]

Separately, Mastercard teamed with the United Nations High Commissioner for Refugees (UNHCR) to expand a $27 million cash distribution system in Turkey for more than half a million refugees and asylum-seekers. Debit cards were provided to 108,000 refugee families, including 96,000 Syrian families, through UNHCR's financial services provider, Turkey's Postal and Telegraph Corporation. The cards allowed the recipients to use them at any shop that was part of the Mastercard circuit network. The $27 million winter program included "a personalized SMS [short messaging service] system, an interactive webpage which provides real-time verification of eligibility by applicants, call-centre support and leaflets in several languages."[236]

What does Mastercard's willingness to partner with Soros and his NGO network tell us about the company's political leanings? Actions speak louder than words. As we'll see in chapter 6, Mastercard is now entangled in the business of facilitating the financial blacklisting of those who dare defy the Open Society juggernaut.

- *CREDO Mobile:* It's the cell phone company "with a conscience," otherwise known as "America's progressive carrier." CREDO is a San Francisco-based mobile virtual network powered by Verizon Wireless and founded by privately held Working Assets, a "socially responsible" money market fund that spawned a telecommunications company. The company first launched a credit card that generates donations to progressive nonprofit groups every time the cardholder uses it, then introduced long-distance phone service, and most recently rolled out mobile phones. CREDO claims its donations to left-wing groups have reached over $87 million. Its CREDO Action network of activists has reportedly grown to more than 5.9 million members.[237] Its published list of recipients includes the following Soros-backed and Soros-allied open-borders entities: the American Civil Liberties Union, Color of Change, Center for Media Justice, International Rescue

Mission, Center for Constitutional Rights, Doctors Without Borders/Médecins Sans Frontières, Muslim Advocates, Mercy Corps, Southern Poverty Law Center, and United We Dream.[238] On immigration, CREDO Mobile has stepped up its resistance efforts:

- Distributing free "ABOLISH ICE" and "FREEDOM FOR IMMIGRANTS" posters to members[239]
- Barging into former DHS secretary Kirstjen Nielsen's neighborhood with signs calling her a "child snatcher" and protesting Trump immigration enforcement policies on her front lawn by blaring leaked audio of crying children who were separated from their parents at the border[240]
- Joining the "spontaneous" protests (organized by Soros-backed Make the Road) at airports against President Trump's national security-based restrictions on foreign travelers[241]

In conjunction with Soros, the Obama White House issued its own "Call to Action," urging other private-sector ideological allies to make their own virtue-signaling "commitments to address the global refugee crisis."[242] (See Appendix E for the press release listing the companies.) The list of corporations stepping up to volunteer their time, money, and personnel to support the Trump administration's America First agenda is much, much shorter. So is the list of government-funded nonprofits stepping up to the plate to aid American families, neighborhoods, and workers harmed by immigration anarchy and SorosWorld. Question their patriotism? Hell, yes.

Faith-Based Flunkies

Strange bedfellows can sometimes accomplish great things. When it comes to open borders, however, "bipartisanship" is almost always bad for America. As I reported in my book *Sold Out*,[243] the National Immigration Forum (NIF) was founded by far-left attorney Dale Frederick "Rick" Swartz of the Lawyers Committee for Civil Rights, who opposed tracking and deporting visa overstayers and opposed sanctions against companies that violated immigration laws.[244] Swartz cozied up to open-borders Wall Street whiz and philanthropist Richard Gilder, Grover Norquist, the U.S. Chamber of Commerce, and the libertarian Cato Institute.[245] Swartz also served as an adviser to Microsoft. In 2009, Open Society Foundations gave a $2.5 million grant to NIF for "immigration reform" work.[246] In the spring of 2013, GOP mega-bundler, Mitt Romney supporter, and hedge fund billionaire Paul Singer (net worth: $2 billion) forked over a "six-figure donation" to NIF.[247] Swartz's open-borders, left-right coalition helped sabotage the Immigration Act of 1990, which was intended to impose modest restrictions on immigration, and turned it into "one of the most expansionist immigration bills ever passed."[248] Swartz worked with former Michigan GOP Senator Spencer Abraham's legislative director, Cesar Conda, and former Kansas GOP Senator Sam Brownback's legislative director, Paul Ryan (yes, *that* Paul Ryan), to kill 1996 immigration enforcement measures. Moving forward, NIF allied with religious conservatives to put a holy glow on open borders. Swartz propped up a faux grassroots initiative of religious conservatives, dubbed the Evangelical Immigration Table, to lobby for the infamous Gang of Eight immigration expansion bill.[249] NIF's newly branded initiative, "Bibles, Badges, and Business" (BBB) lobbies for protecting and expanding refugee resettlement, allowing illegal aliens in the military, and expansion of foreign worker programs to maintain the flow of cheap labor to Big Business.[250] While BBB pays lip service to the federal government's need to enforce our immigration laws, NIF's executive director Ali Noorani condemns construction of meaningful border walls[251] and traveled to El Paso, Texas, to declare that "our southern border is more secure than ever."[252] God help us.

Open Society Foundations has forged multiple alliances with left-wing religious groups that support expanding the welfare state and filling their pews with dependent illegal aliens. Faith in Action is a religious charity that runs a radical activist network based in Oakland, California, which crusades for gun control, welfare state expansion, drivers' licenses for illegal aliens, and mass amnesty for all immigration lawbreakers. Formerly known as PICO (Pacific Institute for Community Organization) National, the group was founded by liberal Chicago Catholic priest John Baumann, who studied under community organizing godfather Saul Alinsky, the notorious author of *Rules for Radicals*.[253] In 2016, the group received $750,000 from OSF.[254] The PICO Action Fund is the "social welfare" arm of PICO/Faith in Action. Leaked internal documents obtained by the *Washington Free Beacon* exposed the electoral plans of PICO Action and the $80 million Soros-funded Center for Popular Democracy to "challenge Trump and his dangerous agenda on all fronts—in the streets, in state houses and Congress, and at the ballot box." The strategy aims to elect more Democrats to the United States Senate and House of Representatives and "progressive governors and state legislators who will oversee census and redistricting in 2020–2021."[255]

The "grassroots" nonprofit Faith in Public Life claims to oversee a "national network of nearly 50,000 clergy and faith leaders united in the prophetic pursuit of justice and the common good." In 2010, OSF gave the group $450,000.[256] DCLeaks documents show Faith in Public Life (FPL)and PICO/Faith in Action worked together to capitalize on Pope Francis's 2015 visit to the United States and push Catholic bishops in an even more leftward direction on economics and immigration.[257] Internal minutes revealed the explicitly political aims of the Soros-funded groups: "by harnessing the Papal visit to lift up the Pope's searing critique of what he calls 'an economy of exclusion and inequality' and his dismissal of 'trickle down' theories, PICO and FPL will work to build a bridge to a larger conversation about bread-and-butter economic concerns and shift national paradigms and priorities in the run-up to the 2016 presidential campaign."[258] As Fr. Robert Sirico, a priest and founder of the pro-free market Acton Institute, noted: "Given the efforts evident among some faith-based activist groups, which essentially appear to be about influencing the present presidential campaign and even raising money using images of Pope Francis, I believe Mr. Soros's investment has paid off."[259]

Another Soros-backed partnership with Catholic open-borders crusaders is the World Meeting of Popular Movements. This gathering is an initiative of Pope Francis, organized by Soros-funded PICO National, showcasing radicalized left-wing Catholic leaders working to address the "economy of exclusion and inequality… by working for structural changes that promote social, economic and racial justice."[260] Sounding more like a Democratic presidential candidate than a clergyman, San Diego Bishop Robert McElroy told seven hundred attendees at the 2017 U.S. Regional Meeting of Popular Movements that "we must all become disrupters" on behalf of illegal aliens, the "undocumented," and Muslims in the wake of President Trump's election.[261] Pope Francis chimed in with a support letter declaring, "It makes me very happy to see you working together towards social justice," and decrying the "invisible tyranny of money" as a disability and restriction to human dignity and the common good.[262]

Now that we've amassed and connected hundreds of Open Society satellites around the world all working to remove the "obstacles" to global governance, mass migration, cheap illegal alien labor, and coerced refugee redistribution, we can say "¡Adios!" to the preposterous denial that George Soros and his sovereignty-sabotaging galaxy have nothing to do with the de facto smuggling rings on land and sea dumping unwanted masses on our shores. We've still barely scratched the surface of Open Borders Inc. It's not just a swamp. It's a sinkhole threatening to swallow us all.

But let's venture even deeper into the sinkhole to follow the "tyranny of money" fueling George Soros's allies at the Vatican and the U.S. Conference of Catholic Bishops who are playing the faith card to eliminate our national borders.

CHAPTER THREE

UNHOLY ALLIANCE: THE POPE, CATHOLIC BISHOPS, AND AMNESTY PROFITEERS

"And he built fenced cities in Judah: for the land had rest, and he had no war in those years; because the LORD had given him rest. Therefore he said unto Judah, Let us build these cities, and make about them walls, and towers, gates, and bars, while the land is yet before us; because we have sought the LORD our God, we have sought him, and he hath given us rest on every side. So they built and prospered...."
—2 Chronicles 14:6

Pope Francis lives and lectures like a Hollywood celebrity: He vociferously condemns others for building walls and desiring security, while he is enveloped by barriers, barricades, and bulletproof glass. His Holiness hectors the rest of the world to open our borders to millions of international migrants every year, while zealously sealing off the Catholic Church's sanctuary space in the heart of Rome. The papal center enjoys ironclad independent sovereignty and wealth beyond imagination. No expense is spared to protect it.

The Vatican is the mother of all exclusive gated communities, with fortifications and phalanxes around its 109 acres that make Beverly Hills look like Appalachia. Keeping watch at the entrances to Vatican City are the members of the Pontifical Swiss Guard. More than just a ceremonial force, the 140-man standing army is staffed by highly trained marksmen with expertise in crowd control, VIP protection, lethal and less than lethal weapons employment, and surveillance.[1] They accompany the Holy Father on all his travels, packing the same personal defense weapons that fire armor-piercing small caliber rifle rounds used by SEAL Team Six and presidential protection units around the globe, as well as Sig Sauer pistols and rifles.[2] Vatican City has its own separate police force, the Gendarmerie Corps of Vatican City State, which performs border control, general security, and investigative duties. They, too, are highly trained and highly armed, "with a full range of modern weaponry," including "Glock pistols and Heckler & Koch and Beretta submachine guns" plus "Carbon 15 machine pistols and Heckler & Koch/ FABARM shotguns."[3]

Among the big, beautiful walls that ring the world's smallest nation-state are the sturdy Aurelian Walls of Rome dating back to the third century. In 846, those barriers helped repel Saracen invaders, but the basilicas of Sts. Paul and Peter that lay outside the walls fell prey to the Muslim looters, who carted away every last jewel and gilded treasure, including the altars.[4] After the sacking, Pope Leo IV imposed a levy throughout the empire to pay for a new barricade to protect the basilicas.[5] The thirty-nine-foot-high Leonine Wall, completed in 852, completely encircled Vatican City and successfully prevented another Muslim invasion.[6] From Paul III to Pius IV through Pope Urban VIII in the seventeenth century, church leaders continued to add to and fortify the walls.[7]

Bear all this history in mind as you contemplate the pope's repeated attacks on President Trump's wall-building efforts in America:

- "He who raises a wall ends up a prisoner of the wall he erected. That's a universal law in the social order and in the personal one. If you raise a wall between people, you end up a prisoner of that wall that you raised."[8] —March 2019

- "[T]here is the temptation to a culture of walls, to raise walls, walls in the heart and on earth to prevent this encounter with other cultures, with other people. And whoever raises a wall, whoever builds a wall will end up as a slave inside the walls he has built, without horizons."[9] —March 2019

- "'We know that the father of lies, the devil, prefers a community divided and bickering,' Francis told a crowd of tens of thousands of youth Thursday night at a seaside park in Panama City. 'This is the criteria to divide people: The builders of bridges and the builders of walls, those builders of walls sow fear and look to divide people. What do you want to be?' When the crowd replied 'builders of bridges,' Francis replied, 'You learned well. I like that.' The Pope's remarks seemed to be a clear reference to President Donald Trump's proposal to build a wall along the US-Mexico border."[10] —January 2019

- "I invite you not to build walls but bridges, to conquer evil with good, offence with forgiveness, to live in peace with everyone."[11] —March 2017

- "We need to knock down the walls that divide us: try to boost well-being and make it more widespread but in order to achieve this, we need to knock down walls and build bridges that can lessen inequality and boost freedom and rights.... What we want is a fight against inequality, this is the biggest evil that exists in the world today."[12] —November 2016

- "A person who thinks only about building walls, wherever they may be located, and not building bridges, is not a Christian. This is not in the gospel, the Pope told journalists who asked his opinion on Trump's proposals to halt illegal immigration."[13]—February 2016

I was raised Catholic, but the words of the current pope and past popes on America's immigration policy are not gospel. Pope Francis has issued apostolic exhortations citing the Old Testament to justify open borders, such as Exodus 22:21: "You shall not wrong a stranger or oppress him, for you yourselves were strangers in the land of Egypt." Yet he ignores a multitude of biblical examples of leaders, from King Asa to Nehemiah to David, who built walls to protect their lands and people, with the Lord's approval or at his specific behest. Pope Francis further counsels every other sovereign nation to implement a program of open-ended hospitality for "welcoming the stranger" in the spirit of Saint Benedict.[14] To date, however, the pontiff has not instituted such a policy in his own nation-state and thrown open the gates of Vatican City to any and all strangers seeking refuge. Even worse, His Eminence takes a far more radical position of not only demanding that we admit every asylee and refugee claimant without question, but also that every economic migrant be allowed onto our soil. The "only proper attitude" for a Christian towards illegal aliens, he proselytizes, "is to stand in the shoes of those brothers and sisters of ours who risk their lives to offer a future to their children."[15]

Patriotic Catholics have voiced their opposition to the social justice hijacking of theology for promoting unfettered immigration. The late archbishop Cardinal Giacomo Biffi called for careful vetting of immigrants in Italy to preserve its national culture and character. "The criteria for admitting immigrants can never be just economic," he argued in 2000. "It is necessary to concern oneself seriously with saving the identity of the nation." No one has a "right of invasion," he told two hundred priests, in response to a wave of illegal Muslim immigrants and other non-assimilating foreigners. He warned an Italian minister at the time, "If you really have the good of Italy at heart, and want to spare a lot of suffering, then you can't allow all the immigrants in."[16]

Father Andrew McNair, chaplain for the Office of Black Catholic Ministry of the Diocese of Providence, distinguished "Good Samaritan" open-borders Catholics from "enforcement Catholics" who understand that the "endorsement of lawlessness does not serve the common good of society." Alluding to the church's own catechism on welcoming foreigners, Fr. McNair stated plainly that "the right to immigrate is not absolute"; the "common good of any nation consists of three principles: respect for the person, social well-being and development, and peace"; and "lax immigration policy walks over these principles." The Catechism of the Catholic Church 2241 acknowledges that immigrants "are obliged to respect with gratitude the material and spiritual heritage of the country that receives them, to obey its laws and to assist in carrying civic burdens."[17] He concluded, "Enforcing the law and asking people to obey the law isn't mean or heartless, but charity in its truest sense."[18]

Citing Revelation 21:12 and Luke 13:25, Monsignor Charles Pope of the Archdiocese of Washington, D.C., noted that "even Heaven has walls and gates—and a very strict immigration policy!"[19]

Chaldean Catholic Bishop Bawai Soro in El Cajon, California, an Iraqi Christian refugee who came to the U.S. forty years ago, defended President Trump's border wall and vetting initiatives based on past experience and common national interest. Rejecting the open-borders orthodoxy of the elite bishops, he wrote: "Being delayed as a refugee is not a new thing. All the previous administrations, since President Carter, delayed numerous refugees and migrants not only for months but also for years. If Americans really believed that coming to America was a universal human right, I assure you that by now the US population might have reached three billion, instead of only 325 million." Soro added that our nation needs to protect itself from all manner of intruders, but particularly those in jihad-wracked territories like the one he escaped: "If America needs to build a wall and vet refugees, then it must be so. If a simple house is to be secured, doesn't the owner of the house lock the doors at night?" he asked. "What happens if thieves know the door is unlocked? Open borders and easy-going immigration policies are what could inflict the US with the fire that has been burning in the Middle East for centuries."[20]

Contrary to the pope's radical and selective pronouncements, scripture teaches citizens to honor the rule of law and secular authorities who preserve and defend civil order and safety. Romans 13:1–7 counsels: "Let every person be subject to the governing authorities. For there is no authority except from God, and those that exist have been instituted by God. Therefore, whoever resists the authorities resists what God has appointed, and those who resist will incur judgment." Our laws are clear. 8 U.S. Code Section 1324 makes it a felony to knowingly bring or attempt to bring aliens across the border illegally; to knowingly conceal, harbor or shield them from detection in reckless disregard for the law; and to engage in any conspiracy or to aid and abet such acts. The Catholic leadership's institutional resistance to our sovereignty is an act of treachery, not an act of faith, which destabilizes an ordered society.

There are currently an estimated 1.3 billion Catholics around the world, including 72 million in America. According to Georgetown University's Center for Applied Research in the Apostolate, American Catholics donate an average of $10 to their parish every Sunday. According to the *National Catholic Register* in 2012, average annual parish revenue in the United States is $695,291.[21] Multiply that by the 17,139 parishes in the country and parish income alone totals $11.9 billion, with two-thirds ($8.2 billion) coming from the collection plate. Capital campaigns, one-time gifts, inheritances and other relatively minor sources account for the rest.[22] The Vatican's wealth is shrouded in mystery, but over two thousand years, the Vatican has amassed incalculable treasures ranging from art to buildings to property to gold reserves, commercial concerns, and investments so vast that its own internal audits have accidentally turned up "hundreds of millions of euros" that were "tucked away" and overlooked or misplaced.[23] The Vatican Bank, which manages $7.3 billion in assets, reportedly stores away $20 million in gold reserves at the U.S. Federal Reserve.[24] Avro Manhattan, author of *The Vatican Billions*, documented how the Church transformed from a charitable enterprise into big business—complete with its own investment office advisors, including "J. P. Morgan in New York (mostly for American investments), Hambros of London for British investments, and the Swiss Credit Bank of Zurich for European investments" to maximize profits and manage its liquid financial assets.[25] In 2012, *The Economist* estimated that annual spending by the Church and entities owned by the Church in the U.S. "was around $170 billion in 2010 (the Church does not release such figures). We think 57% of this goes on health-care networks, followed by 28% on colleges, with parish and diocesan day-to-day operations accounting for just 6% and national charitable activities just 2.7%."

So, why is the fabulously wealthy Vatican so hell-bent on foisting millions of illegal aliens, primarily from Hispanic Catholic countries, on us? One answer: in North America, the Catholic Church is losing members at a faster rate than any other denomination, which means less money and less political influence for the Church. Another factor is that illegal alien Catholics in the U.S. earn higher wages than they would at home. Their donations in American collection baskets—and their remittances to family members—mean more money for the Church.

Pew Research determined that some three million American Catholics left the Church between 2007 and 2015; and a total of thirty million Americans identify themselves as *former* Catholics, with nearly 30 percent citing the sex abuse scandals as their reason for abandoning the faith.[26] Settlements and monetary awards paid out by the Church reportedly now total more than $4 billion.[27] It took decades for rank-and-file Catholics to revolt against their Church's worldwide conspiracy to whitewash rampant pedophilia and silence abuse victims. Loyalty, fear, intimidation, shame, denial, and lack of transparency were all major factors. I believe the same is true for the Catholic Church's deplorable open-borders scandal. Although the sex abuse scandal first broke in Boston in 2002, only recently have the faithful stopped filling gilded coffers with their hard-earned dollars. After a Pennsylvania grand jury report in 2018 exposed how three hundred priests sexually abused more than one thousand children, and how bishops coordinated the cover-up, parishioners exploded.[28] "We need to cut off the money," author John Zmirak told the website Church Militant. "Big Catholic donors should create a 'St. Escrow' movement, with escrow accounts for each diocese, where all gifts go instead of to the bishop. Let the money pile up, and have committees of faithful laymen hold bishops accountable, if they want a single dime."[29] One disgusted Catholic even tweeted a video of herself burning her church's tithe envelopes on a backyard grill and did not mince words: "Burn in hell you despicable, evil, scumbag pieces of shit."[30]

"Stop donating to corrupt bishops and clerics," Beverly Stevens, editor in chief of *Regina Magazine*, urged. "Why? Because you are enabling them."[31]

Legions of Catholics have been similarly deceived, duped, and left in the dark about how their donations are enabling human trafficking, violent crime, and exploitation of cheap, illegal alien labor in America. The Good Samaritan Catholics have been exhorted to marginalize the Enforcement Catholics based on phony, self-serving theological fictions concocted by walled-off elites driven to fill pews and replenish collection plates. It's one thing to show compassion to legal immigrants, legitimate refugees and asylees, and those abused and mistreated by smugglers. It's quite another to support the systematic undermining of an orderly immigration and entrance system that imposes limits, eligibility requirements, criminal background checks, medical screening, and a commitment to assimilation. Since 1986, when open-borders lobbyists were hammering out the disastrous Reagan amnesty on Capitol Hill, Catholic leaders in the U.S. and abroad have moved from fighting against legislation that enhances American immigration enforcement to actively undermining enforcement and violating immigration laws. Catholic bishops vigorously fought the employer sanction provisions of the Immigration Reform and Control Act, California's anti-illegal immigration Proposition 187, and Arizona's anti-illegal immigration SB 1070. Liberal priests and cardinals in Chicago and Los Angeles have promoted sanctuary policies for decades. Disgraced leftist cardinal Roger Mahony, censured and banned for his role in covering up sexual abuse,[32] was booted from his post in

Los Angeles, yet continues to advocate that Catholic clergy and other Americans brazenly defy deportation orders and harbor DREAMers.[33] Catholic lawyers, relief workers, and volunteers aid and abet illegal aliens every day in the name of "charity."

The Vatican donated at least $20,000 in 2009 through the Pontifical Commission for Latin America to erect a shelter for Central American illegal aliens sneaking through Ixtepec, Mexico, where they hopped on freight trains into our country.[34] Mexican Catholic priest Father Alejandro Solalinde Guerra established Brothers on the Path (Hermanos en el Camino) in 2007 to run the shelter, which lies at a "strategic point of convergence between the Pacific Ocean and the Gulf of Mexico, with migration flows coming from the south, primarily Central America. The majority of the migrants arrive by riding on top of freight trains coming from the neighboring state of Chiapas."[35] Another papal society, Catholic Extension, poured more than $12 million dollars into ministries along our southern border over five years "to ensure that those who are on a journey are protected by the Church and that we advocate on their behalf," according to the Catholic News Agency.[36] In April 2019, Pope Francis donated $500,000 through his Peter's Pence Collection fund to fund twenty-seven projects associated with sixteen Mexican dioceses and congregations for 75,000 migrants who arrived in Mexico in 2018 as part of six caravans. The first round of funding went to Mexican bishops in the dioceses of "Cuautitlán, Nogales, Mazatlán, Querétaro, San Andrés Tuxtla, Nuevo Laredo, and Tijuana; as well as for the Scalabrinians, the congregation of the Sacred Hearts of Jesus and Mary and the Josefinas Sisters."[37]

We're diving into the shocking finances and unpatriotic perfidy of these top four Catholic entities colluding against America:

- U.S. Conference of Catholic Bishops
  - Migration and Refugee Services
  - Justice For Immigrants
  - Catholic Campaign for Human Development

- Catholic Legal Immigration Network
- Catholic Relief Services
- Catholic Charities

Catholic or not, all citizens who work hard and play by the rules will be shocked to learn how much of the Vatican-directed sabotage of our borders is funded not by collection-plate cash or tithes—but by your tax dollars and mine.

Radical Bishops, Alien Pawns

The U.S. Conference of Catholic Bishops grew out of the National Catholic War Council, created in 1917 to take care of American servicemen during World War I. Americans of faith demonstrated their compassion and love for Americans in uniform. "Standing firmly upon our solid Catholic tradition and history from the very founding of the Nation," Cardinal James Gibbons of Baltimore declared at the time, "we reaffirm in this hour of stress and trial our most sacred and sincere loyalty and patriotism toward our country, our government, and our flag."[38]

Now, contrast that legacy with USCCB's politicized activity since President Trump was elected. The group has released scores of statements regarding immigration. Every single one of those missives opposes rational immigration limits, condemns sovereignty enforcement, and puts global interests above America's. Archbishop José Gomez, head of the Los Angeles archdiocese, penned a CNN op-ed blasting President Trump's workplace enforcement actions, blanket-condemning any and all deportations of illegal aliens, and bemoaning the plight of outlaws "who live in the shadows."[39] He refused to acknowledge their lawbreaking, instead referring to their "status" as "irregular." Similarly, Bishop Nicholas DiMarzio of Brooklyn rejected any distinction between legal and illegal, excusing criminal border trespassing, criminal visa violations, and criminal document fraud by rationalizing that "undocumented immigrants have either entered without inspection or, more commonly in recent years, have overstayed or otherwise violated the terms of their temporary visas by working with false documents. As human beings, they cannot be 'illegal.' Moreover, they do honest work that is needed by our society."[40] Which means money to fill collection plates and bodies to fill church pews.

Bishop Thomas Joseph Tobin of the Providence, Rhode Island, diocese issued a declaration of support for drivers' licenses for illegal aliens in his state, citing the pope's call "to welcome immigrants into our midst" because "these immigrants will enrich America and its Church."

Key words: "Enrich" its "Church."[41]

Rev. Joe S. Vásquez, chairman of USCCB's Committee on Migration and bishop of the Diocese of Austin, Texas, condemned President Trump's plans for the border wall in January 2017 and staked out the church's extreme position of opposing all increased immigration detention and deportation efforts. While paying disingenuous lip service to a nation's right to enforce its borders, Vásquez decried the separation of families and made the Church's priorities clear: "We will continue to support and stand in solidarity with immigrant families."[42] Reunification of unaccompanied minors with family members is not just an emotional rallying cry or hashtag. For USCCB's Catholic Charities, it's a "ministry" and an ever-expanding cash cow totaling more than $104 million between 2008 and 2018, according to the Capital Research Center.[43] (As I'll explain more in chapter four, Catholic Charities serves as a prime contractor for the unaccompanied alien children racket created by President Obama and exploited by tax-funded religious charities and immigration lawyers during the southern border surges under his watch.)[44]

In November 2018, Vásquez condemned the Trump White House plan to end asylum abuse and stem the Central American caravan floods. The USCCB again made its allegiances clear: "the Catholic Church will continue to serve, accompany and assist all those who flee persecution, regardless of where they seek such protection and where they are from."[45] When the Trump administration moved to enforce long-standing rules requiring that foreigners seeking entrance into the country demonstrate that they will not become public charges (dependent on welfare),[46] Vásquez protested that guarding American citizens and law-abiding immigrants already here from those unwanted costs of illegal immigration would "be very harmful to families, raising fear among immigrant families already struggling to fulfill the American Dream. Further, it is likely to prevent families from accessing important medical and social services vital to public health and welfare."[47]

How did such a once-noble and patriotic organization of Catholics who coalesced to support American soldiers transmogrify into an anti-American, open-borders juggernaut for cheap, illegal alien workers and worshipers?

The USCCB now describes itself as "an assembly of the hierarchy of the United States and the U.S. Virgin Islands who jointly exercise certain pastoral functions on behalf of the Christian faithful of the United States" to "promote the greater good" that its 264-member organization "offers mankind."[48] Ministering to American soldiers fell by the wayside in favor of lobbying for refugees, economic migrants, deportation evaders, and other immigration outlaws. The USCCB is incorporated as a tax-exempt 501(c)(3) charity in Washington, D.C., with 315 employees who "organize and conduct religious, charitable and social welfare work at home and abroad," "aid in education," and "care for immigrants."[49] Under canon law, "the Christian faithful are obliged to assist with the needs of the Church," the USCCB dictates, "for divine worship, for the works of the apostolate and of charity, and for the decent support of ministers." The elite Catholic conference counsels its flock that followers "are also obliged to promote social justice" and assist the "poor."

The Church does quite well for itself by doing supposed good. According to the group's 2017 financial records prepared by KPMG that I examined, $11.6 million filled the USCCB's treasury from diocesan assessments. The USCCB's total operating revenues, gains, and other support have swelled to an eye-popping $274,096,328.[50]

Migration and Refugee Services

Nearly $144 million poured in from "national collections," which refers to contributions from parishioners solicited throughout the year by their local clergy. These funds are funneled to specific programs and "subordinate" arms of the USCCB, including the Catholic Communication Campaign (public relations), Catholic Relief Services Collection; Catholic Campaign for Human Development, Catholic Home Missions Appeal, Collection for the Church in Central and Eastern Europe, Collection for the Church in Latin America, Peter's Pence Collection (subsidizing the needs of the pope), Retirement Fund for Religious, Solidarity Fund for the Church in Africa, and Trinity Dome Collection. Government contracts and grant revenue total more than $72 million, and more than $3.5 million came from collection fees on refugee loans.

Holy guacamole. Let's tackle the $72 million from government contracts and grants revenue first. Government money means tax money. That means *your* money and *my* money. Get out your pencils for some easy back-of-the-envelope calculations: $72 million out of $123 million in total unrestricted operating revenue means that this "religious charity" depends on government subsidies for 59 percent of its revenue base. It also spells a screaming financial conflict of interest for an increasingly radicalized faith-based organization that spends a considerable amount of its efforts issuing barbed political statements opposing the Trump administration's immigration enforcement policies. (And don't forget, as a 501(c)(3), the USCCB enjoys huge tax benefits: the group and its subordinates are exempt from paying federal income taxes; donations are deductible for federal income, gift, and estate tax purposes; and diocesan priests are exempt from paying Social Security taxes.)[51] This $72 million mountain of our tax dollars goes to the USCCB's refugee resettlement program and other related services to illegal aliens, purported asylum seekers, and anti-trafficking efforts. Since 1975, the USCCB has contracted with the feds to perform resettlement activities financed by government agencies led by the U.S. Department of Health and Human Services and the U.S. Department of State under the authority of the amended Immigration and Nationality

Act. It is the "largest nongovernmental refugee resettlement agency in the world," working with more than one hundred local refugee resettlement programs to help transport and relocate twenty thousand refugees each year into the interior of the U.S. Moreover, it is the single largest of the nine non-governmental organizations anointed by the State Department to carry out the refugee resettlement boondoggle, having resettled nearly one-third of all refugees since 1980.[52] (We'll plunge into the other eight volunteer agencies—"VOLAGs"—which rake in hundreds of millions each on refugee resettlement in the next chapter.) The USCCB was reimbursed $11,415,905 and $11,504,703 for direct administrative costs and program services provided for resettlement activities for the full years at the end of 2017 and 2016.[53]

Investigative blogger and journalist Ann Corcoran of Refugee Resettlement Watch determined that the charity had soaked up more than $534 million of taxpayer dollars for refugee resettlement programs between 2008 and 2017.[54] Bear in mind that this figure does not include the public costs of subsidized housing, education, health care, criminal justice and the courts, food stamps, cash, and other welfare aid. We'll get into the nuts and bolts of how the USCCB and Catholic Charities collaborate to distribute refugees across the country without the input—or against the will—of unsuspecting communities shortly.

For now, let's note that on top of receiving more than half a billion taxpayer dollars for refugee resettlement programs, the USCCB also gets travel agent benefits, raking in "collection fees" on refugee travel loans. Here's how it works: Refugees are flown to the U.S. through a contractor known as the International Organization for Migration (IOM; see chapter 4). IOM makes loans to the refugees to purchase airline tickets and cover other travel and resettlement costs, and the State Department's Bureau for Population, Refugees, and Migration forwards the money for the loans—which means, once again, you and I as taxpayers foot the bill. The USCCB "sponsors" the refugees, which means the refugees repay the loans through the USCCB, which, in turn, pockets a "collection fee." How convenient, and profitable, for the USCCB!

So you see, the USCCB's fervent calls for America to absorb thousands of Syrian Muslims and its heated condemnations of the Trump administration's slowdown of refugee intake can't just be taken at face value. When Bishop Vásquez decried the White House executive order in 2017 which cut refugee admissions from 110,000 to 50,000, imposed increased security vetting, and barred new entrants from dangerous countries, the clergyman asserted that the group's heated and repeated opposition to rational immigration control was "living out our Christian faith as Jesus has challenged us to do" as an "act of love and hope."[55] But the open-borders business of the Catholic Church is less about love, hope, faith, or charity than it is about cold, hard cash.

Justice for Immigrants

During the George W. Bush years, Catholic leaders joined forces with open-borders Democrats and cheap-labor Republicans to push for an "immigration reform" package in Washington. One of the agitating groups was Justice for Immigrants (JFI). In the early 2000s, JFI was a lobbying group, supporting the legalization of an estimated 2.1 million unlawful border-trespassers, visa overstayers, and deportation evaders, mostly from Mexico and Latin America. Through groups like JFI, the USCCB wanted to make "legalization" a "major public policy priority" and "create political will for positive immigration reform."[56] Today, JFI's "action alerts" mimic the hysterical tone of far-left demagogic movements such as Abolish ICE—inciting opposition to all immigration enforcement, condemning all border walls (except the Vatican's), and attacking detention reform as "inhumane."[57]

JFI's national manager at the USCCB, Tony Cube, is a former staffer for left-wing Democratic Senator Patty Murray of Washington, and JFI's partners have been tasked with Democratic resistance-style activism and public relations propagandizing against President Trump's immigration agenda. "[P]ositive examples of migrants and their communities should be promoted and fear based narratives that prey on the insecurities of the native population, condemned," a JFI document advises, to decrease opposition to amnesty and refugee resettlement.[58] The JFI Twitter account tweets out heartstring-tugging memes of illegal aliens every #MigrationMonday and urged followers to help "resettle 30,000 refugees in 2019."[59] The action alert did not disclose the amount of money the USCCB stands to reap from its demand, nor did it acknowledge that Pope Francis himself—the loudest preacher of "welcoming the stranger"—has yet to resettle a single refugee inside the walls of the Vatican. A few families brought by the pope to Rome from a Greek detention center for a widely disseminated photo op in 2016 were dumped in the community of Sant'Egidio outside the Vatican walls and are given living expenses "every now and then."[60] Another forty were brought over in 2018 and will be spread across Italy—but none will be resettled inside the Vatican walls.[61]

In total, the USCCB spent $19,470,670 in 2017 on what it calls "communications, policy, and advocacy activities."[62] It is difficult to determine how much of that is political advocacy, because churches are exempt from filing tax returns with the IRS, their lobbyists are exempt from disclosure requirements, and the USCCB stopped voluntarily disclosing such information to Pew Research in 2010, according to Ian Smith of the Immigration Reform Law Institute.[63]

Catholic Campaign for Human Development

The Catholic Campaign for Human Development (CCHD) is the bishops' social justice grant-making arm, ostensibly operating as an "anti-poverty program" for the church. In practice, it's a political radicalization and social justice recruitment program. CCHD is funded through a national collection taken up at more than seventeen thousand American parishes the Sunday before Thanksgiving; 75 percent of the receipts are remitted to the USCCB and the remainder is retained by the dioceses.[64] In 2017, CCHD's national collections windfall (plus other grants and income on investments) totaled $18.1 million.[65]

The group boasts that it "works on the margins" of society, but the margins of left-wing political ideology would be more accurate. Founded in 1969, its roots trace back to *Rules for Radicals* author/organizer Saul Alinsky. He allied with then–Chicago bishop Bernard J. Shiel to create the Industrial Areas Foundation (IAF), which continues to train community organizers for "social change."[66] Back in 1994, author Paul Likoudis published *The Legacy of CHD: A Critical Report and Analysis of the U.S. Bishops' Campaign for Human Development*, a devastating investigation that exposed how CCHD was "a political mechanism bonding the American Church to the welfare state."[67] In Alphonse J. Matt Jr.'s foreword to the book, he described Catholic Campaign for Human Development projects in which "collective membership is routinely coerced. Class and ethnic divisions are utilized to mobilize group action groups. Project organizers and leaders often spout Marxist rhetoric as justification of their objectives."[68]

Likoudis showed how Catholic bishops created CCHD to "set up a permanent funding mechanism for IAF" two years before Alinsky died.[69] The primary goal was not spiritual ministering, but political organizing—with a special focus on southwestern states. IAF regional coordinator Ernesto Cortes received an $80,000 CCHD grant for twelve groups in Texas participating in an "Immigrant Leadership Project" and supervised efforts to register 750,000 new voters comprised of new immigrants.[70] He spoke to Catholic bishops about organizing for political power: "Power! Power comes in two forms: organized people and organized money."[71] IAF trainers schooled activists on Alinsky-inspired tactics of protesting, picketing, threatening lawsuits, sit-ins, and "overloading the system."[72] IAF organizers were explicitly hostile towards limited-government Republicans and the "religious right." One trainer outlined "strong-arm" tactics to "create conflict" in pursuit of power by exploiting "class envy and race" and stirring discontent. If harassing "the enemy" at his workplace, kids' school, or health club doesn't work, the trainer advised, "call a meeting and enrage the citizens into a mob."[73]

Naturally, Barack Obama cut his teeth at the intersection of the Catholic Church and Alinsky world. Obama ran a CCHD-funded outfit called Developing Communities Project from an office inside Holy Rosary Church of Chicago.[74] "I got my start as a community organizer working with mostly Catholic parishes on the Southside of Chicago that were struggling because the steel plants had closed," Obama told the *Catholic Digest*. "The Campaign for Human Development helped fund the project and so, very early on, my career was intertwined with the belief in social justice that is so strong in the Church."[75] No wonder, then, that CCHD also funded the notorious Alinsky acolytes at ACORN to the tune of $7.3 million over ten years before embezzlement, voter fraud, and Project Veritas's undercover prostitution smuggling sting brought the group down in 2008.[76]

Among CCHD's earliest grant recipients in 1970 and 1971, Catholic investigative journalist Stephanie Block found:[77]

- "$50,000 to the Universidad de Aztlán, an alternative educational initiative spawned from Plan Espiritual de Aztlán (Spiritual Plan of Aztlán), a 'manifesto' that insisted 'economic control of our lives and our communities can only come about by driving the exploiter out of our communities, our pueblos, and our lands.... Lands rightfully ours will be fought for and defended.'"
- "$25,000 to Interreligious Foundation for Community Organizations for Alinskyian organizing. The Foundation was a deliberate attempt to circumvent 'internal debates over Alinsky's intentions and methods and over the role the churches should be playing in political affairs.' In other words, to filter money less visibly, and therefore less controversially, into Alinsky's work, supporters created an 'ecumenical front' to 'shield the churches supporting community organizations from the growing anti-Alinsky' sentiments of their congregations."

- "$100,000 to Los PADRES, an association of priests who, among other things, established the Mexican American Cultural Center, a hub of liberation theology."

CCHD currently funds "restorative justice" efforts in public schools to chip away at effective discipline for disruptive students; "environmental justice" campaigns for "green jobs"; and a "Social Justice League" at St. Mary's University that welcomes illegal alien DREAMers to campus and sells T-shirts to fund DACA applications.[78] During the Bush amnesty battles, CCHD collaborated with the lawyers' arm of USCCB, the Catholic Legal Immigration Network Inc. (CLINIC; more on them below), to "empower" purportedly "grassroots" pro-illegal immigration activists and agencies. CCHD spent upwards of $3.5 million on amnesty-promoting efforts "to intensify the campaign for comprehensive immigration reform in 2013 by strategically promoting education in parishes and mobilizing the political support of Catholics across the country."[79] In 2014, CCHD issued grants of $4 million "to empower immigrant communities."[80]

Source: CCHD

In 2016, CCHD issued "strategic national grants" of $500,000 to the pro-DREAMer Hope Border Institute in El Paso, Texas, and $500,000 to the PICO National Network to provide "training and support to leaders and pastors in dioceses across the country to put Catholic teaching on immigration into practice." The Hope Border Institute relied on statistics generated by the Soros-funded, Obama operative-staffed Center for American Progress to argue that granting amnesty to millions of illegal alien DREAMers was good for the American economy.[81] I remind you again that all of this stems from the same organization, the USCCB, which originally formed to advocate for American soldiers.

Appendix F takes a closer look at recipients dedicated to "immigrants' rights" who soaked up CCHD funds in 2016–2017 and 2018–2019.

Catholic Legal Immigration Network Inc. (CLINIC)

You can thank the disastrous 1986 illegal alien amnesty for the existence of CLINIC. After President Reagan signed the law, 2.7 million illegal aliens became eligible for legalization, and as the USCCB put it, "demand for low-cost immigration legal services skyrocketed." The bishops created CLINIC as a legally distinct 501(c)(3) that has now expanded into a network of 2,300 attorneys and Department of Justice–accredited paralegals in 330 programs in 47 states and the District of Columbia. By CLINIC's own account, this legal racket is up to its eyeballs in work on behalf of amnesty nation. In 2017, the network conducted "an estimated 276,000 consultations, more than half of which became cases for network agencies." The bureaucracy of resettlement, appeals, adjustments of status, deportation proceedings, and visa renewals and extensions keeps the lawyers of CLINIC busy and fed. CLINIC has filed upwards of 250,000 applications, petitions, motions, and waivers on behalf of aliens. Its volunteers devoted more than 84,000 hours to legal assistance in 2017, with legal presentations to nearly 325,000 people. Invoking the Church's "welcome the stranger" mantra, CLINIC trains lawyer activists to agitate for open borders and help illegal immigrants stay in the U.S. and avoid deportation. The group joined with the smear merchants of the SPLC (see chapter 6) to sue over President Trump's detention policies involving minors, because such policies were "serving as a deterrent to migrants who want to travel to the United States."[82]

CLINIC's practice areas and projects span every aspect from resistance to immigration enforcement: political advocacy for illegal aliens and interminable extensions of the Temporary Protected Status program; lobbying and grant-making on behalf of amnesty legislation through the Center for Citizenship and Immigrant Communities; a Religious Immigration Services program to assist foreign religious workers trying to enter the country; a Defending Vulnerable Populations Project to equip attorneys to represent immigrants in immigration hearings; training and legal support to expand the corps of open-borders advocates and volunteers nationwide; and an alliance of illegal alien activists and lawyers focused on providing free lawyers to caravan families at the border in Texas, originally known as the CARA Family Detention Pro Bono Representation and Advocacy Project (now known as the Dilley Pro Bono Project).The other members of that group are the American Immigration Council, the Refugee and Immigrant Center for Education and Legal Services, and the American Immigration Lawyers Association. In addition, CLINIC assists with the Church's lucrative refugee resettlement practice.

In March 2018, CLINIC, the USCCB, and Catholic Charities USA (more below) united to file a friend-of-the-court brief with the Supreme Court opposing President Trump's national security-related travel restrictions on foreigners attempting to come into the U.S. from terror-enabling and terror-sponsoring countries.[83] CLINIC and its allies argued that all foreign Muslims have First Amendment rights to emigrate to America and practice their religion. The amicus brief's closing paragraph reveals the Catholic leaders' true concern and motive: "If allowed to stand," they hyperventilated, those "starting a new life with the help of resettlement services from organizations like the Conference" would be prevented from entering.

The accusation that President Trump's actions were motivated by "un-Catholic," "un-American," "unconstitutional," and "anti-religious bias" invites the obvious question of what the USCCB and CLINIC's actions are motivated by. Hint: Cha-ching. Cha-ching. Cha-ching.

According to audit records CLINIC made publicly available, the organization's total assets grew from $9,598,079 in 2016 to $12,767,172 in 2017. The USCCB pitched in $2,323,215 in 2017, up slightly from $2,065,308 in 2016.[84] As always, there are Soros fingerprints all over this endeavor, too. Between 2000 and 2014, Influence Watch reports, Soros donated more than $1.4 million to CLINIC, and in 2015 his Foundation to Promote Open Society doled out $970,000 to the group. A constellation of other leading left-wing foundations have pitched in, with millions coming from the Carnegie Foundation, the Ford Foundation, and the MacArthur Foundation.[85]

Catholic Relief Services

It's difficult to distinguish where one Catholic nonprofit begins and another one ends. Catholic Relief Services (CRS), based in Baltimore, identifies itself as the church's international humanitarian arm assisting "the poor and vulnerable overseas" in 110 countries, as well as serving Catholics in the United States "as they live their faith in solidarity with their brothers and sisters around the world."[86] CRS began as a World War II refugee relief program. Later, it supported Mother Teresa's work in India, worked on vaccination and disease eradication programs, and provided food aid to the world's hungry.[87] But eventually, its traditional charitable work expanded into providing "critical support" to Syrian Muslim refugees in southeastern Europe by renovating shelters and providing monthly cash assistance through prepaid debit cards.[88] Since

2011, Catholic Relief Services boasts, it has provided more than 1.25 *million* Syrian refugees with such aid.[89]

CRS voluntarily releases its IRS Form 990 to the public.[90] It's an enlightening read for those under the impression that the agency known for its humble rice bowl collections lives on a shoestring budget. CRS's total revenue reported in 2017 was more than $1 billion with a "B" as in "Bless their hearts." Its president, Sean Callahan, earned nearly $500,000 in salary and compensation. According to its 2017 annual report, CRS's operating revenue totaled $979 million, with $738 million of it—three-quarters of the pie—coming from government sources.[91] That includes $38 million from the U.S. government for education and job programs in three countries, according to Rick Jones, El Salvador-based youth and migration policy adviser for CRS.[92] By contrast, contributions from the CRS Rice Bowl campaign amounted to one percent of the group's take.[93]

Naturally, CRS was among the loudest voices squawking in opposition to President Trump's proposal to cut foreign aid to Latin American countries failing to control the caravan trekkers swamping our borders. "U.S. foreign assistance is a moral and practical imperative. Poverty not only causes unnecessary suffering, but also breeds instability. Aid empowers local leadership, builds local capacity and supports a community on its journey to self-reliance," CRS executive vice president for Mission, Mobilization, and Advocacy Bill O'Keefe testified before Congress in March 2019.[94] In April 2019, CRS president Sean Callahan said, "We oppose the administration's decision to cancel foreign assistance for the Northern Triangle of Central America. With bipartisan support, targeted U.S. assistance has improved prosperity for the poor and vulnerable in Central America."[95] Of course, the burning question arises: if all the billions that have been poured into Catholic relief efforts to increase safety, self-reliance, and wealth for the poor in Central America were as effective as CRS claims, why are hundreds of thousands of migrants from the region still dragging themselves and their children to our border?

Catholic Charities

As you can see, Catholic charity is yuuuuge business—and Catholic Charities USA (CCUSA) is no exception. Founded in 1910, its stated mission is "Reducing Poverty in America." That goal is accomplished by raising billions of dollars to fund the work of more than 65,000 employees engaged in affordable housing, health, welfare, employment, and immigration and refugee resettlement. At one point in fiscal year 2012, an overwhelming 98 percent of the Catholic Charities refugee resettlement budget ($69 million out of $70 million) came from the federal government.[96] According to Georgetown University's Center for Applied Research in the Apostolate (CARA):[97] 66 CCUSA agencies involved in refugee resettlement reported having 1,020 full-time paid staff members; 31 agencies reported having 214 full-time service volunteers; and 31 agencies reported having 1,666 other volunteers. In 2016 alone, Catholic Charities' members served 413,050 immigrant and refugee clients.[98] Immigrants (no distinction is made between legal and illegal) received help with DACA applications, detention and removal hearings, visa applications, and citizenship services. Refugees received "interpreter services, job placement, employment training, outreach, counseling, legal services, and matched savings programs."[99]

What every Catholic who believes in a sovereign America needs to understand is that the radicalized leaders of Catholic Charities are using your collection-plate contributions to implement Marxist-inspired liberation theology principles—think of it as faith-based socialism for a borderless planet.

What every taxpayer needs to know is how much of this Catholic largesse for open borders has actually been subsidized by *you.*

Forbes ranks Catholic Charities as the thirteenth largest charity in the nation, with total annual revenues of nearly $3.8 billion.[100] According to the group's most recently available financial statements, analyzed by CARA in June 2017, $1.2 billion of CCUSA's revenue came from the government—its largest single source of funding.[101]

But if anything, that understates the level of Catholic Charities' plundering of the taxpayer. *City Journal*'s Brian Anderson reported that Catholic Charities received "nearly a quarter of its funding from government by the end of the sixties, over half by the late seventies, and more than 60 percent by the mid-eighties, where it has remained ever since."[102] Fr. Richard John Neuhaus scathingly roasted the organization's alliance with the "government-subsidized poverty industry" and its redefined role as "chief apologist for a catastrophically destructive welfare system."[103] Then U.S. Senator Daniel Patrick Moynihan saw it coming in 1980. "Private institutions really aren't private anymore," he warned, because "many are primarily supplied by government funds."[104] He singled out Catholic Charities, which had just crossed into the 50 percent mark for public subsidies. "In time, there cannot be any outcome to that encroachment save governmental control."[105]

By one *Washington Times* estimate, some fifty-seven government agencies now contract with the Catholic Church.[106] In 2016, for example, Catholic Charities agencies scooped up $14 million from the federal Corporation for National and Community Service. That year, the U.S. Department of Health and Human Services provided the largest infusion of tax dollars, followed by the U.S. Department of Housing and Urban Development, the U.S. Department of Agriculture, and other major agencies. The federal funding includes both direct government grants as well as "pass-through" money funneled through to Catholic agencies from federal grants to other state and local entities or nonprofit groups (including the USCCB). Catholic Charities has also reaped unknown financial and in-kind contributions from governmental and intergovernmental agencies ranging from the European Union to the United Nations to the governments of Austria, Australia, Canada, Columbia, El Salvador, Germany, Honduras, Sweden, Switzerland, the U.K., and the World Bank.[107]

From Vatican City to European refugee camps to Latin American shelters for caravan marchers to government-subsidized Catholic agencies across America, the wealth-generating network built by the Catholic

Church works around the clock to fill pews and coffers in the name of "welcoming the stranger." Those foreign "clients"—who are prioritized over needy Americans—are then radicalized on our dime to aid and abet the next generation of illegal border-crossers.

In one of his many Trump-bashing lectures in 2019, Pope Francis insisted that "all" migrants must be welcomed by prosperous nation-states (other than his own) because their cultures enrich our own: "Migrants are those who bring us riches, always."[108] But whatever cultural riches migrants allegedly bring, the material riches reaped by the church's open-borders business are far greater. Unfortunately for taxpayers who believe in God *and* country, the Catholic Church is just one of many faith-based profiteers making bank on our backs.

CHAPTER FOUR

WRETCHED REFUSE: THE REFUGEE RESETTLEMENT RACKET

Everyone knows the first two lines from late-nineteenth-century social activist Emma Lazarus's ode to open borders:

> Give me your tired, your poor,
> Your huddled masses yearning to breathe free...[1]

But do you remember what comes next?

> The wretched refuse of your teeming shore.[2]

In other words: Human garbage.

Immigration anarchists incessantly invoke their poetic vision of America as an unbounded refuge for the world's overflowing refuse. They've elevated Lazarus's sentiment on the pedestal of the Statue of Liberty to the highest law of the land. In justifying their opposition to every enforcement measure, every mile of border wall, every screening requirement, every limitation, every exclusion, and every deportation, Open Borders Inc. propagandists sing the same insipid verses.

California Democratic congresswoman Nancy Pelosi convened a press conference in September 2017 to denounce President Trump's immigration reform executive orders by babbling, "Give me your tired, your poor, your huddled masses yearning to breathe free. You know the rest." I doubt *she* does, though. "It's a statement of values of our country," Pelosi insisted. "It's a recognition that the strength of our country is in its diversity, that the revitalization of the United States of America comes from our immigrant population."[3]

Two-time presidential election loser Hillary Clinton fumed in response to President Trump's travel restrictions on foreigners from state sponsors of terror: "I stand with the people gathered across the country tonight defending our values and our Constitution. This is not who we are."[4]

2020 Democratic presidential candidate Julian Castro fretted that President Trump's border wall would "change the notion of America from the Statue of Liberty that stands for freedom and welcomes immigrants to a country that literally walls itself off from the rest of the world.... I don't think it represents the best of what America stands for."[5]

Democratic Representative Dina Titus of Nevada similarly declared, "We cannot let Trump build a wall. That's not who we are."[6]

Former vice president and 2020 Democratic presidential front-runner Joe Biden bemoaned the crackdown on our besieged southern border by proclaiming, "We are in the battle for the soul of this nation. If we give Donald Trump eight years in the White House, he will forever and fundamentally alter the character of this nation, who we are, and I cannot stand by and watch that happen."[7]

At an epic press conference in August 2017, left-wing henchman Jim Acosta of CNN attacked Trump senior adviser Stephen Miller over the administration's support for legislation shifting the nation's priorities away from family reunification and chain migration to skill-based immigration. After sanctimoniously quoting the sappy Lazarus sonnet, Acosta carped that the White House was "trying to change what it means to be an immigrant coming into this country."[8]

And the Rev. Joe S. Vásquez, bishop of Austin, Texas, and chair of the U.S. Conference of Catholic Bishops' Committee on Migration, decried the Trump administration's decision to cap refugee admissions at thirty thousand for fiscal year 2019 as "deeply disturbing"[9] because "[t]o cut off protection for many who are fleeing persecution, at a time of unprecedented global humanitarian need, contradicts who we are as a nation."[10]

Holy bloviation. Under Trump, the U.S. still accepted more refugees than any other country in the world in both 2017 and 2018.[11] Based on the U.N. High Commissioner on Refugees's (UNHCR) release of data for those years, Nayla Rush of the Center for Immigration Studies reported that "[d]espite refugee advocates' constant criticism of the Trump administration's refugee policy, the United States accepted more refugees for resettlement in 2018 than any of the other 29 nations who did so. The United States was, in fact, the top resettlement submission and destination country in 2018 and 2017." On top of that, America forked over nearly $1.6 billion of our money to "support UNHCR's response to historic levels of displacement and humanitarian need."[12] Moreover, as the State Department pointed out in its announcement of refugee levels for 2019, America remains the largest single-country provider of humanitarian assistance worldwide—funding not only UNHCR, but also the United Nations Children's Fund (UNICEF), IOM, the International Committee of the Red Cross (ICRC), the World Food Programme (WFP), and other international and non-governmental partners. Total U.S. humanitarian assistance was more than $8 billion in FY 2017, covering "food, shelter, health care, and access to clean water for millions of displaced and crisis-affected people, including refugees, worldwide."[13] Of course, it's never enough.

Here's a reality-based reminder to the finger-waggers lecturing us all about "who we are": the official name of the Statue of Liberty is "Liberty *Enlightening* the World"[14]—not Liberty *Resettling* the World.

America is not, nor has it ever been, the world's full-service homeless shelter. We are not governed by "The New Colossus" or any other poem.

We are governed by the United States Constitution, the preamble of which binds our federal government to "establish justice, insure domestic tranquility, promote the general welfare, and secure the blessings of liberty to ourselves and our posterity."[15] Our founders, as I've reminded readers repeatedly over the years in my books and columns, asserted their concerns publicly and routinely about the effects of indiscriminate mass immigration. They made it clear that the purpose of allowing foreigners into our fledgling nation was not to recruit millions of new voters or to secure permanent ruling majorities for their political parties. It was to preserve, protect, and enhance the republic they put their lives on the line to establish.

In a 1790 House debate on naturalization, James Madison opined: "It is no doubt very desirable that we should hold out as many induce-ments as possible for the worthy part of mankind to come and settle amongst us, and throw their fortunes into a common lot with ours. But why is this desirable?"[16] No, not because "diversity" is our greatest value. No, not because Big Business needed cheap labor. And no, Madison asserted, "Not merely to swell the catalogue of people. No, sir, it is to increase the wealth and strength of the community; and those who acquire the rights of citizenship, without adding to the strength or wealth of the community are not the people we are in want of." Madison argued plainly that America should welcome the immigrant who could assimi-late, but exclude the immigrant who could not readily "incorporate himself into our society."[17]

George Washington, in a letter to John Adams, similarly emphasized that immigrants should be absorbed into American life so that "by an intermixture with our people, they, or their descendants, get assimilated to our customs, measures, laws: in a word soon become one people."[18]

Alexander Hamilton, relevant as ever today, wrote in 1802: "The safety of a republic depends essentially on the energy of a common national sentiment; on a uniformity of principles and habits; on the exemption of the citizens from foreign bias and prejudice; and on that love of country which will almost invariably be found to be closely connected with birth, education and family." The survival of the American republic, Hamilton maintained, depends upon "the preservation of a national spirit and a national character." He asserted, "To admit foreigners indiscriminately to the rights of citizens the moment they put foot in our country would be nothing less than to admit the Grecian horse into the citadel of our liberty and sovereignty."[19]

When it comes to explaining "who we are," why America was founded, and what criteria should be set for new entrants, the words of the Founding Fathers hold far more weight than that of a bleeding-heart poet whose words were an afterthought on a plaque tacked onto the base of the Statue of Liberty seventeen years after it was dedicated. Lady Liberty was a symbol of friendship between the U.S. and France, two independent and sovereign nations who shared common reverence for individual liberty, not an invitation for every last French peasant to invade our shores. As journalist Steve Sailer observed, Lazarus's poem has been turned into "an all-conquering mind virus that is making impossible intelligent thought about the future of America. The Constitution may not be a suicide pact, but Lazarus's dopey poem is turning into one."[20]

It is most certainly true that America has a history of embracing people from around the world fleeing persecution and war, as opposed merely to poverty. After World War II, the U.S. helped lead efforts to assist more than 650,000 displaced Europeans who had fled in fear, were expelled, and were victims of Nazi crimes and terror. Congress passed the Displaced Persons Act of 1948 to accommodate them. Five years later, the Refugee Relief Act of 1953 aided refugees from southern Europe and those escaping Communist regimes, adding another 250,000 refugees over four years. In the 1950s and 1960s, we welcomed Hungarians, Cubans, and Czechoslovakians escaping Communist oppression. In the 1970s, we opened our doors to an estimated 300,000 political refugees from Vietnam, Cambodia, and Laos.[21] The Refugee Act of 1980 created the Office of Refugee Resettlement and office of U.S. Coordinator for Refugee Affairs;[22] formalized the definition of "refugee" to align with the definition used by the United Nations, which created an eligibility standard that a person outside his or her home country must demonstrate a "well-founded fear of persecution for reasons of race, religion, nationality, membership in a particular social group, or political opinion," to qualify;[23] and raised the annual ceiling of admissions to 50,000 per year.

But past refugee admissions don't obligate America to lock into those same levels now or in the future. America's duty is to Americans first ("ourselves and our posterity"), not to all the millions of "tempest-tost" individuals abroad aspiring to get into America. As I showed you in chapter two, the United Nations and the Soros brigade have stretched the definition of "refugee" so thin that "climate change refugees" seeking relief from allegedly uninhabitable environments are now a phenomenon. Just reach the border, hum "Baby, It's Cold Outside" or "Fever," and you're in!

Question: Where do Americans seek refuge when illegal alien and refugee influxes render *our* climate uninhabitable?

Overall, since 1975, the U.S. has resettled more than three million refugees.[24] But most citizens have no idea how the system works. Nationwide, the refugee influx has transformed urban centers and small towns alike on both coasts and across flyover country—at considerable cost to those communities' health, safety, and welfare. Who decides how many refugees come here, from which countries, and where they resettle? Who profits? Who pays? A tiny cabal of open-borders government contractors perpetuate the refugee resettlement racket. Openly hostile to American sovereignty, they spread their tax-subsidized syndicate's wealth to a vast network of subcontractors, often tied to SorosWorld, who advocate global governance and unfettered migration espoused by the United Nations, the European Union, and the Vatican. They've systematically blurred the lines between legitimate refugees seeking asylum from oppression and economic migrants from Central America clamoring for higher wages or better welfare benefits. And they're indifferent to the national security risks of absorbing large numbers of Muslims whose adherence to repressive sharia and religious jihad are utterly incompatible with our constitutional principles.

The Trump-bashers and border-phobes equate any and all criticism of the refugee program as racist, xenophobic hatred. But it's not all sweetness and light. The "refugees" are not all "yearning to breathe free." Some of them just want free stuff. Some of them want to kill us. Many of them have absolutely no interest in assimilating themselves into our customs, measures, and laws. And many of them have outright contempt for Western civilization. They're not here to strengthen our nation with their "diversity." They're here to destroy it. That's fact, not "hate." We'll follow the money and expose how the scam operates largely out of public view—without the knowledge, consent, or oversight of the communities upon which tens of thousands of unassimilable, dangerous, and ungrateful foreigners are foisted every year.

But first, let's take a closer look at the real-world impact of blindly dumping the world's "wretched refuse" into our backyards with no accountability from the refugee resettlement racketeers when things go wrong.

CRIMBY: Criminal Refugees in My Backyard

When I moved from the Beltway swamp to the Rocky Mountains in 2008, illegal alien gangs had begun to fester in the D.C. suburbs in shockingly ordinary places. The Lakeforest Mall in Gaithersburg, Maryland, where my kids used to frolic at the indoor playland, morphed into an MS-13 stronghold where stabbings and parking lot carjackings drove families away.[25] Teachers and students now live in constant fear in Montgomery County schools, where illegal alien gang recruiters target children as early as fifth grade.[26] "MS dominates the school," one eighth grader, who said she had been raped by a gang member at William Wirt Middle School in Riverdale, Maryland, told the *Washington Post*. "The school is a ticking time bomb," a teacher warned.[27] Out west (but not too west), I figured the quality of life would be vastly improved not only by getting away from the Beltway swamp but also by protecting our children from the weekly barrage of MS-13 gang-ordered robberies, group rapes, stabbings, beheadings, and dismemberments now weaved into the fabric of the community where they spent their toddler years.[28]

But there is no safe space from violent, immigration-related crime.

Not far from a local IHOP in the south part of Colorado Springs, where I used to take my kids for breakfast on weekends, a horrific rape of a middle-aged woman took place in 2012 at a home where five young male Iraqi translators lived. Her injuries were so savage that police said she could have bled to death; police described blood-spattered walls and the "unmistakable odor of feces"[29] after one of the assailants allegedly shoved his fist up the victim's rectum.[30] All five suspects had won Special Immigrant Visas to the U.S. because of the reported risks they took to aid American soldiers. Sarmad Fadhi Mohammed and Jasim Mohammed Hasin Ramadon were arrested and convicted for the sexual assault. Mustafa Sataar Al Feraji, Ali Mohammed Hasan Al Juboori, and Yasir Jabbar Jasim were convicted or pleaded guilty to misdemeanor accounts of accessory crimes.

Ramadon had been hailed as a teen hero by the soldier who sponsored him; they went on a whirlwind book tour together and appeared on Oprah Winfrey's show before settling down in the Springs.[31] Ramadon lived with the soldier's wife while he was on duty, but "cultural differences"[32] (translation: the Iraqi refugee hated women) led to the "hero" moving out. He quickly amassed a long rap sheet: felony menacing charges in 2009; assault charges in 2010; domestic violence charges against his high school girlfriend and mother of his child in 2011. The girlfriend filed a restraining order after telling a judge that Ramadon had "sent to her to the hospital twice—she said he had busted blood vessels in her eyes and face, crushed soft tissue in her arm and bruised tissue and muscles in her neck when he choked her," the *Colorado Springs Gazette* reported.[33] She was too afraid to comment when Ramadon was arrested for the violent rape.

And these were supposed to be the vetted, "good" Iraqi refugees we didn't have to worry about.

Near the Citadel Mall in Colorado Springs, where I took my kids school shopping, another Iraqi refugee with a lengthy criminal record shot Colorado Springs police officer Cem Duzel in the head in August 2018.[34] Duzel, a five-year veteran of the force and thirty-year-old son of Turkish immigrants,[35] survived the cold-blooded attack, but remains in intensive treatment for serious brain and spinal injuries.

Here's what we know about the suspect: According to the Department of Homeland Security, thirty-one-year-old Karrar Noaman Al Khammasi entered the U.S. legally from Istanbul, Turkey, and landed at Chicago O'Hare airport in December 2012. Khammasi is an Iraqi citizen who had secured an RE-1 visa for "principal" refugees—meaning he was the first in his family to get here. The six years between the time he landed in Chicago and ended up in the shoot-out outside my local mall are largely a black hole. But the Department of Homeland Security (DHS) disclosed to the public that Khammasi had racked up a mile-long rap sheet of least nine other encounters with police before his fateful showdown with Duzel, including felony and misdemeanor charges of criminal extortion, trespassing, assault, drunk driving, parole violations and contempt of court, and weapons violations.[36] The Colorado Springs Police Department revealed that Khammasi had been kicked out of a car by an Uber driver who accused him of being "handsy" before he ran into the street and allegedly exchanged gunfire with Duzel.[37] DHS also reported that Khammasi has been a transient living in Colorado Springs since January 2018.[38]

How was this homeless, jobless, RE-1 visa holder allowed to stay here after committing so many crimes that should have made him subject to removal? You can thank the immigration anarchists in our court system, of course. In June 2016, Khammasi was actually ordered to be deported after U.S. Immigration and Customs Enforcement officials made contact with him. But while he was in custody, a Tenth U.S. Circuit Court of Appeals ruling determined that deportation laws were "too vague when it came to defining crimes that rose to the level of getting legal immigrants deported."[39] As a result, President Obama's DHS reversed course and released Khammasi from custody in November 2016.[40] While Khammasi committed more crimes, a separate U.S.

Supreme Court decision in *Sessions v. Dimaya* on the same issue of deportation time limits for violent felonies concluded that the rules were "unconstitutionally vague." That plaintiff, James Garcia Dimaya, was a legal immigrant from the Philippines convicted of two burglaries and ordered deported by the Obama administration. He was represented by the Communist Party member-founded, open-borders National Lawyers Guild. Shockingly, Trump-appointed Justice Neil Gorsuch sided with the far-left majority in the 5 to 4 ruling, which invalidated a long-standing congressional statute on criminal alien removal and created constitutional due process rights for foreign nationals who are not U.S. citizens.

The decision gave a green light to litigate every deportation order against a criminal alien, even though federal deportation orders had been exercised for more than a century, and, as Justice Clarence Thomas noted in his dissent, the Court had "never held that an immigration statute is unconstitutionally vague."[41] Never. That's because there had been long-held deference by the courts to our sovereign nation's power to remove any foreigner it wanted to remove from the country—legal or illegal, green card holder or refugee. Justice Thomas pointed to John Marshall's assertion in 1799, backed by a century of jurisprudence, that "[t]he right of remaining in our country is vested in no alien; he enters and remains by the courtesy of the sovereign power, and that courtesy may at pleasure be withdrawn"[42] without access to the courts.

But thanks to the resistance wing of the federal courts, the floodgates are open. "The ruling significantly undermines our efforts to remove aliens convicted of certain violent crimes, including sexual assault, kidnapping, and burglary, from the United States," a Homeland Security official told the *Washington Times*. "By inhibiting ICE from establishing that such aliens are removable or ineligible for certain immigration benefits, *Sessions v. Dimaya* hampers our national security and allows criminal aliens who prey on our communities to remain in the country, making us more vulnerable as a result."

Sixty of the World's Finest Refujihadis

Open Borders Inc. propagandists will do what they always do when confronted with criminal nightmares that don't fit the Emma Lazarus fantasy narrative: whitewash them. The vast majority of refugees are law-abiding, they'll sputter. Only xenophobes dwell on the negative impacts, they'll seethe. But 9/11 taught us that all it takes is a teeny, tiny minority of foreign menaces to wreak massive havoc on our safety and civil order. An untold number of refugees are not just committing ordinary civilian crimes. They are Islamic oppressors masquerading as the oppressed.

In *Invasion*, I documented multiple examples of Muslim terrorists who entered the U.S. after making phony asylum claims. Ramzi Yousef faked an asylum claim to plot the 1993 World Trade Center bombing. Gazi Ibrahim Abu Mezer, a Palestinian bomb-builder who entered the U.S. illegally through Canada, claimed political asylum based on phony persecution by Israelis. Palestinian jihadist Mir Aimal Kansi, convicted in 1997 of capital murder for the January 1993 shooting spree outside CIA headquarters in McLean, Virginia, claimed bogus political asylum based on his ethnic minority status in Pakistan.[43] (An asylee and refugee must demonstrate the same "credible fear of persecution." The only difference is that an asylee makes his claim while in the U.S.; a refugee makes his claim outside the U.S.)

Since my first book was published, examples of what I call refujihadis—refugee jihadis—have proliferated. Appendix G is a handy list of just sixty of the world's finest refujihadis, derivative asylum and green card beneficiaries, asylum-seekers, and special immigrant visa holders plotting Islamic terror in the U.S. over the past twelve years based on my review of government documents and media reports. The next time you hear treacly paeans to the Unassailable Noble Refugee, feel free to reference my list. Wretched refuse, indeed.

Inside the Refugee Redistribution Bureaucracy

When you read about all these and other refugees gone wrong and realize they live in *your* backyard, I know you have the same burning questions I do. Here are some answers.

How did they get here? Who decides? Anonymous global bureau-crats hold enormous power over how refuges are resettled across the United States; the people who *aren't* consulted are most American citizens.

This is how it all starts: Refugees who have escaped one country and landed in another must file their claims with the U.N. High Commissioner for Refugees (UNHCR) for possible referral to a third country for permanent resettlement with a vast assortment of benefits. Some far-off, foreign U.N. bureaucrat conducts an interview with the refuge-seeker and compiles a dossier. If UNHCR approves the claim and selects the U.S. as the receiving nation, the applicant is referred to the U.S. Refugee Admissions Program (USRAP) for consideration as a refugee by the U.S. State Department's Bureau for Population, Refugees, and Migration (PRM). Contrary to the narrative that the vast majority of refugees referred to the U.S. are the most oppressed people suffering the most dire humanitarian crises on the planet, the U.N.'s own data show the opposite. UNHCR prioritizes refugees using three categories: "Emergency" (refugees with security or medical needs necessitating relocation "within days"); "Urgent" (refugees requiring relocation within "six weeks"); or "Normal" (refugees with no immediate medical, social, or security concerns that would warrant expedited processing; twelve-month waiting times are expected).[44] Virtually all of the 2018 refugee referrals by UNHCR (83 percent) were classified as normal. As Center for Immigration Studies analyst Nayla Rush summed it up: "Resettlement, therefore, is usually not 'a life-saving solution for the most vulnerable refugees in the world' as UNHCR likes to claim."[45]

In other words: Give me your tired, your poor, your non-emergency, non-urgent applicants who can wait a year, give or take, to get here.

How many? From where? Who decides? Under the 1980 Refugee Act, the president of the United States, after consultation with Congress and federal agencies, determines the designated nationalities[46] and processing priorities for refugee resettlement for the upcoming year. Under Obama, at the end of FY 2016, nearly 39,000 Muslim refugees entered the U.S., the highest number on record in our history, according to Pew researchers.[47] Muslims comprised nearly half (46 percent) of refugee admissions, Pew reported, while Christians accounted for 44 percent of refugees admitted.[48] That year, the highest number of refugees came from the Democratic Republic of Congo (16,370 refugees), followed by Syria (12,587), Burma (a.k.a. Myanmar, with 12,347), Iraq (9,880), and Somalia (9,020). During the past decade, the largest numbers of refugees have come from Burma (159,692) and Iraq (135,643). From FY 2008 through March 31, 2019, the top language of refugees was Arabic, followed by Nepali and Somali.[49]

The president also sets annual ceilings on the total number of refugees who may enter the U.S. from each region of the world. On average, as the pro-open borders Refugee Council USA notes, the ceiling has exceeded 95,000 since 1980. Since 2000, the ceiling has ranged from 70,000 to 100,000. Under President Obama's last year in office, the FY 2017 ceiling was set at 110,000, which President Trump cut to 55,000. At the end of FY 2017, 53,716 were admitted[50] and the Trump White House initiated a series of major reductions and reforms to tighten eligibility requirements and screening, including adding more security vetting of refugees from high-risk, terror-friendly nations. In FY 2018, Trump set the ceiling at 45,000; 22,491 were admitted. In FY 2019, the ceiling was lowered to 30,000. As of April 30, 2019, 14,808 had been admitted.[51] Howls of protest ensued from Open Borders Inc. Senate Democrats lambasted the White House, demanding that the ceiling be raised to 80,000 because "admitting refugees to the United States is a moral imperative and reducing the number of people we accept sends the wrong message to other countries."[52] The message of putting Americans first is always the "wrong message" to Open Borders Inc. and its global partners.

Who vets? Who resettles? An army of governmental and non-governmental organizations at five Resettlement Support Centers abroad assist the refugee in applying and preparing for an interview with a U.S. Citizenship and Immigration Services (USCIS) officer. They operate under the State Department's Bureau for Population, Refugees, and Migration (PRM). Biometric data and identification documents are supposed to be screened, but fraud is common among displaced people who abandoned their home countries with few possessions—and that means there are few reliable means to vet their stories.

If the officer approves the refugee, an entire support system kicks in to arrange for medical screening, orientation, visas, travel costs, and loan arrangements. Next, one of nine primary voluntary agencies (VOLAGs) contracted by the Office of Refugee Resettlement (ORR) under the U.S. Department of Health and Human Services' Office for the Administration of Children and Families swoops in to welcome the refugees at U.S. airports and choose where to redistribute them across the country. USCIS selects which agencies will handle each of the new refugee cases. The VOLAGs meet weekly to decide where to place the refugees.[53] Like so many other decisions along the way, the criteria and process for doing so are shrouded in secrecy. The VOLAGs are:

- Church World Service (CWS)
- Ethiopian Community Development Council (ECDC)
- Episcopal Migration Ministries (EMM)
- Hebrew Immigrant Aid Society (HIAS)
- International Rescue Committee (IRC)
- U.S. Committee for Refugees and Immigrants (USCRI)
- Lutheran Immigration and Refugee Service (LIRS)
- United States Conference of Catholic Bishops (USCCB)
- World Relief

For thirty to ninety days after the refugee lands in America, the VOLAGs provide transitional financial and social assistance, including housing and essential furnishings, food, necessary seasonal clothing, orientation, and assistance with access to social, medical, and employment services.[54] When choosing where to move the refugees, we do know that VOLAGs place a priority on locations where there are family, friends, and compatriots of the same nationality and who speak the same language.[55] In other words, resettlement favors creating and reinforcing ethnic enclaves over assimilation. "Diversity" means division.

The Government Accountability Office (GAO) warned in 2012 that the VOLAGs were failing to consult with local communities, even though federal law requires them to do so.[56] Section 2A of the Refugee Act of 1980[57] states that local and state governments shall be consulted regularly, no less than quarterly, concerning the distribution of refugees among the states and localities prior to placement in those states.[58] The resettlement agencies told investigators that they talked to landlords and employers (always eager for cheap labor), but not to schools and health departments. Indeed, one resettlement agency confessed that they avoided talking to those who "might unnecessarily object to the proposed number of refugees to be resettled."[59] That would include American citizens who might object to their neighborhoods becoming refugee dumping grounds.

Meanwhile, the refugees have access to a wide variety of benefits. The VOLAGs subcontract to more than two hundred affiliates to deliver goods and services to the refugees. State welfare services and medical screening costs to refugees are "reimbursed" (by federal taxpayers) via the federal Office of Refugee Resettlement. Taxpayers, of course, also pay the additional education costs borne by local schools. And refugees immediately qualify for work permits. Within one year of arrival, the refugee can file for a green card and start the path to U.S. citizenship. Within two years of arrival, the refugee can petition for his spouse and unmarried children under twenty-one to join him.[60]

Here's another question:

Who's responsible when refugees chosen by the U.N., vetted by the State Department and DHS's USCIS, welcomed and resettled by tax-subsidized VOLAGs, and assisted by hundreds of their subcontractors go bad? No one! After four months, the VOLAGs bear no responsibility for tracking what happens to their cash cows. The VOLAGs just keep on milkin' and movin' on to the next meal ticket.

As I mentioned in chapter one, the VOLAGs run a nice little side business collecting on the no-interest travel loans to refugees covered by the International Organization of Migration through the State Department, which requires refugees to sign promissory notes to pay back the costs within three to nine years, depending on the loan terms and family conditions. Once the refugees cough up the money, the VOLAGs get to pocket 25 percent. In 2015, the Religion News Service reported that the nine resettlement agencies reaped upwards of $5 million a year in commissions as resettled refugees repay loans for their travel costs.[61] In 2018, the State Department reported that the average loan note is $2,740, with costs increasing for large refugee families.[62] In their disingenuous defense, VOLAG flacks claim it's good for refugees to pay back the loans in order to "become financially literate and build up their credit history."[63] Of course, since a significant number of refugees are from the Lazarus-ian "tired and poor" demographic, they default on their loans, thereby ruining their credit history.[64] We don't know how many have defaulted on the loans (Judicial Watch sued the feds in 2017 to try and find out.)[65] Nor do we know how and why the VOLAGs were able to insert themselves into the debt collection business in the first place—while also being paid handsome sums to resettle all the refugees and lobbying for ever higher refugee admissions levels in the name of compassion, humanitarianism, and faith.

For FY 2018, the costs of refugee processing and resettlement totaled $959 million and were expected to rise to more than $1 billion in FY 2019.[66] The share for HHS/ORR, which funds the VOLAGs and a plethora of other refugee grant programs, is $527 million for FY 2018 and $514 million for FY 2019. More than $50 million to $66 million is expected to come from loan collections alone.[67] "It's money-producing, and I do find that troubling," Ronald Simkins, director of the Center for the Study of Religion and Society at Creighton University, fretted in regard to the VOLAGs' loan business. "It adds a perception of conflict of interest. Certainly for their advocacy it can become that.... It becomes in some sense self-serving in the end." Certainly, that applies to the *entire* refugee resettlement racket.[68]

Who pays? You do, of course.

Self-Serving Shakedown of the Soul-Savers

Six of the nine VOLAGs are religious organizations with a vested financial interest in stoking the refugee influx. It's not just about saving the wretched or enriching their souls. It's not just about "welcoming the stranger." It's about welcoming the moolah, the Benjamins, and the sweet, steady flow of resettlement cash cows. I hate government acronyms and the term "VOLAG" embodies everything that's wrong with them. Where, exactly, is the volunteerism when the majority of these faith-based "voluntary agencies" operate as tax-funded social welfare lobbyists doing the bidding of Open Borders Inc?

By the Capital Research Center's count, there are an estimated 350 subcontractors in 190 cities affiliated with the VOLAGs.[69] (In many cases, some VOLAG affiliates act as both prime contractors *and* subcontractors.) Between 2008 and 2018, the nine resettlement agencies collectively hoovered up more than $3.6 billion in government subsidies for their services as primary contractors. James Simpson tallied up each VOLAG's take over the past decade and the percentage of those revenues that came from the government for each entity.[70]

- Catholic Charities/United States Conference of Catholic Bishops (USCCB)—$742.6 million (39 percent)
- International Rescue Committee (IRC)—$846.6 million (67 percent)
- Lutheran Immigration and Refugee Services (LIRS)—$471.6 million (94 percent)
- Church World Service (CWS)—$433.3 million (72 percent)

- U.S. Committee for Refugees and Immigrants (USCRI)— $416.1 million (95 percent)
- World Relief—$215.3 million (65 percent)
- Hebrew Immigrant Aid Society (HIAS)—$186.1 million (54 percent)
- Domestic & Foreign Missionary Service/Episcopal Migration Ministries (EMM)—$146.7 million (22 percent)
- Ethiopian Community Development Council (ECDC)— $129 million (96 percent)

The Center for Immigration Studies' Nayla Rush also determined independently that the VOLAGs are funded, for the most part, by the U.S. government. Her estimates for the share of the VOLAGs' revenues that comes from the U.S. federal government range from a low of 58.5 percent to a high of 97.3 percent. (Some services provided and government funds received by these organizations may be non-refugee related.) For volunteer work, the heads of the VOLAGs sure don't sacrifice much. Nayla Rush estimated that yearly compensation for VOLAG leaders ranged from $132,000 to more than $671,000.[71] Rush's research found that three of the VOLAGs—ECDC, LIRS, and USCRI—clocked in with more than 96 percent of their funding coming from government grants.[72]

How much per refugee do VOLAGs collect? The State Department pays each agency $2,125 per refugee for initial reception and placement;[73] the nonprofits can take up to a 45 percent cut and use the rest for the initial resettlement costs.[74] Subsidies for management costs are negotiated separately. Unknown thousands more per head are collected for post-placement services. Catholic Charities of Central and Northern Missouri divulged that it received about $4,000 per refugee.[75]

In the most recently available annual report to Congress by the Office of Refugee Resettlement (published for 2016), the agency reported that in the year prior, 26.7 percent of refugees received cash assistance from at least one federal program; 66.1 percent of refugees had received non-cash assistance such as SNAP (food stamps).[76]

The Federation for American Immigration Reform crunched the numbers in 2018 and estimated the annual cost of refugee resettlement to U.S. taxpayers at $1.8 billion and $8.8 billion over a five-year period. Using ORR data, FAIR estimated the cost per refugee to American taxpayers at just under $79,600 in the first five years after a refugee is resettled in the U.S. and also found:[77]

- In 2016, the State Department spent nearly $545 million to process and resettle refugees, including $140,389,177 on transportation costs
- Of the $1.8 billion in resettlement costs, $867 million was spent on welfare alone
- In their first five years in the U.S., approximately 54 percent of all refugees will hold jobs that pay less than $11 an hour
- $71 million will be spent to educate refugees and asylum-seekers, a majority of which will be paid by state and local governments
- Over five years, an estimated 15.7 percent of all refugees will need housing assistance, which is roughly $7,600 per household in 2014 dollars

Steven Camarota of the Center for Immigration Studies zeroed in on the heavy costs of resettling Middle Eastern refugees in particular. In their first five years in the United States, he found, "each refugee from the Middle East costs taxpayers $64,370 [or $257,481 per household]—12 times what the UN estimates it costs to care for one refugee in neighboring Middle Eastern countries. The cost of resettlement includes heavy welfare use by Middle Eastern refugees; 91 percent receive food stamps and 68 percent receive cash assistance. Costs also include processing refugees, assistance given to new refugees, and aid to refugee-receiving communities."[78]

Applying the same methodology as Camarota to data from the 2013 Annual Report of Refugees (including all countries sending refugees, not just Middle Eastern ones), Breitbart reporter Michael Patrick Leahy estimated that over a five-year period American taxpayers pay $59,251 per refugee and $4.1 billion a year for resettled refugees in FY 2017.[79] In addition to food stamps and public housing, refugees collect money from Supplemental Security Income (for the elderly and disabled); welfare cash benefits from Temporary Assistance for Needy Families (TANF); Medicaid; the federal school lunch program; and the Women, Infants, and Children program.

Daniel Greenfield of the David Horowitz Freedom Center reported that in Barack Obama's first year in office, the United States resettled three-quarters of Iraqi refugees, with 71 percent of them receiving cash assistance; 82 percent going on Medicaid, and 87 going on food stamps.[80]

Fun fact: Britain-based jihad preacher Anjem Choudary was caught on tape urging his followers to collect welfare benefits while working to destroy infidels' countries. "Claim your Jihad Seeker's Allowance," he advised. "You find people are busy working the whole of their life. They wake up at 7 o'clock. They go to work at 9 o'clock. They work for eight, nine hours a day. They come home at 7 o'clock, watch EastEnders, sleep, and they do that for 40 years of their life. That is called slavery." By contrast, terrorist operatives who mooched off the government only needed to work a few days. "The rest of the year they were busy with jihad (holy war) and things like that. People will say, 'Ah, but you are not working.' But the normal situation is for you to take money from the kuffar [non-Muslim]. So we take Jihad Seeker's Allowance. You need to get support."[81] Choudary practiced what he preached, scooping up the equivalent of $32,000 a year in welfare payments from the U.K. government.[82]

Don't forget: These financial impacts don't include the costs to national security and public safety imposed by untold numbers of the violent refujihadis and other criminal refugees like the ones I introduced to you. One of those refujihadi families, the Boston Marathon bombers Tamerlan Tsarnaev and his wife, received welfare benefits.[83] So did Bowling Green, Kentucky, weapons collector and bloodthirsty Iraqi insurgent

Waad Ramadan Alwan, who quit a briefly held job, enrolled in public housing, and collected welfare payments.[84]

Ann Corcoran, founder of the Refugee Resettlement Watch website (whose body of vigilant work laid the foundation for resettlement watchdogs and citizen activists pushing back against the racket), summed up the scammy symbiosis between the charity racketeers and the expanding refugee welfare state:

> Despite their rhetoric, refugee agencies have steadfastly refused to use their own resources to maintain the U.S. refugee resettlement program. Public money has thoroughly driven out private money. A program known as the Private Sector Initiative allowed sponsoring agencies to bring over refugees if the agencies were willing to cover costs of resettlement and support. It was discontinued for lack of use in the mid-1990s. Today the agencies are on record as opposed to diverting more federal refugee dollars to overseas refugee assistance (where each dollar will go further in helping refugees) because it might mean fewer dollars for them! As with other government-dependent industries, there is a revolving door between the refugee industry and the federal government which pays its bills.[85]

A U.S. Government Accountability Office report in 2012 stated the obvious about the self-serving incentives baked into the refugee resettlement cake: "Because refugees are generally placed in communities where national voluntary agency affiliates have been successful in resettling refugees, the same communities are often asked to absorb refugees year after year. One state refugee coordinator noted that local affiliate funding is based on the number of refugees they serve, so affiliates have an incentive to maintain or increase the number of refugees they resettle each year rather than allowing the number to decrease."[86]

The "welcoming" ethos that these religious and diversity-promoting enterprises promote so zealously may appear to be warmhearted and selfless. But underneath the charitable cover is an open pipeline teeming with human pawns and trafficking revenue.

The Refugee Resettlement Racket Resistance

The good news is that the anti-Trump, open-borders resistance isn't the only resistance game in town. An increasing number of local officials and community leaders are standing up for themselves and their posterity:

- In 2001 and 2002, more than 1,000 Somalian refugees descended on the tiny town of Lewiston, Maine, (population 36,000). Then-mayor Robert MacDonald penned an open letter pleading with Somalian refugees to be considerate to his beleaguered town and dissuade more of their relatives from resettling there: "Please pass the word: we have been overwhelmed and have responded valiantly. Now we need breathing room. Our city is maxed-out financially, physically and emotionally."[87] You'll not be surprised to learn that he was accused of "bigotry." Nor will you be surprised that his entreaty was ignored. A decade later, MacDonald was attacked for telling more truths about the failure of a generation of Somalian refugees to assimilate in his town, where they now made up 10 percent of the population. "I don't care if you're white, you're black, you're yellow. I don't care what color you are, when you come into the country, you have to accept our culture. Don't try to insert your culture into ours.... You come here, you come and you accept our culture and you leave your culture at the door."[88]

- Yet, even after Maine Republican Governor Paul LePage announced in 2016 that he was withdrawing the state from the refugee resettlement program, the refugees kept coming. VOLAG Catholic Charities of Maine worked with the feds to resettle more than 3,400 refugees over the past decade and moved forward with resettling at least 600 more that year. The Catholic group circumvented the state withdrawal by collaborating directly with the feds, as they do in other states. In 2016–2017, Catholic Charities of Maine reported revenue of $27.7 million—with $14.2 million coming from governmental payments, $6.9 million from Medicaid fees, and $2.7 million collected from program service fees.[89]

- In 2011, during a tough economic downturn, the Republican mayor of Manchester, New Hampshire, Ted Gatsas, and the city's Board of Aldermen asked the U.S. State Department to halt resettlements in order to allow the townspeople to "catch our breath." Over a decade, an influx of 2,100 refugees were sent to the town of 109,500 and the schools were inundated with children speaking more than sixty languages.[90] The city's request to put the brakes on another planned resettlement of 300 refugees was ignored; the feds and the local resettlement agency in charge, International Institute of New England, relocated 200 refugees against the town's wishes. In 2016–2017, the International Institute of New England reported annual revenue of $5.1 million.[91]

- Both Fort Wayne, Indiana, and Detroit, Michigan, requested restrictions on refugee resettlement due to poor economic conditions, according to the 2012 GAO report. The State Department limited resettlement to those with family members already in the area.[92]

- In 2013, the Democratic mayor of Springfield, Massachusetts, Domenic Sarno, urged the State Department to stop the flow of refugees into his economically depressed city, citing another key concern: mass relocation had become a "pressing issue of public safety," straining public housing, the schools, code enforcement, and local police.[93] Sarno called out Catholic Charities, Lutheran Social Services, and Jewish Family Services for cutting and running on refugees dumped in vermin-infested housing. He also cited the city's schools being forced to divert resources away from existing pupils to accommodate refugee children who were overwhelming the system's very limited foreign language capabilities. "We have done more than our fair share," Sarno told a local reporter. "It's not fair to the refugees or Springfield. I have to draw the line."[94]

- Providing a candid reality check to Open Borders Inc., Sarno raised his alarm again in 2014 after being ignored: "I have enough urban issues to deal with. Enough is enough. You can't keep concentrating poverty on top of poverty."[95] The Obama White House ignored his pleas.

- After a coordinated series of terror attacks by refujihadis in Paris in 2015 left 130 people dead,[96] American officials finally banded together to send a message: no more. Governors in thirty-one states (all but one of them Republican) voiced concern about the Obama administration's vetting process and registered objections to the mass importation of 10,000 Syrian Muslims. Open Borders Inc. leaped into action to quell the nationwide rebellion. The Council on American-Islamic Relations, indifferent to the clear and present danger posed by refujihadis infiltrating the countryside, slammed elected officials who put security over open borders as "un-American" and "bigots," declaring, "Governors who reject those fleeing war and persecution abandon our ideals and instead project our fears to the world."[97] Miraculously, a spokesman for the U.S. Conference of Catholic Bishops rediscovered the federal government's "plenary power" to decide "who should be allowed in this country" and opposed state efforts to enforce the provision of the Refugee Act requiring local, state, and federal cooperation on refugee resettlement.[98] Funny how the USCCB and other top promoters of sanctuary policies defy federal authority over immigration matters—except when it fills their coffers.

- The state of Indiana withdrew public funds used by the VOLAGs to help refugees find employment and went to court to stop refugee resettlement after the 2015 Paris attacks. VOLAG affiliate Exodus Refugee Immigration, represented by open-borders lawyers at the ACLU, argued that the ban was unconstitutionally discriminatory against Syrians who have no constitutional right to be here. A three-judge panel of the Seventh Circuit Court of Appeals upheld a ruling against Indiana's citizens in favor of the Syrian refugees on foreign soil. Then-governor Mike Pence moved on to the vice presidency; a federal judge upheld a permanent injunction against the ban in 2018. And, naturally, the ACLU celebrated the win because protecting American citizens "was a shameful retreat from our values."[99] In 2015 and 2016, Exodus Refugee Immigration reported annual revenue each year of about $4 million. For the latter year, the nonprofit scored $1.9 million in refugee resettlement and placement revenue, plus nearly $1 million more in other government grants.[100]

- In 2016, the Waterford Township board of commissioners in southeast Michigan voted unanimously to stand against the flood of Syrian Muslims being resettled there. Michigan is the largest recipient of Syrian refugees in the U.S. Of the 4,600 Syrian refugees resettled in the U.S. between 2011 and 2016, 505 were settled in Michigan.[101] The largest refugee resettlement agency in the state, Samaritas (formerly Lutheran Social Services) invoked the spirit of Emma Lazarus as a response to the local officials' concern for taking care of citizens first. "As Americans, our own roots trace back to refugees and immigrants seeking freedom and opportunity," the agency lectured in a statement.[102] What Samaritas didn't mention was its reported annual revenue for 2017 of $98,799,016.[103]

- In Oakland County, Michigan, where many of the Syrian refugees were imposed on citizens, the county executive L. Brooks Patterson led a revolt backed by his county board of commissioners—pressing the feds to follow their own laws on consulting localities before dumping refugees. Remember: the Refugee Act of 1980 requires the resettlement racketeers to consult with community leaders and elected officials before shoving refugees down their throats. "The ORR has already placed hundreds of refugees in Oakland County without that consultation and coordination taking place," the officials warned. "Why is that a concern? The Islamic State has said it is seeding these waves of refugees with its own agents and terrorists. Plus, there have been a number of cases of refugees arriving with communicable diseases, with at least one in Oakland County." Patterson and the board are mulling a lawsuit.

- In April 2016, the mayor of Rutland, Vermont, Chris Louras, announced a plan to import 100 Syrian refugees to the economically depressed town of 16,000. The Vermont Refugee Resettlement Program set up shop and prepared to welcome the influx. But Louras didn't bother to consult elected aldermen about the scheme, and to the chagrin of the refugee resettlement racket, tax-paying citizens pushed back. A "Rutland First" group appeared on Facebook advocating for "Rutland before Refugees" and questioning the financial and security costs of resettlement. Once again, the racketeers ignored federal law requiring them to solicit input from affected communities.[104] Louras protested that allowing aldermen to vote on the issue or putting the question up for a citizen referendum is, you guessed it, "not who we are." In 2017, a majority of aldermen approved a letter to the State Department objecting to Louras's plan.[105] Voters sent their own message to Louras in his bid for a sixth term that year: they voted him out of office.[106]

- One state, Wyoming, has never joined the refugee resettlement machine and has zero VOLAGs and affiliates operating in the state. An additional twelve states—Alaska, Alabama, Colorado, Idaho, Kentucky, Louisiana, Massachusetts, Nevada, North Dakota, South Dakota, Tennessee, and Vermont—had withdrawn from the federal program before 2016. Under Obama that year, Kansas, Maine, New Jersey, and Texas followed through the exit door.[107] But the tentacles of the global refugee resettlement octopus run deep. Open Borders Inc. found a way to circumvent state opposition by arranging for the feds' Office of Refugee Resettlement to contract and subsidize local VOLAG affiliates directly to move foreigners (many of whom go on Medicaid and other welfare programs) into the objecting states. A Clinton-era regulation based on the federal Wilson-Fish Amendment (which was originally meant to curtail prolonged refugee welfare use) created new authority out of whole cloth for ORR to "authorize a replacement designee or designees to administer the provision of assistance and services, as appropriate, to refugees in that State."[108] Bottom line: the refugee dump continues unabated.

- The state of Tennessee, which filed a groundbreaking Tenth Amendment lawsuit against the feds over coercive refugee resettlement, noted: "When Congress enacted the Refugee Resettlement Act of 1980, the explicit intent was to assure full federal reimbursement of the costs for each refugee resettled and participating in benefit programs provided by the states. Eventually, however, federal reimbursements to the states for these benefit programs were reduced and, by 1991, eliminated entirely. The states thereby became responsible for the immense costs of the programs originally covered by the federal government."[109] Instead of honoring Tennessee's decision to withdraw from the program, the federal government (thanks to the Wilson-Fish regulation) went over the heads of its citizens and appointed Catholic Charities of Tennessee to run the program. "Currently, Tennessee State revenues that could otherwise be used for State programs to help Tennesseans are appropriated by the federal government to support the federal refugee resettlement program," lawyers for the Thomas More Law Center, which is representing Tennessee pro bono, pointed out. "This arrangement displaces Tennessee's constitutionally mandated funding prerogatives and appropriations process." In March 2019, a federal district court dismissed the case, but Tennessee has hired a top appellate lawyer to continue the fight.[110]

Are VOLAGs dumping refugees in *your* backyard without your input, knowledge, and consent? See Map B for the FY 2018 map of reception and placement program sites operating across America;[111] Appendix H for top refugee destinations by state and metro area from 2008 to 2017;[112] and Appendix I for a list of so-called Wilson-Fish states and the monopoly VOLAGs that operate refugee resettlement programs in those states.

The Poisoned U.N. Tree

So, who dictates "who we are" and who we let into our country? Ultimately, the refugee resettlement racket is the rotten fruit of the poisoned global governance tree. Behind the deep-pocketed VOLAGs, the State Department, and the International Organization for Migration, the United Nations has been pushing for increasing "collective action" to "protect the rights of refugees and migrants, to save lives and share responsibility for large movements on a global scale."

"Shared responsibility" is elitist speak for: Make America pay. Make America carry the load.

Let's talk about what the U.N. should be doing to "save lives." Islamic jihadists are lopping off infidels' heads; kidnapping young African girls, Christian missionaries, and Western tourists; incinerating Afghan schoolgirls; imposing genital mutilation on Muslim girls and marrying them off to lecherous brutes while they're still in grade school; pushing gays off of rooftops; gang-raping European women; casting fatwas on cartoonists, filmmakers, and authors; and stabbing, shooting, and bombing Jews, Christians, and ex-Muslim apostates all over the world. But the real problem, the U.N. pooh-bahs tell us, is "rising xenophobia" against "migrants" in countries whose citizens are sick and tired of open borders.[113] If only we uneducated heathens who oppose unfettered mass immigration to America from America-hating breeding grounds learned to appreciate "diversity" more, they preach, a rainbow of peace and harmony would reign.

For his final address to the United Nations General Assembly in September 2016, President Obama echoed the chamber's America-bashing and railed against national self-preservation in favor of "global integration."[114] Instead of a full-frontal fusillade against al-Qaeda, the Islamic State, and all the other homicidal spreaders of Allahu Akbar-itis, Obama aimed his sharpest barbs at American supporters of then presidential candidate Donald Trump and U.K. voters who voted to withdraw from the European Union. "A nation ringed by walls would only imprison itself," he lectured.[115] The U.N. Commissioner for Human Rights, Zeid

Ra'ad Al Hussein, ran with Obama's baton, bloviating against "race-baiting bigots, who seek to gain, or retain, power by wielding prejudice and deceit, at the expense of those most vulnerable."[116]

What they didn't talk about: the decades-old corruption, fraud, and abuse perpetrated by the U.N. itself and its vast refugee bureaucracy. Behind the veil of compassion and humanitarianism lies a worldwide ring of shakedown artists and thugs exploiting the destitute and desperate, "wielding prejudice and deceit, at the expense of the most vulnerable," to quote UNCHR chief Zeid Ra'ad Al Hussein's words right back at him. You want an exhibit of "racism?" There isn't a continent of non-white people on the planet that hasn't been infiltrated by and preyed upon by U.N. refugee vultures.

For years, U.N. staff members in Nairobi shook down African refugees seeking resettlement in North America, Europe, and Australia while the U.N. looked the other way.[117] The extortion racket charged up to $5,000 a head for resettlement rights. Belated investigations found that the scandal wasn't the result of a few rogue workers, but of negligent management that created a ripe atmosphere for abuse. "[E]verything had a price in the Kenya branch of the refugee agency," the *New York Times* reported back in 2001. "Guards at the door had to be tipped, they said. One current employee recalled asking about 35 refugees in the Kakuma refugee camp in northern Kenya, where roughly 100,000 refugees live, how many had paid bribes to guards on the way into the refugee agency's offices there. Nearly everyone stood up, the employee said."[118]

In Malaysia, U.N. officials were implicated in black market schemes to sell false identity papers, including identity cards from the United Nations High Commissioner on Refugees, to get refugees resettled in the United States, Australia, and Canada. An undercover Al Jazeera investigation in 2014 found that "refugee communities in the country [had] paid anything from RM 1,700 to RM 3,500 (roughly $500 to $1,000) for" U.N. Refugee Agency identity cards, "allegedly brokered by UNHCR officials in Malaysia."[119] The probe also found fraud involving some 3,000 asylum seekers who allegedly used false identities to gain early interviews with UNHCR staff to determine refugee status; about 1,000 went on to be resettled in the U.S., Canada, and Australia.[120]

On tape, U.N. Refugee Agency officials described themselves as "thieves" for an illegal document brokering scam.[121] "All the money from this activity goes into the pockets of some top guys in the UN," a U.N. translator claimed on Al Jazeera's current-affairs program, *101 East*. "We have been doing this ... for a long time. We are thieves, and we look for thieves above us."[122]

While the U.N. Refugee Agency downplayed the fraud and claimed to have a "zero tolerance policy," the fraud appeared to be global. In Lebanon, Arabic-language news site Al-Monitor reported that "[a]id organizations have become fountains of corruption, while 'humanitarian mafias' accrue massive sums" on the backs of Syrian refugees.[123] Graft is rampant in contract arrangements between the U.N. and private companies and NGOs that serve refugee camps. Al-Monitor described one agency's nutrition and health initiative approved by UNHCR that charged $1 million but "did not employ enough personnel to administer it" and did not provide the required equipment, "like water filters, soap and basic cleaning products." Municipal leaders are paid bribes to cover up mistreatment of refugees. Systemic defrauding follows a well-worn pattern: "A group runs a field study to define the basic necessities for a project that will benefit Syrian refugees, and will request an amount of money to implement the project. Then the group will allocate the money according to a particular time frame. Once UNICEF and UNHCR agree on the project and the requested amount is allocated, the group will alter the allocation to distribute huge amounts of money to non-refugees."[124]

In 2016, fiscal watchdogs blew the whistle on systemic mismanagement of the U.N. Refugee Agency's nearly billion-dollar budget over two years. A U.N. Office of Internal Oversight Services (OIOS) internal audit deemed every measure of financial controls over refugee relief funds "unsatisfactory."[125] The report came just two years after another internal assessment raised red flags over "the lack of adequate managerial control" by U.N. officials contracting with third parties purportedly helping refugees.[126] All that came in the wake of the latest in a string of U.N. rape epidemics involving peacekeepers in the Central African Republic who sexually abused civilians, including more than one hundred girls in one prefecture.[127] That outbreak followed years of brutal exploitation by U.N. staff members in Nairobi[128] and ran parallel to another widespread U.N. peacekeepers' sexual predator ring involving refugees that stretched from the Congo to Bosnia[129] and Eastern Europe.[130]

U.N. brass downplayed the barbaric treatment of refugees in its care as the result of a few rogues. But rape rooms and internet pedophile video productions were run by senior U.N. officials and other civilian personnel, untold numbers of whom fathered babies with young girls and teens held as prostitutes and sex slaves.[131] Nothing has changed since I started chronicling the U.N. sex scandals on my blog nearly fifteen years ago.[132] In April 2019, NBC News published the results of a seven-month investigation into U.N. Refugee Agency employees' refugee shakedowns in Kenya, Uganda, Yemen, Ethiopia, and Libya.[133] Among the investigation's findings:

- "Refugees who are part of the Nakivale settlement in southwest Uganda said UNHCR staffers and officials from organizations that work with them demand bribes for everything from medical referrals to food rations to contacting police, and it can cost $5,000 in bribes to resettle a family."
- "In the Dadaab refugee camp, whose residents are almost all Somalis, 19 refugees said it used to cost as much as $50,000 to resettle a large family, or roughly $3,000 per person, before the Trump administration effectively stopped resettlement of Somalis in the U.S."
- "Refugees who cannot afford to pay bribes report that unscrupulous resettlement workers will sell their case files, often compiled painstakingly over years, to others with more wealth."

The U.N. responded by accusing NBC News of endangering its staff by exposing the fraud. Deny, deflect, defame, demand. Remember, my fellow Americans: These are the sanctimonious corruptocrats making decisions thousands of miles away that are altering our cultural landscape, endangering our safety, draining our pocketbooks, obliterating our borders, and stealing our children's futures. Before the world's policemen denigrate our efforts to protect our home and dictate our immigration policies, they should spare us their refugee sanctimony and clean up their own wretched refuse.

CHAPTER FIVE

THE A-TEAM: ABOLISH ICE, ANTIFA, AND SANCTUARY ANARCHISTS

"**N**o ban. No wall. No borders at all."[1]
    Can the message be any clearer? This is the rallying cry of the Democratic Socialists of America (DSA), the radical leftists leading protests on the ground against the U.S. Immigration and Customs Enforcement agency since President Trump took office. DSA and its subversive allies have taken #AbolishICE from a hashtag to a movement, from extremism to a normalized Democratic Party talking point—inciting hatred, threats, and physical resistance of law and order every step of the way. DSA's *modus operandi* is "direct action"[2]: throwing up roadblocks, fomenting chaos, and shutting down the basic national security of government at all levels in the name of wide, open borders.

Waving desecrated American flags, grubby fists, fetid armpits, and ratty anarchy banners, DSA's professional protesters target Trump administration officials, threaten immigration enforcement agents, and blockade detention facilities and processing centers nationwide. It is a grave mistake to dismiss them as harmless losers and basement dwellers. In June 2018, after online vigilantes had released personal information about thousands of ICE employees, DHS deputy secretary Claire Grady[3] informed employees in a memo that officials had identified a "heightened threat against DHS employees in response to U.S. government actions surrounding immigration" based on "specific and credible threats that have been levied against certain DHS employees and a sharp increase in the overall number of general threats against DHS employees—although the veracity of each threat varies."[4] In May 2019, a leaked FBI report detailed an alleged plot by "anti-fascist activists"—Antifa—to "disrupt U.S. law enforcement and military security operations at the US-Mexican border" by purchasing weapons from a "Mexico-based cartel associate."[5] The group has been on the national security radar of the feds for years.

A joint FBI/Department of Homeland Security intelligence assessment first classified Antifa subversion as "domestic terrorist violence" in 2016, under the Obama administration.[6] In San Jose that year, a bloodthirsty mob of four hundred Antifa thugs targeted Trump supporters—spitting on them, throwing bottles, hurling eggs, vandalizing their cars, burning American flags, and waving Mexican flags.[7] By September 2017, the feds had flagged armed Antifa groups such as Redneck Revolt and the Red Guards, as well as moldy-oldy agitators like Berkeley's militant By Any Means Necessary, which joined Antifa-led riots. Left-wing brawlers instigated attacks against Trump supporters in Austin, Texas, and Sacramento, Orange County, and the bay area in California before aggravating the volatile clash in Charlottesville, Virginia. At least two domestic terrorism suspects have been arrested for threatening ICE agents. One was an illegal alien Mexican "DREAMer," Sergio "Mapache" Salazar,[8] who was deported after the FBI investigated his social media threats against federal employees. The Center for Immigration Studies's Todd Bensman reported that Salazar had posted on Twitter about "how to make bombs to kill federal officers"[9] and continued to demonize ICE and FBI officers as "liars and snakes."[10] The other menace, thirty-three-year old anti-ICE activist Brandon Ziobrowski of Cambridge, Massachusetts, used his Twitter account to offer $500 to "anyone who kills an ICE agent" even though he was "broke." When an ICE agent informed the punk online that he was endangering ICE personnel, Ziobrowski sneered: "Thank you ICE for putting your lives on the line and hopefully dying I guess so there's less of you?" He then endorsed shooting cops, which he said "should get you a medal."[11]

Ziobrowski's Twitter account was suspended only after law enforcement requested it.[12]

These are not just clownish rent-a-mobsters who defecate on police cars[13] and rage ineffectually at the machine. These are not just harmless hammer-and-sickle hipsters. They are public safety menaces, operating in bad faith, who pose a serious threat to our nation's well-being.

You'll be darkly amused (or simply disgusted) to know that despite their bottomless contempt for capitalism, DSA's merchandise store peddles bright red "ABOLISH ICE" T-shirts for twenty dollars a pop and "ABOLISH ICE" fifteen-button packs for twelve dollars.[14] Open Borders Inc. is big business, even for the foaming-at-the-mouth foes of the free market.

The #AbolishICE mantra first surfaced on Twitter in February 2017 thanks to an obscure millennial "socialist researcher" and statistician named Sean McElwee.[15] (He sold his own line of "Abolish ICE" T-shirts, by the way, which raised $4,000 for the Soros-backed open-borders groups Make the Road Action, Detention Watch Network, and United We Dream.[16]) In his March 2018 manifesto for the liberal magazine *The Nation*, McElwee condemned ICE as a "mass deportation strike force" that was "incompatible with democracy and human rights."[17] The agenda is not to defund, reform, or replace the immigration enforcement bureaucracy, but to stop immigration enforcement altogether. The "goal of abolishing the agency is to abolish the function," McElwee declared. "ICE has become a genuine threat to democracy, and it is destroying thousands of lives." He ratcheted up the invective with charges that ICE agents are guilty of racism and "authoritarian saber rattling." Citing a handful of far-left congressional candidates on board with his mission, McElwee called on the Democratic Party to "begin seriously resisting an unbridled white-supremacist surveillance state that it had a hand in creating."[18] He name-checked the anti-Trump Indivisible Project (a Tides

Foundation project)[19] and the Bernie Sanders' staff-founded Brand New Congress PAC[20] as early endorsers.

The movement achieved lift-off when progressive poster girl Alexandria Ocasio-Cortez, an early Abolish ICE promoter, won her primary challenge against incumbent Democrat Congressman Joseph Crowley in New York's Fourteenth District in June 2018. A perfect storm formed that same month as media-manufactured hysteria over President Trump's efforts to clamp down on the illegal alien influx at our southern border reached full tilt. A coalition of malingerers and malefactors—Occupy Wall Street leftovers, amnesty agitators, ethnic activists, cop-haters, and Trump resisters—took to the streets while McElwee basked in BuzzFeed buzz over his success in normalizing open-borders zealotry.[21] He calls himself an "Overton window mover," a reference to conservative think-tanker Joseph Overton's concept of the range of ideas and discourse acceptable in the political mainstream.[22]

"We need to just let it out," McElwee exhorted his fellow smashers of the window of decency. "Fucking abolish ICE!"[23]

(Pardon the profanity. Warning: there will be a lot more of it.)

In June 2018, Oregon-based DSA operatives and their radical partners shut down a U.S. Immigration and Customs Enforcement office in Southwest Portland during a five-week siege. Dubbed Occupy ICE PDX, the self-proclaimed insurrection united militant groups committed to "abolishing the agencies that are the militarized arms of enforcement, abolishing the criminalization of migration, abolishing national borders altogether.[24] In case that wasn't clear enough, a "rebel alliance" of anarchists called CrimethInc. spelled it out further:

> We want to abolish ICE and everything it does completely. We do not want to secure the border. We do not want immigration reform, but to stop all deportations immediately, abolish immigration imprisonment, abolish borders in so-called North America, decriminalize movement, and undermine the logic of "citizen versus migrant." This is not about

simply the abolition of ICE, but the decolonization of North America.[25]

VICE praised the Portland cell's adoption of "Occupy-style tactics, camping out and erecting a quasi-Utopian tent city complete with provisions, communications, legal aid, and other hallmarks of Zuccotti Park circa fall 2011."[26] Weird. Those of us not inhaling illicit substances have far different memories of Occupy Wall Street's Zuccotti Park zoo: the rapists run amok,[27] contagious diseases,[28] overflowing garbage, and rats.[29] But I digress. Occupy ICE PDX's targeting of the Southwest Portland ICE office eventually led to twenty arrests after the sanctuary city's left-wing leaders dragged their feet about enforcing the law. Federal agents were pelted with unknown liquids and objects. Portland's Mayor Ted Wheeler, an open-borders sympathizer, announced a hands-off policy in support of the protesters. Only after demonstrators' filthy camps posed health and safety hazards—and after the protestors tried to block ICE vans from leaving the parking lot—did Wheeler reluctantly approve a police sweep and shutdown of the trespassers.[30]

Inspired by their Pacific Northwest comrades (they seriously do call each other "comrades"), DSA rabble-rousers days later launched their own Occupy ICE New York City operation at a SoHo loading dock used to transport immigrants at an ICE processing center. One giant banner read: "SMASH I.C.E. SMASH THE STATE."[31] Other posters declared: "FUCK ICE"; "ABOLISH ICE, OPEN ALL BORDERS"; and "Freedom to Migrate." Everyone deserves freedom of movement, socialists screech, except for federal agents trying to do their jobs. Overnight DSA campers linked arms to successfully obstruct ICE vans from driving detainees to court. The virtue signaling may have made for viral Twitter and Instagram posts. But for the detainees they claimed to care about so much, the blockade imposed more delay and separation from their families. As a result of the protests, bond hearings for detainees were canceled and the immigrants were forced to spend another six or more weeks in detention.[32]

In Detroit, organizers disrupted ordinary processing and appointments at a downtown ICE field office and declared their intention to park there twenty-four hours a day until the end of the month. "Our short-term goal is to shut down operations at this particular center," ringleader Robert Jay explained. "Our long-term goal is to abolish ICE entirely."[33] The Occupy ICE Detroit cell explains that it is an "extension of the prison abolition movement"[34] whose demands include full release of all illegal alien detainees claiming asylum and a "welcoming, open borders policy absent of xenophobia"[35]—by which they mean an absolute policy of non-enforcement against any aliens from any country for any reason encountered anywhere along any part of the border, at any port of entry, or anywhere on the interior.

The anarchists don't want to reform or reduce the U.S. Immigration and Customs Enforcement agency, which was created by merging existing immigration entities after the 9/11 attacks to better coordinate enforcement against alien lawbreakers inside the country. They want it gone. Zapped. Poof. They've ramped up their rhetoric to create a climate of hate against the entire twenty thousand-person ICE workforce, which handles not only enforcement and removal operations, but also homeland security investigations combating criminal organizations illegally exploiting our travel, trade, financial, and immigration systems. That includes international smugglers of women and children, drugs, weapons, and cash.

So, how exactly do these ICE-melters propose to deal with criminal alien fugitives, such as the estimated 300,000 deportation absconders who've been ordered by immigration judges to leave the country? How about the 40 percent of illegal aliens, from the pool of between 11 million and 30 million immigration lawbreakers, who overstayed their visas and are on the loose doing heaven knows what? And when will these noble twenty-first-century abolitionists be stepping up to open their homes to the members of the ICE Most Wanted list, which includes illegal aliens wanted for murder, aggravated homicide, narcotics and human trafficking, and membership in terrorist organizations? Just ask the liberal organizers of the jihad-coddling, Jew-bashing, race-baiting Women's March,[36] which endorsed the "call to #AbolishICE" and "eliminate the agency that has been terrorizing immigrant communities for 15 years."[37] Their answer: female and child victims of smuggling rings are on their own.

DSA's talking points again drive home for activists that replacement and reform are not their objectives. "It is not enough to reform ICE or even defund ICE. ICE is monstrous to its core and must be abolished." Period.[38]

It follows, of course, that the #AbolishICE radicals also demand the abolition of the Border Patrol. Brooklyn College sociology professor Alex Vitale, author of *The End of Policing*, expounded: "We need to abolish the Border Patrol as much or more than ICE."[39] Author Richard Parker published his own screed on the *Los Angeles Times* op-ed page titled, "Forget ICE, the Real Problem Is CBP [U.S. Customs and Border Protection]."[40] And Mijente, a Latino activist group leading the Abolish ICE movement, coordinated a tour under the battle cry, "*Chinga La Migra*"[41]—which means "Fuck the Border Patrol."[42]

This virulent hatred for ICE and the Border Patrol traces its ideological lineage back to the cop-bashing domestic terrorism of the 1970s that festered in academia and resulted in bloodshed across the country at the hands of the Black Liberation Army and Weather Underground. Investigative journalist and author Bryan Burrough observed that while these left-wing groups "were vehemently anti-war, their core motivation was rallying the black community toward open revolt."[43] Today's Abolish ICE extremists harbor the same seething "Pigs in a blanket, fry 'em like bacon"[44] contempt for immigration enforcement as the "progressive" cop-haters of the 1970s and their heirs in the Bush-era ANSWER and amnesty coalitions, Code Pink, Occupy Wall Street and Black Lives Matter movement. The underlying mission back then as now, as you'll see from our examination of the A-Team anarchists, is three Ds: destabilization, disruption, and destruction of civil order.

The Portland Cell

I lived and worked in the Pacific Northwest in the mid-to-late 1990s as a columnist and editorial writer for the *Seattle Times*. I moved out just in time to miss the infamous 1999 World Trade Organization riots in Seattle. The lame local police in that liberal city failed to protect citizens and business owners, who sustained $2.5 million in damage to stores and offices at the hands of 75,000 resisters run amok. (Fun fact/ side note: my candid critique of the police department over its botched handling of the protests[45] led the *Seattle Times* to drop my syndicated column.) The radical Ruckus Society, which has trained social justice warriors in "guerilla" and "monkey-wrenching" tactics since 1995, spearheaded the Seattle chaos and pulled in operatives from across the country.[46] Ruckus leaders created the Direct Action Network (DAN) to coordinate the demonstrators, hundreds of whom broke off into black bloc units that lit fires, threw rocks, destroyed property, and looted retailers.[47] Anarchists gloated in triumph at the havoc they sowed. "People with the reason to be fucking shit up, people who have the most reason to be breaking the windows of Nike, were doing it. And that was one of the best aspects of it. People who needed shoes were breaking the windows and getting shoes. And that's the way it should be," said one participant.[48]

DAN disbanded in the early 2000s, but radical disrupters are a mainstay in the region. I've covered the Pacific Northwest's criminal anarchist element for more than twenty years[49]—from the animal rights terrorists who have harassed, threatened, and firebombed scientific researchers across the U.S. and Europe[50] through the 1999 "Battle in Seattle," and Occupy Seattle/Occupy Portland "Days of Rage" to shut down ports in 2011–2012[51] as an expression of "solidarity" with union workers' "struggle."[52] On May Day 2012, masked Portland anarchists threw smoke bombs and provoked fistfights with police.[53] After election day in November 2016, the Associated Press dubbed Portland the "epicenter" of anti-Trump resistance when four thousand hoodlums took to the streets smashing windows, hurling firecrackers, and attacking police.[54] Among the early rising stars of the Portland Resistance was Micah Rhodes, who "helped organize day after day of marches and rallies against Trump" after the November 2016 election, according to the

Oregonian. In 2018, he evaded prison for abusing an underage girl and an underage boy; he had earlier been convicted as a minor for sexually abusing four young boys.[55]

For Inauguration Day in January 2017, Portland troublemakers formed the Direct Action Alliance to "respond to the rise of fascism in America" and to organize the Disrupt J20 "Rise Up & Shut It Down" protest. The alliance's partners included Milenio, an Oregon illegal alien community-organizing outfit comprised of DREAMers; MEChistas; labor union activists;[56] Portland Punx Against Fascism; Anarchist Red and Black Block; Portland Committee for Human Rights in the Philippines; and Portland Student Action Network."[57]

Thousands from these groups and more turned out in Portland's Pioneer Courthouse Square, where anarchists burned American flags, threw bottles and flares,[58] and scuffled with police, leading to six arrests.[59] On the anarchist website It's Going Down, one unsatisfied thug posted his after-action critique: "While I was handed an egg to throw, I'd have preferred it to be a rock, and the few hammers I saw earlier never seemed to come into play," he/she griped to comrades. "We should have been gathering projectiles while we were relatively left alone by the cops. It would have been better to throw rocks than to have to make a push, and less costly in terms of injuries to our own. At the Broadway bridge, it would have been good to have larger shields, and perhaps longer flags or poles to hit the cops with...."[60]

Cue the punchline: the American Civil Liberties Union of Oregon still insists on calling these projectile-wielding punks, you guessed it, "peaceful protesters."[61] So did other anarchist apologists like Portland city councilwoman and Abolish ICE supporter Chloe Eudaly. She praised the protest goons as "organized," "peaceful," "collaborative," and "respectful of the neighborhood."[62] Because nothing says "respectful" like assaulting cops with hammers, rocks, and poles.

A few months after the J20 protests, Direct Action Alliance planned to protest the city's 82nd Avenue of Roses Parade. The target of their leaders' ire: the Multnomah County Republican Party.[63] Just days before the event, parade organizers received thug-mail: "You have seen how much power we have downtown and that the police cannot stop us from shutting down roads so please consider your decision wisely." The e-mail threatened that organizers could cancel the Republican group's registration or else face action from protesters. "This is non-negotiable."[64] The organizers canceled the parade, sending a message that in Portland, mobs rule. Direct Action Alliance next connected with DSA to orchestrate the Occupy ICE PDX takeover that sparked Abolish ICE and detention center protests nationwide. Another key partner: the Portland General Assembly, which openly defies any cooperation with law enforcement and espouses a policy of "police non-collaboration" in all matters.[65] The group's resource page cheers radical Zapatistas, armed and masked left-wing revolutionaries in Chiapas, Mexico.[66] The Occupy ICE PDX coalition received legal support from the Communist Party member-founded National Lawyers Guild,[67] which works to "defend and expand the rights of all immigrants in the United States"[68] and partners with Al Otro Lado, the illegal alien caravan's legal advisers who work in Mexico to undermine border and interior immigration enforcement.

While the lawyers put up a non-violent front, Occupy ICE PDX intensified their hate against ICE agents: "We are calling on activists across the country to establish their own occupations to abolish ICE. Wherever ICE agents dare to show their faces, they must be challenged and shamed for carrying out this fascist policy.... It takes ALL of us working together to stop this machine of terror. Fuck La Migra!"[69]

Online-extremism researcher Eoin Lenihan spotlighted the whitewashing of the Portland cell's violent threats by Jason Wilson, a Portland-based writer for the U.K. *Guardian*. Wilson frequently relies on pro-Antifa writer Mark Bray, author of *Antifa: The Anti-Fascist Handbook*, as an "expert" to deflect criticism of the group, and he quoted a "local activist" Luis Marquez who proclaimed that "I think this occupation is a beautiful thing, a wonderful thing. Every single person here is a hero." Marquez, as Lenihan pointed out, "is in fact a prominent Antifa leader in Portland, and has been arrested on numerous occasions due to his militant behavior—including alleged theft and assault."[70]

No one who has followed this long history of anarchists' threats, intimidation, and physical confrontation in the Pacific Northwest will be surprised at what happened to the Portland lawyer who represents the union for ICE officers in the region. In late April 2019, Sean Riddell's law office was vandalized by anonymous anarchists who flooded the entire main floor and basement with a garden hose inserted through his front door mail slot. An e-mail sent to *Willamette Week*,[71] which broke the story, claimed credit for the thuggery, explaining that "our goal was to cause maximum economic damage" to "serve as a warning to all individuals and businesses that profit off the human misery perpetrated by ICE."[72] Signed by "some anarchists," the bullies closed with the usual open-borders, Marxist-inspired sloganeering: "For a world without borders and prisons. For the free movement of all people. Smash ICE."[73]

Riddell remained unbowed. "I'm not a victim," he told *Willamette Week*. "I'm just doing my job."

So was independent investigative journalist and documentarian Andy Ngo, a Portland resident, who reported on the Occupy ICE PDX siege for the *Wall Street Journal* op-ed page in August 2018.[74] Ngo described the fetid "smell of urine and feces" that filled the block around the ICE field office. He interviewed local residents and business owners, like the Hakes family, which owns and operates a food cart in the area. The mob "terrorized" the family, accused one of them of "supporting the pigs," and threatened to burn down their cart. Police ignored their calls for help. Ngo similarly recounted unheeded pleas by federal workers for assistance from local police. ICE agents were harassed and targeted by the mob, which stalked them at their homes and heckled one black ICE officer as a "fucking nigger" and "piece of shit" in a video posted on YouTube.[75] (I told you the profanity and vile bile were going to get worse.) The *Oregonian* reported on internal e-mails documenting further examples of Occupy ICE PDX's racial epithets hurled at a black ICE officer called an "Uncle Tom" and a Hispanic/Native American female

ICE officer[76] taunted as a "traitor." She added that she was "berated for so long I can't even remember everything that was told to me." Another ICE agent reported that the mobsters chanted "that they hope we die, they hope our families die."[77]

In early May 2019, Ngo was "doxxed" by online anarchists who posted his home address and threatened him to "tone down your volume" or face retribution.[78] "Doxxing" is the practice of online harassment through public release of private documents and data—phone numbers, work and residential addresses, family information. Disseminating the information is an open call to fellow troublemakers to cross the line from virtual harassment to stalking and physical confrontation. On May Day, the rabble-rousers' favorite day of the year, Ngo was assaulted by black-clad operatives who pepper-sprayed him in the face.[79] A few days later, a man Ngo recognized from previous reporting on left-wing protests attacked Ngo at his local gym by throwing liquid on him and stealing his phone.[80] Abolish ICE/anarchist agitators focus their hate on law enforcement officers and immigration enforcement officers, but they hate brave citizen journalists and conservative activists just as much.

Antifa: Fascist Anti-Fascists

"Antifa" is short for "anti-fascist" and long on hypocrisy. While its acolytes preach opposition to authoritarian regimes, Antifa itself uses violent and oppressive tactics, coupled with incendiary and inciting rhetoric, to achieve its goal of eradicating ideological foes. The movement festered in Europe for decades, with Germany's Antifascistische Aktion forming post–World War II alliances between Communists and Social Democratic workers ostensibly to fight any remaining Nazis.[81] In modern times, however, Antifa has evolved into a far-flung umbrella group for extreme leftists dedicated to "peace through violence," as the apologists at CNN memorably put it.[82] Thousands of masked Antifa outlaws hijacked the G20 Summit in Hamburg, Germany, in 2017, attacking and injuring two hundred police officers with bottles, iron bars, rocks, and homemade incendiary devices over a two-day siege.[83] Malicious rioters attempted to blind cops with powerful green lasers aimed at their eyes; others looted and burned down shops and cars.[84]

Perhaps the oldest Antifa chapter in the U.S. is the Rose City Antifa group founded in Portland in 2007.[85] The organization "tapped into regional currents of anarchism and latent communism," Portland writer Casey Michel reported, adopting a uniform of "blood-red and black bandanas and hoods" with an explicit and "unapologetic" vow to employ the "physical militancy"[86] embraced by their European comrades. In June 2018, the militants made good on their promise and physically assaulted members of the conservative group Patriot Prayer who had gathered in downtown Portland for a peaceful march to celebrate one of its activists. Patriot Prayer's leader, Joey Gibson, is of Japanese ancestry, but that hasn't stopped Antifa from labeling him a "white supremacist."[87] Antifa had similarly targeted the group in a violent fit a year earlier and again a few months later in October 2018, when masked, black-clad anarchists maced the conservatives and provoked all-out brawls.[88]

As we've already seen with Portland Antifa target Andy Ngo, doxxing is standard operating procedure. In the name of fighting "fascism," Rose City Antifa published the home address of Portland activist Haley Adams,[89] a young female conservative who organized a #HimToo rally protesting false rape allegations against innocent men after Judge Brett Kavanaugh's Supreme Court hearings.[90] Antifa elements chanted, "A-C-A-B. All cops are bastards!" as officers tried to maintain the peace.[91]

The hatred spiraled and spread to the heartland. Anti-Fascist Action Nebraska endangered the lives of nearly 1,600 ICE agents on June 19, 2018, by directing followers of its Twitter account to a massive, aggregated database of the agents' LinkedIn information and other personal data.[92] "Some enterprising hero archived the ICE employees listed on LinkedIn," the tweet gloated.[93] The list included photos of the ICE workers, their titles, and where they live.[94]

The vindictive cop-hating researcher who compiled and posted the dossier was Sam Lavigne, an adjunct professor at New York University[95] whose campus bio describes him as an "artist and educator whose work deals with data, surveillance, cops, natural language processing, and automation."[96] Antifa's "hero" was a designated "Something in Residence" in spring 2018 at NYU's Interactive Telecommunications Program (ITP),[97] funded by Microsoft Research,[98] which supports "people who are doing work at the edge of the leading edge." In a now-deleted tweet on June 19, 2018, Lavigne announced that he had "scraped LinkedIn for people that work for ICE."[99] The tweet linked to his now-deleted essay on Medium, which explained how he had helpfully compiled the personal data for easy use and downloading on a site called GitHub. He also posted the Python code he developed for mining LinkedIn to surveil ICE employees, along with instructions on how to use it.[100] "While I don't have a precise idea of what should be done with this data set," Lavigne wrote, "I leave it here with the hope that researchers, journalists and activists will find it useful."[101]

The dog whistle was loud and clear: come and get it!

On Twitter, which claims that doxxing violates its terms of use,[102] Lavigne still maintains an account—while peaceful, non-harmful conservatives and independent thinkers and writers have been banned for expressing their opinions. ICE-haters immediately started sharing the ICE employee profiles.[103] Bizarrely, Twitter permanently suspended a liberal coder's account (@ICEHRgov) that shared Lavigne's database profiles, but not the originator of the list.[104] Lavigne took his vendetta against ICE employees a step further, tweeting a photo of ICE chief technology officer David Larrimore on Father's Day.[105] One Twitter user responded approvingly: "Nothing wrong with doxxing people who operate concentration camps."[106] Right on cue (or rather, far-left on cue!), the New York City Antifa group piled on Larrimore in a menacing thread that stirred up personal animus against the ICE CTO:

> Thought y'all might want to know that the Chief Technology Officer for ICE, @davidlarrimore, enjoys LARPing [live action role-playing] as Captain America while over 700 children have yet to be reunited with their parents & a judge ordered ICE to stop forcing psychotropic drugs on these kids. #AbolishICE[107]

One Antifa follower raged: "Captain America would punch him right in his stupid face."[108] Another Twitter user (whose *nom de guerre* was the Robespierre-inspired "Litl Guillotine") fumed: "FUCK ICE" with a link to a video titled "SMASH FASCISM."[109] NYC Antifa continually stokes ICE hatred on Twitter, while rising numbers of pro-immigration enforcement conservatives have been silenced on the platform. Other tweets included: "Throw ICE into a goddamn volcano"[110] and "Customs & Border Patrol are absolute scum & no one should extend them the benefit of the doubt."[111]

The Daily Caller reported that the Antifa-endorsed Lavigne list made its way to a far-left subgroup on Reddit called r/ChapoTrapHouse, whose members "encourage doxxing those who they deem Nazis and alt-right,"[112] including ICE agents just doing their jobs. "Doxxing ICE agents is good and moral," one Reddit user on the subgroup applauded. Two days after Lavigne's data dump, WikiLeaks perpetrated its own anti-ICE doxxing by publishing a database called "ICE Patrol"[113] of more than 9,200 employees ranging from low-level interns to senior management, including their names and photos, searchable by location, industry, current position, school attended and field of study.[114] Its Twitter account remains active and verified. The blog Far Left Watch exposed yet more examples of doxxing by "anti-fascist union" Greater Seattle GDC, which shared a blog post on Twitter from the Puget Sound Anarchists that "included the names and home addresses of 37 Immigration and Customs Enforcement (ICE) agents and even included the personal contact information for their spouses."[115] Concerned Twitter users joined Far Left Watch in flagging the Seattle Antifa threats multiple times with no response from Twitter's safety police.[116]

As of May 2019, another incitement against ICE first published on June 18, 2018, by New York environmental agitator Ariel Schwartz, remained on Twitter. "Members of ICE should be outed and ostracized," she ranted. "Hassled at restaurants, malls, when they pick their kids up from school, etc. You should not be able to be a part of the machine separating children from their families and clock out for a peaceful evening."[117]

A *Wired* magazine reporter spotlighted another Antifa sympathizer who employs doxxing against non-leftists, Megan Squire, an Elon University computer science professor. *Wired* hailed her as "Antifa's secret weapon against Far Right Extremists," gushing over her data-mining of alleged white nationalists that she feeds to the Southern Poverty Law Center smear machine (see chapter ten).[118] Squire calls her digital surveillance project "Whack-A-Mole."

Wired ominously explained: "She's an intelligence operative of sorts in the battle against far-right extremism, passing along information to those who might put it to real-world use. Who might weaponize it."[119]

Occupy Wall Street escalated the violent rhetoric further, tweeting a six-point guide on "What To Do If You Encounter An ICE Agent."[120] If an ICE agent tries to take your child at the border, the Occupiers advise in their graphic cartoon, grab the agent "from behind and push your knife into his chest with an upward thrust, breaking through his sternum." Illustrated with an agent gushing blood, the instructions continue: "Reach into his chest and pull out his still beating heart," then "hold his bloody heart out for all other agents to see, and tell them that the same fate awaits them if they fuck with your child again."[121]

It is no coincidence that as Antifa allies cranked up the anti-ICE, anti-right witch hunt online, operatives on the ground were indeed weaponizing hate in the real world. Just one day after Lavigne doxxed ICE workers, former Department of Homeland Security secretary Kirstjen Nielsen was accosted at a Mexican restaurant in Washington, D.C. by Metro DC DSA hecklers shouting "Abolish ICE" slogans.[122] The group whipped up a frenzy on Twitter: "Why should she get to eat in peace while thousands of migrant children sit in cages?"[123] Antifa followers effused: "WOOT! We should be making it impossible for them to exist in public. Thank you, comrades!"[124] And: "This should happen to every republican, every member of the administration, public shaming wherever they go."[125] Among the rabble-rousers who harassed Nielsen: Justice Department paralegal, Allison Hrabar,[126] later exposed by undercover journalists at Project Veritas as one of many DSA moles in the Trump administration abusing their positions to do "inside" work for the resistance.[127] One DSA member spilled the beans on Hrabar, admitting she used her work computer to dig up home addresses on enemies and share them with her comrades.[128] She was fired in late September 2018, raised $11,000 on GoFundMe as a social justice martyr,[129] and is currently listed among Metro DC DSA leadership.[130]

Metro DC DSA, George Soros-backed CREDO Action, and Bend the Arc (a Jewish social justice nonprofit established with the help of Soros's son, Alex) ratcheted up the pressure on Nielsen a week after the Mexican restaurant ambush by marching into her neighborhood. The obnoxious contingent blasted audio of detained children crying on loudspeakers while wielding Satanic-tinged posters of Nielsen labeled "CHILD SNATCHER."[131] The vigilante mob also targeted Trump senior adviser and immigration enforcement stalwart Stephen Miller. His private phone number was spread on Twitter by the same Nebraska Antifa group that promoted the doxxing of ICE employees.[132] Splinter News, a left-wing news outlet owned by open-borders Univision, the Spanish TV conglomerate, impudently headlined an article, "Here's Stephen Miller's phone number if you need it."[133] Other anti-Trump journalists joined the doxxing bandwagon, including *The Nation*'s David Klion[134] and Gizmodo editor Tom McKay.[135] The journalists remained defiant even after temporary Twitter suspensions. Univision's Splinter News went untouched and unpunished.

Emboldened jerks hounded Miller at a Mexican restaurant and a sushi restaurant in D.C. over the next two weeks.[136] White House press secretary Sarah Sanders was booted from the trendy Red Hen restaurant in Lexington, Virginia, by its left-wing owner.[137] Several weeks later, self-identified D.C. Antifa "hooligans" from Smash Racism D.C. chased Texas Republican Senator Ted Cruz and his wife from the D.C. Italian eatery Fiola. "No—you can't eat in peace," the pot-stirrers railed. "Tonight Senator Ted Cruz arrived at Fiola, an upscale restaurant mere steps from the White House, to enjoy a hearty Italian dinner. He could have dined on a lavish four course meal for only $145 while millions of Americans struggle to buy groceries.... He might have sampled from the top shelf wine list as migrant children languish in cages.[138] The group used the spotlight to toss in a gratuitous doxxing of Gavin McInnes, whose phone number they posted to Twitter.[139] McInnes was banned from the social media platform in August 2018[140] for non-violent political views after being targeted by the Southern Poverty Law Center's ideological hitmen (see chapter ten). Meanwhile, Smash Racism D.C. got away with a short suspension and happily returned to tweeting and menacing.

In November 2018, Smash Racism D.C. targeted Fox News primetime anchor Tucker Carlson's home with mob chants and threats, shouting, "You are not safe!" and, "Racist scumbag, leave town!" and "Tucker Carlson, we will fight! We know where you sleep at night!" while his wife hid in a pantry.[141] After spreading his private home address on Twitter, the serial rule-breakers at Smash Racism D.C. were suspended, attempted to evade punishment by creating a new account (which was suspended), and finally received a permanent suspension of the group's official Twitter handle.[142] But Smash Racism D.C.'s former organizer and John Jay College economics professor, Mike Isaacson, remains on the platform after taunting Carlson, threatening law enforcement,[143] and advocating punching Trump supporters: "Bring it, throat punching is probably a good thing."[144]

Friendly reminder: Twitter's own plain and explicit rules state: "You may not make specific threats of violence or wish for the serious physical harm, death, or disease of an individual or group of people."[145]

But threats and wishes for harm have fantastically hyper-elastic definitions when applied to the violence-promoting left. While conservative actor James Woods was suspended from Twitter for paraphrasing Ralph Waldo Emerson's famous verse ("If you try to kill the King, you best not miss' #HangThemAll") with no specific threat aimed at anyone or any group,[146] the politically correct platform condoned specific and violent wishes and threats from Antifa forces aimed at President Trump. Far Left Watch provided more grim examples of toxic speech deemed acceptable by the Twitter overlords of civility:

- A New York City anarchist center called The Base promoted armed revolution daily on its Twitter feed. The Bushwick, Brooklyn–based group peddles a manual on how to "Burn Down the American Plantation,"[147] along with merchandise featuring a graphic image of President Trump with a giant safety pin piercing his head.[148]
- Paramilitary Antifa outfit Redneck Revolt posted a training manual for "urban guerillas" with sections of "kidnapping," "executions," and "terrorism."[149]
- CrimethInc., mentioned at the beginning of this chapter as a leading Abolish ICE rabble-rouser, tweeted a frightening poster of a MAGA hat–wearing man with a large knife pointed at his chest and the caption: "WE BEAT 'EM BEFORE. WE'LL BEAT 'EM AGAIN." Behind the Trump supporter was the shadow of a Nazi.[150]

The Nazi smears against Trump supporters and ICE agents spread like gangrene across social media and the internet. Antifa trashmouth Ulrike

Salazar attacked ICE officers as "shadowy Gestapo agents" and Border Patrol officers as "fascistic...dogs" in a piece for Incendiary News. Wait, that was just a prelude. Salazar rallied his comrades to rise up and "slay" DHS officers with "revolutionary fire and justice."[151] The overthrow will be achieved throughout the country, he inveighed, when revolutionary organizations "such as the Red Guards" band together "among the immigrant masses in forming defense units, rallying around the shared slogan of 'fight ICE with fire!'"[152]

Before you laugh off his bloviations, keep in mind that the Antifa "punch a Nazi" meme online has stoked multiple criminal attacks by a rogue's gallery of violent "peaceful protesters." Let me refresh your memories with the infamous Diablo Valley College professor Eric Clanton, an Antifa assailant who pummeled innocent Trump supporters with a heavy metal bike lock at an April 15 "Patriots Day" event in Berkeley, California. One of the victims, Sean Stiles, had been debating immigration with two liberal women[153] when masked and black-clad Clanton weaponized the U lock to strike a total of seven people in the head, neck, and back. One bled all over the sidewalk and required staples to close his wound. Another, lucky enough to be wearing protection, had a chunk of his bike helmet taken out. When Berkeley police searched Clanton's car and apartment, they found a "canister of bear spray, two flip knives, metal knuckles, Rayban sunglasses...and a Billy club."[154] Clanton received three years of probation.[155] Not even a slap on the wrist, but a tickle.

The proliferation of Antifa/Communist-promoting Red Guards chapters, which celebrate and emulate Chairman Mao's brutal enforcers of the Cultural Revolution,[156] is especially chilling. In Texas, Red Guards Austin moved beyond hammer and sickle hipsterism[157] into physical intimidation of local Republican Party activists by placing bloody severed pigs' heads at five campaign offices.[158] They explicitly advocate armed conflict and "revolutionary violence" because "everywhere is a battlefield."[159] The Austin chapter purports to have dissolved, but has identified other chapters across the country: Red Guards Los Angeles, Red

Guards Kansas City, Red Guards Pittsburgh, and Red Guards Charlotte.

For my timeline of Abolish ICE vigilantism and Antifa violence since the 2016 presidential campaign, see Appendix J.

The New York City Cell

A mishmash of anarchists and "direct action" disrupters form the open-borders resistance in the Big Apple. I've already introduced you to the Soros-funded Center for Popular Democracy and Make the Road organizers. Supplementing their sovereignty-sabotaging work is Rise and Resist, a nonprofit that sprung up after Election Day "to oust the Trump administration, fight for equality, and collaborate on a wide variety of social justice issues." The group's biggest moment in the spotlight: hijacking Independence Day 2018 to unfurl an "ABOLISH I.C.E." banner at the Statue of Liberty while fellow professional protester Patricia Okoumou scaled the monument. The stunt caused an emergency evacuation and three-hour shutdown of the patriotic tourist site on America's birthday. Okoumou was charged with federal trespassing but escaped with probation and community service. A judge expressed concern that her lack of a job was driving her to break the law in order to raise money from the stunts. (Her website protesting immigration enforcement sells headbands emblazoned with "SHERO" and "I CARE.")[160] She held a hysterical press conference outside a Manhattan courthouse screeching: "America you mother f–kers! You drug addicts! You KKK! You fascist USA."[161] Instead of securing non-insane employment, Okoumou continued to climb things and make noise. She somehow scraped together money to travel to Paris to crawl up the Eiffel Tower, then headed back to the U.S. to clamber up the Border Patrol museum in San Antonio and an immigration shelter in Austin, Texas.[162] Among her loyal supporters: the creepy lawyer and anti-Trump nemesis Michael Avenatti, who was busy facing federal wire fraud and extortion charges in March 2019 while Okoumou was sentenced to house arrest for violating her probation during the Austin stunt.[163]

Okoumou's fellow Rise and Resist operative Jay Walker appeared on MSNBC's *Rachel Maddow Show*, labeled as an "immigrants rights activist."[164] In fact, Walker is a leader of Refuse Fascism, a front group for the Revolutionary Communist Party,[165] which is dedicated to "organize daily actions" to "bring down" the Trump "regime."[166]

The Metropolitan Anarchist Coordinating Council (MACC) joined New York's Abolish ICE brigade in June 2018. The nonprofit is "based on the guiding principles of horizontalism, anti-oppression, mutual aid, direct democracy, and direct action" and supports New York City's anarchist movement "through coordination of existing and emerging projects."[167] That translates into mau-mau-ing wacknut Democratic mayor and presidential candidate Bill de Blasio for not being open borders *enough* in a sanctuary city that panders to half a million illegal aliens.

Despite his opposition to President Trump's travel restrictions[168] and vigorous defense of his city's dangerous sanctuary policies, MACC spearheaded a protest against de Blasio for simply speaking at a national homeland security conference. Occupy ICE NYC, the New Sanctuary Coalition, and NYC Shut It Down (motto: "Abolition, Decolonization, Liberation") joined the attack by the far-far-far-left on far-far-leftist de Blasio. "It's telling how little the 'Sanctuary' designation means that that the Mayor of the nation's most ardent Sanctuary City doesn't see a contradiction in delivering the keynote address to a National Homeland Security Conference," spewed MACC's Marisa Holmes.[169]

Thanks, comrade, for confirming the obvious: sanctuary cities and national security are, indeed, completely contradictory.

True to form, the outlaw mayor has resorted to another bribery attempt to prove his bona fides. In May 2019, de Blasio announced a $100 million plan to provide health care to all illegals in the city. He displayed a new card for immigration outlaws at his press conference, beckoning: "We're saying, come get this card, we're going to assign you a doctor, we're going to show you all the services you can get with this."[170] Silly Billy. You can't appease the insatiably unappeasable.

The Intersectionalists

Irked that privileged, white, liberal man Sean McElwee received the lion's share of credit for making the #AbolishICE movement go viral, several racial and ethnic groups in the long fight to obliterate immigration enforcement clamored for attention in the age of Trump. I would be remiss if I didn't give them proper credit—for helping to ruin our country.

Amnesty advocates and identity politics zealots want you to know that they have been fighting to decriminalize border trespassing, document fraud, deportation evasion, and visa overstays for as long as modern immigration enforcement agencies have been in existence. ICE has been their hobby horse since its creation in 2003, when the Bush administration merged the investigative and interior enforcement functions of the U.S. Customs office and the Immigration and Naturalization Service (INS) under one roof. "The demand to abolish ICE has existed almost since the beginning of ICE," Ana Maria Archila, co-executive director of the Soros-funded Center for Popular Democracy, told women's website Refinery29. "Since its creation, there were organizations that were saying that the inclusion of ICE as an agency that is designed specifically to separate families, put people in detention, to deport them is a dangerous development in the way we as a country relate to migration."[171]

As readers of *Invasion* will recall, it was the myriad enforcement failures by the defunct INS that created the conditions for the 9/11 terrorist attacks. For a brief moment, Washington achieved bipartisan consensus that immigration should be treated as a national security issue. That meant implementing secure identification, better vetting of visa applications, reform of the deportation abyss created by catch-and-release policies, and increased cooperation among local, state, and federal authorities. But since then, liberal politicians have reverted to form, Open

Borders Inc. has returned to clamoring for decriminalization of immigration rule-breaking, and a rainbow coalition of leftists bound together by "intersectionality" have redoubled their efforts to turn America into a full-blown sanctuary nation.

Intersectionality is a far-left, quasi-Marxist theory. As Merriam-Webster explains: "Though originally applied only to the ways that sexism and racism combine and overlap, *intersectionality* has come to include other forms of discrimination as well, such as those based on class, sexuality, and ability."[172] The more politicized minority boxes you can check (and being an illegal alien is now one of them), the more oppressed you are, and the more you are welcomed into the great leftist coalition!

Intersectionality explains why original Abolish ICE promoters Mijente call themselves a movement of "Pro-Latinx, pro-Black, pro-woman, pro-queer, pro-poor" (all in favor of staying poor, raise your hands!). All for one and one for all.

Intersectionality explains the existence of the Black Alliance for Just Immigration, which lobbies to carve out a piece of the amnesty-benefits pie created for Latino illegal aliens for black illegal aliens.[173] Similarly, the UndocuBlack Network (whose website features black illegal aliens raising militant black power fists)[174] lobbies for DREAM Act expansions, Temporary Protected Status extensions, and Diversity Visa Lottery protections that benefit black illegal aliens. The network also opposes President Trump's "public charge" reforms to prevent foreigners from entering the country who would abuse our welfare system.[175] In the spirit of intersectionality, the UndocuBlack Network has "facilitated workshops, strategizing, intersectional caucus spaces, and healing spaces, including a 'queer caucus,'" to "advocate for the rights of Black undocumented individuals, provide healing spaces, and community to those with intersecting identities."

Intersectionality also explains why Assata's Daughters, a Chicago, police-bashing collective of "Black women, femmes, and gender non-conforming people"[176] named after convicted cop-killer Assata

Shakur (a.k.a. Joanne Chesimard), joined with Not1More Deportation in 2016 to shut down the Loop in Chicago to block a local ICE field office.[177]

"Undocumented people in Chicago and nationally are living in fear daily of being taken from their homes and away from their families. We, as Black American community organizers, can relate to that fear," members of Assata's Daughters explained in a statement. "Our communities experience that fear when Chicago Police Officers patrol our neighborhoods, stop and frisk us, occupy our schools, and arrest us en masse. Our struggles are distinct but connected. When enforcement is overfunded, that is money that is not being spent on services that actually keep us safe...."[178]

It doesn't matter that illegal immigration has driven down the wages of black workers, most significantly hurting poor and working-class black men for decades, according to the U.S. Commission on Civil Rights[179] and many other scholars.[180] It doesn't matter that illegal alien crime has robbed untold numbers of black families of loved ones like teenager Jamiel Shaw in Los Angeles,[181] police officer Rodney Johnson in Houston,[182] and young Delaware State college friends Dashon Harvey, Terrance Aeriel, and Iofemi Hightower in Newark. Harvey, Aeriel, and Hightower were lined up against a wall and shot execution-style in the summer of 2007 by illegal alien MS-13 gangsters. A fourth friend, Natasha Aeriel, survived and identified the killers. Newark's sanctuary city status aided and abetted the ruthless illegal alien criminals, two of whom had been arrested multiple times and evaded deportation.[183] Hightower's family rejected the nonsensical intersectionalist demand that they support bloody open borders and spoke out in support of Donald Trump's candidacy in 2016:

> Shalga Hightower, 55, Iofemi's mother, said her family endured seven years of legal trials, as well as a period of homelessness and job loss. Asked if she would be supporting Trump for president, she said yes.

Her son, Jamar Hightower, 26, said Trump was the only person paying attention to the problem of crimes committed by people living in the United States illegally.

"I feel as though this man is the only one that's actually standing up to do something about it," Jamar Hightower said. "This is not a problem that just started. They've been here."[184]

Now, compare the Hightower family's reality-grounded stance with that of another intersectionalist Chicago group, the illegal alien advocates at Organized Communities Against Deportation:

Organized Communities Against Deportations (OCAD) is an undocumented-led group that organizes against deportations, detention, criminalization, and incarceration, of Black, brown, and immigrant communities in Chicago and surrounding areas.... We fight alongside families and individuals challenging these systems to create an environment for our communities to thrive, work, and organize with happiness and without fear.... We envision a future without displacement and borders; without incarceration and deportations. A future where people can choose to stay or migrate freely. A future where our bodies will not be commodified or exploited to fulfill quotas, fill cages, and used to generate profit.

It's a future, in other words, where the illegal alien killers of Jamiel Shaw, Rodney Johnson, Dashon Harvey, Terrance Aeriel, and Iofemi Hightower would all be free—and future illegal alien killers would "migrate freely" through all ports of entry and any point along both northern and southern borders in the name of fighting "racism" and "fascism."

The Government Sponsors of Sanctuary Anarchy

Not all open-borders subversives hide behind black bandanas and throw Molotov cocktails. Sometimes, they wear three-piece suits or silk dresses. Sometimes, they wear badges or black robes. Sometimes, the worst enemies of law and order are the very people subsidized by taxpayers to uphold law and order. They are local police chiefs, county executives, district attorneys, mayors, judges, governors, members of Congress, and federal officials whose words, actions, and inaction enable Abolish ICE, Antifa, and anarchists. Walls and border controls are not enough to save America from invasion. The government sponsors of sanctuary anarchy must be exposed, shamed, voted out of office, impeached, and prosecuted.

In May 2018, Obama-appointed federal judge Indira Talwani attacked ICE agents in Massachusetts when they took an alien into custody who had received probation for visa fraud. "I am upset at the notion that ICE thinks a courtroom is a place to go and pick up people," she was quoted complaining in an article for Law360.com. "I see no reason for places of redress and justice to become places that people are afraid to show up."[185] The Center for Immigration Studies' Dan Cadman noted the increasing "progressive-activist bent" of jurists and questioned Talwani's excoriation of the agents: "One wonders, first, why the good judge thinks it is somehow inappropriate to take custody of convicted alien fraudsters in a courtroom when they get off with a slap on the wrist such as probation. One is also left to wonder, would Judge Talwani express such reservations if DEA agents waited quietly during a sentencing hearing so that they might take into custody an individual wanted in a separate criminal probe into, for example, unlawful diversion of prescription opioids? Probably not."[186]

In March 2019, the Suffolk County, Massachusetts, district attorney Rachael Rollins ordered her employees to monitor ICE officers at courthouses. Rollins' sixty-five-page policy memo mandated that "If any [Assistant District Attorney], victim witness advocate, or other [Suffolk County District Attorney's Office] employee observes Immigration and Customs Enforcement officers, Department of Homeland Security officers, or other civil immigration authorities apprehending or questioning parties scheduled to appear in court about residency status in or around the public areas of any Suffolk County courthouse, they are to immediately notify me (the District Attorney), my First Assistant, or my General Counsel." Rollins outlined a radical restorative justice agenda to decrease arrests, detentions, and prosecutions for both citizens and non-citizens. "[L]ocal criminal matters always supersede federal civil matters," she declared, and anyone should be able to arrive at court "without fear of civil immigration authorities."[187] Moreover, she decreed, "our office will begin to factor into all charging and sentencing decisions the potential of immigration consequences."[188] Let me translate that for you: If foreign alien adults commit crimes that would separate them from their families and lead to imprisonment and deportation, D.A. Rollins will drop charges or shorten sentences in the name of social justice—the law-abiding victims of these alien criminals be damned.

Rollins, who is sworn to "bear true faith and allegiance to the Commonwealth of Massachusetts" and support its constitution, defended the creation of her illegal alien, criminal suspect safe space on Boston talk-radio legend Howie Carr's show by complaining that ICE's presence at a courthouse was "chilling."[189] So what? If the presence of law enforcement officers at a courthouse "chills" the repeated criminal behavior of immigration outlaws, that's a good thing. Carr raised the horrific example of West African immigrant Bampumim Teixeira, who avoided deportation after admitting to robbing two banks. His sentence was bargained down to seven months by bleeding heart prosecutors and defense attorneys who agreed on a 364-day sentence.[190] This allowed him to evade ejection from the country, because federal law requires that aggravated felony punishments of a year or more trigger deportation proceedings. Immigration attorney Marisa DeFranco explained the loophole to WBZ-TV: "It's a tactic used by defense attorneys to prevent immigration consequences to somebody's convictions." Teixeira was released early after serving only nine months of the sentence, but barely a month later, in May 2017, he was arrested and charged in the gruesome double murder of two well-regarded Boston doctors, who were themselves productive, law-abiding immigrants.[191]

Why shouldn't immigration outlaws who compound their illegal status by committing even more crimes face "immigration consequences" for every single civil and criminal law they break? When Carr asked Rollins, she grudgingly acknowledged that the Teixeira case was a "horrific situation." She said she would have "no problem" deporting convicted criminal aliens *after* they "shoot or rape or kill somebody." In other words: always look the other way at immigration crimes until it's too late to save the lives of innocent people sacrificed at the altar of open borders.

That is truly chilling.

But Rollins's memo was hailed by social justice warriors. Real Justice PAC, co-founded by Bernie Sanders's staffer and serial false accuser[192]/ Black Lives Matter activist Shaun King, hailed the non-cooperation policy because "it sets the bar for what reform policies should look like." Rollins's election was part of a wave of successful campaign bids to install "progressive prosecutors" to carry out George Soros's[193] plan of undermining the criminal justice system from within. Rollins announced in April 2019, a month after issuing her courthouse sanctuary order, that she was suing ICE "in the defense of the sanctity of our courts and the protection of the public safety"—of illegal alien criminal suspects.[194]

Incredibly, a month later, the case was assigned to none other than Judge Talwani—the ICE-bashing Obama appointee "upset" at immigration agents enforcing immigration law in her courtroom![195]

Yes, we live in Opposite World, my fellow Americans. Joining Rollins was Middlesex district attorney Marian Ryan, who explained that the duo were filing the suit and seeking an immediate injunction against ICE in response to a federal indictment that same week against a Massachusetts district court judge, Judge Shelley M. Richmond Joseph, and a former court officer, Wesley MacGregor, for allegedly helping an illegal alien evade ICE at a Newton courthouse. Federal prosecutors charged the two government subversives with obstruction of justice after they conspired to let Jose Medina-Perez—a fugitive who had been wanted on narcotics possession, deported twice before, and barred from reentering under federal law—out a back door when ICE issued a detainer and warrant of removal. (Detainers are notices from ICE to other agencies that its officers intend to assume federal custody of alien arrestees; the documents include important public safety information, criminal histories, and immigration violations.) MacGregor was also charged with lying to a federal grand jury about the case.[196]

The Newton City Council declared the city a sanctuary city (or "welcoming city," as the new euphemism goes) on a 16-to-1 vote in 2017; the measure forbids local-federal cooperation on immigration enforcement unless a suspect has an outstanding criminal warrant.[197] The Rollins/Ryan lawsuit would force ICE agents to put their lives and citizens' lives at even greater risk by preventing them from making arrests in the safety of a courthouse environment where metal detectors would ensure that illegal alien suspects were not carrying weapons. On the very day that Rollins and Ryan filed their suit, ICE agents arrested two illegal alien criminal suspects (one a reputed MS-13 gang member, the other from the rival 18th Street gang and a triple deportee) at Chelsea and East Boston courthouses in Suffolk County.

As of April 2019, the following cities in Massachusetts are official sanctuaries that hinder and obstruct ICE from enforcing federal immigration laws inside our borders: Amherst, Boston, Cambridge, Concord, Lawrence, Newton, Northhampton, and Somerville. That's news you can *use*, Bay State voters.

On another front in the Bay State, federal judge Mark Wolf ruled in May 2019 that an ACLU lawsuit challenging arrests of illegal alien spouses of American citizens at United States Citizenship and Immigration Services offices in Boston could be extended to all of New England.[198] Judge Wolf declared that the illegal alien spouses "have a constitutional right to the fifth amendment's equal protection," despite being issued judicial orders of removal from the country.

From coast to coast, we are hurtling toward Sanctuary Nation. You have the power to protect your communities at the local battle box. You can't afford to wait for President Trump or feckless Republicans in

Washington, D.C., or our social justice warrior-hijacked courts to do something about it. The vigilant Federation for American Immigration Reform (FAIR) reported in May 2018 that the number of sanctuary jurisdictions around the country "has proliferated in recent years and now stands at 564."[199] In 2000, one year before sanctuary policies in New York and Virginia helped aid and abet the 9/11 legal and illegal alien hijackers, only eleven such outlaw jurisdictions existed. FAIR notes that sanctuary cities, counties, and states exploded by 650 percent under President Obama and the trend continued under President Trump. After his inauguration, government sanctuary anarchists adopted sanctuary policies in another 236 jurisdictions.[200]

In March 2019, Milwaukee County sheriff Earnell Lucas announced his new policy to protect and serve illegal aliens by refusing to cooperate with ICE unless they produce judicial warrants.[201] But there is nothing in federal law justifying the sanctuary anarchists' demand for ICE to produce judicial warrants (as opposed to administrative warrants). If they want to rewrite or nullify Section 236 of the Immigration and Nationality Act (INA), 8 U.S.C. § 1226,[202] which gives the DHS secretary authority to issue detainers when ICE has probable cause to suspect that individuals in state and local law enforcement agency custody on criminal charges are removable aliens, they should lobby Congress and get the law changed. Moreover, as the Center for Immigration Studies points out, police and sheriffs' offices "routinely honor warrants issued by parole boards, which are administrative, not judicial, in nature. Consider also that, when occasion demands, they honor detainers issued for AWOL or deserting military members, which are not backed up by judicial warrants but rather filed under the Uniform Code of Military Justice. Finally, consider that local police routinely undertake enforcement activities authorized by civil process (evictions, arrest for failure to make child support payments, etc.)."[203]

Contrary to the claims of sanctuary sheriff Lucas and other open-borders law enforcement officers that anti-ICE policies enhance public safety by encouraging illegal aliens to report crime, there is no empirical evidence to bolster this standard open-borders talking point.[204] What is irrefutably true is that the dangerous phenomenon of immigration non-enforcement and non-cooperation has resulted in about ten thousand criminal aliens being released into sanctuary jurisdictions—only to be arrested for new crimes between 2014 and 2017.[205] This includes untold numbers of illegal aliens from countries officially designated as sponsors of terrorism. The Immigration Reform Law Institute obtained records from a Freedom of Information Act request revealing that at least twenty-five state and local law enforcement agencies nationwide failed to honor ICE detainer holds on forty-four aliens hailing from Iran, Sudan, and North Korea, thirty-nine of whom had committed threat level 1 and 2 offenses such as homicide, kidnapping sexual assault, and robbery.[206] The majority were released by the mother of all sanctuary outlaw states, California.

I don't want to be a total Debbie Downer (or Michelle Malcontent). There is some resistance by patriotic counties in basket-case California and by the state of Texas to pass anti-sanctuary measures. And the Trump administration has secured some partial legal victories.

In *Nielsen v. Preap*, for example, the Supreme Court reversed an open-borders Ninth Circuit decision banning ICE from detaining criminal aliens without bond hearings who were released by sanctuary cities before ICE recaptured them.[207] But these glimmers of good news are far offset by the open-borders collaborators on city councils and in our criminal justice and court systems fighting tooth and nail to elevate illegal alien criminals' rights over Americans' lives and liberties. The Soros-funded Immigrant Legal Resource Center published a victory lap of a report celebrating "The Rise of Sanctuary" in January 2018. The group credited cities such as Santa Ana, California; Oak Park, Illinois; Santa Fe, New Mexico; Providence, Rhode Island; Lansing, Michigan; Atlanta, Georgia; and counties such as Maricopa, Arizona; Travis, Texas; Baltimore, Maryland; Middlesex, New Jersey; Denver, Colorado; and Marion, Indiana, with scoring "sanctuary wins."[208] At the state level, California, Illinois, Oregon, New York, and Washington each adopted restrictions on cooperation with enforcement, deportation, and inquiries into immigration status. There are now seven total sanctuary states: California, Colorado, Illinois, Massachusetts, New Mexico, Oregon, and Vermont. The largest sanctuary cities—outlaw cities—are New York, Los Angeles, Chicago, Philadelphia, San Diego, San Francisco, and Seattle. In April 2019, a three-judge panel of the odious Ninth Circuit ruled against the Trump administration's challenge of California's sanctuary laws forbidding local law enforcement from notifying ICE of the release dates of criminal aliens.[209] [See MAP A for a handy nationwide map of sanctuary outlaws.]

In the judicial system, six federal courts ruled against Trump White House initiatives to punish sanctuary jurisdictions in 2017.[210] Immigration scholar and *Stolen Sovereignty* author Daniel Horowitz has reported extensively on how sanctuary anarchists in America's lower courts have defiantly practiced civil disobedience against our immigration laws. Individual federal judges have created a First Amendment right out of whole cloth for anyone in the world to immigrate here, turned illegal aliens into a protected class vested with constitutional rights that even American citizens don't have, and thrown immigration statutes that have been on the books for more than a century under the bus. One of them, federal judge Edgardo Ramos of the Southern District of New York, issued a permanent injunction barring the U.S. Justice Department from withholding law enforcement grants from sanctuary jurisdictions that refuse to cooperate with federal immigration agencies![211] One single, unelected black-robed subversive used his power to sabotage the Justice Department's ability to punish localities that flout our laws and endanger our citizens. The ruling applies not only to New York, but across New Jersey, Connecticut, Rhode Island, Washington, Massachusetts, and Virginia.

Similar injunctions impeded President Trump's initiative on extreme vetting of immigrants from dangerous countries and tightening the asylum process for illegal immigrants. The Supreme Court ultimately upheld the Trump travel restrictions, but did not rule on the lower court judge's unilateral exercise of power to expand his injunction beyond his jurisdiction. In San Francisco, federal judge Richard Seeborg of the Northern District of California single-handedly blocked the Trump administration's policy ordering migrant caravan marchers to remain in Mexico while seeking asylum.[212] Established law is clear that Trump and the attorney general have the authority to implement their "Remain in Mexico" policy to safeguard our system from rampant asylum abuse and end catch and release: 8 U.S.C. § 1158(b)(2)(C)[213] sets forth that "the Attorney General may by regulation establish additional limitations and conditions, consistent with this section, under which an alien shall be ineligible for asylum under paragraph (1)." Siding with the ACLU, SPLC, and another open-borders outfit called the Center for Gender and Refugee Studies, Seeborg unilaterally legislated immigration policy from the bench and usurped the president's executive authority to protect our borders. A three-judge panel of the Ninth Circuit overruled Seeborg, but the case was headed back to another lower court and then most likely to the full panel of the Ninth Circuit.[214] Seeborg is the same federal judge who ruled that the Trump administration's attempt to include a question about citizenship on the 2020 U.S. Census questionnaire was "fundamentally counterproductive to the goal of obtaining accurate citizenship data about the public."[215] Yes, we live in Opposite World. There's already such a question on the annual American Community Survey administered by the Census Bureau. It was asked in long-form questionnaires sent to a sample of households in 2000. And it was regularly asked in historical census forms from 1820 to 1950.[216] In April 2019, the case brought by the Soros-funded Lawyers' Committee for Civil Rights Under Law and other open-borders groups went to the U.S. Supreme Court.

Finally in May 2019—more than two years into the Trump presidency and after enduring more than thirty such nationwide injunctions imposed by lower courts[217]—Vice President Mike Pence told lawyers at a Federalist Society gathering that the White House would be stepping up challenges to the sanctuary anarchists who have purposefully judge-shopped to get their open-borders challenges in front of the disrupters of the Ninth Circuit Court of Appeals. An assistant attorney general at the Department of Justice found that the nationwide injunctions against Trump match the total for the first forty-two of the forty-five presidents in American history.[218] In just one district, the Northern District of California, a total of five federal judges, all appointed by Presidents Obama and Clinton, have ruled against Trump on immigration cases.[219] But can the Trump administration actually follow through on its efforts to halt the judicial overreach of these and other courts? House Republicans have twice introduced a bill called the Injunctive Authority Clarification Act that would ban district courts from issuing nationwide injunctions and limit that power to circuit courts or the Supreme Court. That only solves part of the problem, and even this limited, commonsensical reform has gone nowhere.[220]

The open-borders judiciary at all levels is out of control. We have political operatives in the judicial branch writing immigration policies and rewriting established laws from the bench. They've almost limitlessly expanded the definition of asylum and granted illegal aliens greater rights in court than American citizens. A panel of the illegal alien-friendly Ninth Circuit denied the family of Kate Steinle, who was murdered by an illegal alien, standing in court to sue San Francisco over the sanctuary policies that led to her death, while illegal aliens and their abettors are given standing to challenge American immigration law.[221]

This is the anti-American, anti-Trump resistance in action. Black masks, black robes. Incendiary devices, incendiary rulings. Anarchy on the streets, anarchy in court chambers. The inmates are running the asylum.

I want to come back full circle to the Pacific Northwest—ground zero for the Abolish ICE anarchists in masks and of far-left sanctuary anarchists inside the government. Washington's Democratic governor Jay Inslee signed a statewide sanctuary order in 2017 to protest President Trump's "mean-spirited" efforts to regain control of a system run amok.[222] Radical Democrat and self-identified "lifelong organizer" Pramila Jayapal wants taxpayer-subsidized reparations for illegal alien families separated at the border.[223] "Progressive" Seattle mayor Jenny Durkan welcomed President Trump's threat to send border-crossers to sanctuary cities like hers because "Immigrants and refugees are part of Seattle's heritage, and they will continue to make us the city of the future."[224] Seattle and the following counties in Washington state are also official sanctuaries within a sanctuary that hinder and obstruct ICE from enforcing federal immigration laws inside our borders: Chelan, Clallam, Clark, Cowlitz, Franklin, Jefferson, King, Kitsap, Pierce, San Juan, Skagit, Snohomish, Spokane, Thurston, Walla Walla, Wallowa, Whatcom, and Yakima.

All that rain in the Emerald City has turned the brains of Democratic politicians to shapeless, senseless mush. As I mentioned earlier, I am all too familiar with the self-sabotaging saps in my former stomping grounds in Seattle. The police department's failure to protect citizens and businesses during the 1999 WTO riots presaged their current policy of protecting illegal aliens at all costs over the safety and security of Seattle's tax-paying, law-abiding citizens. King County executive Dow Constantine endorsed immigration anarchy with an executive order in April 2019 directing the county's airport "to amend its lease practices in hopes of seeing ICE banned from being able to deport immigration detainees from its runways. The move came a year after the county learned that its airport was being used to deport thousands of immigration detainees out of the country," *Newsweek* reported.[225]

In predictable response, aviation operators in the leftist county vowed to stop serving charter flights carrying immigration detainees being deported out of the country by the U.S. Immigration and Customs Enforcement agency. The companies that announced they would not be providing ground support to ICE deportation flights are Modern Aviation, Kenmore Aero Services and Signature Flight Support.[226] Constantine preached that Seattle is a "welcoming community that respects the rights of all people" and accused ICE of human rights violations. Reminder: illegal alien deportees have exhausted all their "rights" in immigration courts and received multiple bites at the court apple, often with pro bono open-borders lawyers assisting them in evading "immigration consequences" for months, years, and even decades.

As ICE spokeswoman Tanya Roman patiently reminded *Newsweek*: Federal immigration law already "provides extensive and rigorous procedures to be followed before an alien can be ordered removed from the United States, including a full and fair opportunity to pursue asylum and other forms of relief and protection from removal. Once removal is ordered, generally by a federal immigration judge, it is the job of U.S. Immigration and Customs Enforcement (ICE) to efficiently carry out the removal order. ICE removes thousands of aliens each year, and does so humanely and in full compliance with domestic law and U.S. treaty obligations. To suggest that the enforcement of federal immigration laws is somehow a human rights violation is irresponsible and reflects either a profound misunderstanding or willful mischaracterization of those laws and of the proper roles and responsibilities of the federal government and states and localities in ensuring that the laws are properly administered."

The University of Washington Center for Human Rights reported that ICE has deported more than thirty thousand people over the last eight years using King County's Boeing Field.[227] Reminder: deporting people who have no business being here in the first place is not a human rights violation. Forcing law-abiding citizens to expose themselves to untold dangers at the hands of tens of thousands of criminal alien deportees on the loose is the real travesty of justice.

Twelve years ago, in July 2007, I reported on the horrific kidnapping, rape, and murder of twelve-year-old Ukrainian-born Zina Linnik in Tacoma, Washington.[228] She was snatched from her home by forty-two-year-old Terapon Dang Adhahn, a Thailand-born convicted sex offender and permanent legal resident who should and could have been kicked out of the country after his 1992 conviction for intimidation with a dangerous weapon made him deportable. Section 1227(a)(2)(C) of Title 8 provides that "[a]ny alien who at any time after admission is convicted under any law of purchasing, selling, offering for sale, exchanging, using, owning, possessing, or carrying, or of attempting or conspiring to purchase, sell, offer for sale, exchange, use, own, possess, or carry, any weapon, part, or accessory which is a firearm or destructive device (as defined in section 921(a) of Title 18) in violation of any law is deportable." Adhahn had also been convicted of incest in 1990, had failed to register as a sex offender, and had been the subject of another immigration complaint. But no one at any level of government or law enforcement did anything about this removable alien until it was too late for Zina Linnik because, as one official put it at the time, "He escaped our attention."[229]

I will never forget this tragedy because it illustrated how the abject failures of local and federal law enforcement agencies to coordinate and prioritize the deportation of criminal aliens cost innocent life. It also exposed open-borders morons in the media for the useless tools they are. In response to my reporting on the deportation abyss in Zina Linnik's case, Fox News resident reconquistador Geraldo Rivera lost his shizzle. He falsely asserted that the terrible outcome for Zina had "absolutely nothing to do with [the] immigration status"[230] of her kidnapper, rapist, and killer—who was a removable alien, but slipped through the cracks. Rivera falsely reported that Adhahn was a naturalized U.S. citizen. He was not. The amnesty shill followed up that big lie by deflecting criticism of his falsehoods and railing against... me:

> I have to point out how in my view, this awful case was distorted by anti-immigrant radicals like Michelle Malkin to make a cheap point. Michelle said that this tragedy was the result of our open borders policy, that allows creeps like this guy to sneak in. In fact, it has nothing to do with our borders, open or otherwise.[231]

He followed that up by threatening to spit on me because I advocate reporting illegal aliens to federal authorities:[232]

> "Michelle Malkin is the most vile, hateful commentator I've ever met in my life," he says. "She actually believes that neighbors

should start snitching out neighbors, and we should be deporting people. It's good she's in D.C. and I'm in New York," Rivera sneers. "I'd spit on her if I saw her."[233]

Even more stomach-turning, Rivera recklessly and selfishly distorted the words of Zina's uncle, Anatoly Kalchik, whom Rivera tried to turn into an organ for his insane rehabilitation campaign of all criminal alien sex offenders. Rivera read a tease on his show purporting to show how Kalchik rejected emphasizing Adhahn's "immigrant" status and preferred to replace it with the word "monster." He failed to produce any soundbite of Kalchik saying any such thing. But Kalchik *did* tell a local newspaper that he and his family were angry that Adhahn had not been deported: "If someone is a sex offender, or any kind of offender, he has no business being in America." Oops. Didn't fit Rivera's all-immigrants-support-open-borders narrative.[234] (Some of you, by the way, may remember that Rivera feigned an "apology" to me on *The O'Reilly Factor* claiming it was "not like" him to make spitting threats and laughing while he tried to show that he was "really sorry" and had just been filled with "emotion." I, by contrast, do not apologize ever for calling Rivera a fool.)[235]

As I noted at the time, "open borders" is a metaphor for the willful, malign neglect of the entire immigration and entrance system—not just at the physical borders, but on the interior, at our consular offices abroad, on the immigration services side, throughout the investigations and enforcement bureaucracies, and in the detention and deportation offices. But with Gerry One Note, the immigration debate is always and only about one border: the southern border. It's only about one kind of immigrant: Hispanic illegal aliens. And it's all about one cheap set of talking points: all illegal aliens are hardworking angels, all ICE agents are jackbooted thugs, and everyone who believes in enforcing immigration laws is an "anti-immigrant radical"[236] akin to white supremacists and neo-Nazis. Yes, he compared me to a KKK member and neo-Nazi, complaining that he "cringes every time" he sees me on Fox because opposing mass illegal immigration causes violence. Predictably, he cited the smear machine at the Southern Poverty Law Center to bolster his attack on me.[237]

Sound familiar? As I have shown you, those are the same talking points and tactics of the Abolish ICE brigade, Antifa menaces, anarchists, and government sanctuary advocates. When they marginalize reality-based critics of failed immigration enforcement as "white supremacists" who "hate" all immigrants and make it acceptable to incite physical violence against immigration hawks and immigration enforcers, they win. By silencing us, they succeed in obstructing the policy changes and judicial reforms that would actually enhance public safety and promote peace through civil order. Instead of strengthening and expanding the federal 287(g) program to allow state and local enforcement officers to investigate, detain, and arrest aliens on civil and criminal grounds,[238] the bleeding hearts in Washington state and across Sanctuary Nation put the car in complete reverse. Instead of protecting the next Zina Linnik, Jamiel Shaw Jr., Rodney Johnson, Dashon Harvey, Terrance Aeriel, or Iofemi Hightower, the A-Team has mobilized to protect all deportees at all costs and to be "welcoming" of the next generation of illegal alien criminals.

It's insane and suicidal. But as you're about to see, the anarchist fringe is now the center of the Democratic Party, the Never Trump GOP, and the frothing Fourth Estate.

CHAPTER SIX

HATE MACHINE: THE SOUTHERN POVERTY LAW CENTER

Here are some things I am:

- The non-white, brown-skinned daughter of Filipino Catholic immigrants
- The wife of a grandson of Ukrainian Jewish immigrants
- The mother of multiracial, multi-ethnic children

Here are some things I am not:

- A xenophobe
- A racist
- A white supremacist

None of the things I am and am not has stopped the Southern Poverty Law Center and its media handmaidens from attacking me as an "anti-immigration pundit"[1] and "white supremacist threat."[2] Nor does it matter that SPLC's board of directors and leadership members, who have recklessly branded many prominent non-white immigration hawks and conservatives like me as racists, are themselves overwhelmingly white. In fact, a former SPLC writer confessed that one of the progressive organization's black employees, most of whom held administrative or support positions, referred derisively to minorities on staff as "the help."[3] Ain't liberal, pale-faced privilege grand?

Whether they blame whitey or righty, the cogs in SPLC's well-oiled smear machine have attacked their targets with ruthless zeal and reckless disregard. After black conservative scholar Carol Swain criticized the group in October 2009 for its silence over the militantly racist New Black Panther Party and its "mission creep" into anti-conservative political warfare,[4] SPLC national spokesman Mark Potok labeled her an "apologist for white supremacists."[5] The character assassins' pretext for smearing Swain: her use of a documentary on race in her Vanderbilt University classroom, which the SPLC deemed racist because *other* organizations the group deemed racist endorsed it.[6] The guilt-by-association smear "has had a lasting impact on my life and career," Swain poignantly reflected. Such attacks "are harmful and designed to destroy the individual's credibility and ability to have influence in the public square."[7]

Swain is not alone. In 2015, the SPLC's opposition researchers were forced to apologize to famed neurosurgeon and Trump administration secretary of Housing and Urban Development Ben Carson, who is black, after categorizing him as an "extremist." Why? Because he supports the traditional definition of marriage.[8] In June 2018, the Family Research Council won a $3.4 million defamation lawsuit settlement[9] after the SPLC recklessly[10] designated the social conservative organization a "hate group" and "extremist" group. The false accusation was parroted by charity-rating website GuideStar,[11] Human Rights Campaign,[12] *Newsweek*,[13] and countless left-wing activist groups and media outlets. The same week it settled the FRC's defamation claim, SPLC paid a $3.375 million settlement to British human rights activist Maajid Nawaz after sliming him in its "Field Guide to Anti-Muslim Extremists" (co-authored[14] with the George Soros-funded Media Matters for America and sponsored by Soros's $10 million initiative[15] to combat purported "anti-Muslim hate").[16]

Nawaz, founder of the Quilliam Foundation think tank, which counters Islamic extremism, became an SPLC target after renouncing his own radical past as a jihad recruiter. The preposterous "field guide" purported to expose fifteen "propagandists" for the "pernicious brand of extremism and hate they espouse against Muslim communities and the Islamic faith."[17] Facing a formidable lawsuit threat from Nawaz's legal team (Washington, D.C., defamation boutique firm Clare Locke LLP), the SPLC was forced to admit in a public statement that Mr. Nawaz and Qulliam "are most certainly not anti-Muslim extremists" and have "made valuable and important contributions to public discourse, including by promoting pluralism and condemning both anti-Muslim bigotry and Islamist extremism."[18] Only after conducting "more research" and consulting with "human rights advocates we trust" did SPLC acknowledge it was "wrong" to classify Nawaz as a hater.

Shoot first, research later, apologize last.

Nawaz, Swain, Carson, and the Family Research Council are not alone. The remaining fourteen "anti-Muslim extremists" named with Nawaz are all mainstream researchers, critics, and activists who expose the dangers of radical Islam and open borders:

- Refugee Resettlement Watch blogger and citizen journalist Ann Corcoran
- Investigative Project on Terrorism founder and author Steven Emerson
- Lebanese-born Christian and ACT for America founder Brigitte Gabriel
- Former Reagan official and Center for Security Policy president Frank Gaffney
- Jewish anti-jihad activist and founder of the American Freedom Defense Initiative Pamela Geller

- Former FBI agent and Marine veteran John Guandolo of the Strategic Engagement Group
- Somali-born, ex-Muslim activist, feminist, female genital mutilation survivor, and apostate facing global fatwas for leaving Islam, Ayaan Hirsi Ali
- Renowned historian and author David Horowitz
- Clarion Project national security analyst Ryan Mauro
- Scholar and Middle East Forum founder Daniel Pipes
- Palestinian-American ex-jihadist Walid Shoebat
- Scholar, author, and Jihad Watch founder Robert Spencer
- Anti-sharia activists Robert Muise and David Yerushalmi of the American Freedom Law Center

Then there are the twelve women named by the smear machine's "Intelligence Report" in June 2015 as "the most hardline anti-Muslim women activists in America."[19] In addition to Geller and Gabriel (deemed so not-nice they were named twice), the alleged menaces include:

- Texas grandmother and grassroots GOP activist Cathie Adams of the Eagle Forum
- Colorado anti-sharia activist and speaker Ann Barnhardt
- Conservative author and commentator Ann Coulter
- Retired Albany police officer turned counter-jihad researcher and blogger Cathy Hinner
- Lawyer, Fox News host, LifeZette founder, and talk radio veteran Laura Ingraham
- Retired CIA agent and Center for Security Policy senior fellow Clare Lopez
- Former prosecutor and judge and Fox News Channel host Jeanine Pirro

- American Family Association radio host and former president of Concerned Women for America Sandy Rios
- Author and nationally syndicated columnist Diana West
- Lawyer Debbie Schlussel

This wide-ranging group of women, plus Nawaz, Swain, Carson, and the Family Research Council, plus the other sharia critics deemed "anti-Muslim extremists," are not alone. In February 2019, the SPLC's "Intelligence Report" named nine members of Congress "who traffic in hate and extremism"—all of them Republicans, of course, including:

- Florida congressman Matt Gaetz
- Louisiana congressman Clay Higgins
- North Dakota congressman Kevin Cramer
- Texas senator Ted Cruz
- Tennessee senator Marsha Blackburn
- Missouri senator Josh Hawley
- Iowa congressman Steve King
- North Carolina congressman Mark Harris
- Montana congressman Greg Gianforte

Their sins: protesting federal overreach in public lands, displaying a Confederate flag, protecting children from radical social justice propaganda in public schools, speaking to activist groups that demand enforcement of our immigration laws, and defending traditional marriage. In addition to the socially conservative politicians and the Family Research Council, other faith- and family-based groups hit with the "hate" label included:

- Parents Action League
- Illinois Family Institute
- United Families International
- Christian Action Network

- American Defense League
- United States Justice Foundation
- Watchmen Bible Study Group
- Mission to Israel
- Jewish Defense League
- Alliance Defending Freedom
- Ruth Institute

The harm to people of faith doing God's work is real and devastating. The Ruth Institute, for example, is a global Catholic nonprofit run by former economics professor Dr. Jennifer Roback Morse that defends traditional marriage and the nuclear family. The institute provides counseling to children of divorce, women experiencing post-abortion loss, and young men and women who've been victimized by the "toxic sexual culture." The SPLC first designated the peaceful, non-violent organization a "hate group" in 2013 over its alleged "anti-LGBT" hatred.[20] "At that time, no one from the SPLC contacted us about the possibility of being included on their 'hate map,'" the institute noted in a statement. "They made no effort to understand our mission, then or now. No one outside the SPLC knows how organizations come to be included on the list. No one knows how to get off the list. The SPLC sets itself up as judge, jury and enforcer of the charge of hate.'"[21] As a result of the smear, Amazon dropped the pro-family activists from its Amazon Smile charity giving program and Vanco Payment Solutions banned them from its online payment processing system.[22] Ruth Institute board member Walter Hoye blasted the specious lumping of his organization with white supremacists—with which his own family was personally familiar. Hoye's great-grandfather was lynched and his Georgia house burned down with fourteen children inside by the KKK in Georgia.

"I understand what the Klan is," Hoye told the *Washington Times*, "and with that understanding, there is just no way that the Ruth Institute should be on that list."[23]

Phyllis Schlafly's Eagle Forum, the conservative American Principles Project, and yours truly appeared in yet another hysterical SPLC report on "Christian Right culture warriors" and "antigovernment extremists" who opposed the federal Common Core educational testing, curriculum, and technology racket.[24] The hit piece attempts to tie Common Core objectors to the "John Birch society" and other dangerous "conspiracists" in order to delegitimize any criticism of the law. Never mind that the grassroots parent and teacher revolt against the billion-dollar, top-down regime is a movement that crosses party lines, encompassing liberal educators who oppose usurpation of their classrooms, privacy activists who balk at the infiltration of data-mining tablets and software, parents alarmed at the elimination of local control over their schools, and critics in both political parties who object to Silicon Valley's undue influence over federal education policy.

The tsunami of "hate" designations is rendered completely meaningless as SPLC lumps a stadium full of non-extremist public figures together with marginal "extremist" figures nobody ever heard of until the SPLC put them on its lists. Many are long dead or completely powerless, like the loony tune in Nebraska who dresses up as Hitler and rants on a dank, distant, and isolated corner of the internet,[25] or the "vice presidential candidate for the racist American Third Position ticket."[26] Whatever the "American Third Position" party is, the SPLC researchers found the nothingburger entity so useful they listed it on the hate map seventeen different times!

Laird Wilcox, an expert on political extremism across the ideological spectrum, identified the SPLC's cynical "sensationalizing" of "racial conflict issues" early on. His own guides on political groups and movements in the U.S., which included "one-or-two-person outfits" or "Mom-and-Pop operations," were cribbed by SPLC researchers, with a key exception: While Wilcox "tried to be as fair as I could" in accurately describing the scope or influence of the groups he included, the SPLC's lists "had no addresses so it's actually very difficult to check them out.... I concluded that a lot of them were vanishingly small or didn't exist, or could even be an invention of the SPLC."[27] Others, he discovered, were front groups for intelligence-gathering or hoax bait created by "local anti-racist activists." The "smoke and mirrors" created by the hate manufacturers results in what Wilcox described as "a highly developed and ritualized form of defamation... a way of harming and isolating people by denying their humanity and trying to convert them into something that deserves to be hated and eliminated."[28]

Indeed, another terror expert, J. M. Berger, found while scrutinizing the SPLC's 2012 hate map that filtering out names that had been duplicated for inflation, SPLC's 1,007 "hate groups" shrank to 358.[29]

Mixed in with a few true extremists who have minuscule followings, the SPLC's hyperbolic profiles of other alleged "extremists" are usually just smear jobs on popular conservatives. In its "extremist" file on prolific Canadian vlogger-philosopher Stefan Molyneux, the SPLC complains that the popular YouTuber and podcaster employs a "confident radio-host style delivery and liberal use of infographics" to garner an impressive "subscriber count (650,000+)." The SPLC warns that his "charismatic" personality and style of "staring straight at the camera, talking intensely and at length about a subject" provide "an elaborate illusion of expertise."

Actually, he wins followers by speaking deeply, candidly, persuasively, and profoundly on matters of world history, science, race, sex, parenting, immigration and more.[30] The SPLC, beyond parody, concludes by labeling him an "alleged cult leader" of the "alt-right." I have appeared on Molyneux's long-form show to discuss everything from wrongful convictions and modern-day witch hunts to identity politics and favorite childhood Christmas memories. You know, all the stuff extremist cult leaders talk about to brainwash unsuspecting masses.

Has there ever been a more diverse universe of "white supremacists" on the planet than the "1,020 hate groups" identified by the SPLC, covering people from multiple races and religions and ranging from men's rights groups to religious liberty legal foundations, to pro-traditional values organizations, to advocacy projects for families of victims of illegal alien crime?[31] The Remembrance Project, for instance, earned an "SPLC Designated Hate Group" label for daring to oppose sanctuary city policies and amnesty bills in Congress, spotlighting illegal alien drunk drivers and gang members, and making quilts memorializing murder victims.[32] Beware the Designated Quilts of Hate!

The SPLC could save time, money, and bandwidth by publishing a list of anyone to the right of Bernie Sanders who *isn't* labeled an "extremist," "bigot," or "hater."

Truth and decency are no obstacles to the SPLC. Neither is funding. The SPLC was launched as a tax-exempt 501(c)(3) charity in 1971 "to ensure that the promise of the civil rights movement became a reality for all."[33] Founder Morris Dees, the son of Alabama farmers, achieved early success selling pigs, chickens, and cotton gin trash as a youngster.[34] While studying law at the University of Alabama, he applied his entrepreneurial prowess to a birthday cake business and direct mail order gig. Dees bought out his partner and sold the direct mail order company for $6 million in stock from the Times Mirror Company.[35] Dees parlayed the windfall into a litigation shop with fellow liberal Alabama lawyer Joseph Levin Jr. They successfully sued the Ku Klux Klan on behalf of murder victims in civil court for inciting violence, including a landmark $7 million jury verdict in 1987, which became its own fundraising cash cow.

So how did Dees go from peddling livestock, baked goods, and cookbooks to bankrupting the KKK to demonizing patriots of all colors for profit and political power?

How did he go from small-town Southern salesman to king of a half-billion-dollar hate-hoaxing enterprise employing 250 workers in four states with more than $121 million in offshore accounts?[36]

And how on earth has the SPLC remained influential with left-wing journalists and Silicon Valley techies—even after Dees was fired[37] in disgrace in March 2019 and SPLC president Richard Cohen resigned[38] amid an internal employee revolt over alleged sexual harassment and racial discrimination?

Put on your heavy-duty wading boots, because we're about to trudge through the SPLC cesspool, the predatory inhabitants of which found success targeting peaceful, patriotic Americans standing against Open Borders Inc.

The Forbidden Code Words of Hate

I first learned of the SPLC's connection to Open Borders Inc. when a mysterious YouTube channel called "We Can Stop the Hate" popped up out of nowhere as the 2008 presidential campaign season swung into full gear.[39] Beneath a seven-minute video compilation of examples of alleged "hate" speech, titled "Code Words of Hate," a message from this mysterious group expounded:

> When people acting as "experts" or "commentators" on the immigration debate demonize Latino immigrants, either legal or illegal, as a dangerous threat to American society or as subhuman and inherently inferior, they follow a tragic historical pattern which, time and again, has led to extreme civil rights abuses in American history.
>
> Such labels are used to justify extreme action, sometimes even genocide, since the people using those labels claim that the "larger public interest" is at risk. Further, if a group is widely accepted as "inhuman" or "inferior," it allows the rest of society to suspend its normal standards of right and wrong in judging actions taken against the target group.[40]

Nifty trick, huh? If you "demonize" lawbreakers by calling attention to the public safety, national security, health, and welfare risks they pose, you are the real menace to society. If you refuse to look the other way at systemic abuse of our immigration and entrance system, you are undermining "normal standards of right and wrong."

Among the soundbites highlighted by "We Can Stop the Hate" were those of journalist and former presidential candidate Pat Buchanan accurately warning of the "wholesale invasion, the greatest invasion in human history, coming across your southern border"; veteran cable news anchor Lou Dobbs reporting on how "the number of illegal immigrants in our prisons is increasing and the financial burden rising"; and Americans for Legal Immigration spokesman William Gheen noting that Mexican elite military forces working for drug cartels on the southern border "such as Los Zetas... were trained by the U.S. military at Fort Benning, South Carolina."

It's not just right-wing immigration restrictionists who reported the indisputable facts that Gheen illuminated. The far-left *Guardian* newspaper in the U.K. traced the "leakage of Mexican special forces into organized crime" through the Gulf Cartel's recruitment of its own paramilitary enforcement unit. The paper investigated how enlisted defectors from the Mexican military who had been trained in "counter-terrorism, counter-intelligence, interrogation and strategy" by the U.S., France, and Israel joined Los Zetas—ushering in narcoterrorism across the southern border.[41] Exposing the "bloodletting" plaguing our southern border is called "journalism" if it comes from a liberal source overseas. But it's classified as "hate" when American citizens call attention to it and demand that politicians do something about it.

Brown-skinned me and my big ol' mouth also appeared three times in the "Code Words of Hate" video uttering unacceptable phrases during news segments I had done on Fox News with Bill O'Reilly. In the first clip, I described the widespread theory among open-borders radicals "who believe that the Southwest is Aztlan and it belongs to them." In the second excerpt, I criticized the attitude of pro-illegal alien radicals who believe "the culture they live in and place they live in is supposed to assimilate to them as opposed to the other way around." And in the third clip, where the caption highlighted my first book, Invasion (another code word violation!), I commented on the Reconquista movement to overwhelm the Southwest through demographics: "If you look at the Mexican consulates that are active political lobbyists who've entrenched themselves in the American mainstream and who have succeeded in blurring the lines between illegal and legal immigration, yes there's a plan."[42]

The "Code Words of Hate" narrator, Stacy Burdett of the Anti-Defamation League (irony alert!), made no effort to dispute the factual basis of my commentary. The Reconquista ideology is real and deep-rooted across the U.S. The plan (*El Plan Espiritual De Aztlan*)[43] is the foundation of radical ethnic separatist group MEChA (*Movimiento Estudiantil Chicano de Aztlan*), which translates to the Chicano Student Movement of Aztlan. As I've long reported, MEChA has been dismissed by some as a harmless social club, but it operates an identity politics indoctrination machine on publicly subsidized college and high school campuses nationwide that would make David Duke and the KKK turn green with envy.[44] MEChA members in the University of California system have rioted in Los Angeles and editorialized that federal immigration "pigs should be killed, every single one"[45] in San Diego.

MEChA's symbol is an eagle clutching a dynamite stick and machete-like weapon in its claws; its motto is *Por La Raza todo, Fuera de La Raza nada* (For the Race, everything. For those outside the Race, nothing).[46] The MEChA Constitution calls on members to "promote Chican-ismo within the community, politicizing our *Raza* (race) with an emphasis on indigenous consciousness to continue the struggle for the self-deter-mination of the Chicano people for the purpose of liberating Aztlan."[47] Aztlan is the group's term for the vast southwestern U.S. expanse, from parts of Washington and Oregon down to California and Arizona and over to Texas, which MEChA claims as a mythical homeland and seeks to reconquer for Mexico (*reconquista*). MEChA's liberation agenda, outlined in *El Plan de Aztlan*, states defiantly:

> We do not recognize capricious frontiers on the bronze con-tinent. Brotherhood unites us, and love for our brothers makes us a people whose time has come and who struggles against the foreigner "gabacho" who exploits our riches and destroys our culture. With our heart in our hands and our

hands in the soil, we declare the independence of our mestizo nation. We are a bronze people with a bronze culture.[48]

That's what actual racial supremacism looks like. But the "hate" cops turn a blind eye when anti-white nationalists heap identity-based contempt upon inferior, non-bronze people and non-bronze cultures.

Just so we're keeping track, the dread Code Words of Hate and the themes identified by the "We Can Stop the Hate" campaign in 2008, as Congress and presidential candidates battled over illegal alien amnesty proposals, were:

- Aztlan
- Crime
- Demographics
- Disease
- Illegal aliens
- Invaders
- Invasion
- Reconquista

Now, if a white nationalist group calling itself "The Race" inserted itself into the debate, there's no doubt it would make the liberal handbook of Hateful Code Words, right? But what if a Latino group with the same name—"The Race"—exercised widespread influence in America? What if it talked openly of Aztlan and *reconquista*? Would the SPLC sound the alarm? No—actually, the SPLC teamed up with the National Council of La Raza (NCLR) to disseminate "We Can Stop the Hate" propaganda in the mainstream media. To both groups, the idea that we should enforce our borders and immigration laws is "hate." La Raza relied almost exclusively on SPLC data and talking points in its "We Can Stop the Hate Tool Kit For Action." La Raza president Janet Murguia called for TV networks to keep immigration enforcement proponents off the airwaves and argued that hate speech should not be tolerated, "even if such censorship were a violation of First Amendment rights," as the *New York Times* reported.[49] Among those who Murguia said should be stifled: Lou Dobbs, Sean Hannity, and the late Alan Colmes ("and most of their guests"), and former Colorado GOP congressman Tom Tancredo.[50] The NCLR tool kit quoted SPLC "Intelligence Report" director Heidi Beirich linking a purported rise in hate groups directly to GOP politicians and conservatives in the media "pounding the anti-immigration drum."[51] Murguia elaborated:

> Everyone knows there is a line sometimes that can be crossed when it comes to free speech. And when free speech transforms into hate speech, we've got to draw that line.... we need to make sure that network executives will hold their people accountable and not cross that line.[52]

The strategy of tarring all criticism of immigration enforcement as hate in order to stifle opposition to open borders was hatched in a meeting of far-left groups convened by the SPLC in October 2007, according to a *City University of New York Law Review* article co-authored by Heidi Beirich and former senior fellow Mark Potok. The white progressives in the driver's seat of the SPLC enlisted NCLR's "bronze"-hued ethnic separatists to provide politically correct cover.

After outlining a decade's worth of SPLC's opposition research attempting to tie fringe groups to mainstream critics of lax immigration enforcement, Beirich and Potok recounted the formation of their new coalition "with allies in the immigrant rights community to help educate the public on the hate motivating the nativist movement." At the Center for American Progress (CAP) offices in Washington, D.C., SPLC met with staffers from La Raza and something called the Center for New Communities to address (or concoct) a "rising tide of hate against Latinos. Out of the meeting came the NCLR website, wecanstopthehate.org, "which uses materials from the SPLC about nativist groups to educate the public about the rising tide of hate against Latinos and immigrants."

Also featured on the website are videos about the "nativist" movement featuring two SPLC staffers.[53]

The self-referentialism rivals the Hall of Mirrors at the Palace of Versailles: SPLC conjured up "hate" files, coordinated left-wing allies to launch an anti-"hate" website using SPLC's "hate" research, created new claims of "hate" to support a "stop the hate" campaign, and fed open-borders media shills who regurgitated their hit pieces while masquerading as professional journalists.[54]

And the manufactured hate chamber was just getting warmed up.

All's Un-FAIR in "Hate" and War

As a result of the SPLC-convened meeting in 2007, the merchants of smear produced a series of reports providing open-borders ammunition to politicians lobbying for illegal alien amnesty. One paper targeted the Federation for American Immigration Reform (FAIR), a grassroots, non-partisan public interest organization that evaluates public policy and seeks solutions "to help reduce the negative impact of uncontrolled immigration on the nation's security, economy, workforce, education, healthcare and environment."[55] FAIR's core beliefs are clear, reasonable, and unequivocally mainstream:

- Immigration, within proper limits, can be positive. Adhering to the rule of law is central to successful assimilation and citizenship.
- Tough decisions require strong leadership. Strong leadership, in turn, is underscored by defined principles that anchor public policy.
- Immigration can be an emotional topic: we believe in respecting the basic human rights and the dignity of all involved. As such, FAIR opposes policies based on favoritism toward, or discrimination against, any person based on race, color, religion, or gender.

- We understand that under any rational system of ordered entry, the demand will always vastly exceed available slots. Tough decisions will therefore always be necessary.[56]

FAIR argued against the 2007 amnesty package on its merits: Past amnesties adopted by Congress resulted in increased illegal immigration. The 1986 amnesty for agricultural workers signed by President Reagan resulted in rampant document fraud. Ultimately, FAIR asserted, amnesty is unfair to both native-born Americans and law-abiding applicants waiting for approval to enter the country from abroad: "An amnesty says that eventually you will be forgiven, even rewarded, for breaking the law. Furthermore, it makes a mockery of the legal immigration process, wherein those who obey the rules wait years to immigrate (instead of 'jumping the line' and hoping for absolution later)."[57]

But the SPLC, La Raza, the Center for American Progress, and their ground troops were not interested in either a fair debate or an immigration policy in which limits, assimilation, and rationality prevail. Working together, they launched a plan of attack against FAIR as a "hate group" after its millions of members mobilized to help defeat a bipartisan push in Congress for mass illegal alien amnesty.[58] The bitter Big Business lobby lost out on untold hundreds of thousands of low-wage illegal alien laborers who would have been awarded work permits under the bill. The corporatists struck back by helping fund another of SPLC and La Raza's key propaganda partners, America's Voice, whose board of directors includes the U.S. Chamber of Commerce, United Food and Commercial Workers International Union, and the American Nursery and Landscape Association.[59] Longtime open-borders operative Frank Sharry founded the group after the 2007 amnesty loss to establish a new "war room" to "debunk the fear mongering common amongst pundits and politicians" on behalf of eleven million illegal aliens—or as his group puts it, "Americans-in-waiting" (a.k.a. future Democrat voters and low-wage laborers.)[60]

Sharry's prime means of "debunking the fear mongering"? Fear mongering! America's Voice likened FAIR to "the Ku Klux Klan, the American Nazi Party, and the Aryan Nations" and urged politicians and media executives to ban them from the halls of Congress and TV airwaves.[61] In a teleconference with the media, SPLC's Mark Potok openly bragged about the speech-squelching agenda driving his coalition: "What we are hoping very much to accomplish is to marginalize FAIR. We don't think they should be a part of the mainstream media."[62]

Another SPLC report expanded the target range to include two other organizations: the Center for Immigration Studies, a Washington, D.C.-based think tank, and NumbersUSA, a national immigration reduction action group.[63] All three, Potok argued, are "fruits of the same poisonous tree."[64] Roping them together under a purportedly racist umbrella, SPLC briefed Capitol Hill Democrats to smear the trio's work, members, and employees. Potok and Heidi Beirich wrote, "The hope is that their poisoned views will not infect the debate over America's immigration policies."[65]

It was never about stopping the hate. It was and is always about stopping the *debate*.

The Mission: "Destroy Them"

At the Michigan Alliance Against Hate Crimes conference in 2007, Potok snickered about SPLC's ruse of playing watchdog. Captured on video, he acknowledged, "Sometimes, you know, the press will describe us as monitoring hate groups and so on. *I want to say plainly that our aim in life is to destroy these groups, to completely destroy them*" [emphasis added].[66] The tolerance brigade of three hundred attendees (including state and local government officials, "civil rights organizations, community-based groups, educators, and anti-violence advocates")[67] met his Machiavellian declaration with thunderous applause.

Whatever good will the SPLC rightfully earned in its early years as a courtroom crusader against bona fide racism and violence by the KKK was overdrawn long ago. And it's not just conservatives who saw through the sham. Left-leaning *Harper's Magazine* reporter Ken Silverstein called the SPLC "essentially a fraud" that "shuts down debate, stifles free speech, and most of all, raises a pile of money, very little of which is used on behalf of poor people."[68] Alexander Cockburn at *The Nation* dubbed SPLC co-founder Morris Dees the "King of the Hate Business" and mocked his racket of "scaring dollars out of the pockets of trembling liberals aghast at his lurid depictions of a hate-sodden America in dire need of legal confrontation by the SPLC."[69] Another *Nation* writer, JoAnn Wypijewski, ripped Dees as a "millionaire huckster" leading an organization that had abandoned legitimate anti-poverty causes in favor of stirring up terror over marginal "militia nuts ...lurking around every corner." The progressive costuming of the hate marketers was all a ruse. Wypijewski minced no words:

> Hate sells; poor people don't, which is why readers who go to the SPLC's website will find only a handful of cases on such non-lucrative causes as fair housing, worker safety, or health-care, many of those from the 1970s and 1980s. Why the organization continues to keep "Poverty" (or even "Law") in its name can be ascribed only to nostalgia or a cynical under-standing of the marketing possibilities in class guilt.[70]

Undoubtedly recognizing the shrinking market for lawsuits against tin-pot bigots and dwindling white supremacist outfits, Potok told the Michigan crowd that the SPLC had pivoted away from its usual targets and instead towards mainstream anti-illegal immigration groups because that's "where the action is."[71] To maintain relevance, the SPLC needed cash flow. To increase cash flow, the SPLC needed to whip up fear and loathing. To whip up fear and loathing in the modern era, the SPLC needed to manufacture the illusion of a "rising tide of nativism and xenophobia."[72]

Along with FAIR, the Center for Immigration Studies, and NumbersUSA, the SPLC designated pretty much every grassroots immigration group in America an "anti-immigrant hate group," including the American Border Patrol, Americans for Legal Immigration, Californians for Population Stabilization, the Colorado Alliance for Immigration Reform, the Immigration Reform Law Institute, Legal Immigrants for America, Michiganders for Immigration Control and Enforcement, North Carolinians for Immigration Reform and Enforcement, Oregonians for Immigration Reform, San Diegans for Secure Borders, Texans for Immigration Control and Enforcement, and ProEnglish.[73]

Dees reiterated his agenda to annihilate these activists in an interview with Vermont school kids in 2008: "We see this political struggle, right? So you know, I mean, we're not trying to change anybody's mind. We're trying to wreck the groups, and we are very clear in our head: we are trying to destroy them."[74]

Capiche?

Center for Immigration Studies senior research fellow and Pulitzer Prize-winning journalist Jerry Kammer exposed how the SPLC engaged in gross distortions of the founder of FAIR and the Center for Immigration Studies, John Tanton, to impute alleged racism on everyone engaged in activism to limit both mass illegal and legal immigration. Tanton, a Michigan eye doctor, espouses zero population growth and sounds the alarm over the demographic and cultural consequences of uncontrolled migrant waves hitting our shores. As the SPLC itself acknowledged, Tanton arrived at his views from the political *left* and served on the liberal Sierra Club's population committee.

The "hate" police made much hay over Tanton's embrace of Jean Raspail's 1970s dystopian French novel of mass migration run amok, *Camp of the Saints*. Tanton had bought the publishing rights and brought the long-forgotten but prophetic work back into print in 1994.[75] For the SPLC, this was an unconscionable endorsement of a "lurid," "racist," "race war novel" that is "revered by white supremacists."[76] The hate hunters apparently overlooked a 1994 cover story by two mainstream historians in the liberal magazine *The Atlantic*,[77] comparing Raspail's novelistic vision to real-life illegal immigrant floods across the West.[78]

In the 8,400-plus word essay, "Must It Be the Rest Against the West?" Yale historian Paul Kennedy and Yale history PhD student Matthew Connelly explained their academic interest in the novel:

> Why revisit this controversial and nowadays hard-to-obtain novel? The recovery of this neglected work helps us to call attention to the key global problem of the final years of the twentieth century: unbalanced wealth and resources, unbalanced demographic trends, and the relationship between the two. Many members of the more prosperous economies are beginning to agree with Raspail's vision: a world of two "camps," North and South, separate and unequal, in which the rich will have to fight and the poor will have to die if mass migration is not to overwhelm us all. Migration is the third part of the problem. If we do not act now to counteract tendencies toward global apartheid, they will only hurry the day when we may indeed see Raspail's vision made real.[79]

Kennedy and Connelly seriously contemplated the civilizational crisis depicted in *Camp of the Saints*. They called on policymakers and global leaders to think through the "demographic-technological fault lines" emerging "between fast-growing, adolescent, resource-poor, undercapitalized, and undereducated populations on one side and technologically inventive, demographically moribund, and increasingly nervous rich societies on the other." The issue "dwarfs every other issue in global affairs," the historians warned. And, they concluded, "It will take more than talk to prove the prophet wrong."[80]

Alas, in our Trump-deranged, white-guilt-addled era, breathing any word of the book or exhibiting any shred of familiarity with its themes is tantamount to bigotry. K. C. McAlpin, writing on the website The Social Contract, chronicled some of the criticism: "The book has recently been described as 'really racist' (*The Week*), 'staggeringly racist' (*Slate*), 'unbelievably racist' (*Bustle*), 'violently racist' (*Politico*), and 'rabidly racist' (HuffPost)."[81] Or just Google "Steve Bannon, racist, Camp of the Saints," and you'll see what I mean. Instead of making the effort to prove the prophet wrong, it was far easier to assert that the prophet and those who digested his words were evil.

Who needs to debate when you can destroy?

Armed with *prima facie* evidence that Tanton was a racist because he published a racist book (which is racist because SPLC says so), the character assassins unearthed and recycled excerpts from private memos Tanton had written to colleagues. He had pondered tough issues of assimilation, education, and a "two-tiered economic system" in southern California, where large numbers of Hispanics and Asians have settled, which the SPLC twisted into Tanton "questioning Latinos' educability."[82] The SPLC painted Tanton as a "mastermind" and "puppeteer" installing other unrepentant bigots as leaders of the "nativist lobby" who would carry forth his purportedly radical, racist views on immigration,[83] which can be distilled to three fundamental questions that should concern Americans of all races, ethnicities, and socioeconomic backgrounds:[84]

- How many people should we admit?
- Who gets the visas?
- How can we enforce the rules?

For the sake of argument, let's assume Tanton is everything the SPLC claims him to be. If indeed Tanton was the omniscient Gepetto carving all immigration hawks in his image, his marionette skills have failed miserably. For the record, I've spoken at numerous FAIR conferences, received an award from the Center for Immigration Studies (CIS), spoken at several CIS events, and sat for interviews with Roy Beck of NumbersUSA. I've never met Tanton. I vehemently oppose Planned Parenthood, which Tanton supported in the past. At the Center for Immigration Studies, executive director Mark Krikorian, policy studies director Jessica Vaughan, and research director Steven Camarota are all strong pro-lifers.[85] Moreover, I vigorously oppose eugenics, which the SPLC has accused Tanton of espousing because he once accepted money from the Pioneer Fund. Two points about that: 1) As Tanton points out, the list of university and college grantees who received money from the Pioneer Fund between 1937 and 2000 includes Johns Hopkins University, Cornell Medical School, Brandeis University, the University of California-Berkeley, the University of London, the University of Tel Aviv, and many more (not surprisingly, those institutions are omitted from the SPLC's hate profile of the fund[86]); and 2) while the SPLC decries eugenics as promoted by the Pioneer Fund, it unironically attacks pro-life journalists who expose Planned Parenthood's gruesome abortion business—rooted in eugenics-promoter Margaret Sanger's racism[87]—as, you guessed it, "extremists."[88]

The SPLC's hysterical attacks on Roy Beck, a veteran journalist, powerful communicator, and consummate gentleman, prove just how dishonest and unreliable the hate-hunters are. In plain English on the NumbersUSA website is an emphatic message titled: "No to Immigrant Bashing." Beck writes, "Nothing about this website should be construed as advocating hostile actions or feelings toward immigrant Americans; illegal aliens deserve humane treatment even as they are detected, detained and deported."[89] The group's board of directors is dedicated to preserving a peaceful, civil forum for education on immigration issues and advocacy of immigration reduction to enhance "individual liberty, mobility, environmental quality, worker fairness and fiscal responsibility." And if it wasn't already clear in the numerous statements they've previously issued, the board's statement of values lays it out again: "Immigrant bashing, xenophobia, nativism and racism are unacceptable responses to federal immigration policy failures."[90]

Why attack such a message? Remember: The mission of SPLC is not to engage, not to persuade, and not to monitor. The mission is to destroy. NumbersUSA, like the laundry list of other peaceful, law-abiding groups and individuals before them, is effective. Jeff Sessions, former Trump attorney general and GOP senator from Alabama who led opposition to illegal alien amnesties under the Bush and Obama administrations, credited the grassroots activists of NumbersUSA who melted the phone lines to make their voices heard:

> The big lobbies pulled out all the stops, spent millions of dollars, and bore down hard in their push for mass amnesty. But Goliath fell to the grassroots David, whose faxes, e-mails, rallies, visits to our offices, and phone calls registered the clear message that the American people would not accept Washington rewarding lawbreaking. The overwhelming grassroots response actuated by the NumbersUSA coalition was most evident when citizens called Capitol Hill in such volume that it shut down the Senate's telephone system ...[W]ith the click of a button they can send a fax—a technology that, though largely antiquated, still prevails on Capitol Hill.[91]

To paraphrase the old legal aphorism, if the faxes and the laws are against you, pound the table and yell "RACIST!"

SPLC in the Classroom

The hand that rocks the cradle rules the world. The hand that writes the schoolbooks rules the narratives. In the early 1990s, the SPLC launched its "Teaching Tolerance" program to provide educators with "free, anti-bias classroom resources such as classroom documentaries and lesson plans" that teach children "to respect others and help educators create inclusive, equitable school environments."[92] According to the SPLC, 500,000 educators use Teaching Tolerance materials, which "have won two Oscars, an Emmy and scores of honors."[93] Immigration is a key subject area. But instead of balanced reading on the consequences of legislative amnesties dating back to 1986, SPLC goads children with social justice calls to arms, to "take a stand" for illegal alien DREAMers and oppose efforts by Immigration and Customs Enforcement agents to stop illegal employment of low-wage alien workers.[94] Students and teachers are taught how to create sanctuary spaces[95] and obstruct federal law enforcement officers from doing their jobs.[96] Infused in the materials on immigration are emotion-laden anecdotes that blur the lines between legal and illegal immigration:

> Be vocal about your support of undocumented teachers, students and their families. This makes it clear to those with undocumented or mixed-status families that you are a safe person to talk to. Going public also models the value of upstanding to students for whom immigration status isn't a daily concern. Display signs with messages like "Migration Is Beautiful" and "No Human Being Is Illegal."

Students are taught to renounce their "white privilege" as early as third grade,[97] while granting blanket immunity to all "undocumented" students for any public safety threats posed by illegal alien gangs. "Teaching Tolerance" whitewashes MS-13-related kidnappings, violent initiations, rapes, and sex trafficking in the name of diversity. Missing are facts like these:

- In Suffolk County, New York, alone, MS-13 has committed twenty-seven murders since a surge of unaccompanied minors began arriving in 2013.[98] The gang's motto is "Rape, control, kill."
- The infiltration of MS-13 in the predominantly Hispanic William Wirt Middle School in Riverdale, Maryland, was so "out of control" that one teacher called it a "ticking time bomb," at least ten MS-13 gang members had been identified in attendance in its classrooms, and violence prompted the school to call the police more than seventy times in the 2017–2018 school year.[99]
- In 2018, the Northern Virginia Gang Task Force reported that 80 percent of gang recruitment is taking place in middle and high schools in the region.[100]

Instead of confronting these facts, a lesson condemning the "school-to-deportation pipeline" introduces students to an expert who dismisses President Trump's concerns about foreign gang violence in classrooms and on campuses as "national hysteria."[101]

Another lesson for kindergarten to third grade students tells the story of a horrible "Great Wall" built between the "Great North" (evil America) and "Great South" (noble Mexico). Butterflies on either side suffered because of the wall, dropping dead or withering away, until Papalotzin, the Royal Butterfly of the Aztecs, "kicked and crumbled the Great Wall" so the monarch butterflies could come back to life. (How a butterfly "kicks" a wall is a story for another day, but suspension of disbelief is a prerequisite in open-borders ideology.)[102] The story ends: "The Great North and the Great South decided it was best to leave things this way, to let the monarchs, and everything and everyone, migrate back and forth for the rest of time. And Papalotzin thought so, too, as he flapped his great wings and pushed the beautiful rainbows high into the sky."[103]

The SPLC teaches tolerance by stoking intolerance of Republicans and Trump supporters, decrying the "Trump Effect" through a "survey" on the "impact of the 2016 election in classrooms" that features the following comments from teachers and administrators:[104]

- "My immigrant students, illegal and legal, are asking questions that tell me they are scared. The Republican rhetoric about walls and 'keeping them out' is frightening. The lack of tolerance is appalling!"
- "My students are horrified at the spectacle of the Republican candidates shouting insults and insulting American citizens."
- "One student asked if this was how Germany elected Adolf Hitler."
- "In the past two days there has been a group of 8th grade boys coming to school with Trump-emblazoned t-shirts, red-white-and-blue plastic leis, and other 'patriotic' decorations

that are related to this Trump support. These are popular
boys, and the group is growing. There are plenty of teachers
who are saying to them how much they, too, like Trump. I
am appalled."

For indoctrinated middle school and high school students, Teaching Tolerance naturally recommends a trip to the "Anti-Immigration Movement" page from the SPLC's Intelligence Project for a "wealth of information about anti-immigrant bias in the mainstream, as well as among extremist groups that promote xenophobia and nativism."[105]

A featured immigration handout, "Ten Myths About Immigration," itself propounds myths and frames disagreement with the SPLC and its allies as bigotry.[106] The plain fact, for example, that short-term visa holders have included criminals and terrorists—including the 9/11 hijackers[107]—is classified as a "myth." No alternative analysis of immigration issues by think tanks like the Center for Immigration Studies or activist groups like FAIR are provided. Why? Because they offer counterbalancing perspectives.

And counterbalancing perspectives spell H-A-T-E.

The House That (Fake) Hate Built

Peddling hateful hysteria pays.

Hustler Morris Dees went from selling hogs to living high on the hog by monetizing a seemingly bottomless commodity: wealthy liberals' fear and loathing of their political opponents on the "radical right."[108] With slick flyers appealing for money, the Direct Marketing Association Hall of Fame inductee milked tragic cases and sowed racial division. Veteran journalist Carl M. Cannon described the "simple, albeit cynical" business model perfected when Dees and his legal team secured a $7 million judgment against the Ku Klux Klan in a wrongful death suit on behalf of Beulah Mae Donald. Her nineteen-year-old boy, Michael, died in a horrific lynching murder perpetrated by Klan members. Mrs. Donald collected a mere $52,000 after suing the convicted killer—the total value of the only assets the defendants possessed. She died a year later. But Dees hit the jackpot, reaping "$9 million for the SPLC from fundraising solicitations about the case, including one featuring a grisly photo of Michael Donald's corpse," Cannon noted.[109] Talk about a return on investment. Disgusted legal staff members resigned en masse in the mid 1980s in protest of Dees's prioritization of sensational anti-Klan marketing campaigns over the more "mundane" bread-and-butter issues of actually fighting, you know, poverty. But the hate oil salesman prevailed.[110] Grifters gotta grift.

To be sure, Dees has collected a high-minded assortment of honors and plaudits, including the American Civil Liberties Union's Roger Baldwin Award, the Martin Luther King Jr. Memorial Award from the National Education Association, and the Humanitarian Award from the University of Alabama.[111] The real rewards of social-justice scaremongering, however, lie not in the paper plaudits hanging on the wall, but in the piles of Benjamins that coastal elites have shoveled into the gaping maw of the SPLC's junk mail smear machine. According to the nonprofit charity's most recent financial documents and statements, its endowment (humbly named "The Morris Dees Legacy Fund") skyrocketed to $433 million at the end of fiscal year 2018.[112] At the civil rights museum across from SPLC's headquarters in Montgomery, Alabama (properties valued at nearly $30 million), a special interactive kiosk with huge images of Dees invites visitors to search names of donors to the fund, who are recognized for their "willingness to take a stand for justice and tolerance."[113]

Among the glitterati who've filled Dees's coffers: Hollywood royalty George and Amal Clooney, who forked over $1 million to the SPLC in 2017 "to add our voice (and financial assistance) to the ongoing fight for equality."[114] Their donation will help endow a "standing legal fellowship" at the SPLC to contribute to the center's efforts "to combat hate in the U.S." Or manufacture it.

Endowment funds are segregated from operating funds and are reserved "for the future support" of the center's activities. Total operating and action fund assets top $47.5 million, which pushes the value of Dees's empire to more than a half-billion dollars.[115] Awash in cash, the fear profiteers spent just $5.5 million on legal case expenses (its original claim to fame). By comparison, the center spent more than $10 million on postage and printing expenses; nearly $11 million on development; $29 million on employee salaries and benefits; and $45 million for operating expenses.[116]

The "P" in SPLC may stand for poverty, but Saint Dees never took a vow of asceticism. He reportedly parked his Rolls-Royce in a reserved spot at the company parking lot.[117] He basked in "Mediterranean living" at his $1.6 million Mathews, Alabama, manse, complete with horse stables, tennis courts, pool, and gaudy art.[118] Dees and former SPLC president Richard Cohen earned salaries and compensation worth $400,000 each in 2017. One watchdog analysis determined that since 2000, Dees and Cohen separately raked in more than $5 million in pay and benefits.[119] Senior fellow Mark Potok and Intelligence Project director and chief hate monitor Heidi Beirich each earned roughly $200,000 in 2017. Some thirty employees in total are paid six-figure salaries.

Investigative journalist Matthew Vadum was first to report in 2012 that the SPLC maintains bank accounts in offshore tax havens stretching from Bermuda to the Cayman Islands to the British Virgin Islands.[120] Such foreign tax shelter schemes are usually vilified by the left as symbols of greed and evasion. The liberal *Guardian* newspaper excoriated wealthy GOP donors who park their money in offshore accounts "beyond the reach of public scrutiny and tax authorities."[121] Beltway reporters excoriated former GOP presidential candidate Mitt Romney for using tax havens in Bermuda and the Cayman Islands to help eligible investors avoid U.S. taxes and boost profits.[122] A *Huffington Post* scold dubbed it "Bermuda-gate."[123]

"Do you think it's patriotic of you to stash your money away in the Cayman Islands?" a liberal heckler of Romney shouted in a campaign video on Barack Obama's YouTube channel.[124]

Curiously, the usual suspects are nowhere to be found to question the patriotism of the SPLC. The *Washington Free Beacon* dug up IRS forms showing that a private equity firm transferred nearly a million dollars to a pooled investment fund in the Cayman Islands on the group's behalf in 2014 and an additional $100,000-plus transfer the next month to a different foreign entity located in the Caymans. In 2015, millions more were transferred to another entity on the islands. Additional foreign "financial interests" in Bermuda and the British Virgin Islands were noted, but not detailed.[125] As of October 2018, the SPLC's endowment included a whopping total of $121 million in "non-U.S. equity funds," more than $91 million in U.S. equity funds, nearly $60 million in private equity funds, and $132 million in other investments.[126]

That's quite a hefty rainy day fund—or rather, a campaign war chest—for the political destroyers disguised as eradicators of hate. Morris Dees, however, didn't expand his domain on his own. None of it would have been possible without untold thousands of gullible and not-so-gullible donors who failed to do their own due diligence or blithely ignored decades of public warnings about the house that fake hate built.

Revolts at the Poverty Palace

In March 2019, an earthquake hit Montgomery, Alabama, and sent seismic shockwaves across the political landscape. The SPLC announced the firing of Morris Dees with a terse statement from president Richard Cohen: "As a civil rights organization, the SPLC is committed to ensuring that the conduct of our staff reflects the mission of the organization and the values we hope to instill in the world. When one of our own fails to meet those standards, no matter his or her role in the organization, we take it seriously and must take appropriate action."[127] Cohen alluded to the values of "truth, justice, equity and inclusion" without specifying how exactly Dees had transgressed them within the organization. The *Los Angeles Times* fleshed out a few more details of the "stunning" internal revolt laid out in e-mails to employees, which acknowledged "inappropriate conduct," and "complaints of workplace mistreatment of women and people of color."[128] The *Alabama Political Reporter* identified the "spark" of the "near-mutiny" as the resignation of SPLC staffer, Meredith Horton, a black senior attorney who documented discrimination on the basis of race and sex within the SPLC. Staffers followed up with complaints about retaliation and cover-ups, all denied by Dees.[129] A week later, Cohen himself resigned after sixteen years as president as whistle-blowers stepped forward to expose the headquarters' "toxic" environment, "as well as prioritization of marketing and fund-raising over on-the-ground civil rights work," according to the *Montgomery Advertiser.*[130]

The Johnny-come-latelys at the *New York Times*, America's newspaper of delayed record, brought up the rear with a superficial recap of Dees's "troubling reputation" of "inappropriate touching" and "lewd remarks"—compounded by senior leaders' tolerance for "racially callous remarks."[131] While the SPLC's history of gross mismanagement may have been "news" to *Times* readers, it was an old story to local reporters and watchdogs who had boldly and repeatedly called out the scam artist. "He's the Jim and Tammy Faye Bakker of the civil rights movement," anti-death penalty lawyer and Habitat for Humanity founder Millard Fuller told *Harper's* Ken Silverstein back in 2000, "though I don't mean to malign Jim and Tammy Faye."[132] Silverstein noted at the time that SPLC money-grubbers shamelessly misled donors about the apocalyptic "strain" on their operating budget, while holding $60 million in reserves. Another early critic, Yale law professor Stephen Bright, emphatically refused an award named after Dees at the University of Alabama back in 2007:[133]

> Morris Dees is a con man and fraud, as I and others, such as
> U.S. Circuit Judge Cecil Poole, have observed and as has been
> documented by John Egerton, *Harper's*, the *Montgomery
> Advertiser* in its "Charity of Riches" series, and others.... He
> has raised millions upon millions of dollars with various

schemes, never mentioning that he does not need the money.... He has taken advantage of naive, well-meaning people—some of moderate or low incomes—who believe his pitches and give to his [then]-$175-million operation. He has spent most of what they have sent him to raise still more millions, pay high salaries, and promote himself.

The investigation by John Egerton referenced by Professor Bright was first published in a progressive magazine in 1988, thirty-one years ago; the full ten-thousand-word version was published three years later in Egerton's book, *Shades of Gray: Dispatches from the South*, in 1991. Millard Fuller told Egerton: "I was naive at first. I thought [Dees] was sincere. I though the Southern Poverty Law Center raised money to do good for poor people, not simply to accumulate wealth." He soon learned otherwise, saying, "Morris Dees is a skillful but deceptive lawyer who's running a basically dishonest operation."[134] Egerton highlighted the hyperbolic appeals the SPLC sent to targeted liberal areas. One mailer identified the co-founders as "Morris Seligman Dees and Joe Levin, Jr." Then senior staff attorney Ira Burnim explained: "Morris used his middle name in mailings to Jewish zip codes. The intent, I assume, was to boost returns."[135] Egerton also chronicled a staff revolt back in 1986 over Dees's "manipulative, ruthless, autocratic" rule and monomaniacal exploitation of fear of the KKK to the exclusion of actual anti-poverty work—presaging the second staff revolt thirty-three years later that led to Dees's overdue downfall.[136]

The "Charity of Riches" series that Professor Bright mentioned appeared in print in the *Montgomery Advertiser* newspaper back in 1994. The nine-part series (a Pulitzer Prize finalist) reported that "of 13 black former center staffers contacted, 12 said they either experienced or observed racial problems inside the Law Center." Several likened the work atmosphere to a "plantation." The paper also reached out to a "random sampling of donors" to poll them about their knowledge of the ubiquitous junk-mail solicitors and found "they had no idea the Law

Center was so wealthy."[137] A former legal fellow decried the relentless prioritization of easy cash over taking on legal cases. "They're drowning in their own affluence," she warned.

That was a quarter-century and hundreds of millions of dollars ago.[138]

Stop the Smears

So the foundations of the SPLC were rotten from its inception. But it would take forces from both within and without to usher in the fall of the House of Dees. Conservative groups rallied around the Family Research Council after a murder-minded, left-wing domestic terrorist, Floyd Lee Corkins, barged in on the nonprofit charity's Washington, D.C., office with a 9mm pistol in 2012 and shot FRC staffer Leo Johnson. In his taped video confession with FBI agents, Corkins stated he identified the group through Southern Poverty Law lists of "anti-gay groups. I found them online."[139] He planned to smear employees' faces with fifteen Chick-Fil-A sandwiches he brought with him, kill everyone in the building over the Christian group's opposition to gay marriage, and then move on to other organizations on the list. He was convicted of terrorism and sentenced to twenty-five years in prison.[140] In 2014, the Obama Justice Department finally eliminated the SPLC from an online FBI resource list on hate crimes.[141] On the fifth anniversary of the shooting in 2017, nearly fifty conservative activists, scholars, and lawyers released an open letter to the media urging against promotion of the SPLC's hate map and lists: "The SPLC is a discredited, left-wing, political activist organization that seeks to silence its political opponents with a 'hate group' label of its own invention and application that is not only false and defamatory," they warned, "but that also endangers the lives of those targeted with it." [142]

People of good faith similarly urged caution when referencing SPLC's "hate" labels after American Enterprise Institute fellow Charles Murray, a "white supremacist" designee on the hate map, was violently attacked while attempting to give a speech at Middlebury College in Vermont in 2017.[143] Allison Stanger, a Middlebury professor who was injured by the protest mob, condemned the students and faculty for rendering judgment without knowing anything about Murray. She pinned the blame squarely on the smear merchants in Montgomery:

> Intelligent members of the Middlebury community—including some of my own students and advisees—concluded that Charles Murray was an anti-gay white nationalist from what they were hearing from one another, and what they read on the Southern Poverty Law Center website.... The Southern Poverty Law Center incorrectly labels Dr. Murray a "white nationalist," but if we have learned nothing in this election, it is that such claims must be fact-checked, analyzed and assessed. Faulty information became the catalyst for shutting off the free exchange of ideas at Middlebury. We must all be more rigorous in evaluating and investigating anger, or this pattern of miscommunication will continue on other college campuses.[144]

But the pleas for rationality and decency in the press went unheeded. Mainstream media outlets have dutifully regurgitated SPLC's annual alarmist press releases. In February 2019, the SPLC website launched a new fundraising push with the claim that "Hate groups reach record high."[145] With hardly a mention of the smear racketeers' five decades of controversy, overreach, fundraising deceit, defamation liability, statistics inflation, and proclaimed agenda of political destruction, thousands of mainstream news articles parroted the propaganda that "Trump 'fear-mongering' fuels rise of U.S. hate groups to record,"[146] "Number of US hate groups at record high 'and linked to Trump,' study suggests,"[147] and "Report blames Trump for record number of U.S. hate groups in 2018."[148] The tactic is adapted from the Obama years, when the SPLC released a report called "Rage on the Right,"[149] which blamed "nativist extremists" who opposed the new administration for a purported rise in harassment of immigrants. In the same screed invoking "Waco," "racist skinheads," "the Oklahoma City bombing," and "paramilitary wings," the SPLC's Mark Potok incited parallel fear of—wait for it—the Tea Party, politicians who support "Tenth Amendment Resolutions," and immigration enforcement activists who volunteered to patrol the border or monitor and report illegal alien day laborers.[150]

When a Republican is in office, hate crimes spiral out of control. When a Democrat is in office, hate crimes spiral out of control. Nifty trick, right? The SPLC donations from frightened northeastern liberals and paranoid Hollywood celebrities pour in either way, especially during election cycles. Laird Wilcox deconstructed the "post hoc fallacy" at the heart of the SPLC strategy of linking electoral outcomes to "alleged behavior that is by no means established." The fallacy is compounded by "dishonest framing where an attempt is made to construct meaning by associating an event with a false cause. Some people will buy into this kind of thinking but it's not too hard to see through if you think about it."[151]

Fortunately, the defamation settlements in favor of moderate Muslim reformer Maajid Nawaz and the Family Research Council have helped cut through the fog and emboldened other victims to go to court. The Center for Immigration Studies, an early-and-often target of the SPLC's bile, fired its own shot across the bow in January 2019 with a civil lawsuit under the Racketeer Influenced and Corrupt Organizations Act (RICO). CIS is seeking damages and an injunction prohibiting SPLC leaders from repeating the destructive lie that the center is a hate group; a section of the federal RICO law allows for private parties to claim that the racketeers are committing wire fraud in spreading the lie. The complaint points out that SPLC's definition of "hate group" is purportedly "based on its official statements or principles, the statements of its leaders, or its activities" and "beliefs or practices that attack or malign an entire class of people typically for their immutable characteristics."[152] Yet, the immigration status of foreigners in our country is not an "immutable" characteristic by the U.S.

Supreme Court's definition or any other rational definition. The CIS motto is "pro-immigrant, low-immigration" in the national interest. And the SPLC can point to no statements by the organization or its employees attacking or maligning any class of people.

Repeating endlessly that CIS is "anti-immigrant" doesn't make it true. It has, however, cost the group at least $10,000 in donations; access to the Amazon Smile program, which terminated its relationship with CIS based on the SPLC hate designation; and harm suffered after GuideStar temporarily listed it as a SPLC-designated "hate group."[153]

The defiant SPLC doubled down on the smears, telling a Law & Crime reporter that CIS "richly deserves the hate group label" for "making racially inflammatory statements, associating with white nationalists, and circulating the work of racist writers." The speech-stiflers had the gall to accuse the think tank of trying to "silence us from exercising our First Amendment right to express our opinion."[154] Everything is upside-down and backwards in the fun house mirrors of the Poverty Palace.

In February 2019, one month after CIS sued, iconoclastic media entrepreneur, humorist, and founder of the Proud Boys fraternal club, Gavin McInnes, filed suit against the SPLC in Montgomery, Alabama, for:

- defaming him by use of the SPLC hate designations
- publishing other false, damaging, and defamatory statements about him
- its concerted, obsessive, and malicious actions taken to "deplatform" and defund him
- its tortious interference with his economic opportunities
- intentionally interfering with his contractual relationships by causing termination of his employment and subjecting him to employment discrimination based on his lawful non-employment recreational activities[155]

The SPLC had attacked McInnes relentlessly since February 2018, when it put the Proud Boys—a fraternity for like-minded men who meet in a social club setting to drink beer, talk about shared Western values, and plan community fundraising events—on the hate map. Media coverage parroted the hate designation, stoking fear and hatred of a group whose members protested sharia law, conducted toy drives and emergency relief support, and acted as a fraternal organization. SPLC website posts falsely labeled McInnes, a British-born, Canadian immigrant, as "anti-immigrant"; falsely claimed the FBI had designated the Proud Boys a hate group, and falsely attributed violence to Proud Boys members at the Charlottesville, Virginia, "Unite the Right" rally in 2017. What began as a protest over threats to Confederate monuments became a rally of white nationalists that spun out of control when confronted by violent Antifa counter-protesters. *New York Times* reporter Sheryl Gay Stolberg tweeted on-scene that she "saw club-wielding 'antifa' beating white nationalists being led out of the park" (a candid observation that she later deleted after blowback from her narrative-enforcing colleagues).[156] Live video footage showed left-wing protesters hurling objects at the white nationalists.[157] An independent review of the clashes by Timothy J. Heaphy of the Virginia law firm Hunton & Williams, commissioned by the Charlottesville city government, found that the Charlottesville and Virginia State Police "failed to intervene," "did not respond to requests for assistance," were "insufficiently equipped to respond to mass unrest," "failed to protect the points of egress, instead pushing the conflicting groups directly into each other," and "failed to 'stand up' to protect human life."[158] Indeed, three people died—two state troopers in a helicopter crash and one counter-protester rammed by a car.

Police supervisors told Heaphy they were ordered out of their protection zones. One officer said, "We were sitting there with our thumbs up our asses." Another described how "we were prevented from doing police work." And a third officer stated plainly that "we failed this community."[159]

McInnes was not in Charlottesville. He explicitly disavowed violence of any kind. He explicitly forbade his group and its members from participating in any of the events. But through repeated and malicious lies, false labels, and guilt by association, McInnes asserted, the SPLC exposed him, his family, and anyone else associated with him "to public scorn, harassment, intimidation, and potential violence."

In a nine-month span after the hate designation, McInnes was banned from Twitter, kicked off PayPal, fired from his TV show at CRTV/Blaze Media, temporarily banned from YouTube, banned from e-mail marketing service Mailchimp, and banned from iTunes. "I'm suing the SPLC. And it's not just because they destroyed my career and shattered my reputation. It's because they could do the same to you," McInnes told fans and followers on DefendGavin.com, a crowdsourcing site that raised nearly $258,000 by May 2019 from more than seven thousand individual donors for his legal battle. "It's beginning to feel like Eastern Europe where we're all looking over our shoulders petrified of false allegations and infiltrators," he urged. "That's not what this country was built on. We're mad as hell, and we're not going to take it anymore. Let's fight back. Starting right now."

The writing is on the wall and the stakes are high for each and every citizen who defends American sovereignty in any forum, especially online.

SPLC, Silicon Valley, and financial terrorism

Following the firing of Morris Dees and the resignation of Richard Cohen and other top deputies in March 2019, the SPLC may have appeared rudderless and crippled. But the board's hiring of Tina Tchen[160]—Chicago power lawyer, top advisor to former President Barack Obama, and former chief of staff to former First Lady Michelle Obama—to mop up the mess in Montgomery[161] suggests the daunting possibility that the SPLC's half-a-billion-dollar endowment could eventually end up under the direct authority of partisan Democratic operatives. The wrecking crew inside the Poverty Palace forged ahead to new frontiers, partnering with leftists in Silicon Valley to "Change the Terms" on the internet of who can say what in advance of the 2020 election season.

Sound familiar? We're back to where we began this chapter—banning "code words of hate" to suppress the speech, thought, and influence of peaceful Americans participating in the marketplace of ideas.

SPLC's "Change the Terms: Reducing Hate Online" campaign was first launched in October 2018 as "a set of policy recommendations to help social media and other internet companies reduce hateful activities on their platforms."[162] While church ladies in Louisiana, moderate Muslims in Britain, anti-Common Core parents, and think tank scholars are being de-platformed indiscriminately, the SPLC lamented that tech companies aren't doing enough to censor speech. The new initiative rests on the same old tried-and-untrue tactic of other-izing Americans with mainstream political views on immigration and traditional marriage by linking them to "white supremacists." Intelligence Project director (a.k.a. Smear Queen) Heidi Beirich decried "extreme ideas from the fringes" on social media platforms and linked immigration restrictionists and Christian conservatives to "violence in real life, including the tragic events that we saw unfold in Charlottesville, Virginia, last year." The horrific massacre at a mosque in Christchurch, New Zealand, by a lone white-nationalist madman (who was all over the map ideologically) in early spring 2019 breathed new life into the program. As for the violence perpetrated by consumers of SPLC's hatred—like FRC shooter Floyd Lee Corkins or the thugs at Charles Murray's Middlebury College speaking event—Beirich remained mum. Nor did the SPLC say much after GOP white congressman Steve Scalise of Louisiana was shot at a 2017 congressional baseball practice by James Hodgkinson, an online fan of the Soros-supported SPLC, Media Matters, and MoveOn.org.[163]

The "Change the Terms" architects had a plan to track the progress of major tech companies on implementing their "model corporate policies" and the creation of "report cards" (uh-oh!) on their performance. The usual thought police and defamation troopers joined with SPLC to pressure Big Tech, including the Soros-funded Center for American Progress ($10.7 million from Soros's Open Foundations), Free Press ($2 million),[164] National Hispanic Media Coalition (at least $300,000),

Color of Change ($550,000),[165] and forty other groups. The SPLC itself has received at least $75,000 from Soros's Foundation to Promote Open Society.[166] How do the policies define "hateful activity"? On paper, they're described as "activities that incite or engage in violence, intimidation, harassment, threats, or defamation targeting an individual or group based on their actual or perceived race, color, religion, national origin, ethnicity, immigration status, gender, gender identity, sexual orientation, or disability."[167] In practice, it means anything left-wing ideological character assassins want it to mean while trying to win elections and secure power.

The "enforcement" model pushed by the speech bullies naturally gives them a special place with a "trusted flagger program for vetted, well-established civil and human rights organizations." For even more opportunities to meddle (and make money), the hate-hunters recommend that companies "create a committee of outside advisers with expertise in identifying and tracking hateful activities who will have responsibility for producing an annual report on effectiveness of the steps taken by the company."[168] Hmmm. Who could fit that bill?

Here's what my SPLC Silicon Valley Stooge Report looks like so far:

Google/YouTube: As early as February 2018, the Daily Caller learned from a Google spokesperson that the SPLC had been designated a "trusted flagger" along with more than one hundred non-governmental organizations and government agencies (who were required to sign confidentiality agreements). Company monitors and engineers draw on the flaggers' "expertise" (i.e., SPLC's "expert" track record of ruining targets' lives by falsely designating them haters and extremists)[169] to help them design and tweak flagging algorithms. At a House Judiciary Committee hearing in December 2018, Google CEO Sundar Pichai confirmed that "Southern Poverty Law Center is a trusted flagger."[170] Pichai had been caught on tape exposing his political bias after the election of President Trump in 2016, when he vowed to stop "misinformation" by "low-information voters," and cheered an employee's rant about "white privilege."[171] At the same meeting, Google co-founder Sergey Brin praised an employee's suggestion to donate to progressive groups and compared Trump voters to "extremists."[172] In January 2019, *Fortune* magazine reported that Google's philanthropic arm had created a new program to pay employees six months' salary for "pro bono" work for left-wing social justice causes, including the SPLC. Ironically enough, given the center's decades-long internal struggle to address alleged sexual and racial discrimination, Google's volunteers who serve with the SPLC are focused on "inclusion."[173] Google has also donated $250,000 to the intolerant bunch's Teaching Tolerance program since 2016.[174] Conservative legal scholar and former corporate litigator Hans Von Spakovsky warned that the company's entanglements with the SPLC's long-known defamers "opens them up to potential liability. If one of their organizations is working for the SPLC, when the SPLC is sued under defamation or a RICO suit, that could potentially bring Google into the lawsuit."[175] Not if, but when.

PragerU, founded by author and radio legend Dennis Prager, publishes a phenomenally popular five-minute video series on YouTube with more than a billion total views. The organization sued Google in February 2018 and again in January 2019 after suffering repeated, nonsensical restrictions of its educational content. The first lawsuit is on appeal before the Ninth Circuit Court of Appeals; the second action is in state court and challenges the "outright falsehoods" of Google/YouTube's claims that it enforces content policies in a "politically neutral way."[176] The SPLC clowns have targeted the site on Hatewatch as "another node on the internet connecting conservative media consumers to the dark corners of the extreme right."[177] Here are some of the nefarious, extreme topics that PragerU speakers are indoctrinating viewers in: modern art and masculinity, whether to follow your passion or not (with that notorious extremist, Mike Rowe of *Dirty Jobs* fame), parenting, education, religion, history, and yes, immigration (including a by-the-numbers breakdown from yours truly). To the fearmongers, the success of PragerU through peaceful, non-coercive means of enlightenment and persuasion isn't a sign of healthy debate and a thirst for knowledge, but a "dog whistle to the extreme right" that must be stifled.

Facebook: Mark Zuckerberg's empire treats PragerU and countless other conservative content providers the same way Google/YouTube do: as threats to be managed, policed, and throttled. In August 2018, the video publisher reported that nine of its pieces in a row had mysteriously received zero views on Facebook (where PragerU has three million followers) and two videos were deleted as "hate speech."[178] Facebook apologized after being called out and chalked it up to a "mistake."[179] Once or twice could be a mistake. But eleven times? Keep in mind that Facebook informed a conservative group that its posting of the Declaration of Independence—on the 4th of July!—"goes against our standards of hate speech." Of course, the company chalked it up to another "mistake" after the group raised hell.[180] Same with Trump-supporting social media stars Diamond and Silk, whose videos were "mistakenly" classified as unsafe in April 2018.[181] The mistakes keep adding up and skewing in the direction of de-platforming conservatives by "accident." Or design.

As the Daily Caller News Foundation confirmed with a Facebook spokeswoman, SPLC is on an official list of "external experts and organizations" that the tech giant works with "to inform our hate speech policies."[182] The flack denied adopting the exact definitions of "hate" and "hate groups" pushed by the SPLC. But in March 2019, Facebook announced a new policy of banning "white nationalist content" from its platform in the wake of the Christchurch mosque massacre and consistent with the demands of the SPLC's "Change the Terms." After consulting with "experts," the company concluded that no meaningful distinction between "white nationalism and separatism" and "white supremacy and organized hate groups" exists. Users who post what the "experts" tell them is "white nationalism" will now have their content diverted to a Chicago-based website called "Life After Hate" to help them "leave" the hate-filled life.[183] There they can find articles condemning toxic masculinity and offering advice if they're worried about friends and neighbors becoming "extremists."[184]

A day after the Facebook rollout, the SPLC released a new propaganda year-in-review report, "Rage Against Change," which recycled the same old themes and hysteria from "Rage of the Right" and every other year in review: "Surging numbers of hate groups. Rising right-wing populism and antisemitism. Mounting acts of deadly domestic terrorism. Increasing hate crimes. Exploding street violence. That was the landscape of the radical right in 2018." The report linked white supremacy to President Trump, Fox News, Tucker Carlson, Laura Ingraham, FAIR, Brigitte Gabriel, David Horowitz, the Family Research Council, Alliance Defending Freedom, and everyone and anyone who had anything negative to say about jihad, gay marriage, and migrant caravans.

A *New York Times* article trumpeted Facebook's announcement about banning white nationalist content, and cited approvingly Facebook's October 2018 banning of SPLC target Gavin McInnes and the Proud Boys.[185] Oh, and just so the double standards are clear to all, non-white pride is fine and dandy: "Going forward," the company asserted, "while people will still be able to demonstrate pride in their ethnic heritage, we will not tolerate praise or support for white nationalism and separatism."

If you question the regime, you are extreme.

Twitter: The microblogging service with 321 million users worldwide prides itself on transparency and the "open exchange of information."[186] But in the Trump era, conservative users of Twitter, from flyover moms to activists and journalists to prominent Republican officials, are under siege. In March 2019, Republican congressman Devin Nunes of California filed a $250 million lawsuit against Twitter and individual parties for influencing and interfering in his election race and congressional investigations through suppressing tweets without his knowledge, knowingly hosting and monetizing content "that is clearly abusive, hateful, and defamatory," and selectively amplifying the messages of defamers attacking political opponents on the Right (and in Nunes's case, his own mother, as well).[187] Social media guru Nick Short and national security expert David Reaboi sounded the alarm over Twitter's use of a "complex and opaque Quality Filter algorithm that has the effect of disproportionately restricting the voices of conservatives under the guise of limiting harmful or abusive users"—otherwise known as shadow banning. Their concerns were dismissed in meetings with Twitter officials, who scoffed that if followers were not seeing their content, it's because it was not worthy of sharing.[188]

Yet, a former Twitter engineer admitted to an undercover Project Veritas journalist that the shadowy practice goes on all the time: "The idea of a shadow ban is that you ban someone, but they don't know they've been banned," the source said. "They keep posting, but no one sees their content." The strategy, he acknowledged, is to retain "ultimate control."[189]

Who is determining what should be controlled? In 2018, Twitter listed the SPLC as one of its "safety partners" working to combat "hateful conduct and harassment.[190] But Twitter's executives squirmed under the glare of scrutiny when asked about their relationship with the SPLC. Confronted by independent journalist Tim Pool on the Joe Rogan podcast about the group's overreaching hate classifications and unreliability as a neutral arbiter, Twitter co-founder and CEO Jack Dorsey played dumb and the company's "Legal, Policy and Trust and Safety" lead attorney Vijaya Gadde deflected.[191] Asked point-blank whether Twitter uses the SPLC "in their decision-making process" and rule development, Gadde stuttered that the company was aware of "flaws with certain of their research" and was "careful" about "who we take advice from." Pool asked again whether the SPLC advises Twitter, to which Gadde replied: "Um, I, I, think that they have certainly reached out to our team members, but there is certainly nothing definitive that we take from them."[192]

The SPLC would beg to differ, no doubt. Its hate-weaponizers touted Twitter's "long awaited crackdown on hate groups and extremist rhetoric" in December 2017,[193] which Twitter rolled out after consulting its "safety" partners. Tweets "celebrating any violent act in a manner that may inspire others to replicate it or any violence where people were targeted because of their membership in a protected group," are banned according to the new policy.[194] In addition, signal-boosting of "hateful images and symbols" in usernames, profile bios, profile headers, profile images, and display names could also trigger suspensions and de-platforming. Question: Who decides what qualifies as a "protected group" or a "hateful" image or symbol? Answer: biased, vested "experts" who've profited off expanding the definitions into meaninglessness. The SPLC gloated that the policy changes came in response to its pressure campaign to purge Twitter of the "racist alt-right." Like the SPLC, the Twitter hate police only seem concerned about alleged threats from one side of the political aisle. As Pool pointed out to Gadde and Dorsey, the rules were not applied consistently to violent, left-wing "antifa" activists who had threatened him, doxxed law enforcement agents, and threatened the lives of the Covington Catholic high school boys.[195]

After the Christchurch massacre, the hashtag #eggboy trended on Twitter in celebration of a seventeen-year-old Australian punk who smacked an egg at the head of sixty-nine-year-old Queensland senator Fraser Anning during a press conference.[196] The politician had issued a statement condemning the massacre and calling attention to the immigration programs in his country "which allowed Muslim fanatics to migrate to New Zealand in the first place."[197] Virtue signalers around the world demonized Anning for telling the truth as the baying Twitter mob heaped praise on his attacker—egging on more physical attacks approved by the Twitter overlords: "Eggboy is the hero we wanted. But too bad it wasn't something harder. Like a brick," one user gloated.[198]

Novelist Jane Caro, a verified, blue check-marked Twitter celebrity, threatened: "If the thugs and the racists and the misogynists come marching down the streets or the airwaves we will applaud those who take up eggs against them. I only hope I have the courage to do so too. Thank you #EggBoyHero."[199]

Jeremy McLellan, another blue check mark who calls himself a "comedian," enthused: "Props to eggboy for selecting the ideal ammunition for his attack, the humble egg, which is funny, harmless, available everywhere, cheap, easy to transport, nice sound on impact, makes the target change their clothes. The perfect weapon for these times."[200]

Now imagine if a seventeen-year-old MAGA hat-wearer videotaped himself hurling an egg at Bernie Sanders or Ilhan Omar or Beto O'Rourke in protest of their open-borders, sharia-coddling agendas. And imagine if thousands of conservative Twitter users posted the clip endlessly of the act of physical violence. And imagine what the SPLC would tell their friends at Twitter to do.

It doesn't help that Vijaya Gadde, the Twitter decider of trust and safety, is a brazen, Trump-hating leftist who wears her politics on her Twitter feed. In 2014, she gushed about her meeting at company headquarters with Hillary Clinton, whom she called "amazing" and "full of great advice and inspiration"—illustrated with a beaming photo of the two.[201] In 2015, she called for "$30 million" to get Congress to pass gun control.[202] In 2016, she excerpted a caustic column from *New York Times* columnist Nicholas Kristof attacking President Trump as "ill-informed, evasive, puerile and deceptive."[203] Born in India and raised on the Gulf Coast of Texas, she frequently tells an anecdote attributed to her father about a local Klansman requiring him to get permission to sell insurance door-to-door in her neighborhood.[204] The alleged incident took place in the 1970s, but Gadde said it continues to this day to "color my instinctive nature to protect the underdogs. It's why I have the political views that I have." Institutional racism and lurking white supremacists didn't seem to pose much of a barrier to her own success in climbing the corporate ladder. By 2014, after graduating from Cornell and New York University Law School, Gadde ascended to Twitter's general counsel office and owned shares in the company valued at $28 million.[205]

Gadde stubbornly refuses to acknowledge her liberal bias. Consider her response when Tim Pool provided specific examples of Twitter's "pattern and practice of banning only one faction of people." After Pool cited a Quillette analysis showing that "of 22 prominent, politically active individuals who are known to have been suspended since 2005 and who expressed a preference in the 2016 U.S. presidential election, 21 supported Donald Trump,"[206] Gadde exclaimed, "I don't agree with that. I don't believe that's the case."[207] Actions, of course, speak louder than words. In March 2019, Gadde announced new plans to "label" tweets by President Trump and other public figures (but mostly President Trump) that are "a violation of our rules" so users have more "context."[208]

Remember, kids: It's not about transparency or engagement or trust or safety. It's all about control.

Amazon: Billionaire Jeff Bezos, founder of Amazon and owner of the *Washington Post*, is open in his disdain for President Trump and his embrace of liberal Democrats and liberal Republicans. Bezos half-joked about sending Trump to outer space on one of his Blue Origin rockets.[209] He has personally donated to the campaigns of liberal Democrats Patty Murray and Maria Cantwell in Washington state; left-wingers like Vermont Senator Pat Leahy and Michigan Congressman John Conyers; and open-borders Michigan Senator Spencer Abraham.[210] Bezos and his ex-wife also pledged $2.5 million to support a gay marriage referendum in Washington state, which passed by a seven-point margin.[211] Although the *Post* has reported in-depth on the SPLC's "blunders" that "undermined its own credibility,"[212] Amazon proudly partners with the beclowned cops of political correctness to ban conservatives from using its "Smile" program, a charitable donation mechanism used by customers to earmark 0.5 percent of the proceeds from their purchases on Amazon to a participating charity.

There are more than one million charities to choose from, according to the AmazonSmile FAQ,[213] including the smear merchants of the SPLC and several militant Muslim charities linked to Louis "Jews are termites" Farrakhan's Nation of Islam.[214] Yet, several Christian charities and immigration hawks deemed "hate groups" by the Christian-hating SPLC have been kicked off. As mentioned previously, the Center for Immigration Studies and the Ruth Institute were barred from the program. So was D. James Kennedy Ministries, a mainstream Presbyterian offshoot based in Florida. In 2017, they sued SPLC, Amazon, and charity-ranker GuideStar for defamation and trademark violations.[215]

In April 2018, Brother Andre Marie of the tiny Saint Benedict Center learned from a supporter that the New Hampshire-based Catholic charity had also been barred from receiving AmazonSmile donations. Brother Andre received the following response from Amazon after he inquired about the ban: "The AmazonSmile Participation Agreement states that certain categories of organizations are not eligible to participate in AmazonSmile. We rely on the Southern Poverty Law Center to determine which charities are in certain ineligible categories. You have been excluded from the AmazonSmile program because the Southern Poverty Law Center lists Saint Benedict Center Inc in an ineligible category."[216]

The SPLC has repeatedly attacked the leaders of the tiny religious order as a "hate group" since 2007 and maligned the center's "radical traditionalists" because of their opposition to gay marriage, abortion, and liberalization of the church.[217] Brother Andre Marie published a point-by-point refutation of the SPLC's unsubstantiated claims that the Benedict Center condoned antisemitism, stocked up rifles, planned to dragoon children away from public schools, and had a "desire" to "outlaw" government.[218]

A month after the Saint Benedict Center was dropped, Amazon ejected the Alliance Defending Freedom (ADF), the pro bono Christian legal foundation that successfully defended Colorado's Masterpiece Cakeshop baker Jack Phillips for refusing to bake a gay wedding cake, citing his religious liberty rights before the U.S. Supreme Court.[219] ADF's Sarah Kramer revealed that Amazon officials told the group explicitly that SPLC's "hate" designation was the reason for being blacklisted.[220] ADF fellow Michael Farris wrote an open letter to Bezos's company recounting the SPLC's mission of destruction and defamation in which he urged: "If you are going to rely on a discredited partisan organization like the SPLC to determine who is eligible to participate in AmazonSmile, you should disclose that in your policy and to your customers."[221] ADF's Jeremy Tedesco revealed that after being banned by Amazon, his group was "declined nonprofit pricing with Microsoft," and had to "hire plain-clothes police officers to protect our attorneys when they speak on hostile campuses." He has also seen ADF employees "verbally accosted in public places."[222]

Here's something that won't leave you smiling: an Amazon spokes-woman doubled down on the ban by explaining to Peter Hasson of the Daily Caller News Foundation that the company relies on the SPLC to "establish the criteria" for who's violating its policies against hate "because we don't want to be biased whatsoever." Relying on virulent bias to avoid the appearance of bias? Now, *that* is spacey.

Predictably, the speech patrol isn't limiting its aim at participants in Amazon's charity program. In 2018, then-Congressman (now Minnesota Attorney General) Keith Ellison—a radical left-wing Democrat, who proudly wears a T-shirt that reads *Yo No Creo En Fronteras* (I don't believe in borders)—sent a letter to Jeff Bezos demanding that the company commit to "ceasing the sale of all products that promote hateful and racist ideologies," stop doing business with "SPLC-identified hate groups," and "stop publishing physical and digital materials from SPLC-identified hate groups."[223] While Congressman Ellison cited "nazi," "white nationalist," "antisemitic," and "Islamophobic" content as his focus of concern, SPLC target Robert Spencer pointed out the wider threat at issue if Amazon caves to the demand and purges its site of any books and other material sold by groups and individuals named and defamed by the SPLC: "Given Amazon's dominance of the book market, that would be a serious blow to the freedom of speech, as the SPLC is making an all-out attempt to delegitimize the full spectrum of opinion that dissents from the leftist agenda—on Islam, immigration, social issues and more." It could very well be, Spencer rightfully worries, the "nail in the coffin of the freedom of speech in the U.S."[224]

PayPal: PayPal's CEO, Dan Schulman, admitted to the *Wall Street Journal* in February 2019 that the company relied on the Southern Poverty Law Center's smear machine for input on which conservatives or non-leftist groups to blacklist in order to uphold the company's alleged values of "diversity and inclusion."[225] Schulman bragged that he was "born with social activism in his DNA."[226] PayPal had already taken a social justice stand in 2016 by canceling plans to open an operations center in North Carolina after the state passed a law protecting girls and women from being forced to share bathrooms with transgender boys and men.[227] Schulman has also been outspoken about his hostility to guns, and PayPal can't be used to buy firearms and ammunition.[228] Social-justice narratives around the Charlottesville, Virginia, "Unite the Right" rally became a pretext for purging non-violent, non-leftist users from the site. Who decides? Schulman acknowledged that PayPal consulted with "outside groups" on both the "right and the left" to determine whether to terminate a user, but the SPLC was the only one he name-checked.

Among the countless, non-leftist, de-PayPal-ed users: anti-jihad Arab Christian Brigitte Gabriel and her group ACT for America; Gavin McInnes and the Proud Boys; independent journalist, sharia critic, and anti-open borders activist Laura Loomer;[229] Toronto mayoral candidate, Canadian nationalist, and social media personality Faith Goldy; Tommy Robinson, the English anti-jihad activist; VDARE, a nationalist immigration news and commentary site that publishes my syndicated column; free-speech provocateur Milo Yiannopoulos; far-out radio/web host Alex Jones; and free-speech social network Gab (which was punished because a crazed gunman who shot up a Pittsburgh synagogue in October 2018 happened to have posted on the site).[230]

Another conservative kicked off PayPal: Luke Rohlfing, a young reporter for Big League Politics, who had exposed how the payment processor was allowing Open Borders Inc. heavyweight Pueblo Sin Fronteras to raise money for illegal alien caravans conspiring to break our immigration laws—even though PayPal's own terms of service state clearly that users may not engage in any activities that "violate any law, statute, ordinance or regulation."[231] When he contacted a PayPal representative to ask why he had been booted from the service, she told him she had no idea and advised him to "submit a subpoena to our corporate address" to obtain "more details regarding the WHY of this action."[232]

Just call 'em Pay(NotYour)Pal.

Chase Bank: Enrique Tarrio is a young, peaceful, Afro-Cuban free-thinker and chairman of the Proud Boys. In February 2019, the Texas political activist and Trump supporter received a letter from Chase Bank informing him that "after careful consideration," the financial institution could "no longer support" his banking account and was closing it in two months. The notice followed a hit piece against minorities who support the president published by *The Daily Beast,* a dependable amplifier of SPLC propaganda. The article tied young men of Asian, black, and Latino descent to "white supremacists" and derided them because they "proudly identify as 'American' without modifiers."[233] Not long after the piece came out, Tarrio was kicked off Chase's payment processor, which he used to sell patriotic and pro-Trump T-shirts. In quick succession, he was deplatformed from Facebook, Twitter, Instagram, Airbnb, First Data, Square, Stripe, and PayPal before losing his bank accounts. When I asked on Twitter why we can't have just one financial institution that doesn't cave to SJWs,[234] the official Chase Twitter account tweeted me back: "Hi Michelle, this article is inaccurate. We did not close his personal account. We do not close accounts based on political affiliation."[235]

I pointed out that Chase's letter clearly stated that the company had closed his account. "So if not for political reasons," I asked, "why, 'after careful consideration,' did you close his account?"[236] To which the social media manager of Chase's corporate Twitter account replied: "For privacy reasons, we can't say more."[237] An undercover investigation by Project Veritas in April 2019 caught one Chase employee explaining that "Chase is not involved with any like, you know, alt-right people or anything." Those with "no moral character," he told a Project Veritas journalist, are people that the bank usually doesn't get involved with in any "business relationships, period." Chase bankers who looked up Tarrio's case were told the "decision is not reversible."[238] Tarrio announced in May 2019 that the Proud Boys were suing the SPLC over its destructive and defamatory "hate" designation.[239] Tarrio shared this warning with me in an interview: "If this goes unchecked the left will use this to wage war and implement what I believe to be 'financial communism' where conservative Americans will be afraid to express their views and concerns because of fear that they will not be able to put food on the table or provide for their families. Welcome to 1984 and 1939."[240]

Others who received Chase shutdown notices in 2019: conservative Rebel Media contributor Martina Markota,[241] anti-sharia and pro-borders investigative journalist Laura Loomer, and U.S. Army combat vet and vocal Trump supporter Joe Biggs.[242] On Twitter, Eric Weinstein of Thiel Capital publicly questioned whether every Chase customer "whose account is closed by you [is] entitled to know the reasons for the closure and given the opportunity to contest what may be bank error even if only to guard against any possible rogue breach of internal protocols motivated by political reasons?"[243] Weinstein voiced concern[244] that the tactic was similar to "Operation Choke Point," an Obama-era initiative to choke off the financial oxygen of legal small businesses and lenders deemed politically undesirable[245] under the guise of cracking down on "fraud."[246] Weinstein's inquiries went unanswered. Instead, the Chase social media operator once again invoked "privacy" and denied that it would ever "close an account due to political affiliation."[247]

It would, of course, be unseemly for a financial institution to engage in blatant partisan politics. It would be unwise business practice to alienate customers en masse based on ideology. Right? And yet, in the wake of Charlottesville, JPMorgan Chase ponied up $500,000 to the SPLC race racketeers—whose mission is to "destroy" its political enemies on the right—in order "to confront hate, intolerance and discrimination wherever it exists."[248]

I asked whether that commitment includes confronting the hate, intolerance, and discrimination that exists within the walls of the SPLC's Poverty Palace. A Chase spokesperson did not respond to my question.

More Big Banking Bullies: Jihad Watch founder, bestselling author, and longtime SPLC target Robert Spencer announced plans in July 2018 to raise money on the Patreon crowdsourcing website to create educational videos.[249] A month later, he revealed that he had been abruptly cut off from using Patreon because Mastercard notified the crowdfunder to remove his account.[250] Strangely, Spencer doesn't use Mastercard. Patreon repeated its alibi, blaming Mastercard on its Twitter account.[251]

The only crimes Robert Spencer is guilty of are thought crimes—the same ones conservative historian, think tank founder, and perennial SPLC target David Horowitz was found guilty of by the left-wing character assassins. A week after Spencer's cutoff, Horowitz was similarly blacklisted by Mastercard.[252] Officials from the online donation service Worldpay had informed him that Mastercard relied on Soros-funded SPLC ally Color of Change to identify merchants who created "content which is hateful in nature" through a website called bloodmoney.org. Worldpay explained that it was "part of our normal process" to share information about websites "that may have illegal content" with the merchant's bank connecting them to its financial network to accept card payments. "In this case," the bank "advised us that they decided to terminate acceptance."[253] After a massive uproar in conservative media, Mastercard retreated. But as Horowitz warned: "The censorship powers of Social Media are awesome and historically unprecedented. When they are amplified by the arbitrary financial power of corporations such as Mastercard and Visa, the result is a leviathan willing and able to crush our basic freedoms and constitutional guarantees without a moment's remorse."[254]

Amalgamated Bank: Amalgamated Bank bills itself as "America's socially responsible bank," which in practice means that it is more openly left-wing than other banks. For instance, the meltdown at SPLC headquarters in Montgomery did nothing to dissuade Amalgamated from organizing twenty-five donor networks to launch yet another frontal assault on mainstream conservative and Christian groups blacklisted by the SPLC vigilantes. Perhaps it was intended to distract from the SPLC's troubles. Five days after Dees's firing in March 2019, the Amalgamated Bank's foundation spearheaded the "Hate Is Not Charitable" campaign to pressure donor-advised funds to "exercise their legal discretion over grants recommended by their donors and adopt proactive policies to ensure that funds do not flow to organizations that promote hatred."[255]

Among the prominent members of the campaign: the unindicted terror co-conspirators of the Council on American Islamic Relations, who were disavowed by the Federal Bureau of Investigation, disgraced by multiple leaders convicted of terror-related activities, and tied to antisemitic Hamas hatemongers.[256]

The Amalgamated Foundation cited a report by an obscure media outlet with the appropriate name of Sludge, which targeted four major donor-advised funds including Donors Trust, Fidelity Charitable, Schwab Charitable, and Vanguard Charitable. The quartet provided nearly $11 million in grants to thirty-four organizations between 2014 and 2017 "that have been deemed hate groups by the Southern Poverty Law Center," Sludge slimed. Relying on the thoroughly discredited and heavily inflated SPLC hate map, Sludge tallied "12 anti-LGBT groups, 12 anti-Muslim groups, eight anti-immigrant groups, one white nationalist group, and one radical traditional Catholic group."[257]

The pressure campaign against publicity-shy financial institutions is borrowed straight from veteran progressive organizers in the labor movement. As I reported in *Culture of Corruption*, the tactic involves bullying companies ranging from private equity firms to fast food chains into surrendering to the demands of left-wing pressure groups—or else face full destruction of their reputations, often through being painted as hatemongers. Amalgamated is majority-owned by an affiliate of the far-left Service Employees International Union (SEIU).[258] As SEIU's former president and agitator extraordinaire Andy Stern once said: "[W]e prefer to use the power of persuasion, but if that doesn't work we use the persuasion of power."[259] How... charitable.

Apple: The head of the global tech company known for its sleek computers and smartphones thinks consumers want to hear what he has to say about immigration. Apple CEO Tim Cook mouthed off while in Ireland, condemning the Trump administration's handling of the illegal alien invasion at our southern border in June 2018 as "inhumane" and "heartbreaking."[260] Asked why Apple should be delving into partisan politics, Cook defended his diatribe by asserting that the issue was "square in the dignity and respect area, and I felt we needed to say something."[261]

So what about the dignity and respect due to SPLC employees protesting sexual and racial discrimination within the SPLC? Apple donated a whopping $1 million to the "hate" monitors in the wake of the Charlottesville riot and installed special SPLC donation buttons on the iTunes store; 100 percent of the proceeds will go to the SPLC.

Does Cook have something to say about SPLC co-founder Morris Dees's penchant for "hitting on young women"? Or the "multiple reports of sexual harassment by Dees through the years [that] had been ignored or covered up"? Or "the unchecked power of the lavishly compensated white men at the top of the organization"? Or the "highly profitable scam" that has duped thousands of SPLC donors "who believed that their money was being used, faithfully and well, to do the Lord's work in the heart of Dixie" when employees were all "part of the con, and we knew it"?[262] Apple's media relations department did not respond.

Don't take my word for it, Tim. Those were the conclusions of former SPLC staffer Bob Moser in the *New Yorker* following the resignation of Dirty Dees.[263] Ignoring the wreckage of the past half-century inside and outside the Poverty Palace is an affront to the "respect" and "decency" that Apple's CEO and his fellow corporate virtue-ists claim to value. In the name of diversity, equity, and justice, Montgomery's flimflam man and his wrecking crew stirred fear and paranoia, destroyed innocent lives and livelihoods, deepened racial divisions, exploited tragedies, poisoned debate over the gravest threats to America's survival, and demonized nonviolent, law-abiding citizens defending one nation under God.

To borrow Cook's own useful words: "Hate is a cancer, and left unchecked it destroys everything in its path. Its scars last generations."[264]

CHAPTER SEVEN

HOLLYWOOD OR HOLLYWALL? INSIDE THE FORTRESS OF CELEBRITY HYPOCRISY

Let us take a scenic tour, rolling like a celebrity, through the hallowed hills of Hollywood. Or maybe we should call it "Holly*wall*."

First stop: Beverly Hills, 90210. The zip code made famous by the 1990s TV teen drama connotes glitz, glamour, and gates. High atop the Santa Monica Mountains, three exclusive communities lie behind tall, impenetrable, iron bars: The Summit, Beverly Park, and Mulholland Estates.

Pop diva Gwen Stefani's $35 million sweet escape is located in the guard-gated Summit neighborhood, protected by a second gate blocking a 250-foot private driveway, which leads to her 12,000-square-foot compound surrounded by massive concrete walls topped by wire.[1]

Homes average $20 million in Beverly Park, which boasts A-listers Denzel Washington, Mark Wahlberg, and Sylvester Stallone.[2] Denzel's domain is "heavily guarded and is only accessible through a private entrance off Mulholland Drive," according to a map of celebrity homes.[3] Beverly Park is "a super unique enclave that gives you complete security, living among your peers," gushed a local real estate agent.[4]

Mulholland Estates counts Paris Hilton, Kendall Jenner, Christina Aguilera, and Charlie Sheen as homeowners.[5] Many of the multi-multi-million-dollar mega-mansions have their own private residential gates and personal armed bodyguards in addition to the neighborhood's 24/7 guarded stations for added security.

Nearby, Eva Longoria lives in the gated community of Beverly Crest, where her $13.5-million mansion sits sequestered at the end of its own gated driveway and boasts custom steel front doors.[6] It is "custom-lit and protected by a comprehensive security system."[7] One of Longoria's previous compounds was described by *Variety* as a "gated and heavily fortified multi-residence property... perched on a private, 2.75-acre promontory above Laurel Canyon.[8]

Supermodel Chrissy Teigen and musician John Legend nest together in a gated, $14-million Beverly Hills spread at the end of a cul-de-sac for maximum security and privacy.[9] They traded up from a $2-million Hollywood Hills pad, also gated and located at the end of a long driveway safe from prying eyes.[10]

Actor Chris Evans bought his Hollywood Hills hideaway for $3.5 million. It is "completely walled and gated," according to Zillow, which suits the celebrity's thirst for solitude and privacy.[11] A "high wall with locked and secured entry gates zig-zags its way around and completely encloses the front yard," *Variety* added.

Jay-Z and Beyoncé's $88-million Bel Air mansion "sits behind walls and gates," the *Los Angeles Times* reports, with windows and pocketing glass walls that are bulletproof.[12] Renovations include beefed-up security buildings to provide living quarters for bodyguards that will turn the manor into a "fortress."[13] The new structures will be attached to garages and carports facing the front and the back of the property to ensure that all entrances and exits are breach-proof.

Jennifer Lopez has owned multiple properties in L.A.'s most prestigious neighborhoods. While married to Marc Anthony, she owned an $8-million walled-off French farmhouse in the guarded and gated Bel Air community.[14] Another J.Lo abode located in the exclusive, gated

Hidden Hills area sold for $10 million.[15] With latest beau Alex Rodriguez, she purchased actor Jeremy Piven's walled and gated Malibu beach home for the "bargain" price of $6.6 million.[16]

While we're near the beach, we can peek in on Malibu Colony—the gated, guarded enclave of one hundred homes owned by the world's richest and most famous one percenters. Barbra Streisand's beachfront hideaway is here. So are the mansions of Robert Redford, Angelina Jolie, Rob Reiner, and David Geffen.[17] The stars are so zealous about their security that they routinely dispatch private guards to keep people off the *public* beaches. "Executive protection" can cost $500 to $1,000 a day per officer, one security expert told the *Hollywood Reporter.*[18] Fortifying a home with shifts of security guards stationed in a command center, who constantly monitor high-definition video from cameras installed in every nook and cranny of an estate, can run up to $500,000 a year.[19]

Next stop: The lands of make-believe. If you want a glimpse of how Tinseltown works its magic at the Warner Bros. Studio, you'll need a valid, government-issued photo ID, and you'll be required to pass through a metal detector before entering the tour center. Bags are also subject to security screening.[20] At the Sony Pictures Studios lot in Culver City, you'll have to drive through manned gates. The vast complex is equipped with security cameras everywhere and multiple guarded checkpoints in every building.[21] Most of the major studios beefed up barricades and other physical barriers after the 9/11 terrorist attacks, when the FBI warned they could be targets of al Qaeda.[22]

And finally, let's visit the Oscars. In 2019, the organizers took extensive precautions and nearly doubled the law enforcement presence at the Dolby Theatre compared to the year prior. TMZ reported that about 190 uniformed police officers were deployed to patrol the event.[23] The *Hollywood Reporter* cited a Los Angeles Police Department source comparing the presence to a similar deployment reserved for a visit from the president to Los Angeles.[24] Many top celebs brought their own personal guards to the red carpet. Fans vying for bleacher seats were required to supply their Social Security numbers for background checks, display government-issued ID, and sign liability and publicity waivers.[25] In 2018, an estimated 500 armed officers formed "concentric circles" of security outside the theater, *Variety* reported, "along with firefighters, police helicopters and agents from the FBI." Private security guards from Security Industry Specialists worked inside the ceremony venue.[26] Workers constructed ten-foot-high gates and barricades to keep undocumented intruders out.

Are we sensing a theme here yet? The lifestyles of the rich and famous are lined with walls within walls within walls. Of course, Hollywood's brightest stars worked hard for their success (except for the spoiled elites who coasted on their parents' names and the casting-couch connivers, but I digress). Just like you and me, their homes are their castles (well, sometimes their castles *are* castles, but I digress again). They've invested in valuable real estate that must be protected. They've got precious families who deserve comfort and safety. No one should begrudge the Beautiful People the right to be sovereign over their own spaces and beings, right?

Wrong. *I* begrudge.

These elite entertainers cloistered in an impenetrable bubble of protection—armored cars, armed security details, bulletproof windows, twenty-foot-high stone walls, wrought-iron gates, 24/7 manned guard stations, the works—vehemently oppose President Trump's efforts to protect *our* national home. They're using their fortunes to support brazen border saboteurs. They're leveraging their fame to marginalize and demonize political opponents. They're polluting TV, movie, and music airwaves with cultural messages undermining the rule of law, American citizenship, and basic principles of self-determination. What President Trump said about wealthy politicians resisting America's wall holds true for wealthy celebrities as well.

"Some have suggested a barrier is immoral," he observed in an Oval Office address in January 2019.[27] "Then why do wealthy politicians build walls, fences and gates around their homes? They don't build walls because they hate the people on the outside. But because they love the people on the inside. The only thing that is immoral is the politicians who do nothing and continue to allow more innocent people to be so horribly victimized."

Inside the fortress of celebrity hypocrisy, actors, musicians, producers, directors, supermodels, and "comedians" are working to destabilize our peace and prosperity by promoting mass, uncontrolled migration without impediments, limits, or sanctions. They believe in a world without borders, except for the robust barriers around their own sprawling compounds. I'm going to show you how deeply embedded the entertainment industry is in Open Borders Inc. and why America's celebrity worship is suicidal.

But first, let me remind you of a patriotic Californian whom none of these bleeding hearts in Hollywall mourned.

No Tears for Corporal Singh

In the still of the last night of 2018, the silence of Golden State liberals on the brutal shooting death of Newman Police Department corporal Ronil Singh chilled the air and airwaves.

The thirty-three-year-old Singh was a married father of a five-month-old son. He was working an extra shift in the early morning hours after Christmas when he was shot and killed during a routine traffic stop by illegal alien suspect and Mexican alleged criminal gangbanger Pablo Mendoza, a.k.a. Gustavo Arriaga.[28] Singh was a legal immigrant of Indian descent from Fiji, living the American dream. His police chief Randy Richardson called him an "American patriot" who "told me he came to America to become a police officer. That's all he wanted to do. He truly loved what he did."[29] To his fellow officers, he was more than a colleague, Richardson recounted, but also a friend and inspiration: "This is a man that loved his country. This is a man that worked hard for what he believed in. He believed in this community."[30]

Neighbors, friends, and co-workers turned out in full force for a candlelight vigil memorializing the dedicated, compassionate, hardworking Singh.

Reggie Singh, his brother, broke down in tears at a press conference while expressing thanks to local, state, and federal officers upon the arrest of his slain brother's suspected murderer after an intense, multi-agency, fifty-five-hour manhunt. President Trump reached out to Singh's widow to praise his service; his brother Reggie accompanied the commander in chief to the southern border to support immigration enforcement efforts. "[W]hat my family's going through right now, I do not want any other family law enforcement person to go through that," Reggie Singh pleaded. "Whatever it takes to minimize, put a stop to it, my family fully supports it."[31]

So, what were California's most prominent politicians and celebrities doing while Singh's loved ones mourned their hometown hero?

Border wall opponent Congresswoman Nancy Pelosi decried the deaths of two illegal alien children on the same day Corporal Singh was murdered, bashed the government shutdown, and on New Year's Eve promoted her upcoming MSNBC special.

Border wall opponent Senator Kamala Harris tweeted three times between Christmas and New Year's Eve bemoaning the plight of illegal aliens and their children.

Border wall opponent Senator Dianne Feinstein released a public letter to the Customs and Border Patrol agency to voice her "strong concern about the recent deaths and illnesses of children detained in Border Patrol custody, and to request a full accounting and a revised protocol to prevent such tragedies from occurring in the future."[32]

Not a word was heard from Pelosi, Harris, or Feinstein about Corporal Singh, or the illegal alien suspect, or the arrests of a total of seven alleged accomplices—all illegal aliens as well. There was no call from these California politicians for an investigation of how the murder suspect and his illegal alien accomplices arrived in the U.S., were able to evade arrest and detection, and who employed, aided, abetted, and sheltered them. There was no Democratic outrage over the revelations of Stanislaus County sheriff Adam Christianson, who reported that Corporal Singh's illegal alien suspected murderer from Mexico had worked illegally as a laborer, had known gang affiliations, and had two prior drunk driving arrests before his homicidal traffic stop and attempted escape back to Mexico. California's sanctuary laws, supported by every leading Democrat in the state and signed into law by Governor Jerry Brown, barred local authorities from reporting the cop-killing suspect for his prior criminal arrests to ICE.

Not one peep. Not one tweet.

The priorities couldn't be starker: Open-borders Democratic hearts bleed for those bent on undermining our sovereignty, while they turn blind eyes to legal immigrants who honor our institutions and enforce our laws. Corporal Singh was a true example of the American Dream, brought down by the ongoing open-borders nightmare. He cherished his family roots and heritage but embraced the privileges and responsibilities of legally obtained citizenship as a fully assimilated American. And this is precisely why California Democrats refused to say his name, acknowledge his sacrifice, or investigate the policy failures that led to his death.

To speak Corporal Singh's name is to admit the blood on their own hands.

Over in la-la land, leading liberal celebs followed silent suit.

Spotlight on Mindy Kaling:
Not All Separated Children Are Equal

Like Corporal Singh, Mindy Kaling (born Vera Mindy Chokalingam) is of Indian descent. The forty-year-old comedian and actress grew up in New England, the daughter of educated immigrants (her father was an architect, her mother a doctor) and of privilege, attending a prestigious private school (Buckingham Browne & Nichols School) and an Ivy League college (Dartmouth). Now a single mother of a toddler girl and living in the ritzy Hancock Park enclave of Los Angeles, Kaling has plunged into social justice activism because, she told the *Hollywood Reporter,* "I'm Indian, and to think of the millions of babies who look exactly like my daughter, who don't have the same advantages that she does, it is very chilling to me, and it's very personal to me now that I see her face every single morning."[33]

In June 2018, Kaling saw the face of her daughter in the faces of Latino children crossing the border illegally from Mexico into the U.S. "As a mother and a daughter of immigrants, I am heartbroken about children being separated from their families at America's borders," she posted on Twitter."[34] Kaling urged her nearly twelve million followers to donate to the ACLU and directed them to a resource page listing other pro-illegal immigration groups.[35] Her tweet was accompanied by the infamous Getty Images photo of a terrified two-year-old girl purportedly torn from her mother by cruel jackboots enforcing President Trump's family separation policy.

Except, of course, the narrative was faker than tofurkey wrapped in vegan bacon.

Little Yanela Sanchez became an instant poster child for the anti-Trump resistance after Getty photographer John Moore snapped her bawling in front of towering Border Patrol agents in McAllen, Texas. He dubbed her "Crying Girl on the Border." The bright pink-sneakered toddler and her mother, Sandra, had crossed illegally into the U.S. across the Rio Grande River after a three-week trek from Puerto Cortes, Honduras. Moore told CNN that "the mother had to set down her daughter to be body-searched, to be frisked, before she was loaded into a van & taken away."[36] In a dramatic "behind the scenes" interview for *Time* magazine's YouTube channel, Moore called the girl's hysterical condition "an acute case of separation anxiety happening in front of me."[37] *Time* photoshopped Moore's picture of Yanela on its cover with an image of President Trump looming over her and the snarky headline, "Welcome to America"—cunningly manipulated to stoke anger over the administration's efforts to stop that summer's well-orchestrated illegal alien flood. An animated tweet on *Time*'s Twitter account promoting the cover, which garnered more than two million views, lamented: "What kind of country are we?"[38]

As left-wing Vox described it, Yanela's panicked face "embodied the horror of Trump's 'zero tolerance' policy to prosecute all people crossing the border illegally, leading to the separation of families. It helped fuel the public outrage that forced Trump to backtrack by issuing an executive order to end the practice."[39]

Actress Jennifer Lopez devoted an Instagram post to Yanela that garnered nearly 400,000 likes. "Reading the news about the separation of children from their families," she emoted, "I can't help but think about my own children. I cannot fathom a world where they would be ripped from my arms, taken to a place no better than a prison far from home. I feel we will never forget this moment in time.... If you care about children, have concern for the lack of transparency about this disastrous display, in full view to the world in general, I encourage you first to get caught up on the situation." She added the hashtags "#familiesbelong-together" and "#lovenothate."[40]

Lopez didn't bother to "get caught up on the situation." The narrative was as phony as her glam hair and lash extensions.

Yanela was never separated from her mother, never torn from her arms by brutes impervious to her piercing cries for help as they tossed her into a car never to be seen again. Never happened. The girl was sobbing at 11:00 p.m. on the night she and her mother were caught because she was tired, hungry, and wanted to be held while agents searched her mother. They remained together from the second they set foot on American soil. Yanela, was, however forcibly separated from her *father* back in Honduras. Denis Javier Varela Hernandez revealed to a *Daily Mail* reporter that his wife had taken the child from him without notifying him that she was leaving. Sanchez had paid $6,000 to a coyote to smuggle them into America. She had no credible fear of persecution or legitimate asylum claim, as the calcified open-borders narrative goes. In fact, Hernandez said they all lived a "fine" life where he held down a job as a sea captain, but his wife wanted more and didn't bother saying goodbye before abandoning him and her three other children—ages fourteen, eleven, and six.[41] President Trump and the Border Patrol weren't responsible for the cruel family separation of Yanela Sanchez from her loved ones. Sandra Sanchez was. And she had left her husband and other children behind before. Hernandez acknowledged that Sanchez had previously broken the law, broken into the country illegally, and been previously deported from the U.S. in 2013.

Time was forced to issue a correction to its viral cover story, which "misstated what happened to the girl in the photo after she [was] taken from the scene." The once-prestigious publication admitted that "the girl was not carried away screaming by U.S. Border Patrol agents; her mother picked her up and the two were taken away together."[42] Despite the debunking of its big lie, *Time* editor-in-chief Edward Felsenthal stood by the overarching narrative because the "cover and our reporting capture the stakes of this moment."[43] For his part, Moore denied misleading anyone about the manipulated moment and defended *Time*'s fakery because "I believe this image has raised awareness."[44] The *Washington Post* simply stealth-edited out its false reporting that the "young girl [was] crying as her mother was patted down by a Border Patrol agent before the two were separated," without acknowledging the deletion. Now you see it, now you don't![45]

To recap: The iconic image of President Trump's barbaric treatment of illegal aliens depicted a child and her mother who were not poor. Not separated. Not persecuted. Not mistreated. Ready for the plot twist? As of February 2019, Yanela and her mother were still together and still in America. Propaganda photographer John Moore caught up with them living comfortably in an apartment in the "greater Washington, D.C. area" with other illegal aliens after being released from eighteen days total in federal custody. Moore snapped photos of them at the mall and playground, in their living room, and eating a meal. They have yet to be scheduled for their sham asylum hearing. It is unclear how Yanela's mother can afford rent, phone bills, food bills, and other living expenses.[46] But they are alive and together.

Corporal Singh's family, however, has been destroyed by a 100 percent preventable death. His child will never know the simple joy of being pushed on a swing by his daddy or taking a trip to the toy store. When news broke of Corporal Ronil Singh's murder, the ostentatiously compassionate Mindy

Kaling—whose social justice activism was fueled by her new mother-hood—had nothing to say about a fellow young Indian-American family. There was no tweet featuring the last photo of the Singh family together around the Christmas tree on Kaling's Twitter feed. There were no rallying cries to raise funds for Corporal Singh's widow and child. But thousands of ordinary Americans outside of Fortress Hollywood stepped up to the plate. The Tunnel to Towers Foundation, a charity that aids the families of fallen first responders in need, raised $300,000 to pay off the mortgage on the Singh family's home and chipped in an additional $50,000 for his son's education. Donations poured in after the charity's CEO, Frank Siller, personally appealed for help on the *Fox & Friends* morning show.[47]

The Stanislaus Sworn Deputies Association created a memorial fund within hours of Singh's murder in the line of duty.[48] A local restaurant in Turlock, the Tri-Tipery, held a "fly-in" with local law enforcement agencies at the Turlock Municipal Airport, showing off first-responder vehicles, planes, and helicopters, with all proceeds going to the memorial fund. Bay Area breweries chipped in as well,[49] and New York City police officer and Blue Lives Matter co-founder Joseph Imperatrice held a fundraiser in Lower Manhattan for the family.[50]

The America that puts the law-abiding above the lawless rallied around the Singh family. The America that exalts criminal trespassers over our guardians looked the other way.

Spotlight on Alyssa Milano: Putting Americans Last

In the immediate wake of Corporal Singh's senseless murder and preventable death, another left-wing actress and Californian, Alyssa Milano, used her formidable social media platform to raise money—not for a fellow citizen in need, but for an illegal alien agitator. On December 30, 2018, Milano urged her 3.6 million Twitter followers to donate to a GoFundMe campaign on behalf of detained illegal alien Eduardo Samaniego, whom supporters hail as a "powerful immigrant rights leader who has built nationwide networks to support Dreamers, DACA, and comprehensive immigration reform."[51] Milano fretted that "Eduardo is in Irwin Detention Facility which has numerous human rights abuse cases against it. The Southern Poverty Law Center tried to do a wellness check on him & the facility refused to grant access."

Who is Eduardo Samaniego? He says he entered the U.S. from Mexico at age sixteen on a travel visa, overstayed illegally and lived with a pastor after his uncle was deported, enjoyed free public education through high school, and openly organized protests against a Georgia law banning illegal aliens from top public colleges and universities.[52] He defiantly described himself as "undocumented and unafraid" at marches and rallies for so-called DREAMers.[53] Samaniego's activism caught the attention of left-wing Hampshire College in Amherst, Massachusetts, which granted him a full, four-year scholarship. He enrolled while working as an illegal alien organizer for the progressive Pioneer Valley Workers Center, but had moved back to Georgia by the fall of 2018, when he was arrested after failing to pay a taxi cab driver. While in immigration custody, hundreds of campus demonstrators and open-borders Democratic officials in New England lobbied for his release. The law had finally caught up to Samaniego. Time was up, game over. But instead of giving thanks for the time he did have here and leaving graciously after breaking our rules, he and his supporters whined about "due process," complained about his mental health, and demanded that Immigration and Customs Enforcement be defunded ("MELTICE," they tweeted).[54]

Alyssa Milano's championing of Samaniego's case came four days after Corporal Singh's cold-blooded murder at the hands of an illegal alien and ten days after she had mocked an American veteran's efforts to raise citizen funding for a border wall. "Oh, yes, let's #GoFundTheWall," she snarked, "while not caring for our veterans. Cool. Cool. Cool."[55] The #GoFundTheWall campaign, which raised millions of dollars for border wall efforts, was founded by a triple amputee Air Force veteran. Milano had time and energy to disparage the veteran, Brian Kolfage, and thousands of American citizens who contributed to the wall-funding effort. She had time and energy to solicit donations for a defiant illegal alien freeloader whose singular focus was undermining our laws and upending our orderly immigration system.

In fact, Milano tweeted the open-borders hashtag #FamiliesBelong-Together a dozen times between June 3, 2018, and May 23, 2019. She used it in tweets promoting #AbolishIce, calling for the firing of DHS Secretary Kirstjen Nielsen, raising funds for DREAMers, and lashing out at President Trump for "wasting time at the border advocating for a wall no one wants."[56]

"Reminder," she lectured, "children are still separated from their families. That's the real crisis, and he created it. #FamiliesBelongTogether #NoWall"[57]

A comprehensive search of Milano's Twitter feed for any mention of the sacrifice of Corporal Singh and his permanently separated family turned up... nothing.[58]

Spotlight on George and Amal Clooney:
Locked Away on Lake Como

We're going to take a brief jaunt away from Fortress Hollywood to another walled sanctuary for the rich and famous. Imagine boarding a private jet at LAX that whisks us halfway across the world to the lush, eighteenth-century villas on Lake Como in Laglio, Italy, along the border with Switzerland. Deep green hills and crystal blue waters envelop the hamlets that host A-list stars like Madonna, Tom Cruise, Richard Branson, the Versace family, and the biggest kahunas on the block: George and Amal Clooney. Their Villa Oleandra is a thirty-bedroom waterfront summer retreat surrounded by stone walls, spiked wrought-iron fences, and high hedges.[59] The entrance is protected by a massive gate and surveillance cameras. The mayor imposed fines for loitering anywhere near the property and created "no-go zones" to protect the Clooneys (and elite guests, including Victoria and David Beckham and Prince Harry and Duchess Meghan) from prying eyes by land or lake.[60]

It's a welcome escape for the liberal actor and his human rights lawyer wife, who have both been outspoken in their hatred for President Trump and his efforts to improve America's security. In March 2016, Clooney attacked then-candidate Trump as a "xenophobic fascist."[61] The next month, Mrs. Clooney indignantly told the BBC that building walls doesn't represent "U.S. values."[62] (Hosting a $350,000-per-couple campaign fundraiser for Hillary Clinton, as the Clooneys did that spring in walled-off Beverly Hills, on the other hand, is thoroughly red-white-and-blue![63]) But if they thought verdant Villa Oleandra would shield them from "xenophobia," the Clooneys were in for a rude awakening. As hordes of illegal aliens from Africa, Asia, and the Middle East washed up on Italy's shores and took up residence in its parks, piazzas, and railway stations, Lake Como's own besieged residents raised Trumpian objections. Several spoke out in interviews with the *Daily Mail*:

- Tour guide Denise, 67, complained: "Immigration here in Italy is a problem, a big problem because of the huge numbers who are arriving all the time."
- Chauffeur Santi, 26, argued: "We simply don't have the resources to deal with all these new people. Italy has lots of problems of our own without having to try to deal with other people's problems."
- Restaurant owner Maria Grazia declared: "I don't want them here. Italy has enough problems without trying to solve the problems of the world. We [Italy] should not have to deal with these people on our own. Europe [the EU] does nothing to help us. Now they make us—me, my family and other Italian families—pay for them."
- Housewife Federica, 55, said: "A small number of immigrants is not a problem but now they are so many. You see them arriving at the San Giovanni station. They are not poor hungry refugees but they are big and strong. People

here in Como don't like them. There are simply too many
of them."

- Shop worker Simona, 27, put it bluntly: "We don't need
any more immigrants here. They are already all over the
town. I really hope the situation will not get any worse.
Already they sleep in the park. We don't want people all
over the streets."[64]

In 2017, Clooney's Lake Como neighbors elected center-right candidate Mario Landriscina their mayor. A former United Nations medical relief worker, he ran on a platform of cleaning up the city, closing
refugee "reception centers," and taking the idyllic town back from
migrants who refused to assimilate.[65] Landriscina was endorsed by
conservative Italian parliament member Giorgia Meloni, a staunch
opponent of the European Union, global migration pacts, and the
extension of birthright citizenship to foreigners. Open borders, she
told a *New York Times* reporter, "devastates the culture, devastates
tourism, devastates security, devastates everything," she said. "Nothing good comes of it. Not even for the immigrants."[66] In January
2019, Meloni gave an interview to a local Italian TV host in which
she called for a naval blockade along the coast of Libya. The problem
isn't how to stop immigrants from landing in Italy, she insisted, but
preventing them from leaving Libya in the first place.[67] She added
that even closing Italy's ports to migrants failed to address the real
problem: the NGOs (non-governmental organizations) that sponsor
immigrant-laden boats, which are funded by individuals "that work
to destroy nation states" and "import cheap labor useful for big
companies."[68] Meloni did not flinch from naming names, identifying "investor George Soros who wants to give us lessons and often
finances the NGOs."[69] She said the Italian government should confis-
cate the migrant boats and "let's see how many Soros is able to buy."
The studio audience roared its approval.[70]

So is it "xenophobic fascism"—or a rational embrace by Italians of the same principle of self-preservation driving Americans to support serious enforcement of our borders and immigration laws? George Clooney was curiously unavailable for comment.

Instead, as South and Central American caravans crashed our gates in the summer of 2018, the Clooneys announced a $100,000 donation to the Young Center for Immigrant Children's Rights to battle President Trump's immigration enforcement agenda. Like Mindy Kaling, the Clooneys invoked their newborn children, twins Ella and Alexander, as inspirations for their activism. "At some point in the future our children will ask us: 'Is it true, did our country really take babies from their parents and put them in detention centers?' And when we answer yes, they'll ask us what we did about it. What we said. Where we stood. We can't change this administration's policy but we can help defend the victims of it."[71] The Clooneys, of course, spared no compassion, outrage, or cash for the victims of illegal immigrant crime.

The Young Center is ostensibly a support group for unaccompanied minors who cross the border illegally. Child advocates and lawyers accompany them to deportation proceedings, "advocating for their best interests, and standing for the creation of a dedicated children's immigrant justice system that ensures the safety and well-being of every child."[72] But a closer look at the overarching agenda of the center and its sponsors reveals that it is yet another cog in the radical open-borders machine. The ideologues at the Young Center explicitly reject the basic distinction between lawful and unlawful immigration, complaining that "current rhetoric is increasingly anti-immigrant, calling children who come to our borders *illegal*."[73] The organization's FAQ section further explains that its goal since the 2016 election is to oppose enforcement reforms such as "enforcement actions against parents and family members who bring their children to the United States. Enforcement actions include deportation proceedings and even referral for criminal prosecution."[74] Punish parents for breaking the law and risking their children's lives? How monstrous!

The Young Center is housed at the University of Chicago Law School and is a project of the far-left Tides Center. Tides and its parent organization, the Tides Foundation, have subsidized some of the nation's most radical activist groups, including the Communist-friendly United for Peace and Justice, the jihadist-friendly National Lawyers Guild and the grievance-mongering, unindicted terror co-conspirators at the Council on American-Islamic Relations. George Soros has donated millions to the Tides network.[75] Tides' founder, Drummond Pike, bailed out Barack Obama's favorite community organizers at ACORN after the corrupted organization discovered that then-leader Wade Rathke's brother had embezzled $1 million from the group.[76] In fiscal year 2017, the Tides Center raked in total revenue of more than $150 million.[77]

In addition to the Young Center, Tides has funded high-profile illegal alien amnesty projects such as Define American, the propaganda machine run by illegal alien journalist/activist Jose Antonio Vargas. He's the openly defiant lawbreaker who proudly calls himself "the most privileged undocumented immigrant in the country."[78] The former *Washington Post* reporter came here from the Philippines as a child. As an adult he obtained a fake passport with a fake name, a fake green card, and a bogus Social Security number, and committed perjury repeatedly on federal I-9 employment eligibility forms.[79] In 2002, an immigration lawyer told him he needed to accept the consequences of his lawbreaking and return to the Philippines. He ignored the counsel and instead obtained an Oregon driver's license under false pretenses (using a friend's address), which was nearly all the ID he needed to travel by car, board trains and airplanes, work at prestigious newspapers, and even gain access to a state dinner at the White House—where crack Secret Service agents failed to spot his bogus Social Security number.

Vargas's Tides-funded nonprofit media and culture organization "uses the power of story to transcend politics and shift the conversation about immigrants, identity, and citizenship in a changing America."[80] By obliterating the distinction between legal and illegal immigration, Vargas and his employees work to turn America into a sanctuary nation where there are no punishments, only rewards, for jumping the line and repeatedly defying federal law. It's not just about lobbying Congress, where Vargas testified before the Senate Judiciary Committee.[81] It's about implanting pro–illegal immigration themes and messages that saturate pop culture. Define American "has consulted on more than 45 films and television projects, such as *Grey's Anatomy* and *Superstore*, spanning networks like ABC and NBC and streaming platforms such as Netflix and Hulu."[82] Vargas's most notorious propagandizing involved spreading a fake news photo in June 2018 of a little boy crying in a cage as he clutched the wires encasing him.[83] "This is what happens when a government believes people are 'illegal.' Kids in cages," Vargas exclaimed. The post was retweeted more than 24,000 times and liked by more than 36,000 people. Vargas admitted that he did not know the source of the photo, but laid blame on Trump's border policies anyway, while he tried to verify the image. Shoot first, ask questions later, as always: otherwise known as bass-ackwards "journalism."

Resistance celebrity Ron Perlman piled on with his own tweet of the photo: "Trump, Sessions, McConnell, Ryan, this is on YOU!"[84]

Except, well, it wasn't. A freelance journalist informed Vargas that, um, the "photo was taken by Leroy Pena as part of a protest with the Brown Berets"[85] and she helpfully provided a link to other "staged protest" photos taken by the militant, anti-white Chicago group exploiting children placed in chicken-wire pens to raise awareness.[86]

The Clooneys, meanwhile, are crusading for the redistribution of refugees through unfettered expansion of "open door" policies across Europe and into the U.S. Clooney has served as a United Nations "Messenger of Peace" since 2008 and met with German chancellor Angela Merkel in 2016 to encourage her ruinous absorption of an unprecedented two million asylum seekers from Africa and the Middle East into her welfare state.[87] He trashed America because "we are not doing enough" to take on the refugee burden, despite our country's generous admittance of ten thousand Syrian refugees in 2016. To prove his own bona fides, he and his wife invited one Yazidi refugee from Iraq to board in a home he owns in Kentucky[88] and dedicated an estimated $20 million from the proceeds of the sale of his tequila company to the Clooney Foundation's refugee resettlement efforts in the U.S.[89]

As long as the mass resettlement of those refugees doesn't take place in Fortress Hollywood, the Clooneys' compassion is unbounded. The family splits time between a secluded seventeenth-century English manor on the Thames, which features 360-degree CCTV cameras perched atop sixteen-foot poles, installed atop high stone walls around the entire perimeter of the sprawling property,[90] and a secluded mansion in the star-studded, gated Fryman Canyon neighborhood of Studio City, California. The views of the canyon, mountains, and city are spectacular. The hiking trails are endless. To protect the Clooneys' children amid reported threats from ISIS over Amal Clooney's legal work, the couple reportedly spend upwards of $1.5 million a year on twenty-four-hour bodyguards with Secret Service and CIA training.[91]

And there isn't a single refugee reception center or day labor camp in sight of their guarded residences.

Spotlight on Jimmy Fallon: RAICES to the Bottom

Poor Jimmy Fallon. His attempt to remain as above the political fray as possible during the 2016 election cost him ratings—and even more damaging in Fortress Hollywood, his liberal street cred. While other late-night "comedians" morphed into de facto MSNBC political talk show hosts incessantly gunning for Donald Trump, Fallon initially maintained the *Tonight Show* tradition of neutrality. In September 2016, Fallon hosted Trump for a ten-minute softball interview that ended with a famously playful tousling of the mogul's hair; as a fellow NBC star when Trump hosted *The Apprentice*, the two had participated in nearly a dozen comedy bits together.[92] The hair-pawing moment went viral, but not in the way Fallon expected. Allowing Trump to be humanized (and treated like every Democratic politician that sits for these lighthearted gabfests) led to countless public lashings of Fallon in the left-wing entertainment and national press for what the *New York Times* called his "fawning, forgiving tone."[93] A *Variety* TV critic railed at Fallon for giving his "seal of approval" to a "nationalist demagogue."[94] The *Guardian* concluded that his "genuflection toward Trump"[95] led to a ratings slump that saw Fallon lose his longtime demographic edge to the unhingedly partisan, anti-Trump Stephen Colbert.[96] For the past three years, Fallon has issued numerous mea culpas and self-flagellating regrets. In a podcast with the *Hollywood Reporter* in June 2018, Fallon asserted defensively that he "didn't do it to normalize" Trump, confessed that the backlash from his peers gave him depression, and told listeners he was "sorry if I made anyone mad." Pensive and touchy, Fallon confessed he would do it all differently if he had a chance.[97] The self-pitying was too much for President Trump to take; in his usual raw style, he took to Twitter to chastise Fallon for "whimpering" and poked, "Be a man Jimmy!"[98]

His manhood and liberal-hood in jeopardy once again, Fallon responded by announcing a donation to RAICES (Refugee and Immigrant Center for Education and Legal Services).[99] As you know from chapter 1, the radical nonprofit helps enable the illegal alien kiddie smuggling racket by supporting catch-and-release policies at the border.

AWOL on Obama's Kiddie Cages

In the summer of 2014, the Obama administration separated massive waves of Central American border trespassers into detention facilities across the Southwest and distributed them around the country in military bases. I reported in my syndicated newspaper column on the secretive unloading of illegal aliens shipped to Hanscom Air Force Base in Bedford, Massachusetts, in early June that summer. A tipster informed me of a second flight of illegal aliens that had landed at Boston's Logan Airport. Obama officials initially denied my reporting, then grudgingly acknowledged the truth a month later.[100] By that time, Obama had requested $4 billion to deal with "a flood of kids as well as 30,000 illegal immigrants who crossed the border in recent weeks."[101]

Several other military bases across the country had been converted into outposts for tens of thousands of illegal aliens from Central and South America, including San Antonio's Lackland Air Force Base; Port Hueneme Naval Base in Ventura County, California; and the Fort Sill Army post in Lawton, Oklahoma. Another source, working in the Border Patrol in south Texas, told me: "Our station, along with every other station, is flooded with women and small children. One lady yesterday had a baby as young as 8 months. And they're coming over with pink eye and scabies. So getting them medically cleared becomes a priority. They'll be here for almost a week, so we provide them with formula and diapers. We have a catering service contracted to feed them because it's too many for us to feed on our own. And of course they end up being released because every family housing facility is full. They're supposed to show up for immigration court at a later date, but they don't."[102]

As I further reported at the time, a makeshift detention center in Nogales, Arizona, was being used as the central clearing station for the illegal alien surge. The *Arizona Republic* snapped a series of photos of teenage boys covered with foil blankets, sleeping on floor mats in cages, at this very center. There were no hashtag rallies from celebrities and Democrats excoriating the Obama White House for separating families and locking up children. No entourages of stars headed down to the border to deliver water or livestream visits to the border facilities or military bases.

But four years later, with President Trump in office, former Obama speechwriter Jon Favreau disseminated the old photos from Nogales and falsely claimed that President *Trump* had caged the children that his own boss had put there: "Look at these pictures. This is happening right now, and the only debate that matters is how we force our government to get these kids back to their families as fast as humanly possible."[103] Instead of correcting his lie, Favreau deleted the tweet and spun furiously as he tried to explain why Obama's cages were noble and defensible, while Trump's detention policies were "cruel" and "inhumane."[104]

Actress Mia Farrow fell for the hoax, tweeting: "Children of immigrants are being held in cages like animals at @ICEgov detention centers. Tell ICE and your elected officials that this is horrifyingly unacceptable. In addition to tearing children from their mothers arms- ICE has LOST 1500 kids. #WhereAreTheChildren"[105]

Actress Rosanna Arquette was so upset that she seemed unable to punctuate her tweet: "How can we as human beings allow this. ? This cannot continue or we are not human. this is evil ... sick crime against Humanity ..we are responsible .. we must stop this now."[106]

Actress Reese Witherspoon woke up after ignoring the border crisis under Obama for four years and sounded the alarm: "Attn ALL U.S. Senators & U. S. Representatives: Please support the Keep Families Together Act. This atrocity must end. Please Support S. 3036."[107]

Entertainment mogul Oprah Winfrey mustered up belated outrage in a tweet to her forty-two million followers: "Babies torn from their parents. Can't stand it!"[108]

TV host Ellen DeGeneres exclaimed: "I don't care what your politics are, we can't be a country that separates children from their parents."[109]

Supermodel Gigi Hadid, actress Natalie Portman, and actress Gina Rodriguez tossed in caring tweets of their own. Supermodel Chrissy Teigen and singer John Legend tossed in a bit more, donating nearly $300,000 to the American Civil Liberties Union on President Trump's birthday in June 2018 to defend the "rights and humanity" of illegal alien families.[110] (Just for context, their combined net worth has been estimated by one website to be $71 million.)[111] Teigen's followers pitched in $1 million more to help pay for ACLU lawyers to defend non-citizens.[112] Actor Judd Apatow threw in $10,000. (One website estimated his net worth at $90 million.[113]) The virtue signaling train picked up steam with a "Families Belong Together" nationwide protest in late June 2018 announced on MSNBC by radical leftist and Abolish ICE instigator, Democratic congresswoman Pramila Jayapal of Washington. She made no pretense about the event's real agenda. It wasn't about kids. It was all about hard-line partisan politics: "The end game is really to say, 'This is about Trump.'"[114]

Families Belong Together is run by Jessica Morales Rocketto, a Democrat operative who worked for the Democratic National Committee, Hillary Clinton, and Barack Obama.[115] Pop star Selena Gomez offered her expert take on immigration policy, promoting the Families Belong Together demonstration on Twitter by arguing that "Families seeking safety in our country need protection, understanding and opportunity, not detention. This is a moral choice, not a political one."[116] A search of Gomez's Twitter feed for the entirety of 2014 found zero posts on the border or immigration.[117] Anti-Trump celebrities America Ferrera, Alicia Keys, and Lin-Manuel Miranda left their walled mansions and condos for a brief moment to speak at the D.C. Families Belong Together March. Ferrera had first unleashed her militant ethnicity-based advocacy in an open letter to Trump before the election, lashing out at him for being "bigoted" for telling hard truths about illegal alien crime imported from Mexico and Central America onto American soil.[118] With the self-unawareness that only Hollywood starlets can get away with, she railed at Trump's "racial politicking" while whipping up the outrage of the entire "Latino community" voting bloc against immigration enforcement.

Teigen and Legend headlined the L.A. event. Marketed as a mass gathering of "everyday people across the country," the anti-Trump protests were actually organized by the same old, moldy network of Soros-funded agitators, labor unions, amnesty lobbyists, and identity politics grievance-mongers, led by MoveOn, CAIR, the SPLC, SEIU, Define American, MALDEF, Voto Latino, and UnidosUS (a.k.a. the National Council of La Raza, a.k.a. "The Race").[119]

On Broadway, musical theater veterans Chita Rivera, Idina Menzel, and others staged a benefit concert to raise money for four open-borders groups: Al Otro Lado, the Texas Civil Rights Project, the ACLU Foundation of Texas, and the Florence Project.[120] Unironically, the special event to support non-citizens was called a "Concert for America."

An earnest-seeming young actress named Evan Rachel Wood did more than the usual preening and posturing. She drove her pickup truck down to McAllen, Texas, loaded up supplies, delivered shoes and toys to detention centers, and played with kids at the border—all captured on Twitter and Instagram, of course, with a publicity-friendly hashtag: #EvaninTX. She also claimed to have participated in a twenty-four-hour fast to honor the "work done by Cesar Chavez."[121] Of course, in Hollywood, a twenty-four-hour fast is just another work day in the world of rail-thin leading ladies and fitness fanatics. But more important, Cesar Chavez would certainly *not* be honored by Hollywood self-promoters protesting immigration enforcement. Chavez opposed illegal alien labor for driving down the earnings of citizen farm workers.

"It's frustrating to be a citizen of this country and see that your government, because of inaction of some bureaucrats, are not living up to the law," Chavez vented. "What the heck's going on? It's just, it's a complete breakdown of the law."[122]

When ranchers and other citizens at our border echo similar sentiments, they're racists and xenophobes. Rather than inform herself of Chavez's true beliefs, Wood gave media interviews and vowed to return to Texas. *People* magazine featured her in a splashy photo spread.[123] "I want to go back because there's so much more to be done and to learn and I could only be there for a weekend," she told comicbook.com in July 2018.[124] As of June 2019, Wood had not used the #EvanInTx hashtag since her weekend jaunt.

Several other made-for-Instagram contingents flew down to Tornillo, Texas, from Fortress Hollywood to hoist their virtue flags, including unemployed actress Lena Dunham, singer Sia, supermodel Amber Heard, and actresses Bella Thorne and Mira Sorvino. The sign-waving caravan was organized by Voto Latino, the Democrat-promoting lobbying vehicle funded by the Ford Foundation, Knight Foundation, and George Soros's ubiquitous Open Society Institute. Voto Latino pushes for illegal alien driver's licenses, illegal alien health care coverage, DREAM Act benefits, and tuition breaks for illegal aliens.[125] Another Hollywood caravan led by America Ferrera, Kerry Washington, Eva Longoria, and Wilmer Valderrama descended on a migrant shelter tour in the Mexican border city of Tijuana, across from San Diego, in March 2019.

"It is easy for me to look at these human beings and see myself," Ferrera, a child of Honduran immigrants, told reporters.[126]

Amazing, isn't it, that not a single one of these bleeding hearts has ever looked at ICE agents, Border Patrol officers, Angel Moms and Dads, or the children of victims of illegal alien crime and identified with their plight.

Lights, Cameras, Open-Borders Action!

Let's return to Tinseltown's most coveted red carpet—the paparazzi-lined pathway, guarded by blockades and armed police, that leads to the Academy Awards ceremony. In 2019, the gala was littered with open-borders demagogues inveighing against President Trump's efforts to secure the borders and improve vetting of short-term visa holders. With ostentatious paeans to "diversity" (the skin-deep kind only, of course), the Oscars paid affirmative action tribute to as many liberal non-white actors, producers, and films as possible. They returned the favor by embroidering their acceptance speeches with identity politics pabulum.

Rami Malek, who played Queen lead singer Freddie Mercury in *Bohemian Rhapsody*, used his Best Actor victory speech to babble about "struggling with his identity" and his "curly haired little mind" (huh?). He paid tribute to Mercury as a "gay man, an immigrant, who lived his life just unapologetically himself. And the fact that I'm celebrating him and this story is proof that we're longing for stories like this. I am the son of immigrants of Egypt. I'm a first-generation American and part of my story is being written right now."[127] What Malek's immigration identity has to do with Mercury's rock star legacy is beyond me. Such is the logic of Hollywood narcissism.

Spanish actor Javier Bardem, presenter of the foreign language award, seized the moment to share his own deep thoughts on walls. Not that anyone asked him. "There are no borders or walls that can restrain ingenuity and talent," he philosophized in Spanish. "In any region of any country of any continent, there are always great stories that move us, and tonight we celebrate the excellence and importance of the cultures and languages of different countries."[128] Bardem was cheered on by the anti-Trump press. "Javier Bardem trolled Trump," Business Insider exulted. VICE effused: "Javier Bardem sent Trump a low key f*ck you— ¡y en espanol!"[129]

Not everyone was impressed.

"I have a lot of talent but the wall around the Oscars prevented me from getting in," one viewer jeered, "along with the heavily armed guards and police."[130]

"Meanwhile everyone there lives in gated communities" with "fortresses around their homes," another Twitter user responded. "They are completely out of touch, the majority of Americans want our borders secure."[131]

My favorite? "Javier Bardem drops a political speech about borders during #Oscars, but there's one problem," astute Trump supporter and TV producer Giacomo Knox tweeted. "If the Aztecs and Mesoamericans had walls to protect themselves against the Spanish conquistadors (like Javier's ancestors), they wouldn't be speaking Spanish today."[132]

Intent on grabbing his own anti-Trump spotlight, celebrity chef José Andrés paid tribute to the foreign film award winner, Roma, by praising its championing of "the invisible people in our lives—immigrants and women—who move humanity forward."[133] The movie, by Oscar-winning Mexican director Alfonso Cuarón, celebrates a live-in housekeeper in Mexico City whose white, middle-class employer's family is falling apart. Based on childhood memories of his own nanny, to whom the film is dedicated, Cuarón said he made the film to "heal family wounds."[134] He told Variety he "never intended it to be a political film. I was doing a film about a specific character." But anti-Trump Hollywood was all too happy to hijack the story for its own political ends. Eva Longoria, a prodigious Hillary Clinton and Barack Obama fundraiser who donated more than $40,000 in 2018 alone to Democrats, gushed that the film's portrayal of the Mexican maid would "touch people's hearts to say we must support immigration reform."[135]

Too bad no Hollywood discussion will ensue about how Mexico itself has long treated "undesirable" foreigners who break its laws or threaten its security. Despite widely touted immigration "reforms" adopted in 2011, Mexico still puts Mexico first—as any country that is serious about protecting its sovereignty should and would. Article 33 of Mexico's Constitution establishes the right of the president to detain and deport "any foreigner" and prohibits foreigners from participating "in any way" in the political affairs of the country:

> Foreigners are those who do not possess the qualifications set forth in Article 30. They are entitled to the guarantees granted by Chapter I, Title I, of the present Constitution; but the Federal Executive shall have the exclusive power to compel any foreigner whose remaining he may deem inexpedient to abandon the national territory immediately and without the necessity of previous legal action. Foreigners may not in any way participate in the political affairs of the country.[136]

Article 32 of Mexico's Constitution unapologetically bans non-native-born residents from holding sensitive jobs and joining the country's military. Preference is given unabashedly to Mexicans over foreigners:

> Mexicans shall have priority over foreigners under equality of circumstances for all classes of concessions and for all employment, positions, or commissions of the Government in which the status of citizenship is not indispensable. In time of peace no foreigner can serve in the Army nor in the police or public security forces.
>
> In order to belong to the National Navy or the Air Force, and to discharge any office or commission, it is required to

be a Mexican by birth. This same status is indispensable for captains, pilots, masters, engineers, mechanics, and in general, for all personnel of the crew of any vessel or airship protected by the Mexican merchant flag or insignia. It is also necessary to be Mexican by birth to discharge the position of captain of the port and all services of pratique and airport commandant, as well as all functions of customs agent in the Republic.[137]

Until the vast caravans of 2018 and 2019 hit Mexican soil, the country fiercely maintained laws against illegal border crossings; "verification visits" to enforce visa conditions; requirements that foreigners produce proof of legal status on demand; and enforcement and cooperation between and among immigration officials and law enforcement authorities at all levels in Mexico. Native-born Mexicans are also empowered to make a citizen's arrest of illegal aliens and turn them in to authorities.

Mexico's National Catalog of Foreigners tracks all outside tourists and foreign nationals. A National Population Registry tracks and verifies the identity of every member of the population, who must carry a citizen's identity card. Visitors who do not possess proper documents and identification are subject to arrest at any time. And for those seeking permanent residency or naturalization, Mexico requires that they must not be economic burdens on society and must have clean criminal histories. Those seeking to obtain Mexican citizenship must show a birth certificate, provide a bank statement proving economic independence, pass an exam, and prove they can provide their own health care. Applicants are assessed based on a point system using factors such as level of education, employment experience, and scientific and technological knowledge. Property acquisition and ownership by foreigners is still severely restricted. Mexican corporations are banned from hiring illegal aliens.[138]

Mexican citizens have vigorously supported strict immigration enforcement on their side of the border. So when Tijuana became overrun by illegal alien caravan marchers in the fall of 2018, local citizens took to the streets holding signs that read "Mexico First," "No illegals," and "No to the invasion."[139] Disgusted protester Magdalena Baltazar told NPR: "Tijuana is a place that welcomes anyone, but you must have papers, you must identify yourself. We work hard here. We don't get handouts. The government shouldn't be giving things to migrants when plenty of Mexicans are in a difficult position."[140]

Now, that's what flipping the liberal script is all about. But Tinseltown won't be reflecting those diverse voices any time soon. The 2018 Oscars were as rife with pro-illegal alien propaganda as was 2019's Hollywood celebration of itself. Immigrant actors Kumail Nanjiani and Lupita Nyong'o hijacked the best production design award presentation to announce they stood in solidarity with "Dreamers." During his musical performance, rapper/poet Common interjected: "We stand up for the Dreamers. We stand up for the immigrants." And Mexican director Guillermo del Toro, who won an Oscar for *The Shape of Water*, prattled on about his vision for a borderless world: "I am an immigrant" like "many, many of you and in the last 25 years, I've been living in a country all of our own. Part of it is here, part of it is in Europe, part of it is everywhere. I think the greatest thing the industry does is erase the lines in the sand. We should continue doing that, when the world tells us to make it deeper."[141]

Try using that excuse with Mexican custom officials or Saudi Arabian airport officers or Japanese police. Good luck with that, pal!

Not to be left out, social justice warriors who write for the boob tube staked their claim on pro-illegal alien activism and open-borders story lines in preparation for the 2020 election cycle. Hollywood writers' rooms for TV shows including ABC's *Fresh Off the Boat*, Netflix's *One Day at a Time* and *Orange Is the New Black*, and NBC's *This Is Us* united to raise money for immigrant aid group RAICES. So did the co-executive producer of the kids' TV show, *Duck Tales,* who endorsed donations "to support legal services for separated families."[142] A total of eighty Hollywood writers' rooms participated; in total, the campaign raised a whopping $20 million.[143]

When they're not assisting illegal aliens, the denizens of Fortress Hollywood are normalizing them in comedies, dramas, and on prime-time's most-watched shows.

Hollywood's ICE-Bashing-Capades

A half-dozen shows in development by major studios in 2018 revolved around sympathetic portrayals of illegal aliens, including a reboot of the popular 1990s *Party of Five* drama about orphans—this time featuring a parentless family helmed by a young DACA recipient who must become the breadwinner for his brothers and sisters after their parents are deported to Mexico.[144] ABC signed on to *Sanctuary Family*, a comedy about a married couple that shields the family's illegal alien nanny and her relatives from law enforcement (what a hoot!).[145] Actress Gina Rodriguez of *Jane the Virgin* TV fame is overseeing two open-borders entertainment projects: *Have Mercy*, about an illegal alien doctor in Florida, and *Illegal*, about a teenage DREAMer.[146]

Jose Antonio Vargas's Soros-funded Define American outfit collaborated with powerhouse showrunner Shonda Rimes to weave a DREAMer sob story into ABC's hit show *Grey's Anatomy,* which garners an estimated eight million viewers per episode. The special propaganda episode, "Beautiful Dreamer," tells the back story of El Salvadoran Dr. Sam Bello, a medical intern who came to the U.S. as a one-year-old. When an ICE agent arrives at the hospital to interview her after she ran a red light, Bello's colleagues concoct various schemes to help her evade arrest and deportation. Meanwhile, the nefarious ICE agent is struck by a heart condition, leading him to confess on the operating table that he doesn't "know what we're doing anymore." The fantasy monologue has him bashing himself and his honorable profession:

> I don't like doing my job at all. I don't even like wearing the jacket. Some guys like wearing the jacket. I used to. I used to feel good about it. I believe in law and order. You know, I...

I grew up watching Westerns. I wanted to be the sheriff that rode in at the last minute and saved everyone. Now… I don't know what we're doing. Staking out schools, taking kids… doctors… I don't know what we're doing anymore.[147]

Thousands of ICE agents—of all colors and backgrounds—are proud to wear their uniforms as they perform their duties: tracking down deportation evaders, drug cartel thugs, human traffickers, child exploiters, and yes, lawbreakers of all kinds who violate the terms of their stay. But good luck getting representation of their diverse views on the airwaves. ICE-bashing has become a go-to plotline:

- On Fox, the drama *Star*, featured a brutal ICE agent beating a woman at a detention center.[148]
- After killing off Roseanne Barr and throwing her hit show under the bus, the season finale of ABC's spin-off *The Conners* whipped up hatred of ICE, with one character's baby daddy, Emilio, taken into custody after a restaurant raid. "This is ridiculous. These people are just trying to have a better life,"[149] liberal actress Sara Gilbert's character laments. No attempt was made to depict the perspective of ICE agents trying to preserve law-abiding citizens' way of life or the perspective of American workers displaced by cheap illegal alien labor.
- Foulmouthed "comedian" Samantha Bee, who called First Daughter Ivanka Trump a "c*nt" in response to the president's immigration enforcement initiatives, starred in a December 2018 holiday special on the Turner Broadcasting System called "Christmas on I.C.E." The show took direct aim at the twenty-thousand men and women in uniform who are responsible for interior enforcement and removal operations and homeland security investigations combating criminal organizations illegally exploiting our travel,

trade, financial, and immigration systems—including international smugglers of women and children, drugs, weapons, and cash. One skit depicted a Christmas Nativity set raided by ICE agent action figures; another featured Samantha Bee in a festive rink surrounded by "Abolish ICE" skaters.[150] She encouraged donations to actress Angelina Jolie's nonprofit group KIND (Kids in Need of Defense), which provides legal and social services to illegal alien families, strengthening the magnets drawing them here and endangering the lives of the children they claim to want to protect.[151]

- On CBS's *Murphy Brown*, two ICE agents on a routine workplace enforcement assignment are bullied by Trump-hating actress Candice Bergen, playing her old fictional journalist character. While illegal alien employees are cooking Thanksgiving dinner in a food truck, the federal officers show up in response to a complaint about the truck's owners. Turns out they have evaded deportation and have an outstanding order of removal, which as *Invasion* readers know, means that our court system bent over backwards to give them due process from which many citizens would never benefit. The illegal alien workers are repeat lawbreakers who have entered illegally, worked illegally, committed other civil violations, and ignored deportation orders. But outraged Bergen spits fire at the agents for doing their jobs and threatens them with violence: "You cannot barge in here like this. I know you're used to dealing with people who are scared and vulnerable, but if you don't get out of this truck, I will spatchcock you."[152]

"Spatchcock" dates back to eighteenth-century Ireland and refers to a brutal method of preparing poultry for cooking by removing the backbone from tail to neck, cracking open the breastbone, slicing off the wingtips, and laying out the butchered bird flat for quick roasting.

Of course, if conservatives used such language against politically correct targets—illegal border crossers or journalists, for example—we'd be accused of creating a climate of hate and inciting violence. Imagine if I wielded a spatula or carving knife and joked about my desire to spatchcock CNN twerp Jim Acosta or open borders propagandist Jorge Ramos. What happened to toning it down? What happened to "the children are watching" virtue signalers worried about harsh language? What happened to the civility brigade? Where's Michelle Obama to lecture us about going high and refraining from going low?

Jose Antonio Vargas was too busy exulting over the success of his propaganda efforts on TV. While thanking Shonda Rimes for incorporating his ICE-bashing, DREAMer-promoting storyline into *Grey's Anatomy*, he opined: "More than ever, we need STORIES to humanize people and liberate them from the limits of partisan politics."[153]

Irony detector malfunction alert!

Unsatisfied with the pace of Hollywall's open-borders makeover, Vargas issued "groundbreaking new research" in October 2018 conducted with the liberal Norman Lear Center "showcasing that immigrant characters are disproportionately tethered to crime and incarceration, with over one-third of immigrant characters being associated with crime." With the Hollywood writers' rooms dominated by left-wingers, who exactly is to blame for that? Not Fox News pundits! Vargas's study also found that "deportation and ICE-related storylines focused overwhelmingly on Latinx immigrants." Complain to your own mirror, Jose. The "study," another self-perpetuating piece of propaganda that will be used by Define American to secure more consulting gigs, then laid the groundwork for developing more open-borders storylines reflecting "diversity" of skin color.[154]

How about nuanced, sensitive portrayals of ICE agents and Border Patrol members who risk their lives to enforce our laws?

How about putting viewers in the shoes of law enforcement officials' families who wonder every night whether their loved ones will return home in one piece?

How about depicting the terror experienced by ICE families "doxxed" by WikiLeaks and the left-wing domestic terrorists of Antifa?[155]

Naaaaaah. In la-la-land, "humanizing people and liberating them from the limits of partisan politics" only ever works in one direction. Leftward.[156]

Until, that is, the privileged elites who live privately behind walls while publicly denouncing they need the vital protection that only ICE agents can provide.

Kendall Jenner's Alien Invader

The most talented screenwriters couldn't make this one up. In March 2019, ICE officials detained thirty-eight-year-old John Ford, a Canadian creep caught twice trying to sneak into model Kendall Jenner's $8.5-million Beverly Hills home. As I told you at the beginning of our journey into Hollywall, the celebrity community is gated and guarded. No wall is 100 percent foolproof, of course. The alien invader penetrated security by entering the estate's backyard, which was unfenced because it faces a mountainside.[157] Fortunately, Jenner's security guards spotted the culprit, who had trespassed several times before. "I was crying. I was screaming. I was freaking out. I didn't know what his intentions were. I was freaking out," the Kardashian sister testified at a court hearing.[158] Ford was sentenced to 180 days in jail; he served half the term before being released in early March 2019. A few weeks later, ICE agents acting on a tip picked up Ford in New Mexico and sent him to a Texas detention center where he awaited a deportation hearing for illegally overstaying his B-2 visa.

New Mexico, unlike California, is not a full-blown sanctuary state, so ICE agents could do their job without the normal open-borders heckling and obstruction that became the law of the land in the land of lawlessness under Democratic Governor Jerry Brown. The feds worked to stop a crime before it happened by simply enforcing visa rules. "This timely arrest could very well have prevented a violent crime," an ICE spokesperson said in the statement. "Our special agents acted quickly on this tip to ensure that this obsessive behavior didn't escalate to become a tragedy." When the gates, guards, and walls fail to protect Hollywood elites, they depend on the very men and women in uniform they routinely vilify in scripts, on studio sets, and on their Twitter feeds.

Just eight months before ICE preemptively detained her menacing stalker, Kendall Jenner was chiming in with all her ICE-bashing celebrity friends and condemning border enforcement. She urged her fans to donate to the ACLU, which vigorously opposes the very kind of local-federal law enforcement partnerships that helped put her stalker back in custody and on the deportation track.[159] Newly woke to the benefits of such cooperation, the relieved Kardashian-Jenner family told TMZ: "We are extremely appreciative of the hard work by the Los Angeles Police Dept. and ICE, whose swift response and professionalism led to this man's apprehension. His actions have not only had a severe impact on Kendall's life, but the entire family's sense of security, causing us to fear for Kendall's safety as well as our own. Knowing this individual is in custody gives us peace of mind."

Begrudge the bilious bigwigs of Beverly Hills? You're damned right I do. When you watch their TV shows, buy their movie tickets, and perpetuate their monolithic cult of celebrity, you give them license to strip us of our sovereignty, insult us while they barricade themselves in their gated enclaves, and brainwash our children to feel guilt and loathing for wanting the same standards of living and security that they enjoy.

Kendall Jenner got her happy ending. Lucky her. Corporal Singh's widow and fatherless child, by contrast, must endure an ongoing open-borders nightmare—a permanent family separation—that no one in Fortress Hollywood wants or dares to bring to the silver screen.

CHAPTER EIGHT

FACT CHECK: TRUE, THE LIBERAL MEDIA HATES AMERICA

While media pooh-bahs blame President Trump for the "death of civility in America,"[1] it is the truth-trampling pot-stirrers of the press who incite a climate of hate.

We've already encountered a quartet of the most prominent media propagandists in our deep dive of Open Borders Inc.: the obstreperously obnoxious Jim Acosta of CNN, former *Washington Post* reporter and illegal alien fraudster Jose Antonio Vargas, the spittle-flecked Geraldo Rivera, and the liars of *Time* magazine. Acosta embodies the disingenuous sanctimony of Emma Lazarus utopianists. Vargas represents the insatiable entitlement of amnesty mongers. Rivera personifies ethnic identity narcissism. *Time* epitomizes Trump-deranged Fake News.

But if I had to name just one America-sabotaging mouthpiece who symbolizes the foulest of the Fourth Estate, it would be Ana Navarro-Cárdenas.

Everything about this woman is phony, feckless, and treacherous. She is billed as a "Republican strategist," but voted for Hillary Clinton, cuddled up to Bill Clinton on a Florida golf course, and climbed up the pundit ladder bashing mainstream Republicans at every turn. It's the only winning strategy this made-for-TV "strategist" has ever had. The Nicaraguan-born loudmouth came to the U.S. with her family in 1980 and was amnestied under Ronald Reagan's 1986 mass pardon for law-breakers.[2] She fought alien deportations as a law student and worked for foreign special interests busting open our borders even wider. In 1997, she was literally a foreign agent: "a special advisor to the Government of Nicaragua and in that role, she was one of the primary advocates for NACARA (Nicaraguan Adjustment and Central American Relief Act)."[3] Under the law, Nicaraguans who had lived in the U.S. illegally since 1995, along with their spouses and unmarried children, were automatically granted permanent resident status (and the coveted path to American citizenship) as long as they applied by April 1, 2000.[4] Certain Cubans, El Salvadorans, Guatemalans, and Eastern Europeans who had entered illegally and/or faced deportation were also tossed into the amnesty. NumbersUSA projected that the number of NACARA beneficiaries over ten years would reach 966,000.[5]

Navarro-Cárdenas served on the Hispanic Advisory Council for amnesty traitor John McCain's failed 2008 presidential bid, and she secured a National Hispanic co-chair position for liberal Republican Jon Huntsman's 2012 flameout of a presidential bid. She served as a "confidante" of former Florida governor Jeb Bush (the nitwit who proclaimed that illegal immigration is an "act of love"[6]) and held a position as his state director of immigration policy "until it was discovered that she did not have a law license."[7] Then she "advised" Jeb's low-energy 2016 presidential campaign until it ran out of gas. Far-left outlets describe her as a "moderate." ¡Ay, Dios mío! She's a camera-hogging opportunist whose "willingness to criticize Republicans on same-sex marriage and immigration issues make her a favorite of TV bookers," as the Fishwrap of Record (that's the New York Times) gushed.[8] Rude and crude, she racked up paid gigs at CNN, CNN en Español, Telemundo, and ABC's The View (affectionately known in my household as The Spew).

You may remember one of her most infamous stunts: Pulling out a nail file and feigning boredom during an immigration debate on CNN's

Cuomo Prime Time show.[9] On January 9, 2019, host Chris Cuomo introduced the segment by accusing President Trump of "creating the fiction of a brown menace" and concocting the bloody consequences of open borders.[10] Exactly two weeks earlier, Corporal Singh had been killed by an illegal alien gangbanger. When Trump supporter Steve Cortes called attention to the victims of illegal alien crime, Navarro-Cárdenas sighed and rolled her eyes. She exploded when Cortes had the audacity to call her a "leftist." Ignoring Singh's sacrifice, she whined: "I'm so tired of you calling me leftist just because you want to compromise your values."

Playing the victim while disrespecting the real victims is par for the Open Borders Inc. course.

In 2014, Amnesty Ana's "Dem hubby" (her words)[11] was seventy-one-year-old liberal Gene Prescott.[12] He's the wealthy proprietor of the Biltmore Hotel, where she held court for years schmoozing with political and media elites to advance her career.[13] Five years later, she switched horses, tying the knot with establishment Republican bigwig and former Florida Republican Party chairman Al Cárdenas in a lavish wedding covered by *People*.[14] They're a Trump-bashing match made in open-borders hell—two illegal alien amnesty stooges and sharia surrenderists for the price of one!

Al Cárdenas is a Florida-based lawyer/lobbyist who shills for open-borders billionaire Michael Bloomberg's No Labels front group.[15] From 2011 to 2014, Cárdenas helmed the American Conservative Union, which runs the Conservative Political Action Conference (CPAC). But don't let the "conservative" part fool you into thinking that Cárdenas actually works for conservatives. Like his wife, Cárdenas has made a handsome career for himself undermining movement conservatives fighting for American sovereignty. In 2013, the Cuban immigrant admitted that the ACU had banned anti-jihad activist Pamela Geller from speaking after she had battled for years to sponsor independent, standing-room-only events[16] on the outskirts of CPAC related to the spread of jihad and mass Muslim immigration across the West.[17] Cárdenas told the *Washington Post* that she was blacklisted over "comments she made at CPAC critical of our officers."[18] At the same time, under Cárdenas's tenure, Robert Spencer—stalwart Islam scholar, founder of Jihad Watch, and author of nineteen books on jihad, Islam, and terrorism—was cautioned not to speak critically of CPAC officials at an acceptance ceremony for winning the conference's People's Choice blog award.[19] Also banned for several years beginning under Cárdenas's reign: Center for Security Policy founder and former Reagan official Frank Gaffney.[20]

Gaffney, Spencer, and Geller had all spoken critically of Grover Norquist, who was then on the ACU board of directors, and whose alliances with Muslim radicals I've spotlighted since 2003.[21] In the wake of 9/11, I and others helped expose Norquist's lobbying firm, which had served as a registered lobbying organization for American Muslim Council (AMC) founder and Council on American-Islamic Relations' northern Virginia director Abdurahman Alamoudi.[22] Alamoudi was convicted in 2004 on terror-funding conspiracy charges focused on Saudi-backed Islamic foundations and businesses based in Herndon, Virginia. Alamoudi provided seed money for Norquist's Islamic Institute, which shared office space with Norquist's Americans for Tax Reform group. The institute was run by Alamoudi deputy and former AMC government relations director Khaled Saffuri. Saffuri and Norquist worked closely with Bush senior adviser Karl Rove to give radical Muslim activists access to the White House. Chillingly, Alamoudi had been scheduled to meet at the Bush White House on 9/11, as the Clarion Project first reported,[23] and Alamoudi was invited to a White House prayer service just three days after the September 11 attacks.[24] Norquist and Rove worked tirelessly to pass a mass illegal alien amnesty under Bush; Norquist, Rove, and Cárdenas continue to advocate[25] for various forms of Big Business–supported pipelines for cheap labor—from the Gang of Eight bill to DREAMer legislation. In addition to spurning Geller and Spencer, Cárdenas and CPAC open-borders tools stacked immigration panels with pro-amnesty advocates 3-to-1 in 2014.[26] When Soros-funded People for the American Way whinged about a panel on multiculturalism featuring former *Forbes* senior editor and VDARE founder Peter Brimelow in 2012, a jelly-spined Cárdenas denied awareness of the prescient *Alien Nation* author's work and blubbered that his "staff" would "delve" into the "controversy"[27]—manufactured by left-wing character assassins allied with the Southern Poverty Law Center smear machine[28] and amplified by CBS News and other "mainstream" outlets.

Like his wife, Cárdenas saves his most toxic venom for immigration hawks and sovereignty defenders. Outraged that President Trump released a 2018 midterm ad attacking Democrats' sanctuary policies that featured convicted illegal alien cop-killer Luis Bracamontes, Cárdenas called the commander in chief a "despicable divider" with a "bigoted legacy" who represented the "worse [*sic*] social poison to afflict our country in decades."[29] Mrs. Cárdenas echoed her hubby on CNN, hissing that President Trump was a "racist pig"[30] for memorializing the dead American cops slain by Bracamontes, who laughed upon his conviction and bragged: "I wish I had killed more of the motherfuckers."[31]

The next time the mouthpieces of Open Borders Inc. heckle you about civility, compassion, and "who we are," remember Luis Bracamontes. Remember the smirks, snarls, sighs, and sneers directed at President Trump and the memory of Corporal Singh. And never forget who the Cardenas clan thinks is the despicable pig.

Triggered by a Hero's Tattoo[32]

Talia Lavin, a former "fact-checker" for the *New Yorker,* graduated with a degree in comparative literature from Harvard University in 2012, won a Fulbright Scholar fellowship to study in Ukraine, "worked in all realms" of the Jewish Telegraphic Agency news and wire service,[33] and contributed stories and translations for the HuffPost.[34] Lavin held the coveted position of "fact-checker" at the revered *New Yorker* for three years. The publication brags that its "fact-checking department is known for its high standards."[35] It demands the ability "to quickly analyze a manuscript for factual errors, logical flaws, and significant omissions."[36]

The editorial department requires "a strong understanding of ethical reporting standards and practices" and prefers "proficiency or fluency in a second language."[37] Lavin speaks four languages (Russian, Hebrew, Ukrainian, and English). But her abdication of ethical reporting standards in baselessly smearing an ICE agent raised fundamental questions not only about her competence, but also about her integrity—not to mention the *New Yorker*'s journalistic judgment.

With a single tweet, the *New Yorker*'s professional fact-checker smeared Justin Gaertner, a combat-wounded war veteran and computer forensic analyst for the U.S. Immigration and Customs Enforcement agency. Amid the national media hysteria over President Trump's border enforcement policies in June 2018, Lavin derided a photo of Gaertner shared by ICE, which had spotlighted his work rescuing abused children.[38] Scrutinizing his tattoos, she claimed an image on his left elbow was an Iron Cross—a symbol of valor commonly and erroneously linked to Nazis.[39] The meme spread like social media tuberculosis: *Look! The jackboots at ICE who cage children and families employ a real-life white supremacist!*

Only it wasn't an Iron Cross. It was a Maltese Cross, the symbol of double amputee Gaertner's platoon in Afghanistan, Titan 2. He lost both legs during an IED-clearing mission and earned the Navy and Marine Corps Achievement Medal with Combat Valor and the Purple Heart before joining ICE to combat online child exploitation. When actual military veterans, whom Lavin failed to consult before defaming Gaertner so glibly, pointed out that the image looked more like a Maltese Cross, Lavin sheepishly deleted her original tweet "so as not to spread misinformation."[40] Too damned late. As ICE noted in a statement responding to Lavin's smear, she had "essentially labeled" Gaertner a "Nazi."[41] The harm to Gaertner's name and honor was irreparable and could not be unseen, unread, or unpublished.

Lavin resigned[42] and the *New Yorker* issued an obligatory apology, acknowledging that "a staff member erroneously made a derogatory assumption about ICE agent Justin Gaertner's tattoo."[43] The magazine editors claimed "we in no way share the viewpoint expressed in this tweet," yet the abject ignorance of, and knee-jerk bigotry against, law enforcement, immigration enforcement, and the military underlying Lavin's tweet is rampant in New York media circles. Just days before her attack on Gaertner, Lavin had penned a screed for the New York City-based *Forward* magazine titled: "No, We Don't Have to Be Friends With Trump Supporters," replete with Nazi allusions and more hatred for ICE agents.[44] Rejecting calls for decency in public debate over these contentious matters, she spat: "tough nuts, sugar. When they go low, stomp them on the head."

She further raged:

> It is high time, when you find yourself next at a dinner party with someone who has gone Trump, to smash your glass to shards and leave. It is time to push yourself away from the table. It is time to cease to behave with subservient politesse towards those who embrace barbarity with unfettered glee.[45]

A month later, Lavin was hired as an "extremism researcher" for the Soros-backed Media Matters for America goon squad.[46] In January 2019, after she had locked down her social media account, she was back on Twitter publicly whining about being victimized by ICE. "[I]'m still processing" the incident "as a trauma," the smear merchant complained, citing "death threats," "antisemitic abuse," "reputational shredding," and "absolute wall to wall bad faith."[47] Boo-freaking-hoo. Playing the victim while savaging the real victims is, as we've seen, par for the Open Borders Inc. course. So is capitalizing on the attacks. In March 2019, Lavin was hired by New York University to teach a journalism class called "Reporting on the Far Right."[48] The perks of Abolish ICE media thuggery are boundless. Two months later, NYU canceled the course, citing a lack of interest among students and not because of anything to do with her irresponsible smear-mongering, writing, or tweets.[49]

In Bed with Antifa

As I mentioned in the introduction, online extremism researcher Eoin Lenihan was suspended from Twitter in May 2019 after exposing social media ties between Antifa members and left-wing journalists. Lenihan and his team pinpointed 962 verified Twitter accounts that had at least eight connections to known Antifa leaders. One of them had been a credentialed journalist at CPAC—the HuffPost's Christopher Mathias ("senior writer" who specializes in covering the "far right").[50] According to Lenihan, Mathias had falsely accused a man of being a "prominent white supremacist" and taken information from "an Antifa news outlet" to disclose private information about individuals serving in the military whom he accused of being European white nationalists, despite having "no idea of their innocence or guilt," according to Lenihan.[51]

Lenihan's report on the connections between left-wing journalists and Antifa menaces found that Mathias "harvests info from his Antifa network to cast serious allegations against individuals with potentially career shattering consequences and through doxxing, opens up the real chance of violence and serious harm against them."[52] Conservative journalists and activists have been banned for life from Twitter with no chance of appeal for far less than this, yet Mathias remains on Twitter with a verified blue check mark.

Another top Twitter media personality with strong online connections to Antifa is *The Guardian*'s Jason Wilson, who frequently cites Mark Bray (author of *Antifa: The Anti-Fascist Handbook*) as an authoritative source on why Antifa is not a threat to peaceful people. Lest you think Bray is a neutral and objective expert, Lenihan pointed out that Bray donated half of the profits from his book to the Antifa International Defence Fund.[53]

As of June 1, 2019, Lenihan remains kicked off Twitter. My requests for comment from Twitter's public relations department went unanswered.

The anti-conservative conspiracy is real.

Promoting Toxic Food Terrorism

While Antifa bullies hounded Trump administration officials and prominent conservatives at their homes and Beltway restaurants, keyboard social justice warriors posing as journalists did their best to whip up the tolerance mob from the comfort of their newspaper cubicles. Shirley Leung was appointed interim editorial page editor of the *Boston Globe* in August 2018 during the Open-Borders Summer of Rage. Her op-ed page colleague, Marjorie Pritchard, spearheaded a campaign by one hundred newspapers across the country to publish coordinated editorials decrying President Trump's "dirty war on the free press."[54] But the unhinged press doesn't need any outside forces undermining its credibility. The media's worst and dimmest are doing a fine job themselves. To demonstrate her idea of exemplary discourse, Leung approved publication of a putrid column on the *Globe*'s commentary page calling for waiters to poison the food of Trump officials. The original title of the piece: "Keep Kirstjen Nielsen Unemployed and Eating Grubhub over Her Kitchen Sink."[55]

Freelance author Luke O'Neil tweeted the piece out on April 10, 2019, with a link to the *Globe* and a delighted comment on his opening sentence: "'One of the biggest regrets of my life is not pissing in Bill Kristol's salmon.' lol this is one my favorite ledes I've ever written."[56]

The diatribe recounted how O'Neil served as a waiter to neoconservative (and Never Trumper) Kristol ten years ago in Cambridge, Massachusetts, and regretted, to his "eternal dismay," that "some combination of professionalism or pusillanimity prevented me from appropriately seasoning his food."[57] He then exulted in open-borders mobs stalking former Trump DHS secretary Nielsen, White House press secretary Sarah Sanders, senior adviser Stephen Miller, Florida attorney Pam Bondi, and Senate Majority Leader Mitch McConnell in restaurants and other public spaces. "It was the last time I remember being proud to be an American," he gloated. Praising further efforts by protesters to pressure corporations to deny jobs to former Trump administration officials, O'Neil suggested even more radical and unmistakable action:[58]

Invariably the bad guys, like the rest of us, will have to eat. And when they show up in our restaurants, you have my permission, as an official member of the mainstream media, to tell them where to go and what they can do with themselves when they arrive there, but, you know, said in a more specific and traditional Boston colloquialism.

As for the waiters out there, I'm not saying you should tamper with anyone's food, as that could get you into trouble. You might lose your serving job. But you'd be serving America. And you won't have any regrets years later.

Editorial page editor Shirley Leung initially had no regrets about the vicious call to poison the food of political opponents. The morning the op-ed was published, she tweeted out the headline, link, and O'Neil's Twitter handle. Nobody tricked her into promoting this call for domestic terrorism. Remember: the mainstream media prides itself on its "layers and layers" of fact-checkers and editors.[59] O'Neil didn't bypass all those layers and publish the piece directly himself like a personal blog post. Multiple editors read his article, prepared it, copyedited, formatted it, and uploaded it—and Leung willingly and deliberately highlighted it on her blue-checkmarked Twitter account followed by fifteen thousand people.[60] So did Rachel Slade,[61] interim editor of the "Ideas" section of the newspaper, as well as the blue-checkmarked Twitter account of the *Globe* newspaper itself.[62] Only after a widespread, bipartisan backlash across social media reached the attention of Leung's bosses—the owners of the *Boston Globe*—did she exhibit her own pusillanimity.

First, she changed "pissing" to "defiling" (as if this made advocacy of food poisoning more tolerable) without transparently acknowledging the edit. Defiling means "contaminating," of course, so the backtrackers made a second change caught by Boston talk radio legend Howie Carr: "One of the biggest regrets in my life was serving Bill Kristol salmon and not telling the neoconservative pundit and chief Iraq War cheerleader what I really thought about him."[63]

Then, Leung and her colleagues made a third attempt to blunder their way back to their bosses' good graces with an "editor's note" that informed readers that a "version of this column as originally published did not meet Globe standards and has been changed. The Globe regrets the previous tone of this piece."[64] On Boston's public radio station, WGBH, Leung (who is a contributor there) then explained how the piece was ultimately pulled after newspaper owners John and Linda Pizzuti Henry read the story amid the brewing controversy. "When the Henrys read the column, they felt that even after changing the column—and I ultimately agree with them on this—this is a kind of piece that should never been published on our website to begin with," Leung admitted. Another editorial note added that O'Neil's piece "did not receive sufficient editorial oversight and did not meet Globe standards. The Globe regrets its lack of vigilance on the matter. O'Neil is not on staff."[65]

Leung praised O'Neil's "provocative writing style," but condemned him for "crossing the line." What a self-serving careerist. Leung knew exactly what she was getting: a vicious provocateur who hates conservatives and Trump as much as she does. Long before Leung greenlighted his tribute to food terrorism, O'Neil had publicly advocated harming conservatives. In October 2013, he tweeted: "Punch a Republican in the fucking face. Go to jail for it. It's worth it."[66] In November 2016, he repeated the sentiment: "If someone is Trumpy to you, you can still punch them in the fucking face. That is the same amount of barely illegal as it was the other day."[67] Repeatedly endorsing political violence is the "provocative writing style" that attracted Leung to publish O'Neil's toxic column in the first place. She's not sorry she did it. She's only sorry she got called out.

In May 2019, Leung disclosed that she would be returning to the newsroom to write a column for the business section.[68]

Amazon-ian Generosity for Aliens

Amazon founder Jeff Bezos purchased the *Washington Post* for $250 million in 2013.[69] A month before Election Day in 2016, the tech mogul slammed GOP candidate Donald Trump for "eroding" American democracy because he had the audacity to criticize the hallowed Beltway press.[70] Barely a week after President Trump's inauguration, Bezos mouthed off against the White House executive order tightening travel restrictions on individuals coming from terror-sponsoring and terror-enabling nations. "This executive order is one we do not support," he wrote in an open letter to Amazon employees, which was, of course, headlined in Bezos's *Washington Post*.[71] "Our public policy team in D.C. has reached out to senior administration officials to make our opposition clear. We've also reached out to congressional leaders on both sides of the aisle to explore legislative options."

Not only that, Bezos disclosed, but he was taking his protest against Trump even further. "Our legal team has prepared a declaration of support for the Washington State Attorney General who will be filing suit against the order." Next came the obligatory paean to Emma Lazarusian utopia: "We're a nation of immigrants whose diverse backgrounds, ideas, and points of view have helped us build and invent as a nation for over 240 years," Bezos waxed rhapsodically. "No nation is better at harnessing the energies and talents of immigrants. It's a distinctive competitive advantage for our country—one we should not weaken."[72]

Unconcerned with putting young *American* college students at a competitive disadvantage, Bezos stepped up his Open Borders Inc. advocacy again in 2018 by donating an Amazon-ian $33 million contribution to create college scholarships for illegal alien DREAMers. He and his wife steered their massive contribution to TheDream.US, a nonprofit group founded by another pro-illegal alien media mogul—the former owner of the *Washington Post*, Don Graham.[73] Bezos says he plays no role in the editorial direction of the newspaper, but he "holds one-hour conference calls with executives every two weeks, and brings them into Seattle twice a year for longer meetings."[74] Leveraging his business empire, he pushed discounted *Washington Post* subscriptions on Amazon Prime users and had *Washington Post* apps installed on Amazon Fire tablets. Those products deliver a steady stream of pro-DREAMer content. A *Washington Post* website search for "protect DREAMers" yields nearly 1,800 hits.

Bash-the-Border-Patrol Bias

If you got your news exclusively from the *New York Times*, *Washington Post*, *Time* magazine, the *New Yorker*, and CNN, you'd likely oppose the wall, the Border Patrol, ICE, President Trump, and America, too. The elite media's "sovereignty kills" sermonizing is second only to the Russia collusion hoax in its corrosive effect on rational thought. Imagine restricting your diet to a daily binge of "Trump Cages Babies," "All DREAMers Are Saints," "All ICE Agents Are Racists," "All Border Patrol Officers Are Nazis," "No Muslim Refugee Does Harm," and "Pro-Immigration Enforcement Is Anti-Immigrant" narratives.

Let's look at the dog-whistle headlines of child deaths at the border during the caravan surges of 2018–2019.

- *The Washington Post*: "7-Year-Old Migrant Girl Taken into Border Patrol Custody Dies of Dehydration, Exhaustion"[75]
- The HuffPost: "7-Year-Old Migrant Girl Dies of Dehydration in Border Patrol Custody"[76]
- The Daily Beast: "8-Year-Old Child Dies in Border Patrol Custody on Christmas Day"[77]
- PBS: "Juan de León Gutiérrez, a 16-Year-Old Who Died on April 30, Was the Third Guatemalan Child To Die in U.S. Custody since December, Heightening Scrutiny of the U.S. Government's Ability to Care for Migrant Families and Children Crossing the Border."[78]

- Daily Kos: "A Two-Year-Old Boy Is Now the Fourth Guatemalan Child in the Past Six Months To Die after Being
Taken into Federal Immigration Custody. Border Network
for Human Rights: 'This Is an Appalling Pattern of Immorality and Inhumanity.'"[79]

Are we sensing a theme here? Children dead. Border Patrol to blame.
Custody equals danger. Ergo: end all detention, back to catch and release!
The unhinged responses to these headlines attacking Border Patrol agents
and Trump officials as "murderers,"[80] "fucking monsters,"[81] "Nazis"
and "war criminals"[82] are too numerous to mention. So are the reckless
misrepresentations of how the Border Patrol has handled sick children
they have encountered in treacherous conditions.

Let's look at one representative example: Border Patrol agents came
into contact with Jakelin Caal, the seven-year-old Guatemalan girl who
died in December 2018, at a remote forward operating base nearly one
hundred miles from the nearest Border Patrol station in the El Paso Sector. A total of 163 illegal aliens were taken into custody, interviewed,
and received initial medical screening. Jakelin's father, Nery Caal, signed
a form claiming his daughter's health was fine. Several hours after boarding a bus, the girl began vomiting. Her temperature spiked past 105
degrees; agents mobilized emergency care as quickly as possible. She was
transported by air ambulance to the nearest children's hospital, but died
of cardiac arrest and liver failure.[83]

An autopsy report released in March 2019 revealed that Jakelin had
died of streptococcal sepsis that had spread to her lungs, spleen, and
liver.[84] Her father had initially acknowledged the humane and immediate
treatment by the Border Patrol. According to Tekandi Paniagua, the
Guatemalan consul in Del Rio, Texas, the father told him he had "no
complaints about how they were treated."[85] But once in the U.S., he soon
changed his story and lawyered up, because no eye-on-the-cash-prize
lawyer would want him to face questions about exactly when he knew
his daughter was sick without expert legal counsel in place.[86]

Despite the ambiguities, complexities, and shared responsibilities of each of these tragedies, the open-borders media keeps stoking open season on Border Patrol agents through its biased framing of child deaths. NPR piled on in May 2019 with this immigration enforcement–bashing bait:

> JUST IN: A 2-Year-Old Migrant Child Died on Wednesday in El Paso, Texas. This Is the Fourth Guatemalan Minor To Die after Crossing the Border and Being Apprehended by the Border Patrol since December.[87]

To which I responded on Twitter with the appropriate narrative correction:

> Fixed it for you: "This Is the 4th Guatemalan Minor to Die after Being Dragged 1,200 Miles by Reckless Adults, Who Likely Paid Coyotes, Who Likely Paid Drug Cartels, To Cross the Border, Lured by Dem-Sponsored Amnesty Magnets, Cheap Labor-Hungry Employers & Sanctuary Enablers."[88]

The Fact-Chucking Fishwrap of Record

Linda Qiu, "fact-checker" for the *New York Times*, wants you to believe that Democrats do not support open borders. The Fishwrap of Record's designated arbiter of truth rated President Trump's claim that "Democrats want open borders" to be "false." She pointed to Democrats' past Kabuki-theater support of border security funding legislation as proof positive that they don't want unrestricted illegal immigration. "Mr. Trump is grossly exaggerating Democrats' positions when he conflates their opposition to his signature campaign promise and immigration priorities as "open borders," Qiu prattled. "And there is no evidence that they 'want anybody,' including MS-13, to enter the United States freely."[89]

No evidence? News flash, Ms. Qiu.

At a May Day 2018 parade in his district, former Democratic congressman and Democratic National Committee chairman (and now Minnesota attorney general) Keith Ellison, proudly sported a T-shirt emblazoned with "*Yo No Creo En Fronteras*"—Spanish for "I don't believe in borders."[90] Can the truth be spelled out any more clearly?

Democrat California Attorney General Xavier Becerra called for illegal immigration to be decriminalized, telling the HuffPost that southern border trespassers "are not criminals," "haven't committed a crime against someone," and "are not acting violently or in a way that's harmful to people." He made no distinction between gangbangers, traffickers, smugglers, and ordinary "migrants who cross without authorization."[91]

2020 Democratic presidential candidate and former San Antonio, Texas, mayor Julián Castro also proposes abolishing the federal statute[92] under 8 U.S. Code § 1325[93] that makes illegal entry into the country a crime—a de facto recipe for open borders.[94] Two of Castro's fellow liberal Texans—2020 Democratic presidential candidate Beto O'Rourke and Congresswoman Veronica Escobar—along with Arizona Democratic Congressman Raul Grijalva support similar decriminalization efforts on behalf of asylum claimants and border trespassers.

Minnesota Democrat Congresswoman Ilhan Omar railed that we "need to abolish ICE and end all inhumane deportation and detention programs. We need to fight back against the criminalization of immigrants and those crossing the border. We need to create a fair and accessible path to legal status and citizenship for all undocumented people in the United States."[95]

What part of "end all" deportation and detention programs and legalize "all undocumented people" does Ms. Fact-Checker not understand? The business of journalism has morphed into selective interpretation in defense of Democratic radicalism. Qiu's work is not about debunking falsehoods; it is about deflecting political broadsides against her ideological allies. The "fact" that some Democrats supported border security funding at some moment in time does not offset their systematic enabling of open borders and mass illegal immigration through sanctuary cities, free education, in-state college tuition discounts, driver's licenses, work permits, a dozen legislative amnesties, Obama-era administrative amnesties, and expansive legal rights.

It is worth noting that Mexican billionaire Carlos Slim, formerly the largest shareholder[96] in the *New York Times* who loaned the newspaper $250 million during the 2009 financial crisis, slammed our border fences as "absurd," demanded that the U.S. build more hospitals in his country, and dictated that our immigration policies show preference for all of his country's unskilled workers, "not just for highly qualified people."[97] Beware of all designated Fact Checkers of the Fourth Estate. Fact *Chuckers* is more like it.

Angels vs. Demons

Angel Moms and Dads are the brave parents of victims of illegal immigrant crime who keep the legacies of their lost loved ones alive by fighting for secure borders and immigration enforcement to prevent more needless suffering. If these families were advocates for gun control, or expanding the DREAM Act, or protesting Chick-fil-A, they'd be regular commentators on CNN every night and honored guests at the GRAMMYs, Oscars, and White House Correspondents' Dinner.

Instead, they are regularly mocked, smeared, or ignored.

After President Trump spotlighted Angel Moms on the campaign trail in 2016, left-wing wacknut "journalist" Mark MacKinnon of Canada's *Globe and Mail* attacked the parents as a "hate group" and an event they held in Phoenix as a "hate rally."[98] Liberal freelance journalist Rania Khalek also described the families as "like a hate group."[99] Never mind the fact that many are legal immigrants and naturalized citizens themselves.

During his State of the Union address in 2018, President Trump honored parents of murdered children who died at the hands of illegal alien criminals—including Evelyn Rodriguez and Freddy Cuevas (whose daughter Kayla Cuevas was slain by MS-13 gangbangers on Long Island)

and Elizabeth Alvarado and Robert Mickens (parents of Kayla's teenage friend Nisa Mickens, who was brutally murdered with her). Democrats in the audience initially had booed the mention of illegal alien crime. Reporters callously carped and pouted about the president's focus on a violent criminal organization that has murdered, raped, beheaded, kidnapped, robbed, and ruined the lives of innocent Americans and their families from coast to coast:

- CBC Radio's Tom Harrington: "MS-13 Getting More Mentions Than Infrastructure_#SOTU"[100]
- *Young Turks* host John Iadarola: "Multiple References to MS-13. No Mention of Climate Change. #SOTU[101]
- MSNBC's Joy Reid: "MS-13 (Which Most Americans Who Don't Mainline Fox News Likely Have Never Heard of) Has Been Mentioned Tonight More Than Russia. Actually, Has Russia Been Mentioned at All? #SOTU"[102]

Infrastructure, climate change, and Russia. Anything to avoid talking about the bloody consequences of open borders. Joy Reid poured more salt into the wounds of the grieving by adding on MSNBC that Trump gave "a speech tonight, in which he makes it sound like the biggest issue in the United States, the biggest threat is MS-13, a gang nobody that doesn't watch Fox News has ever heard of.[103] So he makes it sound like they're the biggest threat."[104] Tell that to the FBI, which labeled the safety threat of MS-13 "high" more than a decade ago with operations identified in at least forty-two states and thousands of members engaged "in a wide range of criminal activity, including drug distribution, murder, rape, prostitution, robbery, home invasions, immigration offenses, kidnapping, carjackings/auto thefts, and vandalism. Most of these crimes, you'll notice, have one thing in common—they are exceedingly violent."[105]

Ho hum. Just an insignificant little gang nobody has heard of outside Fox. Nothing to see here, move along.

Diminishing the illegal alien criminal threat is bad enough. Demeaning the parents of children sacrificed to open borders is incivility on steroids. The personal animus against the Angel Moms spread to the appropriately named St. Louis-based Contemptor, whose writer Gary Legum tweeted after a White House event in February 2019: "Oh for fuck's sake, is Trump using the Angel Moms as props for this announcement?"[106] Immigration reporter Tina Vasquez of Rewire.News cursed: "Ugh. The 'angel moms' are so fucking blatantly racist."[107] HuffPost contributor and PoliticsUSA.com writer Sarah Reese Jones attacked Republicans and Trump for "using 'angel moms' to (misleadingly) defend the need for a wall, while they ignore the parents who have lost children to gun violence."[108] To the HuffPost huffer, all parents who promote gun control do so of their own volition and free will, while all parents who advocate border control are being "used." Such are the "absolute moral authority" double standards of the media enemies of the people, who welcome the prerogative of liberal parents to participate in politics on behalf of their loved ones, but ostracize moms and dads who have lost their children to Democratic incompetence, corruption, and open-borders treachery.[109]

CNN's Jim Acosta belongs in an angels vs. demons category all his own. At a February 2019 White House event on the southern border emergency, Acosta accused President Trump of "manufacturing" the invasion crisis. Acosta referred to Angel Moms as "parents of victims who were allegedly killed by undocumented immigrants" and cynically accused the president of "trying to drum up some emotional energy on this occasion here, to try to sell this wall."[110] *Allegedly?* All of the Angel Parents who have spoken up for the president endured grueling trials, graphic descriptions of the execution of their children, and convictions of the illegal alien criminals who should have never been here in the first place. Unable to avoid interviewing one of the Angel Moms surrounding him with photos of their loved ones, Acosta grudgingly gave a few seconds of air time to Agnes Gibboney, mother of American Ronald Da Silva, slain in 2002 by an illegal alien gangbanger who had been previously deported.[111] Obliterating Acosta's tired and tireless narrative that only racists support a border wall, deportation, and strict immigration enforcement, the soft-spoken Hungarian-born Gibboney told him: "I'm a legal immigrant. This is my son. We need to secure our borders to protect American citizens. President Trump is completely correct on this issue. We need to protect this country."

Acosta glibly ended the interview to report on GOP squishes who disagreed with Trump that any emergency existed. Just a reminder: when it comes to illegal alien parents being separated from their children, Acosta's fury knows no limits. He infamously raged at White House press secretary Sarah Sanders in June 2018 with a grandstanding monologue demanding, "How is it a moral policy to take children away from their parents? Can you imagine the horror these children must be going through, when they come across the border and they're with their parents and then suddenly they're pulled away from their parents? Why is the government doing this?"[112] But not even a "sorry for your loss" from selective bleeding-heart Acosta to Angel Mom Agnes Gibboney, who was permanently and fatally separated from her son by a convicted illegal alien gangster scheduled to be released in 2020.[113]

As the trenchant William McGowan diagnosed in his book *Coloring the News*:[114]

> Two things appear to be driving immigration reporting. The first is a failure of confidence in America and its history—a "punitive liberalism," as James Piereson has called it, or "penitential narcissism" in Oriana Fallaci's phrase. The second driver is an intellectual and journalistic framework that romanticizes "the Other" and shrugs off the question of a Latinization or Islamization of American culture as if it were meaningless. Like other liberal institutions, the *Times* puts the "human rights" of illegal immigrants ahead of the collective right of ordinary American citizens to decide who should be allowed to immigrate and who should

not—thereby essentially voiding one of the most fundamental aspects of any country's sovereignty.

That is why not all separated families are equal to the Open Borders Inc. propagandists. From Corporal Singh's family, to the family of the police officers killed by maniac Lucas Bracamontes, to the parents of MS-13 murder victims Kayla Cuevas and Nisa Mickens, to Ronald Da Silva's family, Americans always come last.

CONCLUSION

BORDER DEFENDERS' ACTION PLAN

When you follow the money, you find the truth. The truth is we face overwhelming odds in the fight to reclaim our borders and our country. But we cannot despair. We must act by first using the power of our own purses to ensure that we are not subsidizing our own worst enemies. Defending the sovereignty of our collective home begins in our individual homes. For starters:

Not one more cent for churches, nonprofits, and international non-governmental organizations that conspire to aid and abet illegal immigration and indiscriminate refugee resettlement in our backyards.

Because of everything I have uncovered about the Vatican, its border-bashing bishops, and sprawling open-borders network, I can no longer trust that donations I make to the Catholic Church will be used in a lawful manner that protects our freedom and posterity. I refuse to put my hard-earned money in collection baskets whose contents will end up in the hands of Trump-deranged cultural Marxists in white collars. Use the information in this book to help you do your own due diligence with the religious institutions and charities that you have supported in the past. If you want to save your children, boycott Save the Children.

Cut off Catholic Charities. Give instead to patriotic nonprofit legal foundations, activists, and independent journalists who uphold our Constitution, laws, and borders (see my acknowledgments for the pro-America groups and individuals to whom I pay tribute). Exercise your checkbook as a check and balance against corrupted church and "humanitarian" leaders.

Not one more dime to Hollywood celebrities, producers, and studios that encourage violence against Border Patrol and ICE agents and contempt for our country.

Of all the reasons to boycott the entertainment industry, Tinseltown's treacherous assault on immigration enforcement looms as the largest threat to our safety and security. How can we sit in movie theaters, lining the pockets of celebrities who live behind high walls, while our fellow Americans on the border remain under siege—and hypocritical Hollywood stars incite hatred of our Border Patrol and ICE officials?

No more campaign contributions to politicians in either party who support deportation protection and deferral; work permits, driver's licenses, and tuition discounts for illegal aliens; immigration enforcement obstruction, or amnesty in any shape or form.

Grassroots conservatives, independents, and patriots of any political ideology must send a message to the cheap vote/cheap labor lobby in Washington: American lives matter and American jobs matter. If Beltway swamp creatures won't put their votes where their mouths are, stop putting your money in their grubby, duplicitous hands.

Two words: Stop Soros.

If Hungary can put an end to the Soros open-borders racketeers, why can't America? If Italy can block Soros-tied NGOs from enabling the migrant invasions in Europe, why not America? Taxpayers must demand full and vigorous prosecution of Title 8, U.S.C. § 1324(a) felony offenses involving alien smuggling and harboring, encouraging, inducing, conspiring, or aiding and abetting illegal immigration. Soros-sponsored nonprofits that collaborate with Silicon Valley companies to discriminate against sovereignty activists should be investigated by the IRS and state attorneys general. Patriotic citizens should support the legal defense funds of peaceful nationalists and anti-open borders groups suing to stop the de-platforming conspiracy and fight the censors.

Putting America First means a judiciary and legal profession that serves American interests, not the rest of the world.

Demand that Congress impeach open-borders judges who sneak illegal aliens out of their courtrooms, protect them from ICE arrests, and impede the president's plenary powers over immigration enforcement. Vote out district attorneys who side with the illegal alien bar association over Americans. Stop supporting law schools cranking out sovereignty saboteurs.

Putting America First means resisting coercive and secretive refugee resettlement without full transparency, reimbursement, and consent.

Federal law requires government-funded resettlement agencies to consult with local communities affected by refugee relocation. Informed and engaged citizens must form what Refugee Resettlement Watch founder Ann Corcoran called "pockets of resistance" to ensure that their neighborhoods, schools, hospitals, and streets are protected. Pressure your state officials to (literally) follow suit in Tennessee's footsteps and assert our Tenth Amendment rights to withhold tax dollars from any and all refugee resettlement schemes.

Putting America First means a financial sector that puts American interests and American customers ahead of immigration outlaws.

Petition the Trump White House to follow through on its threat to tax remittances. Billions of dollars, which create one of the most powerful economic magnets pulling foreign workers to migrate here legally or illegally, are at stake. Pressure the feds to prosecute banks that conspire to aid and abet illegal aliens, investigate the de-banking of sovereignty champions, and terminate the Federal Reserve's Directo a México program. Don't do business with businesses that bank on illegals and discriminate against Americans.

Putting America First means defeating the Abolish ICE/Antifa/ anarchist movement online, on the ground, and in the courts.

The A-Team of Open Borders Inc. constitutes a domestic terrorist threat. If you can't put your own body on the front lines against the sowers of chaos, support those who will. Hold Silicon Valley social media giants accountable for amplifying violence-promoting leftists: Expose them. Protest them. Sue them. Replace them. Keep them away from children.

Putting America First means purging American classrooms of SPLC-manufactured propaganda.

The SPLC's "Teaching Tolerance" curriculum undermines the rule of law, our civil order, and common culture. It is anti-assimilationist propaganda that has no place in government-funded schools.

Putting America First means countering radical community organizers with an independent army of nation organizers.

Establishment Democrats have prioritized illegal aliens and refugees over native-born veterans, homeless citizens, elderly citizens, and law-abiding families struggling to make ends meet. Establishment Republicans have failed to defund and destroy Sanctuary Nation despite repeated promises. This bipartisan abdication dishonors the memories of American citizens sacrificed in the name of "diversity" and safe spaces for immigration outlaws. Open Borders Inc. has spent four decades and tens of billions of dollars in public and private funds on the global migration machinery, starting with radical community organizers spread across the country working tirelessly to replace Sovereign America with Sanctuary America. Where are the nationalist organizers united in demanding that politicians once and for all cut off taxpayer funding from sanctuary cities, counties, and states whose non-cooperation policies risk American lives? Where is a nationalist movement of candidates, independent of both parties and their corporate donors, deeply and singularly focused on our country's self-determination and preservation? It's time for grassroots activists to start raising money and laying the foundation needed to build a new party, not just a new wall. Knowledge is power. Money is power. Use them.

If citizens sit back and wait for others to do the work that American politicians, CEOs, and other purported leaders won't do, we have no one to blame but ourselves for the demise of our country and the destruction of our children's future.

APPENDIX A

PUEBLO SIN FRONTERAS PRESS RELEASE AND DEMAND LETTER

Pueblo Sin Fronteras
March 23, 2018
FOR IMMEDIATE RELEASE
Tapachula, Mexico
To the governments of Central America, Mexico, and the United States of America,
To the media,
To human rights organizations,
To civil society,

We are a group of people from different nations, religions, genders, gender expressions, and sexual orientations migrating and seeking refuge. We seek to become one collective, supporting each other shoulder to shoulder and demonstrating that by uniting we can abolish borders.

We Central Americans have formed a caravan of many united in struggle. We leave Tapachula, Chiapas on March 25.

If all goes well we will be in Puebla, Mexico from April 5 to 9 to participate in legal preparation and workshops. From there we will hope for the blessing of solidarity from the Mexican people and human rights organizations, who we hope will join our struggle and assist us with the supplies and resources that they have available. We appreciate the support and collaboration of the people of Mexico and the United States. We hope to be an example of solidarity and struggle to the world.

We demand of our Central American countries:

- An end to political corruption
- An end to violence against women and the LGBTQIA community
- An end to failures of justice for victims of domestic violence, extortion, threats, and homophobia
- An end to corruption between gangs, the police, and governments
- An end to murder with impunity and gang recruitment of youth

We demand of Mexico and the United States:

- That they respect our rights as refugees and our right to dignified work to be able to support our families
- That they open the borders to us because we are as much citizens as the people of the countries where we are and/or travel
- That deportations, which destroy families, come to an end
- No more abuses against us as migrants
- Dignity and justice
- That the US government not end TPS for those who need it
- That the US government stop massive funding for the Mexican government to detain Central American migrants and refugees and to deport them
- That these governments respect our rights under international law, including the right to free expression

- That the conventions on refugee rights not be empty rhetoric

"The border is stained red!"
"Because there they kill the working class!"
"Why do they kill us? Why do they murder us. . ."
"If we are the hope of Latin America?"
Sincerely,
2018 Refugee Caravan "Migrantes en la Lucha"
Pueblo Sin Fronteras

APPENDIX B

SOROSWORLD: INTERNATIONAL ALPHABET SOUP OF NGOs

(B-1) Key global grantees of International Migration Initiative (IMI)[1]:

- Columbia Global Policy Initiative (CGPI)
- Central European University's School of Public Policy
- European Program on Integration and Migration (EPIM)
- Georgetown Law School—International Migrants Bill of Rights (IMBR) Initiative
- Global Coalition on Migration (GCM)—co-funded with MacArthur Foundation
- Migrant Forum in Asia (MFA)—Asia/Middle East corridor
- Alianza Americas—Central American/Mexico corridor
- International Catholic Migration Commission (ICMC)
- Platform for Cooperation on Undocumented Migrants (PICUM)
- Global Forum on Migration and Development (GFMD)
- The International Detention Coalition (IDC)

- Sin Fronteras—Mexico
- Tamkeen—Jordan
- The Migration Policy Institute (MPI)
- MPI-Central American Migration Study Group
- MPI-Europe
- MPI Transatlantic Council on Migration

(B-2) Migration and Development Civil Society Network partners:

- African Foundation for Development (AFFORD UK)
- Alianza Americas
- American Federation of Labor and Congress of Industrial Organizations (AFL-CIO)
- Amnesty International—Regional Office for the Americas
- Bangladesh Support Group (BASUG)
- Brot für die Welt
- Caritas Sénégal
- Caritas Sweden
- Cordaid
- Consortium for Refugees and Migrations in South Africa (CoRMSA)
- Education International
- Federación Zacatecana A. C.
- Forum des Organisations de Solidarité Internationale Issues des Migrations (FORIM)
- Himilo Relief and Development Association (HIRDA)
- International Detention Coalition (IDC)
- International Federation of Red Cross and Red Crescent Societies (IFRC)
- International Network on Migration and Development (INMD)
- Migrant Forum in Asia (MFA)

- Migration Working Group, Malaysia
- National Network for Immigrant and Refugee Rights (NNIRR)
- NGO Committee on Migration
- One Third Sweden
- Pan African Network in Defense of Migrants Rights (PANiDMR)
- Transnational Migrant Platform (TMP)
- Verband Entwicklungspolitik und humanitäre Hilfe (VENRO)
- WARBE Development Foundation
- AFFORD—African Foundation for Development
- Building and Woodworkers International (BWI)
- Caritas Internationalis
- Global Coalition on Migration (GCM)
- International Catholic Migration Commission (ICMC)
- Migrant Forum in Asia (MFA)
- NGO Committee on Migration
- Platform for International Cooperation on Undocumented Migrants (PICUM)
- Scalabrini International Migration Network (SIMN)
- International Council of Voluntary Agencies (ICVA)

(B-3) European refugee travel agents and public relations propagandists:

- *Watch the Med/PRO ASYL.* This Germany-based outfit describes itself as an "online mapping platform to monitor the deaths and violations of migrants' rights at the maritime borders of the EU." But "Watch the Med" does far more than passively watch and map Mediterranean migrant activity from the sidelines. It operates "Alarm-Phone," a special hotline for "boat people in distress" (you'd be amazed at how many poor, oppressed asylum seekers can afford cell phones while destitute on the high waters). Watch the Med also protests enforcement of maritime borders, decries "pushbacks" by governments refusing to consider asylum claims of obvious economic migrants on smuggling ships, assists in legal cases to sue countries defending their sovereignty; and "[pressures]" authorities "into respecting their obligations at sea."[2] Watch the Med lists "PRO ASYL" as one of its three main supporters/sponsors. PRO ASYL, a partner of the OSF-led donor collaborative known as the European Programme for Integration and Migration (EPIM),[3] is Germany's "largest pro immigration advocacy organization."[4] PRO ASYL was founded in 1986 "to counteract the rightwing, racist incitement to ill feeling against asylum seekers and to campaign for the protection of victims of persecution."[5] Pretty much any restrictions or requirements mandating that foreigners abide by Germany's laws counts as "rightwing, racist incitement," of course.

- *W2Eu/PRO ASYL.* "W2Eu" stands for Welcome to Europe. Its website—a clearinghouse for borderless tourism—crusades for "freedom of movement" and "provides information to refugees and migrants that might be useful on their journey to and through Europe." These open-borders travel agents, who partner with Watch the Med and Soros-sponsored PRO ASYL, provide access to detailed step-by-step guides on navigating asylum, detention, deportation, the social welfare bureaucracy, health care, and employment.[6] They also advertise the Alarm-Phone in seven languages. A Sky News reporter discovered a bound, printed copy of the W2Eu/Watch the Med guide written in Arabic that washed up on a beach on the Greek island of Lesbos.[7] "It's a life-saving service we give to refugees," a Watch The Med volunteer explained to the reporter who asked about the W2Eu booklet. "They are going to go anyway, so it's better if we give them advice."[8]

- **Panos Europe Institute/ United Nations Alliance of Civilizations (UNAOC).** As you can see, obliterating the difference between "illegal" and "legal" immigration is not just a key agenda item for the open-borders lobby in America. It's job number one for liberal activists and media editors in chief across Europe. Panos Europe Institute is a political correctness enforcer committed to "social justice" through dissemination of "unbiased information."[9] The United Nations Alliance of Civilizations (UNAOC) is a political initiative co-sponsored by the governments of Spain and Turkey that aims to "reduce cross-cultural tensions and to build bridges between communities, with a focus on education, youth, migration, and media."[10] What better way to "reduce tensions" between citizens and foreign lawbreakers than to convince reporters to stop describing illegal behavior as illegal? After meeting with European journalists in Paris in 1993, Panos Europe and UNAOC collaborated on a "Media Friendly Glossary on Migration" funded through Open Society's European "Fund to Counter Xenophobia." (In its other main projects, the so-called "Xen Fund" manufactures claims of racism by European police against minorities[11] and pushes "diversity migration."[12]) Accordingly, the migration glossary redefines accuracy and neutrality as "xenophobia" and "unacceptable." The guide explains that public opinion in favor of immigration control is a problem because focusing on behavior that paints migration in a "negative light" leads to increasing support for "restrictions on asylum claims" and "access to basic services."[13] The glossary advises journalists to always use the word "child" instead of the perfectly accurate and legal term "minor" and to substitute the obfuscating terms "irregular" and "undocumented" for illegal. "The term 'illegal migrant' should never be used," the language cops assert, and "it is never appropriate to refer to asylum-seekers or refugees as 'illegal migrants.'"[14] (As I reported in 2013, the Associated Press banned the term "illegal immigrant"[15] and ordered reporters to only use the term "illegal" to "refer to an action, not a person"[16] and to only use the terms "illegal alien, an illegal, and illegals" in direct quotations. Never mind that "illegal alien" is the accurate phrase used in federal immigration law to describe anyone who is in the U.S. unlawfully.)[17] The Soros glossary gods have ordained that "irregular" is "preferable to 'illegal'" because the latter "is seen as denying migrants' humanity[18]—which is apparently a worse crime than denying reality. The Panos Europe/ UNAOC glossary was adapted for the Middle East; a #SpreadNoHate initiative soon followed to combat "hate speech against migrants and refugees in the media" with Facebook and Google in attendance.[19]

• *International Metropolis Project.* The Canadian government's citizenship and immigration bureaucracy created the Metropolis Project in 1996 to provide research on "international migration and integration." The participating agencies added "diversity" to their mission and expanded internationally into a global network of sixty-eight partner organizations in twenty-three countries. Open Society-funded entities MPI and IOM are partners, along with the European Commission, UNESCO, the International Center for Migration Policy Development, and a Canadian-based outfit (also supported by the Open Society Foundations[20]) called Cities of Migration that promotes radical sanctuary city policies[21] and "inclusivity" ratings to measure whether your neighborhood is politically correct enough when it comes to welcoming illegal aliens.[22] The co-founder of the Metropolis Project, Demetrios G. Papademetriou, is an MPI co-founder, former president, and fellow; chair of the World Economic Forum's Global Agenda Council on Migration (2009–2011); and founding chair of the advisory board of the Open Society Foundations' International Migration Initiative (2010–2015).[23]

- *International Rescue Committee (IRC)*. Former British secretary David Miliband, head of the IRC, penned a book whose "message is simple: rescue refugees and we rescue ourselves." He's certainly speaking for *himself*. After suffering political humiliation and defeat at the hands of his own brother for the Labour Party's top leadership slot, Miliband was powerless and jobless. He resigned from parliament in 2013 and moved to New York City's Upper West Side, where he collects a rather generous $840 million annual salary and oversees the top American refugee-centered NGO. The committee raked in more than $727 million in revenue at the end of fiscal year 2017; $415 million (57 percent) came from government grants.[24] Open Society Foundations contributed $500,000+ to IRC in 2017.[25] It's a mutual admiration society. IRC awarded Soros its top humanitarian award in 2013;[26] in turn, Soros picked IRC to "create principles" that will guide his new $500 million investment initiative in migrant and refugee initiatives.[27] IRC has plenty of experience dispensing cash to like-minded open-borders nonprofits. In 2017, it handed out more than $16.8 million to refugee resettlement operations in the U.S., including hundreds of thousands of dollars to Catholic Charities chapters across the country.[28] The money reportedly assisted more than 31,000 refugees, asylees, and immigrants of unknown legal status already here, plus facilitated the resettlement of more than 10,600 other new aliens here. Abroad, the charity reports that it helped nearly 23 million people "access primary health care" and "provided cash and asset transfers to 179,491 households of refugees and vulnerable people."[29] Milliband's tenure, however, has been stained by allegations of corruption and abuse. In 2016, USAID's inspector general found that several Turkey-based companies had "violated federal or state antitrust statutes by having colluded with each other in order to win an award to provide supplies to displaced persons under IRC's Syrian aid program and another NGO. IRC fired two staffers who had accepted money from vendors in exchange for steering contracts to them.[30] In a separate scandal reported by the British press in 2018, leaked government documents revealed that IRC had an estimated $7 million in public funding frozen by U.K. authorities in 2016 "based on direct reporting of sexual harassment and fraud" in the Congo.[31] The IRC confirmed three cases of sexual abuse under its watch and closed off several other fraud related cases without further comment.[32] Not only did it receive its U.K. funds back, but the cash flow from U.S. taxpayers remains unabated without any independent investigation of how the organization is managing our money. According to the Capital Research Center, the IRC has received $846.6 million from the federal government for refugee resettlement since 2008 and a total of $1.5 billion from the feds over the same period.[33] For Miliband, the IRC, and the other refugee resettlement agencies, "charity" doesn't begin at home. It begins and ends in your bank account and mine.

APPENDIX C

SOROS'S ALIEN BAR ASSOCIATION

- American Immigration Lawyers Association (AILA)/American Immigration Council (AIC). As I first reported in *Invasion* in 2002, AILA—or as I call them, the Alien Bar Association—has obstructed tighter borders and immigration enforcement every step of the way over the past half-century.[1] The merchandise section of the organization's website once sold a $10 poster with the slogan, "No human being is illegal," along with a slew of guides and brochures on evading and undermining our immigration rules and regulations.[2] After the 9/11 terrorist attacks, AILA balked at the federal government's plans to track foreign student visa holders, deport visa overstayers, and locate hundreds of thousands of deportation absconders. AILA's public policy arm is the AIC,[3] which files lawsuits challenging immigration enforcement, disseminates pro-amnesty propaganda, lobbies Congress for amnesty, and operates a J-1 Exchange Visitor visa consulting and referral service for businesses. AIC's research arm is the Immigration Policy

Center. In 2015, Soros's Foundation to Promote Open Society donated $150,000 to AIC to support its immigration litigation activities.[4] According to its 2017 financial statement, AIC reported $6.1 million in total assets.[5] AILA and AIC formed a new campaign in the Trump era, the Immigration Justice Campaign, to "vigorously defend immigrants facing removal."[6] AIC's cases include suing the Trump administration "seeking monetary damages on behalf of six asylum-seeking mothers and their children for the trauma they suffered when torn apart under the Trump Administration's family separation policy"; suing on behalf of Temporary Protected Status aliens seeking legal permanent residence instead of returning home as their status requires; challenging the Trump national security travel ban; and combating extreme vetting of alien benefits applications. AIC joined the Soros-supported Southern Poverty Law Center (see chapter ten) and Soros-supported Center for Constitutional Rights (CCR) in a class action lawsuit on behalf of economic migrants turned away at the southern border by Border Patrol officers exercising their discretion to prevent asylum fraud and protect our sovereignty.[7] CCR received $530,000 in 2016 to support its "Human Rights Movements and Institutions" program.[8] It is the same outfit of jihadi-sympathizing lawyers who helped spring suspected Benghazi terror plotter Abu Sufian bin Qumu from Guantanamo Bay in 2010.[9]

- **CARA Family Detention Pro Bono Project a.k.a. Dilley Pro Bono Project.** A partner of the Immigration Justice Campaign, CARA (Catholic Legal Immigration Network, the American Immigration Council, the Refugee and Immigrant Center for Education and Legal Services, and the American Immigration Lawyers Association) is now known as the Dilley Pro Bono Project serving border-trespassing mothers and children at the South Texas Family Residential

Center in Dilley, Texas. Mexican-American immigration lawyer and past AILA president Victor Nieblas Pradis, a leader of the Dilley project, makes the agenda of the campaign clear: "There is simply no humane way to detain families. Asylum seeking families should be given due process, not expedited removal. And the end of the road must be the end of family detention entirely." The goal, in other words, is not merely "catch and release, "but unfettered migration, decriminalization of the border, and abolition of "family" detention (translation: any group of people claiming to be a "family") entirely.

- **Immigration Advocates Network.** AIC is a member of the Immigration Advocates Network (IAN), whose members harness the "power of technology and collaboration to support immigrants and their allies."[10] One project funded by Open Society Foundations and the Grove Foundation allows illegal aliens to "Make a Plan" for potential detention or deportation online[11] on a website dedicated to defending illegal aliens' rights and putting them on the path to citizenship.[12]
- The **ACLU** is a repeat Open Society grantee, notably receiving $75,000 to represent Muslims detained or deported after 9/11[13] and a gargantuan $50 million to end mass incarceration.[14] The group's Idaho chapter won $100,000 in 2017 to "conduct outreach, strengthen protections, and empower immigrant, refugee, Muslim, and indigenous communities in Idaho who are feeling threatened in a culture of rising hate."[15]
- The **Catholic Legal Immigration Network** received $150,000 in 2016.[16]
- The **Immigrant Legal Resource Center** received $80,000 from OSF in 2016 "to promote promising practices that successfully reach, provide legal screenings for, and assist immigrants with applications for immigration relief."[17]

- The **National Immigration Law Center (NILC)** received $200,000 from OSF in 2009,[18] another $630,000 in 2012,[19] $500,000 in 2016 for the legal defense of President Obama's executive amnesty orders, $450,000 more specifically for DACA, and $625,000 for "general support."[20] By Capital Research Center senior vice president Matthew Vadum's calculations, the NILC has received a total of at least $4.6 million from Soros-related non-profits, and the ACLU and its affiliates have received at least $35.5 million. One other co-litigant in the ACLU's lawsuit against President Trump's travel restrictions order is also a Soros grantee: the **International Refugee Assistance Project** (formerly Iraqi Refugee Assistance Project) at the Urban Justice Center ($621,000 from Open Society). The executive director of IRAP is also on the advisory board of the OSF's IMI (see above).[21]
- **ProBono.Net** snagged $240,000 in 2016 "to support and build technology capacity in the immigration field."[22]
- **Unidos US** (a.k.a. **National Council of La Raza**) received $400,000 in 2016.[23]
- Another entity outside the Immigration Advocates Network, the **Lawyers Committee for Civil Rights Under Law**, has filed its own raft of lawsuits and amicus briefs against President Trump's immigration enforcement and screening measures, repeal of DACA, and termination of a temporary amnesty program called Deferred Enforced Departure for 4,000 Liberian immigrants fighting to stay here permanently in defiance of the program's intentions.[24] The Lawyers' Committee reported total revenue of more than $9.5 million in 2017.[25] In 2016–2017, the nonprofit received seven grants from the Open Society Foundations totaling $3.3 million.[26]

AMERICAN SJWs, SHARIA ENFORCERS, AND SPEECH POLICE

- Center for Community Change
- Color of Change
- Genders & Sexualities Alliance Network (GSA Network)
- Hollaback!
- Lawyers' Committee for Civil Rights Under Law
- Leadership Conference Education Fund
- Muslim Advocates
- National Council of La Raza
- National Network for Arab American Communities (NNAAC)
- New York City Anti-Violence Project
- Transgender Law Center
- Arab American Institute
- Asian Americans Advancing Justice-Atlanta
- Bend the Arc Jewish Action
- Center for Human Technology
- Center for Media Justice
- Community Responders Network

- CreaTV San Jose
- CREDO
- Emgage
- Equality Labs
- Freedom From Facebook
- HOPE not Hate
- Interfaith Center on Corporate Responsibility,
- Muslim Community Network (MCN)
- Media Matters for America
- Million Hoodies Movement for Justice
- MomsRising
- MoveOn
- MPower Change
- Muslim Youth Collective
- NAACP
- National LGBTQ Task Force
- National Network for Arab American Communities
- The Campaign to TAKE ON HATE
- South Asian Americans Leading Together (SAALT)
- Southern Poverty Law Center
- The Sikh Coalition
- UltraViolet
- United We Dream
- Urbana-Champaign Independent Media Center
- Voting Rights Forward
- Women's Alliance for Theology, Ethics, and Ritual (WATER)

APPENDIX E

CORPORATE HANDMAIDENS[1]

Barack Obama announced on September 20, 2016, in conjunction with George Soros's same-day announcement of $500 million in refugee-related investments, that the following private companies had pledged their fealty to the U.N./NGO resettlement agenda:

- 180LA pledges to provide its advertising, digital, social media, and design services to raise awareness of the refugee crisis and welcome resettled refugees.
- Accenture commits to providing over $3 million in financial support and in-kind strategic consulting, program management, and digital services to support the Partnership for Refugees and Upwardly Global. Regarding Upwardly Global, Accenture is expanding its refugee workforce programs in the United States and globally as aligned to its global Skills to Succeed program. Accenture is also collaborating with UNHCR to launch a connectivity strategy for refugees and with USA for UNHCR through the Accenture Innovation Challenge to increase

its impact on refugees while raising awareness among graduate students nationally.

- Airbnb commits to developing a program that enables existing Airbnb hosts temporarily to accommodate refugee families when long-term housing is not immediately available, expand its initiative to host relief workers through the travel credits program, develop a job creation strategy for Syrian refugees in Jordan through a livelihoods pilot program, and create a social media campaign to allow its hosts and guests to raise funds for the UNHCR.

- Alight Fund pledges to raise $100 million in micro-loan capital to invest in 50,000 refugee and host community small-business entrepreneurs. The pilot program will be launched in Iraqi Kurdistan.

- Autodesk pledges to make an estimated $2 million software donation to UNHCR, offering 141 subscription licenses of Autodesk Infrastructure Design Suite Ultimate and 141 subscription licenses of Autodesk InfraWorks to support UNHCR's physical settlement planning and design capacity, and also to recommend a financial grant of $50,000 to support the adoption of technical solutions to help refugees in conjunction with Microdesk.

- BanQu, Inc. commits to creating mobile phone-based block chain economic profiles through its Economic Identity Platform for approximately 1.5–2.0 million refugees by the end of 2017.

- Bloom Five commits to providing 10 hours per month of professional development services—including technical assistance and workshops on resume and cover letter writing, written and oral presentations, seminars, mock interviews, and employment-related networking—to resettled refugees in the United States.

- BRCK commits to providing digital access and developing digital educational content and resources for children, youth, and women in refugee camps.
- Citigroup pledges to collaborate with its public and private sector clients as well as with its strategic partners to focus on sustainable solutions that are responsive to the needs of refugees. These solutions include youth education and employability initiatives, as well as collaboration with sovereigns and the international development community to unlock funding to address the needs of displaced persons. Citi will continue to optimize its relationships with the supranational agencies and NGOs that operate in conflict and refugee zones.
- Chobani pledges to continue its ongoing commitment to welcoming into the company people from all over the world, including those in its local communities who are resettled refugees. It will look for ways to support the broader business community by sharing its experiences and learnings, and work with the Partnership for Refugees to help ensure this insight is incorporated into research and materials to improve cross-sector knowledge.
- Coursera pledges to launch and support Coursera for Refugees in conjunction with the Department of State. Coursera for Refugees enables an unlimited number of non-profits that work with refugees to apply for at least one year of group financial aid. Partner non-profit organizations will be able to support refugees quickly, build career skills, and gain recognizable certificates through access to the 1,000+ Coursera courses offered by leading universities. Coursera for Refugees also includes organizational support services for partner non-profit organizations.
- DSM pledges to develop programs enabling refugees to obtain employment; develop employee volunteer programs to facilitate the development of language and cultural skills

of refugees resettling in the United States; offer programs to refugees on nutrition improvement and education; and continue to work with leading organizations such as Upwardly Global, WFP, UNICEF, Global Health Corp, and World Vision to ensure that refugees have opportunity, nutrition, and healthcare.

• Facebook pledges to bring Wi-Fi connectivity to 35 locations across Greece, in partnership with NetHope; develop a strategy for bringing internet connectivity to individuals living in refugee camps and surrounding communities, in partnership with UNHCR and local partners; leverage the Facebook social media platform to raise awareness and funds for the refugee crisis; and donate advertising credits and creative services support to UNHCR and other refugee-serving organizations.

• Figure 8 Investment Strategies pledges to recruit, hire, and train refugees and provide refugee employees with access to key industry licenses and certifications (CFA, CFP, Series 7, 63, 65); partner with Global Talent Idaho and the Idaho Department of Labor to provide skilled refugees with internship and apprenticeship opportunities in financial analysis and investment advising; support refugee communities in Idaho with pro bono financial literacy training and advice; and source goods and services from refugee-owned business wherever possible.

• Goldman Sachs pledges to donate $7.5 million to support refugees in partnership with leading NGOs, including UNHCR. Specifically, Goldman will: provide support to organizations delivering critical humanitarian aid, including food, shelter, urgent medical care, and trauma support; help ensure refugee children have access to consistent education and safe learning facilities throughout camps in and around Syria; create a new online 10,000 Women program that will teach entrepreneurial and business skills; and support positive refugee integration in European host countries by providing English language, employability skills, and other training opportunities.

- Google pledges to provide new funding and technical expertise to organizations enabling 10,000 out-of-school primary school-aged refugees in Lebanon to access free formal education through a new primary school classroom model in 2017.
- Henry Schein pledges, over the next three years, to donate $350K in essential health care products to an international aid organization to support volunteer physicians providing care to Syrian refugees in Europe and the Middle East. Henry Schein will also donate $100,000 in oral care products to support volunteer dentists treating refugees, and 7,500 health and hygiene kits for refugees living in camps, including specialized kits for women and girls.
- HP pledges to establish 6 HP Learning Studios in Lebanon and Jordan to engage refugee youth in developing skills and help to give refugee students access to the latest education technology while providing adults the opportunity for employment re-skilling. HP also pledges to expand the HP Learning Initiative for Entrepreneurs (HP LIFE) with additional free online courses and curated content to help refugees develop essential business and IT skills; connect Girl Scouts in the Washington D.C. area with young Syrian refugee girls for one-to-one peer learning and mentoring; actively pursue the purchase of online freelance services from refugees; enable access to technology and HP LIFE e-learning for refugees at the International Medical Corps Livelihoods Center pilot in Turkey; and explore IT infrastructure solutions.
- IBM pledges to continue its ongoing commitment in support of migrants and refugees, with a focus on the crisis in Europe. IBM intends to continue actively seeking grant

partnerships, volunteerism opportunities, and other avenues to leverage IBM's capabilities in support of this humanitarian crisis.

- IKEA U.S. pledges to introduce a national community involvement activity in Fiscal Year 2017 in partnership with select refugee non-profit organizations, and to use IKEA's furniture and home furnishing expertise to help refugees in the United States. This estimated in-kind donation will be worth approximately $500,000.

- Johnson & Johnson pledges to donate an additional $1.75 million to Save the Children, earmarked for refugees, to be spent in 2016 and 2017; to expand programmatic efforts to Turkey and Egypt; to shift its program focus to refugee education, mental health support, and community building initiatives for refugee parents; and to launch a public awareness-campaign in support of refugees.

- Karp Randel pledges to leverage their corporate network and expertise to garner more support for the Partnership for Refugees and encourage others to submit pledges and to support the future host organization.

- Kleiman International Consultants commits to establishing a multisector taskforce and organizing a Private Sector Financing Forum to develop innovative financial market projects, including sovereign refugee bonds and stock exchange company investment funds, that will enable frontline state capital markets to raise funds for their crisis response, employment, infrastructure, and development needs.

- Libra Group commits to continue providing monetary support, resources, and technologies to nongovernmental organizations (NGO) working directly with refugees in Greece, and to extend its focus on education, mental health and security for unaccompanied minors and women. Activities will include purchase and installation of security cameras; hiring and deployment of mental health professionals; and provision of funds, shelter, and educational scholarships for unaccompanied minors and women entering Greece.

- LinkedIn is committed to expanding its refugee initiative, Welcoming Talent, to additional countries beyond Sweden. LinkedIn is taking a different strategy in expanding to Canada by integrating LinkedIn training curricula into economic empowerment and employment programs, in collaboration with the Prime Minister's office and two local NGOs, and scaling this approach with the IRC to expand in global markets.
- Lynke pledges to open a second tech center in Jordan by the end of 2017, expanding their partnership with Microsoft, MasterCard, HP, UNHCR, Coursera, and others to replicate their facilities in a second economic zone. This will double the number of refugee employees building apps or conducting outsourcing work for Lynke's partners and double the number of graduates for partners to hire.
- MasterCard pledges to expand the reach of its MasterCard Aid Network, humanitarian prepaid, and remittance services to 2 million aid recipients; to mobilize and partner with other private and public sector organizations to build "smart communities" that seek to integrate refugee populations; to assist refugee-serving organizations with information safety and security workshops and guidance; and to convene a multisector working session to determine how refugees can more easily access financial services.
- McKinsey & Co. pledges to conduct and publish new research, which will seek to understand the root causes, economic, social, and environmental impacts of migration and to develop a toolkit for policymakers, executives, and social leaders; lead activities to improve education for Syrian refugee children in Lebanon; and partner with a leading

international humanitarian organization to develop inter-
ventions to create meaningful job opportunities for Syrian
refugees in Jordan.

- Microsoft pledges to build upon existing partnerships with
the U.N. and NGOs such as UNHCR to invest in technology that provides refugees with broader access to education, professional skills, and economic opportunity. This
includes support for UNHCR's Connectivity for Refugee
initiative; donation of cloud technology services to NGOS
engaged in refugee relief; expansion of an Arabic to German language training program; support for a 12-month
counseling and psychosocial assistance program; and an
Innovation Hub where refugees can develop technology
and entrepreneurial skills.

- Newton Supply Company pledges to increase the percentage
of refugee-made products outsourced by Open Arms from
30 percent to 90 percent over the next 12 months, to employ
more female refugees, and to focus their marketing efforts
on raising awareness of their refugee-made products.

- Not Impossible Labs pledges to establish "maker labs" in
refugee camps and settlements. These labs will be focused
on innovative thinking and "maker" skill sets, and will
provide refugee youth with tools, trainings, and skills-
building workshops to develop breakthrough solutions to
local needs and challenges. Not Impossible plans to launch
the inaugural lab in Q4 of 2016.

- Nova Credit Inc. is building the world's first cross-border
credit reporting agency, enabling immigrants to access
their credit. Nova pledges to prioritize and develop data
partnerships with countries that have a high refugee population in the United States, including Iran, Bhutan, and
countries in Sub-Saharan Africa. Many of these nations
have limited financial infrastructure, and the company

pledges to pursue alternative data partnerships to help drive financial inclusion for these populations in need.

- Oliver Wyman pledges to recruit qualified refugees in Europe, use their partner network to explore solutions for enhancing entrepreneurial activities and developing job-related skills for refugees, raise the issue of providing employment with clients, and provide a central website where clients can access information on organizations that can help them support refugees.

- Pearson pledges to extend its partnership, Every Child Learning, doubling its initial investment of $2.2 million and working with partners to develop and provide digital educational solutions and programs for Syrian refugees and vulnerable Jordanian children.

- PIMCO pledges to host a panel discussion on September 20, titled "The Frontlines of the Global Refugee Crisis: Human Flight Beyond Comparison," and invite a panel of experts to speak to the broader PIMCO population about refugees' emergency needs, the legal assistance refugees seek, and resettlement efforts more broadly. PIMCO will then form action teams in each PIMCO office to dig in, identify needs and nonprofit partners, and give time and financial resources to determine the best way to support the crisis.

- SAP pledges to educate 10,000 refugee youth across four nations with coding skills during their inaugural "Refugee Code Week," October 15–23, 2016; to address the education shortage in the refugee population by creating a full life cycle of skills support for young people in refugee camps; to empower adults and youth with critical, job-relevant coding tools and skills; to create computer literacy by introducing young refugees to coding basics through playful workshops; and to facilitate the integration of coding education within school curriculums of the hosting nations.

- Singhal & Co. pledges to offer corporate internships to two refugees a year until 2020; donate up to $10,000 a year in educational scholarships for refugees until 2020; and provide $20,000 in funding toward assisting refugees through the U.S. Committee for Refugees and Immigrants until 2020.
- SkillSmart is pledging to provide their skills matching and skills capacity building platform to refugee resettlement agencies to allow refugees to connect to available jobs as well as to tailored training courses.
- Sparrow Mobile commits to expand its RefugeeMobile program from 250 families (est. 700 individuals) to 1,000 or more families (est. 2,800 individuals) by 2018; to expand to another geographic region; and to target at least 50 percent women as primary smartphone recipients.
- Synthesis Corp. plans to identify and work with refugee entrepreneurs in the Northeast United States to develop an innovation hub for refugees seeking to either launch or grow an on-going business. The hub will serve as a clearinghouse for materials and will seek to develop an ecosystem of mentors, funders, and cross-business activity.
- Tetra Tech commits to hire one locally-based qualified refugee as a paid intern for at least 2 months over the course of 2017; to host one mock interview workshop that includes refugee jobseekers; and to interview qualified refugees for any vacancies listed during 2017 in the San Francisco and Washington, D.C. offices.
- TransparentBusiness pledges to donate $1 million in TransparentBusiness.com technology for U.S. companies, including those who have answered the Call to Action, to use for hiring and managing qualified refugees remotely.
- TripAdvisor will commit at least $5 million, over the next three years, from the TripAdvisor Charitable Foundation to aid the humanitarian refugee crisis, expanding its

partnerships with the International Rescue Committee and Mercy Corps, and by providing in-kind support through its TripAdvisor Media Group.

- Twilio pledges to offer credits and discounts for refugee-serving organizations to access Twilio's communication platform; to launch a Call-to-Action campaign to recruit and deploy developers to provide pro bono support to refugee-serving organizations; and to donate an additional product donation, cash grant, and dedicated developer team to a leading NGO.
- Twitter pledges to support NGOs that directly assist refugees with an "Ads for Good" advertising grant of $50,000, and to provide best practices trainings to refugee-serving organizations in Europe and the United States.
- Uber pledges to work with U.S. resettlement agencies to provide independent work opportunities to refugees through its platform and connect potential refugee drivers with affordable, low-risk leases and auto discounts. Uber also pledges to support local organizations that provide critical goods and services to refugee families through the UberGIVING donation campaign.
- Udemy pledges to leverage the Udemy platform and audience to create economic empowerment opportunities by onboarding refugees as course instructors, and to deliver educational content to displaced people to help them qualify for market-relevant jobs.
- UPS pledges to leverage funding, expertise, company resources, and UPS volunteers to expand its partnerships with UNHCR, UNICER, WFP, Care, the Salvation Army, and others, investing up to an additional $1 million to provide relief to refugee communities and support to displaced people around the world.
- Western Union pledges to support economic opportunities for refugees and displaced persons over the next three

years through a new company-wide global initiative. Specifically, Western Union will help expand educational opportunities for refugee children and youth; provide refugees with internships, freelance and traditional employment opportunities at Western Union and with key corporate partners; and leverage Western Union's core assets—including its financial technology and global network of 35 million members to support refugee crisis response initiatives and shift the global conversation about refugees to one of economic opportunity.

- Zynga pledges to work proactively with resettlement agencies globally to make Words with Friends EDU, the educational version of Words with Friends, focused on teaching English academic vocabulary, readily and freely available to displaced people who are looking to develop their English language skills. Zynga will also provide three Expert Advisors to mentor the finalists of the Edu-App4Syria competition, an international innovation competition to develop an open source smartphone application that can help Syrian children learn how to read in Arabic.

CATHOLIC CAMPAIGN FOR HUMAN DEVELOPMENT'S AMNESTY PROMOTERS

Nationwide CCHD grant recipients for 2016/2017 and 2018/2019:

2016-2017	
Archdiocese of Boston Essex County Community Organization	$50,000
Archdiocese of Boston Merrimack Valley Project	$60,000
Diocese of Newark Archdiocese of Newark	$50,000
Archdiocese of Baltimore Immigration Outreach Service Center, Inc.	$35,000

Diocese of Lansing ACTION of Greater Lansing	$50,000
Diocese of Toledo Farm Labor Research Project	$30,000
Diocese of Alexandria Northern Louisiana Area Interfaith Sponsoring Committee, Inc.	$50,000
Diocese of Des Moines Ethnic Minorities from Burma Advocacy and Resource Center	$35,000
Diocese of Saint Cloud Asamblea de Derechos Civiles de Minnesota	$55,000
Diocese of Brownsville Arise Support Center	$55,000
Diocese of Austin Brazos Interfaith Immigration Network (BIIN)	$35,000
Archdiocese of Galveston and Houston Gulf Coast Leadership Council Inc.	$45,000
Diocese of Stockton Congregations Building Community	$65,000
Diocese of San Diego Justice Overcoming Boundaries in San Diego County	$55,000
Dioces of San Jose Latinos United for a New America (LUNA)	$35,000

Diocese of San Diego San Diego Organizing Project	$40,000
Archdiocese of Denver Together Colorado Metro Organizations for People	$50,000
Archdiocese of Seattle Intercommunity Peace & Justice Center	$60,000
Archdiocese of Chicago Centro de Trabajadores Unidos; Immigrant Workers' Project	$40,000
Total	**$895,000**

2018/2019

Archdiocese Boston Essex County Community Organization	$75,000
Archdiocese Boston Merrimack Valley Project	$75,000
Archdiocese of Newark Archdiocese of Newark Faith in Essex County	$50,000
Diocese of Brooklyn Cidadao Global, Global Citizen, Inc.	$30,000
Diocese of Ft. Wayne and South Bend Faith in Indiana, Northeast	$40,000

Archdiocese of Baltimore Immigration Outreach Service Center, Inc.	$30,000
Archdiocese of Baltimore People Acting Together in Howard	$40,000
Diocese of Toledo Farm Labor Research Project	$40,000
Diocese of Milwaukee SOPHIA	$55,000
Archdiocese of Miami South Florida Interfaith Committee For Worker Justice, Inc.	$50,000
Archdiocese of Miami WeCount!, Inc.	$35,000
Diocese of Palm Beach People Engaged in Active Community Efforts (PEACE)	$50,000
Archdiocese of New Orleans New Orleans Workers' Center for Racial Justice	$50,000
Diocese of Raleigh NC Latino Coalition	$35,000
Diocese of Saint Cloud Asamblea de Derechos Civiles de Minnesota	$65,000
Archdiocese of Omaha Heartland Workers Center	$50,000

Diocese of Brownsville Arise Support Center	$65,000
Archdiocese of Los Angeles Inland Empire Sponsoring Committee	$50,000
Diocese of Monterey Communities Organized for Relational Power in Action	$75,000
Diocese of San Diego San Diego Organizing Project	$40,000
Diocese of San Diego Justice Overcoming Boundaries in San Diego County	$55,000
Diocese of San Jose PACT: People Acting in Community Together	$25,000
Diocese of San Jose Latinos United for a New America AKA LUNA	$50,000
Archdiocese of Denver Together Colorado Metro Organizations for People	$50,000
Archdiocese of Seattle Intercommunity Peace & Justice Center	$60,000
Total	$1,240,000

APPENDIX G

60 OF THE WORLD'S FINEST REFUJIHADIS

- Somali national and al Qaeda operative *Nuradin Abdi*, the Ohio shopping mall bomb plotter convicted in 2007, first entered the U.S. illegally in 1995 using a false passport, entered again illegally from Canada in 1997, and then secured asylum on false grounds. He fraudulently obtained a refugee travel document by telling authorities he was going on religious holiday in Germany, but instead flew to Ethiopia and Chechnya for jihad training. After returning, Abdi hatched a plan to bomb a local shopping mall.[1] Columbus, Ohio, Abdi's home base, is home to more than 60,000 Somalis—the second largest Somali community in the United States, after Minneapolis.[2]
- Convicted Fort Dix (N.J.) jihad plotters and ethnic Albanian illegal alien brothers *Dritan, Shain, and Eljvir Duka*, snuck into the country through Mexico with their parents, who applied for asylum in 1984. The feds ignored them for two decades. In the meantime, as America showed the Dukas' refugee community unmatched compassion and

generosity, the Muslim trio returned the favor by planning to massacre U.S. soldiers in 2007.[3]

- *Mohanad Shareef Hammadi* was an Iraqi refugee who landed in Las Vegas before resettling in Bowling Green, Kentucky, in 2009. He was not being hunted or oppressed by anyone. He was, in fact, a bomb-maker insurgent for al Qaeda in Iraq who had targeted American soldiers on the battlefield. He sought to amass high-powered weapons and ship them from his adopted home back to the front lines to assist his terrorist brethren. In 2013, he was sentenced to life in prison for providing material support to terrorists and "conspiring to transfer, possess, and export Stinger missiles," not to mention making a false statement in an immigration application.[4]

- *Waad Ramadan Alwan* was Hammadi's co-conspirator and fellow Iraqi refujihadi in Bowling Green, Kentucky. His fingerprints were found on unexploded IEDs in Iraq. During a sting operation, Alwan and Hammadi loaded money and weapons together on five occasions, including "five rocket-propelled grenade launchers, five machine guns, five cases of C4 explosive, two sniper rifles, one box of 12 hand grenades, two Stinger surface-to-air missile launchers, and what they believed to be a total of $565,000." According to the DOJ, Alwan spoke of his efforts to kill U.S. soldiers in Iraq, stating "lunch and dinner would be an American." Alwan received a 40-year prison sentence.

- *Abdow Munye Abdow*, a Somalian refugee who spent six years in a refugee camp before landing in the U.S. and obtaining a green card and eventually American citizenship, pleaded guilty in 2011 to obstruction of justice charges related to his role in renting a car for al Shabaab recruits driving from Minnesota to San Diego.[5]

- *Farah Mohamed Beledi* was a Somalian child refugee who arrived in the Twin Cities in 1996 and racked up a violent criminal and drug record in his teens and early twenties.[6] After joining the Abubakar as-Saddique mosque, he traveled to Mexico with an al Shabaab recruiter and fellow Minnesota Muslim radical with U.S. citizenship, *Cabdulaahi Ahmed Faarax*, and headed back to Somalia. Beledi and Faarax were in the car rented by Abdow Munye Abdow. Beledi died in 2011 after attempting to blow himself up in a Mogadishu suicide attack. Family members identified his voice in a tape released after his death: "I would like to talk to my brothers and sisters out there in the West, or wherever you are," he beckoned. "Brothers, come. Come to jihad. I welcome you and call you to jihad."[7] Faarax remains at large but was spotted in a photograph with a top al Shabaab leader in 2012 by jihad trackers from the *Long War Journal* website.[8]

- *Shirwa Ahmed*, a Somalian refugee, moved to the U.S. in 1995 at age 12 or 13, landing in Portland, Oregon, before resettling in the Twin Cities, Minnesota. He became radicalized at the Abubakar as-Saddique mosque,[9] the largest mosque in the state, amid a hotbed of anti-American and pro-jihad sentiment. In 2007, he left to study in Yemen. A year later, he blew himself up in northern Somalia.[10] Ahmed was part of a ring of Somalian refujihadis in Minnesota that included Beledi and Faarax, who were exposed by the FBI's Operation Rhino counterterror investigation. Somalian-born janitor *Mahamud Said Omar*, who worked at the Abubakar as-Saddique mosque, was convicted at trial on five terror counts related to his role as a refujihadi recruiter and sentenced to 20 years in prison.[11] Also named in terror indictments unsealed by the Justice Department in 2009 were Somalian Muslim refugee recruits *Abdiweli Yassin Isse, Kamal Hassan, Salah Osman Ahmad, and*

Adarus Abdulle Ali, who all pleaded guilty to offenses ranging from providing material support to terrorists to perjury to conspiring to kill, maim, or injure persons outside the U.S. Five additional Somalian-born Minnesotans who left the U.S. to wage jihad—*Ahmed Ali Omar, Khalid Mohamud Abshir, Zakaria Maruf, Mohamed Abdullahi Hassan and Mustafa Ali Salat*—were charged *in absentia.* Maruf had a lengthy rap sheet and ran with a Somali street gang. In 2009, after praising Shirwa Ahmed's martyrdom, Maruf was killed in combat fighting for al Shabaab jihadists.[12]

- Anzor Tsarnaev, an ethnic Chechen Muslim and father of Boston Marathon bombers *Tamerlan and Dzhokhar Tsarnaev* visited America on a short-term visa along with his wife. While here, he claimed he was fearful of persecution if he returned to Russia and won asylum for himself and his wife. He then petitioned for his boys to come to America; they received "derivative" asylum status. Younger son Dzhokhar obtained U.S. citizenship. Older son Tamerlan, whose naturalization application was pending, travelled freely between the U.S. and the jihad recruitment zone of Dagestan, Russia, before hatching his sick terrorist plot with his brother. The Tsarnaev parents were back in Russia in 2013 when news hit of the Boston Marathon bombing, even though their asylum claim rested on them fearing for their lives if they went back.[13] Authorities will not reveal any details of the sob stories the Tsarnaevs originally spun to win asylum benefits for the entire family.

- *Issa Doreh* was a Somalian refugee who worked at a money-transmitting company (*hawala*), Shidaal Express, in southern California. In 2013, Doreh was sentenced to ten years in prison for conspiracy to provide material support to al-Shabaab, the violent militia group designated a terrorist organization in 2008. Money raised by a ring of

Somalian refugees in the U.S. who were urged by al Shabaab leaders to "finance the jihad." Doreh obtained a green card and U.S. citizenship while plotting against America[14]

- *Basaaly Saeed Moalin*, a cab driver in San Diego, was a Somali refugee who conspired with Doreh to subsidize al Shabaab's terrorist activists. Intercepted phone conversations revealed Moalin, who became a U.S. citizen after obtaining his green card, offered his house in Mogadishu to enable al Shabaab to hide weapons and aid its broader terrorist agenda. A top leader of the jihad group who had personally lobbied Moalin for money was killed in a missile strike in 2008.[15]

- *Mohamed Mohamed Mohamud*, another Somalian refugee in the al Shabaab fundraising scheme, was imam at Masjid Al Ansar mosque. He was sentenced to 13 years in prison for his role in using his mosque connections to help raise money to provide material support to terrorists.[16]

- *Ahmed Nasiri Taalil Mohamud*, a cab driver from Anaheim, was the fourth member of the San Diego refujihadis' terror fundraising ring. He had become a legal permanent resident in 2004 after arriving from Somalia as a refugee. In 2016, he was returned to Somalia after serving part of a 6-year prison term.[17]

- In 2015, a ring of Bosnian Muslim refugees and naturalized Bosnian-American citizens were indicted on criminal charges for sending money and supplies to terrorists in Syria and Iraq. *Ramiz and Sedina Hodzic,* refugees who had resettled in St. Louis, were charged in a criminal conspiracy involving fellow Bosnian immigrants *Mediha Medy Salkicevic, Armin Harcevic, Jasminka Ramic, and Nihad Rosic*. They raised money and purchased U.S. military uniforms, combat boots, tactical gear, and rifle scopes, which they sent to *Abdullah Ramo Pazara*—a

Bosnian Muslim refugee who had lived in St. Louis and became a U.S. citizen just days before traveling to Syria in 2013 to fight for al Qaeda and the Islamic State.[18] Pazara rose up the ranks of ISIS; he was reportedly killed on the Turkey-Syria border.[19] Ramiz Hodzic, Harcevic, Salkicevic, and Ramic pleaded guilty to their charges in 2019.[20] As of May 2019, Sedina Hodzic and Rosic had pleaded not guilty and were awaiting trial.

- *Fazliddin Kurbanov* was born in Uzbekistan to a Muslim family that claimed to be victims of persecution after converting to Orthodox Christianity. Although he remained a Muslim, he was allowed to accompany his family to the U.S. in 2009 as a refugee. He resettled in Boise, Idaho, with a wife and son, where he made his anti-American, pro-militant Islamic views known on Facebook and YouTube, where he posted more than 100 jihad videos. (Facebook and YouTube were apparently too busy deplatforming and demonetizing non-violent conservatives to remove Kurbanov's videos.) In 2015, he was found guilty of conspiring and attempting to provide material support to an Uzbek terrorist group. He had plotted a bomb attack to rival the 1995 OKC bombing, which resulted in 168 deaths.[21]

- *Liban Haji Mohamed* arrived in the U.S. from Somalia as a child refugee. He was working as a cab driver in the Northern Virginia suburbs before he returned to his native land to join al Shabaab in 2012.[22] He reportedly was an associate of American Zachary Chesser, who pleaded guilty to threatening the producers of the TV show, South Park, over their cartoon depiction of Mohammed in a bear suit.[23] In 2015, Mohamed was detained in Somalia.[24]

- *Mohamed Abdullahi Hassan* is a top online terror recruiter for al Shabaab and the Islamic State of Iraq and the Levant (ISIL) who lived in the Twin Cities, Minnesota, as a child and left after high school in 2008 to return to Somalia. He was indicted by a federal grand jury in 2009 for conspiracy to support terrorism and is on the FBI's Most Wanted list of terrorists. He used Twitter to stoke the shooting attack[25] on the Garland, Texas, Mohammed Cartoons exhibit in 2015, which resulted in the wounding of one security officer.[26]

- *Abdinassir Mohamud Ibrahim* was sentenced to 15 years in federal prison for conspiring to provide material support to al Shabaab in 2015. A Somalian refugee, he had lied on his application claiming he was a member of a persecuted minority clan—when in fact he was a member of the majority clan he falsely asserted had victimized him.[27]

- *Mohamud Ali Yusuf* pleaded guilty to using a remittance business in St. Louis to raise and transfer $6,000 to al Shabaab.[28] Yusuf was a Somalian refugee taxi driver.[29]

- *Nima Yusuf,* a Somalian refugee in San Diego who came here as a child, pleaded guilty in 2011 to sending $1,450 to al Shabaab operatives and lying about it.[30]

- Nine Somalian refugees ages 19-21 who resettled in the jihad hotbed of Minnesota—*Zacharia Yusuf Abdurahman, Adnan Farah, Hanad Mustafe Musse, Guled Ali Omar, Abdirahman Yasin Daud, Mohamed Abdihamid Farah, Abdirizak Warsame, Hamza Ahmed, and Abdullahi Yusuf*—were convicted of, or pleaded guilty to, plotting to travel to Syria to join the terrorists of the Islamic State.[31] At his sentencing in 2016, Musse declared: "I am a terrorist, your honor."[32] Omar, the ringleader, received the longest sentence: 35 years. He was born in a Kenyan refugee camp and came to the U.S. when he was two.[33]

- Guled Ali Ombar's older brother and fellow refujihadi, *Ahmed Ali Omar,* left Minnesota to join al Shabaab in 2007 and hasn't been seen since. Minnesota boasts the largest concentration of Somalian refugees and immigrants—over 70,000 have settled there. In 2009, the FBI told National Public Radio that it had tracked, arrested, and charged a total of 14 Somalians from the Twin Cities refugee enclave who had moved out of the country to join terror operations.[34] Reporting on Muslim refugee and Minnesota Democrat Rep. Ilhan Omar's congressional district as the terror recruiting capital of the world, Fox News updated the FBI stats in 2019: 45 Somalian refugees and family members have now abandoned their Minnesota haven to join al Shabaab or ISIS, and a dozen more had been arrested with the intention of leaving to support ISIS.[35]

- Also in 2015, the material support convictions of another pair of Somalian refugees from Minnesota were upheld by a federal appeals court. Two women, *Amina Farah Ali and Hawo Mohamed Hassan,* had been convicted of raising money for al Shabaab and routing the funds through a "deadly pipeline" to support the terrorists. They duped fellow Muslims by posing as "humanitarians." At trial, Ali refused to stand for the judge in court and spewed through a court-appointed translator that "she said she was happy because she knew she was going to heaven. Those who were against Muslims, she said, were going to hell."[36]

- *Abdul Razak Ali Artan* was a Somali refugee who left his homeland with his family in 2007 for Pakistan and landed in Dallas before resettling in Ohio. In 2014, he became a legal permanent resident. At Ohio State University, where he was a student,[37] Artan raged against America and invoked radical Muslim cleric and spiritual adviser to jihadists Anwar al-Awlaki. In 2016, he plowed his car into a group of students and then broke out a knife and stabbed innocent bystanders. Eleven were injured before police shot Artan dead.[38]

- Somali refugee *Dahir Ahmed Adan* went on a stabbing spree at a St. Cloud, Minnesota, mall in 2016, injuring ten people before an off-duty police officer shot him dead. Police told local media Adan quizzed at least one person on whether the individual was Muslim and made references to Allah while carrying out the stabbings.[39] A local chapter leader of the unindicted terror co-conspirators of CAIR-Hamas disseminated an obligatory condemnation of Adan's jihad before wailing about "the potential backlash to this community."[40]

- *Omar Abdulsattar Ameen* traveled from Iraq to Turkey in 2012 and wove the usual tale of fleeing persecution and violence. In 2014, after passing screening interviews with U.N. and U.S. officials, he snagged refugee status and settled in Sacramento. Turned out Ameen had nothing to fear. According to the feds, he had lied to everyone in the refugee resettlement racket about being targeted because his father had been "shot dead" for serving in the Iraqi military. FBI investigators discovered that Ameen's father, identified as a supporter of jihadist Abu Musab al Zarqawi, had died of a natural cerebral blood clot. Ameen not only hid his ties to al Qaeda and ISIS from interviewers; he took a quick trip back to the country he was allegedly so afraid to live in and allegedly killed a police officer in Rahwah before packing his bags for America.[41] Iraq requested his extradition to stand trial for premeditated murder in 2018. After his arrest, the Justice Department revealed that the FBI's Joint Terrorism Task Force had been secretly investigating him since 2016 for visa fraud and other suspected violations, interviewed eight individuals with knowledge of his wealthy family's terror ties, and had "received documents from Iraq, which corroborate Ameen's involvement" with terrorist organization al Qaeda in Iraq and the Islamic State of Iraq.[42]

- *Omar Faraj Saeed Al Hardan*, a Palestinian born in Iraq, was a lucky refugee who resettled in Houston in 2009 and obtained a green card. In December 2017, he was sentenced to 16 years in prison for attempting to provide material support to the Islamic State of Iraq and the Levant (ISIL), a designated terrorist group.[43] Al Hardan pledged loyalty to ISIS, spread jihad propaganda online, kept an ISIS flag in his apartment, taught himself to build IEDs, plotted to bomb Houston malls, and told an undercover informant he planned to travel abroad to kill Americans. "I want to blow myself up. I want to travel with the Mujahidin. I want to travel to be with those who are against America. I am against America," Al Hardan declared.[44]

- *Aws Mohammed Younis Al-Jayab*, a friend of Al Hardan, was an Iraqi refugee who lived in Sacramento. On Facebook, they committed to armed jihad together and discussed traveling together to Al-Jayab's native Syria for weapons training. Al-Jayab had arrived in the U.S. in 2012 as a refugee purportedly fleeing persecution, but he was soon jetting off to Turkey and Syria, where he joined Ansar Al Islam. He lied to U.S. Customs officials about where he had been and what he had been doing ("visiting his grandmother"). In October 2018, he admitted he had lied and provided material support to terrorists.[45]

- *Abdullatif Ali Aldosary* was admitted to the U.S. as an Iraqi refugee in 1997 and settled in Arizona. A decade later, he served prison time for felony harassment, had his probation revoked, and served more time. In 2011, he sought help acquiring a green card from the office of Rep. Paul Gosar (R-Arizona). DHS told Gosar that Aldosary had fought with anti-government forces in Iraq. In 2013, Aldosary was indicted for setting off a bomb outside a Social Security office in Casa Grande *and* charged with first-degree murder of a co-worker at a grain processing plant in Maricopa.[46] In 2014, he was convicted on felony weapons charges.[47] All that and he *still* wasn't deportable.[48] Five years later, in 2018, Aldosary was still in the U.S. After being ordered to wear a mask during court proceedings because he spat on people, he was determined to be incompetent and committed to a mental institution in exchange for the bombing and murder charges being dropped.[49]

- *Bilal Abood* was a translator in Iraq for the U.S. Army during the Gulf War who resettled in Mesquite, Texas. He was awarded a Special Immigrant Visa designated for Iraqi and Afghan translators and interpreters who assisted American forces, joined the U.S. military for a short stint, and became a naturalized U.S. citizen.[50] The oath of citizenship, which requires swearing off any foreign allegiances, apparently didn't mean much to Abood, who swore allegiance instead to the Islamic State. He lied to immigration officials and claimed he was going to Iraq to visit family (sensing a theme here?) but journeyed to Mexico to get to Syria to wage jihad. He was sentenced to four years in prison.[51] Abood the ungrateful refujihadi declared America the "enemy of Allah."[52]

- *Jamshid Muhtorov*, a Muslim refugee from Uzbekistan who resettled in Aurora, Colorado, in 2007, was convicted of aiding terrorism in 2018 after he swore allegiance to the Islamic Jihad Union and told his daughter to pray that he died a martyr for Allah. "We'll raise the banner of jihad with a weapon in one hand and a Koran in the other," he told a co-conspirator.[53] That collaborator and fellow Uzbek refugee, Bakhityor Jumaev, was found guilty on two terror-related counts.[54]

- *Mahad Abdiaziz Adbiraham* pleaded guilty to stabbing two people at the Mall of America in Minnesota in January 2018. Initially, the crime was reported as an "interrupted theft" in which two men had spotted Adbi-raham attempting to steal merchandise at a Macy's.[55] But Adbiraham made his intent clear in the courtroom when he entered his plea. His attack was a "call for jihad by the Chief of Believer, Abu-bakr Al-baghdadi, may Allah protect him, and by the Mujahiden of the Islamic State," he wrote in a statement. "I understand that the two men I stabbed know and have explained the reason for my attack, and I am here reaffirming that it was indeed an act of Jihad in the way of Allah."[56] Any questions? Adbiraham entered the U.S. with "derivative status," meaning he came here with a relative legally (most likely a refugee or green card recipient).[57]

TOP 10 REFUGEE DESTINATIONS BY STATE AND METRO AREA (2008–2017)[1]

Derived from Fiscal Policy Institute and U.S Department of State (DOS) Bureau of Population, Refugees, and Migration (PRM)Worldwide Refugee Admissions Processing System data

By State

1.	California	69,429
2.	Texas	67,552
3.	New York	39,930
4.	Michigan	34,452
5.	Florida	31,012
6.	Arizona	30,504
7.	Georgia	27,171
8.	Pennsylvania	25,819
9.	Washington	25,781
10.	Ohio	24,845

By Metropolitan Area

1. Dallas-Fort Worth, Texas   26,772
2. San Diego, California   26,552
3. Atlanta, Georgia   25,900
4. Phoenix, Arizona   22,022
5. Los Angeles, California   20,154
6. Houston, Texas   19,220
7. Chicago, Illinois   18,003
8. Detroit, Michigan   17,988
9. Seattle, Washington   16,811
10. Minneapolis-St. Paul, Minnesota 14,779

APPENDIX I

REFUGEE RESETTLEMENT HIJACKERS

Under the 1980 Refugee Act, the federal government was supposed to reimburse states for 100 percent of the costs of refugee resettlement. When the feds reneged on the promise, creating a swelling unfunded mandate, 12 states and one county withdrew from the program altogether. (In bureaucratese, they are known as "Wilson-Fish" states after a congressional amendment to immigration law.[1] But the refugee resettlement racket found a way to circumvent the will of the people and steered resettlement subsidies directly to selected private contractors (the "voluntary agencies" or VOLAGs) who facilitated refugee dumps in the very states that had rejected them. Is your state held hostage to the refugee resettlement hijackers? Here they are:[2]

- Alabama: USCCB-Catholic Social Services
- Alaska: USCCB-Catholic Social Services
- Colorado: Colorado Department of Human Services
- Idaho: Janus Inc. (formerly Mountain States Group), Idaho Office for Refugees

- Kentucky: USCCB-Catholic Charities of Louisville, Kentucky, Office for Refugees
- Louisiana: USCCB-Catholic Charities Diocese of Baton Rouge, Louisiana, Office for Refugees
- Massachusetts: Office for Refugees and Immigrants
- Nevada: USCCB-Catholic Charities of Southern Nevada
- North Dakota: LIRS-Lutheran Social Services of North Dakota
- San Diego County, CA: USCCB-Catholic Charities Diocese of San Diego
- South Dakota: LIRS-Lutheran Social Services of South Dakota
- Tennessee: USCCB-Catholic Charities of Tennessee, Tennessee Office for Refugees
- Vermont: USCRI-Vermont Refugee Resettlement Program

TIMELINE OF ANTIFA VIOLENCE AND ABOLISH ICE VIGILANTISM

2016	
April	Costa Mesa, Calif., pro-Trump rally overrun by open-borders protesters and anarchists throwing rocks, vandalizing police cars, provoking bloody assaults
March	Trump cancels Chicago rally amid threats of violence
June	San Jose Convention Center riot at pro-Trump rally as left-wing mob hurled eggs and ambushed GOP attendees
August	West Hollywood pro-Trump rally ends in the arrest of two female protesters accused of assault
November	Three days of Election Week riots in Portland; highways shut down in Los Angeles, Chicago, San Francisco, Denver, and Minneapolis; Oakland in flames amid calls to "Kill Trump"
2017	
January 20	("J20") Violent Inauguration Day riots in Washington, D.C., New York, Seattle, and Portland

February 1	Berkeley, Calif., Antifa and Black Bloc anarchist mayhem at canceled Milo Yiannopoulos speech
March 4	Antifa assaults occur at pro-Trump rally at MLK Park near University of California at Berkeley; Son of Sen. Tim Kaine (D-Va.) arrested at Minnesota Antifa protest after throwing smoke bomb
March 25	Violent outbreak at Philadelphia Antifa protest of pro-Trump event, forcing cancellation
April 15	More Antifa masked mobsters at Tax Day protest and counter-protest; Portland's Avenue of the Roses parade canceled after Antifa threats against Multnomah County Republican party participants
May 1	May Day arsons, vandalism, and fist fights in Portland, Oregon, and Olympia, Washington
June	Pro-Trump free speech event in Portland disrupted by masked Antifa, police attacked, bricks thrown
August 11/12	Charlottesville, Virginia, deadly chaos and anarchy at "Unite the Right" counter-protest exacerbated by de facto police stand-down orders and withdrawal that pushed alt-right protesters into Antifa mob
August 19	"Free speech rally" at Boston Common marred by violent left-wing assaults perpetrated by black-clad protesters who spat on, punched, and dragged an elderly woman by the American flag she was holding
August 27	Pro-Trump/anti-Marxism rally in Berkeley hijacked by thousands of violent anarchists; Left-wing thug caught on camera beating an elderly Trump supporter with a sign that read: "NO HATE" Patriot Prayer rally canceled amid threats of Antifa violence

September	Hundreds of anarchists, Antifa members, and Brown Berets march in Austin, Texas, to protest a "white suremacist rally" that never transpired. Two radicals were arrested for assaulting police
2018	
June	New York University adjunct professor Sam Lavigne doxxes nearly 1,600 ICE agents online; Wikileaks doxxes 9,200 ICE employees; Seattle-area Antifa groups doxx nearly 40 ICE agents and their spouses; Occupy PDX shuts down Portland ICE office, minority ICE agents stalked, harassed by racists; Occupy ICE New York City shuts down SoHo ICE processing center; Occupy ICE Detroit members shut down Detroit ICE facility, disrupt immigration enforcement for five days; Former DHS Secretary Kirstjen Nielsen mobbed at D.C. restaurant, home; White House senior adviser Stephen Miller doxxed, stalked at two D.C. restaurants; Sen. Ted Cruz (R-Tx.) and wife mobbed at D.C. restaurant; Proud Boys founder Gavin McInnes doxxed
August	Felony charges dropped against Antifa vigilante and Diablo Valley College professor Eric Clanton, who bloodied Trump supporters by thrashing them in the head with a heavy metal bike lock at a 2014 "Patriots Day" rally in Berkeley, California
October	Austin, Texas, Antifa celebrate Mao's cultural revolution, hang severed pigs' heads at polling stations and campaign offices

November	Fox News host Tucker Carlson's home targeted; family doxxed; Antifa operatives arrested after allegedly assaulting and robbing U.S. Marine reservists in Philadelphia near a Proud Boys gathering; three charged with assault awaiting trial, including D.C. Antifa leader and Democratic Party-tied activist Joseph Alcoff
2019	
April	Anonymous thugs vandalize Portland ICE union workers' attorney Sean Riddell's law office
May	Independent Portland journalist Andy Ngo doxxed by online anarchists, pepper-sprayed at protest, attacked at local gym
July	Andy Ngo beaten and hospitalized after assault by Portland Antifa mob; eight total treated by medics, including three police officers; Puget Sound anarchist Willem Van Spronsen shot and killed by police after attacking Tacoma, Washington, ICE detention center armed with rifle and incendiary devices. Antifa members celebrate "hero" and "martyr" Spronsen on Twitter

OUTLAW NATION: MAP/ LIST OF SANCTUARY CITIES, COUNTIES, & STATES

Map A

Source: Center for Immigration Studies/ICE data

States

California
Colorado
Illinois
Massachusetts
New Jersey
New Mexico
Oregon
Vermont

Cities and Counties

California

Alameda County
Berkeley
Contra Costa County
Los Angeles County
Los Angeles
Monterey County
Napa County
Oakland
Riverside County
Sacramento County
San Bernardino County
San Diego County
San Francisco
San Francisco County
San Mateo County
Santa Ana
Santa Clara County
Santa Cruz County
Sonoma County
Watsonville

Colorado

Arapahoe County
Aurora
Boulder County
Denver
Denver County
Garfield County
Grand County
Jefferson County
Larimer County
Mesa County
Pitkin County
Pueblo County
Routt County
San Miguel County
Weld County

Connecticut

East Haven
Hartford

Florida

Alachua County

Georgia

Clayton County
DeKalb County

Iowa

Benton County
Cass County
Fremont County
Greene County
Ida County

Iowa City
Iowa City, Johnson County
Jefferson County
Marion County
Monona County
Montgomery County
Pottawattamie County
Sioux County

Illinois

Chicago
Cook County

Kansas

Butler County
Harvey County

Louisiana

New Orleans

Massachusetts

Amherst
Boston
Cambridge
Concord
Lawrence
Newton
Northhampton
Somerville

Maryland

Baltimore
Montgomery County
Prince George's County

Michigan

Ingham County
Kalamazoo County
Kent County
Wayne County

Minnesota

Hennepin County

Mississippi

Jackson

Nebraska

Hall County
Sarpy County

New Jersey

Newark

New Mexico

Bernalillo County
New Mexico County Jails
San Miguel

Nevada

Washoe County

New York

Albany
Franklin County
Ithaca
Nassau County
New York City
Onondaga County

St. Lawrence County
Wayne County

North Carolina

Buncombe County
Durham County
Forsyth County
Mecklenburg County
Orange County
Wake County

Ohio

Franklin County

Oregon

Baker County
Clackamas County
Clatsop County
Coos County
Crook County
Curry County
Deschutes County
Douglas County
Gilliam County
Grant County
Hood River County
Jackson County
Jefferson County
Josephine County
Lane County
Lincoln County
Linn County
Malheur County
Marion County

Marlon County
Multnomah County
Polk County
Sherman County
Springfield
Tillamook County
Umatilla County
Union County
Wallowa County
Wasco County
Washington County
Wheeler County
Yamhill County

Pennsylvania

Bradford County
Bucks County
Butler County
Chester County
Clarion County
Delaware County
Erie County
Franklin County
Lehigh County
Lycoming County
Montgomery County
Montour County
Perry County
Philadelphia
Pike County
Westmoreland County

Rhode Island

Providence, Rhode Island

Rhode Island Department of Corrections

Virginia

Arlington County
Chesterfield County
Fairfax County

Vermont

Burlington
Montpelier
Winooski

Washington

Chelan County
Clallam County
Clark County
Cowlitz County
Franklin County
Jefferson County
King County
Kitsap County
Pierce County
San Juan County
Skagit County
Snohomish County
Spokane County
Seattle
Thurston County
Walla Walla County
Wallowa County
Whatcom County
Yakima County

WRETCHED REFUSE: REFUGEE RESETTLEMENT SITES ACROSS AMERICA

Map B

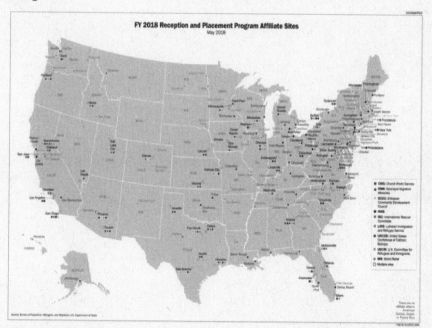

Source: Bureau of Population, Refugees, and Migration, U.S. Department of State

ACKNOWLEDGMENTS

Thank you, Marji Ross, Harry Crocker, John Caruso, Alyssa Cordova, and the rest of the Regnery team for welcoming me "home" and taking on my latest labor of love.

Thank you, SABO, for your creative dissent, righteous rebellion, and the perfect cover art to both embody and trigger Open Borders Inc. (Support SABO's work at unsavoryagents.com.)

Thank you to the following individuals and organizations whose work is saving the West from destruction: Capital Research Center and Influence Watch; FAIR; Mark Krikorian and everyone at Center for Immigration Studies; Roy Beck and NumbersUSA; Tom Fitton and Judicial Watch; Daniel Horowitz; Breitbart.com's John Binder, Neil Munro, Allum Bokhari, and Brandon Darby; Ann Corcoran's Refugee Resettlement Watch and Frauds, Crooks, and Liars; Far Left Watch; Fight The Censors; David Horowitz, the Freedom Center, and Discover the Networks; Church Militant; James Simpson; Jim Edwards; Matthew Vadum; Pajamas Media's Tyler O'Neil and David Steinberg; Brigitte Gabriel and ACT for America; James O'Keefe and Project Veritas; the Thomas More Foundation; the Immigration Reform Law Institute; Pat

Buchanan; Peter Brimelow and VDARE.com; Gavin McInnes; Robert Spencer and Jihad Watch; and all my friends and allies on the SPLC/CAIR/Silicon Valley "hate" lists and hit lists.

Thank you, William Amos, Nick Short, Jason Killian Meath, Patricia Jackson, and Rick Newcombe/Creators Syndicate, for your excellence, dedication, and friendship over the years.

Thank you, Jesse, Veronica, and J.D., for your unfailing support, encouragement, inspiration, and feedback that keep me grounded and laughing every day—especially the imitations and Quote Board reminders. RAH!

Thank you, Mom and Dad, for everything.

NOTES

Epigraph

1. "Naturalization Oath of Allegiance to the United States of America," U.S. Citizenship and Immigration Services, https://www.uscis.gov/us-citizenship/naturalization-test/naturalization-oath-allegiance-united-states-america.

Preface

1. "Syrian Man Arrested on Terrorism Charges after Planning Attack on Christian Church," U.S. Department of Justice Office of Public Affairs, June 19, 2019, https://www.justice.gov/opa/pr/syrian-man-arrested-terrorism-charges-after-planning-attack-christian-church.

2. Christina Morales, "Conservative Writer Andy Ngo Details Attack at Portland Protest," *Oregonian*, July 2, 2019, https://www.oregonlive.com/news/2019/07/conservative-writer-andy-ngo-details-attack-at-portland-protest.html.

3. Stephen Dinan, "ICE Officers Demand Portland Mayor Apologize for 'Occupy ICE' Chaos," *Washington Times*, July 30, 2018, https://www.washingtontimes.com/news/2018/jul/30/ice-officers-demand-portland-mayor-apologize/.

4. Tyler Dumont, "Following Reported ICE Raids, Local Advocacy Group Warns of Unconfirmed ICE Activity in Oregon," Fox 12, July 15, 2019, https://www.kptv.com/news/following-reported-ice-raids-local-advocacy-group-warns-of-unconfirmed/article_082e5924-a773-11e9-8e5b-1b2fdaeaab9c.html.

5. Travis Fedschun, "Washington ICE Detention Center Attacker Willem Van Spronsen Wrote 'I Am Antifa' Manifesto before Assault," Fox News, July15, 2019, https://www.foxnews.com/us/washington-man-killed-at-ice-detention-center-manifesto.

6. Brian Flood, "CNN Recently Glorified Antifa Terrorist Killed in ICE Detention Centre Attack," news.com.au, July 15, 2019, https://www.news.com.au/finance/business/media/cnn-recently-glorified-antifa-terrorist-killed-in-ice-detention-centre-attack/news-story/6cd07befd58b8f08dad31449e2b6f48f.

7. "On Willem Van Spronsen & His Final Statement," It's Going Down, July 14, 2019, https://itsgoingdown.org/on-william-van-spronsen/.

8. Andy Ngo (@MrAndyNgo), "Seattle Antifa Action has posted a eulogy & the ICE firebomber's alleged manifesto on its Facebook page that was sent to friends before the attack. In it, he allegedly wrote: 'I am antifa, I stand with comrades around the world,'" Twitter, July 14, 2019, https://twitter.com/MrAndyNgo/status/1150498054321012736.

9. David Rutz, "Ellison Posts Photo of Himself Posing with 'Antifa' Handbook, Says It Will 'Strike Fear' in Trump," Washington Free Beacon, January 3, 2018, https://freebeacon.com/politics/ellison-posts-photo-of-himself-posting-with-antifa-handbook/

10. Robert Kraychik, "Mitt Romney Tweets Support for Antifa," Daily Wire, August 15, 2017, https://www.dailywire.com/news/19777/mitt-romney-tweets-support-antifa-robert-kraychik.

11. Kate Cronin-Furman, "The Treatment of Migrants Likely Meets the Definition of a Mass Atrocity,'" *New York Times*, June 29, 2019, https://www.nytimes.com/2019/06/29/opinion/immigration-children-detention.html.

12. Sophia Tareen, "Churches Jump into Action with Threat of Immigration Sweeps," *Chicago Tribune*, July16, 2019, https://www.chicagotribune.com/sns-bc-us—trump-immigration-enforcement-20190714-story.html.

13. Eric Garcetti (@MayorOfLA), "A message for all Angelenos: Here is Los Angeles, we will not be coordinating with ICE," Twitter, July 13, 2019, https://twitter.com/MayorOfLA/status/1150138702233911296.

14. Todd Bensman, "The Next Influx: The Entire World's Poor and Dispossessed," Center for Immigration Studies, July 1, 2019, https://cis.org/Bensman/Next-Influx-Entire-Worlds-Poor-and-Dispossessed.

15. John Tufts, "Border Patrol Agents in Del Rio Arrest More Than 1,000 Haitians in Less Than a Month," *San Angelo Standard-Times*, July 5, 2019, https://www.gosanangelo.com/story/news/crime/2019/07/05/border-patrol-arrests-more-than-1-000-haitians-june-2019-texas-del-rio-sector-us-customs-protection/1657318001/.

Introduction

1. MPR News Staff, "Trump Points Finger at Ellison's 'I Don't Believe in Borders' T-shirt," MPR News, May 11, 2018, https://www.mprnews.org/story/2018/05/11/trump-dnc-chair-keith-ellison-i-dont-believe-in-borders-tshirt-may-day-minneapolis-rally.

2. George Soros, *The Crisis Of Global Capitalism: Open Society Endangered*, Greenwood Press, 1998, 227.

3. CAN/EWTN News, "Pope on Trump: Person Who Thinks Only About Building Walls, Not Building Bridges, Is Not Christian," *National Catholic Register*, February 18, 2016, http://www.ncregister.com/daily-news/pope-person-who-thinks-only-about-building-walls-not-building-bridges-is-no.

4. Jake Johnson, "Countering Trump's Inhumane Proposal, Ilhan Omar Presents 'Only Immigration Plan Worth Hearing About,'" Common Dreams, May 17, 2019, https://www.commondreams.org/news/2019/05/17/countering-trumps-inhumane-proposal-ilhan-omar-presents-only-immigration-plan-worth.

5. Johnson, "Countering Trump's Inhumane Proposal."

6. Hollie McKay, "How Minneapolis' Somali Community Became the Terrorist Recruitment Capital of the US," Fox News, February 16, 2019, https://www.foxnews.com/us/how-rep-ilhan-omars-minnesota-district-became-the-terrorist-recruitment-capital-of-the-us-officials-highly-concerned.

7. Julia Delacroix and Coshandra Dillard, "This Is Not a Drill," *Teaching Tolerance* (Fall 2018), https://www.tolerance.org/magazine/fall-2018/this-is-not-a-drill.

8. Crimethinc. Ex-Workers Collective, "Occupy ICE Portland: Lessons from the Barricades," It's Going Down, July 12, 2018, https://itsgoingdown.org/occupy-ice-portland-lessons-from-the-barricades/.

9. Allison Manning and Susan Zalkind, "How Violent Street Gang MS-13 Operates in Massachusetts," Boston.com, January 29, 2016, https://www.boston.com/news/local-news/2016/01/29/how-violent-street-gang-ms-13-operates-in-massachusetts.

10. Allum Bokhari, "Michelle Malkin Censored on Facebook for Opposing Censorship," Breitbart, May 10, 2019, https://www.breitbart.com/tech/2019/05/10/michelle-malkin-censored-on-facebook-for-opposing-censorship/.

11. "Hate Speech Policy," YouTube Help, June 5, 2019, https://support.google.com/youtube/answer/2801939?hl=en.

12. See, e.g., Matthew Yglesias, "The Pernicious Myth of 'Open Borders,'" Vox, June 22, 2018, https://www.vox.com/2018/6/22/17488272/open-borders-myth.

13. Patrick Buchanan, "Is the Liberal Hour Ending in the West?" Creators.com, May 29, 2019, https://www.creators.com/read/pat-buchanan/05/19/is-the-liberal-hour-ending-in-the-west.

14. Tyler O'Neil, "'He Took a Hard Punch in the Face for All of Us'—Berkeley Victim Joins Trump on CPAC Stage," PJ Media, March 2, 2019, https://pjmedia.com/trending/trump-has-hayden-williams-on-stage-at-cpac/.

15. Nick Muscavage, "MAGA Hat Assault: 19-Year-Old NJ Man Charged in Assault of Elderly Man," *Bridgewater Courier News*, February 27, 2019, https://www.mycentraljersey.com/story/news/crime/2019/02/27/nj-man-19-arrested-assault-elderly-man-wearing-maga-hat/3008538002/.

16. Amazing Top News, "Trump Supporter in MAGA Hat Gets Kicked Off Plane for Standing Up for Himself," Youtube, May 9, 2019, https://www.youtube.com/watch?v=qnIscnjDl6I.

17. Stephen A. Crockett Jr., "Black Oklahoma Student Knocks MAGA Hat Off White Teen's Head. Now He's Facing Charges," The Root, February 27, 2019, https://www.theroot.com/black-oklahoma-student-knocks-maga-hat-off-white-teens-1832937828.

18. Crockett Jr., "Black Oklahoma Student Knocks MAGA Hat Off."

19. Public Affairs, UC Berkeley, "Milo Yiannopoulos Event Canceled After Violence Erupts," February 1, 2017, https://news.berkeley.edu/2017/02/01/yiannopoulos-event-canceled/.

20. Daniel Greenfield, "Yes, Amymek Was Doxxed," FrontPage Mag, June 12, 2018, https://www.frontpagemag.com/point/270429/yes-amymek-was-doxxed-daniel-greenfield.

21. Michelle Malkin, "CPAC at the Bridge," Michellemalkin.com, March 1, 2019, http://michellemalkin.com/2019/03/01/cpac-at-the-bridge/.

22. Jason Lemon, "Donald Trump Is the 'Antichrist' and Is 'Going to Hell,' Immigrant from Caravan Says," *Newsweek*, October 21, 2018, https://www.newsweek.com/donald-trump-anti-christ-and-going-hell-immigrant-caravan-says-1180151.

23. Associated Press, "The Latest: Honduran Migrant Says He Wants to Return Home," NBC 12, October 20, 2018, https://www.nbc12.com/2018/10/20/latest-migrants-wait-cross-border-with-mexico/. This article includes an AP photo by Fernando Antoni showing two people burning an American flag. The photo caption states: "Two people burn a United States flag during a protest in favor of the caravan of migrants that is currently stuck on the Guatemala-Mexico border, in front of the American embassy, in Tegucigalpa, Honduras, Friday, Oct. 19, 2018."

24. Cher (@cher), "I Understand Helping Struggling Immigrants, but MY CITY (Los Angeles) ISNT TAKING CARE OF ITS OWN. WHAT ABOUT THE 50,000+ Citizens WHO LIVE ON THE STREETS.PPL WHO LIVE BELOW POVERTY LINE,& HUNGRY? If My State Can't Take Care of Its Own(Many Are VETS)How Can it Take Care Of More," Twitter, April 14, 2019, 11:14 a.m., https://twitter.com/cher/status/1117491420934365185?lang=en.

25. Caroline Linton, "New York Post Cover Features Ilhan Omar Quote and 9/11 Terror Attack," CBS News, April 12, 2019, https://www.cbsnews.com/news/new-york-post-cover-featuring-ilhan-omar-quote-and-911-terror-attack-hit-stands-thursday-2019-04-12/.

26. Megan Olson, "Ilhan Omar Calls to Abolish ICE in Response to Trump's Immigration Proposal," Alpha News, May 23, 2019, https://alphanewsmn.com/ilhan-omar-calls-to-abolish-ice-in-response-to-trumps-immigration-proposal/.

27. Joel B. Pollak, "Ilhan Omar: I Bring 'Perspective of a Foreigner' to U.S. Foreign Policy," Breitbart, May 28, 2019, https://www.breitbart.com/national-security/2019/05/28/ilhan-omar-i-bring-perspective-of-a-foreigner-to-u-s-foreign-policy/.

28. Michelle Malkin, "Question: Did Ilhan Omar Commit Federal Tax Fraud?" Michellemalkin.com, June 6, 2019, http://michellemalkin.com/2019/06/06/question-did-ilhan-omar-commit-federal-tax-fraud/.

29. Scott Johnson, "Ilhan Omar's 'Disgusting Lies,'" *Power Line* (blog), October 23, 2018, https://www.powerlineblog.com/archives/2018/10/ilhan-omars-disgusting-lies.php.

30. David Steinberg, "New Photos Corroborate Perjury Claims Against Rep. Ilhan Omar, as She Deletes Social Media Evidence," PJ Media, November 5, 2018, https://pjmedia.com/davidsteinberg/new-photos-corroborate-perjury-claims-against-rep-ilhan-omar-as-she-deletes-social-media-evidence/.

31. David Steinberg, "Official School Records Support Claims That Rep. Ilhan Omar (D-MN) Married Her Brother," PJ Media, October 23, 2018, https://pjmedia.com/davidsteinberg/official-school-records-support-claims-that-rep-ilhan-omar-d-mn-married-her-brother/.

32. Christine Bauman, "Take A Walk Through Ilhan Omar's Controversial Marriage History," Alpha News, August 8, 2018, https://alphanewsmn.com/take-a-walk-through-ilhan-omars-controversial-marriage-history/.

33. "Findings, Conclusions, and Order in the Matter of the Complaint of Steve Drazkowski Regarding the Neighbors for Ilhan (Omar) Committee," State of Minnesota Campaign Finance and Disclosure Board, June 6, 2019, https://docs.google.com/viewerng/viewer?url=http://michellemalkin.com/wp-content/uploads/2019/06/218_Signed-Findings-1.pdf&hl=en.

34. Amy Forliti, "Minnesota House Hopeful Calls Marriage, Fraud Claims 'Lies,'" Associated Press, October 17, 2018, https://apnews.com/cc2ccd70de56405098d2f259bf0e46c5.

35. "Alliance Member Profile: ACER's Pathway to Citizenship Campaign," The Alliance, https://thealliancetc.org/alliance-member-profile-acers-pathway-to-citizenship-campaign/.

36. Rachel Scott, "State of the Union's Dueling Guest Lists Highlight Trump's Priorities, Democrats' Opposition," ABC News, February 5, 2019, https://www.yahoo.com/gma/state-unions-dueling-guest-lists-highlight-trumps-priorities-220514929.html.

37. Avery Anapol, "Ilhan Omar Bringing Liberian Immigrant Facing Deportation Threat to State of the Union," Hiiraan Online, February 5, 2019, https://www.hiiraan.com/news4/2019/Feb/162158/ilhan_omar_bringing_liberian_immigrant_facing_deportation_threat_to_state_of_the_union.aspx.

38. U.S. Citizenship and Immigration Services, "Temporary Protected Status," June 7, 2019, https://www.uscis.gov/humanitarian/temporary-protected-status.

39. U.S. Citizenship and Immigration Services, "38.2 Deferred Enforced Departure," https://www.uscis.gov/ilink/docView/AFM/HTML/AFM/0-0-0-1/0-0-0-16606/0-0-0-16764.html.

40. Congressional Research Service, "Temporary Protected Status: Overview and Current Issues," March 29, 2019, https://fas.org/sgp/crs/homesec/RS20844.pdf.

41. The Alliance, "Alliance Member Profile: ACER's Pathway to Citizenship Campaign."

42. Alianza Americas, "Save TPS," https://www.alianzaamericas.org/save-tps/.

43. National TPS Alliance, "*Updated* TPS Lawsuit Information," https://www.nationaltpsalliance.org/tps-lawsuit/.

44. Chris Mills Rodrigo, "Trump Extends Deportation Protections for Liberians," The Hill, March 28, 2019, https://thehill.com/homenews/administration/436297-trump-extends-deportation-protections-for-liberians.

45. Rafael Bernal, "DHS Extends Immigration Protection for Four Countries amid Court Battles," The Hill, February 28, 2019, https://thehill.com/latino/432068-dhs-extends-immigration-protection-for-four-countries-amid-court-battles.

46. Andrew R. Arthur, "Judge Halts Termination of TPS for Sudan, Haiti, El Salvador, and Nicaragua," Center for Immigration Studies, October 5, 2018, https://cis.org/Arthur/Judge-Halts-Termination-TPS-Sudan-Haiti-El-Salvador-and-Nicaragua.

47. Ian Mason, "Citing 'Sh*thole Countries' Remark, Federal Judge Extends 'Temporary' Protected Status Indefinitely," Breitbart, October 3, 2018, https://www.breitbart.com/politics/2018/10/03/citing-shthole-countries-remark-federal-judge-extends-tempoary-protected-status-indefinitely/.

48. Chris Cuomo (@ChrisCuomo), "Let's not forget," Twitter, August 16, 2017, https://twitter.com/chriscuomo/status/897820041273626626.

49. Luis Alonso Lugo, "Mexico Asks US to Hasten $5.8 Billion Aid to Central America," Associated Press, May 24, 2019, https://apnews.com/b57693f0926a464aa6316bcf65811056.

50. Anne Speckhard and Ardian Shajkovci, "ISIS Fighter Claims Attack Plot Via Mexico, Underscoring Border Vulnerability," International Center

for the Study of Violent Extremism, June 4, 2019, https://www.icsve.org/isis-fighter-claims-attack-plot-via-mexico-underscoring-border-vulnerability/.

51. Linda Qiu, "No, Democrats Don't Want 'Open Borders,'" *New York Times*, June 27, 2018, https://www.nytimes.com/2018/06/27/us/politics/fast-check-donald-trump-democrats-open-borders.html.

52. Steve Guest (@SteveGuest), "Joe Biden says the US should provide healthcare to people 'regardless of whether they are documented or undocumented,'" Twitter, May 8, 2019, https://twitter.com/SteveGuest/status/1126309940937789440.

53. Mike Lillis, "Biden: Illegal Immigrants Are 'Already Americans,'" *The Hill*, March 27, 2014, https://thehill.com/blogs/blog-briefing-room/news/201972-biden-illegal-immigrants-already-americans.

54. RNC Research (@RNCResearch), "Kamala Harris says she supports illegal immigrants getting Medicare youtu.be/0BR-NsriOVs," May 12, 2019, https://twitter.com/RNCResearch/status/112758447527205273.

55. "Harris, Cortez Masto, Durbin Introduce Bill to Lift Ban on DREAMers Working for Congress," Kamala D. Harris Senate website, April 3, 2019, https://www.harris.senate.gov/news/press-releases/harris-cortez-masto-durbin-introduce-bill-to-lift-ban-on-dreamers-working-for-congress.

56. Ian Snively, "'It Is Radical': Immigration Expert Slams Julian Castro's Open Borders Plan," *Townhall*, April 3, 2019, https://townhall.com/tipsheet/iansnively/2019/04/03/it-is-radical-immigrations-expert-slams-julian-castros-open-borders-plan-n2544216.

57. Roque Planas, "It's Time to Decriminalize Immigration, Say Top Texas Dems," HuffPost, August 23, 2018, https://www.huffpost.com/entry/time-to-decriminalize-immigration-top-texas-democrats_n_5b7c3985e4b0348585fb0db5.

58. "Freshman Democrats Say They Will Not Fund Trump's Immigration Agenda," *Washington Post*, February 7, 2019, https://www.washingtonpost.com/video/national/freshman-democrats-say-they-will-not-fund-trumps-immigration-agenda/2019/02/07/2f686a5b-f6a0-4a0c-a923-47a8ee1da6df_video.html?utm_term=.dbbb4c9c754a.

59. Jessica Kwong, "Alexandra Ocasio-Cortez Sheds Tear, Says 'We Are Standing on Native Land' as She calls to Defund ICE," *Newsweek*, February 7, 2019, https://www.newsweek.com/alexandria-ocasio-cortez-ice-native-land-1322850.

60. Jose Vargas (@joseiswriting), "This is what happens when a government believes people are 'illegal.' Kids in cages," Twitter, June 12, 2018, 9:45 p.m., https://twitter.com/joseiswriting/status/1006397160622055429.

61. Jose Antonio Vargas, "My Life as an Undocumented Immigrant," *New York Times Magazine*, June 26, 2011, https://www.nytimes.com/2011/06/26/magazine/my-life-as-an-undocumented-immigrant.html?pagewanted=all&_r=1&.

62. Charles Koch Institute, "Interesting Leaders In Immigration Reform," BuzzFeed, May 9, 2013, https://www.buzzfeed.com/charleskochinstitute/interesting-leaders-in-immigration-reform.

63. Tim Cook and Charles Koch, "Congress Must Act on the 'Dreamers,'" *Washington Post*, December 14, 2017, https://www.washingtonpost.com/opinions/congress-must-act-on-the-dreamers/2017/12/14/3dc0ab98-e053-11e7-bbd0-9dfb2e37492a_story.html.

64. Philip Elliott, "The Koch Brothers Are Helping More Immigrants Get Help," *Time*, April 13, 2017, http://time.com/4737792/immigration-koch-brothers-citizenship-classes/.

65. Tim Mak, "Breaking With Trump's GOP, Koch Brothers Praise Democrats On Immigration," NPR, May 17, 2018, https://www.npr.org/2018/05/17/611798012/breaking-with-trumps-gop-koch-brothers-praise-democrats-on-immigration.

66. Rollcall Staff, "Schlapp Joins Koch Industries," *Roll Call*, January 31, 2005, https://www.rollcall.com/news/-7951-1.html.

67. "Matt Schlapp," ACU Foundation, http://acufoundation.conservative.org/board-member/matt-schlapp/.

68. Max Greenwood, "Mercedes Schlapp Joins White House as Senior Communications Adviser," *The Hill*, September 12, 2017, https://thehill.com/homenews/administration/350383-trump-names-conservative-commentator-as-senior-adviser-for-strategic.

69. "Cove Strategies," Open Secrets website, Center for Responsive Politics, https://www.opensecrets.org/lobby/firmsum.php?id=D000049818&year=2017.

70. "Cove Strategies," Open Secrets website, Center for Responsive Politics, https://www.opensecrets.org/lobby/firmsum.php?id=D000049818&year=2018.

71. "Cove Strategies," Open Secrets website, Center for Responsive Politics, https://www.opensecrets.org/lobby/firmsum.php?id=D000049818&year=2019.

72. "About," Seasonal Employment Alliance, https://sealabor.com/about/.

73. "Seasonal Employment Alliance H-2B D.C. Fly-In 2/15 and 2/16," EventBrite, https://www.eventbrite.com/e/seasonal-employment-alliance-h-2b-dc-fly-in-215-and-216-tickets-42604382856#.

74. Zach Everson, "Trump's D.C. Hotel Gave a Sweetheart Rate to a Pro-Immigrant Worker Group," The Daily Beast, May 21, 2018, https://www.thedailybeast.com/trumps-dc-hotel-gave-a-sweetheart-rate-to-a-pro-immigrant-worker-group.

75. Peter D'Abrosca, "EXCLUSIVE: Mulvaney, Schlapp Denied Angel Moms Meeting with Trump Over Budget Bill," Big League Politics, February 14, 2019, https://bigleaguepolitics.com/exclusive-mulvaney-schlapp-denied-angel-moms-meeting-with-trump-over-budget-bill/.

76. Preston Huennekens, "Latest Trump H-2B Increase Again Betrays American Workers," Center for Immigration Studies, March 29, 2019, https://cis.org/Huennekens/Latest-Trump-H2B-Increase-Again-Betrays-American-Workers.

77. "Report: Trump's Mar-a-Lago Hiring Foreigners on H-2B Visas," Newsmax, December 6, 2016, https://www.newsmax.com/Politics/H-2B-visa-Donald-Trump-Mar-a-Lago/2016/12/06/id/762541/.

78. Aidan McLaughlin, "Trump Ad-Libs That He Wants Legal Immigration to Reach 'Largest Numbers Ever,'" Mediaite, February 5, 2019, https://www.mediaite.com/tv/trump-ad-libs-that-he-wants-legal-immigration-to-reach-largest-numbers-ever/.

79. Of course, money in politics is nothing new. See, e.g., Brooks Jackson, *Honest Graft: Big Money and the American Political Process* (Knopf, 1990).

80. Will Sommer, "Anti-Muslim Activist Laura Loomer Banned From CPAC After Harassing Reporters," The Daily Beast, March 2, 2019, https://www.thedailybeast.com/anti-muslim-activist-laura-loomer-banned-from-cpac-after-harassing-reporters?ref=home.

81. Sommer, "Anti-Muslim Activist Laura Loomer Banned."

82. Author correspondence, May 9, 2019.

83. Michelle Malkin, "Don't Do Business with Progressive Appeasers," creators.com, April 11, 2012, https://www.creators.com/read/michelle-malkin/04/12/don-t-do-business-with-progressive-appeasers.

84. Malkin, "Don't Do Business with Progressive Appeasers."

85. Eoin Lenihan, "It's Not Your Imagination: The Journalists Writing About Antifa Are Often Their Cheerleaders," Quillette, May 29, 2019, https://quillette.com/2019/05/29/its-not-your-imagination-the-journalists-writing-about-antifa-are-often-their-cheerleaders/.

86. Ian Miles Cheong, "Twitter Bans Analyst Who Revealed AntiFa Connections With Journalists," Human Events, May 29, 2019, https://humanevents.com/2019/05/29/twitter-bans-analyst-who-revealed-journalists-antifa-connections/.

87. John Aidan Byrne, "JPMorgan Chase Accused of Purging Accounts of Conservative Activists," *New York Post*, May 25, 2019, https://nypost.com/2019/05/25/jpmorgan-chase-accused-of-purging-accounts-of-conservative-activists/.

88.   Megan Chuchman, Brian Ross and Joseph Rhee, "JPMorgan Chase To Spend Millions on New Jets and Luxury Airport Hangar," ABC News, March 23, 2009, https://abcnews.go.com/Blotter/WallStreet/jpmorgan-chase-spend-millions-jets-luxury-airport-hangar/story?id=7146474.

89.   Dan Stein, "New from the FAIR Archives – the Previously Unheard Audio of Dick Lamm's Famous 'My Secret Plan to Destroy America,'" Immigration Reform, March 27, 2014, https://www.immigrationreform.com/2014/03/27/new-from-the-fair-archives-the-previously-unheard-audio-of-dick-lamms-famous-my-secret-plan-to-destroy-america/.

90.   Julia Delacroix and Coshandra Dillard, "This Is Not a Drill," *Teaching Tolerance* (Fall 2018), https://www.tolerance.org/magazine/fall-2018/this-is-not-a-drill.

By the Numbers

1.   The phrase "majority minority future" comes from Stef W. Kight, "America's Majority Minority Future," Axois, April 29, 2019, https://www.axios.com/when-american-minorities-become-the-majority-d8b3ee00-e4f3-4993-8481-93a290fdb057.html Stef W. Kight.

2.   "Nativity and Citizenship Status in the United States," Fact Finder, U.S. Census Bureau, 2017 American Community Survey 1-Year Estimates, https://factfinder.census.gov/faces/tableservices/jsf/pages/productview.xhtml?pid=ACS_17_1YR_B05001&prodType=table.

3.   Jie Zong, Jeanne Batalova, and Micayla Burrows, "Frequently Requested Statistics on Immigrants and Immigration in the United States," Migration Policy Institute, March 14, 2019, https://www.migrationpolicy.org/article/frequently-requested-statistics-immigrants-and-immigration-united-states.

4.   "Table 7. Persons Obtaining Lawful Permanent Resident Status by Type and Detailed Class of Admission: Fiscal Year 2017," 2017 Yearbook of Immigration Statistics, Department of Homeland Security, https://www.dhs.gov/immigration-statistics/yearbook/2017/table7.

5.   "20 Million Immigrants Admitted Over 35 Years Through Chain Migration," NumbersUSA, September 27, 2017, https://www.numbersusa.com/news/20-million-immigrants-admitted-over-35-years-through-chain-migration.

6.   Pew Research estimates 10.7 million. See Jeffrey S. Passel and D'Vera Cohen, "U.S. Unauthorized Immigrant Total Dips to Lowest Level in a Decade," Pew Research Center–Hispanic Trends, November 27, 2018, https://www.pewhispanic.org/2018/11/27/u-s-unauthorized-immigrant-total-dips-to-lowest-level-in-a-decade/; FAIR and the Migration Policy Institute estimate 11 million as the base number of illegal aliens. See Spencer Raley, "How Many Illegal Aliens Are in the US?" FAIR.us, October 23, 2017, https://www.fairus.org/issue/illegal-immigration/how-many-illegal-immigrants-are-in-us; and Jie Zong, Jeanne Batalova, and Micayla Burrows, "Frequently Requested Statistics on Immigrants and Immigration in the United States," *op cit*, https://www.migrationpolicy.org/article/frequently-requested-statistics-immigrants-and-immigration-united-states#Unauthorized.

7.   See Mohammad Fazel-Zarandi, Jonathan S. Feinstein, and Edward H. Kaplan, "Yale Study Finds Twice as Many Undocumented Immigrants as Previous Estimates," *Yale Insights*, September 21, 2018, https://insights.som.yale.edu/insights/yale-study-finds-twice-as-many-undocumented-immigrants-as-previous-estimates; and Rafael Bernal, "Yale, MIT Study: 22 Million, Not 11 Million, Undocumented Immigrants in US," *The Hill,* September 21, 2018, https://thehill.com/latino/407848-yale-mit-study-22-million-not-11-million-undocumented-immigrants-in-us.

8.   "End Visa Overstays," NumbersUSA, https://www.numbersusa.com/solutions/end-visa-overstays.

9.   Matt O'Brien and Spencer Raley, "The Fiscal Burden of Illegal Immigration on United States Taxpayers," FAIR, September 27, 2017, https://www.fairus.org/issue/publications-resources/fiscal-burden-illegal-immigration-united-states-taxpayers.

10. Jason Richwine, Ph.D. and Robert Rector, "The Fiscal Cost of Unlawful Immigrants and Amnesty to the U.S. Taxpayer," The Heritage Foundation, May 6, 2013, https://www.heritage.org/immigration/report/the-fiscal-cost-unlawful-immigrants-and-amnesty-the-us-taxpayer.

11. United Nations Office on Drugs and Crime, "Global Study on Smuggling of Migrants 2018," June 2018, p. 22; https://www.unodc.org/documents/data-and-analysis/glosom/GLOSOM_2018_web_small.pdf.

12. *Ibid.*

13. Office of Refugee Resettlement, "Unaccompanied Alien Children," https://www.acf.hhs.gov/orr/programs/ucs.

14. National Immigration Forum, "The President's Budget Request for Refugee and Asylum Services: Fiscal Year (FY) 2019," April 4, 2018, https://immigrationforum.org/article/presidents-budget-request-refugee-asylum-services-fiscal-year-fy-2019/.

15. "Refugees in America," *USA for UNHCR*, https://www.unrefugees.org/refugee-facts/usa/.

16. *Ibid.*

17. "Proposed Refugee Admissions for Fiscal Year 2019," U.S. State Department Bureau of Population, Refugees, and Migration, September 24, 2018, https://web.archive.org/web/20190331085127/https://www.state.gov/j/prm/releases/docsforcongress/286157.htm. From the report: "The largest single country provider of humanitarian assistance worldwide, we fund the programs of UNHCR, the United Nations Children's Fund (UNICEF), IOM, the International Committee of the Red Cross (ICRC), the World Food Programme (WFP), and a number of other international and non-governmental partners. Total U.S. humanitarian assistance was more than $8 billion in FY 2017, including funding from PRM and the U.S. Agency for International Development's (USAID) Bureau for Democracy, Conflict and Humanitarian Assistance (DCHA). Our assistance provides urgent, life-saving support and services, including food, shelter, health care, and access to clean water for millions of displaced and crisis-affected people, including refugees, worldwide."

18. U.S. Department of State, "FY 2019 Notice of Funding Opportunity for Reception and Placement Program," March 15, 2018, https://web.archive.org/web/20181209132519/https://www.state.gov/j/prm/funding/fy2019/279289.htm; and Clare Roth, "Cuts to Refugee Admissions Hit Columbia Resettlement Agency," *Missourian*, October 12, 2018, https://www.columbiamissourian.com/news/local/cuts-to-refugee-admissions-hit-columbia-resettlement-agency/article_24e8f6f6-cb2c-11e8-9f13-33bceaee21af.html.

19. Matthew O'Brien and Spencer Raley, "The Fiscal Cost of Resettling Refugees in the United States," FAIR, February 5, 2018, https://www.fairus.org/issue/legal-immigration/fiscal-cost-resettling-refugees-united-state.

20. *Ibid.*

21. "Affirmative" asylum claims are claims made immediately upon arrival in the U.S. Defensive asylum claims are made by aliens in removal or deportation hearings.

22. "Proposed Refugee Admissions for Fiscal Year 2019," U.S. State Department Bureau of Population, Refugees, and Migration, *op cit.*

23. *Ibid.*

24. "George Soros," *Wall Street Insiders Guide*, Inside Philanthropy, https://www.insidephilanthropy.com/wall-street-donors/george-soros.html.

25. Juliet Chung and Anupreeta Das, "George Soros Transfers $18 Billion to His Foundation, Creating an Instant Giant," *Wall Street Journal*, October 17, 2017, https://www.wsj.com/articles/george-soros-transfers-18-billion-to-his-foundation-creating-an-instant-giant-1508252926.

26. "Open Society Foundations Announce $10 Million Initiative to Confront Hate," Open Society Foundation press release, November

22, 2016, https://www.opensocietyfoundations.org/newsroom/ foundations-announce-10-million-initiative-confront-hate.

27. Open Society Foundations, "2018 Budget Overview," https://www. opensocietyfoundations.org/sites/default/files/open-society-foundations-2018-budget-overview-20181107.pdf.

28. *Ibid.*

29. *Ibid.*

30. John L. Allen Jr., "The Church's Deep Pockets, the Butler Did It, and Myths about Atheism," *National Catholic Reporter*, August 17, 2012, https://www.ncronline.org/blogs/ all-things-catholic/churchs-deep-pockets-butler-did-it-and-myths-about-atheism.

31. KPMG, "United States Conference of Catholic Bishops and Affiliate, Consolidated Financial Statements with Supplemental Schedules, December 31 2017 and 2016," June 20, 2018, http://www.usccb.org/about/financial-reporting/upload/financial-statements-2016-2017.PDF.

32. Catholic Relief Services, "Form 990 for the 2017 Tax Year," March 14, 2019, https://www. crs.org/sites/default/files/fy2018_2017_form_990_-_web_version_03.14.19.pdf.

33. Forbes, "#13 Catholic Charities USA," https://www.forbes.com/companies/ catholic-charities-usa/#55d4324032b6.

34. World Bank Group and KNOMAD, "Migration and Remittances; Recent Developments and Outlook," December 2018, https://www.knomad.org/sites/default/files/201812/ Migration%20and%20Development%20Brief%2030%20advance%20copy.pdf.

35. Daniel Horowitz, "April Was Another Record Month for Illegal Immigration," *Conservative Review*, May 9, 2019, https://www.conservativereview.com/news/ april-another-record-month-illegal-immigration/.

36. *Ibid.*

37. *Ibid.*

38. Jonathan Vespa, David M. Armstrong, and Lauren Medina, "Demographic Turning Points for the United States: Population Projections for 2020 to 2060," *Population Estimates and Projections–Current Population Reports*, P25-1144, U.S. Census Bureau, March 2018, https://www.census.gov/content/dam/Census/library/publications/2018/demo/P25_1144. pdf.

39. *Ibid.*

40. Mike Maciag, "A State-by-State Look at Growing Minority Populations," *Governing*, June 25, 2015, https://www.governing.com/topics/urban/gov-majority-minority-populations-in-states.html.

41. Dudley L. Poston, Jr. and Rogelio Sáenz, "U.S. Whites Will Soon Be the Minority in Number, But Not Power," *Baltimore Sun*, August 8, 2017, https://www.baltimoresun.com/ news/opinion/oped/bs-ed-op-0809-minority-majority-20170808-story.html.

42. Ruy Teixeira, William H. Frey, and Robert Griffin, "States of Change: The Demographic Evolution of the American Electorate, 1974–2060, Center for American Progress, February 2015, https://cdn.americanprogress.org/wp-content/uploads/2015/02/SOC-report1.pdf.

43. John Binder, "Democrats Winning 90 Percent Congressional Democrats with Large Foreign-Born Populations," Breitbart.com, February 7, 2019, https://www.breitbart.com/politics/2019/02/07/ democrats-winning-90-congressional-districts-with-large-foreign-born-populations/.

44. John Binder, "Pew Research: Hispanics to Outpace Black Americans as Largest Voting Minority in 2020," Breitbart.com, April 16, 2019, https://www.breitbart.com/politics/2019/04/16/ pew-research-hispanics-to-outpace-black-americans-as-largest-voting-minority-in-2020/.

45. John Binder, "Pew Research: 1 in 10 U.S. Voters in 2020 Election Will Be Foreign-Born," Breitbart.com, February 20, 2019, https://www.breitbart.com/politics/2019/02/20/ pew-research-1-in-10-u-s-voters-in-2020-election-will-be-foreign-born/.

46. William H. Frey, "The US Will Become 'Minority White' in 2045, Census Projects," The Brookings Institution, March 14, 2018, https://www.brookings.edu/blog/the-avenue/2018/03/14/the-us-will-become-minority-white-in-2045-census-projects/.

Chapter 1

1. Daniel González, "Why a U.S. Citizen Helps Coordinate the Migrant Caravans That Trump Condemns as Invaders," *Arizona Republic*, November 9, 2018, https://www.azcentral.com/story/news/politics/immigration/2018/11/09/irineo-mujica-u-s-citizen-who-helps-coordinate-migrant-caravans/1910712002/.
2. "#DEFENDMIGRANTS," Frontline Defenders, https://www.frontlinedefenders.org/en/campaign/defendmigrants.
3. Curt Prendergast, "Prosecutors in Border-Aid Trial in Tucson Shift Focus to Behind-Scenes Figure," *Arizona Daily Star*, June 4, 2019, https://tucson.com/news/local/prosecutors-in-border-aid-trial-in-tucson-shift-focus-to/article_0004f5dd-3ddf-5cd5-87b3-d9d774a2dc15.html.
4. Madeleine Wattenbarger (@madeleinewhat), "Migration activists Cristóbal Sanchez and Irineo Mujica were just arrested in Mexico—more human rights defenders being criminalized," Twitter, June 5, 2019, 3:28 p.m., https://twitter.com/madeleinewhat/status/1136399439126335488.
5. Fred Lucas, "What Trump Could Learn From the Reagan Immigration Amnesty," Daily Signal, October 8, 2017, https://www.dailysignal.com/2017/10/08/what-trump-could-learn-from-the-reagan-immigration-amnesty/.
6. Michelle Malkin, "Assimilation, Not Amnesty," Michellemalkin.com, November 12, 2012, http://michellemalkin.com/2012/11/12/assimilation-not-amnesty/.
7. "Frequently Asked Questions: The Obama Administration's DAPA and Expanded DACA Programs," National Immigration Law Center, March 2, 2015, https://www.nilc.org/issues/immigration-reform-and-executive-actions/dapa-and-expanded-daca-programs/.
8. Zuzana Cepla, "Fact Sheet: Temporary Protected Status (TPS)," National Immigration Forum, https://immigrationforum.org/article/fact-sheet-temporary-protected-status/.
9. Gonzalez, "Why a U.S. Citizen Helps Coordinate the Migrant Caravans."
10. Ibid.
11. Author correspondence via Facebook Messenger, May 4, 2019.
12. George Ramos, "Fraud Charged as Disputed Amnesty Program Closes," *Los Angeles Times*, December 1, 1989, https://www.latimes.com/archives/la-xpm-1989-12-01-mn-143-story.html.
13. David North, "Lessons Learned From the Legalization Programs of the 1980s," Center for Immigration Studies, January 1, 2005, https://cis.org/Report/Lessons-Learned-Legalization-Programs-1980s.
14. Michelle Malkin, *Invasion: How America Still Welcomes Terrorists Criminals & Other Foreign Menaces to Our Shores* (Washington D.C.: Regnery Publishing, 2002), 58.
15. Sasha Aslanian, "Human Rights Advocate Documents Journey of Central Americans to U.S. Border," MPR News, February 1, 2013, https://www.mprnews.org/story/2013/02/01/human-interest/human-rights-central-americans.
16. Nancy San Martin, "Migration Maze: Samaritans on the Central American Migrant Route," WRLN website, November 24, 2015, https://www.wlrn.org/post/migration-maze-samaritans-central-american-migrant-route.
17. "Fear for Safety," Amnesty International press release, April 25, 2008, https://www.amnesty.org/download/Documents/52000/amr410142008eng.pdf.
18. Roberto Barboza and Maria de Jesus Peters, *"Caravana Se Sube a La Bestia,"* El Universal, July 27, 2011, http://archivo.eluniversal.com.mx/notas/781827.html.

19. Emilio Godoy, "MEXICO: The Long March to Justice for Migrants" IPS News, July 29, 2011, http://www.ipsnews.net/2011/07/mexico-the-long-march-to-justice-for-migrants/.
20. Godoy, "MEXICO: The Long March to Justice."
21. Wendy Cole, "Elvira Arellano," *Time*, December 25, 2006, http://content.time.com/time/specials/packages/article/0,28804,2019341_2017328_2017183,00.html.
22. "Reverend Walter Coleman," DACA Seminar, Harvard University, https://dacaseminar.fas.harvard.edu/people/walter-slim-coleman.
23. Brooke Binkowski, "Activist Deportee Elvira Arellano Released In San Diego," KPBS website, March 21, 2014, https://www.kpbs.org/news/2014/mar/21/activist-deportee-elvira-arellano-released-san-die/.
24. Manya Brachear Pashman, "Son of Immigration Activist Who Sought Sanctuary in Chicago Church To Graduate High School," *Chicago Tribune*, June 14, 2017, https://www.chicagotribune.com/news/immigration/ct-saul-arellano-graduates-high-school-met-20170614-story.html.
25. "Elvira Arellano," Influence Watch, https://www.influencewatch.org/person/elvira-arellano/.
26. Rosa Flores, "Chicago 'Sanctuary Church' Shelters Immigrants, Endures Hate Speech," CNN, February 14, 2017, https://www.cnn.com/2017/02/14/us/sanctuary-church-chicago-immigrants/index.html.
27. Vice News, "Protesting Migrants Recreate the 'Way of the Cross' Through Mexico," Vice News, April 25, 2014, https://news.vice.com/en_us/article/qvae9q/protesting-migrants-recreate-the-way-of-the-cross-through-mexico.
28. Vice News, "Protesting Migrants Recreate the 'Way of the Cross.'"
29. Jane Brundage, "Migrants Crossing Mexico: 'Stop the Humanitarian Tragedy'–Alejandro Solalinde to Peña Nieto," Mexico Voices, June 6, 2014, https://mexicovoices.blogspot.com/2014/06/migrants-crossing-mexico-stop.html.
30. Brundage, "Migrants Crossing Mexico."
31. Alex Mensing, "The Making of 'Danger: Journalists Crossing,'" The Narco News Bulletin, April 29, 2015, https://www.narconews.com/Issue67/article4803.html.
32. "#DEFENDMIGRANTS," Frontline Defenders.
33. Alex Mensing, "The Making of 'Danger: Journalists Crossing.'"
34. "#DEFENDMIGRANTS," Frontline Defenders.
35. "Donors," Frontline Defenders, https://www.frontlinedefenders.org/en/donors.
36. Pueblo Sin Fronteras Twitter page (@PuebloSF), Twitter, https://twitter.com/PuebloSF.
37. Pueblo Sin Fronteras press release, Facebook, March 23, 2018, https://www.facebook.com/PuebloSF/posts/for-immediate-releaseespañol-abajomarch-23-2018tapachula-mexicoto-the-government/2103600996333257/.
38. Kirk Semple, "What Is the Migrant Caravan and Why Does Trump Care?" *New York Times*, October 18, 2018, https://www.nytimes.com/2018/10/18/world/americas/trump-migrant-caravan.html.
39. Nancy San Martin, "Migration Maze: Samaritans on the Central American Migrant Route," WLRN website, November 24, 2015, https://www.wlrn.org/post/migration-maze-samaritans-central-american-migrant-route.
40. International Organization for Migration, "IOM Signs Cooperation Agreements with Migrant Shelters on Mexico's Southern Border," reliefweb.int, March 23, 2012, https://reliefweb.int/report/mexico/iom-signs-cooperation-agreements-migrant-shelters-mexicos-southern-border.
41. Scalabrini Migration Network, "About Us," Casa del Migrante en Tijuana, A.C., https://casadelmigrantetijuana.com/en/quienes-somos/.
42. "Centro de Derechos Humanos Fray Matías de Córdova," Art, Migration, and Human Rights website, https://chiapas2015.tome.press/tome_place/centro-de-derechos-humanos-fray-matias-de-cordova/.

43. "Centro de Derechos Humanos Fray Matias de Cordova, A.C.," MacArthur Foundation website, https://www.macfound.org/grantees/1635/.
44. Jesuit Refugee Service/USA, "The Migrant Caravan: Your Questions Answered," November 9, 2018, https://www.jrsusa.org/story/the-migrant-caravan-your-questions-answered/.
45. Kino Border Initiative, "Who We Are," https://www.kinoborderinitiative.org/who-we-are/.
46. "World Refugee Day: Mexico Not Safe for Thousands of Migrants Fleeing Violence in Central America," Médecins Sans Frontiéres, June 20, 2018, https://www.doctorswithoutborders.ca/article/world-refugee-day-mexico-not-safe-thousands-migrants-fleeing-violence-central-america.
47. Médecins Sans Frontiéres, "World Refugee Day."
48. San Martin, "Migration Maze."
49. Arzu Güler, Maryna Shevtsova, and Denise Venturi, eds., *LGBTI Asylum Seekers and Refugees from a Legal and Political Perspective; Persecution, Asylum and Integration* (Springer, 2018), 265.
50. Emma Buckhout, "'More Migrants Are Coming, and They're Arriving More Hurt': Tales from Mexico City Migrant Shelters," Latin American Working Group, https://www.lawg.org/more-migrants-are-coming-and-theyre-arriving-more-hurt-tales-from-mexico-city-migrant-shelters/.
51. Nina Lakhani, "The Casa de Migrantes: A Light in the Dark," Al Jazeera, February 27, 2014, https://www.aljazeera.com/indepth/features/2014/02/casa-de-migrantes-light-dark-2014225212349719741.html.
52. Reuters, "There Is Now a 'Trip Advisor' for Migrants so They Can Avoid Falling into Slavery," September 2, 2015, https://www.businessinsider.com/r-could-tripadvisor-style-ratings-save-migrant-workers-from-slavery-2015-9.
53. Thomas Lothar Weiss and Pedro Arturo López Chaltelt, "Mexico: Public Policies Benefiting Migrants," International Organization for Migration (2011), https://publications.iom.int/fr/system/files/pdf/oim_pp_en.pdf.
54. Weiss and López Chaltelt, "Mexico: Public Policies."
55. "Guia del Migrante Mexicano," http://www.fairus.org/sites/default/files/2017-08/GuiaDelMigranteMexicano.pdf.
56. "Guia del Migrante Mexicano."
57. "Migrant Caravan: Mexico Bus Transportation Offer Withdrawn," BBC News, November 3, 2018, https://www.bbc.com/news/world-latin-america-46082886.
58. Elisabeth Malkin, "Fact Checking Trump's Claim That Mexico Sent Migrants to the Border," *New York Times*, February 6, 2019, https://www.nytimes.com/2019/02/06/world/americas/trump-state-union-migrants-border.html.
59. "Our Story," Al Otro Lado website, https://alotrolado.org/who-we-are/.
60. "Border Rights Project," Al Otro Lado website, https://alotrolado.org/wp-content/uploads/2018/12/Refugee-Program-Overview-5.pdf.
61. Ryan Devereaux, "Journalists, Lawyers, and Activists Working on the Border Face Coordinated Harassment from U.S. and Mexican Authorities," *The Intercept*, February 8, 2019, https://theintercept.com/2019/02/08/us-mexico-border-journalists-harassment/.
62. Devereaux, "Journalists, Lawyers and Activists Working."
63. Ibid.
64. "8 U.S. Code § 1324. Bringing In and Harboring Certain Aliens," Legal Information Institute, https://www.law.cornell.edu/uscode/text/8/1324.
65. "About RAICES," RAICES website, https://www.raicestexas.org/about/.
66. Friends Peace Committee, "Sanctuary: For Refugees from El Salvador and Guatemala: A Resource Guide for Friends" (August 1985), https://www.afsc.org/sites/default/files/documents/1985%20Sanctuary-%20for%20refugees%20from%20El%20Salvador%20and%20Guatemala%20-%20A%20resource%20guide%20for%20Friends.pdf.

67. Darcy Sprague, "Old-School Activism: The Story of Jack Elder," Folo Media, July 28, 2017, https://webcache.googleusercontent.com/search?q=cache:Y5dZUi-P7z8J:https://www.folomedia.org/old-school-activism-the-story-of-jack-elder/+&cd=1&hl=en&ct=clnk&gl=us.

68. In January 2019, U.S. prosecutors announced charges against eight No More Deaths activists suspected of assisting illegal aliens in the Cabeza Prieta National Wildlife Refuge area spanning 800,000 acres of desert along the Arizona-Mexico border. Four were convicted in a bench trial. See Kristine Phillips, "They Left Food and Water for Migrants in the Desert. Now They Might Go to Prison," *Washington Post*, January 20, 2019, https://www.washingtonpost.com/nation/2019/01/20/they-left-food-water-migrants-desert-now-they-might-go-prison/?utm_term=.f294d551c2b8. A fifth No More Deaths volunteer, Scott Warren, went on jury trial in June 2019 as this book was headed to press.

69. "No More Deaths: An Interview with John Fife," *Reflections: A Magazine of Theological and Ethical Inquiry from Yale Divinity School* (2008), https://reflections.yale.edu/article/who-my-neighbor-facing-immigration/no-more-deaths-interview-john-fife.

70. Samantha Schmidt, "Crying Immigrant Girl: The Truth behind Iconic Photo," *Washington Post* / San Jose *Mercury News*, June 22, 2018, https://www.mercurynews.com/2018/06/22/crying-immigrant-girl-truth-behind-photo/.

71. David Yaffe-Bellany, "A Viral Facebook Fundraiser Has Generated More Than $20 Million for Immigration Nonprofit RAICES," Texas Tribune, July 27, 2018, https://www.texastribune.org/2018/06/27/viral-facebook-fundraiser-has-generated-more-20-million-immigration-no/.

72. Felix Salmon, "How Is RAICES Handling Its $30 Million Windfall?" Slate, July 23, 2018, https://slate.com/business/2018/07/immigration-nonprofit-raices-took-in-usd20-million-from-a-facebook-donation-drive-what-now.html.

73. See, for example, Washington Post photo at: https://www.washingtonpost.com/resizer/A8xCd3OjIjxO2xo1Mdt4dURB5Bs=/742x0/arc-anglerfish-washpost-prod-washpost.s3.amazonaws.com/public/ULCFTUWYQYI6RA4EXTCUSL7PJE.jpg.

74. Associated Press, "Cubans, No Longer Preferred, Are Stuck at US-Mexico Border," March 27, 2017, https://apimagesblog.com/blog/2017/3/27/tales-from-the-border-day-5.

75. Maria Verza and Marcos Aleman, "How Does a Central American Migrant Caravan Form?" Associated Press, April 19, 2019, https://www.apnews.com/77e346d48eee42dc9ffce43c92bb261f.

76. "Empowering Migrants: MigApp," IOM website, https://www.iom.int/migapp.

77. Alex Tabarrok, "Should Apple and Google Ban Gab?" Marginal Revolution, August 23, 2017, https://marginalrevolution.com/marginalrevolution/2017/08/mind-the-gab.html.

78. ICRC press release, "Mexico: Migrants Using WhatsApp Can Get Advice on How To Stay Safe and Avoid Illness, Sickness," International Committee of the Red Cross website, April 3, 2019, https://www.icrc.org/en/document/mexico-migrants-using-whatsapp-can-get-advice-avoiding-illness-sickness.

79. "Frequently Asked Questions," Notifica website, https://notifica.us/faq/.

80. Alex Dunbar, "Crossing the Border Illegally? There's an 'App' for That: A Q+A With Ricardo Dominguez," *Vice*, May 9, 2011, https://motherboard.vice.com/en_us/article/z44m53/the-transborder-immigrant-tool-helps-mexicans-cross-over-safely.

81. Dunbar, "Crossing the Border Illegally?"

82. Ivy Kaplan, "How Smartphones and Social Media Have Revolutionized Refugee Migration," UNHCR Blogs, https://www.unhcr.org/blogs/smartphones-revolutionized-refugee-migration/.

83. Jenny Lisette Flores et al., Stipulated Settlement Agreement, December 7, 2001, https://www.aclu.org/sites/default/files/field_document/flores_settlement_final_plus_extension_of_settlement011797.pdf.

84. Tom Cohen, "Unintended Consequences: 2008 Anti-Trafficking Law Contributes to Border Crisis," CNN, July 15, 2015, https://www.cnn.com/2014/07/15/politics/immigration-unintended-consequences/index.html.

85. William Wilberforce Trafficking Victims Protection Reauthorization Act of 2008, §235, Pub. L. 110-457 (2008).

86. William Wilberforce Trafficking Victims Protection Reauthorization Act of 2008, §235, Pub. L. 110-457 (2008).

87. Administration for Children and Families, "Unaccompanied Alien Children Program" fact sheet, U.S. Department of Health and Human Services, December 2018, https://www.acf.hhs.gov/sites/default/files/orr/unaccompanied_alien_children_program_fact_sheet_december_2018.pdf.

88. Office of Refugee Resettlement, "Unaccompanied Alien Children," Administration for Children and Families, https://www.acf.hhs.gov/orr/programs/ucs.

89. Office of Refugee Resettlement, *Annual Report to Congress FY 2014*, U.S. Department of Health and Human Services, Administration for Children and Families, https://www.acf.hhs.gov/sites/default/files/orr/orr_annual_report_to_congress_fy_2014_signed.pdf, 70.

90. "The President's Budget Request for Refugee and Asylum Services: Fiscal Year (FY) 2019," National Immigration Forum website, April 4, 2018, https://immigrationforum.org/article/presidents-budget-request-refugee-asylum-services-fiscal-year-fy-2019/.

91. Office of Refugee Resettlement, "Facts and Data," U.S Department of Health and Human Services, Administration for Children and Families, https://www.acf.hhs.gov/orr/about/ucs/facts-and-data.

92. Robert Stilson, "Government-Funded Nonprofits Being Paid Millions to House Unaccompanied Minors," Capital Research Center, March 15, 2019, https://capitalresearch.org/article/government-funded-nonprofits-being-paid-millions-to-house-unaccompanied-minors/.

93. "BCFS Health and Human Service," TAGGS website, https://taggs.hhs.gov/Detail/RecipDetail?arg_RecipId=5rtTb1pwLL838sfHg3U02Q%3D%3D.

94. "Southwest Key Programs Inc.," TAGGS website, https://taggs.hhs.gov/Detail/RecipDetail?arg_RecipId=06BHspu4p3T4AaCcnSxzaA%3D%3D.

95. Robert Stilson, "Government-Funded Nonprofits Being Paid Millions."

96. Repatriations have been rare. The Center for Immigration Studies' Jessica Vaughan testified before Congress in February 2015 that "Only a few hundred of the Central American families and unaccompanied juveniles who arrived in recent years have been repatriated" out of tens of thousands allowed to stay and await hearings. See: Jessica Vaughan, "A Review of the Department of Homeland Security Policies and Procedures for the Apprehension, Detention, and Release of Non-Citizens Unlawfully Present in the United States," Center for Immigration Studies, February 25, 2015, http://discuss.ilw.com/articles/articles/383513-article-a-review-of-the-department-of-homeland-security-policies-and-procedures-for-the-apprehension-detention-and-release-of-non-citizens-unlawfully-present-in-the-united-states-by-jessica-vaughan#3.

97. Yolo County Agreement with the Office of Refugee Resettlement, https://yoloagenda.yolocounty.org/docs/2017/BOS/20170425_1755/6201_Skinner%20Report%20with%20Exhibits.pdf.

98. William A. Kandel, "Unaccompanied Alien Children: An Overview," Congressional Research Service, January 18, 2017, https://fas.org/sgp/crs/homesec/R43599.pdf.

99. Amy Taxin, "Immigrant Kids Placed with Adults Who Are in US Illegally," Associated Press, April 19, 2016, https://static1.businessinsider.com/ap-immigrant-kids-placed-with-adults-who-are-in-us-illegally-2016-4.

100. United States Conference of Catholic Bishops and Lutheran Immigration and Refugee Service, "Post-Release Services: Family Preservation Services for Immigrant Children Released From Federal Custody, Frequently Asked Questions," http://www.usccb.org/

about/children-and-migration/upload/LIRS-and-USCCB-Post-Release-Services-FAQs-Final.pdf.

101. General Accounting Office, "Unaccompanied Children; HHS Can Take Further Actions to Monitor Their Care," February 2016, https://www.gao.gov/assets/680/675001.pdf, 24.

102. Young Center for Immigrant Children's Rights, "Young Center for Immigrant Children's Rights Thanks Our Funding Partners," https://www.theyoungcenter.org/funding-partners.

103. General Accounting Office, "Unaccompanied Children," 24.

104. Influence Watch, "Vera Institute of Justice (VIJ)," https://www.influencewatch.org/non-profit/vera-institute-of-justice/.

105. Guidestar, "The U.S. Committee for Refugees and Immigrants, Inc.," https://www.guidestar.org/profile/13-1878704.

106. Daniel Horowitz, "Don't Be Fooled by the Lies about 'Unaccompanied Alien Children,'" Conservative Review, April 5, 2018, https://www.conservativereview.com/news/dont-fooled-lies-unaccompanied-alien-children/.

107. U.S. Citizenship and Immigration Services, "2014 Executive Actions on Immigration," https://www.uscis.gov/archive/2014-executive-actions-immigration.

108. Maria Sacchetti, "Kelly Revokes Obama Order Shielding Immigrant Parents of U.S. Citizens," Washington Post, June 15, 2017, https://www.washingtonpost.com/local/social-issues/kelly-revokes-obama-order-shielding-immigrant-parents-of-us-citizens/2017/06/15/d3b4db62-5244-11e7-91eb-9611861a988f_story.html?utm_term=.1e54ba563b61.

109. Gustavo Lopez and Jens Manuel Krogstad, "Key Facts about Unauthorized Immigrants Enrolled in DACA," Pew Research Center, September 25, 2017, https://www.pewresearch.org/fact-tank/2017/09/25/key-facts-about-unauthorized-immigrants-enrolled-in-daca/.

110. Lopez and Krogstad, "Key Facts about Unauthorized Immigrants."

111. ACLU, "Court Rules Trump Policies Denying Asylum Protections to People Fleeing Domestic and Gang Ciolence Are Illegal," December 19, 2018, https://www.aclu.org/news/court-rules-trump-policies-denying-asylum-protections-people-fleeing-domestic-and-gang-violence.

112. USA for UNHCR, "Central America Refugee Crisis," https://www.unrefugees.org/emergencies/central-america/.

113. Vic Kolenc, "Beto O'Rourke Rallies in Texas Kick-Off in El Paso, Blocks from Migrant Families under Bridge," El Paso Times, March 30, 2019, https://www.elpasotimes.com/story/news/2019/03/30/beto-orourke-rallies-texas-kick-off-el-paso-challenges-trump-border-immigration/3314197002/.

114. David Gagne, "InSight Crime's 2016 Homicide Round-up," Insight Crime, January 16, 2017, https://www.insightcrime.org/news/analysis/insight-crime-2016-homicide-round-up/.

115. Matthew Sussis, "No Relationship Between Homicide Rates in Central America and Illegal Border Crossings," Center for Immigration Studies, March 4, 2019, https://cis.org/Sussis/No-Relationship-Between-Homicide-Rates-Central-America-and-Illegal-Border-Crossings.

116. Kausha Luna, "91.1% of Guatemalans Migrate to the U.S. for Economic Reasons," Center for Immigration Studies, August 7, 2017, https://cis.org/Luna/911-Guatemalans-Migrate-US-Economic-Reasons

117. Richard Pollock, "Guatemala's Human Smuggling Network Is Big Business for 'Coyotes,'" Washington Examiner, August 21, 2014, https://www.washingtonexaminer.com/guatemalas-human-smuggling-network-is-big-business-for-coyotes.

118. Pollock, "Guatemala's Human Smuggling Network Is Big Business."

119. United Nations Office on Drugs and Crime, "Global Study on Smuggling of Migrants 2018," June 2018, https://www.unodc.org/documents/data-and-analysis/glosom/GLOSOM_2018_web_small.pdf, 22.

120. United Nations Office on Drugs and Crime, "Global Study on Smuggling of Migrants 2018," 94.

121. Ibid., 99.

122. Jay Root, "How One Migrant Family Got Caught between Smugglers, the Cartel, and Trump's zero-tolerance policy" Texas Tribune, March 7, 2019, https://www.texastribune.org/2019/03/07/migration-us-border-generating-billions-smugglers/.

123. Root, "How One Migrant Family Got Caught between Smugglers," 98–99.

124. Andrew R. Arthur, "Unaccompanied Alien Children and the Crisis at the Border," Center for Immigration Studies, April 1, 2019, https://cis.org/Report/Unaccompanied-Alien-Children-and-Crisis-Border.

125. Victoria A. Greenfield, Blas Nunez-Neto, Ian Mitch, Joseph C. Chang, Etienne Rosas, "Human Smuggling from Central America to the United States," RAND Corporation (2019), https://www.rand.org/pubs/research_briefs/RB10057.html.

126. United States of America v. Mirtha Veronica Nava-Martinez Order, December 13, 2013, https://www.scribd.com/document/192557927/Judge-Hanen-Order-on-Child-Smuggling#from_embed.

127. United States of America v. Mirtha Veronica Nava-Martinez Order, 3.

128. Ibid., 6–8.

129. Ibid.

130. Ron Nixon, "U.S. Campaign Against Migration Goes Unheard, or Unheeded, in Guatemala," *New York Times,* October 7, 2018, https://www.nytimes.com/2018/10/07/world/americas/guatemala-immigration-usa-mexico-border.html.

131. D'Vera Cohen, Jeffrey S. Passel, and Ana Gonzalez-Barrera, "Rise in U.S. Immigrants From El Salvador, Guatemala and Honduras Outpaces Growth From Elsewhere," Pew Research Center, December 7, 2017, https://www.pewhispanic.org/2017/12/07/recent-trends-in-northern-triangle-immigration/.

132. Daniel Horowitz, "Survey: One-Third of Guatemala's Population Would Like To Come to the US," Conservative Review, May 6, 2019, https://www.conservativereview.com/news/survey-one-third-guatemalas-population-like-come-us/.

133. Homeland Security Digital Library, "Securing the Border: Understanding and Addressing the Root Causes of Central American Migration to the United States," U.S. Senate Committee on Homeland Security and Governmental Affairs, March 25, 2015, https://www.hsdl.org/?view&did=767505.

134. Washington Times, "ICE: 87% of Illegal Alien Families Are No-Shows for Hearings," May 9, 2019, gopusa.com, http://www.gopusa.com/ice-87-of-illegal-alien-families-are-no-shows-for-hearings/.

135. Scott Neuman, "Obama: U.S., Central America Share Responsibility For Influx Of Minors," NPR, July 25, 2014, https://www.npr.org/sections/thetwo-way/2014/07/25/335363959/obama-u-s-central-america-share-responsibility-for-influx-of-minors.

136. Zach Silberman, "Foreign Aid Is Part of the Solution to the Central American Border Crisis," U.S. Global Leadership Coalition, August 8, 2014, https://www.usglc.org/blog/foreign-aid-is-part-of-the-solution-to-the-central-american-border-crisis/.

137. U.S. Citizenship and Immigration Services, "In-Country Refugee/Parole Processing for Minors in Honduras, El Salvador and Guatemala (Central American Minors – CAM)," https://www.uscis.gov/CAM.

138. U.S. Immigration and Citizenship Services, Refugee, Asylum and International Operations Directorate, "Humanitarian Parole Program," February 2011, https://www.uscis.gov/sites/default/files/USCIS/Resources/Resources%20for%20Congress/Humanitarian%20Parole%20Program.pdf.

139. U.S. Immigration and Citizenship Services, "EB-4: Permanent Workers – Special Immigrants," https://my.uscis.gov/exploremyoptions/eb4_permanent_workers.

140. U.S. Immigration and Citizenship Services, "Number of I-360 Petitions for Special Immigrant with a Classification of Special Immigrant Juvenile (SIJ) by Fiscal Year, Quarter and Case Status Fiscal Year 2019," (based on data queried April 2019) https://www.uscis.

gov/sites/default/files/USCIS/Resources/Reports%20and%20Studies/Immigration%20 Forms%20Data/Victims/I360_sij_performancedata_fy2019_qtr2.pdf.

141. U.S. Immigration and Citizenship Services, "Green Card Based on Special Immigrant Juvenile Classification," https://www.uscis.gov/green-card/special-immigrant-juveniles/ green-card-based-special-immigrant-juvenile-classification.

142. Austin Rose, "For Vulnerable Immigrant Children, A Longstanding Path to Protection Narrows," Migration Policy Institute, July 25, 2018, https://www.migrationpolicy.org/ article/vulnerable-immigrant-children-longstanding-path-protection-narrows.

143. Daniel Horowitz, "HHS Reprogramming Department Funding To Facilitate Resettling 'Unaccompanied' Central American Teens," Conservative Review, April 5, 2019, https:// www.conservativereview.com/news/hhs-reprogramming-department-funding-facilitate- resettling-unaccompanied-central-american-teens/.

144. "Southwest Border Migration FY 2019," U.S. Customs and Border Protection, June 7, 2019, https://www.cbp.gov/newsroom/stats/sw-border-migration.

145. Nick Miroff, (@NickMiroff), "ICE has released 168,000 family members in past 4 months, acting director Matt Albence says on conf call. The agency is making 40,000 'at large arrests' per year. 'We've released four times as many people as we're able to arrest on annual basis,' he said," Twitter, May 7, 2019, 1:12 p.m., https://twitter.com/NickMiroff/ status/1125855973917196291.

146. American Immigration Lawyers Association, Documents Relating to *Flores v. Reno* Settlement Agreement on Minors in DHS Custody, October 10, 2018, https://www.aila. org/infonet/flores-v-reno-settlement-agreement.

147. Flores v. Lynch, 828 F. 3d 898–Court of Appeals, 9th Circuit 2016, https://scholar.google. com/scholar_case?case=12780774456837741811.

148. Neil Munro, "Senate Hearing: Obama's DACA and Flores Orders Spiked Illegal Migration," Breitbart, May 23, 2019, https://www.breitbart.com/politics/2019/05/23/ senate-hearing-obamas-daca-and-flores-orders-spiked-illegal-migration/.

149. Jefferson B. Sessions, "Memorandum for All Federal Prosecutors," Office of the Attorney General, April 11, 2018, https://www.justice.gov/opa/press-release/file/956841/download.

150. Stephen Dinan, "African Migrants Discover U.S. Immigration Loopholes," *Washington Times*, May 31, 2019, https://www.washingtontimes.com/news/2019/may/31/ african-migrants-discover-us-immigration-loopholes/.

151. U.S. Customs and Border Protection, "U.S. Border Patrol Southwest Border Apprehensions by Sector Fiscal Year 2019," May 8, 2019, https://www.cbp.gov/newsroom/stats/ sw-border-migration/usbp-sw-border-apprehensions.

152. U.S. Customs and Border Protection, "U.S Border Patrol Southwest Border Apprehensions by Sector Fiscal Year 2019."

153. Curt Prendergast, "Feds in Southern Arizona Turn Attention to Family Fraud at Border," *Arizona Daily Star*, May 4, 2019, https://tucson.com/news/local/feds-in-southern-arizona- turn-attention-to-family-fraud-at/article_ff63b096-8381-5233-b7a5-e2be066163c3.html.

154. Pendergast, "Feds in Southern Arizona Turn Attention to Family Fraud at Border."

155. Bob Price, "EXCLUSIVE: 3 in 10 Migrant Family Interviews Result in False Claim Findings, Says ICE," Breitbart, May 7, 2019, https://www.breitbart.com/border/2019/05/07/ exclusive-3-in-10-migrant-family-interviews-result-in-false-claim-findings-says-ice/.

156. Aaron Montes, "'Recycled' Migrant Children Used by Unrelated Adults To Look like Family, US officials Say," *El Paso Times*, May 4, 2019, https://www.elpasotimes.com/story/news/immigration/2019/05/04/ border-patrol-migrant-caught-using-child-skirt-immigration-process/1104522001/.

157. Nomaan Merchant, "Border Patrol Expands Fingerprinting of Migrant Children" NBC San Diego, April 26, 2019, https://www.nbcsandiego.com/news/national-international/ Border-Patrol-Fingerprinting-Migrant-Children-509125761.html?amp=y.

158. John Burnett, "More Than 3,100 Migrants Found with Fake Documents In Past Year, Federal Agents Say," NPR, April 10, 2019, https://www.npr.org/2019/04/10/711850056/fake-documents-a-growing-problem-among-migrants-crossing-u-s-mexico-border.

159. Anna Giaritelli, "DNA Tests Reveal 30% of Suspected Fraudulent Migrant Families Were Unrelated," *Washington Examiner*, May 18, 2019, https://www.washingtonexaminer.com/policy/defense-national-security/dna-tests-reveal-30-of-suspected-fraudulent-migrant-families-were-unrelated.

160. CBP Arizona (@CBPArizona), "For the first half of FY2019, #YumaSector Border Patrol spent over $1 million on humanitarian costs for families and unaccompanied alien children in our custody, compared to $340K+ for all of FY2018. These costs include food, diapers, clothes, baby formula and other items. @CBP," Twitter, May 9, 2019, 5:55 p.m., https://twitter.com/CBPArizona/status/1126651930728484864.

161. "Iowa, Nebraska Senators: Who was Monitoring Edwin Mejia?" Joni Ernst Senate website, April 27, 2016, https://www.ernst.senate.gov/public/index.cfm/2016/4/iowa-nebraska-senators-who-was-monitoring-edwin-mejia.

162. U.S. Immigration and Customs Enforcement, "Wanted," https://www.ice.gov/most-wanted/mejia-edwin.

163. Andrew R. Arthur, "Most UACs Released to Sponsors Without Status: U.S. Government Completing the Conspiracy to Smuggle Minors," Center for Immigration Studies, April 29, 2019, https://cis.org/Arthur/Most-UACs-Released-Sponsors-Without-Status.

164. Arthur, "Most UACs Released to Sponsors Without Status."

165. Author communication with confidential source, February 20, 2017.

166. Victoria Rocha, "Can Undocumented Immigrants Become Foster Parents in Your State? It Depends.," Chronicle of Social Change, September 21, 2017, https://chronicleofsocialchange.org/analysis/undocumented-families-face-barriers-becoming-caregivers-many-states.

167. Horowitz, "HHS Reprogramming Department Funding To Facilitate Resettling."

168. Jessie Hellman, "HHS To Divert up to $385M from Health Programs to Shelter Migrant Children," *The Hill*, March 8, 2019, https://thehill.com/policy/healthcare/433264-hhs-to-divert-up-to-385-from-health-programs-to-shelter-migrant-children.

169. Michelle Malkin, "Banking on American Stupidity," Jewish World Review, November 30, 2001, http://www.jewishworldreview.com/michelle/malkin113001.asp.

170. Michelle Malkin, "Bank of Illegal Aliens in America," Michellemalkin.com, February 13, 2007, http://michellemalkin.com/2007/02/13/bank-of-illegal-aliens-in-america/.

171. Miriam Jordan and Valerie Bauerlein, "Bank of America Casts Wider Net For Hispanics," *Wall Street Journal*, February 13, 2007, http://online.wsj.com/article/SB117133501870406767.html?mod=home_whats_news_us.

172. U.S. Department of Justice, "1907. Title 8, U.S.C. 1324(A) offenses," https://www.justice.gov/jm/criminal-resource-manual-1907-title-8-usc-1324a-offenses.

173. Kelsey Sheehy and Amber Murakami-Fester, "How Undocumented Immigrants Can Get Bank Accounts," NerdWallet website, April 23, 2018, https://www.nerdwallet.com/blog/banking/undocumented-immigrants-bank-accounts/.

174. "Global Remittances (Money Transfer) Market Analysis & Outlook (2019-2023) with PayPal, Western Union, Euronet, and MoneyGram International Dominating," MarketWatch, February 20, 2019, https://www.marketwatch.com/press-release/global-remittances-money-transfer-market-analysis-outlook-2019-2023-with-paypal-western-union-euronet-and-moneygram-international-dominating—-researchandmarketscom-2019-02-20.

175. World Bank Group and KNOMAD, "Migration and Remittances: Recent Developments and Outlook," December 2018, https://www.knomad.org/sites/default/files/2018-12/Migration%20and%20Development%20Brief%2030%20advance%20copy.pdf.

176. Ivan Pentchoukov, "White House Considers Restricting Remittances to Mexico to Stop Illegal Migration," *Epoch Times*, April 10, 2019, https://www.theepochtimes.

com/white-house-considers-restricting-remittances-to-mexico-to-stop-illegal-migration_2874015.html.

177. Matthew O'Brien, Spencer Raley and Casey Ryan, "The United States Loses $150 Billion Annually in Remittances," fairus.org, May 2019, https://www.fairus.org/issue/workforce-economy/united-states-loses-150-billion-annually-remittances.

178. Tristan Grimble, "Growth of the U.S.-Mexico Remittance Corridor," BBVA, November 8, 2017, https://www.bbva.com/en/growth-u-s-mexico-remittance-corridor/.

179. Grimble, "Growth of the U.S.-Mexico Remittance Corridor."

180. Western Union, "Western Union Announces $0.175 Quarterly Dividend," December 7, 2017, http://ir.westernunion.com/news/archived-press-releases/press-release-details/2017/Western-Union-Announces-0175-Quarterly-Dividend-1272017/default.aspx.

181. SaveonSend, "Western Union: Permanent Leader of International Money Transfer?" June 15, 2019, https://www.saveonsend.com/blog/western-union-money-transfer/.

182. Zacks Equity Research, "Western Union Expands in Mexico With Digital Money Transfer," Nasdaq website, September 13, 2018, https://www.nasdaq.com/article/western-union-expands-in-mexico-with-digital-money-transfer-cm1022502.

183. Money & Banking, "The Stubbornly High Cost of Remittances," February 19, 2018, https://www.moneyandbanking.com/commentary/2018/2/18/the-stubbornly-high-cost-of-remittances.

184. Migration Data Portal, "Remittances," April 30, 2019, https://migrationdataportal.org/themes/remittances.

185. As you'll see in chapter 10, PayPal refuses to do business with Americans critical of open borders while actively pursuing illegal aliens. Priorities!

186. Ben Schiller, "The Fight for the $400 Billion Business of Immigrants Sending Money Home," *Fast Company*, April 28, 2017, https://www.fastcompany.com/3067778/the-blockchain-is-going-to-save-immigrants-millions-in-remittance-fees.

187. Matthew Di Salvo, "Report: Use of Cryptocurrencies for Remittance Is Growing in Popularity," bitcoin.com, December 25, 2018, https://news.bitcoin.com/report-use-of-cryptocurrencies-for-remittance-is-growing-in-popularity/.

188. Saagar Enjeti, "White House Plans to Target Remittance Payments,"Daily Caller, April 9, 2019, https://dailycaller.com/2019/04/09/white-house-plans-target-remittance-payments/.

189. Directo a Mexico, "Frequently Asked Questions," https://www.frbservices.org/assets/resources/financial-services/directomexicofaq.pdf.

190. Molly Hennessy-Fiske, "Illegal Immigrants Wiring Money Have an Amigo: The Fed," *Los Angeles Times*, February 26, 2007, https://www.latimes.com/world/la-fg-migrant-archive26feb26-story.html.

191. Judicial Watch, "Most of the $33 Billion in Remittances to Mexico Flow Via U.S. Govt. Banking Program," April 9, 2019, https://www.judicialwatch.org/blog/2019/04/most-of-the-33-billion-in-remittances-to-mexico-flow-via-u-s-govt-banking-program/.

192. Matt Bakker, *Migrating into Financial Markets: How Remittances Became a Development Tool*, University of California Press, 2015, https://www.jstor.org/stable/10.1525/j.ctt1ffjncm.8?refreqid=excelsior%3A9a5b34eadee2afbcb5165c920510d678&seq=1#metadata_info_tab_contents, 177.

193. Bakker, *Migrating into Financial Markets*.

194. Ibid., 179.

195. Ibid.

196. "Directo a México – (CF311)," Banxico website, http://www.banxico.org.mx/SieInternet/consultarDirectorioInternetAction.do?accion=consultarCuadro&idCuadro=CF311&sector=21&locale=en.

197. Ami Horowitz, "The Truth About the Caravan," YouTube, November 12, 2018, https://www.youtube.com/watch?v=BFbiqlExkfo.

198. See Influence Watch, "Pueblo Sin Fronteras," https://www.influencewatch.org/non-profit/pueblo-sin-fronteras/ and Jorge Butrón, "Activistas Acusan a Pueblo Sin

Fronteras," *La Razón*, November 27, 2018, https://www.razon.com.mx/mexico/activistas-acusan-a-pueblo-sin-fronteras/.

199. "Some Migrants Heading Home: 'They Tricked Us; Our Dreams Have Gone to Hell,'" *Mexican News Daily*, November 28, 2018, https://mexiconewsdaily.com/news/some-migrants-heading-home/.

200. Ana Rosa Quintana and David Inserra, "Managing the Central American Caravans: Immediate Enforcement Corrections and Regional Engagement Strategy Required," Heritage Foundation, January 25, 2019, https://www.heritage.org/sites/default/files/2019-01/BG3372.pdf.

201. Ana Quintana, "Caravan Activists Are Weaponizing Poor Central Americans," Heritage Foundation, October 18, 2018, https://www.heritage.org/americas/commentary/caravan-activists-are-weaponizing-poor-central-americans.

202. "Immigrant Caravan Organizer Held After Trump Threatens Honduras," VOA News website, October 16, 2018, https://www.voanews.com/a/immigrant-caravan-organizer-held-after-trump-threatens-honduras/4616337.html.

203. Mexico News Daily, "What Caravan? Honduras Asks; NGO Claims 'Mother of All Caravans' a Ploy," March 29, 2019, https://mexiconewsdaily.com/news/what-caravan-honduras-asks/.

204. Mexico News Daily, "What Caravan? Honduras Asks."

Chapter 2

1. Open Society Foundations (@OpenSociety), "Neither our founder George Soros nor Open Society is involved in the migrant caravan. We have never funded nor directed people to migrate. We support humane approaches to immigration that respect the law and borders: osf.to/2QILcdu," Twitter, November 5, 2018, 5:17 p.m., https://twitter.com/OpenSociety/status/1059615748207845376.

2. Talia Lavin, "Conspiracy Theories about Soros Aren't Just False. They're Anti-Semitic," *Washington Post*, October 24, 2018, https://www.washingtonpost.com/outlook/2018/10/24/conspiracy-theories-about-soros-arent-just-false-theyre-anti-semitic/.

3. The original version of Lavin's article was posted on the *Washington Post*'s Medium account at the following link and omits any disclosure of Lavin's ties to Media Matters: https://medium.com/thewashingtonpost/conspiracy-theories-about-soros-arent-just-false-they-re-anti-semitic-f22a2577a8f6. The amended article on the *Washington Post* website, which failed to inform readers of a stealthy, post-publication edit, parenthetically included this disclosure from Lavin: "(I worked at Media Matters for America, which received a $1 million donation from Soros in 2010, eight years before I joined.)" See Talia Levin, "Conspiracy theories about Soros aren't just false. They're anti-Semitic."

4. Jon Levine, "Media Matters Hires Ex-New Yorker Fact Checker Who Falsely Said ICE Agent Had Nazi Tattoo," The Wrap, July 20, 2018, https://www.thewrap.com/media-matters-ex-new-yorker-fact-checker-talia-lavin-ice-agent-false-nazi-tattoo/.

5. Michelle Malkin, "Weapons of Mass Manipulation," Michellemalkin.com, June 19, 2018, http://michellemalkin.com/2018/06/19/weapons-of-mass-manipulation/.

6. See more about this sordid episode in chapter eight.

7. Adam Serwer, "Trump's Caravan Hysteria Led to This," *The Atlantic*, October 28, 2018, https://www.theatlantic.com/ideas/archive/2018/10/caravan-lie-sparked-massacre-american-jews/574213/.

8. James S. Robbins, "Synagogue Shooter Hated Donald Trump and Shows What Real Hatred, Anti-Semitism Looks Like," *USA Today*, October 29, 2018, https://www.usatoday.com/story/opinion/2018/10/29/donald-trump-robert-bowers-racist-anti-semitic-synagogue-shooting-column/1800755002/.

9. Serwer's articles for Media Matters for America are available online at: https://www.mediamatters.org/authors/adam-serwer/45.

10. Iga Mergler and Neil McLaughlin, "Scapegoating George Soros: How Media-Savvy Far-Right Activists Spread Lies," Salon.com, June 4, 2019, https://www.salon.com/2019/06/04/scapegoating-george-soros-how-media-savvy-far-right-activists-spread-lies_partner/.

11. Open Society Foundations, "Who We Are—Financials," https://www.opensocietyfoundations.org/about/expenditures-budget.

12. Open Society Foundations, "Open Society U.S. Programs Board Meeting," May 15–16, 2014, https://www.investigativeproject.org/documents/misc/892.pdf.

13. Juliet Chung and Anupreeta Das, "George Soros Transfers $18 Billion to His Foundation, Creating an Instant Giant," *Wall Street Journal*, October 17, 2017, https://www.wsj.com/articles/george-soros-transfers-18-billion-to-his-foundation-creating-an-instant-giant-1508252926.

14. Open Society Foundations, "2018 Budget Overview," https://www.opensocietyfoundations.org/sites/default/files/open-society-foundations-2018-budget-overview-20181107.pdf.

15. Open Society Foundations, "2018 Budget Overview," 4.

16. Michelle Malkin, "Who's Funding the Obamacare Astroturf Campaign?" Michellemalkin.com, June 24, 2009, http://michellemalkin.com/2009/06/24/whos-funding-the-obamacare-astroturf-campaign/.

17. "Open Society Foundations Announce $10 Million Initiative to Confront Hate," Open Society Foundation press release, November 22, 2016, https://www.opensocietyfoundations.org/newsroom/foundations-announce-10-million-initiative-confront-hate.

18. See, for example, Jamie Glazov, "The 'Hate-Crime' Victims of Trump Who Weren't," Daily Caller, November 18, 2016, https://dailycaller.com/2016/11/18/the-hate-crime-victims-of-trump-who-werent/; Ashe Schow, "Mississippi Man Pleads Guilty To Hate Crime Hoax SPLC Used To Slam Trump," Daily Wire, March 30, 2019, https://www.dailywire.com/news/45335/mississippi-man-pleads-guilty-hate-crime-hoax-splc-ashe-schow; and Elizabeth Nolan Brown, "There Is No Violent Hate-Crimewave in 'Trump's America,'" *Reason*, November 11, 2016, https://reason.com/2016/11/11/election-night-hijab-attack-false.

19. "Open Society Foundations Announce $10 Million Initiative to Confront Hate," Open Society Foundations Press Release.

20. Nonprofit Explorer, Foundation to Promote Open Society, Form 990 for period ending December 2015, ProPublica, https://projects.propublica.org/nonprofits/display_990/263753801/2016_11_PF%2F26-3753801_990PF_201512.

21. Joseph Rossell, "Soros, Ford Foundations 'Lavish' $196 Million to Push Internet Regulations," MRC Business, February 25, 2015, http://archive2.mrc.org/articles/soros-ford-foundations-lavish-196-million-push-internet-regulations.

22. Open Society Foundations Grants Database, http://archive.li/FDg3w.

23. Activist Facts, "Color of Change," https://www.activistfacts.com/organizations/524-color-of-change/.

24. Open Society Foundations, "2018 Budget Overview."

25. Avery Anapol, "Fox Business Drops Guest Who Blamed Migrant Caravan on 'Soros-Occupied State Department,'" *The Hill*, October 28, 2018, https://thehill.com/homenews/media/413542-fox-business-exec-condemns-rhetoric-of-guest-who-blamed-migrant-caravan-on.

26. Judicial Watch, "Judicial Watch: Documents Show State Department Links to George Soros' Open Society Foundation—Romania," October 30, 2018, https://www.judicialwatch.org/press-room/press-releases/judicial-watch-documents-show-state-department-links-to-george-soros-open-society-foundation-romania/.

27. Judicial Watch, "Judicial Watch: Documents Show State Department Links."

28. Ibid.

29. Ibid.

30. David D. Kirkpatrick, "Group Fined by F.E.C. for Campaign Violations," *New York Times*, August 30, 2007, https://www.nytimes.com/2007/08/30/washington/30donate.html.

31. Michelle Malkin, "Big Labor's Investment in Obama Pays Off," Michellemalkin.com, May 13, 2009, http://michellemalkin.com/2009/05/13/big-labors-investment-in-obama-pays-off/.

32. Sam Stein, "Patrick Gaspard: Obama's Glue Man," *HuffPost*, January 4, 2009, https://www.huffpost.com/entry/obamas-glue-man-the-best_n_148415.

33. Lachlan Markay, "Read the Confidential Document Left Behind at the Democracy Alliance Meeting," *Washington Free Beacon*, May 5, 2014, https://freebeacon.com/politics/jonathan-soros-left-a-confidential-document-at-his-donor-conference/.

34. FindLaw, "Major Provisions of the Personal Responsibility and Work Opportunity Reconciliation Act of 1996," https://corporate.findlaw.com/law-library/major-provisions-of-the-personal-responsibility-and-work.html.

35. Open Society Institute, "Keeping America Open," 2006, https://www.opensocietyfoundations.org/sites/default/files/tenth_20061116.pdf.

36. George Soros, "Relighting a Lamp Outside America's Darkening Door," *Los Angeles Times*, October 2, 1996, https://www.latimes.com/archives/la-xpm-1996-10-02-me-49536-story.html.

37. 142 U.S. 651 (12 S.Ct. 336, 35 L.Ed. 1146), Nishimura Ekiu v. United States et al., Legal Information Institute, https://www.law.cornell.edu/supremecourt/text/142/651.

38. Open Society Institute, "Keeping America Open."

39. George Soros, *The Crisis of Global Capitalism: Open Society Endangered*, Greenwood Press, 1998, 217.

40. Soros, *The Crisis of Global Capitalism*, 227.

41. George Soros, "The People's Sovereignty," *Foreign Policy*, October 28, 2009, https://foreignpolicy.com/2009/10/28/the-peoples-sovereignty/.

42. Andras Gergely, "Orban Accuses Soros of Stoking Refugee Wave to Weaken Europe," Bloomberg, October 30, 2015, http://www.bloomberg.com/news/articles/2015-10-30/orban-accuses-soros-of-stoking-refugee-wave-to-weaken-europe.

43. George Soros, "Rebuttal of the October 9 National Consultation in Hungary," Georgesoros.com, November 20, 2017, https://www.georgesoros.com/rebuttal/.

44. Karen Gilchrist, "Hungarian Government Faces Anti-Semitism Claims Amid Vilification of George Soros," CNBC, July 12, 2017, https://www.cnbc.com/2017/07/10/hungarian-government-faces-anti-semitism-claims-amid-vilification-of-george-soros.html.

45. Christian Keszthelyi, "Hungary's Government Puts Laughing Soros on Billboards," *Budapest Business Journal*, July 3, 2017, https://bbj.hu/politics/hungarys-government-puts-laughing-soros-on-billboards_135194.

46. Christian Keszthelyi, "Orbán Rails against Soros's 'Brussels Kingdom,'" *Budapest Business Journal*, July 3, 2017, https://bbj.hu/politics/orban-rails-against-soross-brussels-kingdom_135011.

47. Keszthelyi, "Orbán Rails against Soros's 'Brussels Kingdom.'"

48. Marton Dunai, "Hungary Approves 'STOP Soros' law, Defying EU, Rights Groups," Reuters, June 20, 2018, https://www.reuters.com/article/us-hungary-soros-idUSKBN1JG1VN.

49. Open Society Foundations, "The Open Society Foundations to Close International Operations in Budapest," May 15, 2018, https://www.opensocietyfoundations.org/press-releases/open-society-foundations-close-international-operations-budapest.

50. Kersty McCourt and Natacha Kazatchkine, "EU Must Strip Hungary of Voting Rights. Helping Migrants Is Not a Crime," Euronews, June 21, 2018, https://www.euronews.com/2018/06/20/eu-must-strip-hungary-of-voting-rights-helping-migrants-is-not-a-crime-view.

51. Reuters, "Soros Foundation Turns to Strasbourg Court To Get Hungary's NGO Law Repealed," Yahoo News, September 24, 2018, https://news.yahoo.com/soros-foundation-turns-strasbourg-court-hungarys-ngo-law-125109070.html.

52. Reuters, "Soros Foundation Turns to Strasbourg Court."

53. Raphael Ahren, "In Meeting with Netanyahu, Hungary's PM Acknowledges 'Sin' of WWll," Times of Israel, July 18, 2017, https://www.timesofisrael.com/in-meeting-with-netanyahu-hungarys-pm-cites-sin-of-wwll/.

54. Jeffrey Heller, "Hungary's Orban Tells Israel That Jews in His Country Can Feel Safe," Reuters, July 19, 2018, https://www.reuters.com/article/us-israel-hungary-orban-netanyahu-idUSKBN1K919F.

55. Cristina Maza, "Donald Trump Praises Hungary Leader Viktor Orbán's Record on Immigration after Repeated Human Rights Violations," Newsweek, May 13, 2019, https://www.newsweek.com/donald-trump-viktor-orban-immigration-1424310.

56. Chris Tomlinson, "Orban: Hungary Is Defeating Anti-Semitism While Western Europe Imports It," Breitbart, March 6, 2019, https://www.breitbart.com/europe/2019/03/06/orban-hungary-is-defeating-anti-semitism-while-western-europe-imports-it/.

57. Viktor Orbán, "Orbán Viktor's Ceremonial Speech on the 170th Anniversary of the Hungarian Revolution of 1848," Website of the Hungarian Government, March 16, 2018, http://www.kormany.hu/en/the-prime-minister/the-prime-minister-s-speeches/orban-viktor-s-ceremonial-speech-on-the-170th-anniversary-of-the-hungarian-revolution-of-1848.

58. Brett Samuels, "George Soros at Davos: Trump 'A Danger to the World,'" The Hill, January 25, 2018, https://thehill.com/policy/technology/370757-soros-calls-for-stricter-regulations-on-facebook-google.

59. Michael Kranish, "'I Must Be Doing Something Right': Billionaire George Soros Faces Renewed Attacks with Defiance," Washington Post, June 9, 2018, https://www.washingtonpost.com/politics/i-must-be-doing-something-right-billionaire-george-soros-faces-renewed-attacks-with-defiance/2018/06/09/3ba0e2b0-6825-11e8-9e38-24e693b3-8637_story.html?noredirect=on&utm_term=.8ab9d103109f.

60. Anna Berry, "Don't Stop Believing, George Soros," Nonprofit Quarterly, July 20, 2018, https://nonprofitquarterly.org/2018/07/20/dont-stop-believing-george-soros/.

61. Peter Hasson, "Soros Chalks Up Aneother DA Win after Dropping Nearly $1 Million in Texas Race," Daily Caller, March 6, 2018, https://dailycaller.com/2018/03/06/soros-district-attorney-win-texas/.

62. Joe Schoffstall, "Confidential Memo: Secretive Liberal Donor Club Plots $275 Million Spending Plan for 2020," Washington Free Beacon, April 11, 2019, https://freebeacon.com/politics/confidential-memo-secretive-liberal-donor-club-plots-275-million-for-2020/.

63. Kenneth P. Vogel, Scott Shane and Patrick Kingsley, "How Vilification of George Soros Moved From the Fringes to the Mainstream," New York Times, October 31, 2018, https://www.nytimes.com/2018/10/31/us/politics/george-soros-bombs-trump.html.

64. Donald J. Trump (@realDonaldTrump), "The very rude elevator screamers are paid professionals only looking to make Senators looks bad. Don't fall for it! Also, look at all of the professionally made identical signs. Paid for by Soros and others. These are not signs made in the basement from love! #Troublemakers," Twitter, October 5, 2018, 6:05 a.m., https://twitter.com/realDonaldTrump/status/1048196883464818688.

65. Paul Krugman (@paulkrugman), "One thing about the lie that Kavanaugh protestors are Soros-funded: it's anti-Semitic and rejects the legitimacy of dissent. But it's also projection: This is in fact what Republicans have done, e.g. in the 'Brooks brothers riot' against a Florida recount politico.com/gallery/2012/0 … ," Twitter, October 5, 2018, 9:13 a.m., https://twitter.com/paulkrugman/status/1048244783687327745.

66. Jamelle Bouie (@jbouie), "the 'soros-funded protestors' thing should be understood as both an anti-semitic dogwhistle and an attack on the idea of legitimate opposition itself, a tactic

imported from european far-right parties," Twitter, October 5, 2018, 7:26 a.m., https://twitter.com/jbouie/status/1048217781072801795.

67.   E.J. Dionne (@EJDionne), "This is truly horrific. The Soros conspiracy theory is now a staple of anti-Semitic politics in Europe. A president of the United States should not want to be associated with it in any way," Twitter, October 5, 2018, 7:36 a.m., https://twitter.com/EJDionne/status/1048220290810089472.

68.   Frank Dale, "Trump Promotes Anti-Semitic Conspiracy Theory on Twitter," ThinkProgress, October 5, 2018, https://thinkprogress.org/donald-trump-george-soros-anti-semitic-conspiracy-theory-7962b3d02a86/.

69.   Aaron Rupar (@atrupar), "REPORTER: Do think somebody is funding the caravan? TRUMP: 'I wouldn't be surprised, yeah. I wouldn't be surprised.' R: George Soros? T: 'I don't know who, but I wouldn't be surprised. A lot of people say yes," Twitter, October 31, 2018, 2:12 p.m., https://twitter.com/atrupar/status/1057742231937912833/video/1.

70.   Mayors Migration Council website, https://www.mayorsmigrationcouncil.org/.

71.   Julian Hattem, "Thousands of Soros Docs Released by Alleged Russian-Backed Backers," *The Hill*, August 15, 2016, https://thehill.com/policy/national-security/291486-thousands-of-soros-docs-released-by-alleged-russia-backed-hackers.

72.   Peter Hasson, "Leaked Soros Memo: Refugee Crisis 'New Normal,' Gives 'New Opportunities' for Global Influence," Daily Caller, August 15, 2016, https://dailycaller.com/2016/08/15/leaked-soros-memo-refugee-crisis-new-normal-gives-new-opportunities-for-global-influence/.

73.   Raheem Kassam, "UN 'Expert' Calls Britain 'Xenophobic' for Border Control, Media Fails to Report His 'Credentials,'" Breitbart, July 31, 2015, https://www.breitbart.com/europe/2015/07/31/un-expert-calls-britain-xenophobic-for-border-control-media-fails-to-report-his-credentials/.

74.   Brian Wheeler, "EU Should 'Undermine National Homogeneity' Says UN Migration Chief," BBC News, June 21, 2012, https://www.bbc.com/news/uk-politics-18519395.

75.   Open Society Foundations, "Maria Teresa Rojas," https://www.opensocietyfoundations.org/people/maria-teresa-rojas.

76.   International Organization for Migration, "IOM History," https://www.iom.int/iom-history.

77.   Concordia, "The Private Sector Forum on Migration and Refugees," https://www.concordia.net/the-summit-2016/the-private-sector-forum-on-migration-and-refugees/.

78.   Elena Holodny, "SOROS: The Refugee Crisis 'Has No Simple Solution,'" Business Insider, September 20, 2016, https://www.businessinsider.com/george-soros-says-europes-refugee-crisis-has-no-simple-solution-2016-9.

79.   International Organization for Migration, "About Us," https://unofficeny.iom.int/about-us.

80.   International Organization for Migration, "IOM Snapshot," updated May 2019, https://www.iom.int/sites/default/files/about-iom/iom_snapshot_a4_en.pdf.

81.   International Organization for Migration, "United States of America," https://www.iom.int/countries/united-states-america.

82.   Marrakech Mayors Declaration, "Cities Working Together for Migrants and Refugees," The 5th Mayoral Forum on Human Mobility, Migration and Development, Presented at the Intergovernmental Conference to adopt the Global Compact for Safe, Orderly and Regular Migration December 10–11, 2018 And United Nations General Assembly to adopt the Global Compact on Refugees December 17, 2018, http://www.migration4development.org/sites/default/files/en_mf_declaration.pdf.

83.   Marrakech Mayors Declaration, "Cities Working Together for Migrants and Refugees."

84.   William Holt, "Liberal Mega-Donor George Soros Backs Bill de Blasio for NYC Mayor," Yahoo News, August 6, 2013, https://news.yahoo.com/liberal-mega-donor-george-soros-backs-bill-de-blasio-for-nyc-mayor-152925507.html.

85.   Mayors Migration Council website, https://www.mayorsmigrationcouncil.org/.

86. Seth Borenstein, "UN Report: Extreme Weather Hit 62 Million people in 2018," Associated Press, March 28, 2019, https://www.foxnews.com/us/un-report-extreme-weather-hit-62-million-people-in-2018.

87. Borenstein, "UN report: Extreme Weather Hit 62 million."

88. International Organization for Migration, "Migration, Environment and Climate Change (MECC) Division," https://www.iom.int/migration-and-climate-change.

89. David Martosko and Associated Press, "We're Doomed! Beto O'Rourke Starts Presidential Campaign by Claiming the World Faces 'Catastrophe' and Warns 'Hundreds of Millions' of Climate Refugees Will Overwhelm Borders and Humanity Could Go EXTINCT Unless We Fix the Planet in 12 years," *Daily Mail*, March 14, 2019, https://www.dailymail.co.uk/news/article-6808207/Beto-ORourke-announces-running-president-2020.html.

90. Yessenia Funes, "Jay Inslee Is Actually Taking the Climate Refugee Crisis Seriously," Gizmodo, June 6, 2019, https://earther.gizmodo.com/jay-inslee-is-actually-taking-the-climate-refugee-crisi-1835293779.

91. Save the Children USA, "JD Malkin Performs "Feel Again" at the Social Good Summit," YouTube, September 23, 2012, https://www.youtube.com/watch?v=bRWulmOLmfM.

92. Save the Children, "SEARCH. RESCUE. SAVE," https://www.savethechildren.org/us/what-we-do/emergency-response/rescue-at-sea.

93. Save the Children, "SEARCH. RESCUE. SAVE."

94. Nicholas Farrell, "Madness in the Med: How Charity Rescue Boats Exacerbate the Refugee Crisis," *The Spectator*, July 22, 2017, https://www.spectator.co.uk/2017/07/migrants-and-madness-in-the-med/.

95. Nicholas Farrell, "Madness in the Med."

96. Save the Children, "Our Valued Partners," https://www.savethechildren.org/us/about-us/resource-library/annual-report/valued-partners.

97. Open Society Foundations, Grants Database search, https://www.opensocietyfoundations.org/grants-database?filter_keyword=save#OR2016-30304.

98. Doctors without Borders, "Global Refugee and Migration Crisis," https://web.archive.org/web/20180801165216/https://www.doctorswithoutborders.org/global-refugee-and-migration-crisis.

99. Giovanna Castagna and Magdalena Majkowska-Tomkin, "In the Mediterranean, Standing Back Is Not an Option," Open Society Foundations, April 7, 2017, https://www.opensocietyfoundations.org/voices/coast-libya-standing-back-not-option.

100. Nikolaj Nielson, "EU Migrant Mission Will Not Replace Mare Nostrum," EUobserver, September 3, 2014, https://euobserver.com/justice/125456. Note: Pushback by open-borders NGOs and academics who called the magnet effect of search and rescue operations a "myth" led some EU leaders to walk back their conclusion. See: Kate Ferguson, "EU leaders 'killing migrants by neglect' after cutting Mediterranean rescue missions," *Independent*, April 18, 2016, https://www.independent.co.uk/news/world/europe/eu-leaders-killing-migrants-by-neglect-after-cutting-mediterranean-rescue-missions-a6988326.html.

101. AFP, "France Joins Italy's Criticism of NGO Migrant Rescue Ships," The Local, June 28, 2018, https://www.thelocal.it/20180628/france-italy-ngo-ships-migrant-rescue.

102. AFP, "Italy Steps Up Investigation into Charity-Funded Migrant Rescue Boat," The Local, March 23, 2017, https://www.thelocal.it/20170323/italy-steps-up-investigation-into-charity-funded-migrant-rescue-boats.

103. Onize Ohikere, "Aid Groups Defend Their Role in Europe's migration Crisis," World, April 27, 2017, https://world.wng.org/2017/04/aid_groups_defend_their_role_in_europe_s_migration_crisis.

104. Joanne Liu, "'Migration Is Not a Crime. Saving Lives Is Not a Crime,'" Doctors Without Borders website, December 11, 2018, https://www.doctorswithoutborders.org/what-we-do/news-stories/news/migration-not-crime-saving-lives-not-crime.

105. Open Society Foundations, "Partnerships," https://www.opensocietyfoundations.org/sites/default/files/partners_20090720_0.pdf.
106. Avaaz, "About Us," https://secure.avaaz.org/page/en/about/.
107. Avaaz, "Our Victories!" https://secure.avaaz.org/page/en/highlights/.
108. Avaaz Foundation, IRS Form 990 for the year 2015, https://avaazimages.s3.amazonaws.com/AVAAZ+2015+FORM+990+-+PUBLIC+DISCLOSURE+COPY.pdf.
109. NGO Monitor, "Avaaz, Soros, Israel and the Palestinians," March 6, 2013, https://www.ngo-monitor.org/reports/19/.
110. NGO Monitor, "Avaaz, Soros, Israel and the Palestinians."
111. Avaaz Foundation, IRS Form 990 for the year 2017, https://avaazimages.avaaz.org/AVAAZ_2017_FORM_990_Public_Disclosure_Copy.pdf.
112. Avaaz Foundation, IRS Form 990 for the year 2017.
113. Ibid.
114. MADE, "Donors and Partners," http://www.madenetwork.org/donors-and-partners.
115. MADE, "Now and How: TEN ACTS for the Global Compact," http://madenetwork.org/ten-acts.
116. MADE, "European Regional Civil Society Consultation," http://madenetwork.org/european-rcsc.
117. Hermione Garelli, "Civil Society Models of Engagement in a New Era of Migration Governance," February 2019, https://docs.wixstatic.com/ugd/9f35df_5df7011f83e94913bedbdd3596f0894f.pdf.
118. Garelli, "Civil Society Models of Engagement," 20.
119. Castagna and Majkowska-Tomkin, "In the Mediterranean, Standing Back Is Not an Option."
120. UNHCR, "Carta di Roma," https://www.unhcr.it/risorse/carta-di-roma.
121. Anna Meli, ed., "Guidelines for the Application of the Rome Charter," https://www.cartadiroma.org/wp-content/uploads/2014/10/Guidelines-English.pdf, 7, 10, 12, 19.
122. Meli, ed., "Guidelines for the Application of the Rome Charter," 21.
123. ANSA, "Media on Migration: More Attention to Correct language," InfoMigrants, July 27, 2017, https://www.infomigrants.net/en/post/4343/media-on-migration-more-attention-to-correct-language.
124. HOPE not hate, "About Us," https://www.hopenothate.org.uk/about-us/.
125. Matthew Collins (@MattHopeNotHate), "And now for some good news…," Twitter, August 16, 2016, 12:39 a.m., https://twitter.com/MattHopeNotHate/status/765452788662988800.
126. Open Society Foundations, "The Leadership Conference Education Fund, Lawyers' Committee for Civil Rights Under Law & Nine Partner Organizations Launch Communities Against Hate National Initiative," March 13, 2017, https://www.opensocietyfoundations.org/press-releases/leadership-conference-education-fund-lawyers-committee-civil-rights-under-law-nine.
127. "Retailers Quietly Remove Hate Material from Sites," HOPE not hate, March 21, 2018, https://www.hopenothate.org.uk/2018/03/21/retailers-quietly-stop-profiting-hate/.
128. Bruce Bawer, "Sweeney Agonistes: Tommy Robinson Turns the Tables on the BBC," PJ Media, February 26, 2019, https://pjmedia.com/trending/sweeney-agonistes-tommy-robinson-turns-the-tables-on-the-bbc/.
129. Bawer, "Sweeney Agonistes: Tommy Robinson Turns the Tables."
130. Lizzie Dearden, "Tommy Robinson Permanently Banned by Facebook and Instagram," The Independent, February 26, 2019, https://www.independent.co.uk/news/uk/home-news/tommy-robinson-facebook-ban-instagram-permanent-far-right-edl-racism-a8797451.html.
131. Dan Hodges, "Matthew Collins' War against Hate," Labor Uncut, October 21, 2011, http://labour-uncut.co.uk/2011/10/21/matthew-collins-war-against-hate/.

132. Human Rights Watch, Inc. and Subsidiaries, "Consolidated Financial Report," June 30, 2018, https://www.hrw.org/sites/default/files/supporting_resources/financial_statement_fy18.pdf.

133. Human Rights Watch, "George Soros to Give $100 million to Human Rights Watch," September 7, 2010, https://www.hrw.org/news/2010/09/07/george-soros-give-100-million-human-rights-watch.

134. Jonathan Foreman, "Explosive Claims Engulf Human Rights Watch," *The Times*, March 25, 2010, https://www.thetimes.co.uk/article/explosive-claims-engulf-human-rights-watch-39x573mfp9n.

135. NGO Monitor, "Expert or Ideologues?: HRW's Defense of Marc Garlasco's Nazi Fetish," September 10, 2009, https://www.ngo-monitor.org/reports/expert_or_ideologues_hrw_s_defense_of_marc_garlasco_s_nazi_fetish/.

136. Jeffrey Goldberg, "Fundraising Corruption at Human Rights Watch," *The Atlantic*, July 15, 2009, https://www.theatlantic.com/international/archive/2009/07/fundraising-corruption-at-human-rights-watch/21345/.

137. Goldberg, "Fundraising Corruption at Human Rights Watch."

138. Human Rights Watch, "US: Arizona Violating Human Rights Treaty," April 30, 2010, https://www.hrw.org/news/2010/04/30/us-arizona-violating-human-rights-treaty.

139. Human Rights Watch, "US Harassing Journalists, Lawyers, Activists at Border," March 8, 2019, https://www.hrw.org/news/2019/03/08/us-harassing-journalists-lawyers-activists-border.

140. Human Rights Watch, "Human Rights Watch Letter to Congress Regarding Decreasing Immigration Enforcement Funding in FY 2020 Budget," March 22, 2019, https://www.hrw.org/news/2019/03/22/human-rights-watch-letter-congress-regarding-decreasing-immigration-enforcement.

141. Eli Rosenberg, "Protest Grows 'Out of Nowhere' at Kennedy Airport After Iraqis Are Detained," *New York Times*, January 28, 2017, https://www.nytimes.com/2017/01/28/nyregion/jfk-protests-trump-refugee-ban.html.

142. Asawin Suebsaeng, "These Are the Groups Behind Those 'Spontaneous' Anti-Trump-Ban Protests," Daily Beast, February 2, 2017, https://www.thedailybeast.com/these-are-the-groups-behind-those-spontaneous-anti-trump-ban-protests.

143. Jake Offenhartz, "Multiple Arrests During Immigration Protests Outside Jamie Dimon's UES Home," Gothamist, July 25, 2018, http://gothamist.com/2018/07/25/jamie_dimon_chase_protest.php.

144. Yara Simón, "30 Powerful Images & Videos From This Year's May Day Protests You Need to See," Remezcla, https://remezcla.com/lists/culture/may-day-2017/.

145. The New York State Senate, "Senate Passes the José Peralta New York State DREAM Act," January 23, 2019, https://www.nysenate.gov/newsroom/press-releases/senate-majority-passes-jose-peralta-new-york-state-dream-act.

146. Jenni Fink, "Rejecting Gold Star Family Free Tuition After Approving DREAM Act Funding is 'Not the Right Message,' says NY Assemblyman," *Newsweek*, April 10, 2019), https://www.newsweek.com/gold-star-family-free-tuition-rejected-ny-assembly-1392521.

147. Open Society Foundations, "OSI Grantees Ensure Stimulus Brings Opportunity to All," November 12, 2009, https://www.opensocietyfoundations.org/press-releases/osi-grantees-ensure-stimulus-brings-opportunity-all.

148. Make the Road New York, 2011 Annual Report, http://www.maketheroad.org/pix_reports/MRNY%202011%20Annual%20Report.pdf.

149. Open Society Foundations grants database, https://www.opensocietyfoundations.org/grants-database?filter_keyword=Make%20the%20Road#OR2016-32153.

150. The New York Community Trust, "10/3/17–Fund to Help Immigrants Awards Nearly $1 Million to 15 NYC Groups for Emergency Planning, DACA Advocacy, and Know-Your-Rights Trainings," October 3, 2017, https://www.nycommunitytrust.org/newsroom/fund-to-help-immigrants-awards-nearly-1-million-to-15-nyc-groups/.

151. Joe Schoffstall, "Soros-Funded Groups Behind Anti-Trump Corporate Targeting Campaign," *Washington Free Beacon*, May 10, 2017, https://freebeacon.com/issues/soros-funded-groups-behind-anti-trump-corporate-targeting-campaign/.

152. The Center for Popular Democracy, "Ana Maria Archila Confronts Senator Jeff Flake Ahead of Supreme Court Vote," September 28, 2018, https://populardemocracy.org/blog/ana-maria-archila-confronts-senator-jeff-flake-ahead-supreme-court-vote.

153. Foundation to Promote Open Society Form 990-PF for 2014, http://www.guidestar.org/FinDocuments/2014/263/753/2014-263753801-0c022036-F.pdf.

154. Foundation to Promote Open Society Form 990-PF for 2015, http://www.guidestar.org/FinDocuments/2015/263/753/2015-263753801-0d1efdad-F.pdf.

155. Open Society Policy Center, "OSPC Summary of Lobbying Activities: 2016, Third Quarter," November 1, 2016, https://opensocietypolicycenter.org/uncategorized/ospc-summary-of-lobbying-activities-2016-third-quarter/.

156. Gregory Krieg, "Progressive Activists To Unveil New $80 Million Network," CNN, May 23, 2017, https://www.cnn.com/2017/05/23/politics/new-progressive-fund-fight-trump/index.html.

157. The Center for Popular Democracy, "Board," https://populardemocracy.org/about-us/board.

158. Influence Watch, "Make the Road New York (MRNY)," https://www.influencewatch.org/non-profit/make-the-road-new-york/.

159. CASA, "Our Impact, Active Membership Snapshot 2018 Fiscal Year Demographic Data," https://wearecasa.org/our-impact/.

160. Michelle Malkin, "Open-Borders DOJ vs. America," Michellemalkin.com, July 7, 2010, http://michellemalkin.com/2010/07/07/open-borders-doj-vs-america/.

161. Open Society Foundations grants database, https://www.opensocietyfoundations.org/grants-database/?filter_keyword=Casa#OR2017-32520.

162. Nonprofit Explorer, Form 990 for fiscal year ending June 2017, ProPublica, https://projects.propublica.org/nonprofits/organizations/521372972/201801359349308395/IRS990.

163. Influence Watch, "CASA de Maryland," https://www.influencewatch.org/non-profit/casa-de-maryland/.

164. Associated Press, "Citgo Gives $1.5 Million to Casa," *Washington Times*, August 5, 2008, https://www.washingtontimes.com/news/2008/aug/05/citgo-gives-15-million-to-casa/.

165. Dr. Steven Allen, "The Racist: Labor Secretary Tom Perez Is Said To Be Near the Top of Hillary Clinton's VP List," Capital Research Center, July 18, 2016, https://capitalresearch.org/article/the-racist-labor-secretary-tom-perez-is-said-to-be-near-the-top-of-hillary-clintons-vp-list/.

166. Tim Hains, "New DNC Chair Tom Perez: Republicans Don't Give A Shit About You," RealClearPolitics, April 18, 2017, https://www.realclearpolitics.com/video/2017/04/18/new_dnc_chair_tom_perez_republicans_dont_give_a_shit_about_you.html.

167. Ted Goodman, "DNC Chairman Claims 'No Human Being Is Illegal,'" Daily Caller, May 1, 2017, https://dailycaller.com/2017/05/01/dnc-chairman-claims-no-human-being-is-illegal/.

168. MALDEF, "ICE Out of Communities," October 5, 2017, https://www.maldef.org/2017/10/ice-out-of-communities/.

169. MALDEF, "MALDEF Statement on Recent ICE Enforcement Activity," February 11, 2017, https://www.maldef.org/2017/02/maldef-statement-on-recent-ice-enforcement-activity/.

170. Ricardo Lopez, "NHMC Protests Lack of Latino Representation in Studios Ahead of Oscars," *Variety*, March 3, 2018, https://variety.com/2018/biz/news/nhmc-protests-latino-representation-1202716782/.

171. Kartikay Mehrotra, "DACA Recipient Sues Bank of America After Being Denied Advisory Job," Bloomberg, May 3, 2018, https://www.bloomberg.com/news/articles/2018-05-03/bank-of-america-sued-for-refusing-job-to-dreamer-raised-in-u-s.

172. Bonfire, "United We Dream Action," https://www.bonfire.com/store/united-we-dream-action/.

173. United We Dream (@UNITEDWEDREAM), "PRESS RELEASE The Deportation Force Must Be Stopped unitedwedre.am/2tf5rRe #AbolishICE #AbolishCBP #DACA #HereToStay," Twitter, June 20, 2018, 5:30 p.m., https://twitter.com/UNITEDWEDREAM/status/1009594428720340993.

174. Nonprofit Explorer, United We Dream Form 990 for fiscal year ending Dec. 2017, ProPublica, https://projects.propublica.org/nonprofits/organizations/462216565/201823189349302677/IRS990.

175. Nonprofit Explorer, United We Dream Form 990, Schedule I, for fiscal year ending Dec. 2017, ProPublica, https://projects.propublica.org/nonprofits/organizations/462216565/201823189349302677/IRS990ScheduleI.

176. Ballotpedia, "United We Dream," https://ballotpedia.org/United_We_Dream.

177. Laura B. Whitmore, "Watch Now: Kesha Partners with United We Dream and Releases Video for 'Hymn,'" *Parade*, June 4, 2018, https://parade.com/675972/laurawhitmore/watch-now-kesha-partners-with-united-we-dream-and-releases-video-for-hymn/.

178. MacArthur Foundation, "Cristina Jiménez Moreta," https://www.macfound.org/fellows/989/; Patricia Guadalupe, "Immigrant Advocate Cristina Jiménez Moreta Hopes Genius Award Inspires Others to Take Stand," NBC News, October 12, 2017, https://www.nbcnews.com/news/latino/immigrant-advocate-cristina-jim-nez-hopes-genius-award-inspires-others-n810031.

179. United We Dream, "Cristina Jiménez," July 17, 2017, https://unitedwedream.org/dvteam/cristina-jimenez/.

180. Joe Schoffstall, "Soros-Tied Networks, Foundations Joined Forces to Create Trump 'Resistance' Fund," *Washington Free Beacon*, April 1, 2017, https://freebeacon.com/issues/soros-tied-networks-foundations-joined-forces-create-trump-resistance-fund/.

181. Open Society Policy Center, "OSPC Summary of Lobbying Activities: 2018, Third Quarter," November 12, 2018, https://opensocietypolicycenter.org/reporting/ospc-summary-of-lobbying-activities-2018-third-quarter/.

182. Michelle Malkin, "Never Forget CAIR's Dirty Deeds," Michellemalkin.com, March 20, 2019, http://michellemalkin.com/2019/03/20/never-forget-cairs-dirty-deeds/.

183. Open Society Foundations Grants Database, https://www.opensocietyfoundations.org/grants-database?filter_keyword=islamic#OR32098.

184. Andrew C. McCarthy, "The 'Peaceful' Jihad in America," *New York Post*, June 1, 2010, https://nypost.com/2010/06/01/the-peaceful-jihad-in-america/.

185. Open Society Foundations Grants Database, https://www.opensocietyfoundations.org/grants-database?filter_keyword=islamic#OR2015-25732.

186. Muslim Advocates, "Annual Report 2017," https://www.muslimadvocates.org/annual-report-2017/.

187. John Rossomando, "Soros Money, Muslim Advocates Leader, Helped Weaken Homeland Security Policies," IPT News, October 7, 2016, https://www.investigativeproject.org/5669/soros-money-muslim-advocates-leader-helped-weaken.

188. Rossomando, "Soros Money, Muslim Advocates Leader."

189. Scott Simpson, "32 Civil Rights Groups Lose Faith in Facebook, Call for Significant Reforms to its Board," Muslim Advocates, December 17, 2018, https://www.muslimadvocates.org/reform-facebook/.

190. Open Society Foundations Grants Database, https://www.opensocietyfoundations.org/grants-database?filter_keyword=lutheran#OR2017-32615.

191. Philanthropy News Digest, "Media Matters Receives $1 Million From George Soros," October 22, 2010, https://philanthropynewsdigest.org/news/media-matters-receives-1-million-from-george-soros.

192. Tucker Carlson and Vince Coglianese, "Inside Media Matters: Sources, Memos Reveal Erratic Behavior, Close Coordination with White House and News Organizations," Daily

Caller, February 12, 2012, https://dailycaller.com/2012/02/12/inside-media-matters-sources-memos-reveal-erratic-behavior-close-coordination-with-white-house-and-news-organizations/.

193. Michelle Malkin, "Fox News Derangement Syndrome Strikes Again," Michellemalkin.com, October 13, 2009, http://michellemalkin.com/2009/10/13/fox-news-derangement-syndrome-strikes-again/.

194. Media Matters (@mmfa), "Laura Ingraham's anti-immigrant rant is ripped from white supremacists mm4a.org/Zt9," August 9, 2018, 1:57 p.m., https://twitter.com/mmfa/status/1027660077753397248?lang=en.

195. Media Matters for America, "Fox News Pushes for Voter Suppression With A Guest Who Has Ties to White Supremacy," February 13, 2017, http://mm4a.org/2koXWQv.

196. Media Matters for America, "Tucker Carlson Guest Defends White Supremacists and Claims That Hispanics in Arizona Represent the End of American Society," January 18, 2018, http://mm4a.org/ZP5.

197. Media Matters for America, "Tucker Carlson Defends Gab, a Social Media App Dubbed 'a Haven for White Nationalists,'" September 5, 2017, https://www.mediamatters.org/blog/2017/09/05/tucker-carlson-defends-gab-social-media-app-dubbed-haven-white-nationalists/217848.

198. Media Matters (@mmfa), "On CNN, @GoAngelo highlights the rise of white nationalist rhetoric on Fox News," Twitter, August 8, 2018, 8:29 p.m., https://twitter.com/mmfa/status/1027758919110848512.

199. Media Matters (@mmfa), "The source for Fox News' anti-refugee fear-mongering is a white nationalist writer mm4a.org/1rgrUJB," Twitter, June 11, 2016, 7:00 p.m., https://twitter.com/mmfa/status/741812290626850816.

200. Lis Power (@LisPower1), "Hey @FoxNews, while you're covering your ass and pretending to be outraged by people using your network to spread conspiracy theories about George Soros can we also get Jeanine Pirro off the air!? This was her linking Soros to the caravan a week ago," Twitter, October 28, 2018, 10:40 a.m., https://twitter.com/lispower1/status/1056601687186661376?lang=en.

201. Media Matters (@mmfa), "Fox personalities repeatedly pushed conspiracy theories about George Soros and migrant caravans. Will the network do anything about them? mm4a.org/4pn," Twitter, October 29, 2018, 2:32 p.m., https://twitter.com/mmfa/status/1057022443716513792.

202. Media Matters (@mmfa), "Fox News has spent years launching bigoted attacks on George Soros," Twitter, October 30, 2018, 11:20 a.m., https://twitter.com/mmfa/status/1057336329854431232 and "After Pittsburgh synagogue shooting and mail bomb spree, pro-Trump media defend anti-Semitic attacks on George Soros," Twitter, October 29, 2018, 2:53 p.m., https://twitter.com/mmfa/status/1057027768767131648.

203. Carlson and Coglianese, "Inside Media Matters."

204. Solange Uwimana, "Study: Fox News Viewers Hold More Anti-Immigrant, Anti-Latino Opinions," Media Matters for America, September 14, 2012, https://www.mediamatters.org/blog/2012/09/14/study-fox-news-viewers-hold-more-anti-immigrant/189907.

205. Open Society Foundations Grants Database, http://archive.li/FDg3w.

206. Center for Media Justice, "About Us," https://centerformediajustice.org/about/.

207. Color of Change, "Facebook Must Answer For Dangerous Embrace of Anti-Semitism, Racist Targeting of Color Of Change," November 15, 2018, https://www.commondreams.org/newswire/2018/11/15/facebook-must-answer-dangerous-embrace-anti-semitism-racist-targeting-color; Center for Media Justice, "Demand Accountability From Facebook," https://actnow.io/BI0LY3L.

208. MAG-Net, "Covering Race," https://mag-net.org/issues/covering-race/.

209. Center for Media Justice, "Facebook can't be trusted to regulate itself," December 18, 2018, https://centerformediajustice.org/2018/12/18/facebook-cant-be-trusted-to-regulate-itself/.

210. Open Society Foundations Grants Database, https://www.opensocietyfoundations.org/grants-database?filter_keyword=Media%20Justice#OR2015-23716.

211. Michelle Malkin, "Don't do business with progressive appeasers," Michellemalkin.com, April 11, 2012, http://michellemalkin.com/2012/04/11/dont-do-business-with-progressive-appeasers/.

212. Color of Change, "Rashad Robinson, Executive Director of Color of Change on Facebook's Announcement To Conduct an Independent Audit of Its Only Hate Groups," https://colorofchange.org/press_release/rashad-robinson-facebook-independent-audit-hate/.

213. Jareyah Bradley, Balestra Media, "New AP Guidance: Avoid Use of 'Chain Migration' Language on Family Migration Following Grassroots Campaign," Immigrant Legal Resource Center, May 25, 2018, https://www.ilrc.org/new-ap-guidance-avoid-use-%E2%80%9Cchain-migration%E2%80%9D-language-family-migration-following-grassroots-campaign.

214. Jareyah Bradley, Balestra Media, "New AP Guidance: Avoid Use of 'Chain Migration' Language."

215. Kristen Hare, "AP Style Change: Two Objects Don't Have To Be in Motion before They Collide," Poynter, April 27, 2018, https://www.poynter.org/news/ap-style-change-two-objects-dont-have-be-motion-they-collide.

216. Blood Money website, https://www.bloodmoney.org/.

217. Activist Facts, "Color of Change," https://www.activistfacts.com/organizations/524-color-of-change/.

218. Open Society Foundations, "Open Society-U.S.," https://www.opensocietyfoundations.org/about/programs/us-programs/grantees/free-press.

219. Free Press, "About," https://www.freepress.net/about.

220. Joseph Rossell, "Soros, Ford Foundations 'Lavish' $196 Million to Push Internet Regulations," MC Business, February 25, 2015, http://archive2.mrc.org/articles/soros-ford-foundations-lavish-196-million-push-internet-regulations.

221. Tony Romm, "The Trump Administration Just Voted To Repeal the U.S. Government's Net Neutrality Rules," Vox, December 14, 2107, https://www.recode.net/2017/12/14/16771910/trump-fcc-ajit-pai-net-neutrality-repeal.

222. Dell Cameron, "FCC Faces Off in Net Neutrality Lawsuit Against Consumer Advocates and Internet Giants," Gizmodo, February 1, 2019, https://gizmodo.com/fcc-faces-off-in-net-neutrality-lawsuit-against-consume-1832269448.

223. Collette Watson, Diego Barrera, Timothy Karr, "How Journalists Can Avoid Exploitative 'Caravan' Coverage," Free Press, November 28, 2018, https://www.freepress.net/our-response/expert-analysis/explainers/how-journalists-can-avoid-exploitative-caravan-coverage.

224. Watson, Barrera, and Karr, "How Journalists Can Avoid Exploitative 'Caravan' Coverage," Free Press, November 28, 2018, https://www.freepress.net/our-response/expert-analysis/explainers/how-journalists-can-avoid-exploitative-caravan-coverage.

225. Ibid.

226. George Soros, "Why I'm Investing $500 Million in Migrants," Wall Street Journal, September 20, 2016, https://www.wsj.com/articles/why-im-investing-500-million-in-migrants-1474344001.

227. L. Gordon Crovitz, "In Praise of Huddled Masses (Cont'd)," Wall Street Journal, July 6, 2014, https://www.wsj.com/articles/gordon-crovitz-in-praise-of-huddled-masses-contd-1404683839.

228. Soros, "Why I'm Investing $500 Million in Migrants."

229. Dennis Price, "A Growing Community of Investors Steers Capital to Solutions That Benefit Refugees," ImpactAlpha, October 25, 2018, https://impactalpha.com/a-growing-community-of-investors-steer-capital-to-solutions-that-benefit-refugees/.

230. Dennis Price, "A Growing Community of Investors Steers Capital."

231. Mastercard, "About Mastercard," https://www.mastercard.us/en-us/about-mastercard.html.

232. Mastercard, "Mastercard and George Soros to Explore Private Sector Solutions to Societal Challenges," January 19, 2017, https://newsroom.mastercard.com/press-releases/mastercard-and-george-soros-to-explore-private-sector-solutions-to-societal-challenges/.

233. Mastercard, "Mastercard and George Soros to Explore Private Sector Solutions."

234. MercyCorps, "Foundation and Corporate Partners," August 8, 2005, https://web.archive.org/web/20170602205949/https://www.mercycorps.org/articles/foundation-and-corporate-partners.

235. Marisa Grimes, "MasterCard Prepaid Debit Cards Provide Refugees with Mobility, Flexibility and Dignity," Mastercard website, June 20, 2016, https://newsroom.mastercard.com/2016/06/20/mastercard-prepaid-debit-cards-provide-refugees-with-mobility-flexibility-and-dignity/.

236. UNHCR, "Programmes for Direct Cash-Aid to the Displaced Reaches Record $430m in 2016," December 16, 2016, https://www.unhcr.org/news/briefing/2016/12/5853b3ed4/unhcr-programmes-direct-cash-aid-displaced-reaches-record-430m-2016.html.

237. "CREDO Mobile — The Carrier with a Conscience," CREDO Mobile, http://www.credomobile.com/mission/history.

238. "30+ Years of Progressive Partnerships," CREDO Mobile, http://www.credomobile.com/mission/donations.

239. Trish Tobin, "Download Free Progressive Posters from CREDO," CREDO Blog, August 30, 2018, https://blog.credomobile.com/2018/08/march-on-new-protest-posters-now-available/.

240. Josh Nelson and Heidi Hess, "CREDO Leads Protest at DHS Secretary Kirstjen Nielsen's House in Alexandria, Virginia," CREDO, June 22, 2018, https://blog.credomobile.com/2018/06/credo-leads-protest-dhs-secretary-kirstjen-nielsens-house-alexandria-virginia/.

241. Heidi Hess, "The Resistance Is Strong. Here Are Your CREDO Protest Posters," CREDO, January 31, 2017, https://blog.credomobile.com/2017/01/the-resistance-is-strong-here-are-your-credo-protest-posters/.

242. The White House, "Private Sector Participants to the Call to Action," September 20, 2016, https://obamawhitehouse.archives.gov/the-press-office/2016/09/20/private-sector-participants-call-action.

243. Michelle Malkin and John Miano, *Sold Out: How High-Tech Billionaires & Bipartisan Beltway Crapweasels Are Screwing America's Best & Brightest Workers* (Washington D.C.: Regnery Publishing, 2016), 274–5.

244. Discover the Networks, "National Immigration Forum (NIF)," June 24, 2019, http://www.discoverthenetworks.org/groupProfile.asp?grpid=6506.

245. John Heilemann, "Do You Know the Way To Ban Jose," *Wired*, August 1, 2016, https://www.wired.com/1996/08/netizen-11/.

246. Open Society Foundations, "Open Society-U.S.," https://www.opensocietyfoundations.org/about/programs/us-programs/grantees/national-immigration-forum-0.

247. Maggie Haberman, "GOP Mega-Donor Backs Immigration Reform," *Politico*, April 29, 2013, http://www.politico.com/story/2013/04/gop-donor-paul-singer-immigration-reform-90726.html.

248. Nicholas Laham, *Ronald Reagan and the Politics of Immigration Reform* (Westport, Conn.: Praeger Publishers, 2000).

249. Matthew Boyle, "National Immigration Forum Funded by Soros and the Left," Breitbart, June 2, 2013, http://www.breitbart.com/big-government/2013/06/02/national-immigration-forum-lead-evangelical-jim-wallis-funded-by-george-soros-other-bastions-of-institutional-left/.

250. National Immigration Forum, "Natural Allies for Immigration Reform," https://immigrationforum.org/landing_page/bibles-badges-business/; National Immigration

Forum, "Bibles, Badges and Business Principles," August 14, 2018, https://immigrationforum.org/article/bibles-badges-and-business-principles/.

251. National Immigration Forum, "Trump's Wall a Symbol, Not a Solution," February 15, 2019, https://immigrationforum.org/article/trumps-wall-a-symbol-not-a-solution/.

252. National Immigration Forum, "Trump's Wall a Symbol, Not a Solution."

253. Holy Names University, "Father John Baumann, SJ, Discusses PICO and Community Organizing for Passionate Leaders in Social Entrepreneurship Speaker Series," October 31, 2014, https://hnu.edu/about/news/father-john-baumann-sj-discusses-pico-and-community-organizing-passionate-leaders-social.

254. Open Society Foundations Grants Database, https://www.opensocietyfoundations.org/grants-database?filter_keyword=PICO#OR2016-27062.

255. Brent Scher and Joe Schoffstall, "Resistance Royalty: Pelosi, Soros Headline Left's Biggest Dark Money Conference," *Washington Free Beacon*, November 17, 2017, https://freebeacon.com/politics/resistance-royalty-pelosi-soros-headline-lefts-biggest-dark-money-conference/.

256. Open Society Foundations, "Open Society-U.S.," https://www.opensocietyfoundations.org/about/programs/us-programs/grantees/faith-public-life.

257. Robert A. Sirico, "Soros' Catholic Useful Idiots," *Washington Times*, August 30, 2016, https://www.washingtontimes.com/news/2016/aug/30/george-soros-catholic-useful-idiots/.

258. Kevin Jones, "Soros Money Tried To Exploit Pope's US Visit To Influence 2016 Elections," Catholic News Agency, September 1, 2016, https://www.catholicnewsagency.com/news/soros-money-tried-to-exploit-popes-us-visit-to-influence-2016-elections-15985.

259. Sirico, "Soros' Catholic Useful Idiots."

260. Popular Movements, "World Meeting of Popular Movements," http://popularmovements.org/.

261. Deal Hudson, "San Diego Bishop Tells Catholics to 'All Become Disrupters,'" Newsmax, February 20, 2017, https://www.newsmax.com/dealhudson/san-diego-bishop-robert-mcelroy/2017/02/20/id/774572/#ixzz5m9y49eNX.

262. Catholic News Agency, "Pope Francis Encourages Meeting of Popular Movements in California," February 17, 2017, https://www.catholicnewsagency.com/news/pope-francis-encourages-meeting-of-popular-movements-in-california-89704.

Chapter 3

1. Tyler Rogoway, "The Pope Has A Small But Deadly Army Of Elite Warriors Protecting Him," Jalopnik, September 28, 2015, https://foxtrotalpha.jalopnik.com/the-pope-has-a-small-but-deadly-army-of-elite-warriors-1733268646.

2. Rogoway, "The Pope Has A Small But Deadly Army."

3. Ibid.

4. William Mclaughlin, "Arab Raids on Rome: The Eternal City Saved by 600-Year-Old Wall," War History Online, August 14, 2016, https://www.warhistoryonline.com/ancient-history/arab-raids-rome-eternal-city-saved-600-year-old-wall.html.

5. "The Passetto," Virtual Roma (website), http://roma.andreapollett.com/S1/roma-c7.htm.

6. Atlas Obscura, "Vatican City Walls," https://www.atlasobscura.com/places/vatican-city-walls.

7. Atlas Obscura, "Vatican City Walls."

8. Inés San Martín, "Trump's Border Wall Will Make US a 'Prisoner' of Isolation, Pope Says," Crux, March 31, 2019, https://cruxnow.com/vatican/2019/03/31/trumps-border-wall-will-make-us-a-prisoner-of-isolation-pope-says/.

9. Emma R., "Pope on Multiculturalism: 'Migrants Always Bring Riches,'" Voice of Europe, April 12, 2019, https://voiceofeurope.com/2019/04/pope-on-multiculturalism-migrants-always-bring-riches/.

10. Rosa Flores, "In Apparent Shot at Trump, Pope Says 'Builders of Walls' Sow Fear and Divide," CNN, January 26, 2019, https://www.cnn.com/2019/01/25/americas/pope-walls-panama/index.html.

11. Pope Francis (@Pontifex), "I invite you not to build walls but bridges, to conquer evil with good, offence with forgiveness, to live in peace with everyone," Twitter, March 18, 2017, 5:30 a.m. https://twitter.com/pontifex/status/843077028656136193?lang=en.

12. Josephine McKenna, "Pope Francis Reminds Donald Trump Not To Forget the Poor," *National Catholic Reporter*, November 11, 2016, https://www.ncronline.org/news/politics/pope-francis-reminds-donald-trump-not-forget-poor.

13. Daniel Burke, "Pope Suggests Trump 'Is Not Christian,'" CNN, February 18, 2016, https://www.cnn.com/2016/02/18/politics/pope-francis-trump-christian-wall/index.html.

14. Pope Francis, "Apostolic Exhortation *Gaudete et Exultate* of the Holy Father Francis on the Call to Holiness in Today's World," Vatican website, http://w2.vatican.va/content/francesco/en/apost_exhortations/documents/papa-francesco_esortazione-ap_20180319_gaudete-et-exsultate.html.

15. Pope Francis, "Apostolic Exhortation *Gaudete et Exultate* of the Holy Father Francis."

16. Ibid. See also Reuters, "Cardinal Causes Controversy," *Irish Times*, September 15, 2000, https://www.irishtimes.com/news/cardinal-causes-controversy-1.1103017.

17. Catechism of the Catholic Church, http://www.scborromeo.org/ccc/para/2241.htm.

18. Father Andrew McNair, "Immigration's 2 Catholic Camps," *National Catholic Register*, June 26, 2006, http://www.ncregister.com/site/article/immigrations_2_catholic_camps.

19. Msgr. Charles Pope., "Is There a Catholic View on the Border Wall?" *National Catholic Register*, January 9, 2019, https://www.ncregister.com/blog/msgr-pope/is-there-a-catholic-view-on-the-border-wall.

20. Bawai Soro, "Trump Right To Protect Nation with Travel Ban," *San Diego Union-Tribune*, February 17, 2017, http://www.sandiegouniontribune.com/opinion/commentary/sd-utbg-muslims-ban-trump-soro-20170217-story.html.

21. John L. Allen Jr., "The Church's Deep Pockets, the Butler Did It, and Myths about Atheism," *National Catholic Reporter*, August 17, 2012, https://www.ncronline.org/blogs/all-things-catholic/churchs-deep-pockets-butler-did-it-and-myths-about-atheism.

22. Allen Jr., "The Church's Deep Pockets."

23. Shane Croucher, "How Rich Is the Vatican? So Wealthy It Can Stumble across Millions of Euros Just 'Tucked Away,'" International Business Times, December 5, 2014, https://www.ibtimes.co.uk/how-rich-vatican-so-wealthy-it-can-stumble-across-millions-euros-just-tucked-away-1478219.

24. Croucher, "How Rich Is the Vatican?"

25. Avro Manhattan, "The Vatican Billions: Origin of the Current Colossal Wealth of the Catholic Church," Christian Assemblies International (excerpt from *The Vatican Billions*, published October 1, 1983), https://www.cai.org/bible-studies/vatican-billions.

26. Michael O'Loughlin, "Pew Survey: Percentage of US Catholics Drops and Catholicism Is Losing Members Faster Than Any Denomination," Crux, May 12, 2015, https://cruxnow.com/church/2015/05/12/pew-survey-percentage-of-us-catholics-drops-and-catholicism-is-losing-members-faster-than-any-denomination/.

27. Jack Ruhl and Diana Ruhl, "NCR Research: Costs of Sex Abuse Crisis to US Church Underestimated," *National Catholic Reporter*, November 2, 2015, https://www.ncronline.org/news/accountability/ncr-research-costs-sex-abuse-crisis-us-church-underestimated; "Sexual Abuse by U.S. Catholic Clergy: Settlements and Monetary Awards in Civil Suits," BishopAccountability.org, http://www.bishop-accountability.org/settlements/.

28. Jeremy Roebuck, Angela Couloumbis, and Liz Navratil, "Pa. Catholic Church Sex Abuse Report Names Hundreds of Priests, Accuses Leaders of Cover-Up: 'They Hid It All,'" *Philadelphia Inquirer*, August 14, 2018, https://www.philly.com/philly/news/catholic-church-sex-abuse-clergy-pennsylvania-grand-jury-report-released-names-20180814.html.

29. Christine Niles, "Catholic Heavyweights Demand Bishop Accountability," Church Militant, July 26, 2018, https://www.churchmilitant.com/news/article/catholic-heavyweights-demand-bishop-accountability.

30. WonEyeBri (@WonEyeBri), "#papriestreport Ironically, just received these Catholic tithe envelopes in the mail today. Burn in hell you despicable, evil, scumbag pieces of shit," Twitter, August 14, 2018, 4:13 p.m., https://twitter.com/WonEyeBri/status/1029506381349437441.

31. WonEyeBri (@WonEyeBri), "#papriestreport Ironically, just received these Catholic tithe envelopes in the mail today."

32. Claire Chretien, "Disgraced Cardinal Cancels Appearance Representing Pope after Locals Vow To Protest," LifeSite, February 19, 2018, https://www.lifesitenews.com/news/disgraced-cardinal-cancels-appearance-representing-pope-after-locals-vow-to.

33. "I Believe Americans Will Not Cooperate with Mr. Trump's Administration," California Catholic Daily, December 24, 2016, https://cal-catholic.com/i-believe-americans-will-not-cooperate-with-mr-trumps-administration/.

34. Chris Hawley and Sergio Solache, "Vatican Immigrant Aid Stirs Ire in USA," USA Today, April 15, 2008, https://usatoday30.usatoday.com/news/religion/2008-04-15-popeshelter_N.htm.

35. "Migrant Shelter Hermanos en el Camino," Hermanos en el Camino, http://www.hermanosenelcamino.org/english.html.

36. Courtney Grogan, "How Catholic Extension Supports Migrants along the US-Mexico Border," Catholic News Agency, January 11, 2018, https://www.catholicnewsagency.com/news/how-catholic-extension-support-migrants-along-the-us-mexico-border-44412.

37. "Aid from the Pope To Assist Migrants in Mexico," Peter's Pence, http://www.peterspence.va/en/opere-realizzate/messico.html.

38. "The National Catholic War Council," The Great War and Catholic Memory, http://omeka.archnyarchives.org/exhibits/show/archnyww1/fundraising/ncwc.

39. Archbishop José H. Gomez, "The Moral Urgency of Immigration Reform," CNN, January 27, 2016, https://www.cnn.com/2016/01/27/politics/gomez-immigration-column/.

40. Bishop Nicholas DiMarzio, "The Facts About Immigration," The Tablet, May 19, 2016, https://thetablet.org/the-facts-about-immigration/.

41. "Statement from Bishop Tobin on Proposal for Special Licenses for Undocumented Individuals," Roman Catholic Diocese of Providence, March 9, 2016, https://dioceseofprovidence.org/news/030916-statement-from-bishop-tobin-on-proposal-for-special-licenses-for-undocumented-individuals.

42. "Committee on Migration Chair Strongly Opposes Administration's Announcement to Build a Wall at U.S.-Mexico Border, Increase Detention and Deportation Forces," United States Conference of Catholic Bishops, January 25, 2017, http://www.usccb.org/news/2017/17-023.cfm.

43. Capital Research Center, "Selected HHS Refugee Resettlement/ UAC Grants," Department of Health and Human Services Tracking Accountability in Government Grants System, https://capitalresearch.org/app/uploads/Selected-HHS-Refugee-Resettlement-Grants.jpg.

44. "Catholic Charities Is Committed to Helping Immigrants & Refugees," Catholic Charities USA, https://www.catholiccharitiesusa.org/our-ministry/immigration-refugee-services/.

45. "Statement Regarding Their Deep Concern About Restricting Access to Asylum," United States Conference of Catholic Bishops, November 14, 2018, http://www.usccb.org/news/2018/18-183.cfm.

46. "DHS Announces New Proposed Immigration Rule to Enforce Long-Standing Law that Promotes Self-Sufficiency and Protects American Taxpayers," Department of Homeland Security, September 22, 2018, https://www.dhs.gov/news/2018/09/22/dhs-announces-new-proposed-immigration-rule-enforce-long-standing-law-promotes-self.

47. "Statement in Response to Notice of Proposed Rulemaking on Immigrants and Public Benefits," Justice for Immigrants, September 23, 2018, https://justiceforimmigrants.org/

statements/statement-in-response-to-notice-of-proposed-rulemaking-on-immigrants-and-public-benefits/.

48. "About Us," United States Conference of Catholic Bishops, https://usccb.site-ym.com/page/aboutus.

49. "About Us," United States Conference of Catholic Bishops.

50. United States Conference of Catholic Bishops and Affiliate, "Consolidated Financial Statements with Supplemental Schedules, December 31, 2017 and 2016," KPMG LLP, June 20, 2018, http://www.usccb.org/about/financial-reporting/upload/financial-statements-2016-2017.PDF.

51. Anthony Picarello, "2018 Group Ruling," Office of the General Counsel, December 6, 2018, http://www.usccb.org/about/general-counsel/upload/Group-Ruling-2018-Memo-FINAL-2.pdf.

52. Ann Corcoran, "US Catholic Bishops Launch Campaign To Pressure Trump To Admit Large Number of Refugees," Refugee Resettlement Watch, August 19, 2018, https://refugeeresettlementwatch.wordpress.com/2018/08/19/us-catholic-bishops-launch-campaign-to-pressure-trump-to-admit-large-number-of-refugees/.

53. Ann Corcoran, "US Catholic Bishops Launch Campaign To Pressure Trump."

54. Lisa Bourne, "Why Are US Bishops So Concerned about Trump's Refugee Orders? Follow the Money Trail," LifeSite, April 11, 2017, https://www.lifesitenews.com/news/a-conflict-of-interest-for-us-bishops-bashing-trump-on-refugees.

55. "USCCB Committee on Migration Chair Strongly Opposes Executive Order Because It Harms Vulnerable Refugee and Immigrant Families," United States Conference of Catholic Bishops, January 27, 2017, http://www.usccb.org/news/2017/17-026.cfm.

56. "The Justice for Immigrants Campaign," Justice for Immigrants, March 2019, https://justiceforimmigrants.org/wp-content/uploads/2019/03/JFI-March-2019.pdf.

57. "Tell Congress to Reject Inhumane Funding Requests for Immigration Enforcement," Justice for Immigrants, https://justiceforimmigrants.org/action-alerts/tell-congress-to-reject-inhumane-funding-requests-for-immigration-enforcement/.

58. "Responding to Refugees and Migrants: Twenty Action Points," Justice for Immigrants, https://justiceforimmigrants.org/wp-content/uploads/2018/02/20-points-_simplified.pdf.

59. Justice for Immigrants (@USCCBJFI), "A reminder to Urge Our Government to Resettle 30,000 Refugees in 2019 an sign the action alert. Do so today!" Twitter, April 13, 2019, 4:15 p.m., https://twitter.com/i/web/status/1117204579190439936.

60. Paula Cocozza, "What Happened to the 12 Syrian Refugees Rescued by the Pope?" *The Guardian*, May 25, 2016, https://www.theguardian.com/world/2016/may/25/what-happened-pope-francis-syrian-refugees-rescued-lesbos-vatican-rome.

61. John L. Allen Jr., "'Pope's Favorite Movement' Welcomes Syrian Refugees to Rome," Crux, March 28, 2018, https://cruxnow.com/global-church/2018/03/28/popes-favorite-movement-welcomes-40-new-syrian-refugees-to-rome/.

62. United States Conference of Catholic Bishops and Affiliate, "Consolidated Financial Statements with Supplemental Schedules."

63. Ian Smith, "Amnesty advocates turn on each other: the ACLU versus the U.S. Catholic Bishops," Daily Caller, May 26, 2015, https://dailycaller.com/2015/05/26/amnesty-advocates-turn-on-each-other-the-aclu-versus-the-u-s-catholic-bishops/.

64. National Collections Schedule for 2018/19, United States Conference of Catholic Bishops, http://dev.usccb.org/about/national-collections/upload/2018-2019-Collections-Schedule-FINAL.pdf.

65. United States Conference of Catholic Bishops and Affiliate, "Consolidated Financial Statements with Supplemental Schedules," 37.

66. Julie Leininger Pycior, "Odd Couple? U.S. Catholic Bishops and Community Organizers," HuffPost, November 21, 2014; updated December 6, 2017, https://www.huffpost.com/entry/odd-couple-us-catholic-bi_b_6196292; "History," Industrial Areas Foundation (IAF), http://www.industrialareasfoundation.org/content/history.

67. Paul Likoudis, *The Legacy of CHD: A Critical Report and Analysis of the U.S. Bishops' Campaign for Human Development* (The Wanderer Press, 1996), 37.

68. Likoudis, *The Legacy of CHD*, 4–5.

69. Ibid., 21.

70. Ibid., 56.

71. Ibid., 49.

72. Ibid., 53.

73. Ibid., 66–67.

74. Matthew Vadum, "Left-Wing Radicalism in the Church: CCHD and ACORN," *Human Events*, October 26, 2009, https://web.archive.org/web/20181222100909/humanevents. com/2009/10/26/leftwing-radicalism-in-the-church-cchd-and-acorn/.

75. Vadum, "Left-Wing Radicalism in the Church."

76. Dennis Sadowski, "CCHD Ends Funding to ACORN over Financial Irregularities," *National Catholic Reporter*, October 17, 2008, https://www.ncronline.org/news/ cchd-ends-funding-acorn-over-financial-irregularities.

77. Stephanie Block, "What Is the Catholic Campaign for Human Development Trying to Do?" Catholic Media Coalition, http://www.catholicmediacoalition.org/ cchd_what_is_it_trying_to_do.htm.

78. "Catholic Campaign for Human Development," United State Conference of Catholic Bishops, http://www.usccb.org/about/catholic-campaign-for-human-development/.

79. "Comprehensive Immigration Reform Grants," United States Conference of Catholic Bishops, http://www.usccb.org/about/catholic-campaign-for-human-development/grants/ cchd-immigration-reform-grants.cfm.

80. "Catholic Campaign for Human Development Supports Justice for Immigrants," United States Conference of Catholic Bishops, http://www.usccb.org/about/catholic-campaign-for- human-development/grants/upload/immigration-grants-map-2014.pdf.

81. "DACA and Dreamer Quick Facts," Hope Border Institute, September 14, 2017, https:// www.hopeborder.org/ff-daca-and-dreamers-quick-facts.

82. "Trump Administration's Policy between ORR and ICE Keeps Families Separated," Catholic Legal Immigration Network Inc., January 23, 2019, https://cliniclegal.org/news/ trump-administrations-policy-between-orr-ice-keeps-families-separated.

83. *Amici Curiae* brief by United States Conference of Bishops in *Donald Trump, et al. vs. State of Hawaii, et al.*, March 30, 2018, http://www.usccb.org/about/general-counsel/ amicus-briefs/upload/usccb-scotus-amicus-brief-20180330-as-filed.pdf.

84. Catholic Legal Immigration Network Inc., "Financial Statements and Independent Auditor's Report, December 31, 2017 and 2016," May 10, 2018, https://cliniclegal.org/ sites/default/files/2017-CLINIC-Financial-Statements-.pdf.

85. "Catholic Legal Immigration Network (CLINIC)," Influence Watch, https://www. influencewatch.org/non-profit/catholic-legal-immigration-network/#note-26.

86. "Mission Statement," Catholic Relief Services, https://www.crs.org/about/ mission-statement.

87. "Through the Years," Catholic Relief Services, https://impact.crs.org/timeline/.

88. "CRS in Greece," Catholic Relief Services, https://www.crs.org/our-work-overseas/ where-we-work/greece.

89. CRS Staff, "Providing Lifesaving Support for Syrian Refugees," Catholic Relief Services, March 1, 2017, https://www.crs.org/stories/providing-lifesaving-support-syrian-refugees.

90. Catholic Relief Services, Form 990 for the 2017 tax year, March 14, 2019, https://www. crs.org/sites/default/files/fy2018_2017_form_990_-_web_version_03.14.19.pdf

91. Catholic Relief Services Annual Report (2017), https://www.crs.org/sites/default/files/2017. pdf, 8.

92. Mark Pattison, "Border Crisis Declarations Mask Misery of Immigrants," *The Tablet*, April 10, 2019, https://thetablet.org/ border-crisis-declarations-mask-misery-of-immigrants/.

93. Mark Pattison, "Border Crisis Declarations Mask Misery of Immigrants," 9.

94. Tom Zolper, "Catholic Relief Services to Congress: 'Protect U.S. Foreign Aid,'" Catholic Relief Services, March 12, 2019, https://www.crs.org/media-center/news-release/catholic-relief-services-congress-protect-us-foreign-aid.

95. CNA Daily News, "Cutting Central American Aid Will Make Matters Worse, Critics Say," Catholic World Report, April 3, 2019, https://www.catholicworldreport.com/2019/04/03/cutting-central-american-aid-will-make-matters-worse-critics-say/.

96. Ann Corcoran, "How Much of Your Tax Dollars Are the Federal Refugee Resettlement Contractors Receiving?" Refugee Resettlement Watch, January 16, 2015, https://refugeeresettlementwatch.wordpress.com/2015/01/16/how-much-of-your-tax-dollars-are-the-federal-refugee-resettlement-contractors-receiving/.

97. Mary L. Gautier, Ph.D. and Jonathon L. Wiggins, Ph.D., "Catholic Charities USA 2016 Annual Survey Final Report," Center for Applied Research in the Apostolate, Georgetown University, June 2017, https://cara.georgetown.edu/qtn/ccusa16.../CCUSA_2016_Annual_Survey_Report.pdf.

98. Gautier and Wiggins, "Catholic Charities USA 2016 Annual Survey Final Report."

99. Ibid.

100. "#13 Catholic Charities USA," Forbes, December 11, 2018, https://www.forbes.com/companies/catholic-charities-usa/#55d4324032b6.

101. Gautier and Wiggins, "Catholic Charities USA 2016 Annual Survey Final Report," 15.

102. Brian C. Anderson, "How Catholic Charities Lost Its Soul," City Journal (Winter 2000), https://www.city-journal.org/html/how-catholic-charities-lost-its-soul-12150.html.

103. Richard John Neuhaus, "A Mirror of the National Soul," First Things (March 1997), https://www.firstthings.com/article/1997/03/a-mirror-of-the-national-soul.

104. Scott Walter, "Conquering the Private Sector," Philanthropy Daily, December 21, 2011, https://www.philanthropydaily.com/conquering-the-private-sector/.

105. Walter, "Conquering the Private Sector."

106. Kelly Riddell, "Catholic Church Collects $1.6 Billion in U.S. Contracts, Grants since 2012," Washington Times, September 24, 2015, https://www.washingtontimes.com/news/2015/sep/24/catholic-church-collects-16-billion-in-us-contract/#!.

107. Catholic Relief Services Annual Report (2017), 25.

108. "INCONTRO DEL SANTO PADRE FRANCESCO CON I DOCENTI E CON GLI STUDENTI DEL COLLEGIO SAN CARLO DI MILANO," Vatican website, April 6, 2019, http://w2.vatican.va/content/francesco/it/speeches/2019/april/documents/papa-francesco_20190406_istitutosancarlo-milano.html.

Chapter 4

1. Emma Lazarus, "The New Colossus," The Poetry Foundation, https://www.poetryfoundation.org/poems/46550/the-new-colossus.

2. Lazarus, "The New Colossus.".

3. Nancy Pelosi, "Pelosi Remarks at Bicameral Press Event on President Trump's Anti-Immigrant, Anti-Refugee Executive Orders," January 30, 2017, https://pelosi.house.gov/news/press-releases/pelosi-remarks-at-bicameral-press-event-on-president-trump-s-anti-immigrant-anti.

4. Brooke Seipel, "Clinton: 'This is not who we are,'" The Hill, January 28, 2017, https://thehill.com/blogs/blog-briefing-room/news/316717-hillary-clinton-condemns-immigration-ban-this-is-not-who-we-are.

5. Tim Hains, "Julian Castro: Trump's Wall Would Replace Statue Of Liberty As The Symbol Of America," RealClear Politics, January 27, 2019, https://www.realclearpolitics.com/video/2019/01/27/julian_castro_trumps_wall_would_replace_statue_of_liberty_as_symbol_of_america.html.

6. Rep. Dina Titus (@dinatitus), "We cannot let Trump build a wall. That's not who we are. Stand with Democrats to pass immigration reform that protects our #Dreamers and #TPS recipients," Twitter, January 29, 2019, 4:02 p.m., https://twitter.com/dinatitus/status/1090399871322927106.

7. Ken Thomas, "Joe Biden Joins 2020 Democratic Presidential Race," *Wall Street Journal*, April 25, 2019, https://www.wsj.com/articles/joe-biden-enters-2020-democratic-presidential-race-11556186638.

8. Josiah Ryan, "CNN's Acosta, White House aide clash over immigration at briefing," CNN, August 2, 2017, https://money.cnn.com/2017/08/02/media/jim-acosta-stephen-miller-immigration/index.html?iid=hp-toplead-dom.

9. Brandon Sanchez, "Trump Administration's Record-Low Refugee Resettlement 'Contradicts Who We Are as a Nation,'" *American Magazine*, September 20, 2018, https://www.americamagazine.org/politics-society/2018/09/20/trump-administrations-record-low-refugee-resettlement-contradicts-who.

10. Sanchez, "Trump Administration's Record-Low Refugee Resettlement."

11. Nayla Rush, "U.S. Resettled More Refugees than Any Other Nation in 2017 and 2018," Center for Immigration Studies, March 14, 2019, https://cis.org/Rush/US-Resettled-More-Refugees-Any-Other-Nation-2017-and-2018.

12. Rush, "U.S. Resettled More Refugees Than Any Other Nation in 2017 and 2018."

13. "Proposed Refugee Admissions for Fiscal Year 2019," U.S. Department of State, September 24, 2018, https://web.archive.org/web/20190331085127/https://www.state.gov/j/prm/releases/docsforcongress/286157.htm.

14. "Liberty Enlightening the World," National Park Service, https://www.nps.gov/stli/index.htm.

15. U.S. Constitution preamble, https://www.law.cornell.edu/constitution/preamble.

16. James Madison, *The Writings of James Madison* (1790), https://books.google.com/books?id=sGGGs3reve0C&pg=PA437&lpg=PA437&dq=%E2%80%9CIt+is+no+doubt+very+desirable+that+we+should+hold+out+as+many+inducements&source=bl&ots=DLllU8U0nx&sig=gIFnHUz8rEHnGJFs6ooAnCKKH3A&hl=en&sa=X&ved=0ahUKEwiu0er2k-rRAhXCrFQKHUhgBm#v=onepage&q=%E2%80%9CIt%20is%20no%20doubt%20very%20desirable%20that%20we%20should%20hold%20out%20as%20many%20inducements&f=false.

17. Madison, *The Writings of James Madison*.

18. John C. Fitzpatrick, ed., *Writings of George Washington* (Washington DC: Government Printing Office), http://www.vindicatingthefounders.com/library/washington-to-adams.html.

19. William G. Chrystal, "Alexander Hamilton and Immigration," The Federalist Papers, June 19, 2013, http://www.thefederalistpapers.org/current-events/alexander-hamilton-and-immigration.

20. Steve Sailer, "The Highest Law of the Land: Emma Lazarus's Poem," iSteve, May 7, 2013, https://isteve.blogspot.com/2013/05/the-highest-law-of-land-emma-lazaruss.html.

21. Dennis Sawyers, "How Many Refugees Are in the US? Facts, Figures, & History," The Borgen Project, https://borgenproject.org/how-many-refugees-are-in-the-us/.

22. Refugee Act of 1980, https://www.archivesfoundation.org/documents/refugee-act-1980/.

23. The wording is borrowed from the U.N. Convention on the Status of Refugees adopted in 1951 and its 1967 Protocol, which defined refugees and the rights they are entitled to. *See* "The 1951 Refugee Convention," UNHCR, https://www.unhcr.org/1951-refugee-convention.html.

24. "History," Office of Refugee Resettlement, https://www.acf.hhs.gov/orr/about/history.

25. Anjali Hemphill, "MS-13 Teen Gang Member Convicted for Ordering Attack on 2 People at Mall," FOX 5 DC, June 30, 2017, https://www.fox5dc.com/news/local-news/ms-13-teen-gang-member-convicted-for-ordering-attack-on-2-people-at-mall.

26. Stephanie Ramirez, "Gang Recruiting Seen as Early as Elementary School," WUSA 9, February 16, 2017, https://www.wusa9.com/article/news/local/gang-recruiting-seen-as-early-as-elementary-school/409171264.

27. Michael E. Miller, "'A Ticking Time Bomb': MS-13 Threatens a Middle School, Warn Teachers, Parents, Students," *Washington Post*, June 11, 2018, https://www.washingtonpost.com/local/a-ticking-time-bomb-ms-13-threatens-a-middle-school-warn-teachers-parents-students/2018/06/11/7cfc7036-5a00-11e8-858f-12becb4d6067_story.html?utm_term=.79f26688ce62.

28. Penny Starr, "Maryland Teachers, Students Live in Fear of MS-13 Middle Schoolers," Breitbart, June 13, 2018, https://www.breitbart.com/politics/2018/06/13/maryland-teachers-students-live-fear-ms-13-middle-schoolers/.

29. Lance Benzel, "Clashing Portrayals in Colorado Springs Trial for Iraqi Immigrant Accused in Brutal Rape," *Colorado Springs Gazette*, January 9, 2014, https://gazette.com/crime/clashing-portrayals-in-colorado-springs-trial-for-iraqi-immigrant-accused/article_30c04e5a-c233-5352-97e2-8b07432b6da3.html.

30. Maria St. Louis-Sanchez, "Witnesses Told Police Rape Victim Sought Help during Attack," *Colorado Springs Gazette*, September 4, 2012, https://gazette.com/news/witnesses-told-police-rape-victim-sought-help-during-attack/article_ada652b3-89df-52dd-af2d-25a28f3c2413.html.

31. Michael Roberts, "Jasim Ramadon, Former Teen Iraqi Hero, Charged in Horrific Rape," Westword, August 15, 2012, https://www.westword.com/news/jasim-ramadon-former-teen-iraqi-hero-charged-in-horrific-rape-5909053.

32. Diana West, "The Peril of Ignoring Cultural Differences," TRIB Live, January 31, 2014, https://archive.triblive.com/opinion/featured-commentary/the-peril-of-ignoring-cultural-differences/.

33. Anna Staver, "Homeland Security Says Man Accused of Shooting Colorado Springs Officer is Iraqi Refugee," *Colorado Springs Gazette*, August 6, 2018, https://gazette.com/news/suspect-once-hailed-as-war-hero-has-history-of-violence/article_154c5e89-8edb-5d64-9a5b-d4339dabc798.html.

34. Associated Press, "2 Wounded in Shooting at Colorado Springs Mall," December 18, 2018, https://kdvr.com/2018/12/18/2-wounded-in-shooting-at-colorado-springs-mall/.

35. "Turkish American Police Officer Cem Duzel Recovering from Traumatic Head Injury Needs Your Help!" Assembly of Turkish American Associations, https://www.ataa.org/press-releases/turkish-american-police-officer-cem-duzel-recovering-from-traumatic-head-injury-needs-your-help.

36. Staver, "Homeland Security Says Man Accused of Shooting Colorado Springs Officer is Iraqi Refugee."

37. Lance Benzel, "Case against Accused Colorado Springs Cop Shooter Enters Legal Limbo," *Colorado Springs Gazette*, May 3, 2019, https://gazette.com/news/case-against-accused-colorado-springs-cop-shooter-enters-legal-limbo/article_60fbb60e-6dcc-11e9-8545-53e28cac2c86.html.

38. I reached out to Khammasi's lawyer, Jennifer Chu, to find out more about how Duzel got here and what specific claim of persecution he made abroad that persuaded the United Nations to approve his refugee status and send him off to America. I also wanted to know who met him in Chicago, what services he was provided between 2012–2018, and what VOLAGs and subcontractors assisted him on his journey from Chicago to Colorado Springs. Chu did not return my call.

39. Stephen Dinan, "Refugee Charged with Murder Was in ICE Custody in 2016," *Washington Times*, August 6, 2018, https://www.washingtontimes.com/news/2018/aug/6/refugee-charged-with-murder-was-in-ice-custody-in-/.

40. Dinan, "Refugee charged with murder was in ICE custody in 2016."

41. Supreme Court of the United States, Sessions, Attorney General, v. Dimaya, Certiorari to the United States Court of Appeals for the Nine Circuit No. 15–1498, https://www.supremecourt.gov/opinions/17pdf/15-1498_1b8e.pdf.

42. Supreme Court of the United States, Sessions, Attorney General, v. Dimaya, 10.

43. Michelle Malkin, *Invasion: How America Still Welcomes Terrorists Criminals & Other Foreign Menaces to Our Shores* (Washington, D.C.: Regnery Publishing, 2002), 222–25.

44. "UNHCR Resettlement Handbook," UNHCR, 2011, https://www.unhcr.org/46f7c0ee2.html.

45. "Resettlement Facts," UNHCR, February 2019, https://www.unhcr.org/en-us/resettlement-in-the-united-states.html.

46. Designated nationalities are nationalities deemed of particular humanitarian concern for the U.S. resettlement program. Applicants from these groups do not need UNHCR referrals.

47. Jens Manuel Krogstad and Jynnah Radford, "Key Facts about Refugees to the U.S.," Pew Research, January 30, 2017, https://www.pewresearch.org/fact-tank/2017/01/30/key-facts-about-refugees-to-the-u-s/.

48. Krogstad and Radford, "Key Facts about Refugees to the U.S."

49. "Top Ten Refugee Native Languages," U.S. Department of State, March 31, 2019, https://www.wrapsnet.org/s/Top-Ten-Refugee-Native-Languages.xls.

50. "Admissions by Month," U.S. Department of State, April 30, 2019, https://www.wrapsnet.org/s/Graph-Refugee-Admissions-FY2019_04_30.xls.

51. "Admissions by Month," U.S. Department of State.

52. "Menendez Leads Democrats in Urging Secretary Pompeo To Improve Refugee Admissions as Key Foreign Policy Priority," U.S. Senate Committee on Foreign Relations Ranking Member's Press, May 1, 2018, https://www.foreign.senate.gov/press/ranking/release/menendez-leads-democrats-in-urging-secretary-pompeo-improve-refugee-admissions-as-key-foreign-policy-priority.

53. "The Reception and Placement Program," U.S. Department of State, https://web.archive.org/web/20190510003042/http://www.state.gov/j/prm/ra/receptionplacement/index.htm.

54. "United States Refugee Admissions Program," U.S. Citizenship and Immigration Services, August 31, 2018, https://www.uscis.gov/sites/default/files/USCIS/Refugee,%20Asylum,%20and%20Int'l%20Ops/USRAP_FlowChart.pdf.

55. "The Reception and Placement Program," U.S. Department of State.

56. "Refugee Resettlement: Greater Consultation with Community Stakeholders Could Strengthen Program," U.S. General Accounting Office, July 2012, https://www.gao.gov/assets/600/592975.pdf, 12–13.

57. "The Refugee Act," Office of Refugee Resettlement, August 29, 2012, https://www.acf.hhs.gov/orr/resource/the-refugee-act.

58. "The Refugee Act," Office of Refugee Resettlement.

59. Ibid., 14.

60. "Refugees," U.S. Citizenship and Immigration Services, https://www.uscis.gov/humanitarian/refugees-asylum/refugees.

61. G. Jeffrey MacDonald, "Faith-Based Groups Earn Millions on Refugee Loan Commissions," Religion News Service, December 1, 2015, https://religionnews.com/2015/12/01/faith-based-refugees-loans-commissions-congress-syrian-crisis/.

62. Bureau of Population, Refugees, and Migration, "Proposed Refugee Admissions for Fiscal Year 2019," U.S. Department of State, September 24, 2018, https://web.archive.org/web/20190316151447/https://www.state.gov/j/prm/releases/docsforcongress/286157.htm.

63. Fabrice Robinet, "Welcome, Refugees. Now Pay Back Your Travel Loans," *New York Times*, March 15, 2019, https://www.nytimes.com/2019/03/15/nyregion/refugees-travel-loans.html.

64. Robinet, "Welcome, Refugees. Now Pay Back Your Travel Loans."

65. Judicial Watch, "Judicial Watch Files Suit For 'Refugee Travel Loans' Information," February 7, 2017, https://www.judicialwatch.org/press-room/press-releases/judicial-watch-files-suit-refugee-travel-loans-information/.

66. "Proposed Refugee Admissions for Fiscal Year 2019," U.S. Department of State.

67. "Proposed Refugee Admissions for Fiscal Year 2019," U.S. Department of State.

68. Robinet, "Welcome, Refugees. Now Pay Back Your Travel Loans."

69. CRC Staff, "Refugee Resettlement: The Lucrative Business of Serving Immigrants," Capital Research Center, July 28, 2015, https://capitalresearch.org/article/refugee-resettlement-the-lucrative-business-of-serving-immigrants/.

70. James Simpson, "Resettling Refugees: Social and Economic Costs," Capital Research Center, September 14, 2018, https://capitalresearch.org/article/resettling-refugees-part-3/.

71. Nayla Rush, "'Private' Refugee Resettlement Agencies Mostly Funded by the Government," Center for Immigration Studies, August 10, 2018, https://cis.org/Rush/Private-Refugee-Resettlement-Agencies-Mostly-Funded-Government.

72. Rush, "'Private' Refugee Resettlement Agencies Mostly Funded by the Government."

73. U.S. Department of State, "FY 2019 Notice of Funding Opportunity for Reception and Placement Program," March 15, 2018, https://web.archive.org/web/20181209132519/https://www.state.gov/j/prm/funding/fy2019/279289.htm.

74. James Simpson, "The Refugee Resettlement Program Is Not the Refugee Resettlement Program," *Social Contract Journal* (Fall 2018), https://www.thesocialcontract.com/artman2/publish/tsc_29_1/tsc-29-1-simpson.shtml.

75. Clare Roth, "Cuts to Refugee Admissions Hit Columbia Resettlement Agency," *Missourian*, October 12, 2018, https://www.columbiamissourian.com/news/local/cuts-to-refugee-admissions-hit-columbia-resettlement-agency/article_24e8f6f6-cb2c-11e8-9f13-33bceaee21af.html.

76. Office of Refugee Resettlement, "Office of Refugee Resettlement Annual Report to Congress 2016," June 14, 2018, https://www.acf.hhs.gov/orr/resource/office-of-refugee-resettlement-annual-report-to-congress-2016.

77. Matthew O'Brien and Spencer Raley, "The Fiscal Cost of Resettling Refugees in the United States," FAIR, February 5, 2018, https://www.fairus.org/issue/legal-immigration/fiscal-cost-resettling-refugees-united-states.

78. Steven A. Camarota, "The High Cost of Resettling Middle Eastern Refugees," Center for Immigration Studies, November 4, 2015, https://cis.org/Report/High-Cost-Resettling-Middle-Eastern-Refugees.

79. Michael Patrick Leahy, "Refugees Will Cost Taxpayers an Estimated $4.1 Billion in FY 2017," Breitbart, February 19, 2017, https://www.breitbart.com/politics/2017/02/19/refugees-will-cost-taxpayers-an-estimated-4-billion-in-fy-2017/.

80. Daniel Greenfield, "Enough Iraqi refugee terrorists and rapists," Frontpage, February 9, 2017, https://www.frontpagemag.com/fpm/265742/enough-iraqi-refugee-terrorists-and-rapists-daniel-greenfield.

81. Melanie Hall, "Muslim Preacher Urges Followers To Claim 'Jihad Seeker's Allowance,'" *Telegraph*, February 17, 2013, https://www.telegraph.co.uk/news/9875954/Muslim-preacher-urges-followers-to-claim-Jihad-Seekers-Allowance.html.

82. "'Claim Jobseeker's Allowance and Plan Holy War': Hate Preacher Pocketing £25,000 a Year in Benefits Calls on Fanatics To Live Off the State," *Daily Mail*, February 17, 2013, https://www.dailymail.co.uk/news/article-2279972/Anjem-Choudary-Hate-preacher-pocketing-25-000-year-benefits-calls-fanatics-live-state.html.

83. Colleen Curry, "Tamerlan Tsarnaev and Family Used Welfare," ABC News, April 24, 2013, https://abcnews.go.com/blogs/headlines/2013/04/tamerlan-tsarnaev-and-family-used-welfare/.

84. James Gordon Meek, Cindy Gakki, and Brian Ross, "Exclusive: US May Have Let 'Dozens' of Terrorists Into Country As Refugees," ABC News, November 20, 2013,

https://abcnews.go.com/Blotter/al-qaeda-kentucky-us-dozens-terrorists-country-refugees/story?id=20931131.

85. "Refugee Resettlement Fact Sheet," Refugee Resettlement Watch, https://refugeeresettlementwatch.wordpress.com/refugee-resettlement-fact-sheets/.

86. "Refugee Resettlement: Greater Consultation with Community Stakeholders Could Strengthen Program," U.S. General Accounting Office, 12.

87. Pam Belluck, "Mixed Welcome as Somalis Settle in a Maine City," *New York Times*, October 15, 2002, https://www.nytimes.com/2002/10/15/us/mixed-welcome-as-somalis-settle-in-a-maine-city.html.

88. Daniel Lippman, "Robert Macdonald, Maine Mayor, Tells Immigrants To 'Leave Your Culture At The Door,'" *HuffPost*, September 27, 2012, https://www.huffpost.com/entry/robert-macdonald-maine-mayor-immigrants-culture_n_1920630?guccounter=1.

89. "Nonprofit Explorer," ProPublica, https://projects.propublica.org/nonprofits/organizations/10280225.

90. Abby Goodnough, "After Taking In Refugees for Years, a New Hampshire City Asks for a Pause," *New York Times*, November 26, 2011, https://www.nytimes.com/2011/11/26/us/manchester-new-hampshire-seeks-halt-in-refugee-resettlement.html.

91. "Nonprofit Explorer," ProPublica, https://projects.propublica.org/nonprofits/organizations/42104325.

92. "Refugee Resettlement: Greater Consultation with Community Stakeholders Could Strengthen Program," U.S. General Accounting Office, 24.

93. Peter Goonan, "Springfield Mayor Domenic Sarno Urges State Department To Stop Influx of Refugees into City," Mass Live, August 13, 2013, https://www.masslive.com/news/2013/08/springfield_mayor_domenic_sarn_78.html.

94. Goonan, "Springfield Mayor Domenic Sarno Urges State Department To Stop Influx."

95. "New England Mayors Call for Refugee Resettlement Freeze," Fox News, June 23, 2014, updated December 20, 2015, https://www.foxnews.com/politics/new-england-mayors-call-for-refugee-resettlement-freeze.

96. James Rothwell, "Majority of Paris Attackers Used Migration Routes To Enter Europe, Reveals Hungarian Counter-Terror Chief," *Telegraph*, October 2, 2016, https://www.telegraph.co.uk/news/2016/10/02/majority-of-paris-attackers-used-migration-routes-to-enter-europ/.

97. "CAIR Warns Against Increasing Hate Crimes against Muslims in US," Kuwait News Agency, November 18, 2015, https://www.thefreelibrary.com/CAIR+warns+against+increasing+hate+crimes+against+Muslims+in+US.-a0434887157.

98. Ashley Fantz and Ben Brumfield, "More Than Half the Nation's Governors Say Syrian Refugees Not Welcome," CNN, November 19, 2015, https://www.cnn.com/2015/11/16/world/paris-attacks-syrian-refugees-backlash/.

99. Fatima Hussein, "Federal Court Deals Final Blow to Pence's Ban on Aid to Syrian Refugees," KHOU 11, March 1, 2018, https://www.khou.com/article/news/nation-now/federal-court-deals-final-blow-to-pences-ban-on-aid-to-syrian-refugees/465-7ac5bb56-a628-4000-bb60-8e60449e239a.

100. "Nonprofit Explorer," ProPublica, https://projects.propublica.org/nonprofits/organizations/351900090/201733079349300643/IRS990.

101. Beth Dalbey, "Michigan Leads U.S. States Syrian Refugee Resettlement," Patch, June 9, 2016, https://patch.com/michigan/troy/michigan-leads-u-s-states-syrian-refugee-resettlement.

102. Beth Dalbey, "SE Michigan Township Shuts Door on Syrian Refugees," Patch, October 25, 2016, https://patch.com/michigan/troy/se-michigan-township-shuts-door-syrian-refugees.

103. "Nonprofit Explorer," ProPublica, https://projects.propublica.org/nonprofits/organizations/381360553.

104. Elizabeth Hewitt, "Resettlement of Syrian Refugees Riles Rutland Residents," VTDigger, May 26, 2016, https://vtdigger.org/2016/05/26/rutland-aldermen/.

105. Jess Aloe, "Rutland Reels after Halt to Refugee Program," *Burlington Free Press*, January 26, 2017, https://www.burlingtonfreepress.com/story/news/2017/01/26/rutland-reels-after-halt-refugee-program/97097782/.

106. Wilson Ring, "Vermont Mayor: Refugee Resettlement Cost Me My Job," Associated Press, March 8, 2017, https://www.mercurynews.com/2017/03/08/mayor-believes-his-syrian-refugee-plan-cost-him-re-election/.

107. Brittany Blizzard and Jeanne Batalova, "Refugees and Asylees in the United States," Migration Policy Institute, June 13, 2019, https://www.migrationpolicy.org/article/refugees-and-asylees-united-states.

108. Michael Patrick Leahy, "Why 12 States Hold Key to Constitutional Challenge to Refugee Resettlement Program," Breitbart, December 8, 2015, https://www.breitbart.com/politics/2015/12/08/12-states-hold-key-constitutional-challenge-refugee-resettlement-program/.

109. "First in the Nation — Tennessee Files Lawsuit Challenging Constitutionality of the Federal Refugee Resettlement Program," Thomas More Law Center, https://www.thomasmore.org/news/first-nation-tennessee-files-lawsuit-challenging-constitutionality-federal-refugee-resettlement-program/.

110. Michael Patrick Leahy, "Legal Heavyweight Will Represent Tennessee in Appeal of Refugee Resettlement Lawsuit," Breitbart, March 14, 2019, https://www.breitbart.com/politics/2019/03/14/legal-heavyweight-will-represent-tennessee-in-appeal-of-refugee-resettlement-lawsuit/.

111. "FY 2018 Reception and Placement Program Affiliate Sites," U.S. Department of State, May 2018, http://www.wrapsnet.org/s/1789-PRM-RPP-Affiliate-Sites-LARGEFY18.pdf.

112. David Dyssegaard Kallick, "Squeezing Refugees: Numbers for 2018 by State and Metro Area," Fiscal Policy Institute, November 2, 2018, http://fiscalpolicy.org/squeezing-refugees-numbers-for-2018-by-state-and-metro-area.

113. "Amid Rising Xenophobia, Violence, States Must Do More to Protect Migrants' Rights, General Assembly Hears on International Day for Ending Racial Discrimination," United Nations, March 21, 2017, https://www.un.org/press/en/2017/ga11895.doc.htm.

114. Katie Reilly, "Read Barack Obama's Final Speech to the United Nations as President," *Time*, September 20, 2016, http://time.com/4501910/president-obama-united-nations-speech-transcript/.

115. Reilly, "Read Barack Obama's Final Speech to the United Nations."

116. Carole Landry, "Warnings of Xenophobia at UN Refugee Summit," AFP, September 19, 2016, https://news.yahoo.com/un-refugee-summit-hears-call-confront-race-baiting-160001414.html.

117. Michelle Malkin, "Hey, UN Corruptocrats: Spare Us Refugee Sanctimony," michellemalkin.com, September 21, 2016, http://michellemalkin.com/2016/09/21/hey-un-corruptocrats-spare-us-refugee-sanctimony/.

118. Ian Fisher, "Refugees in Kenya Tell of Shakedown by U.N. Agency," *New York Times*, February 19, 2001, https://www.nytimes.com/2001/02/19/world/refugees-in-kenya-tell-of-shakedown-by-un-agency.html.

119. "Refugee Status Being Sold for up to RM3,500 in Malaysia, Claims Al-Jazeera Report," The Malay Mail Online, November 21, 2014, https://www.malaymail.com/news/malaysia/2014/11/21/refugee-status-being-sold-for-up-to-rm3500-in-malaysia-claims-al-jazeera-re/787237.

120. "Refugee Status Being Sold for up to RM3,500 in Malaysia, Claims Al-Jazeera report," The Malay Mail Online.

121. "Myanmese Refugees Made To Pay US$1,000 To Stay in Malaysia," South China Morning Post, November 23, 2014, https://www.scmp.com/news/asia/article/1646449/myanmese-refugees-made-pay-us1000-stay-malaysia.

122. "Myanmese Refugees Made To Pay US$1,000 To Stay in Malaysia," South China Morning Post.

123. Viviane Akiki, "Corruption Creeps into Refugee Aid in Lebanon," Al-Monitor, March 8, 2015, https://www.al-monitor.com/pulse/politics/2015/03/lebanon-corruption-syrian-refugees-aid.html.

124. Akiki, "Corruption Creeps into Refugee Aid in Lebanon."

125. Office of Internal Oversight Services, Internal Audit Division, "Report 2016/034," April 25, 2016, https://oios.un.org/page/download/id/487, 3.

126. George A. Bartsiotas and Sukai Prom-Jackson, "Review of the Management of Implementing Partners in United Nations System Organizations," 2013, https://www.unjiu.org/sites/www.unjiu.org/files/jiu_document_files/products/en/reports-notes/JIU%20Products/JIU_REP_2013_4_English.pdf.

127. Nick Cumming-Bruce, "Peacekeepers Accused of Sexual Abuse in Central African Republic," *New York Times*, January 30, 2016, https://www.nytimes.com/2016/01/30/world/africa/un-peacekeepers-central-african-republic.html.

128. "UN Inquiry: UNHCR Agents Took Bribes," UPI, January 25, 2002, https://www.upi.com/Defense-News/2002/01/25/UN-inquiry-UNHCR-agents-took-bribes/34521012001043.

129. Nisha Lilia Diu, "What the UN Doesn't Want You to Know," *Telegraph*, February 6, 2012, https://www.telegraph.co.uk/culture/9041974/What-the-UN-Doesnt-Want-You-to-Know.html.

130. Michelle Malkin, "The U.N.'s Rape of the Innocents," Jewish World Review, February 16, 2005, http://jewishworldreview.com/michelle/malkin021605.php3.

131. Nicole Einbinder, "French Police to Investigate New Abuse Claims Against Former UN Peacekeeper," *Frontline*, July 24, 2018, https://www.pbs.org/wgbh/frontline/article/french-police-to-investigate-new-abuse-claims-against-former-un-peacekeeper/.

132. Michelle Malkin, "Results for 'U.N. Sex Scandal,'" michellemalkin.com, http://michellemalkin.com/?s=u.n.+sex+scandal.

133. Sally Hayden, "Asylum for sale: Refugees say some U.N. workers demand bribes for resettlement," NBC News, April 6, 2019, https://www.nbcnews.com/news/world/asylum-sale-refugees-say-some-u-n-workers-demand-bribes-n988351.

Chapter 5

1. Miami DSA (@MiamiDSA), "This IS the America we know, but it doesn't have to be. Another world is possible, let's build it together! #AbolishICE #NoBorders #NoMuslimBanEver #NoBanNoWall #AbolishICE #AbolishCBP #TrySocialism #FreeOurFuture #AbolishPrisons #EndImmigrationDetention," Twitter, 1:12 p.m., June 26, 2018, https://twitter.com/miamidsa/status/1011703786400813056?lang=en.

2. "#AbolishICE Resources," Democratic Socialists of America, June 27, 2018, https://www.dsausa.org/organize/abolish_ice_end_muslimban_resources/.

3. Erich Wagner, "Homeland Security Warns of Increased Threats to Employees," Government Executive, June 25, 2018, https://www.govexec.com/management/2018/06/homeland-security-warns-increased-threats-employees/149257/.

4. Wagner, "Homeland Security Warns of Increased Threats."

5. Wendy Fry, "Feds Investigating Alleged Armed Disruption Attempt at U.S.-Mexico Border in December: Report," *San Diego Union-Tribune*, April 28, 2019, https://www.sandiegouniontribune.com/news/border-baja-california/story/2019-04-28/feds-investigating-alleged-armed-disruption-attempt-at-u-s-mexico-border-in-december-report.

6. Josh Meyer, "FBI, Homeland Security Warn of More 'Antifa' Attacks," *Politico*, September 1, 2017, https://www.politico.com/story/2017/09/01/antifa-charlottesville-violence-fbi-242235.

7. John Hinderaker, "Videos and Photos of Fascist Violence in San Jose," Power Line, June 3, 2016, https://www.powerlineblog.com/archives/2016/06/videos-and-photos-of-fascist-violence-in-san-jose.php.

8. Guillermo Contreras, "S.A. Activist Drops Immigration Fight and Agrees To Be Deported," *San Antonio Express-News*, September 14, 2018, https://www.expressnews.com/news/local/article/SA-activist-drops-immigration-fight-and-agrees-to-13230576.php.

9. Todd Bensman, "The Domestic Terror Threat Against ICE," Center for Immigration Studies, January 23, 2019, https://cis.org/Bensman/Domestic-Terror-Threat-Against-ICE.

10. Todd Bensman and Bryan Griffith, "Immigration Brief: Domestic Extremists Target ICE Officers," Center for Immigration Studies, January 23, 2019, https://cis.org/Immigration-Brief/Immigration-Brief-Domestic-Extremists-Target-ICE-Officers.

11. *United States of America v. Brandon James Ziobrowski*, U.S. District Court, District of Massachusetts, Indictment, https://cis.org/sites/default/files/2018-08/Ziobrowski%20indictment.pdf.

12. Tom Winter and Joe Valiquette, "Massachusetts Man Arrested for Threatening ICE Agents on Twitter," NBC News, https://www.nbcnews.com/news/crime-courts/boston-area-man-arrested-threatening-ice-agents-twitter-n899146.

13. Hunter Walker, "Cops Release Surveillance Footage of Occupy Wall Street Poop Pouring Protest [Video]," Observer, March 21, 2012, https://observer.com/2012/03/cops-release-surveillance-footage-of-occupy-wall-street-poop-pouring-incident-video/.

14. DSA Store, Abolish Ice T-Shirt #TS61371, https://store.dsausa.org/abolish-ice-t-shirt-ts61371.html.

15. Sean McElwee (@SeanMcElwee), "abolish ICE abolish ICE abolish ICE abolish ICE abolish ICE," Twitter, February 23, 2017, 7:14 a.m., https://twitter.com/SeanMcElwee/status/834783586574286852.

16. Sean McElwee (@SeanMcElwee), "First printing of Abolish ICE shirts raised more than $4,000 for frontline groups @MaketheRoadAct, @UNITEDWEDREAM and @DetentionWatch. Shirts available at http://abolishice.org. Send me pics of yours! I especially want to see the baby onesies :)," July 11, 2018, 8:18 a.m., https://twitter.com/seanmcelwee/status/1017065673384701952.

17. Sean McElwee, "It's Time To Abolish ICE," *The Nation*, March 9, 2018, https://www.thenation.com/article/its-time-to-abolish-ice/.

18. McElwee, "It's Time To Abolish ICE."

19. "The Indivisible Project (Indivisible)," Influence Watch, https://www.influencewatch.org/non-profit/the-indivisible-project-indivisible/.

20. Samantha Lachman, "Former Bernie Sanders Staffers Seek To Elect A 'Brand New Congress,'" HuffPost, April 29, 2016, https://www.huffpost.com/entry/bernie-sanders-congress_n_5720e608e4b0b49df6a9c933.

21. Steven Perlberg, "How 'Abolish ICE' Went From Twitter Slogan To Winning Over Progressives And Dividing Politics," BuzzFeed, July 28, 2018, https://www.buzzfeednews.com/article/stevenperlberg/abolish-ice-sean-mcelwee.

22. Ali Breland, "How Twitter Vaulted 'Abolish ICE' into the Mainstream," *The Hill*, July 29, 2018, https://thehill.com/policy/technology/399303-how-twitter-vaulted-abolish-ice-into-the-mainstream.

23. Breland, "How Twitter Vaulted 'Abolish ICE' into the Mainstream."

24. "Occupy ICE Portland: Lessons from the Barricades," CrimethInc., July 11, 2018, https://crimethinc.com/2018/07/11/occupy-ice-portland-lessons-from-the-barricades-another-perspective.

25. "Occupy ICE Portland: Lessons from the Barricades," CrimethInc.

26. Matt Taylor, "Occupy Is Back and It's Coming for ICE," VICE, June 26, 2018, https://www.vice.com/en_us/article/xwmjzz/occupy-is-back-and-its-coming-for-ice.

27. Alyssa Newcomb, "Sexual Assaults Reported in 'Occupy' Camps," ABC News, November 3, 2011, https://abcnews.go.com/us/sexual-assaults-occupy-wall-street-camps/story?id=14873014.

28. "Protesters Coming Down With the 'Zuccotti Lung,'" NBC New York, November 12, 2011, https://www.nbcnewyork.com/news/local/Zuccotti-Lung-Park-Sickness-Demonstrators-Protesters-Illness-133669113.html.

29. Antonio Antenucci, "Health Expert Condemns Park Rats," *New York Post*, October 22, 2011, https://nypost.com/2011/10/22/health-expert-condemns-park-rats/.

30. Lydia Gerike, "Occupy ICE PDX: A Timeline of the Portland Encampment," *The Oregonian*/OregonLive, July 25, 2018, https://expo.oregonlive.com/news/erry-2018/07/62ee150670182/occupy-ice-pdx-a-timeline-of-t.html.

31. Ellen Moynihan, "Occupy ICE Protesters Swarm Facility in SoHo," *New York Daily News*, June 22, 2018, https://www.nydailynews.com/new-york/ny-metro-occupy-ice-protest-20180622-story.html.

32. Jeff Offenhartz, "'Occupy ICE' Protesters Shut Down Manhattan Immigration Hearings," Gothamist, June 25, 2018, http://gothamist.com/2018/06/25/occupy_ice_protest_immigration_hearings.php.

33. "Occupy ICE Protesters Continue Weeklong Demonstration at Detroit Office," WXYZ Detroit, June 25, 2018, https://www.wxyz.com/news/occupy-ice-protesters-continue-weeklong-demonstration-at-detroit-office.

34. Occupy ICE Detroit Facebook page, https://www.facebook.com/OccupyICEdetroit/.

35. Occupy ICE Detroit Facebook post, July 26, 2018, https://www.facebook.com/OccupyICEdetroit/posts/402421740282691.

36. Abigail R. Esman, "Behind The Civil Rights Masks Of The Women's March Leaders," The Investigative Project on Terrorism, April 24, 2018, https://www.investigativeproject.org/7417/behind-the-civil-rights-masks-of-the-women-march.

37. Women's March (@womensmarch), "The call to #AbolishICE is a call to eliminate the agency that has been terrorizing immigrant communities for 15 years. Women from all backgrounds must take up @conmijente's call to #FreeOurFuture," Twitter, June 24, 2018, https://twitter.com/womensmarch/status/1011043143490433024.

38. "#AbolishICE Resources," Democratic Socialists of America, June 27, 2018, https://www.dsausa.org/organize/abolish_ice_end_muslimban_resources/.

39. Alex S. Vitale (@avitale), "We need to abolish the Border Patrol as much or more than ICE: nytimes.com/2018/10/12/us/…#NoBordersNoWalls," Twitter, October 15, 2018, 11:21 a.m., https://twitter.com/avitale/status/1051900932810821633.

40. Richard Parker, "Forget ICE, the real problem is CBP," *Los Angeles Times*, August 19, 2018, https://www.latimes.com/opinion/op-ed/la-oe-parker-cbp-20180819-story.html.

41. Chinga La Migra website, http://www.chingalamigratour.com/.

42. hacerle la lucha, "chingra la migra," Urban Dictionary, April 24, 2006, https://www.urbandictionary.com/define.php?term=chinga%20la%20migra.

43. Bryan Burrough, "The Untold Story Behind New York's Most Brutal Cop Killings," *Politico*, April 21, 2015, https://www.politico.com/magazine/story/2015/04/the-untold-story-behind-new-yorks-most-brutal-cop-killing-117207.

44. "'Pigs in a Blanket' Chant at Minnesota Fair Riles Police," CBS News, August 31, 2015, https://www.cbsnews.com/news/pigs-in-a-blanket-chant-at-minnesota-fair-riles-police/.

45. Michelle Malkin, "Amateur Hour in Seattle," Jewish World Review, December 6, 1999, http://www.jewishworldreview.com/michelle/malkin120699.asp.

46. "Ruckus Society," Discover the Networks, May 13, 2019, https://www.discoverthenetworks.org/organizations/ruckus-society/.

47. "1999 Seattle WTO Shutdown," Anarchy in Action, https://anarchyinaction.org/index. php?title=1999_Seattle_WTO_shutdown.
48. "1999 Seattle WTO Shutdown," Anarchy in Action.
49. Michelle Malkin, "Sponsors of Anarchy," Michellemalkin.com, January 18, 2017, http:// michellemalkin.com/2017/01/18/sponsors-of-anarchy/.
50. Michelle Malkin, "Sponsors of Anarchy."
51. Kim Murphy, "Occupy Protests Shut Down 2 Portland Terminals, Spread to Seattle," *Los Angeles Times*, December 12, 2011, https://latimesblogs.latimes.com/nationnow/2011/12/ portland-port-shutdown-occupy-seattle.html.
52. Michelle Malkin, "Port Strike Update: Talks Resume, Occupy Roots for Chaos," Michellemalkin.com, September 17, 2012, http://michellemalkin.com/2012/09/17/ port-strike-update-talks-resume-occupy-roots-for-chaos/.
53. "May Day Portland: Protesters Mix It Up with Police As They March in Downtown Streets," *The Oregonian*/OregonLive, May 1, 2012, https://www.oregonlive.com/ portland/2012/05/arrests.
54. Terrence Petty and Robert Jablon, "Oregon Is Epicenter As Trump Protests Surge across Nation," Associated Press, November 11, 2016, https://apnews.com/2a936aa6a71b4238b d9a463f142e027c.
55. Aimee Green, "Portland Protest Leader Micah Rhodes Avoids Prison for Sex Abuse," *The Oregonian*/Oregon Live, July 2, 2018, https://www.oregonlive.com/portland/2018/07/ portland_protest_leader_micah.html
56. Milenio Facebook page, https://www.facebook.com/milenio.org/.
57. Shut it Down, "Direction Action Alliance–Protest Info," Portland Independent Media Center, January 19, 2017, ww.portland.indymedia.org/en/2017/01/434120.shtml.
58. FOX 12 Staff, "May Day March Becomes Riot after Anarchists Clash with Police," May 1, 2017, https://www.kptv.com/news/may-day-march-becomes-riot-after-anarchists-clash- with-police/article_f0a28635-dd06-52c1-b4e9-c176ad951298.html.
59. Laurie Isola, Amelia Templeton, Kristian Foden-Vencil, and Rob Manning, "6 People Arrested During J20 Protests In Downtown Portland," OPB, January 20, 2017, https:// www.opb.org/news/article/portland-oregon-j20-protest-inauguration/.
60. Anonymous Contributor, "Reflection on the tactics of the Portland J20 black bloc," It's Going Down, January 21, 2017, https://itsgoingdown.org/ reflection-tactics-portland-j20-black-bloc/.
61. "Portland's Protest Problem," ACLU of Oregon, January 25, 2017, https://aclu-or.org/en/ news/portlands-protest-problem.
62. Chloe Eudaly, "Statement from Commissioner Chloe Eudaly on Immigration & Customs Enforcement Facility 4310 SW Macadam," Office of Commissioner Chloe Eudaly, July 23, 2018, https://www.portlandoregon.gov/eudaly/article/691975.
63. Jamie Hale, "Organizers Cancel 82nd Avenue of Roses Parade, after Protesters Threaten To Shut It Down," *The Oregonian*/OregonLive, April 25, 2017, https://www.oregonlive. com/rosefest/2017/04/organizers_cancel_82nd_avenue.html.
64. Hale, "Organizers Cancel 82nd Avenue of Roses Parade."
65. "Statement of Police Non-Collaboration," Portland Assembly, https://portlandassembly. com/about/statement-police-non-collaboration/.
66. "Literature," Portland Assembly, https://portlandassembly.com/resources/lit/.
67. "National Lawyers Guild (NLG)," Discover the Networks, May 13, 2019, https://www. discoverthenetworks.org/organizations/national-lawyers-guild-nlg/.
68. "Who We Are," National Immigration Project, https://nationalimmigrationproject.org/.
69. Occupy ICE website, https://occupyice.org/.
70. Eoin Lenihan, "It's Not Your Imagination: The Journalists Writing About Antifa Are Often Their Cheerleaders," Quillette, May 29, 2019, https://quillette.com/2019/05/29/ its-not-your-imagination-the-journalists-writing-about-antifa-are-often-their-cheerleaders/.

71. Katie Shepherd, "Anarchists Flooded the Offices of a Portland Lawyer Who Represents the Union for ICE Agents," *Willamette Week*, April 30, 2019, https://www.wweek.com/news/courts/2019/04/30/anarchists-flooded-the-offices-of-a-portland-lawyer-who-represents-the-union-for-ice-agents/.

72. E-mail from "some anarchists" to Katie Shepherd at *Willamette Week*, April 29, 2019, https://s3.amazonaws.com/arc-wordpress-client-uploads/wweek/wp-content/uploads/2019/04/30104714/Anarchists-Flood-the-Offices-of-ICE-Union-Attorney_Redacted2.pdf.

73. E-mail from "some anarchists" to Katie Shepherd at *Willamette Week*.

74. Andy Ngo, "Anarchy Breaks Out in Portland, With the Mayor's Blessing," *Wall Street Journal*, August 3, 2018, https://www.wsj.com/articles/anarchy-breaks-out-in-portland-with-the-mayors-blessing-1533331454.

75. Airliner World & More, "Occupy ICE Protesters Call DHS Officers the N-Word," YouTube, July 12, 2018, https://www.youtube.com/watch?time_continue=1&v=xpFONsJlHtg.

76. Gordon R. Friedman, "Feds: Portland ICE Protesters Spewed Racist Insults," *The Oregonian*/OregonLive, July 24, 2018, https://expo.oregonlive.com/news/erry-2018/07/3c121acf878231/feds-portland-ice-protesters-s.html#incart_target2box_default_#incart_target2box_targeted_.

77. Friedman, "Feds: Portland ICE Protesters Spewed Racist Insults."

78. Andy Ngo (@MrAndyNgo), "I've been doxxed by Antifa supporters on Twitter and am now getting threats via DM," Twitter, May 4, 2019, https://twitter.com/MrAndyNgo/status/1124631208476823552.

79. Brenna Kelly, "Two Victims Come Forward after May Day Brawl," Fox 12 Oregon, May 2, 2019, https://www.kptv.com/news/two-victims-come-forward-after-may-day-brawl/article_bed05136-6d5e-11e9-b37a-17ed4424a79f.html.

80. Andy Ngo (@MrAndyNgo), "Was just assaulted & had my phone stolen at @24hourfitness Hollywood Portland by someone I recognize at Antifa rallies. He first dumped liquid on me then stole my phone. Reporting to @PortlandPolice. I don't know his identity & gym wouldn't tell me. They got my phone back," Twitter, May 7, 2019, 3:50 p.m., https://twitter.com/MrAndyNgo/status/1125895659008155648.

81. Loren Balhorn, "The Lost History of Antifa," *Jacobin*, May 8, 2017, https://jacobinmag.com/2017/05/antifascist-movements-hitler-nazis-kpd-spd-germany-cold-war.

82. Kristine Marsh, "Actual CNN Headline: Antifa Seeks 'Peace Through Violence,'" NewsBusters, August 21, 2017, https://www.newsbusters.org/blogs/nb/kristine-marsh/2017/08/21/actual-cnn-headline-antifa-seeks-peace-through-violence.

83. Sebastian Kettley, "Hamburg G20 Protests: What Is Antifa? Who Are the 'Welcome to Hell' Protestors?" Express, July 9, 2017, https://www.express.co.uk/news/world/826336/Hamburg-g20-protests-what-is-Antifa-demonstrations-protestors-Welcome-to-Hell.

84. Darren Boyle and Dave Burke, "Black-Clad Anarchists Try To Blind G20 Riot Police and Helicopter Pilots with Lasers As Fires Are Lit across Hamburg and Nearly 200 Officers Are Injured," *Daily Mail*, July 7, 2017, https://www.dailymail.co.uk/news/article-4674100/G20-protestors-FIREBIOMB-police-station-Hamburg.html.

85. Rose City Antifa website, https://www.rosecityantifa.org.

86. Casey Michel, "How Liberal Portland Became America's Most Politically Violent City," *Politico Magazine*, June 30, 2017, https://www.politico.com/magazine/story/2017/06/30/how-liberal-portland-became-americas-most-politically-violent-city-215322.

87. Brian Ke, "Controversial Rally Leader Denies Being a White Supremacist Because He's Japanese American," NextShark, August 21, 2017, https://nextshark.com/joey-gibson-controversial-patriot-prayer-leader-identifies-as-japanese-american/.

88. Penny Starr, "Patriot Prayer Rally for 'Law and Order' Faces Antifa Violence," Breitbart, October 14, 2018, https://www.breitbart.com/politics/2018/10/14/patriot-prayer-rally-law-order-faces-antifa-violence/.

89. I am not linking the post that disclosed Adams's private home address, but it still exists on the internet.

90. Amanda Morris, "#HimToo: Left And Right Embrace Opposing Takes On Same Hashtag," NPR, October 11, 2018, https://www.npr.org/2018/10/11/656293787/-himtoo-left-and-right-embrace-opposing-takes-on-same-hashtag.

91. Mike Bivins (@itsmikebivins), "counterprotesters chant "a-c-a-b, all cops are bastards" as Portland police in riot gear follow. These are stragglers, theres a bigger group out front. im still following as are police," Twitter, November 17, 2018, 4:35 p.m., https://twitter.com/itsmikebivins/status/1063953840276303872.

92. Matthew Vadum, "Antifa Doxxes 1,600 ICE Agents," The American Spectator, January 22, 2018, https://spectator.org/antifa-doxxes-1600-ice-agents/.

93. Nebraska Antifa (@antifa_ne), "Some enterprising hero archived the ICE employees listed on linkedin," Twitter, June 19, 2018, 3:46 p.m., https://twitter.com/antifa_ne/status/1009205750617575424.

94. Nebraska Antifa (@antifa_ne), "Some enterprising hero archived the ICE employees listed on linkedin."

95. I contacted Dan O'Sullivan, chairperson of the NYU Tisch School of the Arts' ITP program, and asked: "Does the ITP program support doxxing of federal employees? Was this project conducted under the auspices of the ITP program? Did Lavigne make ITP/SIRS aware of his database and promotion of the list prior to posting on social media?" Sullivan did not reply to my written inquiry.

96. "Sam Lavigne," New York University, Tisch School of the Arts, https://tisch.nyu.edu/itp/itp-people/faculty/somethings-in-residence-sirs/sam-lavigne.

97. "Humans in Residence (HIRS)," New York University, Tisch School of the Arts, https://tisch.nyu.edu/itp/itp-people/faculty/somethings-in-residence-sirs.

98. I contacted Microsoft media relations to ask if the company supports doxxing federal employees. Microsoft Media Relations account executive Alexis Bridgewater sent the following reply: "Thank you for your patience as I looked into your request. I have connected with my most appropriate colleagues, and unfortunately, we are unable to accommodate your request at this time. I apologize for any inconvenience this may cause." New York University's ITP program did not respond to my inquiries.

99. Sam Lavigne tweet has been deleted; previously was available online at: https://twitter.com/sam_lavigne/status/1009050062264176641. Screenshot preserved here: Eric Lieberman, "Twitter, Medium, GitHub Suspend Accounts and Posts Sharing ICE Agents' Personal Information," Daily Caller, June 20, 2018, https://dailycaller.com/2018/06/20/twitter-medium-github-ice-suspend-doxxing/.

100. Sam Lavigne, "Downloading the Profiles of Everyone on LinkedIn Who Works for ICE," Medium, June 19, 2019, https://web.archive.org/web/20180619140914/https://medium.com/@samlavigne/downloading-the-profiles-of-everyone-on-linkedin-who-works-for-ice-c4e0ff6b065e.

101. Lavigne, "Downloading the Profiles of Everyone on LinkedIn Who Works for ICE."

102. Glenn Fleishman, "Twitter Suspends Accounts That Posted Trump Advisor Stephen Miller's Phone Number," Fortune/Yahoo, June 20, 2018, https://finance.yahoo.com/news/twitter-suspends-accounts-posted-trump-001016962.html.

103. Vadum, "Antifa Doxxes 1,600 ICE Agents."

104. Caroline O'Donovan, "Medium Just Took Down A Post It Says Doxed ICE Employees," BuzzFeed, June 19, 2018, https://www.buzzfeednews.com/article/carolineodonovan/heres-why-medium-and-github-just-took-down-a-post.

105. Sam Lavigne tweet has been deleted; previously was available online at: https://twitter.com/sam_lavigne/status/1008746480029634561.

106. Pierce Nichols (@nocleverhandle), "Nothing wrong with doxxing people who operate concentration camps," Twitter, June 21, 2018, 10:13 a.m., https://twitter.com/nocleverhandle/status/1009846759894409216.

107. New York City Antifa (@NYCAntifa), "Thought y'all might want to know that the Chief Technology Officer for ICE, @davidlarrimore, enjoys LARPing as Captain America while over 700 children have yet to be reunited with their parents & a judge ordered ICE to stop forcing psychotropic drugs on these kids. #AbolishICE," Twitter, August 1, 2018, 8:42 p.m., https://twitter.com/NYCAntifa/status/1024862903839600641.

108. AlwaysAngryInNJ Prosecute ICE (@JerseyRedRevolt), "Captain America would punch him right in his stupid face," Twitter, August 1, 2018, 9:38 p.m., https://twitter.com/JerseyRedRevolt/status/1024876956414824459.

109. Lil Guillotine (@litlGuillotine), "ugggghhhh Captain America is nationalist propaganda too. Fuck ICE!" Twitter, August 2, 2018, 6:01 p.m., https://twitter.com/litlGuillotine/status/1025184815149182977.

110. New York City Antifa (@NYCAntifa), "Throw ICE into a goddamn volcano," October 8, 2018, 10:12 p.m., https://twitter.com/NYCAntifa/status/1049527952503795712

111. New York City Antifa (@NYCAntifa), "Customs & Border Patrol are absolute scum & no one should extend them the benefit of the doubt. There is a video of them working w/ these militias. There is an *undercover* report by Mother Jones, that shows CPB passing info to these groups. #ChingaLaMigra," Twitter, April 20, 2018, 3:51 p.m., https://twitter.com/NYCAntifa/status/1119735287867957248.

112. Kyle Perisic, "Antifa Spreads List of ICE Agents Compiled Using LinkedIn and Blasts It over Twitter," Daily Caller, June 19, 2018, https://dailycaller.com/2018/06/19/antifa-spreads-ice-agents-identities/.

113. Wikileaks (@wikileaks), "ICEPatrol is an important public resource for understanding ICE programs and increasing accountability, especially in light of the actions taken by ICE lately, such as the separation of children and parents at the US border," June 21, 2018, 5:51 p.m., https://twitter.com/wikileaks/status/1009962132824305665.

114. Lia Eustachewich, "WikiLeaks Shares Personal Info of ICE Agents," *New York Post*, June 22, 2018, https://nypost.com/2018/06/22/wikileaks-shares-personal-info-of-ice-agents/.

115. "Twitter Allows Antifa To Dox ICE Agents and Their Families Despite Being Reported Numerous Times," Far Left Watch, October 17, 2018, https://farleftwatch.com/twitter-allows-antifa-to-dox-ice-agents-and-their-families-despite-being-reported-numerous-times/.

116. "Twitter Allows Antifa To Dox ICE Agents and Their Families Despite Being Reported Numerous Times," Far Left Watch.

117. Tweet has been deleted; previously was available online at: https://twitter.com/ArielleSchw/status/1008770866.

118. Doug Bock Clark, "Meet Antifa's Secret Weapon against Far-Right Extremists," *Wired*, January 16, 2018, https://www.wired.com/story/free-speech-issue-antifa-data-mining/.

119. Bock Clark, "Meet Antifa's Secret Weapon."

120. Joy Pullman, "Leftist Agitators Run DHS Secretary Out of Restaurant, Call for Children to Be Raped and Border Agents Murdered," The Federalist, June 20, 2018, https://thefederalist.com/2018/06/20/leftist-agitators-run-dhs-secretary-out-of-restaurant-call-for-children-to-be-raped-and-border-agents-murdered/

121. The tweet was deleted, but originally published here: https://twitter.com/OccupyWallStNYC/status/1008885853488340999?ref_src=twsrc%5Etfw.

122. Harriet Sinclair, "Shame: DHS Chief Nielsen Hounded from Mexican Restaurant over Border Policy," *Newsweek*, June 20, 2018, https://www.newsweek.com/video-dhs-chief-kirstjen-nielsen-driven-mexican-restaurant-protesters-chanting-985724.

123. Metro DC DSA (@mdc_dsa), "Members of Metro DC DSA Confronted DHS Secretary Kirstjen Nielsen at Dinner. Why Should She Get To Eat in Peace While Thousands of Migrant Children Sit in ages? See the video here: https://www.facebook.com/MetroDCDSA/posts/803611493171511 … #abolishice #abolishcbp #FamilySeparation #FamilesBelongTogether," Twitter, June 19, 2018, 5:25 p.m., https://twitter.com/mdc_dsa/status/1009230659729215489.

124. Nandini B. (@nandelabra), Twitter, June 19, 2018, https://twitter.com/nandelabra/status/1009233978761588742.

125. Sue Stroud (@suestroud), "this should happen to every republican, every member of the administration, public shaming wherever they go. Non-violent civil disobedience is a powerful tool," Twitter, June 19, 2018, 6:18 p.m., https://twitter.com/suestroud/status/1009243986265980928.

126. Steven Nelson, "Who Are the Protesters Who Crashed Kirstjen Nielsen's Dinner and What Are They Planning Next?" *Washington Examiner*, June 20, 2018, https://www.washingtonexaminer.com/news/dhs-secretary-kirstjen-nielsen-protesters-dinner.

127. Staff Report, "Deep State Unmasked: Leaks at HHS; DOJ Official Resists 'From Inside,' DOJ: 'These Allegations Are Deeply Concerning…Referred to Inspector General,'" Project Veritas, September 19, 2018, https://www.projectveritas.com/2018/09/19/breaking-deep-state-unmasked-doj-official-resists-from-inside-cant-get-fired-leaks-at-hhs/.

128. Staff Report, "Deep State Unmasked: Leaks at HHS; DOJ Official Resists 'From Inside,' DOJ."

129. Allison Hrabar, "Activist Fired for Protesting Trump," GoFundMe, September 25, 2018, https://www.gofundme.com/activist-fired-for-protesting-trump.

130. "Allison Hrabar," KeyWiki, last modified May 14, 2019, https://keywiki.org/Allison_Hrabar.

131. Brittany Shepherd, "'Let's Wake Her Up': How the Protest at Kirstjen Nielsen's House Came Together So Quickly," *Washingtonian*, June 25, 2018, https://www.washingtonian.com/2018/06/25/how-the-protests-at-kirstjen-nielsens-alexandria-home-came-to-be/.

132. Nebraska Antifa (@antifa_ne), "Take notice: this is how you write a headline," Twitter, June 20, 2018, 10:29 a.m., https://archive.fo/juowz. The phone number was in the original tweet, but has been scrubbed.

133. Nebraska Antifa (@antifa_ne), "Take notice: this is how you write a headline"

134. Jon Levine, "The Nation Contributor Thrown in Twitter Jail After Doxxing Stephen Miller: 'This is War,'" The Wrap, June 20, 2018, https://www.thewrap.com/the-nation-contributor-defends-doxxing-of-stephen-miller-this-is-war/.

135. Levine, "The Nation Contributor Thrown in Twitter Jail."

136. Greg Morabito, "Stephen Miller Threw $80 of Sushi in the Garbage After Getting Heckled," Eater, July 9, 2018, https://www.eater.com/2018/7/9/17548194/stephen-miller-trump-adviser-sushi-run.

137. Sarah Sanders (@PressSec), "Last night I was told by the owner of Red Hen in Lexington, VA to leave because I work for @POTUS and I politely left. Her actions say far more about her than about me. I always do my best to treat people, including those I disagree with, respectfully and will continue to do so," Twitter, June 23, 2018, 7:53 a.m., https://twitter.com/PressSec/status/1010536237457924096.

138. Smash Racism DC Facebook post, September 24, 2018, https://www.facebook.com/AntifaDC/videos/304033500184029/.

139. Nick Kangadis, "Pro-Antifa Group Doxxes Conservative Review's Gavin McInnes, Threatens 'Right-Wing Scum' on Twitter," MRCTV, September 25, 2018, https://www.mrctv.org/blog/pro-antifa-group-doxxes-conservative-reviews-gavin-mcinnes-twitter.

140. Rob Shimshock, "Twitter Suspends Libertarian Commentator Gavin McInnes and His Activist Group," Daily Caller, August 11, 2018, https://dailycaller.com/2018/08/11/twitter-suspends-gavin-mcinnes/.

141. Joe Concha, "Activists Converge on Home of Fox's Tucker Carlson: 'You Are Not Safe,'" *The Hill*, November 8, 2018, https://thehill.com/homenews/media/415662-activists-converges-on-home-of-foxs-tucker-carlson-you-are-not-safe.

142. Amber Athey, "The Mob That Doxxed Tucker Carlson Is Already Back on Twitter," Daily Caller, November 14, 2018, https://dailycaller.com/2018/11/14/smash-racism-dc-back-twitter-tucker-carlson/.

143. Debra Heine, "Twitter Suspends 'Smash Racism' Account after Tucker Protest, But What About 'Antifa Prof.' Mike Isaacson?" PJ Media, November 8, 2018, https://pjmedia.com/trending/twitter-suspends-smash-racism-account-after-tucker-protest-but-what-about-antifa-prof-mike-isaacson/.

144. Project Veritas (@Project_Veritas), "Throat punching is just a joke, huh? @lacymacauley seems to think so, but our footage seems to say differently. What do you think?" January 19, 2017, 2:23 p.m., https://twitter.com/Project_Veritas/status/822207912646938624.

145. Twitter, "The Twitter Rules," https://help.twitter.com/en/rules-and-policies/twitter-rules.

146. P. Gardner Goldsmith, "Twitter Bans Actor James Woods for Quoting Emerson," MCRTV, May 6, 2019, https://www.mrctv.org/index.php/blog/twitter-bans-actor-james-woods-quoting-emerson-seemingly-shows-vast-double-standard.

147. "Flags and Books," The Base, https://thebasebk.org/store/.

148. "Antifa Is Using Twitter and Facebook To Advocate for the Assassination of Trump," Far Left Watch, September 12, 2018, https://farleftwatch.com/antifa-groups-are-using-twitter-and-facebook-to-advocate-for-the-assassination-of-president-trump/.

149. "Antifa Is Using Twitter and Facebook To Advocate for the Assassination of Trump," Far Left Watch.

150. Ibid.

151. Ulrike Salazar, "Killers in Brown-Shirt Uniforms: How the U.S. Border Patrol Brutalizes the Masses," Incendiary News Service, September 20, 2018, https://archive.fo/TACgr#selection-429.20-441.366.

152. Salazar, "Killers in Brown-Shirt Uniforms."

153. Alan Feuer, "Antifa on Trial: How a College Professor Joined the Left's Radical Ranks," *Rolling Stone*, May 15, 2018, https://www.rollingstone.com/culture/culture-features/antifa-on-trial-how-a-college-professor-joined-the-lefts-radical-ranks-630213/.

154. Feuer, "Antifa on Trial."

155. John Sexton, "Antifa Goon Who Hit People with a Bike Lock Gets 3 Years Probation (Update)," Hot Air, August 8, 2018, https://hotair.com/archives/2018/08/08/bike-lock-toting-antifa-goon-gets-3-years-probation-felony-charges-dropped/.

156. "Election Boycott Speech on the Occasion of the 69th Anniversary of the Chinese Revolution," Red Guards Austin, October 10, 2018, https://archive.fo/5ryPk.

157. Red Guards Austin website, https://redguardsaustin.wordpress.com/.

158. "Antifa Puts Severed Pig Heads at Campaign Offices, Calls for 'People's War,'" Far Left Watch, October 12, 2018, https://farleftwatch.com/antifa-puts-severed-pig-heads-at-campaign-offices-calls-for-peoples-war/.

159. "Everywhere a Battlefield," Red Guards Austin, August 27, 2017, https://redguardsaustin.wordpress.com/2017/08/27/everywhere-a-battlefield/.

160. Patricia Okoumou, "Orders," https://patriciaokoumou.com/orders.

161. Priscilla DeGregory, "Statue of Liberty Climber Spews Anti-American Chant outside Court," *New York Post*, August 3, 2018, https://nypost.com/2018/08/03/statue-of-liberty-climber-spews-anti-american-chant-outside-court/.

162. Avery White, "Statue Of Liberty Climber Patricia Okoumou: 'Walls Will Not Stop Me,'" Gothamist, March 18, 2019, http://gothamist.com/2019/03/18/patricia_okoumou_statue_of_liberty_climber.php.

163. Stefan Becket, "Michael Avenatti Arrested on Federal Charges of Wire Fraud and Extortion," CBS News, March 26, 2019, https://www.cbsnews.com/news/

michael-avenatti-charged-arrested-federal-wire-bank-fraud-charges-live-updates-today-2019-03-25/.

164. Rachel Maddow, "How Patricia Okoumou Decided To Climb the Statue of Liberty," MSNBC, July 6, 2018, http://www.msnbc.com/rachel-maddow/watch/patricia-okoumou-explains-immigrant-rights-for-donald-trump-1271931971777.

165. "Why We Have Taken Up the Fight to Build Refuse Fascism and to Drive Out the Trump/Pence Fascist Regime," Refuse Fascism, July 24, 2017, https://refusefascism.org/2017/07/24/why-we-have-taken-up-the-fight-to-build-refuse-fascism-and-to-drive-out-the-trumppence-fascist-regime/.

166. manhattannews, "Refuse Fascism Opens the Door to Closing the Book on Trump/Pence," The Villager, November 8, 2017, https://www.thevillager.com/2017/11/refuse-fascism-opens-the-door-to-closing-the-book-on-trumppence/.

167. Metropolitan Anarchist Coordinating Council (MACC) website, https://macc.nyc/.

168. Laura Figueroa, "De Blasio to Demonstrators: Keep Protesting Trump's Travel Ban," *Newsday*, February 12, 2017, https://www.newsday.com/news/new-york/de-blasio-to-demonstrators-keep-protesting-trump-s-travel-ban-1.13111434.

169. Metropolitan Anarchist Coordinating Council, "#AbolishICE Protests Target National Homeland Security Conference & Mayor DeBlasio to Demand ICE Out of NYC," https://macc.nyc/blog/.

170. Julia Marsh, "De Blasio Rolls Out Health Care Plan for Illegal Immigrants," *New York Post*, May 7, 2019.

171. Andrea Gonzalez-Ramirez, "Here's How The #AbolishICE Movement *Really* Got Started," Refinery29, July 30, 2018, https://www.refinery29.com/en-us/2018/07/205854/abolish-ice-origins-twitter-undocumented-immigrants.

172. "Words We're Watching: Intersectionality," Merriam-Webster.com, https://www.merriam-webster.com/words-at-play/intersectionality-meaning.

173. "Who We Are," Black Alliance for Just Immigration, http://blackalliance.org/who-we-are/.

174. UndocuBlack Network website, http://undocublack.org/.

175. "Proposed Public Charge Rule Is a Black Issue and We Must Fight Back," UndocuBlack Network, http://undocublack.org/publiccharge.

176. "Our Herstory," Assata's Daughters, http://www.assatasdaughters.org/our-herstory-2019.

177. "BREAKING: Chicagoans Halt Loop Traffic with 'Defund Police, Dismantle ICE' Blockade," #Not1More, February 16, 2016, http://www.notonemoredeportation.com/tag/assatas-daughters/.

178. "BREAKING: Chicagoans Halt Loop Traffic with 'Defund Police, Dismantle ICE' Blockade," #Not1More.

179. "The Impact of Illegal Immigration on the Wages and Employment Opportunities of Black Workers," Briefing before the United States Commission on Civil Rights, https://www.usccr.gov/pubs/docs/IllegImmig_10-14-10_430pm.pdf.

180. John Binder, "Evaluating the Damage: Immigration's Impact on Black Americans," Breitbart, January 15, 2018, https://www.breitbart.com/politics/2018/01/15/evaluating-the-damage-immigrations-impact-black-americans/.

181. "Support Jamiel's Law," http://jamielshaw.com/.

182. "Officer Rodney Joseph Johnson," Officer Down Memorial Page, https://www.odmp.org/officer/18510-officer-rodney-joseph-johnson.

183. "Victim: Iofemi Hightower," Foreign National Crime Information Center–Victims of Illegal Alien Crime Memorial, http://www.fncic-voiacm.org/victims.php?id=375.

184. Emily Stephenson, "Trump, Pushing Immigration Plan, Meets with Family of Woman Killed in 2007," Reuters, September 2, 2016, https://www.reuters.com/article/us-usa-election-trump-immigration-idUSKCN1182OF.

185. "I am upset at the notion that ICE thinks a courtroom is a place to go and pick up people," the judge said on Wednesday. She later added, "I see no reason for places of redress and justice to become places that people are afraid to show up."

186. "The ICE Courthouse Arrest Controversy Continues to Swirl," Center for Immigration Studies, https://cis.org/Cadman/ICE-Courthouse-Arrest-Controversy-Continues-Swirl

187. "The Rachael Rollins Policy Memo," Suffolk County District Attorney, March 2019, http://www.suffolkdistrictattorney.com/wp-content/uploads/2019/03/The-Rachael-Rollins-Policy-Memo.pdf.

188. "The Rachael Rollins Policy Memo," Suffolk County District Attorney.

189. Howie Carr, "Suffolk DA Rachael Rollins Wrong on Blocking ICE from Courthouses," *Boston Herald*, March 28, 2019, https://www.bostonherald.com/2019/03/28/rollins-wrong-on-blocking-ice-from-courthouses/.

190. Ryan Kath and Beth Germano, "Why Wasn't South Boston Murder Suspect Deported?" CBS Boston, May 10, 2017, https://boston.cbslocal.com/2017/05/10/south-boston-murder-suspect-loophole-deported/.

191. Crimesider Staff, "Disturbing Details Emerge in Court about Last Moments of Slain Boston Doctors," CBS News, July 10, 2017, https://www.cbsnews.com/news/disturbing-details-emerge-in-court-about-last-moments-of-slain-boston-doctors/.

192. Michelle Malkin, "False Accuser Shaun Lying King's Record of Harm," Michellemalkin.com, April 10, 2019, http://michellemalkin.com/2019/04/10/false-accuser-shaun-lying-kings-record-of-harm/.

193. Matt Watkins, "Misdemeanors Matter #3: Rachael Rollins Reboots Low-Level Justice," Center for Court Innovation, https://www.courtinnovation.org/publications/rachael-rollins.

194. Dialynn Dwyer, "Here's What Marian Ryan and Rachael Rollins Said about Their Lawsuit against ICE," Boston.com, April 29, 2019, https://www.boston.com/news/local-news/2019/04/29/marian-ryan-rachael-rollins-ice-lawsuit.

195. "Tipping the Scales of Justice," Center for Immigration Studies," https://cis.org/Cadman/Tipping-Scales-Justice?&utm_source=twitter&utm_medium=social-media&utm_campaign=addtoany.

196. Arianna MacNeill, "A Mass. Judge and Court Officer Allegedly Helped a Defendant Evade ICE. Now Both Are Facing Federal Charges," Boston.com, April 25, 2019, https://www.boston.com/news/local-news/2019/04/25/judge-shelley-richmond-joseph-wesley-macgregor-charged.

197. Felicia Gans, "City Measure Makes Newton a Sanctuary for Immigrants," *Boston Globe*, February 21, 2017, https://www.bostonglobe.com/metro/2017/02/21/newton-city-council-vote-welcoming-city-proposal/7KaZNRvu7LCEhNSKpGfsNJ/story.html.

198. Jacqueline Tempera, "Federal Judge Allows ACLU's Class Action Suit on Behalf of Undocumented Spouses To Extend to All of New England," MassLive, May 16, 2019; updated May 17, 2019, https://www.masslive.com/boston/2019/05/federal-judge-allows-aclus-class-action-suit-on-behalf-of-undocumented-spouses-arrested-during-citizenship-interviews-to-extend-to-all-of-new-england.html.

199. "Sanctuary Jurisdictions Nearly Double Since President Trump Promised to Enforce Our Immigration Laws," FAIR, May 2018, https://www.fairus.org/issue/publications-resources/state-sanctuary-policies.

200. "Sanctuary Jurisdictions Nearly Double Since President Trump Promised to Enforce Our Immigration Laws," FAIR, 2.

201. Associated Press, "Milwaukee County Jail To Stop Cooperating with ICE Agents," March 9, 2019, https://apnews.com/c477ccf3166d44d2b11baf07043e1955.

202. 8 USC 1226: Apprehension and detention of aliens, http://uscode.house.gov/view.xhtml?req=granuleid:USC-prelim-title8-section1226&num=0&edition=prelim.

203. "Sanctuary Cities," Center for Immigration Studies, November 7, 2018, https://cis.org/Fact-Sheet/Sanctuary-Cities.

204. "Sanctuary Cities," Center for Immigration Studies.

205. Jessica M. Vaughan and Bryan Griffith, "Immigration Brief: Sanctuary Cities," Center for Immigration Studies, November 5, 2017, https://cis.org/Vaughan/Immigration-Brief-Sanctuary-Cities.

206. IRLI Staff, "California Leads the Way—In Shielding Terror State Illegal Aliens from Justice," Immigration Reform Law Institute, May 9, 2019, https://www.irli.org/single-post/2019/05/09/California-Leads-the-Way%E2%80%94In-Shielding-Terror-State-Illegal-Aliens-from-Justice.

207. *Nielsen v. Preap*, No. 16-1363, U.S. March 19, 2019, https://casetext.com/case/nielsen-v-preap-2.

208. "The Rise of Sanctuary," Immigrant Legal Resource Center, January 25, 2018, https://www.ilrc.org/rise-sanctuary.

209. Kristin Lam, "US Appeals Court Rejects Trump Administration Lawsuit, Upholds Most of California's Sanctuary Laws," *USA Today*, April 18, 2019, https://www.usatoday.com/story/news/nation/2019/04/18/california-sanctuary-law-appeals-court-upholds-immigration-laws/3514813002/.

210. Lam, "US Appeals Court Rejects Trump Administration Lawsuit."

211. Corinne Ramey, "Federal Judge in New York Bans U.S. from Punishing States Over Immigration," *Wall Street Journal*, November 30, 2018, https://www.wsj.com/articles/federal-judge-in-new-york-bans-u-s-from-punishing-states-over-immigration-1543614558.

212. Ross Todd, "Meet the Federal Judge Who Blocked Trump's Policy to Force Asylum-Seekers to Wait in Mexico," law.com, April 8, 2019, https://www.law.com/therecorder/2019/04/08/meet-the-federal-judge-who-blocked-trumps-policy-to-force-asylum-seekers-to-wait-in-mexico/?slret urn=20190410151604.

213. 8 U.S. Code § 1158.Asylum, https://www.law.cornell.edu/uscode/text/8/1158.

214. Associated Press, "Trump Can Make Asylum Seekers Wait in Mexico, Appeals Court Rule," *Los Angeles Times*, May 7, 2019, https://www.latimes.com/local/lanow/la-me-ln-stay-in-mexico-ruling-aslym-20190507-story.html.

215. Richard Wolf, "Trump Can Make Asylum Seekers Wait in Mexico, Appeals Court Rule," *USA Today*, March 6, 2019, https://www.usatoday.com/story/news/politics/2019/03/06/2020-census-citizenship-question-struck-down-second-federal-judge-trump/3082281002/.

216. Jason Richwine, "A History of the Census Bureau's Birthplace and Citizenship Questions in One Table," Center for Immigration Studies, June 8, 2018, https://cis.org/Richwine/History-Census-Bureaus-Birthplace-and-Citizenship-Questions-One-Table.

217. Fred Lucas, "Federal District Judges Have Blocked Trump Actions 30 Times, a Record Rate," *Daily Signal*, February 4, 2019, https://www.dailysignal.com/2019/02/04/federal-district-judges-have-blocked-trump-actions-30-times-a-record-rate/.

218. Lucas, "Federal District Judges Have Blocked Trump Actions 30 Times."

219. Richard Wolf, "Second Federal Judge Thwarts Trump Administration Plan To Ask about Citizenship in 2020 Census," *USA Today*, March 6, 2019, https://www.usatoday.com/story/news/politics/2019/03/06/2020-census-citizenship-question-struck-down-second-federal-judge-trump/3082281002/.

220. H.R. 77: Injunctive Authority Clarification Act of 2019, https://www.govtrack.us/congress/bills/116/hr77.

221. U.S. Court of Appeals for the Ninth Circuit, James Steinle, individually and as heir to Kathryn Steinle, deceased; Elizabeth Sullivan, individually and as heir to Kathryn Steinle, deceased, Plaintiffs-Appellants, v. City and County of San Francisco, a government entity,

et al., No. 17-16283 D.C. No. 3:16-cv-02859- JCS, http://cdn.ca9.uscourts.gov/datastore/opinions/2019/03/25/17-16283.pdf.

222. Daniel DeMay, "Inslee Order Makes Washington a 'Sanctuary State,'" Seattle PI, February 23, 2017, https://www.seattlepi.com/seattlenews/article/Inslee-exec-order-makes-Washington-sanctuary-state-10954517.php.

223. Rep. Pramila Jayapal (@RepJayapal), "I'm proud of my passion, Mr. Whitaker. We all should show real passion and a real commitment to fixing what was done to these families and these children. This is lasting trauma for thousands of children—we must make reparations," Twitter, February 8, 2019, 5:58 p.m., https://twitter.com/RepJayapal/status/1094052768837443584.

224. Samantha Michaels, "Seattle's Mayor Had the Perfect Response to Trump's Threat to Send Immigrants to Sanctuary Cities," Mother Jones, April 13, 2019, https://www.motherjones.com/politics/2019/04/seattles-mayor-had-the-perfect-response-to-trumps-threat-to-send-immigrants-to-sanctuary-cities/.

225. Chantal Da Silva, "Washington Airport Operators Applauded for Refusing To Serve ICE Deportation Flights," Newsweek, May 3, 2019, https://www.newsweek.com/washington-airport-operators-applauded-refusing-serve-ice-deportation-flights-1413867.

226. Da Silva, "Washington Airport Operators Applauded for Refusing To Serve ICE Deportation Flights."

227. University of Washington Center for Human Rights, "Media Advisory: 'ICE Air' Report Release Event at UW Seattle, April 24," April 16, 2019, https://jsis.washington.edu/humanrights/2019/04/16/media-advisory-ice-air-report-and-event-at-uw-seattle-april-24/.

228. Michelle Malkin, "Bloody Consequences of Open Borders: The Kidnapping and Murder of Zina Linnik," michellemalkin.com, July 13, 2007, http://michellemalkin.com/2007/07/13/bloody-consequences-of-open-borders-the-kidnapping-and-murder-of-zina-linnik/.

229. Malkin, "Bloody Consequences of Open Borders."

230. Allahpundit, "Video: Geraldo Spins Zina Linnik Suspect's Immigration Status," Hot Air, July 14, 2007, https://hotair.com/archives/2007/07/14/video-geraldo-spins-zina-linnik-suspects-immigration-status/.

231. Michelle Malkin, "Geraldo Rivera's Breathless Tease," Michellemalkin.com, July 16, 2007, http://michellemalkin.com/2007/07/16/geraldo-riveras-breathless-tease.

232. Michelle Malkin, "Geraldo Rivera Unhinged," Michellemalkin.com, September 1, 2007, http://michellemalkin.com/2007/09/01/geraldo-rivera-unhinged/.

233. Malkin, "Geraldo Rivera Unhinged."

234. Malkin, "Geraldo Rivera's Breathless Tease."

235. Malkinisanidiot, "Geraldo Apologizes to Michelle Malkin on The Factor," YouTube, September 14, 2007, https://www.youtube.com/watch?v=-Dmyk7Uv1fE

236. Malkinisanidiot, "Geraldo Apologizes to Michelle Malkin on The Factor."

237. Johnnydollar, "Geraldo Rivera: 'I Cringe Every Time I See Her Here!'" YouTube, August 17, 2007, https://www.youtube.com/watch?v=jdJUaIKhUic.

238. James Carafano, "Section 287(g) Is the Right Answer for State and Local Immigration Enforcement," Heritage Foundation, March 2, 2006, https://www.heritage.org/homeland-security/report/section-287g-the-right-answer-state-and-local-immigration-enforcement.

Chapter 6

1. Susan Buchanan and Tom Kim, "The Nativists," Intelligence Report, November 2, 2006, https://www.splcenter.org/fighting-hate/intelligence-report/2006/nativists-0.

2. Alex Koppelman, "Michelle Malkin's White Supremacist Ties," HuffPost, May 12, 2006, https://www.huffingtonpost.com/alex-koppelman/michelle-malkins-white-su_b_20873.html.

3. Bob Moser, "The Reckoning of Morris Dees and the Southern Poverty Law Center," *New Yorker*, March 21, 2019, https://www.newyorker.com/news/news-desk/the-reckoning-of-morris-dees-and-the-southern-poverty-law-center.

4. Carol M. Swain, "Mission Creep and the Southern Poverty Law Center's Misguided Focus," *HuffPost*, May 25, 2011, https://www.huffingtonpost.com/carol-m-swain/mission-creep-and-the-sou_b_255029.html.

5. Janell Ross, "Vanderbilt Professor Slammed for Backing Film That Calls Racism a Myth," *The Tennessean*, October 17, 2009.

6. Sonia Scherr, "A Slick DVD Defends Racism," Southern Poverty Law Center Hatewatch, October 8, 2009, https://www.splcenter.org/hatewatch/2009/10/08/slick-dvd-defends-racism.

7. Carol M. Swain, "What It's Like to Be Smeared by the Southern Poverty Law Center," *Wall Street Journal*, September 11, 2017, https://www.wsj.com/articles/what-its-like-to-be-smeared-by-the-southern-poverty-law-center-1505171221.

8. Southern Poverty Law Center Statement on Dr. Ben Carson, February 11, 2015, https://www.splcenter.org/sites/default/files/d6_legacy_files/downloads/publication/splc_statement_carson_feb2015.pdf.

9. "Southern Poverty Law Center's $3.4 Million Settlement Validates What Conservatives Have Been Saying All Along," Family Research Center, October 18, 2018, https://www.frc.org/newsroom/southern-poverty-law-centers-34-million-settlement-validates-what-conservatives-have-been-saying-all-along.

10. "Family Research Council," Southern Poverty Law Center, https://www.splcenter.org/fighting-hate/extremist-files/group/family-research-council.

11. Tyler O'Neil, "GuideStar Marks Family Research Council as a 'Hate Group,'" PJ Media, June 10, 2017, https://pjmedia.com/faith/2017/06/10/guidestar-marks-family-research-council-as-a-hate-group/.

12. "10 Facts about the Family Research Council," Human Rights Campaign, https://www.hrc.org/resources/10-facts-about-the-family-research-council.

13. Harriet Sinclair, "Donald Trump To Speak at Hate Group's Annual Event, a First for a President," *Newsweek*, October 12, 2017, https://www.newsweek.com/donald-trump-speak-anti-lgbt-hate-groups-annual-event-first-president-683927.

14. "Field Guide to Anti-Muslim Extremists," Southern Poverty Law Center, October 2016, http://www.tmoamerica.org/images/article_data/splc_field_guide_to_antimuslim_extremists_0.pdf.

15. See Asra Q. Nomani, "Billionaire George Soros Has Ties to More Than 50 'Partners' of the Women's March on Washington," Women in the World, January 20, 2017, https://womenintheworld.com/2017/01/20/billionaire-george-soros-has-ties-to-more-than-50-partners-of-the-womens-march-on-washington/; Eric Lichtblau, "George Soros Pledges $10 Million to Fight Hate Crimes," *New York Times*, November 22, 2016, https://www.nytimes.com/2016/11/22/us/politics/george-soros-hate-crimes.html.

16. Richard Cohen, "SPLC Statement Regarding Maajid Nawaz and the Quilliam Foundation," Southern Poverty Law Center, June 18, 2018, https://www.splcenter.org/news/2018/06/18/splc-statement-regarding-maajid-nawaz-and-quilliam-foundation.

17. "Field Guide to Anti-Muslim Extremists," Southern Poverty Law Center.

18. "Settlement Agreement and Release," Quilliam, https://www.quilliaminternational.com/wp-content/uploads/2018/06/20180617-splc-final-executed-settlement-agreement.pdf.

19. Mark Potok and Janet Smith, "Women Against Islam," Intelligence Report, June 10, 2015, https://www.splcenter.org/fighting-hate/intelligence-report/2015/women-against-islam.

20. "Ruth Institute," Southern Poverty Law Center, https://www.splcenter.org/fighting-hate/extremist-files/group/ruth-institute.

21. "The Ruth Institute's Statement on Being Included on the SPLC 'Hate Map'" Ruth Institute, August 23, 2017, http://www.ruthinstitute.org/press/the-ruth-institute-s-statement-on-being-included-on-the-splc-hate-map.

22. Valerie Richardson, "Southern Poverty Law 'Hate Map' Label Proves Costly to Pro-Family Ruth Institute," *Washington Times*, September 5, 2017, https://www.washingtontimes.com/news/2017/sep/5/southern-poverty-law-hate-map-listing-costly-ruth-/.

23. Richardson, "Southern Poverty Law 'Hate Map' Label Proves Costly."

24. "Public Schools in the Crosshairs: Far-Right Propaganda and the Common Core State Standards," Southern Poverty Law Center, May 1, 2014, https://www.splcenter.org/20140430/public-schools-crosshairs-far-right-propaganda-and-common-core-state-standards.

25. "Gary 'Gerhard' Lauck," Southern Poverty Law Center, https://www.splcenter.org/fighting-hate/extremist-files/individual/gary-gerhard-lauck.

26. "Virginia Abernethy," Southern Poverty Law Center, https://www.splcenter.org/fighting-hate/extremist-files/individual/virginia-abernethy.

27. Peter B. Gemma, "Interview: Expert on Political Extremism Discusses the $PLC," Politics & Policy, December 31, 2011, http://www.peterbgemma.com/2011/12/expert-on-political-extremism-talks-discusses-the-plc/.

28. Gemma, "Interview: Expert on Political Extremism Discusses the $PLC."

29. J. M. Berger, "The Hate List," Foreign Policy, March 12, 2013, https://foreignpolicy.com/2013/03/12/the-hate-list/.

30. "Stefan Molyneaux," Southern Poverty Law Center, https://www.splcenter.org/fighting-hate/extremist-files/individual/stefan-molyneux.

31. "Hate Map," Southern Poverty Law Center, https://www.splcenter.org/hate-map.

32. "The Remembrance Project," Southern Poverty Law Center, https://www.splcenter.org/fighting-hate/extremist-files/group/remembrance-project.

33. "Our History," Southern Poverty Law Center, https://www.splcenter.org/about-us/our-history.

34. Biography, "Morris Dees," https://web.archive.org/web/20181118053936/https://www.biography.com/people/morris-dees-21415735.

35. Jonathan Kirsch, "Book Review: A Lawyer's Attack on Underbelly of Racism: A Season for Justice: The Life and Times of Civil Rights Lawyer Morris Dees by Morris Dees with Steven Fiffer," *Los Angeles Times*, May 22, 1991, http://articles.latimes.com/1991-05-22/news/vw-1979_1_morris-dees.

36. Joe Schoffstall, "Southern Poverty Law Center Has More Than $90 Million In Offshore Funds," *Washington Free Beacon*, June 20, 2018, https://freebeacon.com/politics/southern-poverty-law-center-90-million-offshore-funds/.

37. Matt Pearce, "Southern Poverty Law Center Fires Co-Founder Morris Dees amid Employee Uproar," *Los Angeles Times*, March 14, 2019, https://www.latimes.com/nation/la-na-splc-morris-dees-20190314-story.html.

38. Matt Pearce, "Southern Poverty Law Center Chief Richard Cohen Announces Resignation amid Internal Upheaval," *Los Angeles Times*, March 22, 2019, https://www.latimes.com/nation/la-na-splc-richard-cohen-resigns-20190322-story.html.

39. Wecanstopthehate, "Code Words of Hate," YouTube, January 29, 2008, https://www.youtube.com/watch?v=iGgKBY61X0Y.

40. Wecanstopthehate, "Code Words of Hate."

41. Falko Ernst, "'The Training Stays with You': The Elite Mexican Soldiers Recruited by Cartels," *The Guardian*, February 10, 2018, https://www.theguardian.com/world/2018/feb/10/mexico-drug-cartels-soldiers-military.

42. Wecanstopthehate, "Code Words of Hate."

43. M.E.Ch.A. de WSU, "El Plan Espiritual de Aztlan," http://studentinvolvement.orgsync.com/org/mechadewsu/el_plan_espiritual_de_aztlan.

44. Michelle Malkin, "Bustamante, MEChA and the media," *Townhall*, August 20, 2003.

45. Jeff Ristine, "Rep. Hunter demands apology; student editorial said border agents should die," *San Diego Union-Tribune*, July 6, 1995, https://www.thefire.org/double-standards-at-ucsd/.

46. "MEChA." *Conspiracies and Secret Societies, Second Edition*, 2013, https://encyclopedia2.thefreedictionary.com/MEChA.

47. M.E.Ch.A. de WSU, "El Plan Espiritual de Aztlan."

48. Ibid.

49. "A Call to End Hate Speech," The Caucus, *New York Times*, February 1, 2008, https://thecaucus.blogs.nytimes.com/2008/02/01/a-call-to-end-hate-speech/?mtrref=undefined&gwh=8BB087157439343049E50F692077E6B9&gwt=pay.

50. "A Call to End Hate Speech," The Caucus.

51. "We Can Stop the Hate," NCLR, http://c0458192.cdn.cloudfiles.rackspacecloud.com/toolkit-wecanstopthehate.pdf.

52. "A Call to End Hate Speech," The Caucus.

53. Heidi Beirich and Mark Potok, "Countering Anti-Immigration Extremism: The Southern Poverty Law Center's Strategies," *The City University of New York Law Review* (Summer 2009), https://academicworks.cuny.edu/cgi/viewcontent.cgi?referer=https://www.google.com/&httpsredir=1&article=1239&context=clr.

54. The Editorial Board, "The Nativist Lobby," *New York Times*, February 4, 2009, http://theboard.blogs.nytimes.com/2009/02/04/the-nativist-lobby.

55. "About FAIR," FAIR, http://fairus.org/about-fair.

56. "About FAIR," FAIR.

57. "Why Amnesty Isn't the Solution," FAIR, August 2007, https://www.fairus.org/issue/amnesty/why-amnesty-isnt-solution.

58. "Nation's Most Prominent Anti-Immigration Group Has History of Hate," Southern Poverty Law Center, https://www.splcenter.org/news/2015/07/27/nations-most-prominent-anti-immigration-group-has-history-hate.

59. Jerry Kammer, "Immigration and the SPLC," Center for Immigration Studies, March 11, 2010, https://cis.org/Immigration-and-SPLC.

60. "America's Story," Carnegie Corporation, https://www.carnegie.org/interactives/immigration-reform/#!/#new-pull-quote.

61. "Tell Congress, 'Don't Meet with FAIR!'" America's Voice, https://web.archive.org/web/20140521170630/http://act.americasvoiceonline.org/page/content/fightfair/.

62. Adolfo Flores, "Southern Poverty Law Center Adds FAIR to 'Hate Group' List," Blogdolfo, December 18, 2007, http://www.csun.edu/elnuevosol/Blogdolfo/Story5_FAIR.html.

63. "The Nativist Lobby: Three Faces of Intolerance," Southern Poverty Law Center, February 20, 2009, https://web.archive.org/web/20100202152449/http://www.splcenter.org/pdf/static/splc_nativistlobby_022009.pdf.

64. Beirich and Potok, "Countering Anti-Immigration Extremism: The Southern Poverty Law Center's Strategies," 415.

65. Ibid., 416.

66. Bonnie Bucqueroux, "Mark Potok Speech 1," September 11, 2007, http://www.youtube.com/watch?v=fnTz2ylJo_8&feature=relmfu.

67. *The Michigan Advocate*, Volume 8, Issue 2, Fall 2007, Michigan Crime Victim Services Commission, https://www.michigan.gov/documents/mdch/Fall2007_389323_7.pdf, 11.

68. Ken Silverstein, "'Hate,' Immigration, and the Southern Poverty Law Center," *Browsings: The Harper's Blog*, March 22, 2010, https://harpers.org/blog/2010/03/hate-immigration-and-the-southern-poverty-law-center/.

69. Alexander Cockburn, "King of the Hate Business," *The Nation*, April 29, 2009, https://www.thenation.com/article/king-hate-business/.

70. JoAnn Wypijewski, "Letters," *The Nation,* February 8, 2001, https://www.thenation.com/article/you-cant-get-there-here/.

71. Bucqueroux, "Mark Potok Speech 1."

72. Beirich and Potok, "Countering Anti-Immigration Extremism: The Southern Poverty Law Center's Strategies," 416.

73. "Anti-Immigrant," Southern Poverty Law Center, https://www.splcenter.org/fighting-hate/extremist-files/ideology/anti-immigrant.

74. "Mark Potok," Recorded by Bill Holiday, https://archive.org/details/MarkPotok/WeAreTryingToDestroyThem-8.aif.

75. John Tanton, "The Camp of the Saints Revisited," The Social Contract Press, (Winter 1994–95), https://www.thesocialcontract.com/artman2/publish/tsc0502/article_410.shtml.

76. "Racist Book, *Camp of the Saints,* Gains in Popularity," Southern Poverty Law Center, March 21, 2001, https://www.splcenter.org/fighting-hate/intelligence-report/2001/racist-book-camp-saints-gains-popularity.

77. Matthew Connelly and Paul Kennedy, "Must It Be the Rest Against the West?" *The Atlantic,* December 1994, https://www.theatlantic.com/past/docs/politics/immigrat/kennf.html.

78. Tanton, "The Camp of the Saints Revisited."

79. Connelly and Kennedy, "Must It Be the Rest Against the West?"

80. Ibid.

81. K. C. McAlpin, "'The Camp of the Saints' Revisited" *The Social Contract,* Summer 2017, https://www.thesocialcontract.com/pdf/twentyseven-four/tsc_27_4_mcalpin.pdf.

82. Jerry Kammer, "Immigration and the SPLC," Center for Immigration Studies, March 11, 2010, https://cis.org/Immigration-and-SPLC, 2.

83. "John Tanton Is the Mastermind behind the Organized Anti-Immigration Movement," *Intelligence Report,* Southern Poverty Law Center, June 18, 2002, https://www.splcenter.org/fighting-hate/intelligence-report/2002/john-tanton-mastermind-behind-organized-anti-immigration-movement.

84. John Tanton, "The Puppeteer Replies—John Tanton Replies to The Puppeteer SPLC Racist Nativist Hate Attacks," https://www.johntanton.org/answering_my_critics/puppeteer.html#pioneer.

85. John Fonte, "Smearing the Center for Immigration Studies," *National Review,* February 20, 2013, https://www.nationalreview.com/corner/smearing-center-immigration-studies-john-fonte/.

86. "Pioneer Fund," Southern Poverty Law Center, https://www.splcenter.org/fighting-hate/extremist-files/group/pioneer-fund.

87. Carole Novielli, "Planned Parenthood's Ties to Eugenics Go Far beyond Margaret Sanger," Live Action, September 6, 2016, https://www.liveaction.org/news/planned-parenthoods-connections-to-eugenics/.

88. Mark Potok, "Group Attacking Planned Parenthood Linked to Extremists" Hatewatch, Southern Poverty Law Center, August 31, 2015, https://www.splcenter.org/hatewatch/2015/08/31/group-attacking-planned-parenthood-linked-extremists.

89. Roy Beck, "'No' to Immigrant Bashing," NumbersUSA, https://www.numbersusa.com/about/no-immigrant-bashing.

90. "About Us," NumbersUSA, https://www.numbersusa.com/about.

91. "Sen. Jeff Sessions Recognizes NumbersUSA in the Congressional Record," NumbersUSA, May 8, 2012, https://www.numbersusa.com/content/news/may-8-2012/sen-jeff-sessions-recognizes-numbersusa-congressional-record.html.

92. "Teaching tolerance," Southern Poverty Law Center, https://www.splcenter.org/teaching-tolerance.

93. "About Teaching Tolerance," Teaching Tolerance, https://www.tolerance.org/about.

94. Julia Delacroix and Coshandra Dillard, "This is Not a Drill," *Teaching Tolerance* 60, (Fall 2018) https://www.tolerance.org/magazine/fall-2018/this-is-not-a-drill.

95. "Supporting Students from Immigrant Families" Teaching Tolerance website, https://www.tolerance.org/moment/supporting-students-immigrant-families.

96. Bryan Christopher, "Walking Undocumented," *Teaching Tolerance* 56, (Summer 2017) https://www.tolerance.org/magazine/summer-2017/walking-undocumented.

97. Mccoyje, "White Privilege," Teaching Tolerance website, https://www.tolerance.org/learning-plan/white-privilege-26.

98. Michael E. Miller, "MS-13's Invasion of a New York School Reveals Politics of Protection" *Albuquerque Journal*, March 9, 2018, https://www.abqjournal.com/1144175/ms-13s-invasion-of-a-new-york-school-reveals-politics-of-protection.html.

99. Michael E. Miller, "'A Ticking Time Bomb': MS-13 Threatens a Middle School, Warn Teachers, Parents, Students," *Washington Post*, June 11, 2018, https://www.washingtonpost.com/local/a-ticking-time-bomb-ms-13-threatens-a-middle-school-warn-teachers-parents-students/2018/06/11/7cfc7036-5a00-11e8-858f-12becb4d6067_story.html?utm_term=.b1da4b0c9018.

100. Tisha Lewis, "Northern Va. Regional Gang Task Force: 80 Percent of Gang Recruitment Occurs in Middle, High Schools," FOX 5 DC, May 9, 2018; updated May 10, 2018, http://www.fox5dc.com/news/local-news/northern-va-regional-gang-task-force-80-percent-of-gang-recruitment-occurs-in-middle-high-schools.

101. Coshandra Dillard, "The School-to-Deportation Pipeline" *Teaching Tolerance* 60, (Fall 2018) https://www.tolerance.org/magazine/fall-2018/the-school-to-deportation-pipeline.

102. Rigoberto González, "Papalotzin and the Monarchs: A Bilingual Tale of Breaking Down Walls," Teaching Tolerance website https://www.tolerance.org/classroom-resources/texts/papalotzin-and-the-monarchs-a-bilingual-tale-of-breaking-down-walls.

103. González, "Papalotzin and the Monarchs."

104. "The Trump Effect: The Impact of the 2016 Election on Our Nation's Schools," Teaching Tolerance website, http://www.tolerance.org/sites/default/files/general/Trump%20Effect%20Comments_0.pdf.

105. "The Immigration Debate: A Lesson from Viva La Causa," Teaching Tolerance website, https://www.tolerance.org/classroom-resources/tolerance-lessons/the-immigration-debate-a-lesson-from-viva-la-causa.

106. Teaching Tolerance Staff, "Ten Myths About Immigration," *Teaching Tolerance* 39, (Spring 2011) https://www.tolerance.org/magazine/spring-2011/ten-myths-about-immigration.

107. Michelle Malkin, *Invasion: How America Still Welcomes Terrorists Criminals & Other Foreign Menaces to Our Shores* (Washington, D.C.: Regnery Publishing, 2002).

108. John Lilyea, "SPLC Wants your $$$ To Protect Morris Dees," This Ain't Hell But You Can See It From Here, October 20, 2010, https://thisainthell.us/blog/?p=20909&cpage=1.

109. Carl M. Cannon, "The Hate Group That Incited the Middlebury Melee," RealClearPolitics, March 19, 2017, http://www.realclearpolitics.com/articles/2017/03/19/the_hate_group_that_incited_the_middlebury_melee_133377.html.

110. Melissa Brown and Brian Edwards, "'Civil Rights' Movement Television Evangelist': Dees Weathered Criticism for Decades amidst SPLC's Groundbreaking Legal Work," *Montgomery Advertiser*, March 16, 2019, https://www.montgomeryadvertiser.com/story/news/2019/03/16/morris-dees-splc-southern-poverty-law-center-martin-luther-king-jr-levin-hatewatch-klan-tracy-larkin/3173039002/.

111. Clarence Spigner, "Morris Dees," Encyclopedia of Alabama, July 6, 2009; last updated May 10, 2015, http://www.encyclopediaofalabama.org/article/h-2333.

112. Jackson Thornton, "Southern Poverty Law Center Inc. and SPLC Action Fund Consolidated Financial Statements," October 31, 2018, https://freebeacon.com/wp-content/uploads/2019/03/SPLCAudited2018statement.pdf.

113. "Assignment," A + L Development, LLC, https://aplusldevelopment.com/our-work/the-morris-dees-legacy-fund-kiosk.

114. Ryan Parker, "Clooney Joins Forces with Civil Rights Group: 'No Two Sides to Bigotry and Hate,'" *Hollywood Reporter*, August 22, 2017, https://www.hollywoodreporter.com/news/clooney-foundation-justice-partners-southern-poverty-law-center-1031522.

115. Thornton, "Southern Poverty Law Center Inc. and SPLC Action Fund Consolidated Financial Statements."

116. Ibid, 9.

117. Ray Jenkins, "Metzger Verdict Unsettling," *The Bulletin*, October 31, 1990, https://news.google.com/newspapers?nid=1243&dat=19901031&id=INU9AAAAIBAJ&sjid=hoYDAAAAIBAJ&pg=7076,521678.

118. Originally featured at "Mediterranean living: Couple's Renovated Showplace Reflects Owners' World Travels, Varied Tastes," April 1, 2010, http://atmore.localspur.com/2010/04/01/mediterranean-living-couples-renovated-showplace-reflects-owners-world-travels-varied-tastes/.

119. Family Research Council, "Southern Poverty Law Center: Preliminary Report," July 3, 2017, http://splcexposed.com/wp-content/uploads/2017/08/2017-07-03-SPLC-Report.pdf.

120. Matthew Vadum, "BREAKING: SPLC Amasses Half a Billion Dollars," Capital Research Center, April 20, 2018, https://capitalresearch.org/article/breaking-splc-amasses-half-a-billion-dollars/; Matthew Vadum, "Smearing Conservatives, Raking in Cash," FrontPage Mag, August 19, 2012, https://www.frontpagemag.com/fpm/140983/smearing-conservatives-raking-cash-matthew-vadum.

121. Ed Pilkington and Jon Swaine, "The Seven Republican Super-Donors Who Keep Money in Tax Havens," *The Guardian*, November 7, 2017, https://www.theguardian.com/news/2017/nov/07/us-republican-donors-offshore-paradise-papers.

122. Bob Drogin, "Romney Utilized Offshore Tax Havens To Help Investors," *Los Angeles Times*, December 19, 2007, http://archive.boston.com/news/nation/articles/2007/12/19/romney_utilized_offshore_tax_havens_to_help_investors/.

123. Sanjay Sanghoee, "Romney's 'Bermuda-Gate': Why His Offshore Bank Accounts Really Matter," *HuffPost*, July 11, 2012, https://www.huffingtonpost.com/sanjay-sanghoee/romney-offshore-tax-havens_b_1664722.html.

124. BarackObamadotcom, "Mitt Romney's Offshore Tax Havens" YouTube, October 2, 2012, https://www.youtube.com/watch?v=nfou37zkiJA.

125. Southern Poverty Law Center IRS Form 8879-EO, December 23, 2015, https://www.splcenter.org/sites/default/files/990-10-31-15.pdf.

126. Joe Schoffstall, "Southern Poverty Surpasses Half Billion in Assets, $121 Million Now Offshore," *Washington Free Beacon*, March 12, 2019, https://freebeacon.com/issues/southern-poverty-surpasses-half-billion-in-assets-121-million-now-offshore/.

127. Melissa Brown and Brian Edwards, "Southern Poverty Law Center Fires Co-Founder Morris Dees," *Montgomery Advertiser*, March 14, 2019, https://www.montgomeryadvertiser.com/story/news/2019/03/14/southern-poverty-law-center-fires-co-founder-civil-rights-lawyer-morris-dees/3164839002/.

128. Matt Pearce, "Southern Poverty Law Center Fires Co-Founder Morris Dees amid Employee Uproar," *Montgomery Advertiser*, March 14, 2019, https://www.latimes.com/nation/la-na-splc-morris-dees-20190314-story.html.

129. Josh Moon, "SPLC Fires Founder Morris Dees; Internal Emails Highlight Issues with Harassment, Discrimination," Alabama Political Reporter, March 15, 2019, https://www.alreporter.com/2019/03/15/splc-fires-founder-morris-dees-internal-emails-highlight-issues-with-harassment-discrimination/.

130. Brian Lyman, Melissa Brown, and Andrew J. Yawn, "Southern Poverty Law Center President Richard Cohen To Step Down," *Montgomery Advertiser*, March 22, 2019, https://www.montgomeryadvertiser.com/story/news/2019/03/22/southern-poverty-law-center-president-richard-cohen-step-down/3251224002/.

131. Audra D. S. Burch, Alan Blinder and John Eligon, "Roiled by Staff Uproar, Civil Rights Group Looks at Intolerance Within," *New York Times*, March 25, 2019, https://www.nytimes.com/2019/03/25/us/morris-dees-leaves-splc.html.

132. Silverstein, "'Hate,' immigration, and the Southern Poverty Law Center."

133. Ken Silverstein, "The Southern Poverty Law Center Business Model," *Browsings: The Harper's Blog*, https://harpers.org/blog/2007/11/the-southern-poverty-business-model/.

134. John Egerton, *Shades of Gray: Dispatches from the Modern South* (Baton Rouge: Louisiana State University Press, 1991), https://books.google.com/books?id=O6YFL YjAgcQC&pg=PA211&dq=egerton+splc+dispatches&hl=en&sa=X&ved=0ahUKEwi o6Ifq8J7hAhVl34MKHRcaCgQQ6AEIKjAA#v=onepage&q=egerton%20splc%20d-ispatches&f=false, 222.

135. Egerton, *Shades of Gray*, 233.

136. Ibid, 235.

137. Dan Morse, "Equal Treatment? No Blacks in Center's Leadership," *Montgomery Advertiser*, February 16, 1994, 1A, 6A; Dan Morse, "Black Former Workers Question Treatment," *Montgomery Advertiser*, February 16, 1994, 1A, 7A.

138. Dan Morse, "Law Center Raised $4.2 Million for Each Suit Filed in Past 5 Years," December 31, 1994, *Montgomery Advertiser*, 1A.

139. Family Research Council, "Confessed Terrorist Floyd Corkins Admits to Using SPLC Target List," YouTube, April 24, 2013, https://www.youtube.com/watch?v=hgjI3wavx-I.

140. Tal Kopan, "FRC Shooter Sentenced to 25 Years," *Politico*, September 19, 2013, https://www.politico.com/story/2013/09/frc-shooter-sentenced-to-25-years-097069.

141. Paul Bedard, "'Shocked' Anti-Defamation League Slaps FBI 'Diss on Hate Crimes," *Washington Examiner*, March 26, 2014, https://www.washingtonexaminer.com/shocked-anti-defamation-league-slaps-fbi-diss-on-hate-crimes.

142. Open letter to members of the media by L. Brent Bozell et al., September 6, 2017, http://downloads.frc.org/EF/EF17I05.pdf.

143. Peter Beinart, "A Violent Attack on Free Speech at Middlebury," *The Atlantic*, March 6, 2017, https://www.theatlantic.com/politics/archive/2017/03/middlebury-free-speech-violence/518667/.

144. Alison Stanger, "Understanding the Angry Mob at Middlebury That Gave Me a Concussion," *New York Times*, March 13, 2017, https://www.nytimes.com/2017/03/13/opinion/understanding-the-angry-mob-that-gave-me-a-concussion.html.

145. "Hate Groups Reach Record High," Southern Poverty Law Center, February 19, 2019, https://www.splcenter.org/news/2019/02/19/hate-groups-reach-record-high.

146. Katharine Jackson, "Trump 'Fear-Mongering' Fuels Rise of U.S. Hate Groups to Record: Watchdog," *U.S. News and World Report*, February 20, 2019, https://www.usnews.com/news/us/articles/2019-02-20/number-of-us-hate-groups-hits-all-time-high-watchdog-says.

147. James Morris, "Number of US Hate Groups at Record High 'and Linked to Trump', Study Suggests," *Evening Standard*, February 21, 2019, https://www.standard.co.uk/news/world/number-of-us-hate-groups-at-record-high-and-linked-to-trump-study-suggests-a4073196.html.

148. Gigi Sukin, "Report Blames Trump for Record Number of U.S. Hate Groups in 2018," Axios, February 20, 2019, https://www.axios.com/trump-us-hate-groups-record-2018-a01bf2a2-a347-4551-848f-4ec6b75ff19c.html.

149. Mark Potok, "Rage on the Right," *Intelligence Report*, Southern Poverty Law Center, March 2, 2010, https://www.splcenter.org/fighting-hate/intelligence-report/2010/rage-right.

150. Heidi Beirich, "The Year in Nativism" *Intelligence Report*, Southern Poverty Law Center March 2, 2010, https://www.splcenter.org/fighting-hate/intelligence-report/2010/year-nativism.

151. Peter B. Gemma, "Interview: Expert on Political Extremism Discusses the SPLC," December 31, 2011; last revised January 21, 2017, http://www.peterbgemma.com/2011/12/expert-on-political-extremism-talks-discusses-the-plc/.

152. "Frequently Asked Questions about Hate Groups," Southern Poverty Law Center, October 4, 2017, https://www.splcenter.org/20171004/frequently-asked-questions-about-hate-groups.

153. Center for Immigration Studies v. Richard Cohen and Heidi Beirich, Complaint, filed January 16, 2019, https://cis.org/sites/default/files/2019-01/Stamped-CenterforImmigrationStudies-vs-RichardCohen-and-Heidi-Beirich.pdf.

154. Matt Naham, "Southern Poverty Law Center Slapped with Racketeering Suit Over 'False Hate Group Designation,'" Law & Crime, January 16, 2019, https://lawandcrime.com/lawsuit/southern-poverty-law-center-slapped-with-racketeering-suit-over-false-hate-group-designation/.

155. Gavin McInnes v. The Southern Poverty Law Center, Inc., complaint filed February 4, 2019, https://www.courtlistener.com/docket/14533180/1/mcinnes-v-the-southern-poverty-law-center-inc/.

156. Sheryl Gay Stolberg originally posted to https://twitter.com/SherylNYT/status/896575560650035200 but the tweet has since been deleted; screenshot available at Rob Eno, "Did a NY Times Reporter Get Bullied into Changing her Reporting?" Conservative Review, August 15, 2017, https://www.conservativereview.com/news/did-a-nyt-reporter-get-bullied-into-changing-her-reporting/. See also Matt Vespa, "Wait–Did The Left Force This NYT Reporter To Retract Her Remarks On Antifa In Charlottesville?" Townhall, August 15, 2017, https://townhall.com/tipsheet/mattvespa/2017/08/15/waitdid-the-left-force-this-nyt-reporter-to-retract-her-remarks-on-antifa-in-cha-n2368946.

157. News2Share, "Raw Footage of the Violence at Lee Park, Charlottesville," YouTube, August 14, 2017, https://www.youtube.com/watch?v=Thhd-VM6mW4&feature=youtu.be&t=161.

158. Timothy J. Heaphy, "Independent Review of the 2017 Protests in Charlottesville, Virginia," Hunton & Williams, https://docs.wixstatic.com/ugd/c869fb_a573de9ad4f04b0491b927ca9d48252c.pdf, 160–62

159. Heaphy, "Independent Review of the 2017 Protests in Charlottesville, Virginia," 135.

160. Yep, this is the same Tina Tchen who meddled in the Jussie Smollett "hate crime" hussle. See Michelle Malkin, "Crony State: Obamas' Chicago Fixer Tina Tchen," Michellemalkin.com, March 27, 2019, http://michellemalkin.com/2019/03/27/crony-state-obamas-chicago-fixer-tina-tchen/.

161. Matt Pearce, "Southern Poverty Law Center Picks Former Michelle Obama Aide To Investigate Workplace Complaints," Los Angeles Times, March 18, 2019, https://www.latimes.com/nation/la-na-splc-inclusion-tina-tchen-20190318-story.html.

162. Change the Terms website, http://www.changetheterms.org/.

163. Paul Bedard, "Support for Southern Poverty Law Center Links Scalise, Family Research Council shooters," Washington Examiner, June 14, 2017, https://www.washingtonexaminer.com/support-for-southern-poverty-law-center-links-scalise-family-research-council-shooters.

164. Joseph Rossell, "Soros, Ford Foundations 'Lavish' $196 Million to Push Internet Regulations" MRC Business, February 25, 2015, http://archive2.mrc.org/articles/soros-ford-foundations-lavish-196-million-push-internet-regulations.

165. "Color of Change," Activist Facts, https://www.activistfacts.com/organizations/524-color-of-change/.

166. Foundation to Promote Open Society, IRS Form 990-PF for calendar year 2015, ProPublica, https://projects.propublica.org/nonprofits/display_990/263753801/2016_11_PF%2F26-3753801_990PF_201512.

167. "Adopt the Terms," Change the Terms, https://www.changetheterms.org/terms.

168. "Adopt the Terms," Change the Terms.

169. Peter Hasson, "Exclusive: YouTube Secretly Using SPLC to Police Videos," *Daily Caller*, February 27, 2018, https://dailycaller.com/2018/02/27/google-youtube-southern-poverty-law-center-censorship/.

170. Tyler O'Neil, "Louie Gohmert Slams Google for Making the SPLC a 'Trusted Flagger' on YouTube," *PJ Media*, December 11, 2018, https://pjmedia.com/video/louie-gohmert-slams-google-for-making-the-splc-a-trusted-flagger-on-youtube/.

171. Allum Bokhari, "The Google Tape: Google CEO Sundar Pichai Promised to Fight Fake News, Educate 'Low Information Voters,'" *Breitbart*, September 12, 2018, https://www.breitbart.com/tech/2018/09/12/the-google-tape-google-ceo-sundar-pichai-promised-to-fight-fake-news-educate-low-information-voters/; Allum Bokhari, "Bokhari: 5 Whoppers Google CEO Sundar Pichai Told Congress," *Breitbart*, December 12, 2018, https://www.breitbart.com/tech/2018/12/12/bokhari-5-whoppers-google-ceo-sundar-pichai-told-congress/.

172. Allum Bokhari, "Leaked video: Google Leadership's Dismayed Reaction to Trump Election," *Breitbart*, September 12, 2018, https://www.breitbart.com/tech/2018/09/12/leaked-video-google-leaderships-dismayed-reaction-to-trump-election/.

173. Tyler O'Neil, "Google May Face RICO, Defamation Lawsuits Due to SPLC Partnership, Lawyers Say," *PJ Media*, January 28, 2019, https://pjmedia.com/trending/google-may-face-rico-defamation-lawsuits-due-to-splc-partnership-lawyers-say/.

174. Meira Svirsky, "Google Donated $250,000 to the Southern Poverty Law Center," *Clarion Project*, January 24, 2019, https://clarionproject.org/google-donated-250000-to-the-southern-poverty-law-center/.

175. Tyler O'Neil, "Google May Face RICO, Defamation Lawsuits Due to SPLC Partnership, Lawyers Say," *PJ Media*, January 28, 2019, https://pjmedia.com/trending/google-may-face-rico-defamation-lawsuits-due-to-splc-partnership-lawyers-say/.

176. Prager University v. Google LLC, filed January 8, 2019, https://www.scribd.com/document/397065400/Prageru-State-Law-Complaint-Filed-1#, 5.

177. "5-Minute Videos," PragerU, https://www.prageru.com/5-minute-videos/.

178. PragerU (@prageru), "BREAKING: We're being heavily censored on @Facebook. Our last 9 posts are reaching 0 of our 3 million followers. At least two videos were deleted last night for 'hate speech' including our recent video with @conservmillen. SHARE to spread awareness about big tech censorship," Twitter, August 17, 2018, 9:32 a.m., https://twitter.com/prageru/status/1030492451146846208.

179. Facebook (@facebook), "We mistakenly removed these videos and have restored them because they don't break out standards. This will reverse any reduction in content distribution you've experienced. We're very sorry and are continuing to look into what happened with your Page," Twitter, August 17, 2018, 5:31 p.m., https://twitter.com/facebook/status/1030613023268855808.

180. Casey Stinnett, "Facebook's Program Thinks Declaration of Independence Is Hate Speech," The Vindicator, July 2, 2018, https://www.thevindicator.com/news/article_556e1014-7e41-11e8-a85e-ab264c30e973.html.

181. Avi Selk, "Facebook Told Two Women Their Pro-Trump Videos Were 'Unsafe,'" *Washington Post*, April 10, 2018, https://www.washingtonpost.com/news/the-intersect/wp/2018/04/10/facebook-accused-of-deeming-black-pro-trump-sisters-unsafe/.

182. Peter Hasson, "Exclusive: Facebook, Amazon, Google and Twitter all work with left-wing SPLC," *Daily Caller*, June 6, 2018, https://dailycaller.com/2018/06/06/splc-partner-google-facebook-amazon/.

183. Life After Hate website, https://www.lifeafterhate.org/.

184. Life After Hate media coverage, https://www.lifeafterhate.org/press.

185. Liam Stack, "Facebook Announces New Policy to Ban White Nationalist Content," *New York Times*, March 27, 2019, https://www.nytimes.com/2019/03/27/business/facebook-white-nationalist-supremacist.html.

186. "Twitter Transparency Report," Twitter, https://transparency.twitter.com/en.html.

187. Devin G. Nunes v. Twitter Inc. et al., complaint, March 18, 2019, https://www.scribd.com/document/402297422/Nunes-Complaint-3-18-19.

188. David Reaboi and Nick Short, "Despite Twitter's Protests, the Stifling of Conservative Speech On the Platform Is Real," The Federalist, August 24, 2018, https://thefederalist.com/2018/08/24/the-stifling-of-conservative-speech-on-twitter-is-very-real/.

189. James O'Keefe (@JamesOKeefeIII), "One strategy is to shadow ban so that you have ultimate control. The idea of a shadow ban is that you ban someone but they don't know they've been banned, because they keep posting, but no one sees their content." – says former Twitter engineer," Twitter, August 20, 2018, 11:57 a.m., https://twitter.com/JamesOKeefeIII/status/1031616332209577985.

190. Hasson, "Exclusive: Facebook, Amazon, Google and Twitter all work with left-wing SPLC."

191. Lucas Nolan, "The 5 Best Moments of Twitter Execs Squirming over Questions on 'Joe Rogan Experience,'" Breitbart, March 6, 2019, https://www.breitbart.com/tech/2019/03/06/the-5-best-moments-of-twitter-execs-squirming-over-questions-on-joe-rogan-experience/.

192. JRE Clips, "Tim Pool Asks Twitter Execs if They Take Cues from the SPLC | JRE Twitter Special," YouTube, March 5, 2019, https://www.youtube.com/watch?v=PJVes1pYyec.

193. Ryan Lenz, "Twitter Begins Long-Awaited Crackdown on Hate Groups and Extremist Rhetoric," Southern Poverty Law Center, December 18, 2017, https://www.splcenter.org/hatewatch/2017/12/18/twitter-begins-long-awaited-crackdown-hate-groups-and-extremist-rhetoric.

194. Twitter Safety, "Enforcing New Rules To Reduce Hateful Conduct and Abusive Behavior," Twitter, December 18, 2017, https://blog.twitter.com/official/en_us/topics/company/2017/safetypoliciesdec2017.html.

195. Nolan, "The 5 Best Moments of Twitter Execs Squirming."

196. Briana Ellison, "Trending: And Over Here, We Have a Totally Composed Senator Definitely Not Hitting a Teenager," Washington Post, March 17, 2019, https://www.washingtonpost.com/express/2019/03/17/trending-over-here-we-have-totally-composed-senator-definitely-not-hitting-teenager/?utm_term=.7603567a762d.

197. Felicity Caldwell (@fel_caldwell), "After the devastating attacks on mosques in Christchurch today, this is Queensland Senator Fraser Anning's response #auspol," Twitter, March 14, 2019, 10:52 p.m., https://twitter.com/fel_caldwell/status/1106432989011959808.

198. Katie Holland (@MemyselfandI536), "#eggboy is the hero we wanted. But too bad it wasn't something a little harder. Like a brick," Twitter, March 16, 2019, 12:07 p.m., https://twitter.com/MemyselfandI536/status/1106995533363793920.

199. Jane Caro (@JaneCaro), "If the thugs and the racists and the misogynists come marching down the streets or the airwaves we will applaud those who take up eggs against them. I only hope I have the courage to do so too. Thank you #EggBoyHero," Twitter, March 18, 2019, 2:19 a.m., https://twitter.com/JaneCaro/status/1107572178952699904.

200. Jeremy McLellan (@JeremyMcLellan), "Props to eggboy for selecting the ideal ammunition for his attack, the humble egg, which is funny, harmless, available everywhere, cheap, easy to transport, nice sound on impact, makes the target change their clothes. The perfect weapon for these times," Twitter, March 16, 2019, 12:45 p.m., https://twitter.com/JeremyMcLellan/status/1107004956614127616.

201. Vijaya Gadde (@vijaya), "Such an honor to meet @HillaryClinton today. Amazing talk at @twitter – full of great advice and inspiration," Twitter, July 21, 2014, 7:05 p.m., https://twitter.com/vijaya/status/491403551508160512.

202. Vijaya Gadde (@vijaya), "If money is the only thing that works with congress, we need $30m to pass gun control laws in America," December 2, 2015, 8:36 p.m., https://twitter.com/vijaya/status/672273120099569666.

203. Vijaya Gadde (@vijaya), "I've never met a national politician in the U.S. who is so ill informed, evasive, puerile and deceptive as Trump," March 26, 2016, 5:21 p.m., https://twitter.com/vijaya/status/713883500982767620.

204. Shalene Gupta, "Twitter's top female exec on discrimination and overcoming adversity," *Fortune*, October 24, 2014, http://fortune.com/2014/10/23/vijaya-gadde/; Women's Leadership Network, "Vijaya Gadde: 'From Texas to Twitter,'" NYU School of Law, https://www.law.nyu.edu/centers/birnbaum-womens-leadership-network/podcasts/gadde.

205. David Lat, "Just How Rich Is Twitter's General Counsel?" Above the Law, May 13, 2014, https://abovethelaw.com/2014/05/fun-fact-of-the-day-twitters-general-counsel-owns-how-many-millions-in-twtr-stock/.

206. Richard Hanania, "It Isn't Your Imagination: Twitter Treats Conservatives More Harshly Than Liberals" Quillette, February 12, 2019, https://quillette.com/2019/02/12/it-isnt-your-imagination-twitter-treats-conservatives-more-harshly-than-liberals/.

207. JRE Clips, "Tim Pool Tells Twitter Exec They Have a Liberal Bias | JRE Twitter Special," YouTube, March 5, 2019, https://www.youtube.com/watch?v=EbTXqrS9l5E.

208. Washington Post Live, "Twitter's Vijaya Gadde Says Twitter Is Working on a Way To Label Tweets That Violate Terms," *Washington Post*, March 27, 2019, https://www.washingtonpost.com/video/postlive/twitters-vajaya-gadde-says-twitter-is-working-on-a-way-to-label-tweets-that-violate-terms/2019/03/27/29dfc960-05bf-4baf-ab8c-ce52f2e51519_video.html?utm_term=.2249abe73056.

209. Bryan Menegus, "Jeff Bezos Still Wants to Send Trump to Space," Gizmodo, October 20, 2016, https://gizmodo.com/jeff-bezos-still-wants-to-send-trump-to-space-1788035764.

210. Readers of *Invasion* will remember that Abraham fought to block the implementation of two different visa tracking databases—one for foreign student visa holders and the other for all temporary visitors (which was mandated by Section 110 of the 1996 Illegal Immigration Reform and Immigrant Responsibility Act). Abraham led efforts to starve the first database of funding and crusaded several times to kill Section 110 altogether. On September 11, 2001, neither of those databases was in place. To this day, they remain incomplete.

211. Michael D. Shear, "Amazon's Founder Pledges $2.5 Million in Support of Same-Sex Marriage," The Caucus Blog (a *New York Times* blog), https://thecaucus.blogs.nytimes.com/2012/07/27/amazons-founder-pledges-2-5-million-in-support-of-same-sex-marriage/#more-224851.

212. David Montgomery, "The State of Hate," *Washington Post Magazine*, November 8, 2018, https://www.washingtonpost.com/news/magazine/wp/2018/11/08/feature/is-the-southern-poverty-law-center-judging-hate-fairly/?noredirect=on&utm_term=.c3d82d08bc2d.

213. "About AmazonSmile," Amazon, https://smile.amazon.com/gp/chpf/about/ref=smi_aas_redirect?ie=UTF8&%2AVersion%2A=1&%2Aentries%2A=0.

214. Peter Hasson, "Prominent Christian Legal Group Barred from Amazon Program While Openly Anti-Semitic Groups Remain," Daily Caller, May 5, 2018, https://dailycaller.com/2018/05/05/amazon-smile-liberal-splc-anti-semitic-groups/.

215. Kate Shellnutt, "D. James Kennedy Ministries Sues SPLC over Hate Map," *Christianity Today*, August 24, 2017, https://www.christianitytoday.com/news/2017/august/d-james-kennedy-southern-poverty-law-center-splc-hate-map.html.

216. Brother André Marie, "Amazon.com Partners with Hate Group to Eliminate Unwanted Charities," Catholicism.org, April 24, 2018, https://catholicism.org/amazon-com-partners-with-hate-group-to-eliminate-unwanted-charities.html.

217. Suzy Buchanan, "Radical Catholic Groups Sour Life in Peaceful New England Town," Intelligence Report, July 1, 2007, https://www.splcenter.org/fighting-hate/intelligence-report/2007/radical-traditionalist-catholic-groups-sour-life-peaceful-new-england-town.

218. Brother André Marie, "Way off Center: The Southern Poverty Law Center on St. Benedict Center" Catholicism.org, August 1, 2007, https://catholicism.org/ad-rem-no-40.html.

219. Debra Cassens Weiss, "Alliance Defending Freedom Gains Influence with Supreme Court Wins," *ABA Journal*, July 9, 2018, http://www.abajournal.com/news/article/alliance_defending_freedom_gains_influence_with_supreme_court_wins.

220. Sarah Kramer, "Amazon Gives ADF the Boot from Its AmazonSmile Program: Here's What You Can Do," Alliance Defending Freedom, May 3, 2015, https://www.adflegal.org/detailspages/blog-details/allianceedge/2018/05/03/amazon-gives-adf-the-boot-from-its-amazonsmile-program-here-s-what-you-can-do.

221. Email from Michael Farris to AmazonSmile, May 3, 2018, https://adflegal.blob.core.windows.net/mainsite-new/docs/default-source/documents/resources/media-resources/letters/adf-letter-to-amazon-(2018-05-03)/adf-letter-to-amazon-(2018-05-03).pdf.

222. Jeremy Tedesco, "Southern Poverty Law Center Wrongly Targets Conservative Groups—Like Mine," Fox News, March 29, 2019, https://www.foxnews.com/opinion/jeremy-tedesco-southern-poverty-law-center-wrongly-targets-conservative-groups-like-mine.

223. Renae Reints, "Rep. Keith Ellison Slams Amazon for Selling 'Hate Group' Merchandise," *Fortune*, July 17, 2017, http://fortune.com/2018/07/17/keith-ellison-jeff-bezos-letter/.

224. Robert Spencer, "Muslim Brotherhood-Linked Rep. Keith Ellison Demands Amazon Stop Selling Books from SPLC-Designated 'Hate Groups,'" Jihad Watch, July 18, 2018, https://www.jihadwatch.org/2018/07/muslim-brotherhood-linked-rep-keith-ellison-demands-amazon-stop-selling-books-from-splc-designated-hate-groups.

225. Peter Rudegeair, "PayPal CEO Grapples With Fringe Groups," *Wall Street Journal*, February 24, 2019, https://www.wsj.com/articles/paypal-ceo-grapples-with-fringe-groups-11551016800?mod=searchresults&page=1&pos=1.

226. Dan Schulman and Patricia R. Olsen, "Teamwork's Rewards," *New York Times*, February 24, 2018, https://www.nytimes.com/2008/02/24/jobs/24boss.html.

227. Rudegeair, "PayPal CEO Grapples With Fringe Groups."

228. David Gelles, "Dan Schulman of PayPal on Guns, Cash, and Getting Punched," *New York Times*, July 27, 2018, https://www.nytimes.com/2018/07/27/business/dan-schulman-paypal-corner-office.html.

229. Citing her de-platforming by Twitter, Paypal, and others, Loomer filed suit in May 2019 against the Council on American-Islamic Relations, which Twitter had given a "special role" along with the SPLC in "deciding what ideas and voices" to silence. See https://freeloomer.com/complaint, 25.

230. Ibid.

231. Luke Rohlfing, "Bad Hombres: PayPal Continues To Help Fund Immigrant Caravans," Big League Politics, May 4, 2018, https://bigleaguepolitics.com/bad-hombres-paypal-continues-help-fund-immigrant-caravans/?utm_source=srp002.

232. Rohlfing, "Bad Hombres: PayPal Continues To Help Fund Immigrant Caravans." I contacted PayPal to follow up and received the following message from Kim Eichorn in the media relations department: "To clarify, this action was related to our company's decision, and ongoing due diligence, in ceasing payment processing for the Proud Boys. It does not pertain to his reporting on other topics or events. We're unable to share additional information or account specifics per company policy." When I asked whether third parties were involved in their "ongoing due diligence," she responded: "All actions taken by the company are independent and based on our own internal review process and analysis."

233. Arun Gupta, "Why Young Men of Color Are Joining White-Supremacist Groups," Daily Beast, September 4, 2018, https://web.archive.org/web/20180904190227/https://www.thedailybeast.com/why-young-men-of-color-are-joining-white-supremacist-groups.

234. Michelle Malkin (@michellemalkin), "Can't we have just one financial institution that doesn't cave to SJWs?!" Twitter, February 9, 2019, 12:59 p.m., https://twitter.com/michellemalkin/status/1094339984704880641.

235. Chase (@Chase), "Hi Michelle, this article is inaccurate. We did not close his personal account. We do not close accounts based on political affiliation," Twitter, February 12, 2019, 8:51 a.m., https://twitter.com/Chase/status/1095364888552181760.

236. Michelle Malkin (@michellemalkin), "The letter clearly states you closed his account. So if not for political reasons, why, after 'careful consideration,' did you close his account?" Twitter, February 12, 2019, 9:13 a.m., https://twitter.com/michellemalkin/status/1095370232212840448.

237. Chase (@Chase), "For privacy reasons, we can't share more. But we didn't close his personal account. You might ask him to share all the facts with you," Twitter, February 12, 2019, 9:33 a.m., https://twitter.com/Chase/status/1095375473809477632.

238. Staff Report, "Debanking: Chase Bank Says 'Moral Character' a Reason Why They Don't Do Business with 'Those Types of People,'" Project Veritas, April 16, 2019, https://www.projectveritas.com/2019/04/16/debanking-chase-bank-says-moral-character-a-reason-why-they-dont-do-business-with-those-types-of-people/.

239. Peter D'Abrosca, "Exclusive: Proud Boys Suing SPLC Over 'Hate Group' Designation," Big League Politics, May 20, 2019, https://bigleaguepolitics.com/exclusive-proud-boys-suing-splc-over-hate-group-designation/.

240. Interview with the author, April 16, 2019.

241. Tyler Durden, "Chase Bank De-Platforms Conservative Performance Artist Martina Markota," Zero Hedge, February 20, 2019, https://www.zerohedge.com/news/2019-02-20/chase-bank-de-platforms-conservative-performance-artist-martina-markota.

242. Joe Biggs (@Rambobiggs), "Chase bank just closed out my account!" Twitter, February 16, 2019, 9:57 a.m., https://twitter.com/Rambobiggs/status/1096830844134662145.

243. Eric Weinstein (@EricRWeinstein), "I really detest this style of (pinned) tweet. Just being direct here. That said, I'm really disturbed to hear that @Chase may have terminated this Vet's account without giving a reason & I have no reason to think he's lying. Why are manners/politics conflated w/our banking now?" Twitter, February 25, 2019, 6:53 p.m., https://twitter.com/EricRWeinstein/status/1100227252665479168.

244. Eric Weinstein (@EricRWeinstein), "I am happy to learn there is another non political story, but I'm hearing a lot of reports of account closures echoing 'Operation Chokepoint' where 'undesirable' operators were denied financial access. If you feel I'm being mislead, I'm eager to learn how & why that is. Thanks!" Twitter, February 25, 2019, 7:02 p.m., https://twitter.com/EricRWeinstein/status/1100229552020672512.

245. Iain Murray, "Operation Choke Point Is Over – Perhaps," National Review, August 22, 2017, https://www.nationalreview.com/corner/operation-choke-point-over-cfpb-continues-its-aims/.

246. Norbert Michel, "Newly Unsealed Documents Show Top FDIC Officials Running Operation Choke Point," Forbes, November 5, 2018, https://www.forbes.com/sites/norbertmichel/2018/11/05/newly-unsealed-documents-show-top-fdic-officials-running-operation-choke-point/#31271df11191.

247. Chase (@Chase), "This is not accurate. We can't discuss specific customer accounts for privacy reasons, as you can understand. But we would never close an account due to political affiliation," Twitter, February 25, 2019, 7:00 p.m., https://twitter.com/Chase/status/1100229088739057664.

248. Kevin Lui, "J.P. Morgan Is Giving $1 Million to Nonprofits Exposing Hate Groups in the Wake of Charlottesville," Fortune, August 22, 2017, http://fortune.com/2017/08/22/jpmorgan-donation-extremism-charlottesville/.

249. Robert Spencer, "Robert Spencer Video: Join Me on Patreon!" Jihad Watch, July 28, 2018, https://www.jihadwatch.org/2018/07/robert-spencer-video-join-me-on-patreon.

250. Robert Spencer, "Patreon and Mastercard Ban Robert Spencer without Explanation," Jihad Watch, August 15, 2018, https://www.jihadwatch.org/2018/08/patreon-and-mastercard-ban-robert-spencer-without-explanation.

251. Patreon (@Patreon), "Hi Robert, we emailed you earlier today which explained that unfortunately Mastercard required us to remove your account. You replied to us but if you have further questions we're happy to keep emailing," Twitter, August 14, 2018, 7:11 p.m., https://twitter.com/Patreon/status/1029551216886341634.

252. Lucas Nolan, "David Horowitz: Visa, Mastercard Cut Off Payments to My Think Tank Based on SPLC 'Hate Group' Label," Breitbart, August 23, 2018, https://www.breitbart.com/tech/2018/08/23/david-horowitz-visa-mastercard-cut-off-payments-to-my-think-tank-based-on-splc-hate-group-label/.

253. Charlie Nash, "Mastercard Forces Patreon to Blacklist Jihad Watch's Robert Spencer," Breitbart, August 15, 2018, https://www.breitbart.com/tech/2018/08/15/mastercard-forces-patreon-to-kick-off-jihad-watchs-robert-spencer/.

254. "David Horowitz Freedom Center Declares Victory over Censorship Attempt," FrontPage Mag, August 27, 2018, https://www.frontpagemag.com/fpm/271154/david-horowitz-freedom-center-declares-victory-frontpagemagcom.

255. Amalgamated Bank, "Amalgamated Foundation Launches Hate Is Not Charitable Campaign," March 19, 2019, https://www.amalgamatedbank.com/news/amalgamated-foundation-launches-hate-not-charitable-campaign.

256. Amalgamated Bank, "Amalgamated Foundation Launches Hate Is Not Charitable Campaign."

257. Alex Kotch, "America's Biggest Charities Are Funneling Millions to Hate Groups From Anonymous Donors," Sludge, February 19, 2019, https://readsludge.com/2019/02/19/americas-biggest-charities-are-funneling-millions-to-hate-groups-from-anonymous-donors/. The groups are: David Horowitz Freedom Center, Center for Security Policy, Proclaiming Justice to the Nations, American Freedom Law Center, American Freedom Defense Initiative, American Freedom Alliance, Cultures in Context, Religious Freedom Coalition, Christians and Jews United for Israel, Florida Family Association, Jihad Watch, Christian Action Network, Alliance Defending Freedom, Family Research Council, American Family Association, Liberty Counsel, Pacific Justice Institute, Probe Ministries International, Indiana American Family Association, Family Research Institute, Illinois Family Institute, Chalcedon, Inc., American Vision, Traditional Values Coalition Education and Legal Institute, American Border Patrol, American Immigration Control Foundation, Californians for Population Stabilization, Center for Immigration Studies, FAIR, Immigration Reform Law Institute, ProEnglish, The Remembrance Project, Saint Benedict Center, and VDARE.

258. Maria di Mento, "Campaign Urges DAF Providers Not to Give to Hate Groups," *The Chronicle of Philanthropy*, March 20, 2019, https://www.philanthropy.com/article/Campaign-Urges-DAF-Providers/245938.

259. Michelle Malkin, "SEIU and the 'persuasion of power;' Update: St. Louis thuggery on tape," Michellemalkin.com, August 6, 2019, http://michellemalkin.com/2009/08/06/seiu-and-the-persuasion-of-power/.

260. Ciara O'Brien, "Apple chief Tim Cook condemns 'inhumane' US detention of children," *Irish Times*, January 19, 2018, https://www.irishtimes.com/news/world/us/apple-chief-tim-cook-condemns-inhumane-us-detention-of-children-1.3536224.

261. Trisha Thadani, "Apple CEO Tim Cook on immigration: 'I felt we needed to say something,'" *San Francisco Chronicle*, June 25, 2018, https://www.sfchronicle.com/business/article/Apple-CEO-Tim-Cook-on-immigration-I-felt-we-13025650.php.

262. Moser, "The Reckoning of Morris Dees and the Southern Poverty Law Center."

263. Ibid.

264. David Choi, "'Hate is a cancer': Read the email Apple CEO Tim Cook sent employees after Charlottesville violence," Business Insider, August 17, 2017, https://finance.yahoo.com/news/hate-cancer-apple-ceo-tim-043103137.html.

Chapter 7

1. Lauren Gega, "Extraordinary Home of the Week: Gwen Stefani's Kelly Wearstler-Designed Estate," California Home, January 25, 2017, https://www.californiahome.me/2017/01/extraordinary-home-week-inside-gwen-stefanis-kelly-wearstler-designed-estate/.

2. Candace Jackson, "L.A.'s Star-Studded Neighborhood," *Wall Street Journal*, January 8, 2015, https://www.wsj.com/articles/l-a-s-star-studded-neighborhood-1420736165.

3. Valery Stone, "Denzel Washington's Dream Home Estate," StarMap, May 24, 2014, https://starmap.com/dream-home-of-actor-denzel-washington-on-starmaps/.

4. Martha Groves, "Stars sue over who may use a gate," *Los Angeles Times*, November 20, 2008, https://www.latimes.com/archives/la-xpm-2008-nov-20-me-beverlypark20-story.html.

5. Zayda Rivera, "Christina Aguilera buys $10 million California home near Charlie Sheen, Paris Hilton," *New York Daily News*, April 15, 2013, https://www.nydailynews.com/life-style/real-estate/christina-aguilera-buys-home-charlie-sheen-paris-hilton-article-1.1317383.

6. Neil J. Leitereg, "Eva Longoria splashes out $13.5 million for Beverly Crest contemporary," *Los Angeles Times*, November 13, 2017, https://www.latimes.com/business/realestate/hot-property/la-fi-hotprop-eva-longoria-beverly-crest-20171113-story.html.

7. Mark David, "Eva Longoria Buys Beverly Hills Estate, Lists Hollywood Hills Compound," *Variety*, November 15, 2017, https://variety.com/2017/dirt/real-estalker/eva-longoria-beverly-hills-estate-hollywood-hills-compound-1202615598/.

8. Mark David, "Eva Longoria Buys Tom Cruise Compound (Exclusive)," *Variety*, October 20, 2015, https://variety.com/2015/dirt/real-estalker/eva-longoria-tom-cruise-compound-1201619953/.

9. Mark David, "John Legend and Chrissy Teigen Pick Up Beverly Hills Mansion Once Owned By Rihanna," *Variety*, January 14, 2016, https://variety.com/2016/dirt/real-estalker/john-legend-and-chrissy-teigen-buy-beverly-hills-mansion-1201680098/.

10. Satinder Haer, "John Legend and Chrissy Teigen's Former Hollywood Hills Home Is for Sale," Zillow, July 7, 2017, https://www.zillow.com/blog/john-legend-former-home-for-sale-218576/.

11. Allison Takeda, "Chris Evans Buys Hollywood Hills Home for $3.52 Million: Pictures," *US Weekly*, May 9, 2013, https://www.usmagazine.com/celebrity-news/news/chris-evans-buys-hollywood-hills-home-for-352-million-pictures-201395/.

12. Neal Leitereg, "Jay-Z and Beyoncé headline L.A.'s most expensive home sales of 2017," *Los Angeles Times*, December 30, 2017, https://www.latimes.com/business/realestate/hot-property/la-fi-hp-top-sales-20171230-story.html.

13. Clare Trapasso, "Why Beyonce and JAY Z Are Building a Fortress Around Their $88M Mansion," Realtor.com, April 10, 2018, https://www.realtor.com/news/celebrity-real-estate/beyonce-jay-z-building-fortress-around-88-million-mansion/.

14. Ann Brenoff, "Jennifer Lopez's Bel-Air home for sale for $8.5 million," *Los Angeles Times*, November 25, 2008, https://www.latimes.com/archives/la-xpm-2008-nov-25-la-hmw-hotproplopez25-2008nov25-story.html.

15. Elijah Chiland, "Jennifer Lopez finds a buyer for her Hidden Hills mansion," Curbed, March 5, 2017, https://la.curbed.com/2017/3/5/14821726/jennifer-lopez-los-angeles-mansion-house-sold.

16. Jason Chester, "Jennifer Lopez and Alex Rodriguez Buy Jeremy Piven's Stunning Malibu Beach House for Bargain $6.6 million… After Actor Slashed Price by Nearly $4 Million during Two-Year Listing," *Daily Mail*, February 8, 2019, https://www.dailymail.co.uk/tvshowbiz/article-6684929/Jeremy-Piven-sells-Malibu-beach-house-6-6-million-slashing-nearly-4-million.html.

17. Elizabeth Day, "Malibu's Celebrity Homeowners Try To Block Public Beach Use," *The Guardian*, September 12, 2015, https://www.theguardian.com/us-news/2015/sep/12/malibu-celebrity-homeowners-beach-battle-public-access.

18. Michael Walker, "The Sky-High Cost of Keeping Stars Safe," *Hollywood Reporter*, October 2, 2013, https://www.hollywoodreporter.com/news/celebrity-bodyguards-sky-high-cost-639496.

19. Walker, "The Sky-High Cost of Keeping Stars Safe."

20. "Arrival Information," Warner Bros Studio Tour Hollywood, https://www.wbstudiotour.com/info/arrival-information/.

21. Anandan Guyomar Amirthanayagam, "Security review of Sony Pictures Entertainment Complex in Culver City, LA," Course Blog for CSCI 1951E S01: Computer Systems Security: Principles and Practice, February 19, 2015, https://blogs.brown.edu/csci-1951e-s01/2015/02/19/security-review-of-sony-pictures-entertainment-complex-in-culver-city-la/.

22. Sallie Hofmeister and James Bates, "Movie Studios React to FBI Warning," *Los Angeles Times*, September 21, 2001, https://www.latimes.com/archives/la-xpm-2001-sep-21-mn-48187-story.html.

23. "Huge Police Presence…To Prevent Terrorism, Oscar Stunts," TMZ, February 24, 2019, https://www.tmz.com/2019/02/24/the-academy-awards-extra-police-oscars-terrorist-attack-thieves-security/.

24. Paul Bond, "Ahead of Oscars, Security Heightened Near Dolby Theatre," *Hollywood Reporter*, February 22, 2019, https://www.hollywoodreporter.com/news/oscars-security-heightened-dolby-theatre-1188824.

25. Bond, "Ahead of Oscars, Security Heightened Near Dolby Theatre."

26. Gene Maddaus, "Oscars Security: LAPD Will Have Over 500 Officers On Hand at Red Carpet," *Variety*, March 2, 2018, https://variety.com/2018/film/awards/oscars-security-2018-red-carpet-1202716110/.

27. Charlie Spiering, "Donald Trump Oval Office Address: Border Security 'A Choice Between Right and Wrong,'" Breitbart, January 8, 2019, https://www.breitbart.com/politics/2019/01/08/donald-trump-oval-office-address-border-security-a-choice-between-right-and-wrong/.

28. Stanislaus County Sheriff's Department Facebook post, Facebook, December 26, 2018, https://www.facebook.com/stansheriff/posts/1999557850121003.

29. ABC 7 News, "Video: Police chief gives emotional statement, calls slain Newman Cpl. Ron Singh an 'American patriot,'" December 27, 2018, https://abc7news.com/chief-calls-slain-newman-cpl-ron-singh-an-american-patriot-/4976092/.

30. Olga R. Rodriguez and Jocelyn Gecker, "Sheriff blames sanctuary law for California officer's death," Associated Press/Yahoo News, December 28, 2018, https://news.yahoo.com/police-california-officer-killing-suspect-us-illegally-064549207.html.

31. Patty Guerra, "Brother of Newman Corporal Ronil Singh appears with President Trump in visit to border," *Modesto Bee*, January 10, 2019, https://www.modbee.com/news/politics-government/article224246380.html.

32. Dianne Feinstein (@SenFeinstein), "Read my letter calling for a hearing on the deaths of two young children in Border Patrol custody this month. We must know more about the care and treatment of these children," Twitter, December 27, 2018, 12:06 p.m., https://twitter.com/SenFeinstein/status/1078381705852080133.

33. Lindsay Weinberg, "Mindy Kaling on How Motherhood Shapes Her Activism," *Hollywood Reporter*, March 20, 2019, https://www.hollywoodreporter.com/news/mindy-kaling-how-motherhood-shapes-her-activism-1196000.

34. Mindy Kaling (@mindykaling), "As a mother and a daughter of migrants, I am heartbroken about children being separated from their families at America's borders. Donate to @ACLU here: aclu.org And find out how you can help here: time.com/

money/5314428/ … ," Twitter, June 19, 2018, 3:36 p.m., https://twitter.com/mindykaling/status/1009203185582395392.

35. Alix Langone, "Thousands of Migrant Children Are Being Separated From Their Families at the Border. Here's How to Help Them," *Money*, June 18, 2018; updated June 20, 2018, http://time.com/money/5314428/how-to-help-immigrant-children-parents-border/.

36. Terri C (@colleen0120), "'The mother had to set down her daughter to be body-searched, to be frisked, before she was loaded into a van & taken away.'—John Moore took photo of young Honduran girl crying at the border cnn.it/2LZOD7C @CNN @FoxNews @womensmarch @SecNielsen," Twitter, June 18, 2018, 2:42 p.m., https://twitter.com/colleen0120/status/1008827369115799553.

37. Time, "Behind The Viral Photo Of The Crying Girl At The Border: Photojournalist John Moore Tells All," YouTube, June 22, 2018, https://www.youtube.com/watch?v=muz8_H150aM.

38. Time (@TIME), "TIME's new cover: A reckoning after Trump's border separation policy: What kind of country are we? Ti.me/2JVINI1," Twitter, June 21, 2018, 4:47 a.m., https://twitter.com/TIME/status/1009764707346075649.

39. Jen Kirby, "Time's crying girl photo controversy, explained," Vox, June 22, 2018, https://www.vox.com/policy-and-politics/2018/6/22/17494688/time-magazine-cover-crying-girl-photo-controversy-family-separation.

40. Jennifer Lopez, Instagram post, June 21, 2018, https://www.instagram.com/p/BkT26byg5Kt/?utm_source=ig_embed.

41. Daniel Bates and Karen Ruiz, "Exclusive: 'They're together and safe': Father of Honduran two-year-old who became the face of family separation crisis reveals daughter was never separated from her mother, but the image of her in tears at U.S. border control 'broke his heart,'" *Daily Mail*, June 21, 2018; updated June 22, 2018, https://www.dailymail.co.uk/news/article-5869829/Father-two-year-old-face-child-separation-crisis-speaks-out.html.

42. The correction is no longer available to the public but is captured in other places, including: Byron York, (@ByronYork), "A pretty big correction from TIME," Twitter, June 22, 2018, 9:37 a.m., https://twitter.com/ByronYork/status/1010200083722317827.

43. Ethan Sacks, "Time issues correction for photo of crying 2-year-old migrant," NBC News, June 22, 2018, https://www.nbcnews.com/storyline/immigration-border-crisis/time-issues-correction-photo-crying-2-year-old-migrant-n885836.

44. Hadas Gold, "Time cover backlash: Magazine stands by illustration of crying girl next to Trump," CNN Business, June 22, 2018, https://money.cnn.com/2018/06/22/media/time-cover-photo-critics/index.html.

45. Amber Athey, "Washington Post Hides Correction on TIME Cover Story," June 22, 2018, Daily Caller, https://dailycaller.com/2018/06/22/washington-post-hides-time-correction/.

46. Valerie Bauman, "The crying migrant girl who became a symbol of Trump's 'zero tolerance' immigration policy–despite never being separated from her mother–is now living in Washington D.C. while seeking asylum," *Daily Mail*, February 14, 2019, https://www.dailymail.co.uk/news/article-6705761/Crying-migrant-girl-symbol-Trumps-zero-tolerance-immigration-policy-living-Washington-D-C.html. *See also* Getty Images photos dated February 13, 2019, https://www.gettyimages.com/photos/john-moore-immigration?family=editorial&phrase=john%20moore%20immigration&sort=newest.

47. Erin Tracy, "Newman Corporal's home paid off after charity CEO appears on Fox News," *Modesto Bee*, January 7, 2019, https://www.modbee.com/latest-news/article224035430.html [accessed May 2, 2019].

48. Tax-deductible donations to the Ronil Singh Memorial Fund can be made online at https://www.stanislaussworn.com/donation.html or by check payable to Corporal Ronil Singh Memorial Fund, Stanislaus Sworn Deputies Association, PO Box 2314, Ceres, CA 95307.

49. "FUNDRAISER CPL. RONIL SINGH," Bay Area Brewers Guild, https://sfbeerweek.org/
events/bibos-fundraiser.

50. David A. Patten, "NYC Police Hold Fundraiser for Fallen Calif. Cpl. Ronil
Singh" Newsmax, January 31, 2019, https://www.newsmax.com/newsfront/
ronil-singh-blue-lives-police-shooting-illegal-immigrant/2019/01/31/id/900667/.

51. Alyssa Milano (@Alyssa_Milano), "Eduardo is in Irwin Detention Facility which has
numerous human rights abuse cases against it. The Southern Poverty Law Center tried to
do a wellness check on him & the facility refused to grant access. This case is being fast-
tracked due to his immigrant right activism," Twitter, December 30, 2018, 11:37 a.m.,
https://twitter.com/Alyssa_Milano/status/1079461449750081536.

52. Karen Morales, "Mass leaders push for DACA legislation," *Bay State
Banner*, January 10, 2018, https://www.baystatebanner.com/2018/01/10/
mass-leaders-push-for-daca-legislation/.

53. Morales, "Mass leaders push for DACA legislation."

54. United We Dream (@UNITEDWEDREAM), "ICE detained and deported Odalis' friend,
Eduardo Samaniego. On their #ICEShamefulSixteen, Congress should CUT funding
from ICE. Text MeltICE to 877877," March 1, 2019, 11:13 a.m., https://twitter.com/
UNITEDWEDREAM/status/1101560993140875264.

55. Alyssa Milano (@Alyssa_Milano), "Oh, yes! Let's #GoFundTheWall while not taking care
of our veterans. Cool. Cool. Cool," Twitter, December 20, 2018, 9:24 a.m., https://twitter.
com/Alyssa_Milano/status/1075804158320492544.

56. Twitter search "#FamiliesBelongTogether from:alyssa_milano," https://twitter.com/search?
l=&q=%23FamiliesBelongTogether%20from%3Aalyssa_milano&src=typd.

57. Alyssa Milano (@Alyssa_Milano), "Why is Trump wasting time at the border advocating
for a wall no one wants!? Reminder: children are still separated from their families. That's
the real crisis, and he created it. #FamiliesBelongTogether #NoWall," Twitter, January 10,
2019, 2:16 p.m., https://twitter.com/Alyssa_Milano/status/1083487743613661184.

58. Twitter search "singh from:alyssa_milano," https://twitter.com/search?l=&q=singh%20
from%3Aalyssa_milano&src=typd.

59. "Clooney's Italian Villa," CBS News, March 16, 2006, https://www.cbsnews.com/
pictures/clooneys-italian-villa/4/.

60. Camilla Turner, "Steer clear of George Clooney's luxury villa, by law," *The Telegraph*,
April 6, 2015, https://www.telegraph.co.uk/news/celebritynews/11517677/Steer-clear-
of-George-Clooneys-luxury-villa-by-law.html; Nick Squires, "George Clooney's villa
protected by 'no-go zone' after paparazzi nuisance," *The Telegraph*, June 24, 2014, https://
www.telegraph.co.uk/news/worldnews/europe/italy/10925551/George-Clooneys-villa-
protected-by-no-go-zone-after-paparazzi-nuisance.html.

61. Alex Ritman, "George Clooney: Donald Trump Is a 'Xenophobic Fascist,'"
Hollywood Reporter, March 3, 2016, https://www.hollywoodreporter.com/news/
george-clooney-donald-trump-is-872492.

62. Kipp Jones, "Amal Clooney Slams Trump: 'Building Walls' Doesn't Represent 'U.S.
Values,'" Breitbart, April 26, 2016, https://www.breitbart.com/entertainment/2016/04/26/
amal-clooney-slams-trump-immigration-building-walls-doesnt-represent-u-s-values/.

63. Corinne Heller and Sarah Kitnick, "George Clooney & Amal Host
Pricey Hillary Clinton Fundraiser, Ellen DeGeneres Among Guests,"
E! News, April 17, 2016, https://www.eonline.com/news/757506/
george-clooney-amal-host-pricey-hillary-clinton-fundraiser-ellen-degeneres-among-guests.

64. Nick Fagge, "EXCLUSIVE – 'We don't want ANY refugees here': George
Clooney's super rich Lake Como neighbours say Italian idyll is being RUINED
by migrants on their doorstep after Switzerland closes its border," *Daily
Mail*, July 14, 2016, https://www.dailymail.co.uk/news/article-3689928/

We-don-t-want-refugees-George-Clooney-s-super-rich-Lake-Como-neighbours-say-Italian-idyll-RUINED-migrants-doorstep-Switzerland-closes-border.html.

65. Jason Horowitz, "Immigration Moves Front and Center in Italy's Local Elections," *New York Times*, June 24, 2017, https://www.nytimes.com/2017/06/24/world/europe/italy-immigration-elections.html.

66. Horowitz, "Immigration Moves Front and Center in Italy's Local Elections."

67. Skogssjön, "A quick & easy fix to the European Migration Crisis #GiorgiaMeloni," YouTube, January 26, 2019, https://www.youtube.com/watch?v=GzK874mthyk.

68. Skogssjön, "A quick & easy fix to the European Migration Crisis #GiorgiaMeloni."

69. Ibid.

70. Ibid.

71. Ryan Parker, "George and Amal Clooney Donate $100,000 to Help Migrant Children," *Hollywood Reporter,* June 20, 2018, https://www.hollywoodreporter.com/news/george-amal-clooney-donate-100000-aid-migrant-children-1121758.

72. "About the Young Center," Young Center for Immigrant Children's Rights, https://www.theyoungcenter.org/about-the-young-center.

73. "About the Young Center," Young Center for Immigrant Children's Rights.

74. "Frequently Asked Questions," Young Center for Immigrant Children's Rights, https://www.theyoungcenter.org/faq.

75. Hayden Ludwig, "Tides' Legal Laundering: An Incubator for the Left," Capital Research Center, March 27, 2018, https://capitalresearch.org/article/tides-legal-laundering-an-incubator-for-the-left-three/.

76. Michelle Malkin, "ACORN Watch: Louisiana Investigates," Michellemalkin.com, August 6, 2009, http://michellemalkin.com/2009/08/06/acorn-watch-louisiana-investigates/.

77. ProPublica Nonprofit Explorer, Tides Foundation Form 990 for the 2017 calendar year, ProPublica, https://projects.propublica.org/nonprofits/organizations/943213100/201803199349319315/IRS990.

78. Jose Antontio Vargas, "Trapped on the Border," *Politico*, July 11, 2014, https://www.politico.com/magazine/story/2014/07/texas-border-trapped-108826#.U8VNe_RDuVN.

79. Jose Antonio Vargas, "My Life as an Undocumented Immigrant," *New York Times Magazine*, June 22, 2011, https://www.nytimes.com/2011/06/26/magazine/my-life-as-an-undocumented-immigrant.html?pagewanted=all&_r=1&.

80. "About", Define American, https://defineamerican.com/about/.

81. Michael Scherer, "Jose Antonio Vargas' Emotional Senate Testimony," *Time*, February 14, 2013, http://swampland.time.com/2013/02/14/jose-antonio-vargas-emotional-senate-testimony/.

82. "About", Define American.

83. Jose Antonio Vargas (@joseiswriting), "This is what happens when a government believes people are 'illegal.' Kids in cages," Twitter, June 11, 2018, 9:45 p.m., https://twitter.com/joseiswriting/status/1006397160622055429.

84. Ron Perlman (@perlmutations), "Trump, Sessions, McConnell, Ryan, this is on YOU!" Twitter, June 12, 2018, 6:30 p.m., https://twitter.com/perlmutations/status/1006710482533617664.

85. Greg Pollowitz, "Busted! The viral photo of the kid in the cage is from a staged protest, not because of Trump," Twitchy, June 13, 2018, https://twitchy.com/gregp-3534/2018/06/13/busted-the-viral-photo-of-the-kid-in-the-cage-is-from-a-staged-protest-not-because-of-trump/.

86. Brown Berets de Cemanahuac -Texas Chapter Facebook page, https://www.facebook.com/pg/Brownberetsofdfw/photos/?ref=page_internal.

87. Scott Roxborough, "Berlin: George, Amal Clooney Meet Angela Merkel to Discuss Refugee Crisis," *Hollywood Reporter*, February 12, 2016, https://www.hollywoodreporter.com/news/berlin-george-amal-clooney-merkel-864588.

88. THR Staff, "George Clooney Reveals a Yazidi Refugee Is Living in His Home," *Hollywood Reporter*, September 6, 2017, 9:30 a.m., https://www.hollywoodreporter.com/news/george-clooney-reveals-a-yazidi-refugee-is-living-his-home-1035726.

89. "Refugee Resettlement," Clooney Foundation for Justice, https://cfj.org/refugee-resettlement/.

90. A report by *Life & Style* magazine that the Clooneys had "abandoned" the home over security concerns proved untrue. *Life & Style Weekly*, "George Clooney Plans to Move Amal and Twins Back to LA for Security Reasons (EXCLUSIVE)," July 10, 2017, https://www.lifeandstylemag.com/posts/george-clooney-twins-135725/.

91. Emmeline Saunders, "Inside Amal and George Clooney's secret battle to protect their family from ISIS," *Daily Mirror*, June 6, 2019, https://www.mirror.co.uk/3am/celebrity-news/inside-amal-george-clooneys-secret-16268250.

92. David Sims, "The Embarrassment of Jimmy Fallon," *The Atlantic*, September 16, 2016, https://www.theatlantic.com/entertainment/archive/2016/09/the-embarrassment-of-jimmy-fallon-by-donald-trump/500354/.

93. David Itzkoff, "Jimmy Fallon Was on Top of the World. Then Came Trump," *New York Times*, May 17, 2017, https://www.nytimes.com/2017/05/17/arts/television/jimmy-fallon-tonight-show-interview-trump.html.

94. Sonia Saraiya, "Jimmy Fallon Gets Trumped by Donald Trump," *Variety*, September 16, 2016, https://variety.com/2016/tv/columns/jimmy-fallon-donald-trump-tonight-show-no-credibility-1201862755/.

95. Jake Nevins, "How Fallon fell: why is the late-night host floundering in Trump's America?" *The Guardian*, October 16, 2017, https://www.theguardian.com/culture/2017/oct/16/how-fallon-fell-why-is-the-late-night-host-floundering-in-trumps-america.

96. 96   John Koblin, "NBC Assigns Veteran Producer to Clean Up Jimmy Fallon's Ratings Mess," *New York Times*/WRAL, October 24, 2018, https://www.wral.com/nbc-assigns-veteran-producer-to-clean-up-jimmy-fallon-s-ratings-mess/17943008/.

97. Scott Feinberg, "'Awards Chatter' Podcast — Jimmy Fallon ('The Tonight Show Starring Jimmy Fallon')," *Hollywood Reporter*, June 19, 2018, https://www.hollywoodreporter.com/race/awards-chatter-podcast-jimmy-fallon-nbc-tonight-show-trump-interview-fallout-1121060.

98. Donald Trump (@realDonaldTrump), ".@jimmyfallon is now whimpering to all that he did the famous 'hair show' with me (where he seriously messed up my hair), & that he would have now done it differently because it is said to have 'humanized' me—he is taking heat. He called & said 'monster ratings.' Be a man Jimmy!" Twitter, June 24, 2018, 5:01 p.m., https://twitter.com/realDonaldTrump/status/1011036519812030467.

99. Jimmy Fallon (@jimmyfallon), "In honor of the President's tweet I'll be making a donation to RAICES in his name," Twitter, June 24, 2018, 7:53 p.m., https://twitter.com/jimmyfallon/status/1011079815057891328.

100. Joe Dwinell and Owen Boss, "Illegal immigrants flown to Bay State," *Boston Herald*, July 13, 2014; updated November 18, 2018, https://www.bostonherald.com/2014/07/13/illegal-immigrants-flown-to-bay-state/.

101. Dwinell and Boss, "Illegal immigrants flown to Bay State."

102. Michelle Malkin, "Military bases: Obama's new illegal alien dumping grounds," Michellemalkin.com, June 10, 2014, http://michellemalkin.com/2014/06/10/military-bases-obamas-new-illegal-alien-dumping-grounds/.

103. Lukas Mikelionis, "Former Obama Official, Liberal Activists Share 2014 Photos from Detention Facility As Swipe at Trump," Fox News, May 28, 2018, https://www.foxnews.

com/politics/former-obama-official-liberal-activists-share-2014-photos-from-detention-facility-as-swipe-at-trump.

104. Jon Favreau (@jonfavs), "2. In 2014, when the Obama Administration dealt with an influx of unaccompanied minors who showed up at the border, fleeing violence from Central America, the agencies charged with sheltering the children were overwhelmed, and the conditions were often atrocious," Twitter, May 29, 2018, 9:45 a.m., https://twitter.com/jonfavs/status/1001504737013809152.

105. Mia Farrow (@MiaFarrow), "Children of immigrants are being held in cages like animals at @ICEgov detention centers. Tell ICE and your elected officials that this is horrifyingly unacceptable. In addition to tearing children from their mothers arms- ICE has LOST 1500 kids. #WhereAreTheChildren," Twitter, May 27, 2018, 11:46 a.m., https://twitter.com/MiaFarrow/status/1000810528078487553.

106. Rosanna Arquette (@RoArquette), "How can we as human beings allow this. ? This cannot continue or we are not human. this is evil… sick crime against Humanity..we are responsible… we must stop this now azcentral.com/picture-galler…," Twitter, May 27, 2018, 2:25 p.m., https://twitter.com/RoArquette/status/1000850485002276864.

107. Reese Witherspoon (@ReeseW), "Attn ALL U.S.Senators & U. S. Representatives: Please support the Keep Families Together Act. This atrocity must end. Please Support S. 3036," Twitter, June 18, 2018, 8:38 a.m., https://twitter.com/ReeseW/status/1008735605746905089.

108. Oprah Winfrey (@Oprah), "Babies torn from their parents. Can't stand it! Will be watching @GayleKing and her colleagues LIVE from Texas. @CBSThisMorning 7am," Twitter, June 17, 2018, 9:10 p.m., https://twitter.com/Oprah/status/1008562641990647808.

109. Ellen DeGeneres (@TheEllenShow), "I don't care what your politics are, we can't be a country that separates children from their parents. Do something about this, here," Twitter, June 18, 2018, 12:11 p.m., https://twitter.com/TheEllenShow/status/1008789401260953601.

110. Chrissy Teigen (@chrissyteigen), "happy birthday, @realDonalTrump," Twitter, June 14, 2018, 10:37 a.m., https://twitter.com/chrissyteigen/status/1007316045793595393.

111. "John Legend & Chrissy Teigen," Celebrity Net Worth, https://www.celebritynetworth.com/couples/john-legend-chrissy-teigen-net-worth/.

112. Chrissy Teigen (@chrissyteigen), "You didn't think your $7.20 would be much. Some of you gave $72 you barely had. In just two days, you guys donated over $1,000,000 to the @ACLU. Over 20,000 of you donated. You. Did. That. I am so grateful, so happy, so humbled and hopeful to live amongst you wonderful beings," Twitter, June 16, 2018, 10:44 a.m., https://twitter.com/chrissyteigen/status/1008042630083514370.

113. "Judd Apatow Net Worth," Celebrity Net Worth, https://www.celebritynetworth.com/richest-celebrities/directors/judd-apatow-net-worth/.

114. Samantha Wilson, "Families Belong Together: Facts About Protest Against Separating Migrant Families At Border," Hollywood Life, June 19, 2018, https://hollywoodlife.com/2018/06/19/what-is-families-belong-together-protest-migrant-children/.

115. Jessica Morales Rocketto LinkedIn page, LinkedIn, https://www.linkedin.com/in/jessica-morales-rocketto-39516015.

116. Selena Gomez (@selenagomez), "Families seeking safety in our country need protection, understanding and opportunity, not detention. This is a moral choice, not a political one. #keepfamiliestogether #june30," Twitter, June 29, 2018, 6:09 p.m., https://twitter.com/selenagomez/status/1012865570629300224.

117. Twitter search "border, OR immigration from:selenagomez since: 2014-01-01 until:2014-12-31," https://twitter.com/search?l=&q=border%2C%20OR%20immigration%20from%3Aselenagomez%20since%3A2014-01-01%20until%3A2014-12-31&src=typd.

118. America Ferrera, "Thank You, Donald Trump!" *HuffPost*, July 2, 2015, https://www.huffpost.com/entry/thank-you-donald-trump_b_7709126.

119. "Families Belong Together — Partners," MoveOn, https://act.moveon.org/survey/families-belong-together-partners/.

120. Hilary Weaver, ""Things Are Off-Kilter": Broadway Unites for Migrant Families at Concert for America," *Vanity Fair*, July 1, 2018, https://www.vanityfair.com/style/2018/07/broadway-unites-for-concert-for-america-to-help-migrant-families?verso=true.

121. Elaine Aradillas, "Evan Rachel Wood Fasts Over Immigration Crisis as Detained Mom Describes Kids 'Crying for Their Mothers,'" *People*, June 24, 2018, https://people.com/human-interest/evan-rachel-wood-fasts-immigration-crisis-detained-mom-living-conditions/.

122. Mark Krikorian, "Happy National Border Control Day," *National Review*, March 31, 2019, https://www.nationalreview.com/2019/03/cesar-chavez-birthday-national-border-control-day/.

123. Aradillas, "Evan Rachel Wood Fasts Over Immigration Crisis."

124. Brandon Davis, "Evan Rachel Wood Opens Up on Border Patrol Hunger Strike, Experience at Detention Centers," comicbook.com, July 6, 2018, https://comicbook.com/2018/07/06/evan-rachel-wood-hunger-strike-us-border-texas-visit/.

125. "Voto Latino (VL)," Discover the Networks, last updated: July 2, 2019 https://www.discoverthenetworks.org/organizations/voto-latino-vl/.

126. Amy Guthrie, "Hollywood Actors Seek Truth at Tijuana Migrant Shelters," NBC 5, March 11, 2019, https://www.nbcdfw.com/news/national-international/Hollywood-Actresses-Seek-Truth-at-Tijuana-Migrant-Shelters-506972261.html.

127. Judy Kurtz, "Rami Malek delivers pro-immigrant message in Oscars speech," *The Hill*, February 24, 2019, https://thehill.com/blogs/in-the-know/431369-rami-malek-delivers-pro-immigrant-message-in-oscars-speech.

128. Judy Kurtz, "Javier Bardem knocks 'borders,' 'walls' during Oscars speech in Spanish," *The Hill*, February 24, 2019, https://thehill.com/blogs/in-the-know/431364-javier-bardem-knocks-borders-walls-during-oscars-speech-in-spanish.

129. Alex Zaragosa, "Javier Bardem Sent Trump a Low Key Fuck You," *Vice*, February 24, 2019, https://www.vice.com/en_us/article/59xwa5/javier-bardem-sent-trump-a-low-key-fuck-you.

130. Thomas Shuck (@geologyguy), "I have a lot of talent but the wall around the Oscars prevented me from getting in.... along with the heavily armed guards and police," Twitter, February 25, 2019, 8:58 a.m., https://twitter.com/geologyguy/status/1100077570941468673.

131. 2Strikes (@OneLateralus), "Meanwhile everyone there lives in gated communities and have fortresses around their homes. They are completely out of touch, the majority of Americans want our borders secure," Twitter, February 25, 2019, 11:39 a.m., https://twitter.com/OneLateralus/status/1100118116598759424.

132. Ethan Sacks, "Javier Bardem's Spanish speech doesn't draw applause from conservative Oscar viewers," NBC News, February 24, 2019, https://www.nbcnews.com/card/javier-bardem-s-spanish-speech-doesn-t-draw-applause-conservative-n975421.

133. Judy Kurtz, "José Andrés Honors Immigrants, Women in Oscars Speech," *The Hill*, February 24, 2019, https://thehill.com/blogs/in-the-know/431366-jose-andres-honors-immigrants-women-in-oscars-speech.

134. Brent Lang, "Alfonso Cuarón on His New Oscars, Netflix and if Trump Should Watch 'Roma,'" *Variety*, https://variety.com/2019/film/features/alfonso-cuaron-roma-oscars-netflix-trump-1203149939/.

135. Latifah Muhammad, "Eva Longoria Reacts to 'Roma's' Historic Wins at 2019 Oscars (Exclusive)," Yahoo Entertainment, February 24, 2019, https://www.yahoo.com/entertainment/eva-longoria-reacts-apos-roma-044212110.html.

136. Constitution of Mexico, https://www.oas.org/juridico/mla/en/mex/en_mex-int-text-const.pdf.

137. Constitution of Mexico.

138. Michelle Malkin, "Reminder: How Mexico Treats 'Undesirable' Foreigners," Michellemalkin.com, March 27, 2013, http://michellemalkin.com/2013/03/27/reminder-how-mexico-treats-undesirable-foreigners/.

139. James Fredrick, "Shouting 'Mexico First,' Hundreds In Tijuana March Against Migrant Caravan," NPR, November 19, 2018, https://www.npr.org/2018/11/19/669193788/shouting-mexico-first-hundreds-in-tijuana-march-against-migrant-caravan.

140. Fredrick, "Shouting 'Mexico First,' Hundreds In Tijuana March Against Migrant Caravan."

141. "Guillermo del Toro at Oscars: 'I Am an Immigrant,'" Yahoo News, March 4, 2018, https://news.yahoo.com/guillermo-del-toro-oscars-am-044132798.html.

142. Frank Angones (@FrankAngones), "The #DuckTale Writers believe families are stronger together. We join with @Vida_Starz @OneDayAtATime and other donating to @RAICESTEXAS to support legal services for separated families. #onevidaatatime #endfamilyseparation #keepfamiliestogether tinyurl.com/onevida," Twitter, June 21, 2018, 12:34 p.m., https://twitter.com/frankangones/status/1009882219018518528?lang=en.

143. Charlotte Willner, "Reunite an immigrant parent with their child; Fundraiser for RAICES by Charlotte Willner and Dave Willner," Facebook, June 16, 2018, https://www.facebook.com/donate/490507544717085/492577791176727/.

144. Ellen Gray, "Get ready for a 'Party of Five' remake that puts immigration—and family separation—front and center," Philadelphia Inquirer, February 6, 2019, https://www.philly.com/entertainment/tv/tv-party-of-five-remake-reboot-freeform-immigration-20190206.html.

145. Nellie Andreeva, "Sanctuary Family Comedy In Works At ABC As Immigration Projects Remain Hot," Deadline, September 20, 2017, https://deadline.com/2017/09/sanctuary-family-comedy-abc-david-feeney-immigration-1202174034/.

146. Joe Otterson, "Gina Rodriguez Developing Pair of Latino Series at CBS, CW," Variety, September 6, 2017, https://variety.com/2017/tv/news/gina-rodriguez-latino-series-cbs-cw-1202548583/.

147. Karen Townsend, "ICE Agent on 'Grey's Anatomy:' 'I Don't Know What We're Doing Anymore,'" NewsBusters, April 12, 2018, https://www.newsbusters.org/blogs/culture/karen-townsend/2018/04/12/greys-anatomy-ice-agent-doesnt-know-what-were-doing-anymore.

148. Karen Townsend, "'Star' Plot Twist: An Illegal Alien Discovers His Status, Told He's Not 'Safe,'" NewsBusters, April 12, 2018, https://www.newsbusters.org/blogs/culture/karen-townsend/2018/04/12/star-plot-twist-illegal-alien-discovers-his-status.

149. Jose Bastidas, "'The Conners': Major Character May Leave Forever in Season Finale Cliffhanger," Pop Culture, February 19, 2019, https://popculture.com/tv-shows/2019/01/22/the-conners-major-character-may-leave-forever-season-finale-cliffhanger-emilio/.

150. Justin Caruso, "Samantha Bee Christmas Special Features 'Abolish ICE' Skaters, Blasts Trump's Immigration 'Cruelty,'" Breitbart, December 20, 2018, https://www.breitbart.com/entertainment/2018/12/20/samantha-bee-christmas-special-features-abolish-ice-skaters-blasts-trumps-immigration-cruelty/.

151. "Family Separation," Kids In Need of Defense, https://supportkind.org/our-work/family-separation-work/.

152. Karen Townsend, "'Murphy Brown' Threatens ICE Agents: 'I Will Spatchcock You,' Tries Intimidation to Stop Raid," NewsBusters, November 22, 2018, https://www.newsbusters.org/blogs/culture/karen-townsend/2018/11/22/murphy-brown-threatens-ice-agents-i-will-spatchcock-you.

153. Jose Antonio Vargas (@joseiswriting), "More than ever, we need STORIES to humanize people and liberate them from the limits of partisan politics. Thank you for your leadership, @shondarhimes: variety.com/2018/tv/news/g…@GreysABC @DefineAmerican," Twitter, April 12, 2018, 6:14 p.m., https://twitter.com/joseiswriting/status/984600733650694144.

154. "Define American Releases Groundbreaking New Research," Define American, October 17, 2018, https://defineamerican.com/blog/define-american-releases-groundbreaking-new-research/.

155. Kyle Perisic, "Antifa Spreads List of ICE Agents Compiled Using LinkedIn and Blasts It Over Twitter," Daily Signal, June 20, 2018, https://www.dailysignal.com/2018/06/20/antifa-spreads-list-of-ice-agents-compiled-using-linkedin-and-blasts-it-over-twitter/.

156. Jose Antonio Vargas (@joseiswriting), "More than ever, we need STORIES to humanize people and liberate them from the limits of partisan politics."

157. "Kendall Jenner stalker ends up by her pool…Ain't No Mountain High Enough," TMZ, October 10, 2018, https://www.tmz.com/2018/10/18/kendall-jenner-stalker-breaks-into-gated-community-pool-porch/.

158. Janice Williams, "Who is John Ford? Kendall Jenner's alleged stalker ordered to stay 100 yards away from model," *Newsweek*, November 9, 2018, https://www.newsweek.com/john-ford-kendall-jenner-stalker-1209811.

159. Marissa G. Muller, "Gigi Hadid and Kendall Jenner Speak Out Against Donald Trump's Immigration Policy," *W Magazine*, June 20, 2018, https://www.wmagazine.com/story/gigi-hadid-kendall-jenner-speak-out-donald-trump-immigration-policy.

Chapter 8

1. Michael Woodward, "Trump and the Death of Civility in America," Psychology Today, August 11, 2016, https://www.psychologytoday.com/us/blog/spotting-opportunity/201608/trump-and-the-death-civility-in-america.

2. Jonathan Vankin, "Ana Navarro: 5 Fast Facts You Need To Know," heavy.com, October 9, 2016, https://heavy.com/news/2016/10/ana-navarro-donald-trump-pussy-scottie-neil-hughes-video-cnn/.

3. "Ana Navarro," Harvard Kennedy School Institute of Politics, Fall 2013, https://iop.harvard.edu/fellows/ana-navarro.

4. "The Seven Amnesties Passed by Congress," NumbersUSA, August 26, 2009, https://www.numbersusa.com/content/learn/illegal-immigration/seven-amnesties-passed-congress.html#4.

5. "The Seven Amnesties Passed by Congress," NumbersUSA.

6. Ed O'Keefe, "Jeb Bush: Many Illegal Immigrants Come out of an 'Act of Love,'" *Washington Post*, April 6, 2014, https://www.washingtonpost.com/news/post-politics/wp/2014/04/06/jeb-bush-many-illegal-immigrants-come-out-of-an-act-of-love/?utm_term=.d73df4850afa.

7. Jason Horowitz, "Jeb Bush, Ana Navarro and the Question That May Have Been Misheard," *New York Times*, May 13, 2015, https://www.nytimes.com/2015/05/13/us/politics/jeb-bush-ana-navarro-and-the-question-that-may-have-been-misheard.html.

8. Horowitz, "Jeb Bush, Ana Navarro and the Question That May Have Been Misheard."

9.   Kyle Moss, "CNN contributor Ana Navarro files her nails on air during debate over border wall," Yahoo Entertainment, January 10, 2019, https://www.yahoo.com/entertainment/cnn-guest-ana-navarro-files-nails-air-debate-border-wall-184738719.html.

10.   CNN, "Navarro files her nails during border wall debate," YouTube, January 9, 2019, https://www.youtube.com/watch?v=1XafNLZrKAo.

11.   Ana Navarro-Cárdenas (@ananavarro), "My Dem hubby, @JebBush workout buddy—/ 'I think it's 60% he runs in '16 and I'll even vote for him.' Did I mention he's a Friend of Bill's?" Twitter, January 7, 2014, 6:28 p.m., https://twitter.com/ananavarro/status/424367614878842880.

12.   Chabeli Herrera, "Biltmore Hotel Staying in Hands of Longtime Operator Gene Prescott," *Miami Herald*, June 24, 2016, https://www.miamiherald.com/news/business/tourism-cruises/article85822242.html.

13.   McKay Coppins, "The Future of the Republican Party Is by the Pool at the Biltmore," BuzzFeed, February 12, 2013, https://www.buzzfeednews.com/article/mckaycoppins/the-future-of-the-republican-party-is-by-the-pool-at-the-bil.

14.   Natalie Stone and Rachel DeSantis, "CNN's Ana Navarro Marries Al Cardenas in Miami Beach: All the Details!" *People*, March 3, 2019, https://people.com/tv/ana-navarro-marries-al-cardenas/.

15.   Jack Martin, "'No Labels' Gets It Wrong," ImmigrationReform.com, July 29, 2016, https://www.immigrationreform.com/2016/07/29/no-labels-gets-it-wrong/.

16.   Breitbart News, "CPAC Turns Away Pamela Geller," Breitbart, March 1, 2013, https://www.breitbart.com/politics/2013/03/01/CPAC-Turns-Away-Pamela-Geller/.

17.   Pamela Geller, "Geller: CPAC Doesn't Deserve Name 'Conservative,'" Freedom Outpost, February 27, 2016, https://freedomoutpost.com/geller-cpac-doesnt-deserve-name-conservative/.

18.   Jennifer Rubin, "CPAC Missteps Again [UPDATED]," *Washington Post*, March 5, 2013, https://www.washingtonpost.com/blogs/right-turn/wp/2013/03/05/cpac-missteps-again/.

19.   911Infidel, "People's Choice Blog Award Now Grover's Choice Blog Award?," The Right Scoop, March 8, 2013, https://therightscoop.com/has-the-peoples-choice-blog-award-morphed-into-the-growers-choice-blog-award/.

20.   Alex Seitz-Wald, "Exclusive: Conservative Board Unanimously Condemned Gaffney's 'Reprehensible' And 'Unfounded' Attacks," Think Progress, February 12, 2012, https://thinkprogress.org/exclusive-conservative-board-unanimously-condemned-gaffneys-reprehensible-and-unfounded-attacks-5d7634e08db5/.

21.   Michelle Malkin, "Alec Baldwin's New Best Friend Is a GOP Strategist—No, Really!" Jewish World Review, October 22, 2003, http://www.jewishworldreview.com/michelle/malkin102203.asp.

22.   Ryan Mauro, "Grover Norquist & Co. Build Islamist Influence in GOP," Center for Security Policy, March 4, 2014, https://www.centerforsecuritypolicy.org/2014/03/04/grover-norquist-co-build-islamist-influence-in-gop/.

23.   Ryan Mauro, "Bush Was To Meet Muslim Brotherhood Affiliates on 9/11," Clarion Project, April 2, 2015, https://clarionproject.org/bush-was-meet-muslim-brotherhood-affiliates-911/.

24.   Fox News, "Some Muslim Leaders Seen With Bush Expressed Support for Terrorist Groups," October 1, 2001; last updated January 13, 2015, https://www.foxnews.com/story/some-muslim-leaders-seen-with-bush-expressed-support-for-terrorist-groups.

25.   Al Cardenas, "To Do Nothing Would Be De Facto Amnesty," *Washington Times*, July 11, 2013, https://www.washingtontimes.com/news/2013/jul/11/decision-time-for-immigration-reform/.

26. Matthew Boyle, "CPAC Immigration Debate Stacked 3-to-1 with Pro-Amnesty Panelists," Breitbart, March 6, 2014, http://www.breitbart.com/Big-Government/2014/03/06/Former-House-Judiciary-Chairman-CPAC-is-liberal-on-immigration.

27. Leigh Ann Caldwell, "Immigration Speaker Sparks Controversy at CPAC," CBS News, February 11, 2012, https://www.cbsnews.com/news/immigration-speaker-sparks-controversy-at-cpac/.

28. "GOP Presidential Candidates Should Denounce Bigotry of White Nationalist Featured at CPAC," People For the American Way, February 8, 2012, http://www.pfaw.org/press-releases/gop-presidential-candidates-should-denounce-bigotry-of-white-nationalist-featured-at-cpac/.

29. Alexandra Hutzler, "Former Florida GOP Chair Says Trump's Attack Ad Will Cement His 'Bigoted Legacy Forever,'" Newsweek, November 1, 2018, https://www.newsweek.com/former-florida-gop-chair-trump-attack-ad-cements-bigoted-legacy-1196918.

30. Pam Key, "Ana Navarro: Trump Is a 'Racist Pig,'" Breitbart, November 5, 2018, https://www.breitbart.com/clips/2018/11/05/ana-navarro-trump-is-a-racist-pig/.

31. Sam Stanton, "'He Shot Them Both,' Defense Lawyer Says of Illegal Immigrant Accused of Killing Two Cops," Sacramento Bee, January 16, 2018; updated January 18, 2018, https://www.sacbee.com/news/local/article194874024.html.

32. Michelle Malkin, "Weapons of Mass Manipulation," Michellemalkin.com, June 19, 2018, http://michellemalkin.com/2018/06/19/weapons-of-mass-manipulation/.

33. Gabrielle Birkner, "JTA Twitter 50: Talia Lavin," Jewish Telegraphic Agency, December 15, 2018, https://www.jta.org/2018/12/15/culture/jta-twitter-50-talia-lavin.

34. "Talia Lavin," Influence Watch, https://www.influencewatch.org/person/talia-lavin/.

35. "Fact Checker," New Yorker, https://www.newyorker.com/home/about/fact-checker.

36. "Fact Checker," New Yorker.

37. Ibid.

38. ICE (@ICEgov), "Justin Gaertner is a combat wounded U.S. Marine who continues to serve his country as an ICE computer forensics analyst, helping solve criminal cases & rescue abused children. The tattoo shown here is the symbol for his platoon while he fought in Afghanistan," Twitter, June 18, 2018, 9:03 a.m., https://twitter.com/ICEgov/status/1008741908091428864.

39. Lia Eustachewich, "New Yorker fact-checker under fire after mistaking ICE worker's tattoo for Nazi symbol," New York Post, June 19, 2018, https://nypost.com/2018/06/19/new-yorker-fact-checker-under-fire-after-mistaking-ice-workers-tattoo-for-nazi-symbol/.

40. Talia Lavin (@chick_in_kiev), "some vets said this ICE agent's tattoo looked more like a Maltese cross than an Iron Cross (common among white supremacists), so I deleted my tweet so as not to spread misinformation," Twitter, June 17, 2018, 10:28 p.m., https://twitter.com/chick_in_kiev/status/1008582302459400192.

41. ICE (@ICEgov), "Read the full ICE statement regarding erroneous attacks on ICE employee for #military tattoo," Twitter, June 18, 2018, 9:03 a.m., https://twitter.com/ICEgov/status/1008741913355276288/photo/1.

42. Lia Eustachewich, "New Yorker Staffer Resigns after Falsely Accusing ICE Agent of Having Nazi Tattoo," New York Post, June 26, 2018, https://nypost.com/2018/06/26/new-yorker-staffer-resigns-after-falsely-accusing-ice-agent-of-having-nazi-tattoo/.

43. Howard Altman, "New Yorker Magazine Apologizes to Combat-Wounded Pasco Veteran over Staffer's Tweet," Tampa Bay Times, June 19, 2018, https://www.tampabay.com/news/military/veterans/New-Yorker-magazine-apologizes-to-combat-wounded-Pasco-veteran-over-staffer-s-Tweet_169286120.

44. Talia Lavin, "No, We Don't Have To Be Friends With Trump Supporters," The Forward, June 12, 2018, https://forward.com/opinion/402990/no-we-dont-have-to-be-friends-with-trump-supporters/.

45. Lavin, "No, We Don't Have To Be Friends With Trump Supporters."

46. Birkner, "JTA Twitter 50: Talia Lavin."

47. Talia Lavin (@chick_in_kiev), "I went to a dinner party and told 'the ICE tweet story' and to be honest, it's a remarkable thing to look back at seven months later. I don't think I'm ready to write about it yet, but someday," Twitter, January 4, 2019, 8:37 p.m., https://twitter.com/chick_in_kiev/status/1081409330241568773; "I also realize I'm still processing it as a trauma (the death threats and antisemitic abuse, the reputational shredding, the absolute wall to wall bad faith from everyone, my face on Fox & Friends) and all its seismic aftershocks," Twitter, January 4, 2019, 8:40 p.m., https://twitter.com/chick_in_kiev/status/1081410178417917953.

48. Jon Levine (@LevineJonathan), "NYU has hired Talia Lavin to teach an undergraduate course called "Reporting on the Far Right" Lavin resigned from the New Yorker last year after falsely accusing a disabled war veteran of having a Nazi tattoo," Twitter, March 20, 2019, 9:16 a.m., https://twitter.com/LevineJonathan/status/1108402007549902851.

49. Jon Levine, "NYU Cancels Former New Yorker Fact-Checker Talia Lavin's Journalism Class," The Wrap, May 30, 2019, https://www.thewrap.com/nyu-cancels-former-new-yorker-fact-checker-talia-lavins-journalism-class/.

50. Brittany Shepherd, "How CPAC 2019 Has Gone for Reporters Who Cover the Far Right," *Washingtonian*, March 2, 2019, https://www.washingtonian.com/2019/03/02/how-cpac-2019-has-gone-for-reporters-who-cover-the-far-right/.

51. Tyler O'Neil, "Report Shows Online Ties Linking HuffPost, the Guardian, and SPLC to Antifa," PJ Media, May 21, 2019, https://pjmedia.com/trending/report-shows-online-ties-linking-huffpost-the-guardian-and-splc-to-antifa/.

52. O'Neil, "Report Shows Online Ties Linking HuffPost, the Guardian, and SPLC to Antifa."

53. Ibid.

54. Brian Stelter, "More Than 100 Newspapers Will Publish Editorials Decrying Trump's Anti-Press Rhetoric," https://money.cnn.com/2018/08/11/media/boston-globe-free-press-editorial/index.html.

55. Archived copy of the now-deleted article is available online at: https://web.archive.org/web/20190410200645/https://www.bostonglobe.com/ideas/2019/04/10/oneil/t0wEh4yEXHTzBttu77AGWK/story.html.

56. Luke O'Neil (@lukeoneil47), "'One of the biggest regrets of my life is not pissing in Bill Kristol's salmon.' Lol this is one of my favorite ledes I've ever written. bostonglobe.com/ideas/2019/04/ ... ," Twitter, April 10, 2019, 7:46 a.m., https://twitter.com/lukeoneil47/status/1115989558418604032.

57. Luke O'Neil (@lukeoneil47), "More context bostonglobe.com/ideas/2019/04 ... ,"April 10, 2019, 7:52 a.m., https://twitter.com/lukeoneil47/status/1115990854353805312.

58. O'Neil (@lukeoneil47), "More context bostonglobe.com/ideas/2019/04 ... "

59. Old-timers in the conservative blogosphere memorialized the "layers and layers" defense of CBS News in the aftermath of the infamous Rathergate/60 Minutes scandal. See John Hinderaker, "It's 2004 All Over Again," Power Line, April 2, 2017, https://www.powerlineblog.com/archives/2017/04/its-2004-all-over-again.php.

60. Shirley Leung (@leung), "Keep Kirstjen Nielsen unemployed and eating Grubhub over her kitchen sink bostonglobe.com/ideas/2019/04/...via @lukeoneil47," Twitter, April 10, 2019, 2:34 p.m. https://archive.is/AQLvy.

61. Rachel Slade (@RachelSlade1), Twitter, https://archive.fo/Jn4kV.

62. Boston Globe (@BostonGlobe), "In @GlobeOpinion: Keep Kirstjen Nielsen unemployed and eating Grubhub over her kitchen sink," April 10, 2019, 9:03 a.m., https://archive.fo/5RiHf.

63. Howie Carr, "Boston Globe's Phony Sanctimony Sounds A Bit Fishy," The Howie Carr Show, April 12, 2019, https://howiecarrshow.com/2019/04/12/boston-globes-phony-sanctimony-sounds-a-bit-fishy/.

64. Carr, "Boston Globe's Phony Sanctimony Sounds A Bit Fishy."

65. Tori Bedford, "Shirley Leung: Globe Owners Pulled Controversial Op-Ed Piece That 'Really Crossed The Line,'" WGBH, April 12, 2019, https://www.wgbh.org/news/local-news/2019/04/12/shirley-leung-globe-owners-pulled-controversial-op-ed-piece-that-really-crossed-the-line.

66. SJW Hunter, "Boston Globe Columnist Luke O'Neil Opines That He Wishes He Urinated In Bill Kristol's Food Because He's Conservative, Disparages 'Retards,' Urges You To Punch Trump Supporters," Turtleboy, April 11, 2019, https://turtleboysports.com/boston-globe-columnist-luke-oneil-opines-that-he-wishes-he-urinated-in-bill-kristols-food-because-hes-conservative-disparages-retards-urges-you-to-punch-trump-supporters/.

67. SJW Hunter, "Boston Globe Columnist Luke O'Neil Opines That He Wishes He Urinated In Bill Kristol's Food."

68. Dan Kennedy, "Shirley Leung To Resume Her Column As Globe Seeks Editorial Page Editor," Dankennedy.net, May 11, 2019, https://dankennedy.net/2019/05/11/shirley-leung-to-resume-her-column-as-globe-seeks-editorial-page-editor/.

69. Paul Farhi, "Washington Post To Be Sold to Jeff Bezos, the Founder of Amazon," *Washington Post*, August 5, 2013, https://www.washingtonpost.com/national/washington-post-to-be-sold-to-jeff-bezos/2013/08/05/ca537c9e-fe0c-11e2-9711-3708310f6f4d_story.html.

70. Kelsey Sutton, "Jeff Bezos: Trump's Treatment of the Press 'Erodes Our Democracy around the Edges,'" *Politico*, October 20, 2016, https://www.politico.com/blogs/on-media/2016/10/jeff-bezos-trumps-treatment-of-the-press-erodes-our-democracy-around-the-edges-230103.

71. Brian Fung and Elizabeth Dwoskin, "Amazon explores legal options against Trump's immigration ban," *Washington Post*, January 30, 2017, https://www.washingtonpost.com/news/the-switch/wp/2017/01/30/amazon-explores-legal-options-against-trumps-immigration-ban/.

72. Fung and Dwoskin, "Amazon Explores Legal Options against Trump's Immigration Ban," *Washington Post*, January 30, 2017, https://www.washingtonpost.com/?utm_term=.c3922d0f3d77.

73. Gary Maher, "Amazon CEO Jeff Bezos Announces $33 Million in Scholarships for 1000 Illegal Immigrants," USA Politics Today, January 12, 2018, https://www.usapoliticstoday.org/amazon-ceo-jeff-bezos-immigrants/.

74. Eugene Kim, "How Amazon CEO Jeff Bezos Reinvented the *Washington Post*, the 140-Year-Old Newspaper He Bought for $250 Million," Business Insider, May 15, 2016, https://www.businessinsider.com/how-the-washington-post-changed-after-jeff-bezos-acquisition-2016-5#in-fact-bezos-liked-the-opportunity-so-much-that-he-didnt-do-any-due-diligence-and-just-signed-the-first-250-million-offer-sheet-that-came-from-graham-3.

75. Nick Miroff and Robert Moore, "7-Year-Old Migrant Girl Taken into Border Patrol Custody Dies of Dehydration, Exhaustion," *Washington Post*, December 13, 2018, https://www.washingtonpost.com/world/national-security/7-year-old-migrant-girl-taken-into-border-patrol-custody-dies-of-dehydration-exhaustion/2018/12/13/8909e356-ff03-11e8-862a-b6a6f3ce8199_story.html.

76. Antonia Blumberg and Roque Planas, "7-Year-Old Migrant Girl Dies Of Dehydration In Border Patrol Custody," *HuffPost*, December 13, 2018; updated December 18, 2018, https://www.huffpost.com/entry/migrant-girl-dehydration-death-border-patrol_n_5c130106e4b0860b8b5cb03b.

77. Nomaan Merchant, "CBP Orders Medical Checks after Second Child's Death," Associated Press, December 25, 2018, https://apnews.com/0a7e7ec16cd743e4840c321a99e005ef.

78. PBS NewsHour (@NewsHour), "Juan de León Gutiérrez, a 16-year-old who died on April 30, was the third Guatemalan child to die in U.S. custody since December, heightening scrutiny of the U.S. government's ability to care for migrant families and children crossing the border," Twitter, May 9, 2019, 10:50 a.m., https://twitter.com/NewsHour/status/1126544863158128645.

79. Gabe Ortíz (@TUSK81), "A two-year-old boy is now the fourth Guatemalan child in the past six months to die after being taken into federal immigration custody. Border Network for Human Rights: "This is an appalling pattern of immorality and inhumanity," Twitter, May 16, 2019, 12:28 p.m., https://twitter.com/TUSK81/status/1129106292876824577.

80. Twitter search using keywords "border patrol murderers child died"; search results available online at: https://twitter.com/search?q=border%20patrol%20murderers%20child%20died&src=typd.

81. Twitter search using keywords "border patrol monsters"; search results available online at: https://twitter.com/search?f=tweets&vertical=default&q=border%20patrol%20monsters%20children&src=typd.

82. Twitter search using keywords "border patrol nazis"; search results available online at: https://twitter.com/search?f=tweets&q=border%20patrol%20nazis%20children&src=typd.

83. "Statement by U.S. Customs and Border Protection on the Death of a Seven-Year-Old Female Child," U.S. Customs and Border Protection, December 14, 2018, https://www.cbp.gov/newsroom/speeches-and-statements/statement-us-customs-and-border-protection-death-seven-year-old.

84. Shannon van Sant, "Autopsy for 7-Year-Old Migrant Who Died in U.S. Custody Shows She Died of Sepsis," NPR, March 30, 2019, https://www.npr.org/2019/03/30/708388844/autopsy-for-7-year-old-migrant-who-died-in-u-s-custody-shows-she-died-of-sepsis.

85. DailyMail.com Reporter, Reuters, and Associated Press, "Heartbreaking Photos of Open Casket Funeral of Guatemalan 7-Year-Old Who Died in Custody of Border Patrol as a SECOND Child Dies in a U.S. Detention Center," Daily Mail, December 25, 2018, https://www.dailymail.co.uk/news/article-6529209/Heartbreaking-photos-open-casket-funeral-Guatemalan-7-year-old-died-U-S-custody.html?fbclid=IwAR1rMH3FTL45ExP3gxFolzOlmkGm_yrOYSxJAtwrTaw_57GAOkvzlrhqsvo.

86. Gina Salamone, "Lawyers for Jakelin Caal, 7-Year-Old Who Died in Border Protection Custody, Say She Wasn't Given Water for Hours," Daily News, December 19, 2018, https://www.nydailynews.com/news/national/ny-news-jakelin-caal-20181219-story.html. I called the father's lawyer, Enrique Moreno, to ask who was paying Nery Caal's bills and where he is now. The law firm referred me to a co-counsel, who did not return my phone call.

87. NPR (@NPR), "JUST IN: A 2-year-old migrant child died on Wednesday in El Paso, Texas. This is the fourth Guatemalan minor to die after cording the border and being apprehended by the border patrol since December," Twitter, May 16, 2019, 7:04 a.m., https://twitter.com/NPR/status/1129024866496262144.

88. Michelle Malkin (@michellemalkin), "Fixed it for you: 'This is the 4th Guatemalan minor to die after being dragged 1,200 miles by reckless adults, who likely paid coyotes, who likely paid drug cartels, to cross the border, lured by Dem-sponsored amnesty magnets, cheap labor-hungry employers & sanctuary enablers," Twitter, May 16, 2019, 7:36 a.m., https://twitter.com/michellemalkin/status/1129032984839970816.

89. Linda Qiu, "No, Democrats Don't Want 'Open Borders,'" New York Times, June 27, 2018, https://www.nytimes.com/2018/06/27/us/politics/fast-check-donald-trump-democrats-open-borders.html.

90. Anna Giaritelli, "Keith Ellison Sports 'I Don't Believe in Borders' T-shirt," *Washington Examiner*, May 7, 2018, https://www.washingtonexaminer.com/news/keith-ellison-sports-i-dont-believe-in-borders-t-shirt.

91. Roque Planas and Angelina Chapin, "California's Attorney General Says Immigration Should Be Decriminalized," *HuffPost*, April 3, 2019, https://www.huffpost.com/entry/california-attorney-general-xavier-becerra-immigration-decriminalized_n_5ca38787e4b0c32979610abc?utm_source=reddit.com.

92. Michael Scherer, "Border Surge Puts Pressure on Democrats To Craft Their Own Immigration Solutions—Not Just Oppose Trump," *Washington Post*, April 2, 2019, https://www.washingtonpost.com/politics/border-surge-pressures-democrats-to-craft-their-own-immigration-solutions—not-just-oppose-trump/2019/04/02/4f074fd6-5494-11e9-8ef3-fbd41a2ce4d5_story.html?utm_term=.085127f44182&noredirect=on.

93. 8 U.S. Code § 1325. Improper entry by alien, https://www.law.cornell.edu/uscode/text/8/1325. "Any alien who (1) enters or attempts to enter the United States at any time or place other than as designated by immigration officers, or (2) eludes examination or inspection by immigration officers, or (3) attempts to enter or obtains entry to the United States by a willfully false or misleading representation or the willful concealment of a material fact, shall, for the first commission of any such offense, be fined under title 18 or imprisoned not more than 6 months, or both, and, for a subsequent commission of any such offense, be fined under title 18, or imprisoned not more than 2 years, or both."

94. Dara Lind, "Julián Castro Wants To Radically Restrict Immigration Enforcement," Vox, April 2, 2019, https://www.vox.com/2019/4/2/18291584/2020-immigration-democrats-policy-castro-abolish-ice.

95. Joseph A. Wulfsohn, "Ilhan Omar Slams Trump's 'Devastating' Immigration Plan, Renews Call To Abolish ICE," Fox News, May 17, 2019, https://www.foxnews.com/politics/ilhan-omar-slams-trumps-devastating-immigration-plan-renews-call-to-abolish-ice.

96. Reuters, "Carlos Slim Becomes Top New York Times Shareholder," January 14, 2015, https://www.reuters.com/article/us-new-york-times-warrants-carlos-slim-idUSKBN0KN2M820150114.

97. Chris Aspin, "Mexico's Slim Tells Bush To Invest in Latin America," Reuters, March 12, 2007, https://www.reuters.com/article/us-bush-latinamerica-slim-idUSN1240076520070313.

98. MacKinnon deleted the tweet, which was originally located at https://twitter.com/markmackinnon/status/771176062185201666. It has been saved at Soopermexican, "Shameless 'Journalists' Said THIS About Moms Whose Children Were MURDERED By Illegals!!" The Political Insider, September 2, 2016, https://thepoliticalinsider.com/shameless-journalists-sneer-angel-moms-whose-children-were-murdered-illegals/.

99. Rania Khalek (@RaniaKhalek), "What the hell is going on? These moms Trump brought on stage are like a hate group," Twitter, August 31, 2016, 7:39 p.m., https://twitter.com/RaniaKhalek/status/771175624085868544.

100. Tom Harrington (@cbctom), "MS-13 getting more mentions than infrastructure #SOTU," Twitter, January 30, 2018, 6:57 p.m., https://twitter.com/cbctom/status/958534573620649985.

101. John Iadorola (@johniadarola), "Multiple references to MS-13. No mention of climate change. #SOTU," January 30, 2018, 6:55 p.m., https://twitter.com/johniadarola/status/958534248423604224.

102. Joy Reid (@JoyAnnReid), "MS-13 (which most Americans who don't mainline Fox News likely have never heard of) has been mentioned tonight more than Russia. Actually, has Russia been mentioned at all? #SOTU," Twitter, January 30, 2018, 6:55 p.m., https://twitter.com/JoyAnnReid/status/958534282921889792.

103. It's a stunning admission, isn't it? Joy Reid is basically admitting that only Fox News viewers are adequately informed about the MS-13 criminal enterprise—and she is admitting that every other media outlet other than Fox News is failing to inform the public about a public safety threat deemed "high" by the FBI.

104. Jessica Chasmar, "Joy Reid: 'Nobody That Doesn't Watch Fox News Has Ever Heard' of MS-13," *Washington Times*, February 1, 2018, https://www.washingtontimes.com/news/2018/feb/1/joy-reid-nobody-doesnt-watch-fox-news-has-ever-hea/.

105. "The MS-13 Threat: A National Assessment," FBI, January 14, 2008, https://archives.fbi.gov/archives/news/stories/2008/january/ms13_011408.

106. Gary Legum (@GaryLegum), "Oh for fuck's sake, is Trump using the Angel Moms as props for this announcement?" Twitter, February 15, 2019, 7:24 a.m., https://twitter.com/GaryLegum/status/1096430032640266241.

107. Tina Vasquez (@TheTinaVasquez), "Ugh. The 'angel moms' are so fucking blatantly racist," Twitter, February 5, 2019, 7:24 p.m., https://twitter.com/TheTinaVasquez/status/1092987327486611462.

108. Sarah Reese Jones (@PoliticusSarah), "Republicans and Trump are using 'angel moms' to (misleadingly) defend the need for a wall, while they ignore the parents who have lost children to gun violence. 2016: 4,648 victims of homicide age 10-24. Average 13/day. 2015: 2,824 children age 0-19 yrs died by gunshot," Twitter, February 15, 2019, 1:04 p.m., https://twitter.com/PoliticusSarah/status/1096515563084546048.

109. See Michelle Malkin, "Who Gets Absolute Moral Authority?" *Townhall*, July 20, 2016, https://townhall.com/columnists/michellemalkin/2016/07/20/who-gets-absolute-moral-authority-n2194961.

110. CNN, "Mother of Slain Son to Jim Acosta: Trump Is Right," YouTube, February 15, 2019, https://www.youtube.com/watch?time_continue=83&v=WicfqYo7MmE.

111. Agnes Gibboney, "My Son Was Murdered by an Illegal Immigrant. Neither He Nor Mollie Tibbetts Deserved To Die," *USA Today*, August 23, 2018, https://www.usatoday.com/story/opinion/voices/2018/08/23/illegal-immigrant-molly-tibbitts-murder-crime-column/1074055002/.

112. Ian Schwartz, "Huckabee Sanders vs. Acosta on Child Migrants: 'I Know It Is Hard for You To Understand Even Short Sentences,'" RealClearPolitics, June 14, 2018, https://www.realclearpolitics.com/video/2018/06/14/huckabee_sanders_vs_acosta_on_child_migrants_i_know_it_is_hard_for_you_to_understand_even_short_sentences.html#!.

113. "Agnes Gibboney," FIGHT Sanctuary State, https://fightsanctuarystate.com/tag/agnes-gibboney/.

114. William McGowan, "Gray Lady Down On Immigration Is Deja Vu All Over Again (Again!)" Coloring the News, February 23, 2019, https://coloringthenews.blogspot.com/2019/02/gray-lady-down-on-immigration-deja-vu.html.

Appendix B

1. Anna Crowley and Kate Rosin, "Migration Governance and Enforcement Portfolio Review," Open Society Foundations, International Migration Initiative, May 12, 2016, https://archive.org/details/321383374OpenSocietyFoundationsInternationalMigrationInitiativeMigrationGovernan.

2. "About WTM," Watch the MED, http://watchthemed.net/index.php/page/index/3.

3. Crowley and Rosin, "Migration Governance and Enforcement Portfolio Review," 9.

4. PRESS TV, "New Integration Draft Bill Requires Refugees To Learn German," April 14, 2016, https://www.presstv.com/Detail/2016/04/14/460798/Germany-Angela-Merkel-PRO-ASYL.

5. "Who We Are," PRO ASYL, https://www.proasyl.de/en/who-we-are/.

6. "About This Site," W2Eu.info, https://w2eu.info/about.en.html.

7. Jonathan Samuels, "Sky Finds 'Handbook' for EU-Bound Migrants," Sky News, September 13, 2015, https://news.sky.com/story/sky-finds-handbook-for-eu-bound-migrants-10346437.

8. Samuels, "Sky Finds 'Handbook' For EU-Bound Migrants."

9. "About the Panos Network," Panos Network, https://panosnetwork.org/about.

10. "Who We Are," United Nations Alliance of Civilizations, https://www.unaoc.org/who-we-are/.

11. Chris Tomlinson, "Soros Group Brags About Pushing Racist Police Agenda In Europe, Undermining Stop And Search," Breitbart, August 16, 2016, https://www.breitbart.com/europe/2016/08/16/soros-group-brags-accusing-european-police-discriminatory-policies/.

12. European Foundation Center, https://www.efc.be/event/for-an-inclusive-europe-european-funders-countering-hatred-and-discrimination-based-on-racial-and-religious-bias/.

13. "Media Friendly Glossary for Migration," United Nations Alliance of Civilizations, 2014, https://www.unaoc.org/resource/media-friendly-glossary-for-migration/, 3.

14. Ibid., 19.

15. Paul Colford, "'Illegal Immigrant' No More," Associated Press, April 2, 2013, https://blog.ap.org/announcements/illegal-immigrant-no-more.

16. Michelle Malkin, "The Open Borders 'Journalists' Who Banned 'Illegal Immigrant,'" Michellemalkin.com, April 3, 2013, http://michellemalkin.com/2013/04/03/the-open-borders-journalists-who-banned-illegal-immigrant/.

17. Hans A. von Spakovsky, "'Undocumented Immigrant' Is a Made-Up Term That Ignores the Law," Heritage Foundation, July 30, 2018, https://www.heritage.org/immigration/commentary/undocumented-immigrant-made-term-ignores-the-law.

18. "ILO Launches Migration Glossary for Middle East Media," International Labour Organization, December 8, 2017, https://www.ilo.org/beirut/media-centre/news/WCMS_608874/lang—en/index.html.

19. "#SpreadNoHate: A Global Dialogue on Hate Speech against Migrants and Refugees in the Media," United Nations Alliance of Civilizations, https://www.unaoc.org/what-we-do/projects/hate-speech/.

20. "About the Project," My City of Migration, https://my.citiesofmigration.org/about-the-program/.

21. "About Cities of Migration," Cities of Migration, http://citiesofmigration.ca/about-2/.

22. "About the Project," My City of Migration.

23. "Experts & Staff," Migration Policy Institute, https://www.migrationpolicy.org/about/staff/demetrios-g-papademetriou.

24. Charity Navigator, "International Rescue Committee," December 1, 2018, https://www.charitynavigator.org/index.cfm?bay=search.summary&orgid=3898.

25. International Rescue Committee, Annual Report 2017, https://www.rescue.org/sites/default/files/document/2813/mkt1801annualreportwebfinal.pdf.

26. Forbes, "Billionaire George Soros Takes Top Honor at International Rescue Committee Benefit," December 2013, https://www.forbes.com/sites/forbeslifestyle/2013/11/26/billionaire-george-soros-takes-top-honor-at-international-rescue-committee-benefit/#377416f82603.

27. Nolan D. McCaskill, "George Soros To Give $500 Million to Migrant, Refugee Businesses," Politico, September 20, 2016, https://www.politico.com/story/2016/09/george-soros-refugee-wsj-228396.

28. Full text of International Rescue Committee's Form 990, Schedule I for fiscal year ending September 2017, ProPublica, https://projects.propublica.org/nonprofits/organizations/135660870/201811809349300506/IRS990ScheduleI.

29.   "The IRC's Impact at a Glance," International Rescue Committee, https://www.rescue.
      org/page/ircs-impact-glance.
30.   "Iraq Syria Complex Crisis," USAID, updated October 6, 2017, https://oig.usaid.gov/sites/
      default/files/2018-06/oig_dashboard_fy17q4_102017.pdf.
31.   Dan Sales, "Charity Fronted by David Miliband Lost Funding Due to 37
      Allegations of Fraud, Sex Abuse, and Bribery—but Public Were Never Told,"
      The Sun, February 13, 2018, https://www.thesun.co.uk/news/5571377/
      david-miliband-charity-cover-up-vice-sex-abuse-bribery-fraud/.
32.   "Aid Group IRC Acknowledges Three Sex Abuse Cases in
      DRC," eNCA, February 14, 2018, https://www.enca.com/africa/
      aid-group-irc-acknowledges-three-sex-abuse-cases-in-drc.
33.   James Simpson, "Resettling Refugees: Social and Economic Costs," Capital Research
      Center, September 14, 2018, https://capitalresearch.org/article/resettling-refugees-part-3/.

Appendix C

1.   Malkin, *Invasion*, 79–81.
2.   Ibid.
3.   The organization formally changed its name from "American Immigration Law Forum" in
      2009.
4.   "Nonprofit Explorer," Foundation to Promote Open Society Form 990 for period
      ending December 2015, ProPublica, https://projects.propublica.org/nonprofits/
      display_990/263753801/2016_11_PF%2F26-3753801_990PF_201512.
5.   American Immigration Council Financial Statements and Independent Auditors' Report,
      December 31, 2017 and 2016, https://americanimmigrationcouncil.org/sites/default/files/
      financial_statements_2017.pdf.
6.   American Immigration Council Financial Statements and Independent Auditors' Report,
      11.
7.   "Litigation," American Immigration Council, https://www.americanimmigrationcouncil.
      org/litigation.
8.   Open Society Foundations, https://www.opensocietyfoundations.org/
      grants-database?filter_keyword=constitutional#OR2016-30969.
9.   Michelle Malkin, "Radical Left-Wing Center for Constitutional
      Rights Represented Abu Sufian bin Qumu," Michellemalkin.
      com, September 20, 2012, http://michellemalkin.com/2012/09/20/
      radical-left-wing-center-for-constitutional-rights-represented-abu-sufian-bin-qumu/.
10.   Immigration Advocates Network website, https://www.immigrationadvocates.org/.
11.   "New Online Tool Created with Support from OSF Helps Immigrants Make a Plan,"
      Philanthropy New York, April 4, 2018, https://philanthropynewyork.org/news/
      new-online-tool-created-support-osf-helps-immigrants-make-plan.
12.   Immi website, https://www.immi.org/en.
13.   Open Society Foundations, "OSI Announces New Fund to Protect Immigrants'
      Rights," January 24, 2004, https://www.opensocietyfoundations.org/press-releases/
      osi-announces-new-fund-protect-immigrants-rights.
14.   "ACLU awarded $50 million by Open Society Foundations to end mass incarceration,"
      American Civil Liberties Union, November 7, 2014, https://www.aclu.org/news/
      aclu-awarded-50-million-open-society-foundations-end-mass-incarceration.
15.   https://www.opensocietyfoundations.org/grants-database/?filter_keyword=American%20
      Civil#OR2017-32635
16.   https://www.opensocietyfoundations.org/
      grants-database/?filter_keyword=Catholic#OR2016-26821.

17. Ibid.
18. https://www.opensocietyfoundations.org/about/programs/us-programs/grantees/national-immigration-law-center.
19. https://www.opensocietyfoundations.org/about/programs/us-programs/grantees/national-immigration-law-center-2.
20. https://www.opensocietyfoundations.org/grants-database?filter_keyword=Immigration#OR2016-30889.
21. Matthew Vadum, "Obama-appointed judge vs. Trump's immigration changes," FrontPage Mag, January 30, 2017, https://www.frontpagemag.com/fpm/265639/obama-appointed-judge-vs-trumps-immigration-matthew-vadum.
22. https://www.opensocietyfoundations.org/grants-database/?filter_keyword=bono#OR2016-28192.
23. https://www.opensocietyfoundations.org/grants-database/?filter_keyword=Raza#OR2015-24081.
24. Lawyers' Committee for Civil Rights Under Law website, https://lawyerscommittee.org/.
25. Lawyers' Committee for Civil Rights Under Law Form 990 for 2017, https://lawyerscommittee.org/wp-content/uploads/2018/11/Our-2017-IRS-Form-990.pdf.
26. https://www.opensocietyfoundations.org/grants-database?filter_keyword=Lawyers%27%20Committee#OR2016-29974.

Appendix E

1. "Private Sector Participants to the Call to Action," Briefing Room, White House, September 20, 2016, https://obamawhitehouse.archives.gov/the-press-office/2016/09/20/private-sector-participants-call-action.

Appendix G

1. "Ohio Man Pleads Guilty to Conspiracy to Provide Material Support to Terrorists," U.S. Department of Justice, July 31, 2007, https://www.justice.gov/archive/opa/pr/2007/July/07_nsd_568.html.
2. "Massive Somali Community Opens Surprising Experiences to Columbus Visitors," Experience Columbus, October 24, 2018, https://www.experiencecolumbus.com/articles/post/massive-somali-community-opens-surprising-experiences-to-columbus-visitors/.
3. Mark Hosenball, "Fort Dix Suspects Illegally in U.S. for 20 Years," Newsweek, May 15, 2017, https://www.newsweek.com/fort-dix-suspects-illegally-us-20-years-100907.
4. "Former Iraqi Terrorists Living in Kentucky Sentenced for Terrorist Activities," U.S. Department of Justice, January 29, 2013, https://archives.fbi.gov/archives/louisville/press-releases/2013/former-iraqi-terrorists-living-in-kentucky-sentenced-for-terrorist-activities#_blank.
5. "Chanhassen Man Sentenced for Obstructing Investigation of Missing Somali Men" FBI, Minneapolis Division, July 16, 2010, https://archives.fbi.gov/archives/minneapolis/press-releases/2010/mp071610.htm.
6. Lauren Yuen, "Family IDs Minn. Man Allegedly behind Somali Suicide Bombing," MPR News, June 7, 2011, https://www.mprnews.org/story/2011/06/07/farah-beledi-minnesota-man-suicide-attack.
7. Ibid.
8. Bill Roggio, "American Fighter Pictured with Shabaab Commander Identified," Long War Journal, January 11, 2012, https://www.longwarjournal.org/archives/2012/01/american_fighter_pic.php.

9.   "Shirwa's Journey," *Minneapolis Star Tribune,* May 6, 2009, http://www.startribune.com/shirwa-s-journey/44231802/.

10. Nicholas Schmidle, "Homegrown Jihad," VQR Winter 2010, https://www.vqronline.org/essay/homegrown-jihad.

11. David Hanners, "Omar Convicted of Aiding Somali Terrorists, Faces Life in Prison," Pioneer Press, October 17, 2010, https://www.twincities.com/2012/10/17/omar-convicted-of-aiding-somali-terrorists-faces-life-in-prison/.

12. "Fourth Twin Cities Somali-American Killed in Homeland Fighting," Pioneer Press, July 12, 2009, https://www.twincities.com/2009/07/12/fourth-twin-cities-somali-american-killed-in-homeland-fighting/.

13. Julia Preston, "F.B.I. Interview Led Homeland Security To Hold up Citizenship for One Brother," *New York Times,* April 21, 2013, https://www.nytimes.com/2013/04/21/us/tamerlan-tsarnaevs-citizenship-held-up-by-homeland-security.html.

14. "San Diego Jury Convicts Four Somali Immigrants of Providing Support to Foreign Terrorists," U.S. Attorney's Office, Southern District of California, February 22, 2013, https://archives.fbi.gov/archives/sandiego/press-releases/2013/san-diego-jury-convicts-four-somali-immigrants-of-providing-support-to-foreign-terrorists.

15.   Abha Shankar, "3 Sentenced for Al-Shabaab Support," Investigative Project, November 19, 2013, https://www.investigativeproject.org/4218/3-sentenced-for-al-shabaab-support.

16. "Three Somali Immigrants Sentenced for Providing Support To Foreign Terrorists," U.S. Attorney's Office, Southern District of California, November 18, 2013, https://www.justice.gov/usao-sdca/pr/three-somali-immigrants-sentenced-providing-support-foreign-terrorists.

17. "Cabbie Who Aided Terror Group Returned to Somalia," Associated Press, November 2, 2016, https://losangeles.cbslocal.com/2016/11/02/cabbie-who-aided-terror-group-returned-to-somalia/.

18. Seamus Hughes and Bennett Clifford, "First He Became an American—Then He Joined ISIS," *The Atlantic,* May 25, 2017, https://www.theatlantic.com/international/archive/2017/05/first-he-became-an-americanthen-he-joined-isis/527622/.

19. *Ibid.*

20. Robert Patrick, "St. Louis County Man Admits Supporting Terrorists, Including Man Who Fought for ISIS," *St Louis Post-Dispatch,* April 3, 2019, https://www.stltoday.com/news/local/crime-and-courts/st-louis-county-man-admits-supporting-terrorists-including-man-who/article_7b18898a-e67b-531e-af6f-296c30033a28.html.

21. John Sowell, "Kurbanov Sent to Prison for 25 Years in Boise Terror Plot," *Idaho Statesman,* January 7, 2016, https://www.idahostatesman.com/news/local/crime/article53610300.html.

22. "Most Wanted: Liban Haji Mohamed," FBI, https://www.fbi.gov/wanted/wanted_terrorists/liban-haji-mohamed.

23. "US Man Gets 25 Years for South Park Threats," AFP, February 25, 2011, https://www.abc.net.au/news/2011-02-25/us-man-gets-25-years-for-south-park-threats/1956682.

24. "FBI 'Most Wanted' Terrorist Liban Haji Mohamed Detained and in Custody of Somali Government," Reuters/ABC, March 3, 2015, https://www.abc.net.au/news/2015-03-03/fbi-most-wanted-terrorist-liban-haji-mohamed-detained/6277706.

25.   Catherine Shoichet and Michael Pearson, "Garland, Texas, Shooting Suspect Linked Himself to ISIS in Tweets," CNN, May 4, 2015, https://www.cnn.com/2015/05/04/us/garland-mohammed-drawing-contest-shooting/index.html.

26. Paul McEnroe and Erin Golden, "Terror Recruiter with Roots in Minn. Linked to Texas Shooting," *Minneapolis Star Tribune,* May 9, 2015, http://www.startribune.com/terror-recruiter-with-roots-in-minn-linked-to-texas-shooting/303188091/.

27. "Somali Citizen Sentenced to 15 Years in Federal Prison for Conspiring To Provide Material Support to Al-Shabaab," U.S. Attorney's Office, Western District of Texas, February 5, 2015, https://www.justice.gov/usao-wdtx/pr/somali-citizen-sentenced-15-years-federal-prison-conspiring-provide-material-support-al#_blank.

28. "Local Man Pleads Guilty to Providing Material Support to Terrorist Organization," FBI, St. Louis Division, November 3, 2011, https://archives.fbi.gov/archives/stlouis/press-releases/2011/local-man-pleads-guilty-to-providing-material-support-to-terrorist-organization.

29. Tim O'Neil, "Somali Here Accused of Sending Money to Terrorists Back Home," *St. Louis Post-Dispatch*, November 4, 2010, https://www.stltoday.com/news/local/crime-and-courts/somali-here-accused-of-sending-money-to-terrorists-back-home/article_42577bc2-bd4f-5665-9bde-7eff44458161.html.

30. "Somali Refugee Admits to Terror Charge," Courthouse News Service, December 2, 2011, https://www.courthousenews.com/somali-refugee-admits-to-terror-charge/.

31. "6 Minnesota Men Sentenced in Islamic State Case," Associated Press, November 15, 2016, https://www.apnews.com/1b2f10455e06449086bb57b7884c7282.

32. Ibid.

33. Laura Yuen, "Guled Omar: The Path to ISIS and the Story You Haven't Heard," MPR News, December 21, 2016, https://www.mprnews.org/story/2016/12/21/path-to-isis-minnesota-guled-omar-mpr-interviews.

34. Dina Temple-Raston, "New Charges In Somali Terror Case," NPR, November 23, 2009, https://www.npr.org/templates/story/story.php?storyId=120709855.

35. Hollie McKay, "How Minneapolis' Somali Community Became the Terrorist Recruitment Capital of the US," Fox News, https://foxnews.com/us/how-rep-ilhan-omars-minnesota-district-became-the-terrorist-recruitment-capital-of-the-us-officials-highly-concerned.

36. Ibid.

37. Pete Williams, Tom Winter, Andrew Blankstein and Tracy Connor, "Suspect Identified in Ohio State Attack as Abdul Razak Ali Artan," NBC News, November 28, 2016, https://www.nbcnews.com/news/us-news/suspect-dead-after-ohio-state-university-car-knife-attack-n689076.

38. Ibid.

39. Nadine Comerford and Alexander Smith, "Dahir Ahmed Adan Named by Police as St. Cloud, Minnesota, Stabbing Suspect," NBC News, September 20, 2016, https://www.nbcnews.com/news/us-news/dahir-ahmed-adan-named-police-st-cloud-minnesota-stabbing-suspect-n651061.

40. Ibid.

41. Ibid.

42. "Memorandum of Extradition Law and Request for Detention Pending Extradition Proceedings," Case No. 2:18-MJ-0152 EFB, https://www.justice.gov/opa/press-release/file/1087556/download.

43. "Iraqi Refugee Sentenced for Attempting to Provide Material Support to ISIL," U.S. Attorney's Office, Southern District of Texas, December 18, 2017, https://www.justice.gov/usao-sdtx/pr/iraqi-refugee-sentenced-attempting-provide-material-support-isil.

44. Ibid.

45. United States of America v. AWS Mohammed Younis Al-Jayab Plea Agreement (undated), https://www.justice.gov/usao-ndil/press-release/file/1106871/download.

46. "Abdullatif Ali Aldosary Indicted on Additional State Charges," Pinal County Attorney, July 22, 2013, http://www.pinalcountyaz.gov/CountyAttorney/Lists/OldNews/DispForm.aspx?ID=12.

47. Shelley Ridenour, "Aldosary Sentenced to Five Years for Weapons Charge," Coolidge Examiner, February 26, 2014, https://www.pinalcentral.com/coolidge_examiner/news/

aldosary-sentenced-to-five-years-for-weapons-charge/article_8860f9a0-9e76-11e3-bab6-0019bb2963f4.html.

48. Brian Skoloff, "Ariz. Bomb Suspect Charged with Previous Murder," Associated Press, July 22, 2013, https://www.usatoday.com/story/news/nation/2013/07/22/arizona-bomb-suspect-charges/2575815/.

49. Kevin Regan, "Criminal Charges against Aldosary To Be Dropped," Maricopa Monitor, January 1, 2019, https://www.pinalcentral.com/maricopa_monitor/news/criminal-charges-against-aldosary-to-be-dropped/article_ff527a4a-0ff8-5689-b622-b111890dd008.html.

50. Kevin Krause, "FBI: Mesquite Man Lied about Islamic State Pledge," *Dallas News*, June 2015, https://www.dallasnews.com/news/crime/2015/06/11/fbi-mesquite-man-lied-about-islamic-state-pledge.

51. "Texan Gets Prison for Lying about Terrorist Group Allegiance," Associated Press, May 25, 2016, https://www.abqjournal.com/780616.

52. Scott Gordon, "Mesquite Man Arrested by FBI Held Without Bond," NBCDFW, May 15, 2015, http://www.nbcdfw.com/news/local/Mesquite-Man-Arrested-by-FBI-Ordered-Held-Without-Bond-303919641.html#_blank.

53. Kirk Mitchell, "Denver Federal Jury Finds Uzbekistan Refugee Guilty of Aiding Terror Group," *Denver Post*, June 21, 2018, https://www.denverpost.com/2018/06/21/denver-jury-jamshid-muhtorov-guilty/.

54. "Jamshid Muhtorov and Bakhtiyor Jumaev Guilty of Providing Material Support to Terrorists," U.S. Department of Justice, June 21, 2018, https://www.justice.gov/opa/pr/jamshid-muhtorov-and-bakhtiyor-jumaev-guilty-providing-material-support-terrorists.

55. Pat Pheifer, "'Interrupted Theft' Led to Stabbings at Macy's in Mall of America," *Minneapolis Star Tribune*, November 13, 2017, http://www.startribune.com/stabbing-reported-at-mall-of-america/457085353/.

56. "Court Records: Mall of America Stabbing Suspect Pleads Guilty, Calls it Act of Jihad," ABC News 5, January 16, 2018, https://kstp.com/news/mahad-abdiaziz-abdiraham-mall-of-america-guilty-plea-jihad/4760698/.

57. John Binder, "Jihadist Responsible for Mall of America Stabbing Spree Entered U.S. with Foreign Relatives," Breitbart, February 5, 2018, https://www.breitbart.com/politics/2018/02/05/jihadist-responsible-for-mall-of-america-stabbing-spree-entered-u-s-with-foreign-relatives/.

Appendix H

1. David Dyssegaard Kallick, "Squeezing Refugees: Numbers for 2018 by State and Metro Area," Fiscal Policy Institute, November 2, 2018, http://fiscalpolicy.org/squeezing-refugees-numbers-for-2018-by-state-and-metro-area.

Appendix I

1. Jim Simpson, "Private Contractors Force Feed Refugees to States that Quit the Program," Daily Caller, March 26, 2017, https://dailycaller.com/2017/03/26/private-contractors-force-feed-refugees-to-states-that-quit-the-program/.

2. "Wilson-Fish Chart," U.S. Department of Health and Human Services, January 25, 2013, https://www.acf.hhs.gov/orr/resource/wilson-fish-chart.

INDEX

A

ACLU, xxvi, 133, 172, 176, 244, 258–59, 244, 271, 215, 271, 315–16

Acosta, Jim, xxvii, 110, 269, 273, 291–92

Adams, Haley, 155

Adhahn, Terapon Dang, 179–81

Alamoudi, Abdurahman, 276

Al Hussein, Zeid Ra'ad, 137–38

Al Otro Lado (AOL), 11–13, 152, 259

Alliance Defending Freedom (ADF), 188, 224, 229

Amalgamated Bank, 234

Amazon Smile, 188, 217, 228–29

American Conservative Union, xxxi, xxxii, 275–76

American Legislative Exchange Council (ALEC), xxxv, 72–73

anarchy, iii, xv, 1, 29, 78, 143, 168–69, 177–78

Angel Moms, xxxiii, 261, 289, 291

Antifa, xii, xiii, xv, xvi, xx, xxi, xxvii, xxxiv, xxxv, xxxvi, 73, 143–57, 159–82, 218, 226, 270, 280–81, 297

B

Apple, xxxii, xxxv, 5, 15, 163, 178, 235–36

Assata's Daughters, 166–67

Avaaz, 57

Azar, Alex, 30

Baptist Child and Family Services (BCFS), 17–18

Becerra, Xavier, 288

Beck, Roy, i, 203–4

Beirich, Heidi, 196, 199, 210

Beverly Hills, 14, 84, 237–38, 250, 270–71

Bezos, Jeff, 228, 230, 284

Biden, Joe, xxx, 110

Border Patrol, ix, xvi, xxxvii, 1, 10, 14–15, 23, 28–29, 62, 67, 149, 157, 162–63, 201, 242–46, 261, 269, 285–87, 296, 314

Bray, Mark, 152, 280

Bright, Stephen, 212

Bush, George W., xxv, 34, 97

C

Caal, Jakelin, 286
Camp of the Saints, 201–3
Cannon, Carl M., 208
Cárdenas, Al, 275–77
Carlson, Tucker, 71, 160, 224
Carson, Ben, 184
CASA de Maryland, 65, 68
Castro, Julián, xxx, 110, 288
Catholic Charities, xxvii, xxxvii, xliii, 68,
    92–93, 96, 103, 106–7, 125–26, 131–
    32, 136, 228, 295–96, 311
Center for Immigration Studies, xvii,
    20–23, 30, 111, 127, 144, 169, 173,
    176, 199–203, 208, 216, 228
Center for Media Justice (CMJ), 72–73, 77,
    317
Center for Popular Democracy (CPD),
    64–65, 80, 163, 165,
Central America, xxviii, xxvii, 7, 17, 20,
    23–24, 32, 55, 91, 105, 114, 301
Central American Minors Refugee/Parole
    Program (CAM), 23–26, 30
Chase Bank, xxxvi, 63, 231–33
Chavez, Cesar, 260
cheap labor, xxii, xxix, xxxiii, xxxiv, 2,
    79, 81, 90, 97, 112, 123, 251, 267, 276,
    287, 296
Choudary, Anjem, 128
Clanton, Eric, 162
Clark, Linda, xxiv, xxv, xxvi
climate change refugees, 53, 114
Clinton, Bill, xxv, xxix, 42, 45, 48, 177,
    273
Clinton, Hillary, 25, 42, 48, 63, 110, 227,
    250, 262, 273
Clooney, Amal, 209, 249, 255
Clooney, George, 209, 249, 251–52
CNN, xvi–vii, xxxiv, 71, 92, 110, 154,
    244, 269, 273–74, 277, 285, 289, 291
Code Words of Hate, 192–95, 220
Cohen, Richard, 191, 210–11, 219
Color of Change, xxxv, 42, 72–74, 77, 117,
    201, 221, 234, 317
Conservative Political Action Conference
    (CPAC), xxxii–xv, 275–76, 280,

Cook, Tim, xxxii, 191, 235–36
Cordero, Olga, 37
Corkins, Floyd Lee, 214, 220
Cuarón, Alfonso, 262
Cuomo, Chris, xxvii, 275

D

Daily Caller News Foundation, 71, 157,
    221, 223, 230
DCLeaks, 50, 69, 80
de Blasio, Bill, 53, 164
Dees, Morris, 191, 200, 208–13, 219, 236
Deferred Action for Childhood Arrivals
    (DACA), xli, 19–20, 32, 101, 106, 247,
    266, 316
Deferred Action for Parents of Americans
    and Lawful Permanent Residents
    (DAPA), 19–20
Deferred Enforcement Departure (DED),
    xxiv, xxvi, 316
Democratic Socialists of America (DSA),
    143, 145–47, 149, 152, 159
Department of Homeland Security (DHS),
    xxvi, xxxiii, 22, 24, 27, 31, 78, 117,
    123, 143–44, 159, 162, 169, 173, 249,
    281
Direct Action Network (DAN), 150
Directo a México, 34–35, 297
Dobbs, Lou, 71, 193, 196
Doctors Without Borders, xxviii, 3, 9, 35,
    55–56, 170. *See also Médecins Sans
    Frontiéres*
Donald, Michael, 208–9
doxxing, xxii, xxxiv, xxxix, 154–57, 159–
    60, 226, 270, 280
DREAMers, xxxii, 102, 151, 205, 247,
    249, 265, 284–85
drug cartels, 144, 193, 267
Durkan, Jenny, 178

E

Egerton, John, 212–13
Ellison, Keith, xvi, xxi, 230, 288
Emma Lazarus Fund, 44–45
Eudaly, Chloe, 151

eugenics, 203–4
European Union, 10, 46, 51, 56, 58, 107, 114, 137, 251
Exodus Refugee Immigration, 133

F

Facebook, xxxi, 2, 6, 14–15, 33, 61, 72–73, 135, 223–24, 232, 310, 318, 322
Faith in Action, 80
Fallon, Jimmy, 255–56
Families Belong Together, 258–59
Family Research Council (FRC), 184–85, 187, 214, 216, 220, 224
Far Left Watch, 157, 161
Farrell, Chris, iii, 43, 71
Favreau, Jon, 267
Federal Communications Commission (FCC), 74
Federal Reserve, 34–35, 88, 297
Federation for American Immigration Reform (FAIR), 32, 127, 173, 197–99, 201, 203, 208, 224, 335
First Amendment. *See also* freedom of speech, xx, 72, 103, 135, 175, 217, 297
Flores v. Reno, 16, 26–27
Flores, Esmeralda, 11
Ford, John, 270
Fox New, xxvii, 43, 70–3, 160, 180–81, 186, 193, 224, 269, 290
Francis, Pope, xix, xxi, 80–81, 83, 85–86, 91, 98, 108
Free Press, 42, 74, 220
Fronteras, Pueblo Sin, 1–2, 5–6, 12, 36–37, 231, 301-3

G

G20 Summit, 154
Gadda, Vijaya, 225
Gaertner, Justin, 40, 278
Gaffney, Frank, 185, 276
Gang of Eight, xxxii, 79, 115, 276
Gatsas, Ted, 131
Gee, Dolly, Judge, 26
Gibboney, Agnes, 291–92
Gorsuch, Neil, 118

Government Accountability Office (GAO), 123, 129, 131
Grady, Claire, 143
Guardian, The, 280

H

H-2B program, xxxiii
Hamilton, Alexander, 112–13
Hanen, Andrew, 21–22
Harris, Kamala, xxx, 242
Hodgkinson, James, 220
HOPE Not Hate (HNH), xxviii, 60, 318
Horowitz, Daniel, iii, 19, 25–26, 175
Huffington Post (HuffPost), 203, 210, 280, 285, 288, 291
Human Rights Watch (HRW), 62–63

I

identity politics, xxix, xxxi–xii, 67–68, 165, 190, 194, 261,
Immigration Act of 1990, xxiv, 79
Immigration and Nationality Act (INA), 173
Immigration Reform and Control Act (IRCA), 2, 90
Influence Watch, 65–66, 104
Inslee, Jay, 54, 177
Internal Revenue Service (IRS), 31, 57, 66, 98, 105, 211, 296
International Migration Initiative (IMI), xxvi, 50–51, 305
International Organization for Migration (IOM), 8, 15, 20, 51–53, 96, 111, 137, 310
intersectionality, 166
Islamic State (ISIS), xv, xxix, 134, 137, 255

J

Jenner, Kendall, 238, 270–71
Jesuit Refugee Service (JRS), 8–9
Jihad Watch, 186, 233, 276
Jiménez, Cristina, 68
Judicial Watch, iii, 34, 43, 71, 124

K

Kalchik, Anatoly, 181
Kaling, Mindy, 243, 252
Kammer, Jerry, 201
Kavanaugh, Brett, xxxii, 48, 64, 155
Koch brothers, xxxi–xiii, xxxv, 84
Ku Klux Klan (KKK), 191, 199, 208

L

Lake Como, 249–51
Larrimore, David, 156
Lavigne, Sam, xxxiv, 155
Lavin, Talia, 39, 277
Lenihan, Eoin, xxxv, 152, 280
Leung, Shirley, 281–82
Linnik, Zina, 179–80
Loomer, Laura, xxxiv, 231, 233
Lucas, Earnell, 173

M

Madison, James, 112
Make the Road, 63–65, 68, 78, 145, 163
Malaysia, 138
Malek, Rami, 261
McElroy, Robert, Bishop, 81
McElwee, Sean, 145, 165
McInnes, Gavin, iii, 160, 217, 219, 224, 231
Médecins Sans Frontiéres, 9, 78. *See also* Doctors Without Borders
Media Matters for America (MMFA), 40, 70–71, 184, 279, 318
Medicaid, 128, 131, 135
Medicare, xxx
Mendoza, Pablo, 241
Merkel, Angela, 254
Metropolitan Anarchist Coordinating Council (MACC), 164
Mexico City, 5, 9–10, 36, 262
Microsoft, xxxiv, xxxv, 79, 156, 229, 326
Middlebury College, 215, 220
Migration and Development Civil Society Network (MADE), 58, 306
Milano, Alyssa, 247–48

Milenio, 151
Miller, Stephen, 110, 159, 281
Molina, Maynor Velasquez, 28
Molyneux, Stefan, 190
Moore, John, 14, 244, 246
Morse, Jennifer Roback, 188
MS-13, xxi, xxvi, xxxix, 26, 35, 115, 167, 172, 206, 287, 289–90, 293
Mujica, Irineo, 1–6, 36
multiculturalism, ii, xxxvii, 276
Murdoch, Rupert, xxix, 57
Murguia, Janet, 195
Murray, Charles, 214–15, 220
Muslim Advocates, 69–70, 73, 78, 317

N

Nairobi, 138, 140
National Hispanic Media Coalition (NHMC), 71, 74, 220
National Immigration Forum (NIF), 44, 69, 79
National Institute of Migration, xxxii, 5, 10, 44, 46, 79-80, 86, 98, 102, 187
national sovereignty, ii, x, xix, xxi, xxviii, xxxviii, 12, 45-47, 51, 56, 81, 83, 88, 92, 113-14, 263, 295, 297, 308, 314
Navarro-Cárdenas, Ana, 273, 275
Nawaz, Maajid, 184, 216
New York Times, xvi, xxx, 49, 138, 157, 196, 206, 212, 218, 224, 227, 251, 256, 274, 285, 287, 289
New Yorker, the, 40, 65, 236, 277-78, 285
Ngo, Andy, xv, 153, 155
Nielsen, Kirstjen, 78, 159, 249, 281
non-governmental organizations (NGOs), xxviii, 43, 46, 96, 221, 251
Norquist, Grover, xxix, 79, 276
Northern Triangle, 20, 24, 32, 105
Nunes, Devin, 224

O

O'Neil, Luke, 281
O'Rourke, Beto, xxx, 20, 53-54, 227, 288
Oakland County, 134

Obama, Barack, ii, xxv, 2, 43, 74, 100, 128, 210, 219, 253, 262
Ocasio-Cortez, Alexandria, xvi, xxx
Occupy ICE PDX, 146-47, 152-53
Office of Refugee Resettlement (ORR), 16, 30, 39, 113, 122-23, 135
Okoumou, Patricia, 163
Omar, Ilhan, xxi, xxiii, xxx, 227, 288
Organized Communities Against Deportation (OCAD), 168

P

Patriot Prayer, 155
PayPal, xxxv, 33, 73-74, 219, 230-32
Perez, Thomas E., 66
Pioneer Fund, 204
Planned Parenthood, 203-04
Pool, Tim, 225-26
Populism, 224
Portland, xv, 53, 146-47, 149-53, 155
Potok, Mark, 184, 196, 199, 210, 216
PragerU, 222-23
Prescott, Gene, 275
Proud Boys, iii, 217-18, 224, 231-32
Pueblo Sin Fronteras, xii, 1-2, 5-7, 36-37, 231, 301-03

R

racial supremacism, 195
Racketeer Influenced and Corrupt Organizations Act (RICO), 216
Red Guards, 144, 162-63,
Refugee Act of 1980, 113, 120, 123, 134
Refugee and Immigrant Center for Education and Legal Services (RAICES), 13, 103, 314
Refugee Council USA, 121
Remittances, xxii, xxviii, 32-34, 37, 297
Republican Party, xxxviii, 151-52, 162, 216, 275
Res Publica, 57
Rise and Resist, 163-64
Rivera, Geraldo, 180, 273
Robinson, Tommy, 61, 231
Rollins, Rachael, 169

Roman, Tanya, 179
Rome Charter, 59-60
Rove, Karl, 276
Ruckus Society, 150
Rush, Nayla, 111, 120, 126
Ruth Institute, 188, 228
Ryan, Paul, xxix, 79

S

Salazar, Sergio "Mapache", 144
Samaniego, Eduardo, 247-48
Sanchez, Yanela, 244-46
sanctuary spaces, 52-3, 166, 205
Sanders, Sarah, 160, 281, 292
Sarno, Domenic, 132
Save the Children, xxviii, 54-55, 76, 295, 324
Schlafly, Phyllis, 189
Schlapp, Matt, xxxii, xxxiv
Seasonal Employment Alliance, xxxiii
Seattle, 53, 149-50, 157, 175, 178, 284, 333, 335
Seeborg, Richard, 176
Service Employees International Union (SEIU), 43, 235
Sessions, Jeff, 204
shadow banning , 225
Silicon Valley, xx-xxi, xxxv, 14-15, 73, 189, 191, 219, 221, 296, 298
Silverstein, Ken, 200, 212
Simpson, James, 125
Singh, Ronil, 241, 246
Sirico, Rober, Fr., 80
Smash Racism D.C., 160
Soros Economic Development Fund, 75
Soros, George, I, xi, xvii, xxi, xxvi, xxx-xxxi, xliii, 3, 6, 19, 39, 42, 47-9, 52, 56, 62, 70-3, 75, 81, 159, 171, 184, 251, 253, 260, 319
southern border siege , xxvii, 42, 49, 110, 146
Special Agricultural Workers (SAW) , 2
Spencer, Robert, I, 186, 230, 233-34, 276
Squire, Megan, 157
Statue of Liberty, xx, 45, 109-11, 113, 163

Steinle, Kate, 177
Sutherland, Peter, 51
Swain, Carol, 184, 187

T

Talwani, Indira, 169
Tanton, John, 201, 204
Tarrio, Enrique, 231
Tchen, Tina, 219
Teaching Tolerance, xx, xxxvii, 205, 222,
    298
Teixeira, Bampumim, 170
Temporary Assistance for Needy Families
    (TANF), 128
Temporary Protected Status (TPS), xxiv, 30
Tenth Amendment, 136, 216, 297
Terry, Ted, 53
Tides Center, 19, 253
Tijuana, 8, 11-13, 91, 261, 264-65
Trump, Donald, xxi, xxx, 69, 85, 110, 130,
    137, 167, 227, 255, 284

U

U.N. Refugee Agency, 138-140
U.S. Citizenship and Immigration Services
    (USCIS), 121
U.S. Committee for Refugees and Immi-
    grants, 19, 122, 126, 311, 328
U.S. custody, 29, 285
United Nations, xxi, xxxviii, 8, 20-21, 33,
    36, 52, 54, 59, 76, 107, 111, 114, 121,
    137-38, 251, 254, 265, 301, 309, 326
United Nations High Commissioner for
    Refugees (UNHCR), 59, 76, 111, 138
United We Dream (UWD), 67-68

V

Vadum, Matthew, 210, 316
Vargas, Jose Antonio, xxxi, 253, 266, 269,
    273
voluntary agencies (VOLAGs), 122, 125

W

Washington, George, 112

welfare benefits, 45, 114, 128, 166
Wheeler, Ted, xv, 147
white supremacy, 70-71, 223-24
Wilcox, Laird, 189, 216
Wilson, Jason, 152, 280
Wilson-Fish Amendment, 135
Wolf, Mark, 172
Women's March, xvii, 148
Wood, Evan Rachel, 260
World Bank, 32, 107
World Trade Organization riots, 150

Y

Young Center, 19, 252-53

Z

Ziobrowski, Brandon, 144